ENVIRONMENTAL DESIGN
AND
HUMAN BEHAVIOR

(PGPS–85)

Related Titles

ENVIRONMENTAL DESIGN AND HUMAN BEHAVIOR

A Psychology of the Individual in Society

Edited by
Leonard Krasner

State University
of New York
at Stony Brook

Pergamon Press

NEW YORK • OXFORD • TORONTO • SYDNEY • FRANKFURT • PARIS

Pergamon Press Offices:

U.S.A.   Pergamon Press Inc., Maxwell House, Fairview Park,
                     Elmsford, New York 10523, U.S.A.

U.K.   Pergamon Press Ltd., Headington Hill Hall,
                     Oxford OX3 0BW, England

CANADA   Pergamon of Canada, Ltd., 150 Consumers Road,
                     Willowdale, Ontario M2J, 1P9, Canada

AUSTRALIA   Pergamon Press (Aust) Pty. Ltd., P O Box 544,
                     Potts Point, NSW 2011, Australia

FRANCE   Pergamon Press SARL, 24 rue des Ecoles,
                     75240 Paris, Cedex 05, France

FEDERAL REPUBLIC Pergamon Press GmbH, 6242 Kronberg/Taunus,
OF GERMANY   Pferdstrasse 1, Federal Republic of Germany

Library of Congress Cataloging in Publication Data

Main entry under title:

Environmental design and human behavior.

   (Pergamon general psychology series)
   Bibliography: p.
   Includes index.
   1. Architecture—Environmental aspects—
Addresses, essays, lectures. 2. Architecture—
Psychological aspects—Addresses, essays, lectures.
3. Environmental psychology—Addresses, essays,
lectures. I. Krasner, Leonard, 1924-
NA2542.35.E58   711   79-13570
ISBN 0-08-023858-0

Printed in the United States of America

To the future in Santa Cassandra.

Contents

Acknowledgments

We, the editor and the authors, wish to express our appreciation and thanks to the following: the students, graduate and undergraduate, and faculty who have been participants in our Environmental Design seminars at the State University of New York, Stony Brook, and at North East London Polytechnic in London, England; the staff in the various community settings in Long Island and in London in which our students have been participant-observers; Ben Reich and Vic Meyer for their assistance to the program in London; Dennis Littky, E. Michael Helmintoller, Shirley Weiss, Evelyn Loveless, and Beth Heyn for their continuing assistance in local schools; Larry Deboer and Ray Jones for their sustained support of our London Program; Rudy Moos for his invaluable critique of the manuscript; Art Houts, Phyllis Bryan, and Maxine Semmel for assistance in various aspects of the manuscript; Grant # OSS 784572 from the National Science Foundation Ethics and Values in Science and Technology Program; and, finally, those environmental designers Wendy, Dave, Linda, Charley, and Stefanie, Krasners all.

Introduction

The function of an introduction to a book usually is to present a foreshadowing of exciting material to come and to establish a relationship with an audience. We are using the term "environmental design" in this book to represent a process and an approach to human behavior which is currently evolving in psychology and related fields. By writing about it and by being participant-observers in the development of the process, we are trying to understand and to enhance its growth and, most important, to train professionals in it.

The focus of this book is upon the elements which enter into the training of individuals for the professional role of "environmental designer." Those who utilize this role implicitly follow a behavioral/environmental/ social-learning paradigm or model of human behavior. The goal of those involved in the preparation of this volume is to illustrate the approach, delineate its parameters, detail the input necessary to train in and evaluate it, describe the sources of scientific and humanistic influences upon it, discuss the social and ethical ramifications of training individuals in it, survey the resources available, and describe the research/training/application process.

The production of this book itself is illustrative of the environmental design process. The book is the product of collaborative efforts of a group of participant-observers in environmental design procedures such as seminars, training programs, research investigations, classroom and community settings, and in an ongoing process of mutual influence. Writing and editing the book have been valuable learning experiences for all participants. We will detail the linkages to the environmental design process and to each other in the introductions to each chapter.

In the context of the influence process we must bring in other labels with which we still identify. The editor and most of the writers in this volume were trained as clinical psychologists and their interest in the training of such professionals and identification with that label has continued to the present. We would prefer labels such as "social change agents," "learning facilitators," or "environmental designers," but current usage, state certifications, and job specifications, enhance the likelihood of the continuation of the "clinical psychology" label. Orienting a volume on environmental design towards, among others, clinical psychologists is intended to affect the direction and emphasis of those involved in this key field of social change.

However, we have focused our material throughout the book toward a wider audience that includes individuals who identify their professional role as educators, community mental health workers, sociologists, nurses, social workers, architects, school psychologists, lawyers, psychiatrists, urban planners, and others involved in the ubiquitous process of designing environments and training others to design their own environment.

Our major interest has been the change process as it involves not only those individuals who have "problems in living," but all of us who are engaged in attempting to live in a complex society. The emerging field of environmental design can be linked with the work of those professionals who function in society as change agents who are called in when there is some individual or group malfunction or unhappiness or simply to help plan an ongoing living process such as building a home or teaching a classroom of elementary school children.

One goal in the development of environmental design is to affect the training of psychologists and other professionals to conceptualize the task of aiding others in terms of educating people in ways of designing and controlling their own environment. In order to do this, the model becomes "educational" − the training of people to help themselves and/or to train others − instead of "medical" − the curing of sickness and disease, or pathology. This development also represents an observation of a process already well underway in the field of psychology. In effect, we would like to accelerate this development.

A further goal in the utilization of an environmental design orientation is to influence the theoretical orientation and research of professional investigators in social, developmental, environmental, and ecological psychology, and related fields such as sociology, architecture, law, and education. We see a greater unity and linkage in theory and purpose between these fields as one result of the environmental design approach. We envision the material in this book being utilized in the training of professional environmental designers (in various programs at the undergraduate and graduate levels) to work in a variety of settings such as schools, community centers, and other similar social institutions where they can bring to bear their value system, orientation, and technology to train people in influencing their own environments.

In offering an environmental design approach to changing human behavior, a basic part of the theoretical orientation requires that the professional continually ask questions as to what changes are to be brought about and who is to bring them about. In effect, there are "for what" and "by whom" questions which are an integral part of the environmental design process and for the basis for considerations of values. We raise and discuss these issues throughout the book.

Our second major goal is to explicate an integrative model of human behavior from the viewpoint of an environmental-behavioral position. This approach emphasizes <u>process</u>, and as such does not offer a finished product but rather <u>a description of an ongoing process</u>, the description of which itself is part of the process.

Thus, this book is conceived of as an attempt at integration of the multitudinous variables of an environmental design model which includes elements derived from history, philosophy, value systems, research methodology, training procedures, analysis of social institutions, and illustrations from other societies.

We will offer an introduction to each of the individual chapters and our rationale for its inclusion in this book. A brief note about the author of each chapter is located at the end of the book. The field and orientation which we are calling environmental design is being defined by the nature of the material which is included herein.

The book is divided into two parts. The first concentrates on theoretical and historical influences; the second, on a wide range of applications. However, the distinction between theory and application is never sharp or clear-cut. Its function in this book is one of convenience, not conviction.

The theoretical model of environmental design comprises a broad set of hypotheses, observations, and research results which bear upon the nature of man and society. These will be described in the first chapter and explicated throughout the book. Issues of values and training (in chapters 2 and 9) are an integral part of this approach to human behavior. The environmental design approach, because of its origins within the behavioral-scientific movement, stresses the importance of "evaluating" the success of the professional in affecting specific behavior. Hence a discussion of assessment issues can be found in chapter 5.

The practitioner of environmental design stands a reasonable chance of influencing the behavior of individuals in certain formal "influencing" institutions. Thus, an important element in the training of environmental designers is exposure to work already done involving those institutions that are relevant to the environmental design model. The specific institutional settings that are currently influential in affecting the "design" of our society include mental hospitals, community mental health centers, and schools. The chapters on these institutions (chapters 6, 7, and 10) relate to the broad model, review studies pertinent to the model, present materials derived from the work of our environmental design group, and attempt to illustrate the "for what" and "by whom" in the particular institutions covered.

The second part of the book offers a wide range of illustrations of environmental design in a variety of settings. In chapter 8, we offer a description of very specific training processes, with which all the participants in the preparation of this book have been involved, used in an ongoing environmental design seminar at SUNY, Stony Brook, since September 1972. From this seminar an environmental design program in London, England, has developed. The seminar, the London Program, and the materials evolving from these activities are discussed as specific illustrations of the application of the broader model. The development of the "participant-observer" role in particular has important implications for training in and application of the environmental design model.

Subsequent chapters describe applications of the environmental design approach in training situations (chapter 9), in the classroom (chapters 10 and 11). Two chapters analyze very different types of alternative societies; the Children's Village in Columbia (chapter 12) and China (chapter 13) within the environmental design framework. Then, in chapter 14, an experienced environmental designer analyzes his own reactions to the power elements in an institution. The Appendix comprises a compendium of resource material, organizations, newsletters, references, etc.

A major point of this book is that environmental design, as a paradigmatic approach to human behavior, involves a wide range of material from a multitude of professional disciplines. To comprehensively cover all of the possible material would require an encyclopedia. However, we have focused on the areas we consider most salient and offer resources for additional materials.

Finally, there is another, and perhaps more subtle, purpose in writing the book. Viewing as we do the behavior influence process as ongoing and interactive, the very writing of the book and attempting to give order and meaning to a wide variety of material is in itself an integral part of training in environmental design. In effect, then, writing the book is a learning experience for its "participant-observers" and, hopefully, its readers will also become "participant-observers" in the learning process. We believe that the material in this book can serve as a text in a wide variety of courses, as well as being useful for related disciplines involving the training of individuals in ways of influencing others to design their own environments. We hope the reader will find widespread applicability from the theories, research, and applications presented herein.

1 Environmental Design in Perspective: Theoretical Model, General Principles, and Historical Context

Leonard Krasner

Professionals in the fields of psychology, psychiatry, education, architecture, sociology, economics, law, and related disciplines, by their theoretical conceptualizations, research investigations, and practical applications are evolving an approach to dealing with their clients (patients, subjects, students) that may be labeled "environmental design." Bringing materials on environmental design together at this time is an attempt to influence future developments of this approach.

In the first chapter, Krasner offers a historical and theoretical framework for this emerging field of environmental design. Krasner was trained as a clinical psychologist, in the Post World War II period, as an "eclectic psychoanalytic psychotherapist." However, a major influence on his clinical behavior was his graduate training at Columbia in the then emerging behaviorism of Skinner as mediated through Keller and Schoenfeld. He then evolved into a "behavioral clinical psychologist," and helped develop an approach to changing human behavior, called "behavior modification," with which he continued to identify until 1976 when there occurred the unfortunate demise of that lamented slogan (Krasner, 1976a). His involvement with token economy studies (Ayllon & Azrin, 1968; Atthowe & Krasner, 1968) convinced him that conceptually and practically behaviorists were going well beyond merely applying reinforcement principles in larger and larger settings into developing more complex principles in training individuals to design their own environments.

The complex interaction between man and environment is nicely captured by the observation of the architect Lars Lerup: "We design things and things design us" (Lerup, 1977, p. 156). This simple statement represents a clear conceptualization of the environmental design position.

Ed.

This chapter presents the basic elements and historical context of the environmental design approach including theoretical principles, definitions, related labels, relevant streams of investigation, and the range of research which has affected this orientation toward human behavior. Although we use "environmental design" as the generic term encompassing this approach, there is a series of other somewhat similar labels around which investigators rally and identify: ecology, behavioral social psychology, social ecology, ethology, population psychology, architectural design, man-environment (the preferable term is person-environment), environmental psychology, functionalism, operant conditioning, behavior-environment congruence, social engineering, spatial patterning of culture, systems analysis, learning environments, and applied behavior analysis.

ENVIRONMENTAL DESIGN AS A LABEL

A reasonable way to approach environmental design is to define the term. We will carefully avoid this temptation by describing the operations involved in devising a model, a training approach, and a system of investigation and assessment. However, we will describe how other investigators use the term and offer the dictionary definition of the two words.

The American Heritage Dictionary defines environment as: "The total of circumstances surrounding an organism or group of organisms. Specifically: a) the combination of external or extrinsic physical conditions that affect and influence the growth and development of organisms; b) the complex of social and cultural conditions affecting the nature of an individual or community" (p 438).

Throughout, we will be offering a variety of material which reinforces the desirability of using the word "environment" in the label. But why combine it with "design"? Why not a combination of words such as that advanced by Goldiamond (1978) of "environmental modification" which would bring together two fine and hallowed terms? Our preference is for the word "design" which has a number of dictionary meanings that allow for a certain amount of flexibility and projection in usage. As a noun, "design" means: "1. A drawing or sketch. 2. The invention and disposition of the forms, parts, or details of something according to a plan. 3. A decorative or artistic work. 4. A visual composition: pattern. 5. The art of creating design. 6. A plan; project; an undertaking. 7. A reasoned purpose; intention." As a verb: "To conceive; invent; contrive. 2. To form a plan for. 3. To draw a sketch of. 4. To have as a goal or purpose; intend" (American Heritage Dictionary, 1969, p. 357).

Each of the above definitions conveys some of the meaning we see in the concept of "design." It fits into the broad paradigmatic model which we will be describing more compactly than "modification" which, as a term, now is carrying considerable excessive and confusing controversy and contradictions.

Environmental design, as the term is used in this volume, has broader implications than merely combining the two words. Colman (1975) phrases this concept in a manner compatible with our orientation.

A more useful definition of environmental design would relate the planning of a coherent program and set of procedures to effect the total human and nonhuman environment in ways that increase the probability that certain goals of 'needs' will be achieved. The goal of environmental design would relate to social behavior, such as planning an educational or therapeutic system, as much as to aesthetics such as constructing an awe-inspiring church. Input into environmental design problems must then include knowledge related to modifying human behavior and social systems as well as structural information from engineering and perceptual psychology. The field would expand toward a new view of man, always powerfully effected by his physical and social environment, now actively developing an environmental design model and methodology that would place the effect of the total environment on his behavior more in his own control, and the responsibility for the design and control of the environment of his behavior, in himself. (P. 411)

Another description of environmental design that reflects the particular orientation used in this book comes from the description of a program in environmental design appearing in the 1978/80 Bulletin of the School of Architecture and Environmental Design, State University of New York at Buffalo. (The Dean of this school of architecture is Harold L. Cohen, an important influence in the behavioral design movement.)

Environmental Design can be understood as a field of study and action, concerned with the conditions which are necessary to initiate, support, and maintain human activities, as well as with developing the means for intervening in such conditions to bring about the desired change . . . . It is important to clarify here that "environment" is understood as those conditions, both physical and social, in which human beings behave and relate, and that "design" is understood as a process of problem solving, decision making, and implementation to bring about a desired change in some current state of affairs. (P. 46)

The view indicated by Colman and by many others reinforces the belief that the behavioral (environmental, social learning) model of man has broadened within the past decade to the point where it now represents a comprehensive approach to human behavior with major social and political ramifications. We are labeling this expanded version of the behavioral model "environmental design," a term which we find both eloquently simple and sufficiently broad to convey the complexities of the approach.

Using a term such as environmental design may be viewed as a kind of territorial growth for the behavioral model in that there are few fields indeed which do not encompass man's involvement with his environment. Heimstra & McFarling (1974) note that, "The relationship between man and his environment is of interest to individuals in many areas, including architecture, urban and regional planning, civil and sanitary engineering, forest and parks management, geography, biology, sociology, and psychology, to name only a few" (p. 3). Wohlwill (1970) succinctly points out that, "There are few, if any, fields that do not at some point touch on the relationship between man and his environment" (p. 303).

Environmental design represents the application of empirically derived principles of behavior influence to the modification and design of environments (Krasner and Ullmann, 1973). Behavior influence principles and the multitude of behavioral and environmental research provide environmental design with both a data base and a philosophy for intervention.

There is an important point about terminology which must be clarified at this point, and repeatedly throughout the book. Expressions such as "planned societies" or "designed environments" abound. At first glance, these terms may sound as if they signify expert designers or planners creating the perfect society for others. This is not how we are using these terms. If there is any point which is central to the approach being presented here as environmental design, it is that the designing and planning should and must come from the participants of the setting in which the design is taking place. This point will be discussed and emphasized again in many of the subsequent chapters (See particularly Chs. 2, 8, 9, 10, and 16).

Note that we utilized the verbs "must" and "should" in referring to the consumer as the designer. We are well aware that most of the studies which we are describing present an orientation of designing for others. Many of the principles of planning environments have developed from studies in which designers have designed for others. This goes to the heart of issues in education, mental health, urban and utopian planning.

HISTORICAL CONTEXTS

The importance of placing their approach to human behavior in broad social and historical perspective is emphasized by most investigators in the environmental field. Moos (1976a) in his "social ecological" approach to "the human context" offers a very comprehensive and broad framework of seven major trends that underlie the recent upsurge of interest in the environment and its impact on human behavior:

1. A broad historical and geographic perspective that attempts to explain the rise and fall of civilizations. Historians and social philosophers such as Toynbee (1962; Halle, 1977) explain the development of civilizations based on interactions of peoples with environments. Moos cites Toynbee's view that

the environment presents a challenge to which man must

respond. If the challenge is too weak (i.e. the environment is too easy) human potential will remain unfulfilled. If the challenge is excessive, human attempts to cope with it will result in failure and decline. When the challenge is optimal, human beings will be stimulated to new creative heights. The challenge of the environment is a necessary condition for man to grow and to develop higher civilizations. It is the stimulus of the battle that allows people to prove their potential . . . . (Moos, pp. 8-9)

2. The development of ecology and the consequent outgrowth of human and cultural ecology. Darwin's evolutionary perspective was the major influence on the development of the human ecology approach. Ecology is defined as "The science of the relationships between organisms and their environments. Also called 'bionomics' " (American Heritage Dictionary). The "human ecology" movement is traceable to the theories of the Chicago school of Sociologists of the 1920s and 1930s (Park, 1961) who believed that competition for environmental resources was the basis of both animal and human ecology. From these views the human ecology approach evolved into analyses of community structures, social areas (based on census and other demographic figures), and the impact of "culture" as an entity on the usage and interpretation of physical environments. Anthropologists, geographers, and sociologists fit their work into context emphasizing the importance of "cultural ecology."

3. The growing recognition of investigators that environmental factors are major determinants in health and in disease. Nutrition, housing, customs, laws, income, and a multitude of other elements of the social and physical environment are acknowledged as affecting the physical and mental health of individuals. These "new" observations can be traced to comments in the Bible, and to philosophers and physicians of Greece (Hippocrates), Rome, and throughout Western civilization. Fields of public health, social medicine, and psychosomatic medicine are based on recognition of the complex interactions between the environment and the health of the individual. (In chapter 6 of this text, McClure places the relationship between the environment and the mental health of individuals in the historic context of the use of mental hospitals as environments designed for alleviating human problems.)

4. The development and emergence of modern organizations such as governmental, corporate, trade union, and university bureaucracies. Moos presents the concept of a complex organized bureaucracy (developed by theorists such as Max Weber and Karl Marx) as itself being a major environmental influence on the behavior of the individuals who are part of the organization.

5. The development within the field of psychology of a large body of theory and research as to environmental influences in human behavior. Psychology can be examined historically as the struggle between inner and outer (heredity vs. environment, nature vs. nurture) theories for the soul of the professional psychologist. Personality theory (Murray and the concept of environmental "press"), Gestalt psychology (Lewin and field theory), ecological psychology (Brunswick and "probablistic func-

tionalism," Barker and "behavior settings"), and experimental psychology (Pavlov and conditioning theory, Skinner and operant conditioning) illustrate some of the environmentally oriented theories.

6. The emphasis within the architectural and building design professions, by the very nature of their functions, on the importance of the design of the space within built environments on human behavior. The philosophy of functionalism ("form follows function") is central to modern architecture. Architectural philosophers such as Gropius, Le Corbusier, Kirkbridge, and Fuller have had influence not only on the construction of buildings, but on the way in which the organization of space affects human behavior. (McClure in chapter 6 details the influence of Kirkbridge on the function of mental hospitals, and Van Wagenberg in chapter 11 describes architectural influences on the classroom.)

7. The recent interest in conservation and the "quality of life" which has become the basis for the ecology movement. Resource depletion, pollution, and population growth are examples of the kinds of environmental concerns which increasingly come to the fore in research, the media, and in publications. Moos credits Rachel Carson's Silent Spring, (1962), as being of seminal importance in arousing public awareness of the consequences of environmental pollution.

These seven trends offer a reasonable, broad and comprehensive framework within which to develop a social ecological approach to the environmental determinants of human behavior.

These seven broad trends, identified by Moos within the developments of western civilization, American society, and the behavioral sciences, offer a reasonable and comprehensive context into which the environmental design approach may be placed.

STREAMS OF DEVELOPMENT

Almost every new approach to human behavior has antecedents that can be traced back to antiquity.

We view environmental design, in the late 1970s, as the melding or confluence of a number of streams of development among professional investigators (both researchers and practitioners) in psychology, psychiatry, architecture, and the social and behavioral sciences.

Behavior Modification

A definition of our main label of "environmental design" has purposely been avoided. Rather, the streams of research and application in the "helping" or "behavior change" professions that have influenced the concept will be described. The first, and perhaps the most influential, is the "behavioral" stream. In the 1950s and 1960s, 15 streams of development in research and application merged to form an uneasy alliance called "behavior modification" or "behavior therapy" (Krasner, 1971). These streams may be briefly summarized as follows:

- The concept of "behaviorism" in experimental psychology, e.g. J.R. Kantor, (1924, 1963);

- The instrument (operant) conditioning concepts of Thorndike (1931) and Skinner (1938);

- The technique of reciprocal inhibition as developed by Wolpe (1958);

- The studies of the group of investigators at Maudsley Hospital in London under the direction of H.J. Eysenck (1960, 1964);

- The investigations (From the 1920s through the 1940s) applying "conditioning" concepts to human behavior problems in the United States (e.g. Watson & Rayner, 1920, Mowrer & Mowrer, 1938);

- Interpretations of psychoanalysis in learning theory terms (e.g. Dollard & Miller, 1950) enhancing learning theory as a respectable base for clinical work;

- Classical conditioning as the basis for explaining and changing normal and deviant behavior (Pavlov, 1928);

- Theoretical concepts and research studies of social role learning and "interactionism," social psychology and sociology;

- Research in developmental and child psychology emphasizing vicarious learning and "modeling" (Jones, 1924; Bandura, 1970);

- Social influence studies of demand characteristics, experimenter bias, hypnosis, and placebo, (Frank, 1961, 1973);

- An environmental social learning model as an alternative to a "disease" model of human behavior (Ullmann and Krasner, 1965; Bandura, 1969);

- Dissatisfaction with psychotherapy and the psychoanalytic model;

- The development of the clinical psychologist as scientist-practitioner;

- A group of psychiatrists emphasizing human interaction (e.g. Adolph Meyer, 1948, Harry Stack Sullivan, 1953);

- A Utopian stream emphasizing the planning of social environments to elicit and maintain the best of man's behavior (e.g., Skinner's Walden Two).

These streams, of course, were not independent of each other and were continually in the process of interacting and developing. The elements of the belief system common to behavior modification adherents include: the statement of concepts so that they can be tested experimentally; the notion of the "laboratory" as ranging from animal mazes through basic human learning studies to hospitals, schoolrooms, homes, and the community; research as treatment – and treatment as research; an explicit strategy of therapy or change.

> The unifying factor in behavior therapy is its basis in derivation from experimentally established procedures and principles. The specific experimentation varies widely but has in common all of the attributes of scientific investigation including control of variables, presentation of data, replicability, and a probabilistic view of behavior. (Krasner, 1971, pp. 457-488)

There are many techniques that derive from behavior modification and they are constantly being expanded and revised. There are now a plethora of excellent textbooks that describe these current techniques and rationale (e.g., Gambrill, 1977; Kanfer & Phillips, 1969; Leitenberg, 1976; O'Leary & Wilson, 1976; Rimm & Masters, 1974).

The most important of these techniques in terms of implications for environmental design are operant conditioning, modeling, and the application of reinforcement and training principles in the form of token economies. This latter procedure, token economy, as eventually applied in classrooms and hospitals, derives from the behavior modification streams of operant conditioning and utopian planning (Ayllon & Azrin, 1968; Atthowe and Krasner, 1968; Skinner, 1948; Kazdin, 1977).

Krasner (1968) has noted that "token economy procedures need a combination of social and economic planning. When an economist (for example Galbraith, 1967) relates a 'general theory of motivation' to the economic structure of society, he is presenting hypotheses that can be tested in small social units, such as hospital wards, by means of a token economy. The research potential of the application of behavioral principles to social affairs is enormous . . ." (p. 160).

A linkage has been growing between economic theorists and behaviorists influenced by token economy research. The pioneering work comes from Winkler's (1971, 1973) dissertation studies at New South Wales which developed from within the behavior modification approach. Psychologists have been developing research programs in conjunction with economists involving ramifications of token economy research (Battalio et al. 1973, 1974; Fisher et al, in press; Kagel, 1972, Kagel & Winkler, 1972). Rachlin's (1976) research with animal behavior has also provided great impetus to the linkage of economic theory with behavior theory.

As the token economy programs have expanded into the realm of testing economic theory, they have become an important precursor to environmental design of large social units. They represent a good illustration of how procedures which started as modification behavior of bar pressing rats expanded further and further into the natural environment.

Behavior modifications in the natural environment

Although there were many hints that foreshadowed this development, it was in the early 1970s that the self-identified behaviorists emerged from the laboratory, the clinic, and the mental hospital to the "natural" social environment guided both by earlier applications of behavioral principles in schoolrooms and hospitals and by the national concerns and debates on the social issues of the 1960s. A new generation of behaviorists began to take on the total natural and manmade environment as the focus for investigation and social change with a purpose – namely, a better environment for members of society.

For example, Nietzel et al. (1977) in a chapter on "environmental problems" (in a book appropriately entitled, Behavioral approaches to Community Psychology) cover the topics of: "litter control, recycling, energy conservation, transportation, architectural design and population change" (p. 310). Of immediate interest here is not so much the specifics of research in these areas, which will be discussed subsequently (below and in chapter 3) but rather the context in which Nietzel and his group place this material. They start their chapter with a quote from Fairweather (1972) who, in part, states that ". . . population growth . . . environmental degradation. . . and human relations crises face man today. He must solve these problems if he is to survive in a liveable environment. He must also find ways of aiding society to adopt the solutions found.   Such problem-solving action requires basic social change" (p. 1).

Nietzel et al. use the Fairweather comments to emphasize "the urgency of finding solutions to these problems" and to accentuate the view that "the amelioration of conditions which degrade the environment may have more to do with maintaining and improving the quality of our life and 'mental health' than much of the current work conducted under the rubric of mental health" (p. 310).

Here, indeed, is a new theme being stated explicitly by the behaviorists; the urgency of the solution of environmental problems of our society and the belief that the behaviorists may have the skill to contribute to the solution. We will return to the question of the goals and values of behavior modifications and environmental design, but at this point we note some behavioral studies as they are applied to solving environmental problems.

Attempts to influence littering behavior has been the first systematic research of the behaviorist in the environmental area and these have become prototypical of later extensions to other environmental problems.   Such studies have generally emphasized either prevention of littering by investigating antecedent events or more generally have focused on reinforcing litter removal. Nietzel et al. (1977) and Cone and Hayes (in press) offer excellent reviews of the basic studies in this area (e.g., those of Burgess, Clark, and Hendee, 1971; Geller, 1973; Kohlenberg and Phillips, 1973; Marler, 1970, and many others).

The related area of recycling (a specific and important aspect of the proper disposal of litter) has also been systematically investigated by the behavior analysis group. Nietzel et al. (1977) confidently conclude that

the research on littering and recycling has focused on procedures that are simple, inexpensive, and can be applied on neighborhood and community levels. Their successful dissemination . . . will depend on both economic considerations and the skillful use of the media to promote such programs. The next step likely will involve the development of more powerful reinforcers and the demonstration that a large-scale environmental protection program can be implemented and supported by communities. (p. 326)

Design stream

Within behavior modification itself there has been an important set of influences from several investigators which warrant the description of "the design stream." Two of the most innovative influencers in the development of behavior modification in the 1950s and 1960s were Harold Cohen and Israel Goldiamond. Both were students at the Chicago School of Design in the late 1940s. The school had been founded on Bauhaus principles. Cohen's description of his peregrinations and future views symbolize the confluences of behavioral with architectural concepts:

Being a hybrid organism, the last three decades have taken me from being a student at the old Institute of Design, through product design, design education, behavioral psychology, environmental psychiatry, and into behavioral architecture. I have taught all forms of behavioral design, both undergraduate and graduate, to design students, psychologists, psychiatrists, social workers and teachers. Presently I administer and teach a new crop of environmental designers, planners and architects in Buffalo, New York. Lazlo Moholy Nagy said, 'Design is not a profession, but an attitude.' Although it may appear that I have changed professions many times, it has only been topographical; for I have always maintained a strong behavioral approach in all my activities. . . Thirteen years ago, almost to the month, I wrote an article for the Architectural Association Journal in London which I called, 'Behavioral Architecture.' (1976)

Goldiamond succinctly summarizes the approach of this group to the design process. "Analyze human behavior regarding object, design it to fit, and also be aesthetic" (1976, p. 142).

Another important influence on the ideas of behavior analysis was Buckminster Fuller, the noted designer, who was a major consultant to the Institute for Behavioral Research, one of the first organizations devoted entirely to behavior research in the early 1950s. Psychologists such as Skinner, Ferster, and Goldiamond, all involved with IBR, interacted with Fuller and mutually influenced each other on concepts of space usage.

Behaviorally engineered environments

One behavioral stream has maintained the approach of the investigators (therapist, "expert") planning, designing, engineering environments for others. In most instances, the "others" are individuals considered unlikely or unable to plan their environment, such as the severely autistic. The Upper Midwest Regional Laboratory (U.M.R.E.L.) has developed "behavioral engineered educational environments" for a wide range of children in a systematic application of behavior analysis to education. They have been particularly influenced by the reinforcement principles developed by Premack (1965) that became the basis for "contingency management techniques" and the development of training programs for teachers (described as "multi-faceted behaviorally engineered and environmentally oriented educational systems").

Brady (1974) uses the term "environmental design" to refer to the research of his colleagues and himself in the setting of 5 designed rooms (at Phipps Clinic of Johns Hopkins School of Medicine). Brady's research links behaviorally engineered or designed environments with broad environmental/behavioral concepts. As Brady describes it:

> A research environment has been designed and constructed for the experimental study of individual and social behavior over extended time periods within the context of a self-contained laboratory programmed for continuous residence by a small group of human volunteers. The environment is composed of several individual living units, a larger social living unit, and a work shop unit. Environmental-behavioral interactions are programmed by contingently scheduled sequential and optional activities, and instrumental measurement techniques provide for both quantitative and qualitative evaluations of adjustment and performance effectiveness. The focus of this laboratory research is upon the experimental analysis of human social interactions as they are related to environmental-behavioral program design factors in the establishment and maintenance of optimal group functioning. (P. 187)

Brady's approach has been influenced by earlier work in the behavioral movement which has attempted to design controlled environments to systematically determine the relationship between environmental influences and human behavior, particularly token economy work (Ayllon and Azrin, 1968), Programmed Environments, (Findley 1966) and "Learning Environments" (Cohen, 1976).

> Perhaps the most significant feature of this research approach to the analysis of social behavior is the high degree of experimental control which is derived from the combined application of environmental design and behavioral programming principles. At least four elements of the laboratory setting as presently designed appear to represent the salient features contributing to such experimental control: 1) functional separation from the

external environment; 2) remote control design of environmental facilities; 3) subdivision of the behavioral repertoire into functional activity units; and 4) sequential scheduling of integrated environmental-behavioral interactions. The resulting experimental methodology promises to provide for a more rigorous analysis of environmental design and behavioral programming as such factors interact to influence human social functioning. (Brady, et al., 1974, p. 207)

The approach of Brady and his colleagues can be contrasted with the less controlled methodology (and somewhat different concept of "control") of investigators from the ecological-environmental stream to be described in the next section whose emphasis is on observations of man-environment relationships in "natural settings."

Human factors

H.M. Parsons, at the Institute for Behavioral Research, offers a course on "Environmental Design: Effects of Environment on Behavior" that covers methodology, residential structures, institutional structures, criminal justice, commercial structures, unusual environments, macro-environments, and environment-dependent behavior. This human factors approach derives from "behavior analysis" and has been influential in training designers of environments.

Systems analysis

Still another stream in the evolution of a broad environmental design approach involves recent linkages between "behavior analyses" and "systems analyses" particularly as they intersect at the concept of accountability. Behaviorists such as Krapfl, Noah & Maley (1975) present a unified field of "behavioral systems analyses." They attempt to expand the notion of control of behavior to include all aspects of an organizational system. They emphasize the reciprocal controlling relationships that exist among the components of systems. They view the application of behavioral technology to broad-scale social problems and to the delivery of human services as clearly involving highly complex environments (Harshbarger and Maley, 1974).

Environmental and Ecological Psychology

Environmental psychology (Proshansky et al., 1970; Sommer, 1959) and ecological psychology (Barker, 1968) represent a major stream of investigation merging into the environmental design approach. Although not synonymous, both of these fields are concerned with the influence of physical and social settings on behavior. Some investigators in these fields may focus on the physical, others on the social, many on both.

The systematic application of architectural space to affect behavior also falls within this stream.

The roots of environmental psychology lie in social, experimental, and clinical psychology; and the major influencers, with quite diverse backgrounds, are people such as Wohlwill, Craik, Moos, Proshansky, Altman, and Sommer. A major impetus to this field was the 1966 issue of the Journal of Social Issues on "Man's response to the Physical Environment." The paper by Studer and Stea in that issue linked the notions of environmental design and architectural programming.

Altman (1973) offers four major models of man that have influenced the work of the environmental psychologist. These are the mechanistic; perceptual-cognitive-motivational; the behavioral; and the "social systems ecological." These models indicate the scope of current environmental psychology and its linkage with the other fields and approaches described in this and other chapters in this volume.

As with other fields, environmental psychology may be conceptualized in three aspects: theoretical (as represented by books which offer a label to the field, e.g., Environmental Psychology, edited by Proshansky, Ittelson, and Rivlin in 1970); research (e.g., Proshansky, 1972, on mental hospitals); and organizational/training (e.g. graduate training programs in environmental/ecological psychology at such institutions as City University of New York, University of California at Irvine, Pennsylvania State University, Michigan State University, and others).

Proshansky's (1976) paper on "Environmental psychology and the real world," presents a description of his own personal development and identity as well as specific suggestions for the "methodological requirements" of an environmental psychology which preserves the "integrity of person/physical-setting events" (p. 306).

Ittelson et al. (1974) represents the viewpoints of the environmental psychologists:

> It should be clear that environmental psychology is not a theory of determinism. It sees man not as a passive product of his environment, but as a goal-directed being who acts upon his environment and who in turn is influenced by it. In changing his world, man changes himself. A guiding principle in this field is what we have called the dynamic interchange between man and his milieu. The traditional conception of a fixed environment to which organisms must adapt or perish is replaced by the ecological view that emphasizes the organism's role in creating its own environment. (P. 5)

Ittelson et al. present environmental psychology as involving elements such as "interactionism," the study of natural environments, multidisciplinary dealings with social problems, and a humanistic value orientation.

A book edited by Craik & Zube (1976), Perceiving Environmental Quality, examines the role "environmental perception" plays in a comprehensive system of indexes for assessing and monitoring trends in environmental quality. (Perception is one concept which behaviorists initially deemphasized or ignored although later developments have brought back an interest in "cognitive processes" such as perception.) Ittelson, Proshansky, and their collaborators stress the impact and meaning of art and literature for environmental theory, thus broadening the scope of such a theory.

Stokols (1978) offers a concise and comprehensive integration of the field of environmental psychology:

> First, the interdisciplinary and problem-oriented nature of the field has fostered a high degree of methodological eclecticism . . . Second, environment-behavioral research reflects an increasing emphasis on the assessment of ecological validity, or the extent to which phenomena studied in one situation are representative of those occurring in other settings . . . Third, in their efforts to integrate diverse theoretical perspectives, researchers in the environment-and-behavior field have increasingly combined existing psychological theories of cognitive development, personality, interpersonal processes and human learning with the assumptions of systems theory . . . Fourth, increasing attention has been paid to the importance of psychological or "perceived" control over the environment and behavioral freedom as determinants of human well-being . . . Fifth, the concept of "behavior-environment congruence" is becoming increasingly important as a theoretical and environmental design tool.
>
> Currently, environmental psychology is comprised of several diverse research areas which vary widely in their respective positions along the theoretical vs. applied continuum, their conceptualizations of the environment, and their emphasis on alternative modes of human-environment interchange. (Pp. 256-57)

Thus, we see a picture of a field that is in the stage of rapid growth characterized by a range of theoretical eclecticism, confusion, controversy, and enormous potential for influencing change in the behavior of those professionally involved in "environmental design" as well as change in the broader society with which these professionals deal. (Pomeranz will extend the discussion of the environmental psychology field in chapter 3 of this text.)

We would tend to agree with Stokols' conclusions about the present status of environmental psychology, which in some ways summarize the trends we will be observing throughout this volume:

> Though the major research areas of the field are rooted in diverse theoretical traditions and emphasize different modes of human-environment transaction, a number of linkages among these areas have been drawn. Such linkages are evident in the combination of behavior setting analysis with the concerns of environmental assessment; the analysis of personality variables as they mediate proxemic behavior and the intensity of stress

reactions; and the combined use of cognitive and behavioral mapping strategies in studies of human response to the physical environment. As for the future, several of the most exciting and promising opportunities for research can be found at the interface of the major substantive areas of the field (e.g. the further integration of ecological and operant perspectives on the analysis of environmentally relevant behavior). (p. 278) (See also chaps. 4,5,9, and 10 this volume.)

In a comprehensive review of the field of environmental psychology, Stokols (1978) sees certain common assumptions or themes which could eventually provide the basis for a more general theory of behavior and environment. "One such theme is the transactional or bi-directional nature of human-environment relations. . . . Transactional views suggest that any attempt to conceptualize the relationship between environment and behavior must account not only for the effects of the environment on people, but also for the reciprocal impact of people on their milieu" (see Chapters 3 and 4 for further discussion).

Altman (1973) views the environmental psychology field as continuing to be characterized by "theoretical, methodological, and substantive diversity, confusion, and controversy." Craik (1973) succinctly summarized the theoretical situation in this field as involving an array of multiple scientific paradigms rather than a conceptually coherent perspective on behavior-environment relations.

Dimensions of environmental assessment

Moos (1974) reviews the dimensions involved in the assessment of social environments in different types of organizations such as elementary schools and psychiatric wards. He describes six "domains" or types of dimensions by which characteristics of environments have been related to indexes of human functions:

1. Ecological dimensions (including geographical, meteorological, and architectural) and physical design variables. The economy of a society, for example, may be affected by environmental characteristics, e.g., terrain (Barry, Child & Bacon, 1959); or geographical influences (Huntington, 1911). Climate is associated with gross national product and indexes of interpersonal and organizational behavior (Russett et al., 1964; Griffitt and Veitch, 1971; Michelson, 1970).

It is clear that human beings increasingly can influence the creation of their own geographic and meteorologic environment. Many of the current ecological impact controversies in our society – such as the SST (Concorde), environmental pollution, use of aerosol cans, energy, pollution, and location of nuclear plants – recognize the impact relationship between man and his environment.

Moos illustrates the use of the following research techniques: behavioral mapping; measures of behavior density; diffuseness; and activity profiles; behavioral measures of work efficiency, comfort, social interaction, interpersonal perception, and exploratory behavior;

environmental description scales (Kasmar, 1970); and large scale planned residential environments along a variety of dimensions (e.g., the work at Reston and Columbia).

2. Behavior settings. A behavior setting is a complex interdependent combination of behavior and milieu. As Barker (1968) reports, "We found, in short, that we could predict some aspects of children's behavior more adequately from knowledge of the behavior character-istics of the drugstores, arithmetic classes, and basketball games they inhabited than from knowledge of the behavior tendencies of particular children."

Barker's behavioral setting concepts are a source of ideas and techniques in observation of behavior in natural or ecological settings. He is also a source of influence, particularly on environmental psychologists such as Wicker (1973) whose concept of "overmanning" offers a linkage of ecological psychology and research on excess population effects.

Patterson moves beyond Barker although citing him as an influence in attempting to identify stimuli in the natural environment. His article on a basis for identifying stimuli which control behaviors in natural settings (1974) describes a methodology of training children and their families to use a coding system of stimuli controlling the interactions.

3. Dimensions of organizational structure. Organizations are assessed on objective dimensions such as size, staffing ratios, salary levels, organizational control structures, population density, and crowd-ing. Such an approach opens the way to a systematic analysis of organizational structure variables.

4. Personal and behavioral characteristics of the milieu inhabitants. Sells (1963) was one of the first to argue that "human aggregate" factors related to the characteristics of individuals (e.g., age, ability level, socioeconomic and educational background) in a particular environment may be considered situational variables; they partly define relevant characteristics of the environment. This point was illustrated by Astin (1968) with an Inventory of College Activities which found that different college environments (based on assessment of these "human aggregate" factors) influence behavior differentially.

5. Psychosocial characteristics and organizational climate. These assessments involve naturalistic descriptions of functioning of different institutions and analyses of organizations along certain dimensions — objective organizational structure dimensions of psychosocial "event-structure" dimensions (e.g., Stern, 1970, talks of environmental "presses"). Moos and his colleagues have studied nine different social environments and have developed a "perceived climate" scale for each: wards; community programs; correctional institutions; military; univ-ersity residences; junior and senior high school classes; social and therapy groups; work milieus; and families.

6. Functional reinforcement analyses of environments. Such assess-ments involve analyses of environments in terms of potential reinforc-ing properties and, thus, clearly link with behavior modification. Illustrations of such analyses are given throughout the behavior modification literature (e.g. token economy).

Moos emphasizes that the six domains listed above are nonexclusive, overlapping, and mutually interrelated. Although we have included these assessment categories within the "environmental" stream, they could just as well have been integrated into the research developments of virtually each of the streams we are describing as belonging within the environmental design rubric.

BEHAVIORAL AND ECOLOGICAL PSYCHOLOGY – A CLOSE RELATIONSHIP?

We have been noting an increasing tendency for an association and interaction between investigators in the behavioral and in the environmental stream. However, there are considerable complexities and, some even suggest, possibly negative consequences to such linkage. The most comprehensive discussion of the issues involved is offered by Rogers-Warren & Warren (1977) in their volume based on the continuing debate and mutual theoretical criticism between self identified ecologists such as Willems (1974) and behavior analysts such as Baer (1974).

A marriage metaphor introduced by Rogers-Warren & Warren opened the door to romantic speculations about the influence process between ecologists and behavior analysts and, perhaps, also communicated the realities of scientific movements.

The "marriage" may have been one of necessity, rather than the culmination of a long, romantic courtship. Behavior analysts admittedly were having difficulties with the environmental aspects of behavior change procedures, and were becoming increasingly aware of the need to consider both the target subject and the setting when formulating interventions. A behavioral ecology was imminent with, or without, a formal union . . . The behavior analysts set forth to specify a marriage contract that would be congruent with their therapeutic objectives and empirical methods. The ecologists, while willing to contribute to the behavioral technology, rightfully demanded recognition for their contribution as describers of natural ecologies and behavior. There were numerous problems of role definition, determining responsibilities for both partners, and selecting a new name (ecobehavioral) to represent the interests of both parties. And of course, there were objections to such a hasty union. (P. IX-X)

Krantz (1977), integrating and reacting to the various positions presented in the Rogers-Warren & Warren collection, expresses concern with what he sees as very real differences between the two movements in the use of the concept "environment" in the theoretical streams from which the two movements evolved (Gestalt-Lewinian versus Behavioral-Skinnerian), and in the theoretical methodology utilized (which Krantz categorizes, perhaps oversimplifying, as "descriptive" design versus "manipulative" design).

I am afraid that I have some concerns about the proposed wedding between ecological psychology and applied behavioral analysis. At times, I wonder whether we are witnessing a marriage, with a sharing between two partners, or an agreed upon rape with applied behavior analysis in the dominating role. (P. 233)

Krantz further questions the desirability of a wedding of these two approaches in that it "could lead to a weakness of both theoretical perspectives. Such a strategy would diffuse the potential confrontation of systems, which in their disharmony could force a clarification and an extension of each" (p. 236).

Krantz concludes that, "I feel that the proposed wedding of ecological psychology and applied behavior analysis could benefit from some premarital counseling to determine if the partners are compatible and if there is any real benefit to their union. Marriage is a holy and sacred institution that should not be entered into lightly" (p. 237).

Other investigators have also attempted to systematically link behavior analysis and the environmental ecological stream. Marston (1977) argues that behavior modification is ready to expand its theoretical and professional base to one which can be described as behavioral ecology. At each operation, from individual therapy to broad social applications, behavioral change involves complex rearrangements in the systems surrounding the focal behavior. Marston, working from a behavioral analysis base offers an interactive model which broadens the base for the behavioral position by incorporating some of the basic ecological viewpoints.

Hursh (1976) views the interface between environmental design and applied behavior analysis in terms of a "complementary relationship between the shaping of human behavior and the shaping of spaces wherein much of that behavior occurs" (p. 1).

In this chapter we are observing the convergence of a number of streams of development into more general environmental design. We have noted that there are considerable complexities and concern about the linkage of two of the major streams we have been discussing. At this point, we note that within the environmental stream there has been a focus on assessment particularly, as one might expect, of environmental variables. A discussion of how an environmentally-oriented investigator conceptualizes the dimensions of the social environment puts this approach into further perspective, and emphasizes its role in developing environmental design.

OTHER STREAMS OF INFLUENCE

At this point, a series of other streams of influence on the evolving concept of environmental design will be briefly noted. These will be expanded upon and further explicated in later chapters. We emphasize the continual interaction and mutual influence between investigators in each of these streams.

The broad context of the influence process involved is illustrated in a paper by Wheater (1975). The author is a librarian analyzing the field of environmental design with its implications for libraries. If, indeed, a new field is emerging, then it is encumbent upon libraries to recognize and appropriately classify material in the field; that is the function of his paper. Wheater proceeds to link architecture, urban planning, and environmental studies as interdisciplinary studies of the environment, part of the "planning and organization of all aspects of the built and natural environment for human ends" (p. 7).

Population Stream

There has been a considerable growth in the study of populations and the relationship between growth of aggregates and their influence on various human behaviors such as disease, poverty, war, death, nutritional patterns, hygiene, recreation, etc. (McKeown, 1976; Academic material presented since 1965 in the journal, Population Studies; Gove et al., 1975)

Demography is the field involved with the systematic study of population. Hauser & Duncan (1959) offer the following widely accepted definition of demography:

> Demography is the study of the size, territorial distribution, and composition of population, changes therein, and the components of such changes, which may be identified as natality, mortality, territorial movement (migration), and social mobility (change of status). (P. 2)

Schnore (1975), working at the Center for Demography and Ecology of the University of Wisconsin, illustrates the growing convergence of research linking population theories and social change. He argues for the salience of demographic thinking for the study of social evolution. Schnore concludes that, because the interconnections between demography and behavior change are so numerous and diverse, "it is the mutual responsibility of demographers and sociologists – not to speak of economists, political scientists, geographers and historians – to undertake the intensive explorations that these fascinating relationships so richly deserve" (p. 51).

Non-Verbal Communication

Another stream of research linking with environmental design is that of non-verbal communication (the use of the initials NVC is an indication of the arrival and acceptance of a new field). In fact, NVC has become a field unto itself with investigators coming in from diverse areas (e.g., the Newsletter of Man-Environment Society, see Appendix, has a section on NVC edited by Robert Deutsch). Deutsch points out (1976) that NVC is still in its infancy and is being hampered by "the lack of a generally accepted framework and methodology." Hence the bits of data collected "often seem to be contradictory or irrelevent to each other."

Birdwhistele (1970) and Goffman (1961) are considered the major influencers on NVC. Deutsch talks of "such behavioral structures as territoriality, dominance hierarchy, courtship, and the regulation of these by nonverbal means." These areas are approached by ethology from a biological/evolutionary point of view. Deutsch emphasizes that "methodologically, ethology stresses systematic observation of naturally occurring behavior. Ethnomethodology seeks to provide accounts of the social order in terms of the procedures participants use to produce social order." This sounds very much like the influence process in the somewhat looser terms of ethnology. The NVC people do use broader units of behavior as functions of environmental contingencies and influences.

Ecology as a Discipline

A major aim of this book is to offer the term environmental design as an integrative concept which can be utilized by investigators in a number of different disciplines such as psychology, sociology, architecture, etc. However, we are living in a period in which there are a number of theoretical concepts (paradigms?) vying for the privilege of super concept. For example, Odum (1977) offers cogent, and logical arguments for the emergence of ecology as a new integrative discipline." Odum argues that science must be both "reductionist" – in trying to understand phenomena by a detailed study of small components – and holistic in trying to understand large components as functional wholes.

> A human being, for example, is not only a hierarchical system composed of organs, cells, enzyme systems, and genes as subsystems, but is also a component of supraindividual hierarchical systems such as populations, cultural systems, and ecosystems. (P. 1289)

Odum emphasizes that the concept of ecology is frequently misused as synonymous with environment. As he uses ecology, it includes man as a part of rather than apart from his natural surroundings. Odum argues that ecology is "a new integrative discipline that deals with the supraindividual levels of organization" rather than as an interdisciplinary concept.

Our tendency is to agree with Odum's emphasis on the interaction between man and his environment in holistic systems, but to disagree with the need for a new discipline. The impression which we have been emphasizing in this chapter is that almost all of the current disciplines are increasingly cognizant of the need to move their efforts in this direction and much of the work we are citing is evidence of this shift. This holistic and naturalistic development is likely to be enhanced by the usual struggles between ideas and ideologies within disciplines rather than by the emergence of a new supradiscipline.

A further usage of "ecology" as a generic term is offered by Michaels (1974) who attempts to systematically link human ecology with behavioral social psychology and behavioral sociology. For Michaels, human ecology involves the study of a population's collective inter-action with its environment. The operant conditioner and the human ecologist both recognize the interaction between behavior and environment, and the need for quantitative and longitudinal analyses.

The Physical Environment

The physical environment has been linked with the broad topic of "mental health." Esser & Deutsch (1975) systematically reviewed the literature in 1974 and arrived at a bibliography of 250 items. For our purposes, the categories used by these authors are of importance in that they denote the general trends in research and delineate the aspects of the environment which influence "mental health." These categories are: physical and chemical pollutants (lead, mercury, insecticide, and air pollution); extremes of sensory stimulation (noise, lighting, microwave, special environments, weather, and geophysical conditions); ecological change (disaster, migration, and acculturation); media influence; and, rational and irrational factors in the design and use of man-built environments.

The Built Environment

Ittelson et al. (1974) offer a fine review of the impact of urban areas on behavior in a chapter appropriately labeled "The City as an Unnatural Habitat." The architectural stream of systematically investigating the impact of built environments on individual behavior is expressed in a number of different models and languages (e.g. Taylor, 1975, and architectural psychology, see chap. 11, this volume).

In 1971, the Philadelphia chapter of the American Institute of Architects and other groups organized a conference on Architecture for Human Behavior: "It was apparently the first conference in this country which sought to bring some understanding of environmental design research to a community of building users and practicing architects as well as to students and draftsmen who are typically unable to afford such learning experiences" (Lan et al., 1971, p. vii). Participants in the conference represented the linkages between psychology and architectural design, and included investigators such as Lawton (Institute of Geriatrics); Proshansky (environmental psychology); Stea (cognitive mapping); Lecompte (a colleague of Barker); Sommer (personal space); Hall (artificial environments); and Patterson (unobstrusive measures).

Environmental Education

A stream of influence derives from the intermixture of scientific ideas with federal funding. We see this in the growth of environmental education initiated by the environmental concerns of the 1960s culminating in the Federal Environmental Education Act of 1970.

The Conservation Education Advisory Committee, in their 1969 Report to the California State Board of Education, used the term conservation education, but expanded its meaning to include broad environmental concerns. In 1970, the Legislature wrote this term into the Education Code, based on the language of the Advisory Committee Report. In 1972, the Conservation Education Advisory Committee recommended to the Department of Education that steps be taken to adopt the term environmental education in an effort to bring state terminology into line with the federal act and in recognition of the general acceptance by the field.

In the Environmental Education Act of 1970 (Public Law 91-516), environmental education is defined as "the educational process dealing with man's relationship with his natural and man-made surrounding, and includes the relation of population, pollution, resource allocation and depletion, conservation, transportation, technology, and urban and rural planning to the total human environment."

Ekistics

The concept of ekistics warrants listing as a separate stream although it, like the others, interacts with and overlaps several other approaches.

Ekistics is defined in the World Book Dictionary (1970) as the study of the ecology of human beings in settlements or communities. The term is often associated with Constantine Doxiadis, a city planner and president of the Institute for the Study of Ekistics in Athens, Greece, but he does not claim to have originated it. The Athens Center of Ekistics was established in 1963 to further research and to foster international cooperation in all fields related to the science of human settlements. The thinking involved in this approach is evidenced by the following introduction to the manual on "Ekistics: A Guide for the Development of an Interdisciplinary Environmental Education Curriculum" :

"For the environment of man is no longer solely the land, sea, and air. Man has made his environment as wide as the cultures which comprise the family of man. Indeed, man's concept of environment is larger than the biological concept of earth, the physical concept of world. Man now needs a larger mind to encompass this new concept of his environment. The cultivation of this larger mind is the function of education." The authors propose the use of the term ekistics which is defined as that field of study, that area of knowledge, and those concepts and values through which man recognizes his interdependence with the environment as well as his responsibility for maintaining a culture that will sustain a healthy and sensitive environment.

Environmental Sociology

Zeisel (1975) reviews what he terms the "new speciality of environmental sociology," the application of social research to architectural design. He observes the increasing attention social scientists focus on the physical environment. He emphasizes the linkages of this current approach with the classic founders of sociology such as Robert Park (1952) and the Chicago School of Sociology, Max Weber (1958) and Georg Simmel (1950), all three of whom had investigated the impact of physical environment on behavior in urban settings.

Two more recent reports by sociologists have extended the earlier work (with its primary emphasis on the physical environment) to the influence of the social environment, and have made major contributions to the emerging environmental sociology field. Michelson in his Man and his Urban Environment (1970) summarized much of the environmental research through 1969. His theoretical model reflected Talcott Parsons' concept of society as being made up of interacting cultural, social, personality, and environmental systems. Robert Gutman in his People and Buildings (1972) structured the field of environmental sociology into 5 major areas: human characteristics necessitating specific requirements to be met in building design; the impact of spatial organization on social interaction; the impact of the environment on physical and mental health; architecture as the expression of social values and cultural patterns; and the use of social science ideas and approaches by designers.

Behavioral Sociology

Another integrative stream is that of behavioral sociology symbolized by a text with that name (1969) edited by Burgess, a sociologist, and Bushell, a psychologist with the Human Development group at Kansas. The editors point out that,

> Behavior analysis is also attracting a growing number of researchers who are sociologists by background and credentials. Twelve of the eighteen contributions to the present collection were written by card-carrying sociologists. These men have found that the orientation and methodologies of the experimental analysis are well suited to the examination of some basic sociological problems. (P. viii)

The general viewpoint of these investigators was expressed by George Homans, a major sociologist influencer:

> My contention is that the propositions of behavioral psychology are the general explanatory propositions not only of sociology but also of all the social sciences . . . I have argued that all existing social behavior is a precipitate of a process of social change, and that the explanation of any social change requires psychological

propositions. (Pp. 13, 20, Homans, 1969)

Utopian or Social Planning Literature and Experience

From Plato's Republic to Thomas More's Utopia to Skinner's Walden Two, men have had visions of ideal societies, either as something impossible, or something that would eventually occur as a natural end result of progress, or as a detailed criticism of current practice and proposal for changes. A related literature of dystopia (1984, Brave New World) projects the disastrous probable or possible future results of current trends. Finally there are the actual experiences of past (e.g. Oneida) and present (Twin Oaks, Children's Village) efforts toward creating ideal communities. This stream of influence provides a sampling of men's ideas of what an ideal society is like, what changes might be made to achieve it, and how well the ideas work in practice.

As indicated in an earlier section, Krasner (1971) argued that the history of behavior therapy included a utopian stream which involved "an ethical concern for the social implications of behavior control, as well as offering blueprints for a better life such as Skinner's Walden Two. This stream can, of course, be traced from Plato's Republic to the setting up of a token economy of a psychiatric ward or in a community setting" (p. 491). Our current view is that the concept of utopia is virtually synonymous with all human efforts to plan or design environments to increase the possibility of a better life.

A systematic study of the concept and history of utopias is reemerging within a number of fields, including psychology. Krasner and Ullmann (1973), in offering a behavior influence approach to human behavior, include a chapter on utopias within the rubric of "planned societies: people controlling their own destinies." They view the designing of utopias as phenomena that do not differ from ordinary living. "Just as there is no dichotomy between personality and behavior, between normal and abnormal, between hypnosis and behavior influence, there is no dichotomy between utopian life and other forms of social learning" (p. 648).

Moos (1976), one of the most systematic investigators of environ-mental attributes, offers an analysis of utopians in terms of the systematic variables (organizational structure, behavior settings, pop-ulations, social climates, etc.) with which environmental psychologists now focus their techniques of analysis. Moos and Brownstein (1977) extend the analyses of environments and utopias to the Oneida community, Israel Kibbutzim, the new town of Columbia, Maryland, and, of course, the ubiquitous Walden Two. These authors offer a synthesis of environmental and utopian perspectives.

Callenbach's Ecotopia (1975) is an illustration of a combination of a utopian novel, political tract, and statement of environmental concerns. There are newspaper reports that it has become the basis of a political movement and a model for planned communes. If so, it would represent the latest in a long line of utopian writing that has influenced the designing of environments.

The integrating of the concept of utopia with all of its ramifications into the mainstream of psychology, sociology, architecture, and other disciplines is a recurring phenomenon. We are currently witnessing an upsurge as manifested by a growing literature (e.g., see Chap. 18).

Open Education

Open education offers still another stream of relevance to environmental design. Krasner and Krasner (1973), link education and the concept of planned environments. Simply put, the classroom is viewed as an environment of which the teacher is the designer or planner. The attraction of the open classroom is that the teacher moves more clearly into this role by virtue of having to use his or her experience and ingenuity in planning 25 individual environments. Further, it is a process which closely links valued behavior or behavioral objectives (which is another way of saying social implications) and the design of the environment to achieve these. More and more, the teacher realizes that he or she must talk in terms of goals and purposes for every design or feature that is put into the environment. The teacher, in effect, is forced to do a functional analysis of behavior. The material on the classroom as a locus for environmental design will be discovered in chapter 10; and chapter 9 describes the use of classrooms in the training of environmental designers.

Phenomenology And All Others

Virtually every model of man with a pretense to a broad scope offers an intellectual view of "the transactions of men and environments." Even phenomenologists such as Wapner, Kaplan, & Cohen (1973) describe human beings who "experience their environments, construe their worlds, and undertake action (or reconstruction of their environments) on the basis of such experience and construals" (p. 256). These authors entitle their later collection of research Experiencing the Environment. (1976) Among the topics covered are: assessment of the individual's experience of the environment in terms of responsibility to pleasantness, arousal quality, and "dominance-eliciting quality of the physical environment"; the categorization of individuals in terms of their specialized, cognitive, effective, and behavioral relations to the persons and things comprising environments; and factors that contribute to the perceptions of environments as hazardous.

ENVIRONMENTAL DESIGN AS A PARADIGM

The environmental design approach can be viewed as a broad paradigm or model of human behavior. Kuhn (1970) has offered a conceptual framework for scientific endeavors in which paradigms are identified according to sociological criteria. A paradigm governs not a subject matter but rather a group of practitioners. A paradigm involves specific solutions to particular puzzles, exemplars, shared values, metaphors, and metaphysical assumptions, all of which make up a "disciplinary matrix."

Some historians of psychology utilize the Kuhnian paradigm in their analysis of psychology yet reject the view that psychology is ready for such an analysis (Watson, 1965, 1971). This view is most clearly stated by Watson in his argument that, "Psychology is still in the pre-paradigmatic stage. Contextually defined and internationally accepted paradigms do not yet exist in psychology" (1965, p. 133). Whether or not the environmental design approach can be conceptualized in Kuhnian paradigmatic terms may well be debatable. At this point, we are merely emphasizing our observation and expectation that this approach is emerging as an alternative to the currently predominant inner, pathology-oriented models of human behavior which hypothesize dichotomist states of health and illness.

Kuhn's views offer a broad philosophy of science which seems compatible with many of the concepts that are basic to environmental design such as that of participant observation.

Hollinger (1976), an historian, goes to the core of Kuhn's impact on the behavioral sciences when he points out that:

> Kuhn's theory of science dispenses with the idea of a fixed, permanent natural order that can function both as a standard for truth in the case of particular theories and as a goal for the progress of science. Kuhn also rejects the a priori methodological unity of science, according to which specific, formalized rules of verification are assumed to attend upon the basic aims of science. (P. 391)

A danger to society occurs when one paradigm has been sold to the point where it no longer is viewed as a paradigm but becomes an accepted reality, an absolute. The importance of the development of new paradigmatic social and behavioral science movements is that they keep the process going of trying to understand, change, and possibly improve human behavior. It's when the process ends and we have an established paradigm that we're in deep trouble.

A major unresolvable issue is whether the environmental design view of the relationship between human behavior and the environment represents a true paradigm shift in Kuhn's sense, or the culmination of the fortuitous and temporary linkage of a number of streams of influence as we have described earlier. We think that a case can be made for both interpretations. However, we are still too close in time to the developments we are describing to get the perspective necessary to resolve this issue. A time perspective would be important not only in terms of understanding environmental design but also in any predictions as to subsequent developments.

Models of Man

The possible determinants of human behavior can be conceptualized along the dimension of an interior/exterior continuum. At the interior extreme, behavior is viewed as the result of inherited characteristics, with the environment exercising minimal influence. For example, there may be certain "basic instincts," "behavior patterns," "needs," "intelligence," "racial consciousness," "developmental stages," etc. Conceiving of "mental illness" as a genetic defect or brain/metabolic disease would be found at this position on the scale.

Moving along the continuum, it could be argued that early learning experiences influence the individual's personality development until a certain age, by which time the person's "basic personality" has been formed. A bit further along the continuum, one could admit the possibility of later personality change. In both of these positions, an individual's personality traits determine his behavior patterns to a very great degree regardless of the situation.

Moving slightly further toward the exterior (environmental) view, evidence is offered that behavior may vary a great deal from situation to situation and is, therefore, a product of the interaction between a person's personality and the immediate situation (Mischel, 1973; Endler, 1975; see also chap. 4). According to these "centrist" positions, behavior change is usually accomplished by changing intrapsychic variables: attitudes, cognition, personality, etc. Applied to larger groups in society such as racial minorities or poor people, this view implies that it was indeed the environment that brought them to where they are, but that the only remedy would be to change them rather than the environmental conditions (Ryan, 1971).

Toward the far environmental end, the immediate environmental situation is seen as by far the most important determinant of behavior, and the utility of the concept of "personality" is questioned (Krasner & Ullmann, 1973). The extreme environmentalist still may use internal or quasi internal concepts such as "learning" history or "expectancy," but will point to evidence that the environment is the most important current influence and is the preferred object for manipulation to produce effective and rapid behavior change.

The preference for an environmentalist position has been well put in pragmatic terms by Skinner (1953), where "inner states" can be interpreted as either cognitions or as personality traits or states:

> The objection to inner states is not that they do not exist, but that they are not relevant in a functional analysis. We cannot account for the behavior of any system while staying wholly inside it; eventually we must turn to forces operating upon the organism from without. Unless there is a weak spot in our causal chain so that the second link is not lawfully determined by the first, or the third by the second, then the first and third links must be lawfully related. If we must always go back beyond the second link for prediction and control, we may avoid many tiresome and exhausting digressions by examining the third link

as a function of the first. Valid information about the second link may throw light on this relationship but can in no way alter it. (P. 35)

Such a position need not imply that man is a passive puppet of the environment. It is obvious that man is active in determining his circumstances; after all, most of us live in houses, not in caves. Man's high levels of intelligence and adaptability prepare him to be very responsive to his environment and creative in confronting problems. A major field of development in psychology is the area of self-control (Bandura, 1977). But self-control is conceptualized as man changing his environment so that it will influence him as he desires. In order to do this effectively, he must understand those processes of influence.

A publisher's statement in the paperback edition of Skinner's Beyond Freedom and Dignity (1971) says: "B.F. Skinner, the great behaviorist and the most influential and controversial psychologist of our time, suggests that what is called for now is a 'technology of behavior – a systematic and scientific program to alter the nature of man. A plan that would take us beyond freedom and dignity." This ominous statement may have its intended effect of influencing people to buy the book, but it is completely misleading in implying that systematic application of behavior influence would alter the nature of man or take away the freedom and dignity that we are now assumed to have. The aim is simply to understand and apply the ubiquitous processes of behavior influence in a more overt, systematic manner in order to solve the major human behavior problems that plague us. Environmental design attempts to do exactly that.

Principles of Environmental Design

The most important implication of these procedures is that they are a process of training people to conceptualize the environment in which they are working in such a way they can apply the general principles of environmental design. Succinctly stated, these principles include:

- A hypothesized model of human behavior which conceptualizes the locus of influence is in the interaction between an individual's behavior and his environment.
- An individual learns by observing and doing.
- Behavior followed by a rewarding event is likely to be repeated.
- Any situation can be analyzed so that the designer can set up specific behavioral goals that are socially desirable, taking into consideration both social and individual needs and desires.
- The sources of social influence are wide and complex, but analyzable.
- Techniques should not be developed in isolation but only in the context of learning environments with which the individual designer is dealing. The broader influences on behavior such as social roles and the impact of institutional rituals and restraints

must be considered.
- The professional influencer is part of the influence process itself, in effect, a participant observer. As such, he must be aware of, and in control of, the influence on him.
- There is a symbiotic relationship between therapist and patient, influencer and influencee, designer and designee – both need each other.
- Research and application, theory and practice are mutually interactive and inseparable.
- One's work as a professional behavioral scientist must be put in the context of a history, philosophy, and sociology of science.
- Social and behavioral science, like environmental design, is a human behavior, subject to the influence process as any other human behavior.
- Behavior is determined by the influence process but only in probabilistic terms.
- Social and personal change is a continuous process.
- The variables of influence lie in the environment (man-built, natural, and social), but they may differentially influence as a function of the history of the individual.
- Meaning or truth are not intrinsic but are imposed currently and repeatedly by the observer, investigator, or designer.
- Man is his own chief product.

On Participant Observation

The concept of participant observation is integral to an understanding of the function of the environment designer as we conceptualize it in this book. Our usage of the term has been influenced by the psychiatrist, Harry Stack Sullivan, for whom the concept was central in his approach to psychotherapy.

Chapman (1976) in one of the first biographies of Sullivan describes how Sullivan utilized this concept in the core of his work.

Sullivan employs the concept of participant observation to define 1) the nature of psychiatry and its allied professions and the data which they study, 2) the basic roles of psychiatrists, clinical psychologists, psychiatric nurses, and other mental health professional workers, and 3) the nature of psychotherapy.

The principle of participant observation states that the basic process in which a psychiatrist, or other mental health worker, is engaged is the informed observation of one or more interpersonal relationships in which he is an active participant. For example, in psychotherapy a therapist is engaged in an interpersonal relationship in which he is alertly observing what is going on between himself and the patient; he is also affecting the nature of that relationship by how he participates in it . . . A further implication of Sullivan's concept of participant observation is that in psychiatry there is no entirely objective information. Psychiatric information is always to some extent distorted by the process of collecting it. (Pp. 111-115)

Chapman then argues that Sullivan was influenced by Heisenberg's "uncertainty principle" as to the limitations of human beings as observers. We feel that this linkage is most appropriate and may well be central to the conception of the environmental designer as a participant observer.

Sarason (1978) clarifies the implications of the role of the professional (scientist, therapist, designer) as participant observer:

We are accountable, and that means that we should feel and nurture the bonds of similarity and communality between ourselves and the people we study. It is the difference between knowing that you are studying people, like yourself, and not "subjects." Society does not exist for the purposes of scientists. It is arrogance in the extreme to look at society from a noblesse oblige stance, expecting that the gifts you give it will be responded to with gratitude, not questions or hesitations. (P. 378)

Influences On The Investigator

As the environmental design approach has evolved, it has become increasingly clear that the professional investigator of the environment is himself/herself an element in the investigation/change process.

Ideally, most books and papers on human behavior, both theoretical and empirical, would start with an analysis of the influences and reinforcers on the individual investigator. Unfortunately, such self-analyses are rare.

For our purposes we once again turn to Moos for his self-analysis. Moos (1975), a leading investigator of environmental influences, illustrates the personal and environmental influences on himself, resulting in his concern for the human environment. His interest developed from a clinical psychology perspective, beginning with his "Rogerian" psychotherapy supervision.

As we have been stressing, the environmental design approach is viewed as a model for training and a means of influencing clinical psychology. The self-observation of Moos that, "I found that I could neither understand nor predict the behavior of my patients in settings other than my office" (p 2), emphasizes the clinical psychology context within which many professionals, now identified as environmental designers, developed.

Moos cites five converging lines of empirical studies which influenced his shift toward emphasizing the importance of situational and environmental forces:

Traits of states: In real life situations, the major proportion of the variance in behavior is generally not accounted for by individual difference variables (Ekehammer, 1974).

- The prediction sound barrier: There appears to be an upper limit to the accuracy of prediction attainable using background and individual difference variables: "The nature of the environment in which behavior is to take place must be considered if more accurate predictions of human performance are to be made" (Moos, p. 3).

- Program outcome studies: The evidence is that there is very little relationship between an individual's behavior in and out of an institution (e.g., Ellsworth, 1968; Sinclair, 1971).

- The impact of enduring environments: The environment exerts potent influence on behavior (e.g., Bloom, 1964; Bronfrenbrenner, 1975; Skeels, 1966).

- Case studies of environments: Moos cites individual cases, real and literary, involving strong environmental influences on individual behavior such as Kozal's Death at an Early Age (1967), Greenberg's I Never Promised You a Rose Garden (1964), and Thomas Mann's, The Magic Mountain (1924).

Moos' self-analysis of influences on him emphasizes the importance of the theoretical orientation (ideology, paradigm) on the behavior of the investigator, the "behavior influencer," the environmental designer.

The Audience As Influence

An additional dimension of environmental evaluation has been introduced within the environmental streams — that of "communication to audiences" (and links with the implications of the investigator as participant observer). Sommer (1971) points out that man-environment relations is such a broad field that the researcher has to choose his audience as well as his problem area. Sommer contends that he himself writes three different kinds of articles for three different audiences. First, he observes that social scientists and sociologists are more receptive to studies of spatial behaviors than psychologists; whereas anthropologists are interested in non-verbal communication. A second audience is made up of architects, landscape people, and others concerned with the design of physical environments. A third audience comprises "space managers" such as hospital administrators, student housing directors, principals, and air terminal managers who are "directly responsible for the furnishing, allocation, and utilization of institutional spaces" (p. 281). Ironically, Sommer notes that animal biologists and ecologists whom he has never tried to reach as an audience are the people "to whom I am most indebted for my theoretical orientation and concepts" (p. 281).

Esser, a psychiatrist, has focused on communicating to a wide audience of professionals interested in the environmental approach. He was responsible for publishing an integrated work on, Behavior and environment: The use of space by animals and man (1971). This book is the report of an international symposium on the use of space by animals and men sponsored by the Animal Behavior Society at an annual AAAS meeting in Dallas, Texas, 1968. The origin of the symposium was Esser's (1965) paper on the use of space by psychiatric patients. Esser offered his paper as a means of enhancing avenues of communication between behavioral science, the design community, and decision makers of our society. Esser describes his work (and that of Calhoun, 1962) as indicating the emergence of a "social biology" or a "behavioral systems approach," which he views as an integration of ethology, ecology, and social psychology.

Esser also initiated a newsletter entitled, Man-Environment Systems in 1970 which has been an important influence in the development of the field as it includes reports by the major investigators in the environmental area. It was the first of numerous newsletters to an ever-expanding professional audience. The following "statement of purpose" reflects the orientation of the newsletter and represents a prototypical orientation of the investigators in this field.

> Man and his social and physical environment, as well as all the relationships between these concepts, are the concern of Man-Environment Systems. A vast spectrum of scientific philosophies, methodologies and disciplines focus upon man's behavior among his fellow man. Categorized into interdependent fields of inquiry dealing with, for instance, man's social, economic, biological, psychological and political life, too often these fields have closed upon themselves, finding it more efficient to generate methods tailored to their specific problems rather than combining efforts toward similar objectives across disciplinary lines. (MES, 1976, P. 224)

Man environment interaction is, of course, not the sole province of the behaviorist or the environmentalist.

The Designer as Interdisciplinarian

Once we start focusing in on the role and influence of the designer as participant observer, the discipline of the designer becomes an element in the design situation. Are we being interdisciplinary in environmental design? Throughout this book we will be describing the work of psychologists, sociologists, psychiatrists, architects, etc. Krasner & Ullmann (1973) noted that:

> Students who read observers in the past such as Freud, Marx, Bentham, and John Stuart Mill are usually astonished by how these writers seem to cut across so many fields. Yet the fault or credit is not these authors'; they covered but one field – that of human behavior and influence. Because of a series of historical events such as the university department structure . . .

information increase, and a tendency by investigators to perpetuate their own kind, we have now reached a stage of
fragmentation and specialization in studying human behavior.

The rewards society offers to the scientific investigator, and any
other kind of influencer, are usually greatest when he stays
within his particular discipline, school, or model – where his work
is more readily 'understood' and its relevance recognized. There
are exceptions, of course, but the general rule for all types of
influencers (as indeed for all citizens) is, 'Don't rock the boat.'
(P. 189)

Design for What and by Whom

Perhaps the most fundamental issue in environmental design is design
for what and by whom? This is not a new issue in that it was expressed
early in the behavioral movement in terms of modification for what and
by whom.

Two important elements of the environmental design approach we
have been describing are relevant to this issue. In eschewing the
medical model we can no longer justify change in behavior of an
individual as a restoration of health, a return to equilibrium. Secondly,
the concept of participant observer implicitly shifts us, as professionals,
away from an elitist concept of expertise.

Thus, the environment designer finds that he has very little room to
maneuver except behind the rationale that he is training others,
everyone in sight, to design their own environment. But there may be a
paradox here. If I plan the situation, be it a classroom, clinic, home, or
industry, so that the individual learns the procedures to design his own
environment, then who is the prime mover, the Grand Designer?

A major point which derives from the social psychological or social
learning model is that the goal of helping individuals is to enable them
to learn how to control, influence, or design their own environments.
Implicit in this is a value judgment that individual freedom is a
desirable goal, and the more an individual is able to affect his
environment the greater is his freedom. Of course, there is no absolute
freedom in this sense. In this context, "environment" is both the people
and physical objects in one's life.

In dealing with people, we are involved in an influence process that
is ubiquitous, not a process of curing or helping unfortunate "sick"
people. By this model, everyone is involved in designing environments.
The individual who seeks help, the therapist, the researcher, the
schoolteacher, the parent, the student, the warden, and the reader of
books on environmental designs.

The traditional focus of change in psychiatry and clinical psychology
has been the one-to-one therapy situation, in which the therapist
attempts to influence the behavior or internal dynamics (depending on
his orientation) of the patient or client by interpersonal or environmental manipulations. An extension of that situation is group therapy

in which a therapist works with a group of people with problems, either for economy over individual therapy or because the group process aids change (or both). The next logical extension has been to go into the community to change faulty environments that are causing behavior problems for an individual or group. Environmental design, while dealing with these situations as well, applies the same principles of influence to achieve behavioral goals in any situation, without the (sometimes) intermediate step of labeling undesired behavior as "sick" or deviant.

The first necessary step in systematic, planned behavior change is specifying the desired behaviors. The fact that value judgments have to be made in choosing desirable behaviors should become very clear. In other models of behavior, it has always seemed possible to escape making value judgments. For instance, in traditional psychotherapy there was no need to question whether a mentally ill person's behavior should be "changed"; the individual was being "healed". In education, there was no hesitation to force children to sit quietly in their seats; how could they learn what they had to learn if they did not sit still and pay attention?

But when any behavior influence program is planned, target behaviors have to be laid out for everyone to view, discuss, and criticize; and the decision process brings questions of values into open debate. It may be a very difficult and painful process, but in bringing the issues and choices into the open it gives a much higher degree of self-control. And while effective behavior influence/control technology presents the possibility of malevolent controllers, the necessity of this decision making process at least suggests the direction to move in "controlling the controllers."

Krasner & Ullmann (1973) present a social behavioral view of the influence process as an alternative approach to explanations of behavior which emphasize a concept of "personality" (internal positions). The basic premises of this approach are explicated throughout this volume. They conclude their presentation of behavior influence approach by suggesting that the way to deal with the very rapidly developing behavior change technology is to "face the hard problems of what procedures may be used by whom to attain what permissible ends" (P. 502).

Krasner & Ullmann end their explication of the behavior influence approach with the following observation which, to this biased writer, represents a useful lead-in to discussions of the goals of environmental design:

> The best way to increase freedom is not merely to say people may choose but to work so that people can choose. Just as humans have gone far in changing their physical environments, we hope the next decade will see humans controlling and changing their psychological environments. The how is being developed rapidly in schools, clinics, families, and formal organizations. An attempt is being made to reduce the gap between decision makers and the populations they affect, especially in the areas of education and consumer affairs and to

a lesser extent in political and industrial settings. Communication among students, parents, and teachers, for example, not
only increases the efficiency of the teacher but becomes
increasingly the best way to help the teacher decide what ends
will best serve all concerned.   We need to foster greater
communication and awareness between influencers (all of us) and
influencees (all of us). (P. 502)

The point is repeatedly made by observers of history that ideas,
philosophy, religion, etc. become transmuted with time and distance –
"as all bodies of belief become transmuted, indeed to the point where
their nominal founders would no longer recognize them" (Halle, 1977, p.
381). Indeed, Karl Marx towards the end of his life is quoted as writing
to his son-in-law "What is certain is that I am not a Marxist" (quoted by
T.B. Bottomore in <u>Karl Marx: Early Writings</u>, London, 1963. p. xiii,
footnote). Can we envision a day when Skinner would say, "I am not a
Skinnerian"?

On Beyond

We would hope that environmental design does not develop to the point
that "behavior modification" did; that is, "it" became an it (reification);
it became virtually ubiquitous and synonomous with any intervention
procedure that the human mind could conceive (success and impe-
rialism) and "it" became senescent and useless as a label ("death"). Our
own view is that the concept of environmental design, as we have been
presenting it in this volume, has in its early stages in terms of
theoretical integration, methodological and social implications. Let it
bloom!

2 Ethical and Value Contexts
William Hutchison

The views of the editor, like those of many clinicians, have evolved from accepting the "medical" model view that ethics were <u>rules</u> or <u>standards</u> separate from the behavior and belief system of the clinician, even a behavioral clinician. In effect, ethical codes were a separate entity independent of the clinician but which we had to abide by. This view evolved to the point where ethics, or the professionals' belief of what "good" behavior is, is considered to be integral to the influence process and is a part of <u>every</u> behavioral sequence.

The usual place for a chapter on ethics in "traditional" books on behavior modification is in the last chapter, if at all (e.g. Krasner chapter on ethics in Leitenberg's 1976 <u>Handbook of Behavior Modification</u>). Yet this kind of placement of material on ethics has not reflected the actual state of evolvement and concern of those identified with behavior modification with the broader social and ethical implications of their theoretical position.

From its early inception, concerns with social and ethical issues (and philosophies of living) have characterized behavior modification as epitomized by Skinner's <u>Walden Two</u> which offered a complex humanistic socioethical value system (Krasner, 1978). Other early investigators (e.g. Bandura, 1969; Goldiamond, 1965; and Kanfer, 1965) emphasized the ethical issues involved when a professional attempted to systematically change another's behavior, especially within the context of clinical psychology.

The broad ethical and value issues then become the first element to discuss, and Hutchinson's chapter puts into focus the various ways in which human beings, particularly those in professional situations, have attempted to answer the "for what" question. In

36

this chapter, Hutchison brings together the recent contributions and theorizing of those identified with the behavioral-environment approach. Clearly it is not an attempt to offer answers, but rather to determine what may be the relevant questions to be asked by environmental designers.

We are defining our terms by the nature of the material we are including in our chapter. Throughout, we are arguing that all behavior of the environment designer is value laden, but this can also become a meaningless statement unless some distinction can be made and implications drawn from specific situations.

The very act of formulating materials, of linking certain ideas or studies with others is, in itself, a value-laden behavior. We are making statements as to what goals are desirable in the design of environments by the nature of what material we include here, which is basically the material we include in the training of environmental designers.

The ethics chapter serves two basic functions: first, to clear up the ethical issue and problems involved in the behavior modification of the past three decades; and second, to extrapolate from them and go beyond into the implications of the newer environmental design approach. It is an ongoing process.

Ed.

As with the other topics in this book, there is enormous current activity in the area of ethics. Of course, philosophers continue their production unabated, but they are not alone in generating excitement. Much activity has been directed toward conceptualizing ethical behavior based on "scientific" views of man. This chapter will examine the spectrum of traditional and more recent ideas in the area of ethics in order to develop a perspective on the topic of ethics and values. Based on this perspective, we will analyze the issues and proposals for solutions that have been made. The underlying belief (and hope) is that we should observe our own behavior as we approach ethical problems.

Environmental designers must face ethical choices at every turn, a point repeatedly and cogently made by Bandura (1969), Kanfer & Phillips (1970), Krasner (1962, 1965, 1969, & 1973), London (1964), and others. This recognition has been facilitated by the development of the behavioral model: the methods are often effective, so discussion of ethical choices is not moot; and the goals which must be explicitly stated in behavior modification programs are starkly exposed for debate. This point has also been well made by the same writers.

Other theoretical approaches tend to obscure the ethical problems involved. The medical model uses "restoration of health" as a justification for change, thereby obscuring the choices involved in the intervention. Likewise at the supraindividual level, the concept of "sick society" of "malfunctioning organization" may be used as justification for intervention.   Use of the term "prevention" in mental health (especially following Caplan, 1964) is yet another attempt to find justification for change, but "preventing mental illness" is a concept within the medical model (Cowen, 1977) which has the same problem as restoration of health.   The behaviorist's frequent use of terms such as behavior problems or deficits is verbal trickery that can be abused in the same way. The change agents are still trying to find intrinsic justification for change.

Behavior influence may also be masked by claiming a "hands off" position. Examples are client centered therapy and other "nondirective" therapies in which the therapist claims to be creating a nurturant environment in which the client matures or self-actualizes, and "free" schools in which the child develops according to his or her own natural needs or predetermined developmental stages. If the environment in such situations is influencing the behavior of the person in it, then claiming "hands off" may be deceptive in masking the ethical choices that are actually made. As Bandura (1969) has pointed out, hands off intervention very often leads to doing a greater amount of global intervention than does explicit goal-directed intervention. Lengthy psychoanalysis or client-centered therapy often results in intervention into all areas of functioning, including conversion to the orientation of the therapist.

Behaviorists are active in self-examination, and are often singled out for criticism or regulation, but it should be clear that the same analysis applies equally to all change attempts. Goldiamond (1975, 1976) discusses this clearly and points out problems in singling out behaviorists. However, there are signs that this discrimination is decreasing (e.g., Friedman et al., 1975; Minnesota Guidelines, 1972). The ethical guidelines being formulated for the Association for the Advancement of Behavior Therapy (Azrin, 1976) exclude terms specific to behavior therapy in order to suggest that the same principles apply to all psychotherapeutic or intervention procedures.

TRADITIONAL ETHICS

Most ethical discussions, even among behaviorists, are based on traditional philosophical views concerning what are problems, solutions, and methods of solution. We will briefly examine philosophical ethics and later will discuss them from a different perspective.

There are three distinct areas that classically come under the heading of ethics, all of which are of interest to environmental designers:

- Normative ethics: What should we do, or how should we behave in specific situations? This is the level at which most discussions of ethics occur, and a level at which all change agents must be fairly proficient.

- Descriptive ethics: How do people actually behave? This is usually approached at the level of the social and behavioral sciences, including cultural anthropology and psychology.

- Meta-ethics or philosophy of ethics: What is the basis for normative ethics? How do we use the terms "good" or "right," and how can we justify ethical decisions? It is at this basic level that a scientific view may provide a more useful framework within which to observe ethical behavior, while enabling us to integrate more traditional viewpoints.

The third area can be seen as the most high-level or basic; it is here that one is analyzing the behavior performed in the first area. We agree with assertions of philosophers that one must be very clear about one's meta-ethics in order to do normative ethics effectively.

Traditional meta-ethical theories are often classified into three categories: Naturalism, Intuitionism, and Noncognitivism (Abelson & Nielsen, 1967; Frankena, 1973). Each of these will be examined briefly for their views on the nature of ethical behavior, as well as what problems are associated with each.

Naturalism

According to naturalism, moral terms are completely definable using nonmoral terms, so that moral judgments are a kind of empirical judgment. Utilitarianism (Mill, 1861), probably the most influential of all ethical theories, is an example of naturalism: That action is best which results in the greatest benefit to the greatest number of people. Ethical choices are, therefore, made by looking at the natural world, as is characteristic of all naturalistic theories.

The important observations derived from these theories are that experience in the natural world does influence moral judgments, and that consequences to people are major considerations in making ethical decisions. However, a critical problem for naturalists is in defining the exact relationship between the empirical facts and the ethical conclusions. For example, how does one measure benefit to people, and how do these units of pleasure for different individuals fit into an equation to determine what is best? A second problem, common to all traditional theories, is that personal preference seems to be the major reason for accepting one theory over another. Even more basically, as will be discussed later, having accepted any theory it is not clear how a person's judgment of what is right is supposed to influence his or her behavior.

Day (1977) claims that Skinner falls squarely in the tradition of naturalism, as all his terms and analyses are based entirely on natural properties. However, naturalism within traditional philosophy (which is essentially dualistic) claims more than this: that one uses the relevant empirical data from the natural realm to decide what is good or right in the ethical realm. That good or right action is the only one that should be done. Skinner's analysis of should and ought statements, discussed in a later section, is very different from what naturalists have in mind.

Intuitionism

According to intuitionists, there must be at least one primitive ethical term representing a non-natural quality, relation, or concept. This term is indefinable and must be perceived directly. Ethical judgments are, therefore, not subject to empirical validation. Some (e.g., Moore, 1912) say we intuit the intrinsic goodness of an act, while other (e.g., Veatch, 1973) say we intuit the obligatoriness of acts.

The useful observations of intuitionism are that we do often have feelings associated with many acts, which we may label guilt, compulsion, etc.; and that we may not be aware of the determinants of those emotions or behaviors. One problem with the theory is that people often disagree about what is good or obligatory. Since there is no natural observation as a basis for these judgments, there is no way to choose among differing intuitions. And as with naturalism, it is not clear what relationship moral judgments have to behavior. What are the consequences of not doing what one intuits as good or obligatory?

Noncognitivism

Noncognitivist philosophers deny that moral utterances are only, or even at all, property-ascribing utterances. For example, emotivists hold that a moral utterance expresses or evokes an attitude or feeling: "X is bad" means "I don't like X." Imperativists hold that they are primarily imperatives: "X is bad" means "Don't do X."

A major observation of the noncognitivists is that moral utterances have certain functions. Feelings or emotional states influence moral statements, and people try to influence others' behavior by making moral statements. Noncognitivists deny that moral judgments are anything more than this, having some sort of "moral imperative force" as the other schools generally hold. In a later section, this functional analysis of ethical verbal behavior will be expanded using Skinner's (1957) ideas. However, in their emphasis upon verbal behavior, non-cognitivists ignore much behavior of interest to us, particularly ethical choice and the development of ethical rules.

PROBLEMATIC ASSUMPTIONS OF TRADITIONAL PHILOSOPHICAL ETHICS

Certain assumptions are common to traditional philosophical views of ethics, primarily that man is autonomous, free, and rational. Skinner has frequently discussed this viewpoint and an alternative behavioral one (see especially his book on the philosophy of behaviorism (1974)). To be consistent with a behavioristic analysis, we will not argue that a deterministic view of man is true or that a traditional view is untrue, since the concept of truth itself can be misleading, as Skinner (1957) has discussed. And as Catania (1976) pointed out, the free will/determinism debate has nothing to do with freedom anyway. Rather, consistent with the view expressed throughout the book, we believe that a behavioristic view is more useful in analyzing and solving the problems humans are facing. (On the point of usefulness, philosophers Abelson and Nielsen, in the influential Encyclopedia of Philosophy (Edwards, 1967, p. 100), make a devastating summary statement: "It would appear from our brief glance over the history of ethics through the nineteenth century that philosophers failed to find any conclusive ethical truths and merely argued, more persuasively and with a more impressive display of learning that most, for whatever way of life and standards of conduct they happened to prefer . . .") This chapter will explain one possible behavioristic view and demonstrate some of its implications.

On the View that Science is Value-Free

The fact that a chapter on ethics appears early in this book is in contrast with the usual position of such a chapter, last, in books and articles on methods of behavior change. Until recently, there was little, if any, discussion of ethics in "scientific" presentations. The underlying belief, which was one direct consequence of traditional philosophical views of ethics, has been that science and technology are value-free, "Science can tell us how to do something, but not whether to do it." A scientist's role involved relentless pursuit of truth, and the technologist's role was to provide service to whomever paid his salary. Ethical/value questions were on a different, perhaps higher level, and they required a different methodology and different language. This value-free view of science and technology is incompatible with the environmental design approach presented herein. An alternative view with different implications is described.

ALTERNATIVE CONCEPTUALIZATIONS

There are several alternative approaches which deal with the realm of behavior called ethics and values wholly within a scientific framework. This section will examine three of these positions which have been the focus of much recent theorizing about the nature of ethical behavior – sociobiology, sociocultural evolution, and behavioral science. A critical examination will lead to formulation of a single consistent viewpoint, which will be used to analyze the practical issues in the section following.

Sociobiology

All human acts – even saving a stranger from drowning or donating a million dollars to the poor – may be ultimately selfish. Morality and justice, far from being the triumphant product of human progress, evolved from man's animal past, and are securely rooted in the genes. These are some of the teachings of sociobiology, a new and highly controversial scientific discipline that seeks to establish that social behavior – human as well as animal – has a biological basis. (Time, August 1, 1977)

The foremost spokesman for this approach is Edward Wilson, whose book (1975) has served as a focus of interest. Following is a brief summary of the position.

Besides physical attributes, such as size and strength, many kinds of behavior may influence the probability of an individual's genes being transmitted. Take, as an example, parents and their offspring, and assume each parent shares half of its genetic makeup with each of its offspring (as with humans). Then any parental behavior (e.g., fighting predators around the nest) which increased the probability of survival of two of his offspring more than it decreased his own chances to survive, would result in the transmission of his genes more effectively than if he had acted in his own "selfish" interest (e.g., fleeing the nest). If there is any genetic mechanism capable of transmitting that behavior, then by accepted Darwinian evolutionary theory, the behavior would tend to become dominant in such species.

An important case relevant to a view of ethics is altruistic versus selfish behavior (Campbell, 1972). If organisms responded in accordance with a biological mechanism favoring group survival over personal survival, then those organisms that were more biologically "altruistic" would tend to die off through greater self-sacrifice, and the mechanism carrying the altruistic tendency would be selected out. At this level of analysis it would seem that biological selection breeds "selfish" individuals, and altruism must be accounted for in some other way.

Much of the opposition to sociobiology has been based on the prediction that it will be used to support social injustices (see Asher, 1975; Wade, 1976), but recent criticism has been directed toward the accuracy of the theory (Sahlins, 1976). The most obvious fault behaviorists would point out is the underestimation of the modifiability of behavior – any behavior which can be seen to change in a few years (or minutes!) cannot be genetic. The many illustrations in this book, reaching to the level of entire cultures such as China (Hoffman, Chap. 13), stand as counterexamples to a sweeping sociobiological view. However, genetic laws will be considered in approaching social behavior later.

Sociocultural Evolution

Campbell (1960, 1965, 1972, 1974a, 1974b, and 1975) is a good spokesman for a sociocultural evolutionary approach within psychology:

By sociocultural evolution we mean, at a minimum, a selective cumulation of skills, technologies, recipes, beliefs, customs, organizational structures, and the like, retained through purely social modes of transmission, rather than in the genes. Given a stability in the selective system, the cumulated culture and social system will become more and more adapted to the selective system. If different social systems are adapting to different ecologies, then divergent speciation will occur. If there are general principles of organizational effectiveness, as in division of labor, then quite independent streams of social cumulation may be shaped by this common selective system so that these streams converge on similar structures, moving from simple social systems to complex social systems along parallel routes. (1975, P. 1104)

Skinner (1953) advocates a similar view:

The evolution of cultures appears to follow the pattern of the evolution of species. The many different forms of culture which arise correspond to the "mutations" of genetic theory. Some forms prove to be effective under prevailing circumstances and others not, and the perpetuation of the culture is determined accordingly. (P. 434)

Since ethical practices are among the human behaviors included in this model, a rather clear meta-ethical viewpoint is asserted. Existing ethical practices have evolved on the basis of their influence on the probability of the carrying cultures' survival. Campbell (1975) as well as Skinnerians such as Michael (1977) urge caution in making changes in practice, because if a practice has evolved over time it may very well have positive or essential functions within the larger culture of which we are as yet unaware. Of course, as Campbell concedes, evolution is based on past conditions which may have changed.

Caution may be an important implication, but does not help very much when considering a proposed change. Skinner (1953) seems to be more helpful. He claims that his analysis does not lead to a prescription, but he says:

A rigorous science of behavior makes a different sort of remote consequence effective when it leads us to recognize survival as a criterion in evaluating a controlling practice . . . A Scientific analysis may lead us to resist the more immediate blandishments of freedom, justice, knowledge, or happiness in considering the long-run consequences of survival. (Pp. 435-36)

Thus, it seems that the model may be used to generate "objective" evaluations of practices, including ethical practices, and many or most behavioral followers of the theory are using it in that way, as becomes clear in reading their recent papers on ethics.

A closer examination of the model shows a number of problems. Campbell (1975) cites a large literature showing that most sociocultural evolutionists use a hard-line neo-Darwinian process as a model for cultural evolution. Skinner (1971) and Hutchison (1975b) argue that the process is more similar to a Lamarckian model, since cultural practices can be acquired and transmitted within a single generation of humans (indeed practices may change many times over a short period of time). However, in such a process, survival — which was our criterion for evaluation — becomes unimportant, since practices can be acquired, transmitted, and replaced by processes other than selective survival. Going further, Hutchison (1975a) asks:

> What does it mean for a culture to die? Obviously it does not mean that all the members of the culture die, since that rarely happens. I believe it is more often taken to mean a massive change in practices. But how many? We could adopt a certain percentage or certain classes of practice changes as arbitrary criteria, but we would not be specifying a clearly recognizable event. Moreover, what if the same amount of change occurred over a longer period of time? In almost no situation does it make sense to say a culture died or survived. (P. 2)

In summary, the posited evolutionary model cannot be the familiar Darwinian one, so the survival criterion is not a useful guide for decisions. Ethical and other practices are obviously changing, but not by any process which we can describe accurately. To call the change evolution is to attach a misleading label which only tends to take our attention away from the important processes in change of practices. In a later section, a basis for an analysis of cultural change will be suggested.

Behavioral Science

The basic assumption of a behavioristic view of ethics/values is that it is possible to analyze ethical behavior using the same concepts and methodology as with other behavior. A three-day conference recently was devoted to such analyses of ethical behavior (Krapfl and Vargas, 1977).

The first basic translation from common to behavioral language is to substitute reinforcers for values, as suggested by Skinner (1953) and well developed by Krasner (1973). Saying that a person values a thing implies that it can be used to reinforce his or her behavior. Saying that individuals have different values translates to saying that individuals differ in what reinforces their behavior. A behaviorist arrives at conclusions about a person's values (reinforcers) by observing the effects of various events on his behavior, regardless of what the person may claim he values. Values may, of course, be conditioned reinforcers, including rather abstract ones (e.g., freedom). As reinforcers, they can and do change over time.

Behavior analysts have come a long way in their ability to conceptualize and measure values. As Schnaitter (1977) expressed it, behavioral psychology moved from a Newtonian to a relativistic view: i.e., from concepts of absolute reinforceability and punishability to the reinforcing and punishing functions of stimuli. Premack (1971) identified the value of a stimulus as the probability that the organism will respond to the stimulus. A given stimulus can be either reinforcing or punishing depending on the relative values involved, and value may be manipulated by operations like deprivation and satiation.

The matching law (Baum, 1973) represents another advance in measuring value: "The relative time spent in two activities equals the relative value of the two activities." These empirical results combine nicely with the work of mathematicians Von Neumann & Morgenstern (1944), who showed that merely demonstrating that people can consistently (even probabilistically) choose between pairs or sets of alternatives guarantees that a scale of values can be constructed. Multi-attribute utility measurement (Edwards, 1971) is a practical application of this approach in social decision making. We believe that the use of behavioral terms associated with values has considerably more clarity and utility than the traditional uses.

FUNCTIONS OF ETHICAL STATEMENTS

The key terms should and ought (used almost interchangeably) are frequently central to ethical discussions. In fact, Brandt (1959) defines ethics as those statements which are or can be stated using those words. There are two major functions of the words, which Vargas (1977) and Day (1977) call the tacting and manding functions, using terms from Skinner (1957).

(a) Tacting. As a statement of contingencies: "You should do X" translates to "If you do X your behavior will be reinforced." "You should take an umbrella" equals "Taking an umbrella, will be reinforced" and "You ought not to kill" means "Killing will be punished."

(b) Manding. As an exhortation or concealed command: "You should go to church more often" is a statement intended to influence the listener to behave in a certain way, regardless of the consequences to the listener. As a mand, moral injunctions fall into the same class as requests, commands, prayers, advice, warnings, permission, offers, and calls (Skinner, 1957, pp 40-41).

In any given statement, it may be difficult to distinguish between these two functions. Many statements indicate contingencies while also attempting to coerce the listener to comply; or, as Begelman (1977) points out, a mand need not be completely tactless. Skinner (1957), Vargas (1977), and Day (1977) have extensively developed this analysis, and have attempted to account for the behavior of both speaker and listener in specific instances. Their analyses represent a very useful advance beyond the noncognitivist formulations of verbal ethical behavior.

RULE-GOVERNED AND PROBLEM-SOLVING
BEHAVIOR IN ETHICS

Ethical behavior in a behavioral view is very often rule-governed behavior, after Skinner's (1969, 1974) analysis. In his analysis, a rule brings to bear sources of control that are more effective (usually more immediate) than the long-term natural consequences, which might be too remote to effectively control behavior. For example, there are rules which recommend or require the wearing of seat belts. The natural contingency – that injuries in an accident are more likely if one does not wear a seat belt – would probably not effectively control seat belt fastening behavior. The rule to wear seat belts, mediated by other people via reinforcement or punishment, may control the behavior more effectively. A rule not to steal may influence behavior because people avoid punishment by complying with the rule, while the long-term consequence of a more orderly society without stealing would be unlikely to control the behavior.

The nature of ethical problems was analyzed by Schnaitter (1977), who develops Skinner's (1953, 1957, 1969) notions of thinking and problem-solving to describe two broad classes of problems. One class is a to-do-or-not-to-do type, such as whether or not to steal an apple. The second class is a which-should-I-do type, in which the person has to choose among alternative choices evoking conflicting ethical rules. Schnaitter shows how a person may learn to discriminate a problem that he had not previously recognized as a problem, and how the ethical rules are evoked and manipulated as verbal stimuli to solve the problem. The problem is "solved" when one of the alternative behaviors becomes highly probable.

BEHAVING FOR THE GOOD OF OTHERS – A PARADOX
FOR BEHAVIORISTS?

Many people interested in ethics may be dissatisfied with the behavioral conceptualization presented, on the grounds that behaviorists assume (and often demonstrate) that each individual is behaving in accordance with laws which depend on personal reinforcement. After all, they say, this seemingly hedonistic theory seems to conflict with the fact that people often behave for the good of others. Is this not a paradox for behaviorists?

This paradox has a very long history. It has often been stated that acting for one's own gain can, at the same time, be behaving for the good of others. Adam Smith, in his classic <u>Wealth of Nations</u> (1776), explained how an "Invisible Hand" operated to make each individual's self-seeking behavior also benefit the community in an optimal way. Philosophers have recognized that:

> Against the conventionalist claim one can point out that there are good Hobbesian reasons for rational and self-interested people to accept the moral point of view. A rational egoist will

naturally desire the most extensive liberty compatible with his own self-interest, but he will also see that this is most achievable in a context of community life where the moral point of view prevails. Thus, in a quite nonmoralistic sense of "reasonable," it is reasonable for men, even self-interested men, to acknowledge that it is better for people to behave morally than amorally or immorally. (Abelson & Nielsen, 1967, p. 132)

Many behaviors are maintained in an individual precisely because they are reinforcing to others and, ironically, aversive contingencies are often used to maintain the behaviors. Far from being incompatible with the facts of "self-sacrifice," a behavioral view is a way to understand human behavior in such situations. The behavioral view of ethics focuses on the capacities of individuals for reinforcement and punishment, including subtle social, token, and other secondary reinforcement processes; on current environmental contingencies, including complex schedules of reinforcement; and on individual learning histories. Each aspect of ethical behavior – rule-following, ethical verbal behavior, accompanying emotions, and other aspects – can be analyzed using this model.

OTHER RELATED CONCEPTS: RIGHTS AND FREEDOM

A great deal of philosophical discussion has centered around the nature of human rights and freedom. Behaviorists have also directed their analyses toward these terms. Skinner (1974) commented on the rights listed in the Declaration of Principles from the Stockholm Conference on the Environment: "No other species has rights and responsibilities in this sense, and it is difficult to see how they could have evolved as fundamental human traits or possessions under natural selection unless we regard them as controlling and counter-controlling practices" (p. 199).

Wood (1975a) analyzes rights as events and activities legally guaranteed to citizens – if a person is denied access to a right there are legal remedies. Thus, rights are a function of social contingencies or rules. Moreover, there are rules to modify the rules, such as the procedure of due process to remove rights, and legislative and judicial processes to modify rights as cultural changes take place. There is also the concept of absolute versus contingent rights (Friedman, 1975; Wexler, 1975) – absolute rights cannot be waived, while contingent rights can be waived by a "competent" person.

The concept of freedom has provided a battleground onto which many behaviorists have charged. In his influential Beyond Freedom and Dignity (1971), Skinner writes:

Man's struggle for freedom is not due to will to be free, but to certain behavioral processes characteristic of the human organism, the chief effect of which is the avoidance of or escape from "aversive" features of the environment. Physical and biological technologies have been mainly concerned with natural aversive stimuli; the struggle for freedom is concerned with stimuli intentionally arranged by other people. (P. 42-43)

According to this analysis of freedom, increasing freedom means decreasing aversive control in favor of positive control. In an alternative analysis Catania (1975a,b) focuses on choice:

> Whatever else is involved in the concept of freedom, it at least involves the availability of alternatives. An organism with no opportunity to choose among alternatives is not called free. In the psychological vocabulary, the availability of alternatives has long been the basis for distinguishing among free choices and forced choices . . . If an organism is free only when alternatives are available, it can be further said to value freedom only if it prefers the availability of alternatives to the unavailability of alternatives. (1975a, p. 89)

Catania has performed a series of experiments (1975a, 1975b) which demonstrate that pigeons prefer a choice among alternatives over no choice, even when the rate of food reinforcement in each case is identical. He suggests that preference for choice may be characteristic of higher-level organisms, whether it arises phylogenetically or onto-genetically. Since a single source of reinforcement may fail occasionally, and different alternative sources may vary in relative rate across time, an organism which has choice is more likely to be reinforced continually and to survive and reproduce; hence, the adaptiveness of the capacity to be reinforced by choice.

Despite these analyses, freedom is not a well defined concept, involving at least both choice and lack of aversive control. We agree with Skinner (1971) that for the present it would be more useful to use terms other than freedom in defining values or goals for ourselves. Choice and reduction of aversive control are good candidates.

HIGHER-ORDER CONCEPTS IN SOCIAL BEHAVIOR

Thus far we have examined a behavioral view as it applied to ethical behavior of individuals and small numbers of interacting individuals; these are the cases which many behavior analysts have already analyzed using their experimental and theoretical approach. However, other concepts may be needed to describe "emergent" social phenomena among larger aggregates of people. Examples of such phenomena are important ones like "cultural change," "group norms," law, professional codes of ethics, dissemination of practices, and many others relevant to ethics. However, most descriptive systems dealing with phenomena at the level of "culture" lead to reification and pseudo-explanatory labeling, just as stage theory sometimes does in developmental psychology. That is, they fail to identify the variables which are functionally related to change so that the process can be controlled. It is not at all unusual to see writers speak of a political state with its own goals, explain a change by calling it evolution, or deplore the growing sickness of society.

There are four general streams of theory and research that are beginning to fill the gap: systems analysis, behavioral sociology (including game and social exchange theory), behavioral economics, and experimental dissemination research. They are all compatible with or based upon a behavioral model of man.

The one that is probably most familiar to behaviorists is systems analysis, popularized by a conference and book called Behavior Analysis and Systems Analysis (Harshbarger & Maley, 1974). The focus of behavioral systems analysis is upon institutions, organizations, and other social structures that involve sometimes complex patterns of contingencies among the people who comprise them. As behaviorists have become administrators in institutions or have tried to make changes in institutional contingencies in the course of simpler interventions, they have become more interested in analyzing such macrocontingency systems. The results have already become indispensable to social change agents in a variety of applications.

A second approach to supraindividual behavior is behavioral sociology (Hamblin & Kunkel, 1977; McGinnies, 1970). This area is attracting a growing number of sociologists, who analyze sociological phenomena using principles straight from behavior analysis. The premise is that social system behavior can be explained in terms of psychological processes, and that no principles beyond those necessary to explain individual behavior are required (Homans, 1974). The origins of behavioral sociology lie in game theory, developed by the coinventor of the hydrogen bomb, John von Neumann, and an economist, Oskar Morgenstern, in a classic volume Theory of Games and Economic Behavior (1944). Social exchange theory, based largely on game theory, developed within social psychology and sociology (Thibaut & Kelley, 1959).

Von Neumann and Morgenstern assumed certain (empirically testable) characteristics of individuals, then analyzed what standards of social behavior would tend to develop when these individuals came together. Predictions about behavior based on the mathematical models developed by game theorists have generated considerable research (esp. see Behavioral Science Journal). However, the rigorously developed mathematics (Von Neumann & Morgenstern, 1944; Symposium on Cardinal Utilities, 1952) depend on assumptions about individual behavior, and research results have modified those assumptions continually. The recent results from research on the matching law (e.g., Davison & Temple, 1974; Herrnstein & Loveland, 1976; H.L. Miller, 1976) and intransitivity (Navarick & Fantino, 1974) are the kind of mathematical input that a game-theoretical approach can utilize.

A related stream of research is behavioral economics, which also traces its roots in part to game theory (Rachlin et al., 1976). Economists have always made important assumptions about individual behavior, many of which seem naive to psychologists. Since economics deals with social behavior at the supraindividual level, and has clear potential for enormous influence on behavior, we are interested in its relationship with behavior analysis. Recent work by behaviorists (e.g., Battalio et al, 1974; Fisher et al., 1978; Rachlin et al., 1976; Winkler, 1973) offers prospects of much more fruitful interaction between behavioral psychology and economics and an NSF-sponsored conference in 1979 will focus attention on the new field.

The fourth stream of research relevant to influencing social behavior is experimental research on the dissemination of social practices, pioneered by Fairweather and colleagues (1974; see also Behavior Analysis and Modification Project Newsletter, 1976 for a recent project). Related empirical approaches in this stream are experimental research on methods of intervention in communities and organizations by Rothman and colleagues (Rothman, 1974; Rothman Erlich, & Teresa, 1976) and "quasi-experimental" social research (e.g., Ross et al., 1970; Schnelle & Lee, 1974). These approaches go well beyond the purely descriptive theory of sociocultural evolution criticized above; they experimentally determine what organizational and intervention variables influence actual change in practices.

The research on dissemination and intervention provides a beginning toward conceptualizing social organizations and change in a way that can interact with and validate the results from systems analysis and behavioral sociology theory. Since many important ethical issues are based on concepts at the social organization/system level, it is important to develop better empirical analyses of these concepts.

A THEORETICAL VIEWPOINT ON VALUES

Based on the foregoing presentation of three major scientific approaches to ethics, we will formulate a conceptualization upon which later discussion of practical issues will depend. We criticized the sociocultural evolutionary position for reifying "culture" and "practice." Practices are said to evolve independently of the organisms' behavior. Worse yet, they are even opposed to the organism's genetic dispositions. Campbell (1975) draws as a model a scale of behavior, with the forces of biological endowment and cultural endowment portrayed as steel springs pulling in opposite directions. "(S)ocial evolution has had to counter individual selfish tendencies which biological evolution has continued to select as a result of the genetic competition among the cooperators" (p. 1115).

A viewpoint which has been clearly stated by Skinner (esp. 1966, 1974) provides a more useful framework for us. According to Skinner, an organism behaves in accordance with its biological endowment, past reinforcement history, and current environment. If an organism is responding in accordance with a cultural practice which seems to be making him act against his biological interest, he is being controlled by means of other biological effects. The cultural practices must be based on the biological characteristics of organisms, rather than opposed to them or independent of them. The error is in taking too narrow a view, focusing on only one behavior or reinforcer rather than looking at the whole organism with its multiple capacities for reinforcement and the whole environment with its multiple contingencies.

Take as an example a member of a family which has a limited supply of food. Taking the narrow view, we would say that the biological tendency to eat until satiated is opposed by the social practice of sharing with one's family. The social practice does seem to be at a different level from, and opposing to, the biological tendency. Now take the larger view. If the person took more than his share, the other members would show signs of disapproval and possibly punish him physically; they would be likely to ostracize him if he continued; and so on. Those family member behaviors are effective influences on his behavior because of his biological capacities to be punished, to acquire responses to conditioned social stimuli which have been paired with more basic reinforcers, and so on. Behavior can be analyzed at different levels, including organismic and cultural, but at each level, the explanatory system should be consistent. Mixing them freely is bound eventually to lead to confusion, although it may be quite convenient at the moment.

Such a behavioral view of social practices is entirely consistent with — indeed dependent on — a kind of sociobiological viewpoint. As we have stressed, social practices must be based on the biological characteristics of organisms rather than opposed to them or independent of them. Neo-Darwinian evolutionary theory is currently the best way to describe the development of such biological properties.

The question then is, what level of properties relevant to behavior of human organisms are genetically transmitted? For example, to what extent is the behavior of sharing food with one's family transmitted full-blown, as opposed to the person inheriting only the capacity to be reinforced by food, human contact, etc., and the capacity to respond to stimuli correlated with these reinforcers? What is inherited in the practice of driving a car on the right (or left) side of the road? Or suckling one's newborn baby? Or maintaining an oppressive prison or racist social practices? (See Herrnstein, 1977a,b,; and Skinner, 1977, for a discussion of the role of what is "inherent" in the reinforcement process).

There are many empirical results which bear on this issue, and much yet to be determined by experiments. At this stage, however, a relatively clear and consistent position based on genetics, personal history, and current environment has been formulated that can deal with behavior at the individual and cultural practice levels. Moreover, on the basis of this formulation, it follows that most behavior we call ethics, and certainly the part that is modifiable, is the result of experience and current environment, based on inherited biological capacities.

Having formulated a position, it remains to see how this will influence our behavior in solving ethical problems. As Campbell (1975) put it: "A descriptive ethics, using biological and social evolution, should also be able to predict which ultimate values animals such as social humankind are likely to choose, even though it would not thereby philosophically justify such normative values" (p. 1109). We agree with Day (1977) that to look for justification of values, i.e., reasons, is essentially mentalistic. Perhaps in belated recognition of this, some of the most modern philosophical meta-ethical writings are concerned with the nature and limits of justification in ethics, as Abelson and Nielsen (1967) observe.

Thus, there will be no final ethic as a result of this analysis. Some may object that this behavioral theory still does not provide any way to decide what we should do in real situations. For example, Begelman (1975) points out that ". . . we ask ourselves the unscientific question: What I have done is socially (professionally, scientifically) approved, but is it right?" (p. 186). People will continue to ask (and answer) the question, but they will not get the kind of answer they seek. A behavioral formulation offers a very different way of looking at ethical choices. In this view, a person in an ethical choice situation is seen to be influenced by the contingencies in effect and by his personal history and genetic endowment. The value of a theory of ethics for him is to make him more aware of the influences on his behavior in order to choose more effectively. This theory may also lead people, individually and collectively, to formulate their problems in terms that will enable them to apply the analyses and methods of a science of human behavior.

APPLYING THE CONCEPTUALIZATION

Professional environmental designers are facing many problems which have come to be identified as ethical problems. Each of these has evoked various proposals for solution, some based on a behavioral analysis of the problem situation. Rather than discuss specific problems, which continually change, the following section will focus on the proffered solutions. In the process of examining them, we will attempt to identify the variables influencing the behaviors of the professionals and others involved, especially the reinforcers (values) involved.

Avoid ethical issues, cease doing controversial research and applications

These proposals can be classed as avoidance and, as such, offer no solution — there are consequences to all behaviors of a professional. If he refuses to make a choice on a controversial area of application or research or to enter an area because there are difficult choices, he has made his decision already, and his values can be inferred from his actions or nonactions.

We do not wish to criticize choosing not to work in certain controversial areas. Critics of sociobiology (discussed above), critics of Herrnstein and Jensen on genetic differences in I.Q., scientists in discussions after the development of the atomic bomb, and biologists who recently imposed a moratorium on their own work with viruses, all have questioned the desirability of certain scientific activities. Scientists may not simply claim an obligation to publish all scientific findings regardless of their implications. Rather, that scientific value must be balanced against the others involved. The structure of scientific organizations, funding agencies, and academic departments all influence choices that are made.

Informed consent,
let the client select
the goal, community involvement
in planning, contracting (informal)

These are proposed as solutions to ethical situations which arise between two parties in which one is generally seen as the influencer and the other is seen as the influencee. These proposals all intend to provide countercontrol to the influencees, so they can "make their own decisions" whether to participate and under what terms. However, a behavioral analysis of the situation sees both parties as influencing and influenced. To the extent one values equality, then making available some countercontrolling behaviors may have some desired effects; but, unless one believes in autonomous and rational free will, these proposals cannot be seen as removing the ethical problems.

A prominent psychologist told the story of a pediatric surgeon he knew who claimed always get permission from parents to do what he wanted by using an authoritative approach. The doctor felt he could get a parent to agree to cutting off the child's head if he put the case strongly enough. A professional dealing with distressed or deprived populations is in an even more influential position.

Informed consent was first specified by the Nuremberg code to rid the medical profession of some of its abusive practices, and the concept has been updated since then (DHEW, 1971, p. 7; See Stolz, in press, for a history). The most recent version specifies that the subject must be given a complete description, including possible risks, alternatives, and information that he or she can withdraw at any time. Good discussions of informed consent are in Atthowe (1975) and Goldiamond (1974).

A problem with informed consent recognized by civil libertarians is that total institutions are inherently coercive, so that inmates cannot exercise free choice. According to this chapter's view, they are only beginning to see the tip of the iceberg of influences involved in informed consent. Maley & Hayes (1977) suggest that people are likely to label as coercive the most obvious and intrusive contingencies, where the control tends to be through punishment, threat of punishment, deprivation of positive reinforcement, the use of positive reinforcement in a barren environment, or where the reinforcers are so strong that compliance is very likely. However, in a behavioral view, client behaviors will always be influenced. Goldiamond (1974, 1975) proposes to eliminate the coercive effect of being in a total institution by removing the promise of early release as an inducement to behave in a certain way. While this may satisfy critics, there are still many other ways to make compliance arbitrarily probable.

Letting clients select their own goals has been strongly urged by Bandura (1969):

> The selection of goals involves value choices. To the extent that people assume major responsibility for deciding the direction in which their behavior ought to be modified, the frequently voiced concerns about human manipulation become essentially pseudo

issues. The change agent's role in the decision process should be primarily to explore alternative courses of action available, and their probable consequences, on the basis of which clients can make informed choices. However, a change agent's value commitments will inevitably intrude to some degree on the goal selection process. These biases are not necessarily detrimental, provided clients and change agents subscribe to similar values and the change agent identifies his judgments as personal preferences rather than purported scientific prescriptions. (P. 112)

But again, there are inevitable influences on the client's choice of goals: 1) the change agent will influence the client by his presentation of alternatives and the predicted outcome of each; 2) the client is continually influenced by others in his life who may have brought him to the professional in the first place; and 3) The client will be influenced by the prevailing ideology in the culture or his subculture. Furthermore, why choose a change agent with similar rather than different values? This suggestion, along with the whole notion of clients choosing "their own" goals, is an attempt at a "hands-off" approach to the problem, which was presented and rejected in the introduction. This is not to say that clients should not select their own goals by some process or other; but this process does not reduce the ethical problem to a pseudo issue.

The "let the client decide" idea has become popular at a different level, with entire organizations and communities as clients. For years, social planners and managers of all types have taken a paternalistic approach to their tasks of providing for people, assuming that as experts they knew best. In recent years, they have begun responding to growing consumer complaints by inviting those affected to participate in the planning and decision-making process (Langton, 1978, Rappaport, 1977, and Rothman et al. 1976). While this is generally a highly laudable change, the individual client analysis earlier in this section suggests several analogous problems with organizations, some of which have been recognized by planners.

- A planner will inevitably influence choices by biasing the presentation of information at his disposal; there is no objective presentation. He will be most influential when his client population is ill-informed or ignorant.

- The community representatives will inevitably fail to "represent" the "community" in many respects.

- The social, economic, historical, and physical environment in which the community exists will influence the decision making process, as will the specific system chosen for participation. A planner/environmental designer will be aware of his influence and other influences in the decision making process, knowing that "hands-off" is impossible.

Contracting between professional and client has been proposed for situations involving unequal control (Schwitzgebel, 1975, in press; Goldiamond, 1974, 1975, 1976). Informal contracts are often very useful, but they are also subject to the same analysis and criticism as was informed consent. Contracts done within the legal system will be discussed in a later section.

Certification
of professionals, ethical guidelines
of professional groups

In the language of game theory (Von Neumann & Morgenstern, 1944), certification and ethical guidelines are practices of coalitions (professional groups). These practices arise because the alternatives are control and punishment by others outside the coalition, resulting in less gain to the members. However altruistic the group may seem to be in its self-control, its behavior is maintained by those outsiders. As a game-theoretical analysis shows, a coalition will try to gain as much as possible, although there are definite limits to how much they can win.

Certification as a procedure has been hotly debated over the years (for the debate among behavior analysts, see Wood, 1975b). As a source of influence on professional behavior, it is only one of many, including economic, educational, legal, professional, social, and institutional (Ford and Hutchison, 1974). There are distinct disadvantages associated with it as a method of control, particularly its rigidifying and divisive/exclusionary effects. As an alternative, the Association for the Advancement of Behavior Therapy decided to offer site visits to deal with questionable practices rather than undertaking to certify behavior therapists.

Ethical guidelines have been developed by a number of organizations for themselves, beginning with the American Psychological Association. Guidelines attempt to control individual behaviors that would have the most adverse effects upon other members of the coalition, and the code may be published widely in order to blunt criticism of a profession. They may also function to pressure other competing coalitions to adopt similar codes and evaluative standards, to the advantage of the initiating group, as Thomson (1977) and Azrin (1975) have advocated for behaviorists.

The Association for the Advancement of Behavior Therapy is in the process of formulating ethical guidelines as this chapter is being written. In soliciting comments and suggestions from AABT members on the draft of principles, Azrin (1976) makes a number of comments directly relevant to points made in various sections of this chapter:

> The phrasing is deliberately interrogatory rather than imperative; to convey the spirit of the guidelines as questions that the therapist should direct to themselves as reminders rather than as legally mandated principles. Also deliberate is the exclusion of terms specific to behavior therapy since we felt these ethical questions should apply to all types of counseling or

treatment. Other objectives were to be very general at this early stage of formulation, to have as few principles as possible for simplicity, to deal only with clinical practice since research guidelines exist in abundance, to avoid specification of the legal obligations because of their ever changing nature, to avoid establishing territoriality of behavior therapy versus other professions and to emphasize cooperation between professions and the clients' interests is desired, to avoid unnecessary practices which would interfere with clinical treatment, to place the burden on the therapist and not solely on a consent by the patient or a committee. Behavior therapy has been accused of late of sometimes being insensitive to the needs of clients. The intent in these guidelines is to provide the means of reminding ourselves of ethical considerations such that our practices will serve as a model for other professions exhibiting human concern for clients. (P. 1)

Even more important than the momentary state of the guidelines is the process of setting up and changing guidelines (Krasner, 1976a). Accounts of such deliberations are furnished by Cook et al. (1971) for APA; Thomson (1977) for the Minnesota Guidelines; and Stolz (1975) for NIMH. Guidelines will change as a result of influences from inside and outside coalitions, and different possible processes will have different consequences to members and nonmembers.

Skill training,
Training in self-control,
Training in counter-control,
Giving psychology away,
Training in environmental design

Goldsmith & McFall (1975) introduce their skill training approach with the assumption that ". . . each individual always does the best he can, given his physical limitations and unique learning history, to respond as effectively as possible in every situation" (p. 51). All of the proposals in this section make the same assumption, and would train people as the preferred way to improve their situation. We approve of this approach, and predict that as training methods improve it will become increasingly influential. More importantly for the purposes of this chapter, skill training can be an approach to many situations seen as ethical problems.

As an example, a colleague of ours explained the ethical dilemma posed to him by youths in his group home: Should you force boys to learn and perform the variety of social skills they teach? Shouldn't a youth be allowed to choose not to learn? Our colleague presented his view that unless a person has acquired the skills, he really has no choice; after a boy acquires the skills and samples the reinforcement available both ways, then he has choice.

A similar and complementary approach has been suggested by Goldiamond (1974) who outlines a "constructional" orientation: "(S)olution to problems is the construction of repertoires (or their reinstatement or transfer to new situations) rather than the elimination of repertoires . . . The focus here is on the production of desirables through means which <u>directly</u> increase available options or extend social repertoires, rather than <u>indirectly</u> doing so as a by-product of an eliminative procedure" (p. 14). Besides the strong appeal of this orientation for other reasons, it removes the necessity for aversive eliminative procedures.

Skill training applies to professional ethical behavior as well. Many cases of unethical professional behavior have occurred because of lack of skills, for which Ford & Hutchison (1974) suggest as a remedy more effective professional training – including in the area of ethics – and provision for continuing education. Skilled and sensitive professionals are less likely to harm clients due to incompetence.

Training in self-control behavior is an important new area of research and application closely related to skill training. Many proponents believe that self-control solves the ethical dilemma by giving clients the capacity to select their own goals. However, this claim to a true hands-off method falls victim to the same reasoning as other hands-off claims. The client's behavior is, and continues to be, influenced by a number of variables, and the result may be desired or undesired.

The most important choice that skill training presents is: What behaviors should be trained? For example, should a trainer teach his students persuasive techniques which are effective only if not per-ceived, or techniques which are completely open but possibly less effective? The process of training increases the strength of the trained behavior relative to alternative behaviors so, in a sense, the trainer is still determining the client's response. Even if he tries to train all alternatives (which is impractical at best) he must choose how much to train each. If trainers are thereby trying to absolve themselves of responsibility, they are victims of the hands-off folly discussed earlier.

Training in counter-control for underprivileged groups has been advocated by Holland (1974), Shaw (1972), and Stolz (1978). A game-theoretical analysis leads to the prediction that underprivileged groups will increasingly form coalitions and exert countercontrol, following the recent examples of civil rights groups, Common Cause, gay rights groups, women's rights groups, coalitions of poor people, and many others. The challenge for professionals adopting this value is to develop processes which will insure adequate reinforcement for maintaining their own helping behavior. The best of intentions does not maintain behavior for long by itself.

Environmental design fits very well in this category (as well as other categories) of approaches. As presented in Krasner & Ullmann (1973) and the present volume, the idea is to train people to most effectively conceptualize and influence the environment which is influencing them. There are many behaviors involved, and we have obviously only begun the process of developing conceptualizations and influence methods.

Replace aversive control with positive control,
Increase available choices

Two proposals have been made which relate closely to our analysis of ethics. The first, to develop positive control procedures to replace aversive control, has long been associated with Skinner (1953). The second, to increase the number of choices available to individuals, has been proposed as the primary criterion for ethical decisions by Kelman (1965) and others.

Positive control generally means offering incentives for desired behavior rather than punishing the undesired behavior. As the efficacy of positive reinforcement has been discovered, it seems possible in more and more situations, although there may still be situations where punishment may be the procedure of choice (Johnston, 1978). Maley & Hayes (1977) point out that positive control techniques are less likely to be blocked for legal reasons (cf. coercion), although in many cases they accomplish the same objective. Maley and Hayes suggest, however, that some people in the legal system are becoming more aware of the implications of positive control.

An increase in available choices is one result of the training proposed in the previous section. However, there are other ways to increase choices: there may be societally imposed restrictions, socially sanctioned discrimination, and self-restraints (such as conditioned fears) which could be removed. One example of approaching an ethical (and practical) problem by increasing choices is the plan for the Butner federal prison for difficult inmates (see Behavior Today, January 26, 1976). Rather than the "behavior modification" approach, the plan is to use the ideas of Morris (1974) to increase options and educational opportunities available to prisoners.

Rather than trying simply to justify why these proposals should be done, the processes will be analyzed more closely. The use of positive control is, by its nature, more reinforcing to the person controlled than is aversive control. Increasing choice is also reinforcing, if the experimental results of Catania (1975a,b) are not contradicted – and there are good evolutionary reasons why they should not be. However, the fact that they are reinforcing to the controllee does not mean they will occur as a natural result. The behaviors of the people controlling are, themselves, under the control of specifiable variables usually including the behavior of those controlled. It is, thus, a two-way process: each controls the other. If a more reinforcing procedure is available than the one being used, the two parties should be able to strike up a bargain in which each side is reinforced for allowing its implementation. Take as example worker participation in management of various productive enterprises, which is increasing rapidly around the world, usually with positive consequences for both sides. The reduction in aversive control used by one side is maintained by more desired behavior on the part of the other. Every effective positive control procedure has the potential for being implemented by this mutual change process and it is likely the use of positive control will increase.

Openness,
Making contingencies explicit,
Accountability

These proposals have become more salient since the beginning of the Watergate era, attacks on the secrecy of intelligence-gathering agencies, "freedom of information" acts, and other movements toward openness and accountability. Behaviorists pride themselves on their openness of methods and goals (Davison & Stuart, 1974, 1975), and the measurement, explicit goal setting, and continual monitoring of progress of behavioral approaches are necessary elements of more open and accountable systems.

Openness in a behavioral view indicates access to information about contingencies in effect. Information used in this sense means verbal statements or other cues about contingencies that humans can utilize to behave almost as if they had been directly in contact with the contingency. Catania (1975a) and earlier experimenters have shown that organisms prefer information about contingencies in effect. The reason for this is clear: one can behave much more effectively with information than without it.

Given this preference, the prediction follows that practices increasing access to information (openness) will continue to increase. Of course, openness is only one value, and in some cases others will outweigh it (e.g., genuine national security intelligence, socially damaging private information, etc.). In the case of deception in experimentation, Kelman (1968) says we must weigh the value of openness with the value of what is to be gained in sacrificing it.

Many behaviorists have advocated the value of being open about our own personal values (Davison & Stuart, 1975) so that clients will be able to resist undue influence. Day (1977) proposed a more comprehensive approach, particularly when the client is seeking advice about a question of values. The professional should analyze the behavior of both the client and himself and the contingencies involved. The three key items are: 1) the reinforcement characteristics of the client, 2) the prevailing contingencies in the environment, and 3) the reinforcement controlling the assertions of the professional analyzer. The first two parts combine to produce a Skinnerian should (See above), i.e., the behavior that will give the client the most reinforcers, as well as can be judged by the professional. The third part enables the client to assess the biases intrinsic to the professional's situation.

Openness by itself is not enough. As Bandura (1974) put it in his analysis, "Awareness alone, however, is a weak countervalence" (p. 868). Rather, awareness of behavioral principles needs to be combined with effective countercontrol, through clients' control of meaningful reinforcers for professionals' behavior. What is needed is accountability, as developed by Krapfl (1975a) and in the systems analysis tradition. A professional voluntarily places himself under the control of those he is supposed to be serving, by means of mechanisms such as public advisory and review boards, feedback systems, and public education. This is more beneficial for the professional than it might initially seem. In the long run, the public controls his reinforcers; the more responsive he can become to them, the more they are likely to benefit from his behavior and continue delivering reinforcers to him.

Accountability based on review and evaluation should be independent, continuous, and publicly reported. The major reason a system may be unresponsive to public wants is that the professionals' reinforcers are controlled by agents not under public control and delivered contingent on behavior not necessarily congruent with good service delivery, such as political loyalty, seniority, number of publications, etc. The methods in systems analysis provide the basis for approaching problems of this type.

Research on consequences of behavior & practices,
Society-wide experimentation,
Combining research and practice

In the previous section we stressed the value of making contingencies explicit. It is obvious that continuing research is necessary in order to discover more remote contingencies in effect, so we can design processes to come under better control of them. Hawkins (1975) advocates (and cites) research into the consequences of alternative behaviors as a basis for deciding what behaviors should be taught (i.e., set up as values). One important example is research on the long-term consequences to children of certain parent and teacher behaviors. He also advocates monitoring a number of other behaviors that may change concomitantly as a result of the independent variable. As examples of this kind of research, he cites Sajwaj, Twardosz, and Burke (1972) and Nordquist (1971).

Research may also be the basis for selecting institutional practices. In rebutting challenges to the ethics of research on involuntary patients and prisoners, Davison & Stuart (1975) told the ACLU that the only ethical alternative is to require research into the effectiveness of various alternative treatments. The alternative of little or no research would result in less than optimal treatments. Of course, research on other populations has value but cannot be generalized without further testing. Azrin (1975) spoke in response to the imposition of cumbersome regulations on behavioral treatments that were being classed as experimental, while traditional techniques were unregulated. Since the old techniques had never been proven effective – and there was considerable doubt about their effectiveness – they should be subject to the same regulations and testing, he argued.

Campbell (1969, 1970, 1971) has been a leading proponent for an experimenting society that utilizes experimental and quasi-experimental research to make decisions about the impact of social programs. There are many naturally-occurring experiments taking place continually, including large scale comparisons across countries, states, or even school districts having different practices. There are certainly many problems in inferences from such comparisons, including nonequivalence of populations and interaction with other practices, as well as problems in applying conclusions across different populations. Frequently, the amount and type of data collected are seriously deficient. The use of quasi-experimental methodology (Campbell & Stanley, 1963) enables a resourceful experimenter to squeeze many valuable results out of the seeming disorder (e.g., Campbell & Ross, 1968; Glass, Tiao, & McGuire, 1971; Ross, Campbell, & Glass, 1970, Schnelle et al. 1975; Schnelle & Lee, 1974), but more effective design and data collection would be very useful. Federal, state, and local support for such experiments has increased dramatically in the last few years, as has support for the dissemination of results of social experiments. Another important development is the beginning of research into the variables influencing adoption of proven procedures (see above). The most grandiose proposal (Fairweather, 1967), called Experimental Social Innovation, would use experimental methods, including random or matched selection, to test the effects of different practices applied to entire communities or regions of the country. An extensive data collection (hundreds of dependent variables) would be monitored to determine all the effects of the different procedures. We seem to be moving in the direction of such a plan.

Another trend we would like to promote is the combining of research and application (Winett, 1976). Behavior modifiers were early practitioners of this idea, which found its purest example in the single-case designs applied to clinical cases (Goldiamond, Dyrud, & Miller, 1965). The experimenter gathers data continually and is thus optimally responsive to (influenced by) the behavior of the subject. In our own program (Chap. 8) we have been developing this model extensively. These designs are highly useful in developing and assessing new practices, all in the course of "delivering services." Too often, practices are adopted on a grand scale, based on their intuitive or political appeal, to be replaced when a more appealing idea comes along. The separation of research and practice into separate activities allows practitioners to ignore the remote consequences of their behavior, and researchers to conduct research that has no practical implications and produces output too late to modify practices anyway. Continuous planned assessment can aid in further development and modification of the practice. There are continuous major and minor changes in practices in our society, but only by combining research with applications can we be most responsive to the consequences of those practices.

Ethical committees,
Law and contracting, social planning

Several proposals for dealing with ethical problems advocate various formal processes. For each of these, we can attempt to analyze the most important controlling variables and the likely outcomes or consequences.

Ethical committees of various types are becoming a feature of research and treatment agencies as major ethical decision making bodies. In research centers, they decide what research is acceptable, usually in conjunction with federal guidelines. In treatment centers, they may act as representatives of persons judged incompetent to make choices for themselves. In community agencies, they may purport to represent the interests of "the community" or various parts of it. In many cases, they have assumed a great deal of power and broad oversight, and their decisions are generally accepted as the product of a fair process (see Friedman, 1975; A.P.A. Guidelines, 1973; NIMH Guidelines in Brown, Wienckowski & Stolz, 1975).

From a behavioral perspective, there is no such thing as objectivity or impartiality (Stolz, 1978). These committees will be composed of individuals, and the behavior in the committee will be the product of those individuals' learning history and current contingencies as they mutually influence each other in the committee. Factors such as the openness of the proceedings and accountability to some population will have a major influence on their behavior. Representatives drawn from a population will almost always be selected in a nonrandom fashion, and can often be converted to the viewpoint of the prestigious professionals or other influential group on the committee. One is deceiving himself to feel "relieved of his ethical responsibility" by referring to a committee his dilemmas about choice of treatment, acceptability of research manipulations, or choice of community activities, in hopes of a balanced and impartial judgment. The ethical guidelines being formulated by AABT (Association for the Advancement of Behavior Therapy) have been influenced by their writers' awareness of this point: "(O)ur intention (is) . . . to place the burden on the therapist and not solely on a consent by the patient or a committee" (Azrin, 1976).

Another very important process is the legal system. In very recent years, an enormous amount of activity has taken place, frequently dragging major ethical questions into courts for arbitration and action – right to treatment (even least restrictive treatment), right to be released if not dangerous (even a restricted view of dangerous), equal right to all kinds of community resources, and many more landmark issues have been taken to court. Articles by Wexler (1973, 1975), Friedman (1975), and newsletters of organizations such as the Mental Health Law Project, Common Cause, Psychology-Law Society, and others (see Appendix) give a strong impression of the influence and potential of this movement.

The value implied in advocating legal remedies is that the consequences will be desirable. This chapter conceptualizes law as a process consisting of a set of relatively well-defined contingencies which influence much behavior of everyone. If there could be such things as well-informed, unbiased, and disinterested decision makers (e.g. judges or legislators) or if a representative democracy (or other system) could represent "the will of the people," then legal processes would offer very neat solutions to many choices. If, however, each person in these processes is seen as subject to historical and environmental influences, and the processes involved are seen as following lawful rules of behavior, then legal decisions are not seen as unbiased. Rather, these decisions have consequences which might be compared with the consequences of other possible processes.

One desirable property of the legal system is that the contingencies are made explicit and usually more reliable. However, the legal system relies primarily on punishment contingencies, and utilizes many concepts which behaviorists challenge as inexact or misleading, such as free will, competence, informed, coerce, etc. (some of which have been analyzed earlier). However, the legal system does change — witness the emergence of class action suits by coalitions as an important force — and new legal concepts emerge. If behavioral concepts and views are effective, they can be adopted. For instance, people in the legal system have recently become more aware of the influence of positive reinforcement, especially with deprived individuals (Maley & Hayes, 1977).

Several issues and processes within the legal system have come to the special attention of professionals. One is the issue of legal guardianship of people judged incompetent. Legal guardians may not be particularly well informed, and often they will have interests which conflict with those of the client (Goldiamond, 1974; Brown et al. 1975). For example, parents of a retarded individual may have to approve a behavioral procedure which would result in the child being capable of moving back into their home, and their desire to avoid this result may influence their decision "on his behalf." Often an attorney may be appointed to represent the interests of a mental patient or prisoner. But as Friedman (1975) discusses, there is often some confusion as to which side he should advocate on behalf of the client. The solution he suggests for legal advocates, as does Stolz (1978) for ethical committees, is to have well-informed advocates for both sides. This would at least allow the major arguments to be made, although it should be clear from a behavioral view that we cannot assume "the truth will win out" in such a confrontation.

Brown et al. (1975), Goldiamond (1974), Holland (1974), and Stolz (1978) claim that it is important to determine and keep clear about who the true client of the professional is. Their common answer is that the client is the one who controls the professional's livelihood. For an institution, the client is not the inmates but the institution: the professional contracts to change the institution's behavior. If he works with an individual, then he establishes a separate contract with him. For a child brought into therapy, the parents are the client, and the therapist contracts to change their behavior. Although this view is consistent with a legal framework, from a behavioral viewpoint it should be extended. To say that a paycheck is the only reinforcer that is (or should be) controlling the professional's behavior ignores the multiple strong sources of control. The true client definition will be important if the professional ends up in court, but as a guide to his likely or desirable behavior in his work it is not too informative.

Informal, nonbinding contracts were discussed under verbal behavior (above). However, if the contract is legally binding, as more and more contracts for services of professionals are being held by courts to be, then the whole set of legal contingencies must be brought into consideration. Although the courts will uphold the right of a "free, competent" person to enter into a contract in which he may not have struck his most advantageous position, there are protections against the most obvious kinds of coercive behavior on the part of the professional.

Because a binding contract is subject to legal contingencies, it can have a much more pronounced influence on behavior.

Schwitzgebel (1975, in press) and Goldiamond (1974) have argued particularly eloquently for the contract as a solution to certain ethical dilemmas. For a prisoner in jail, the argument goes as follows: The prisoner should have the right to enter into a contract with an experimenter (or other person). Since he is in a deprived situation he is more likely to respond to the incentives offered for compliance than he otherwise would be; but to forbid him the right to gain by entering into a contract is reducing his options rather than increasing them. The experimenter can only be seen to provide an increase in options to the prisoners, which is a desirable thing if one considers increased options a value. If people object to the situation, they should be objecting to the original deprivation forced by the prison, not to the experimenter's behavior (Bennett, 1976).

Further analysis of ethics and social systems, Training in ethics

There is wide agreement on the importance of training people in ethics, although this occasionally is a cover for advocating one's own particular values. Such training makes professionals more sensitive to ethical choices and to more remote consequences of their behavior and, hopefully, makes them more effective in performing behaviors involved in making their choices. The last section (v) on training implications will deal with this more fully.

However, there is no finished body of knowledge and analysis to convey to students and professionals. Many highly useful analyses have been made, especially at the individual behavior level, and we have suggested the beginnings of methods for dealing with system behavior. Our understanding of ethics will continue to increase along with our understanding of other behavior. This cannot occur by theoretical analysis alone, but as a function of research on social systems and change discussed previously. Nevertheless, the behavior of theoretically analyzing behavior will continue to be important in ethics, providing eager analysts with exciting prospects of future chapters, papers, and books to write.

TRAINING IMPLICATIONS

We have discussed implications of training for ethics, and in the importance of this training has been stressed throughout the chapter. In this section we will suggest a practical approach to training in ethics, which is used in the program in London described in Chapter 8.

The first step, which occurs very early, is guided exposure to ethical problems, raising awareness of them as problems. As Schnaitter (1977) analyzed this, we could be said to be creating problemswhere there were none before. A problem arises when a person becomes aware of concurrent, incompatible responses. Before he is aware of the competing responses, there is no problem. As contact is made with more contingencies, more conflicts arise, hence more novel "ethical" choices. Trainers can present ethical problems to environmental designers and teach them the skill of discriminating the problems. In this experience, students gain both awareness of the specific important ethical problems presented and skill at recognizing problems as they are encountered.

This training can be accompanied and followed by guided experience in situations where ethical problems occur – both in first-hand practicum work and vicariously in the work of colleagues. The experience should be arranged to put the student in contact with maximum information about the situation and consequences of the choice made. This experience provides the motivation for acquiring the skills, as well as very relevant practice. The students are presented with different approaches to ethical problem solving and given practice using all of them to deal with a variety of situations. The results of such a comparative exercise are a greater perspective on ethical problem solving and the strengthening of the most useful behaviors.

SUMMARY

We have not attempted to provide a method for solving ethical problems, at least in the sense of rules to determine what is right or what one should do in a particular situation. It may seem quite the contrary, that we have done our best to criticize all the suggestions people have proposed as solutions.

Rather than solutions, what we have attempted to present is an environmental design perspective on ethical behavior. This perspective has often led us to identify more sources of influence on professionals and others than we had observed from other perspectives. We hope it will be useful to readers in recognizing and approaching value choices as they design environments.

3 Environmental Psychology

David Pomeranz

The following chapter on Environmental Psychology by David Pomeranz offers a systematic approach to the research in an area of psychology which has virtually become a separate field of its own, environmental psychology (See chap. 1). The environmental design approach places major focus on environmental influences on behavior and utilizes many of the research findings of behavioral scientists in the environmental fields. Hence, a description and incorporation of relevant work in this area is presented in the next chapter.

Designing an environment may range from the construction of a particular item to arranging the elements in a delimited space, to developing a social, political, and economic climate in an environment as small as a classroom to one as large as a total society. Designed environments then have influence on individuals, including those who have been instrumental in their design leading to a systems or ecological approach to understanding the reciprocal nature of the person in the environment. The point is continually emphasized in defining the field of environmental psychology that it is investigating the "effects of continuous physical settings on various aspects of behavior" (Ittelson et al., 1974, p. 2).

This view represents the earlier stated view of one-way influence. These authors, as well as others in other places, realize that what is involved is an interactive and continuous process in which individuals design and influence their physical environment and, in turn, the environment influences their behavior. The environmental design at any given moment was itself influenced by environmental impact. If there has been any major new development in psychology in recent years, it has been the growing cognizance of this highly complex interactive process.

Ed.

During the past decade, an increasing number of theoreticians and researchers have begun to examine the complex interplay of the person and the environment. Investigators from several disciplines have become interested in the interaction of person variables and environmental variables and have developed hypotheses and concepts and generated empirical findings in an attempt to explicate this intricate interaction. Although we will consider inputs from other disciplines, in this chapter our major focus will be on the contributions of psychology.

At this stage in its development, few theorists are willing or able to venture a theoretical or conceptual definition of "environmental psychology." Rather, the area is becoming defined by descriptions of numerous domains of investigation, all of which have some elements in common, and all of which emerge from the attempt to understand the intricate relation between the person and his environmental context.

As such, any definitions or conceptualizations are mainly descriptive in nature and, with the exception of "mini" theories in several sub-areas of environmental psychology, there remains the important task of developing a comprehensive theoretical scheme that will pull together a vast array of hypotheses, speculations, and research findings. This task is all the more difficult because many disciplines are concerned with the person-environment interface, each with its own language, concepts, methodologies, and interests.

The complexity and vastness of the subject matter itself, as emphasized in virtually every chapter of this book, makes it difficult to develop a coherent theoretical schema that will be understandable and useful to society and do justice to the large number of empirical findings that will continue to emerge at an ever expanding rate. Certainly, psychology is not the only, or even primary, discipline which has been interested in the person-environment interaction. As has been emphasized in earlier chapters, architecture, sociology, landscape design, geography, law, etc. have all focused on this issue, and each has contributed important conceptualizations and research.

With psychology itself, there has been shifting emphasis on the role of the environment in human behavior and on the exact nature of the interaction between person variables and environment variables. The emphasis on external determinants of behavior has grown increasingly strong during the past several decades, partly as a function of the behavioristic approach and partly as a function of better methodologies and conceptualizations of the environment. However, this emphasis has been offset by a persistent concern with internal influences, both psychological — traits, states, personality variables, dynamic conceptions — as well as organic and physiological. Psychological theorizing with respect to the relative importance of internal vs. external variables continues to be a hotly debated issue. Recently there has emerged an interactionist model which, while not according equal weight to both sets of variables, at least acknowledges that both are crucial in developing a thorough understanding of behavior and psychological functioning, (See chapter 4).

This chapter, like most of the chapters in this volume, is written from the perspective of a psychologist. As such, the framework is one in which behavior is seen as the dependent variable and the environment as the independent variable. While most of the chapter is addressed to reviewing work from this perspective, brief mention should be made of work which views the environment or influences on the environment as the dependent variable. Before proceeding to this discussion, however, some general considerations concerning methodological and conceptual issues will be mentioned.

METHODOLOGICAL AND CONCEPTUAL ASSUMPTIONS

Regardless of the particular person-environment interaction being considered, certain assumptions pertaining to methods of investigating these relationships exist. While one can find many exceptions, by and large, the research on person-environment interactions is characterized by a number of methodological approaches that emphasize procedures somewhat different from most laboratory investigations.

One emphasis has to do with the importance and, in many cases, the desirability of naturalistic, "real-life," or field studies in contrast to controlled, laboratory methods. Partly because the phenomena of concern are so complex and broad, it is difficult, if not impossible, to adequately bring them into a controlled setting for observation and manipulation. In addition, the ecological nature of the variables often calls for methods too complex to be handled in a typical experimental paradigm. An emphasis on naturally occurring events that characterize many of the issues in environmental psychology precludes, by definition, investigations which depend on artificially manipulating sets of variables in order to determine their effects on other variables.

The emphasis on naturalistic methods has been bolstered by the recent reemergence of the popularity of ethological investigations that has contributed a rich body of literature to understanding the behavior of organisms in their natural setting. (See Chapter 8). From a theoretical, philosophical, and empirical point of view, it is felt that gross injustices are often done to phenomena by subjecting them to laboratory conditions for investigation. Many criticisms and objections have been leveled at research investigators on the following grounds: the reactivity of the subjects being investigated; the biases of the investigator; the artificial and unnatural context of the observations; the nature of the investigation being determined by the methods available; and the difficulty in untangling the web of subject-environment interaction.

While naturalistic observation does not compensate for all of the above difficulties, and while there are problems unique to naturalistic observation itself, nevertheless, it is felt that the issues of concern to environmental psychologists can best be answered by resorting to methodologies not typically utilized in most current psychological studies. While there is no objection to supplementing naturalistic observation with laboratory methods, an exclusive reliance on the latter is rejected.

A second emphasis is in the importance of molar variables in contrast to psychology's "traditional" overemphasis on molecular variables. The area of person-environment interactions includes issues and areas which are too broad and complex to be adequately handled by a molecular approach. Specific responses, specific independent variables, and specific mechanisms are usually too isolated and narrow to account for the behaviors of interest to most investigations in environmental psychology.

Although it is difficult, "messy," and often frustrating for an investigator in environmental psychology to delineate the kinds of relationships considered desirable in current psychological thinking, the natural world and the phenomena we consider important do not lend themselves to the piecemeal approach currently in vogue.

A third assumption concerns an issue discussed above — that the systems or ecological approach to environmental phenomena is the one most likely to result in meaningful theory and applications.

CONCEPTUALIZATIONS OF ENVIRONMENTAL PSYCHOLOGY

A number of theoreticians have attempted to provide a preliminary conceptualization of environmental psychology. These conceptualizations are less definitional than they are schemes of categorizing the intricate relationships between sets of environmental, personal, and interactional variables of concern to investigators. These schemes serve to delimit the areas of primary investigative focus and provide a beginning in defining the field and pointing to the questions which have been answered before a more comprehensive theoretical schema can be offered. Moos (Moos and Insel, 1974) discusses six approaches to person-environment interactions. These are: 1) the effects of objective ecological variables, 2) the influence of behavior setting, 3) the effects of organizational structure, 4) the influence of average individual background characteristics, 5) the effects of psychosocial characteristics and organizational climate, and 6) the effects of maintaining reinforcement contingencies.

Moos feels that each of these approaches or methodologies can generate important data that will contribute to understanding the interaction of environmental and personal variables.

Altman (1973) discusses four models of man which seem to characterize the various approaches taken by investigators and within which various sets of variables have been defined which point to possible aspects of the person-environment interactions. These models of man are: 1) the mechanistic model, 2) the perceptual-cognitive-motivational model, 3) the behavioral model, and 4) the social systems, ecological model.

In addition to these broad approaches, a number of concepts have been postulated, which, while not meant to be comprehensive, serve as organizing schemes for various aspects of the field. For example, Altman (1974) has postulated the concept of privacy; Baum & Valins (1977) discuss the notion of perceived control of social input; Milgram (1970) offers the concept of stimulus overload; Proshansky et al. (1970), the idea of freedom of choice; and Argyle (1969) describes the concept of social intention.

While these theories serve to tie together sets of variables and empirical findings generated by investigations they certainly do not – nor are they intended to – provide a comprehensive definition of theory for the entire area. This is due in part to the complexity, broadness, and diversity of the area as well as to the relative dearth of empirical findings characteristic of all the subareas usually included within the province of environmental psychology.

One of the major difficulties in the development of a theoretical definition of the field concerns the difficulty in analyzing and defining the environment. While psychology has devoted considerable effort and time to developing sets of definitions, instruments, and methods for defining and measuring personality variables, little attention has been directed to a similar effort in terms of environmental variables.

The way the environment is defined depends, to a large extent, on who is doing the defining. Researchers from disciplines such as geography, architecture, and human factors research have concentrated on developing objective, physically-based definitions, while sociologists and anthropologists have concentrated on systems definitions, and psychology on cognitive, emotional, and functional analytic definitions. Before any coherent scheme for relating environmental variables to person variables can be developed, some agreement has to be reached on exactly what environmental variables should be measured and how they should be defined.

Among the current schemes available, the following have received particular attention: 1) objective measurement, 2) cognitive analysis, 3) emotional analysis, 4) functional analysis, 5) systems analysis, and 6) behavioral analysis.

None of these are mutually exclusive, and it is likely that, eventually, a meaningful approach will combine measures from the above categories to arrive at a system that accurately reflects the complexity of environmental impact on individual cognitive, emotional, and behavioral systems. Depending on the particular aspect of person-environment interactions, some approaches might be more meaningful and useful than others, but until such time as more empirical information is forthcoming, investigators will continue to vacillate among the available analytic systems and continue to develop new ones.

While the above discussion has broadly assayed the methodological and conceptual issues in the fields of environmental psychology, the best definition of environmental psychology currently available is a descriptive one. Therefore, the bulk of the remainder of this chapter will describe the major research findings and list some references which more fully delve into the issues. The last part of the chapter will discuss the relationship between environmental psychology and environmental design, the implications for training environmental designers, and the value and ethical issues that permeate the field.

THE ENVIRONMENT AS A DEPENDENT VARIABLE

It is unnecessary to document the recent extensive concern with the deteriorating condition of our ecosphere and other aspects of environmental quality such as overpopulation, the depletion of natural resources, and the changing nature of urban civilizations. These and related areas are sometimes included under the rubric of Environmental Sciences and/or Environmental Psychology. While much of the writing and research in these areas concentrates primarily on the physical aspects of the environment, several investigators have been concerned with the psychological, sociological, political, and economic factors involved in the production of pollution, overpopulation, resource utilization, and other environmental quality factors.

Principles of behavior influence, sociological variables, and other social science writings have concentrated on individual and collective behaviors which interact with natural variables to produce current environmental situations that, in turn, affect many aspects of human functioning. An ecological or systems approach is being applied to this interaction and various speculations, empirical findings, and suggestions are emerging which attempt to clarify and alter the current state of environmental quality. In many of these investigations, therefore, the environment is seen as the dependent variable and various human behaviors and institutions are conceptualized as the independent variables, so that alterations of behavior are investigated as they affect environmental variables. Although Wohlwill (1970) has called for inputs from behavioral scientists in altering the environment, Cone & Hayes (1976) argue that, by and large, most studies done under the rubric of environmental psychology have not considered the environment as the dependent variable. Rather, the environment has been the independent variable, and behavior as the dependent variable. This is not surprising, since the work they review has been done primarily by psychologists, whose orientation and training have been within this framework.

There are, of course, a large number of reports which have focused on environmental quality and the effects on the environment of human activities, but these studies have been done primarily by researchers in other fields. A closer liaison between investigators in areas such as epidemiology, pollution, overpopulation, natural resource utilization, etc. and those in psychology is needed. Some work has already been done in this area by psychologists.

Programs for reducing littering behavior (Geller, Farris, & Post, 1973; Geller, 1973, Geller et al. 1975; Geller, 1975; and Clark et al. 1972), increasing energy conservation (Kohlenberg et al., 1973, Nietzel et al., 1977), increasing birth control measures, and developing an awareness and concern for environmental quality (Buckout, 1972; Swan, 1972) are rapidly being developed. These programs arise from political, economic, and psychological sciences, all of which have as their aim altering people's cognitions, emotions, and behaviors vis-a-vis the environment with the expectation that these altered responses will have a positive effect on the environment.

THE ENVIRONMENT AS AN INDEPENDENT VARIABLE

The remainder of the chapter will summarize a number of areas in which the effects of certain classes of environment variables are investigated in order to better account for the development, maintenance, and alteration of behavior, both with respect to the environment per se, as well as with interpersonal relationships, attitudes, and social functioning.

The Natural Environment

Individuals interested in the effects of the physical, natural, and geographical environment on behavior come primarily from such disciplines as geography, meteorology, landscape design, and architecture.

Their emphasis has been on the influence of large-scale, global features of the ecosystem on molar response of persons and systems. Their approach has been historical and longitudinal and the studies have been, with few exceptions, correlational in nature. Population changes, migrations, economic and social changes, and alterations in natural physical structure have constituted major variables investigated. The effects of changing natural conditions on human behavior have received renewed interest, partly because of the rapidity with which these changes occur now as a result of man's increasing effects on his natural environment.

The recognition that man is part of the ecosystem – not only is he affected by its changes but also increasingly produces these changes through technological activities – has made the study of the reciprocal effects more urgent. Depletion of natural resources, overpopulation, destruction or alteration of the terrain, changing shifts in population concentrations, pollution, stratospheric disturbances, and a multitude of other large-scale effects of man's behavior have awakened increasing concern of the possible outcomes and energized the study of these effects. Much of the literature concerning these areas is technical, highly specialized, and found in sources not readily available to psychologists and other social scientists. Yet the literature and the areas and issues investigated are of extreme importance and relevance to a comprehensive appreciation of the interaction between persons and their environment (Craik, 1968, 1970a, 1975).

There is, however, one research area related to the natural and geographic environment which has emerged as particular interest to social scientists: the perception of the natural and geographic environment. The question here is the way in which people view their environment and the effects of this perception on subsequent behavior.

Methodological and conceptual approaches have been developed that attempt to analyze the variables involved in how people perceive, construe, and react to various aspects of their natural and built environments. This area includes the perceptual as well as cognitive, attitudinal, and emotional reactions to the environment; and these reactions have, in turn, been related to various response variables including liking, attitude formations, responses to and awareness of the environment.

Wilderness use, reactions to environmental quality, vacation-behavior patterns, appreciation, knowledge, and reactions to city-life are all areas of investigation which have recently received increased attention (Stokols, 1978).

The Built Environment

In deciding what variables to investigate, researchers have categorized the built environment into groupings based on the molarity, permanence, and source of the features which may elicit various human reactions.

One set of categories useful in providing a framework from the input side to summarize a number of empirical studies and conceptual speculations divides environmental displays into fixed features, semifixed features and ambient features. While this is not a conceptually-derived scheme, and there are many overlapping elements, it does reflect a meaningful way of defining the environment, since studies and concepts within each category have been attended to by investigators from somewhat disparate fields.

Fixed feature variables refer to large, relatively permanent, and enduring environmental features. They include such person-built structures and configurations as city and town layouts, buildings, roads, and other large-scale and relatively permanent structures.

Semifixed feature variables include person-built artifacts which, while palpable, are relatively easy to manipulate and are subject to structural change with minimal effort. Items of furniture, plants, pictures, movable walls, decorations, etc. are usually included in this category.

Ambient feature variables refer to those less palpable but, nonetheless, objective environmental factors such as lighting, color, temperature, etc. that, while also potentially manipulable, are less substantial than items of a semifixed nature.

In addition to these concrete and objective features of the environment, other sources of inputs have also been delineated that potentially affect the responses of individuals. These variables are more difficult to characterize and include such features as organizational climate and structure; relative size (numerosity, spatiality, and complexity) of institutions, organizations, towns, etc.; social and cultural atmosphere; and setting purposes and goals.

While many of these variables exist simultaneously and interact in any given environmental setting, investigators have usually focused on one or a small number of variables and attempted to develop miniconceptualizations regarding their effects on individuals' reactions and behavior patterns.

Fixed feature variables

Although architects have long been concerned with the effects of buildings, roads, and the layout of towns on behavior, their investigations have not incorporated principles and empirical findings from psychology. Design concepts have often been generated from ideas as to what is functional and esthetic, without being based on existing data from other disciplines concerned with human reactions to the person-built environment. The fact that the design of buildings has important effects on human perception, cognitions, emotions, and behavior has been demonstrated in a variety of studies. Many of these studies, however, have been poorly designed, addressed trivial questions, and have been overly naive leaving many important questions unanswered. Only recently have behaviorally-oriented investigations been conducted, and the early studies focus mainly on a person's perception and evaluation of particular person-built structures (Stokols, 1978). A more recent series of studies, however, have demonstrated the broad effects of architectural design on several aspects of occupant behavior, ranging from feelings of being crowded, to effects on friendship patterns, room usage, avoidance of social interactions, and performance on a variety of tasks (Baum and Valins 1977).

Unfortunately, these results have had little impact on future building plans, partly because the investigators have not had access to or contact with those responsible for design and construction and partly because of economic considerations. It is too often the case that evaluative studies of the effects on user's satisfactions and behavior are not carried out and architects and designers continue to build on the basis of hypotheses without recourse to data about how their buildings really function. Greater communication between individuals in architectural design and those in psychology and sociology would result in products that would better meet the needs of the ultimate users, but unfortunately barriers exist which make it difficult and frustrating for these individuals to cooperate (Altman, 1973).

While the situation described above still exists, there are examples of structures being built or designed which take into consideration not only the variables associated with the building itself, but also with the esthetic, psychological, sociological, and philosophical needs of those who will occupy and use the structure (Mercer, 1975; Sommer, 1974). Such person-oriented structures, require the collaboration of researchers from many different disciplines. The future may see additional attempts at joint development of design ideas.

Semifixed feature variables

Semi-fixed feature variables are those material objects or artifacts which can be fairly easily moved to achieve different configurations in a particular environment. Such items as furniture, partitions, plants, and other objects define, to some extent, the layout or design of a bounded space and this influences certain kinds of behavior. Several researchers have investigated the effects on behavior of the spatial arrangements of such things as desks, chairs, and pictures and the placement of partitions, doors, and windows.

Studies on crowding (Altman, 1974; Loo, 1973; Stokols, 1972), comfortable distances for conversation (Sommer, 1969), and the effects on dyadic and group interactions (Sommer, 1961) have been done to delineate the influence of these variables. For example, the perception of crowding can be altered by dividing up the space in different ways, by rearranging the placements of doorways, walls, and pictures (Baum and Davis, in press; and Desor, 1972). Sommer (1959, 1961, 1962, 1966, 1967 and 1969) has looked at the effects of seating arrangements and distances for comfortable conversation and has made suggestions for structuring particular environments to achieve certain goals (Sommer, 1962, 1969).

Although studies have looked at a variety of semifixed feature space configurations, as with other areas in environmental psychology, few systematic research programs have been instituted, and the studies completed often seem to proceed without any conceptual orientation on the part of the investigators. Without a theoretical base, many empirical studies seem to be haphazard, each investigator pursuing a topic of personal interest, leading to interesting findings but lacking any direction.

As sounder and more comprehensive theoretical systems develop, hopefully, the results of studies in this and other areas can be organized into a conceptually meaningful system.

Ambient feature variables

Research in the area of the effects of the ambient and other physical environmental factors on human behavior has a long history. These studies have investigated the relationships between specific aspects of human functioning and specific aspects of the physical environment. Lighting, room color, temperature, and humidity have been manipulated and their effects on such things as satisfaction, liking, motor performance, fatigue, and emotions have been topics for numerous investigations, usually from a human factors of design perspective. While this literature can be characterized as well done from a methodological point of view, little theoretical formulation has guided the research, and the dependent variables have usually been highly circumscribed aspects of behavior.

These investigations have been primarily within the perspective of man as a machine, responding in structured ways to objective variations in the ambient environment. Little work has been done relating these physical variables to more global aspects of behavior, although recent research has attempted to broaden this perspective (Freedman et al., 1971; Freedman, 1972; 1975).

Other Approaches to Conceptualizing the Environment

Barker and his colleagues (Barker and Gump, 1964; Barker, 1968; 1960; 1963a; 1963b; 1965) have worked for two decades in an area they term behavior setting theory. The major emphasis has been on relating behavior — defined in a particular way — to physical, personal, cultural, and social aspects of the environment, which they term behavioral setting attributes. The research generated has been carefully done and the results have highlighted relationships typically overlooked by psychologists working from a more traditional perspective.

Two subareas which continue to receive research and theoretical attention are size of institution and undermanning-overmanning (Wicker and Kirmeyer, 1975; Wicker, 1973).

The variable of size and/or numbers of individuals participating in an instruction or task, has been the major determinant of whether a setting is undermanned or overmanned. These two states supposedly have implications for a number of important interpersonal, personal, and institutional aspects.

Moos and his colleagues (Moos, R., 1968; 1972; 1973; 1974) have been concerned with the development of measuring instruments which can be used to characterize the social climate of particular institutions. Once these organizational structure and psychosocial climate variables are delineated, they can be used to generate hypotheses which will predict how individuals in those institutions will perceive, respond, and react to the setting. In addition, different institutions can be compared on certain dimensions and these differences related to specific response variables vis-a-vis the setting.

In a similar vein, although utilizing different measuring instruments and a somewhat different conceptual framework, Mehrabian (Mehrabian and Russell, 1974) has offered an approach to characterizing the environment which he feels overcomes the difficulties in developing an objective definition of the environment. Using the semantic differential (Osgood, Succi & Tannenbaum, 1957) and several additional instruments developed specifically for this purpose, Mehrabian feels that one's perception of the environment is a necessary intermediate step in determining how an individual will approach any given environmental display or setting. By focusing on perceptions of the environment, one can compare environments of widely different structures and relate these differences to behaviors toward these situations.

Social and Behavioral Environment

There are five areas which are often considered together by researchers involved in exploring the spatial aspects of behavior. These are personal space, territorality, privacy, crowding, and small group ecology (Altman, 1975; Porteous, 1977; Heimstra & McFarling, 1974). Early theoretical and empirical work focused on each of these areas somewhat independently. Recent investigations, and especially theorizing, has tended toward developing a unified scheme for exploring the way humans use space to achieve certain goals or states (Altman, 1975).

Much of the impetus came from the works of ethologists who were interested in developing theories of the distribution of animals in space and concentrated on the concepts of territoriality and distancing (Wynne-Edwards, 1962).

Anthropologists also contributed early formulations of the distancing of humans from each other and astute observations were made on cultural differences in the use of space. These early formulations were primarily descriptive but provided the initial thrust for other investigators to develop more sophisticated, observational, experimental, and conceptual methods and ideas. In the past decade, numerous studies utilizing field as well as laboratory methods have been carried out, and a reasonable body of data has accumulated explicating the variables involved and providing a data base for more comprehensive and sophisticated themes. In addition, some relationship among these areas has been postulated, so that currently a person's utilization of space is seen as a way of controlling or regulating his relationships with various elements of the environment (Hall 1966; Lyman and Scott 1967; Altman 1970).

While the research in environmental psychology has been variable in sophistication and methodological soundness, and a lack of theory has characterized many of the studies, nevertheless, taken as a whole, the bulk of literature has served to highlight the importance of the environment in accounting for various aspects of personal and interpersonal behavior. Psychology has too long neglected the external, concrete, and material aspects of the environment in the development of psychological theories and the recent spate of studies in environmental psychology has been a needed corrective.

As the conceptualization of environmental design coalesces, it becomes increasingly obvious that students should be trained in substantive and methodological approaches regarding the effects of the environment on human functioning. Individuals who will operate in real settings and who will deal with molar aspects of behavior must be trained in and made aware of these variables in order to develop a broad approach to dealing with society and individuals who function in it.

As described in Chapter 9, we are beginning to develop a program which has as its purpose the training of sophisticated environmental designers who can take into consideration not only principles and strategies of personalistic psychology but also those issues and research strategies described above. Developing an ecological orientation is not an easy task for the typical psychology graduate student whose orientation is usually focused on the individual and his behavior rather than on the intricate relationship between these variables and those of the environment.

In addition to considering environmental inputs, the questions and issues relating to purpose, goals, and ethics become more crucial than ever in providing a framework within which future generations of behavioral scientists will operate. These issues are dealt with in greater detail elsewhere in this volume, but the approach described here makes it obvious that environmental designers will have to consider a broader array of variables than most psychologists are used to handling. This is true not only in terms of theory formation and methodological approaches, but also in the types of problems or issues that behavioral scientists usually consider to be within their province. In some cases, principles and procedures developed by other approaches are being directly applied to problems of environmental quality. In others, new conceptualization will have to be developed and the future will certainly witness a redefinition of what psychology is about and what inputs are appropriate for the psychologically trained individual. Training will have to be broadened to include not only substantive matters, but also a broader variety of methodologies, new definitions, and an expanded consideration of the philosophical, moral, and ethical issues in understanding man's place and role in the ecological system of which he is an integral part.

4 An Interactionist Approach to Environmental Design
James M. Waters

The next chapter by Waters is on interactionist theory. At this point it might even sound axiomatic and trite to contend that the only kind of theory of human nature which makes sense for environmental design is a theory that takes into account the interaction between man and his environment. Waters covers the range of theoretical formulations that are in essence interactionist and their implications for environmental design.

As we have indicated earlier, the orientation which we are offering in this book is not only interactionist in regards to the individual and his environment, but we are also stressing the metalevel interaction between the environmental designer (or behavior modifier) and his theory or model of behavior (the Kuhnian paradigm).

As we have stressed elsewhere (Krasner & Ullmann, 1973) neither personality nor ethics, nor behavior, nor institutions, nor even environments exist in isolation or as entities. Rather, there is a continual ongoing process of interaction and mutual influence between an individual and his environment.

As in most other chapters, stress is placed upon the broad picture and Waters offers a critical overview of the interactionist literature. The reader will note that some of the themes and influencers discussed in other chapters are here but in a somewhat different context.

Ed.

Recently, such terms as "interactionism," "interactionist," and the "situation-by-person interaction" have become increasingly popular among psychologists. Authors of new textbooks (e.g., Goldfried & Davison, 1976; Mischel, 1976) boldly proclaim themselves "interactionists." Endler & Magnusson (1976) have entitled their book

Interactional Psychology and Personality. The literature is filled with studies and reviews of "interactional research." These writers all insist that we must look at both the person and the situation in order to predict or control behavior. In the midst of this apparent reconciliation of person- and situation-oriented approaches, the environmental design approach should not "go it alone."

We agree with Bowers (1973) in asserting that a strict situationist model of behavior is inconsistent with current data. While it is not clear that environmental design is a strict situationist approach, certain aspects of it might benefit from the leavening of a little contemporary interactionism. While this chapter suggests some implications of current interactionism for environmental design, a problem with doing so is the absence of a clear delineation of the limits of environmental design (See Chapter 1). At present, those who apply behavior modification, environmental psychology, and a host of other disciplines may label themselves "environmental designers." Some are already interactional in their approaches, others are not. Rather than trying to deliver blanket criticism unfairly harsh for some and unreasonably kind for others, we will try to emphasize the positive — what would seem to be appropriate behavior for an interactional environmental designer.

BACKGROUND AND DEFINITION OF INTERACTIONISM

For many years, psychology was a science divided against itself. The rift within the field was noted and labeled by many (e.g., Murray, 1938; Cronbach, 1957) as correlationist vs. experimentalist, specifist vs. generalist, centralist vs. peripheralist, and so on. The arguments have largely focused on where to place the locus of control of behavior — within the person or the situation. The obvious answer, suggested by some (e.g., Kantor, 1924), was that both the situation and the person are relevant to behavior. Thus, the fundamental concept of interactionism is not a new one (Shute, 1973 among others, traces it at least to Aristotle), but it was not until the 1950s that researchers began to gather data relevant to the theory.

In all fairness to researchers of the past, however, it should be noted that they were not as naive as the above suggests. Further, interactionism is more complex than the notion that both the person and the situation affect behavior. The personality theory assumption of Guttman scalability (see Wiggins, 1973) is that a particular situation will have essentially the same effect on all individuals, and not that it will have no effect. This implies that by assessing persons, one can predict their rank-ordering on behavioral characteristics in any setting. Unfortunately, the typically low cross-situational correlations (see Hartshorne & May, 1928; Mischel, 1968, 1976) indicate that individuals do not often show the same rank order on behavioral measures across situations. Behaviorists, too, recognized that subject variables were important and, hence, controlled for the state and learning history of the organism. While trait theorists ignored situational effects, situationists such as behaviorists ignored individual differences, though each paid lip-service to the ignored effects. Neither was interactionist, since interactionism focuses on the joint effects of person and situation.

If the expression "joint effects" sounds ambiguous, it may be because the term "interaction" is used ambiguously. Overton & Reese (1973) distinguish between two uses of the term — the organismic, for which they suggest the term "transaction," and the reactive, for which they suggest the term "interaction." The organismic approach (which they advocate) involves the study of the reciprocal cause-effect chain between person and environment. The person's behavior affects the environment, and the (now modified) environment affects the person's behavior. An example of such a transaction is a social "interaction" among people. The reactive approach involves the study of relationships among causes of behavior (for example, the extent to which behavior can be accounted for by the situation and the person). The latter usage of the term (which is slightly more common in the literature) derives from the statistical concept of interaction.

In order to understand statistical interactions, it is important to understand the statistical concept of an effect. An effect is simply a difference between observed and expected scores at different levels of a variable. If the measure is promptness, a simple effect of persons would be observed if different people arrived at different times for a particular seminar. There is, thus, a difference between levels (i.e., different persons) and their expected score (the mean time of arrival) of the variable (persons) on a measure (promptness or time of arrival). Simple effects are those observed when all but one variable is held constant (in this case, situations and day are held constant, since the reference is to only one seminar on a particular day). A main effect is a difference among averages for levels of a variable — if some persons are, on the average, more prompt than others, there is a main effect of persons on promptness; if all persons, on the average, tend to be more prompt for some events than for others, there is a main effect of situations on promptness.

An interaction effect exists if, for a specific combination of variables (e.g., one person attending a particular seminar), the data point can not be predicted from main effects (and simpler interactions). For example, given a seminar for which people average being five minutes late, and a person who averages being two minutes earlier than others, this person is predicted to appear for class three minutes late. If our subject is not three minutes late (if he is earlier or later) that is an interaction effect of person (our subject) by situation (the seminar). Across a group of people, an interaction effect would be observed if for example, those people who are most prompt for a seminar are least prompt for a movie.

Another example may help to elucidate these concepts. Assume that we observe the reading rates of two students — John and Mark — in two situations — a traditional and an open classroom. In a traditional classroom, Mark averages 120 words per minute, while John averages 80. In the open classroom, both average 100 words per minute. There is, then, a simple effect of person in the traditional class — Mark reads more quickly than John — but no simple effect in the open classroom.

The mean reading speed in both classes is 100, so there is no main effect of type of classroom. John's average reading speed is 90, while Mark's is 110, so there is a main effect of person. There is also an interaction of person by situation, since the effect of person depends on the situation (or equivalently, the effect of situation depends on the person).

Researchers often present data in the form of the degree of predictive power associated with particular variables and their inter-actions. There are numerous procedures for making estimates of predictive power (see Endler, 1966b; Meyers, 1973; Argyle & Little, 1972; Golding, 1975) each with advantages and disadvantages. The most common are estimates of total behavior variance accounted for (e.g., "omega-squared"), which are also the most commonly misinterpreted. As Golding (1975) points out, these statistics are often misused as measures of the cross-situational consistency predicted by trait theory. These statistics compare a given source of variance to the total variance — as the magnitude of the effect of situation increases, the total variance increases, and the relative magnitude of the person effect decreases. Trait theory assumes that there will be situation effects, so the magnitude of situation effects should not affect a valid test of trait theory. The appropriate statistic for testing for cross-situational consistency is a "generalizability coefficient" (Golding, 1975).

Interpretative difficulties also arise because the meaning of a statistic is linked to the design of the study. A significant effect of a variable or set of variables reflects some consistency across levels of another variable. For example, assume that talking behavior is observed for a number of people across a number of situations, and the people are observed in each situation a number of times. This study utilizes a person by situation by time factorial design. A substantial person by situation interaction effect would indicate that people who are relatively more talkative in some situations are less so in others, but within a particular situation each person shows substantial consistency from one observation time to the next.

On the other hand, let us examine a study in which we observe two responses — talking and eating — across a number of persons and situations, with one observation per person per situation. We then have a person by situation by response design. In this case, a substantial person by situation interaction would indicate that people who are relatively more talkative and gluttonous in some situations are less so in others, but that within a given situation, eating and talking tend to be correlated. Hence, in two studies, we have substantial person by situation interactions, in one case, the finding reflects a within situation across time consistency, and in the other a within situation across responses consistency. Most authors have not noted this distinction.

The recent history of interactionism has been marked by a number of misinterpretations and misuses of statistics. These problems may be inevitable when mathematically sophisticated analyses are employed by researchers who have not specialized in mathematics. This is not to say that researchers should become better mathematicians — perhaps in some cases the gains from complex statistics may not justify the consequences of mistakes and the loss of research time spent mastering such techniques.

Note that the statistical "interaction" is generally only a description of a pattern of responding across situations; most often there is little indication of the reason for this pattern. Hence, the theoreticians of the area have had to draw heavily on other lines of research. Overton & Reese (1973) suggest that this descriptive data is inadequate, and that a study of the organismic (or reciprocal) transaction between organism and environment would yield information about the processes mediating this interaction; however, as is discussed below, the techniques for such study are currently not well developed (see Endler & Magnusson, 1976), so the bases of contemporary interactionism are the descriptive studies of patterns of response likelihood.

In sum, interactionism refers to a perspective that both the person and the situation are important to behavior, and that the factors must be studied jointly. Bolstering this position is a series of studies of the patterns of behavior, most of which are quite supportive. In addition, there is a body of theoretical literature about processes mediating the interaction (drawn primarily from other psychological theory), and an as yet largely untested assumption that the proper way to study behavior is through examination of the interactions or transactions of people with their environments.

CONTEMPORARY INTERACTIONISM

In most interactionist research, estimates of response likelihood (behavior observation or self report data) are collected for a number of response-situation-person combinations. The data is then analyzed to determine the nature of the pattern of responding.

Interactional data generally indicates that people display a small degree of cross-situational consistency, some within-situation consistency, and a higher degree of consistency for specific person-situation combinations across time (see Mischel, 1968, 1976).(1) This pattern can be illustrated as follows – some people may tend to be noisy and boisterous at most parties they attend, while others are consistently more quiet at parties; these boisterous party people are not necessarily noisy in other, nonparty situations. This descriptive data provides a useful starting point for further research, since it implies where one should look for behavioral determinants. Clearly, since both person and situation contribute significantly to behavior, the breadth of potential variables implied by the data is almost infinite. As Golding (1975) points out, the task of the interactionists at this point is to tie the behavioral data to other variables, to begin narrowing the field of potential determinants of behavior. Few interactional studies have done this; most have merely replicated earlier findings.

Interactional research has also suffered from its use of molar definitions. Though the molar approach is a well-established tradition in psychology, it can work to the researcher's disadvantage. Too broad a view of environment can ignore specific factors relevant to behavior, and too broad a definition of response may ignore crucial differences among responses. The molar view might classify a dayroom in a psychiatric ward as the same situation for all, when the situational determinants of behavior for one individual may be incredibly disparate from those encountered by another. Interactionists must begin to examine such effects if they wish to advance their field.

A further problem with current interactional research is the effect of measurement method on findings. As Campbell & Fiske (1959) pointed out, measurement method may have substantial effects on the data gathered. Bowers (1973) suggests that behavior observation may yield data suggestive of greater situation effects, while paper and pencil measures may yield data more suggestive of person effects. His sample of studies was too small for evaluation of the trend, but this problem may pose a real threat to conclusions based on a particular study.

A final difficulty with this line of research is statistical analysis. As pointed out above, there are substantial difficulties involved in interpretation of the usual statistics. In addition, the use of rating scales and other measures that limit the range of the data may cause artifactual results (see Golding, 1975). In particular, interaction effects may be inflated, because the score predicted from lower level effects can exceed the range of the data. Hence, Golding suggests that interactionists must demonstrate that the effects that they observe are replicable.

With the above caveats, this chapter will explore the state of interactional theorizing. The theorists often overstep the limits of their data, but we feel that, despite the transgressions, much that is worthwhile is contained here.

INTERPRETATIONS OF THE INTERACTION

While there is general agreement on the patterns of responding identified by interactional researchers, various authors have presented different views of the significance or meaning of this data. Some of these views are presented below.

Constraints on Predictive Power

Moos (1974) has suggested that the amount of variance accounted for by a variable will set an upper limit predictive power based on assessment of that variable. He uses this interpretation in an argument for examining the usefulness of environment assessment. Bowers (1973) points out that this constraint argument is applicable to environment assessment as well. Thus, it would seem that an assessment of both kinds of variables is important. A problem with this viewpoint is that unless one has some knowledge of the characteristics of both the situations and the persons of interest, one cannot establish the extent of this predictive constraint. The variation in variance accounted for by different factors is tremendous.

For this reason, some authors (Argyle & Little, 1973; Mischel, 1976) have argued that in some instances behavior may be best predicted from person variables, while in other instances behavior may be best predicted from environment variables. This view implies an interactional approach to assessment. While this seems desirable, the complexities of shifting predictive variables from one situation to the next may make the approach impractical for many applied settings.

Person Effects Dependent Upon the Situation

This view assumes that certain person variables are highly predictive of behavior in a given situation, but which variables are most predictive is situation dependent. For instance, an introversion-extroversion measure may be a better predictor of verbalization at a party, while an intelligence measure may be a better predictor of verbalization in a classroom. Unless one focuses on modifiable person characteristics, however, this view is not particularly useful for an environmental designer. Further, it is not clear that the view can be distinguished from the next view.

Environmental Effects Dependent Upon the Person

This involves the assumption that the environment is the principle controlling agent of behavior, but that its effects depend upon the person. If the same situation has substantial but very different effects on different individuals – e.g., if a bright, sunny day leads one person to go outside to bask in the sun and another to seek a cool, air-conditioned room – then the environment is controlling people's behaviors, but results in different responses. Such a model implies an interactionist assessment with an environmental intervention. This model is consistent with an environmental design approach, since many environmental designers assess both person and situation before instituting an environmental intervention; however, as suggested above, the last view and this are difficult to distinguish from one another. The difference may be one of interpretation rather than representation of process – if person variables modify the effect of environments, then person variables have an effect on behavior. Similarly, if environment variables modify the effects of person variables, then environmental variables have an effect on behavior. This issue could be reduced to a discussion of the meaning of causation, but such a discussion would go beyond the scope of this chapter.

Environmental Idiosyncracies

The basis of this model is that if two people are put in what is truly the same situation, they will exhibit the same behaviors; however, two factors make it difficult to put persons in the same situation.

The first factor relates to subject differences. If one person has experienced a particular situation similar to the one being studied, while the other has not, behavioral differences may be expected. Likewise, the state of the person (e.g., anxious vs. relaxed) may be relevant to the behavior, and persons' states are difficult to control. Hence, situation-determined person variables will contribute to behavioral differences.

The other factor is the difficulty in equating environments. This is particularly a problem with social environments. Two persons in the same room at the same time experience different situations because they must be in different locations in space. In addition, each is a different stimulus to the other, and each will receive different inputs from the other as a result of his/her physical location, and stimulus characteristics (e.g., physical attractiveness). This implies an approach utilizing interactional asssessment and situational intervention.

We believe that there are important factors neglected in this view (e.g., genetic components of behavior); however, we would also argue that it contains much that is worthwhile, and raises issues that have not been addressed adequately by interactional researchers.

The above models, while by no means exhaustive of possible views, are illustrative of approaches to interpreting interactional data. It should be noted that none of these interpretations attempts to take all variables into account. Contemporary interactionist theory, on the other hand, is an attempt at a comprehensive view of human behavior.

CHARACTERISTICS OF CURRENT INTERACTIONIST MODELS

Although a number of theorists (Mischel, 1973, 1976; Bowers, 1973; Endler & Magnusson, 1976) have presented formulations of situation-by-person interaction, there are certain characteristics shared by virtually all models. Endler & Magnusson (1976) summarize these characteristics as follows:

Behavior involves a continuous
interaction between the
person and the situation

Behavior modifies and is modified by the environment in a continuous sequence. This is readily apparent in social interactions, in which a "chain of interchanges" (Rausch, 1965) occurs between or among people, within which each person's responses influence the responses of others. A similar reciprocal influence process occurs in the physical environment. People manipulate objects, turn devices on or off, consume edible, drinkable, and smokeable objects, and change their physical location in space – all of which serve to modify the impinging environment. Likewise, these objects influence behavior, with the nature of the influence modified by each change in the environment. Parenthetically, the reciprocal influence assumption is a feature of behavioral self-control as well as interactionism.

A person is an intentional and active agent, whose
behavior is influenced <u>by his/her cognitions</u>

Endler & Magnusson (1976) present these as two characteristics. We
view them as inseparable. The notion that cognition is relevant to
behavior has gained wide acceptance in psychology and is hardly
exclusive to or necessary for an interactionist position. Further, it is
difficult to interpret the meaning of the terms "intentional" and
"active" within a deterministic framework. Two interpretations of this
seem possible. One is an anti-deterministic, free-will stance, which,
regardless of one's philosophical biases, is counterproductive to a
science of behavior, in that it assumes that behavior is not lawful. The
other is that an individual processes and interprets information and acts
on the basis of the interpretation rather than being a passive recipient
of inputs. The latter interpretation is obvious enough to be trivial —
perception and cognition are quite apparently constructive.

The psychological meaning of the
situation . . . is an essential determinant
of behavior (Endler & Magnusson, 1976; p. 12).

Many researchers in environmental psychology have drawn a distinction
between the "psychological" (or behavioral) and the "physical" (or
geographical) environments. (See Eckehammer, 1974; Craik, 1971; for
discussions of this issue.) The distinction is important inasmuch as it
emphasizes that an individual may respond to what he/she interprets the
situation to be, which interpretation may or may not correspond to
others' perceptions or to measures of the environment. The difficulty
with the distinction is in the definition of the physical environment.
Generally, the "physical" environment is defined by some "objective"
knowledge of the physical environment; there are, however, many ways
of characterizing the environment. Given a particular room, a physicist
might point out that the walls and furniture are mostly empty space
with occasional molecules giving the illusion of solid matter; yet few
others will respond as if the walls and furniture were empty space. The
architect who designed the building (or anyone with a tape measure)
might state the dimensions of the room, but the lighting and furniture
arrangement may yield consensual perception of the room as being
much smaller (or larger). A carpenter might report that the walls are
not quite at right angles to the floor, but the consensus of people in the
room may still be that the walls are perfectly vertical. There may be a
consensus that the room affords a great deal of privacy; this consensus
may not be predictive of the behavior of someone who knows about the
hidden microphones in the ceiling.

The above may be construed as an argument for an emphasis on the
psychological meaning of the situation, but it also points up another
important point — no single conceptualization, regardless of its
"objectivity," captures the "true" physical environment. This is not to
say that there is no environment, but that it may be conceptualized in a

number of ways; and it behooves psychologists to determine which conceptualizations provide optimal prediction of behavior. Interactionists have suggested that "psychological meaning" is the most relevant measure. Some evidence indicates that this may be so, but the issue should remain an open empirical question.

This, then, is the essence of the theoretical framework of contemporary interactionism. It raises some critical questions for environmental designers – particularly the problem of the continuous reciprocal interaction of person and environment, and the question of the roles of "cognition" and "psychological meanings" in behavior. For those who claim that "psychological meaning" is not relevant, the author offers the following example. Bechtel (1967) measured the use of space by two groups of people in a room in an art gallery with microswitches hidden under the rug to record locations. The only difference between the groups was that one group was informed of the presence of the microswitches, while the other was not. The informed subjects spent less time in the room and viewed fewer paintings. Such data is, in our opinion, hard to account for by a situationist interpretation, since the additional information given the one group changed the meaning of the situation without changing its objective characterization.

INTERACTIONISM: EMPIRICAL FINDINGS AND DIRECTIONS

This section is organized with the intent of suggesting directions for research, rather than simply reviewing what has been done before. The focus, thus, will be on some variables that may be relevant to or mediate the situation-by-person interaction.

Person Variables

The term "person variable" refers to a predictor of behavior that may be assessed by measurement of the person only. Much of the literature indicates that person variables account for about ten percent of behavior variance. For example, Mischel (1968) suggests a validity coefficient ceiling for personality measures of .30, which corresponds to nine percent of the variance. Bowers (1973) in his review of the literature, reports a mean of 12.71 percent across 19 comparisons. The actual percentage in a given study may vary considerably (from about 2 to 30 percent in Bowers' survey), so absolute percentages may not be very meaningful. The question might better be asked, as Mischel (1976) puts it, "When do individual differences make a difference?" Following are some person variables.

Adjustment

A number of authors (Bem, 1975; Bem & Allen, 1974; Bowers, 1973; Wachtel, 1973) suggest that better adjusted subjects may show less person variance and more situation and interaction variance. There is some evidence to support this idea.

Rausch and his associates (Rausch, Dittman & Taylor, 1959; Rausch, Farbman & Llewellyn, 1960) found that situation and interaction variance were substantially greater for normal controls than for "hyperaggressive boys"; however, all groups had virtually equivalent subject variance. Moos (1968a) found greater person variance and less situation and interaction variance in psychiatric patients than in members of the ward staff. Subsequent studies (Moos, 1969; 1970) have shown less of a clear pattern. Although in some comparisons there is still a predominance of person over situation effects, the interaction effect is very strong.

Bem (1975) has attacked the question from a slightly different perspective. In her work on sex-role stereotyping, she has found that some people (whom she labels "androgynous") are capable of responding in either a male stereotyped or a female stereotyped manner depending on the situation. As a result of their cross-situational inconsistency, androgynous individuals adjust better to differing situational demands. Wachtel (1973, 1976) adds another dimension to this issue, by suggesting that less adjusted individuals (i.e., those who enter therapy) are, by definition, more cross-situationally consistent. He proposes that people seek therapy because they exhibit behavioral problems that pervade many situations.

Some evidence (albeit inconsistent) and some reasonable speculation thus supports the notion that an individual's degree of adjustment is related to his/her degree of cross-situational consistency. The theory has implications for both research and assessment. Perhaps, as Wachtel suggests, generalization from normals to clinical populations is inappropriate, and perhaps personality assessment instruments should test ability to respond differentially to different situations, rather than general response dispositions.

Cognition

Mischel (1973) has proposed a system with five "cognitive social learning person variables":

1. Cognitive and behavioral construction competencies – abilities to construct (generate) particular cognitions and behaviors.
2. Encoding categories and personal constructs – units for categorizing events and self descriptions.
3. Expectancies – behavior-outcome and stimulus-outcome relations in particular situations.
4. Subjective values – motivating and arousing stimuli, incentives and aversions.
5. Self-regulatory systems and plans: rules and self reactions for performance and for the organization of complex behavior sequences.

Mischel's categories emphasize two loci of behavior variance – the ability to perform a particular act, and the person's interpretation (i.e., psychological meaning) of the environment. The suggested dimensions of these two constructs possess substantial face validity, and there is empirical evidence for the dimensions. (See Mischel, 1976.)

The interrelationships of the variables, and their relative contributions to behavior variance require further investigation. Mischel (1976) offers a final caveat concerning these variables:

> It would be both easy and inappropriate to transform these person variables into general trait-like dispositions by endowing them with broad cross-situational consistency or removing them from the context of the specific conditions on which they depend ... If the above person variables are ... removed from their close interaction with situational conditions they are likely to have limited usefulness. (P. 506)

Locus of control

Since Rotter (1966) proposed the internal-external dimension of locus of behavioral control, numerous authors have investigated this construct. A measure of locus of control may prove a useful variable for determining whether subject (internal) or environment (external) variables will be better predictors of behavior. As usual, Mischel (Mischel, Zeiss & Zeiss, 1974) warns against over-generalizing this dimension – like most "personality" variables, "locus of control" appears to be somewhat situation specific.

Idiographic traits

The case against cross-situational consistency is sufficiently strong to dissuade most researchers from expecting to find Guttman scalable traits; however, Bem & Allen (1974) have proposed a fascinating alternative to the traditional view. In an ingenious study, they asked subjects whether they were consistent across situations on a particular trait (friendliness). Those subjects who answered that they were consistent did show more cross-situational consistency. Hence, Bem & Allen propose that certain traits may be applicable to some people but not others. The degree of cross-situational consistency obtained in those subjects reporting consistency was far from remarkable, but the reliability of the single question used as a moderator variable is most likely unimpressive as well. Determination of the usefulness of this approach awaits attempts to develop empirically validated assessment instruments for determining applicability of a trait to an individual.

Situation Variables

A "situation variable" may be defined as a characteristic of situations that is predictive of behavior. Many recent researchers have pointed to the importance of situational factors in the control of behavior (e.g., Mischel, 1968; Moos, 1973). In supporting these claims, these writers have often invoked the data against cross-situational consistency.

As Bowers (1973) suggests, the available data indicates that situation variables alone are no better predictors of behavior than are person variables (Bowers reports mean proportions of variance for persons and situations as 12.71 percent and 10.17 percent respectively). In fairness to Mischel, it should be emphasized that he has recognized the weaknesses of a strict situationist position (Mischel, 1973, 1976).

Some suggested situation variables include the following:

Ambiguity and "looseness."

A number of authors (e.g., Mischel, 1976) have suggested that some environments are more restrictive of potential responses than others. Mischel (1976) has interpreted this effect in terms of the information provided by the situation. If a situation provides little information – it is ambiguous or unfamiliar – individuals will tend to behave very differently from one another. By Mischel's model, if individuals have similar interpretations of, and expectations in, a particular situation, they will tend to behave similarly.

A comparable characterization of environments is the "looseness-tightness" dimension (Goffman, 1963), which Price & Bouffard (1974) have attempted to quantify in terms of "behavioral appropriateness" and "situational constraint."

To the extent that such variables may be defined strictly as properties of environments, they may be useful as moderator variables which predict whether person or situation variables will yield better prediction. In tighter, less ambiguous situations, the situation may be the best predictor of behavior, while in looser, more ambiguous situations, person variables may be more relevant.

Price (1974), however, has taken the approach that dimensions may be specific to particular response-situation combinations. (See the discussion below on "behavior-environment congruence.") One situation may allow for a wider range of responses than another, but the former may be very restrictive of some responses that are appropriate in the latter. For example, a cocktail party may be a looser environment than a classroom lecture, but may be more restrictive of note-taking behavior.

Situation similarity

Researchers since Hartshorne & May (1928) have suggested that an individual will tend to behave similarly in similar situations. Hartshorne & May defined "similarity" rationally rather than empirically; more recently, researchers have been attempting to isolate dimensions along which to define environmental similarity (see Moos, 1974).

Price (1974) utilizes a cluster analysis approach to classify situations on the dimension of behavioral appropriateness, reasoning that situations are similar if behaviors within them are rated as similar in level of appropriateness. Price is merely proposing and demonstrating a method rather than presenting definitive situation clusters. Hence, the data, while intriguing, is not as relevant as the approach. The usefulness of the approach, of course, is dependent upon the relevance of appropriateness ratings to behavior. Waters (1976) found that behavior appropriateness ratings are highly predictive of behavior likelihood ratings.

There are many other lines of research on dimensions of situations – this is by no means an exhaustive survey. (See, for example, Ecke-hammer, 1973, for research on stressful life events that is relevant to the interactionist approach.)

Contingencies

The relationships among responses and their consequences can be used to characterize environments. If a particular response in a particular situation tends to lead to a particular consequence, regardless of the person emitting the response, then this is a characteristic of that situation. This behavioral view is sufficiently well presented in so many places that it is pointless to reiterate it here. A difficulty with the approach is that in a given situation people often behave differently from one another. The behavioral approach allows for several inter-pretations of this inconsistency. One is that a particular consequence received for a response has different valences; hence, not all persons will work toward attaining that consequence. (Note that consequence valence is then a person variable.) Another is that different previous learning histories have made persons differentially likely to emit particular responses. (Learning history, too, is a person variable.) A third is that different people may receive different consequences for the same response in the same situation. (This is an interactive variable, requiring specification of response, person, and situation.) It should be clear that even within a behavioral model, which is considered the epitome of situationist approaches, it is frequently necessary to consider person and interactive variables and, thus, an over-simplified use of this model for simple situation assessment may be inappropriate.

Interactive Variables

An interactive variable is one that cannot be measured without specification of more than one factor. The interaction that has gained the most attention is the "situation by person" interaction, though many other interactions may be relevant. Bowers' (1973) review of the literature suggests that the situation-by-person interaction effect accounts for an average of 20.77 percent of the variance. Of course, this figure is not particularly meaningful except in pointing out the importance of taking both situation and person into account in psychological theory and practice. Some suggested interactive variables are as follows:

Previous experience in situation

Mischel (1973) has suggested that as people spend more time in a situation, they will begin to behave more and more similarly; a progressive conformity. This makes intuitive sense – as people learn what is expected, rewarded, or appropriate, they will begin to behave more in line with these controlling variables (and will modify these variables in some situations). Endler (1966a) found that this is the case when conformity is reinforced.

A difficulty with this idea is the identification of situations – if someone who has often been in bars enters a new one, will he/she behave as a newcomer or as one who has had many previous experiences? And what is predicted when someone enters a tavern on a Saturday which he/she has frequented only on weekdays? The definition and classification of situations again rears its head. If one defines a situation in a sufficiently molar manner, virtually everyone will have experienced it; while if the same situation is described at an extremely molecular level, almost no one will have experienced it. If the necessary environmental assessment instruments were available, this person-by-situation variable might be expressed as a function of amount of experience in situations similar to the one in question.

Response-environment congruence

This construct represents the degree to which a behavior "fits" (is appropriate or likely in) a particular situation. As an empirical description, response-environment congruence is valid – some responses are more likely than others in a given situation. (See, e.g., Barker's 1968 discussions of behavior settings.) However, as Wicker (1972) points out, psychologists must move beyond the simple description to a study of the processes mediating this relationship. Wicker suggests that the problem may be approached from at least four theoretical standpoints: operant learning, observational learning, behavior setting theory, and social exchange theory. Wicker is not implying that any one approach will account for the phenomenon, but rather that an integration of aspects of each of the approaches may yield a model that accounts for the congruence of behavior with environment. The processes mediating behavior-environment congruence comprise a substantial part of the effects of interest in interactionism. Wicker's model ignores the effect due to persons, and this may prove a serious oversight in this line of research.

The interactional data is very limited and suffers from a number of methodological weaknesses. Little new information has been gained from the interactional stream of research since Rausch and his associates (Rausch, Dittman & Taylor, 1959; Rausch, Farbman, & Llewelyn, 1960) began the collection of this data. Interactional theorists have drawn upon other streams, such as behavioral, personality, environmental, and cognitive psychology, in accounting for their data. There are advantages and disadvantages, however, to trying to account for interactional data with noninteractional research. Certainly, it is more parsimonious to explain new phenomena by established principles. Further, since interactionists have taken on the task of accounting for all behavior in all situations, they should incorporate variables into their theory if these variables have been shown to be relevant. On the other hand, the adoption of principles (such as the importance of the role of cognition) which have been shown to be important in some situations is not equivalent to the demonstration that these principles mediate the situation-by-person interaction. Interactionism poses the ultimate question in human behavior — What factors control all behavior in all situations? We question whether this is an appropriate question given the current state of psychology, and wonder if the complexity and ambitiousness of this question may prove the undoing of interactionism as a unitary line of research. Interactionism must lead to prediction and control of behavior in order to be useful to environmental designers; thus far, the field has provided only description and explanation (see Golding, 1975; Endler, 1975).

IMPLICATIONS FOR ASSESSMENT IN ENVIRONMENTAL DESIGN

To the more hard-nosed workers in the field, the term "assessment" may seem to conjure up demons such as projective tests and personality traits; hence, it is important to make clear what is meant by the term. Assessment, as it is used here, refers to any measurement designed to gain information about a person's or group's behavior. The information may include direct observation of behavior, indirect reports of behavior, measurement of environment characteristics, and measures of person characteristics.

There are many applications of assessment but, for the purposes of this discussion, two general uses will suffice — the measurement of current behavior, and the prediction of future behavior. The measurement of current behavior is necessary for decisions such as when or whether to intervene, and for assessing the effects of an intervention. The prediction of future behavior is crucial to intervention selection — one should know how an individual will respond in a situation in order to decide what intervention is appropriate. Obviously, these are functions necessary to environmental design — if we cannot discover what people are doing, and predict what they will do, we might do best to abandon our endeavors. On the other hand, we offer (without debate) the assumption that Krasner & Ullmann (1973) make: ". . . an assumption that is quite debatable: the more accurate we are in observing phenomena, the more effective we will be in the long run" (p. 15). Unfortunately, many workers have not taken this assumption seriously.

It is now an old saw that behavioral psychologists, who by the nature of their approach are most in need of good assessment instruments, have been the most neglectful of the field of assessment. (Goldfried & Pomeranz, 1968, suggest that it may not be reinforcing enough to them.) Behaviorists, with their target-specific interventions, must identify what their targets should be, and how best to treat them. Environmental designers, who have drawn heavily from the behavioral approach, are at least as much in need of means of identifying how they should intervene. In fairness to the behaviorists, it must be said that in more recent years, at least a few workers have contributed to the field of assessment (Goldfried & D'Zurilla, 1969; Lewinsohn & Shaffer, 1971; numerous workers in the field of behavioral observation). However, Paul's (1967) question, "What treatment, by whom, is most effective for this individual with that specific problem, and under which set of circumstances?" (p. 111) has received less attention than it deserved.

An interactionist perspective implies that this question is very critical – an environment which helps one individual to cope more effectively may have different (possibly detrimental) effects on another.

Assessment: Some Theoretical Considerations

Much of the research in behavioral assessment has involved techniques of behavior observation. There is a sizable literature on effects of various factors on observational data (see Kent & Foster, 1977, for an excellent review), and some of these factors are discussed below. Most readers should be familiar with the usual procedure for designing a behavior observation code – one must define responses in explicit, operational terms, so that one can identify exemplars of a response category unambiguously. Parenthetically, this aspect of the approach is not much different from other methods of behavioral assessment, in that one must find out specifically what the person does. Many have taken to heart the notion that if one measures observable behavior, one is getting the truth – what is really occurring (see Kent & Foster, 1977); however, the problem is really not that simple.

As interactionists (among others) have suggested, behavior is a continuous stream of interaction between person and environment, and not a sequence of discrete responses (see Endler & Magnusson, 1976; Wiggins, 1973). Quantifying behavior requires fractionating the behavior into units, usually responses (see Wiggins, 1973); the definition and categorization of these units is generally treated as arbitrary. To relegate such decisions to the whim of an investigator seems as absurd as leaving the categorization of matter to the whim of the individual chemist. Certainly, there are many ways to categorize matter – element vs. compound, metal vs. nonmetal, fluid vs. solid, inert vs. noninert, and so on – however, there are specific reasons and implications for each categorization. So it is with behavior. If there are laws of behavior, then some approaches to defining behavior should be superior to others in yielding results corresponding to theoretical predictions. Two aspects of the problem are apparent – the definition of the unit of behavior, and the grouping of units into categories.

In studying behavior, researchers have traditionally used the "molar response" as the unit. It is not clear, however, what constitutes a "molar response." If someone is talking, is each phoneme, each word, each sentence, or the entire utterance the response? When does an utterance become a "response chain" instead of a response? If our subject taps his foot while talking, is he emitting two responses at once, or a single talking-and-foot-tapping response? The measure of the response often determines the unit. An operational definition may specify particular movement (leaving the environment out), or the response in an environmental context, or the effect of an act as the criterion. Contrast, for example, the descriptions "the boxer swung his fist," "the boxer swung his fist at his opponent,"(2) and "the boxer bloodied his opponent's nose." All might refer to the same event, but the first could also have occurred with no one else in the ring, and the second would not necessarily cause any damage. Whatever the unit, it seems preferable to assess the situational context and immediate effects of a behavior as well as the motor movements performed – at least on an intuitive level. There seems to be a great difference between the response of swinging one's fist when no one is there to receive the blow, and the same set of movements when the fist strikes another person.

In addition to the problem of characterizing behavior, there is also the problem of characterizing the environment. As discussed above, the specificity with which the environment is defined may be related to the predictive power of the measure. One must also consider how best to characterize an environment. Moos (1973) presents six approaches to the classification of environments: 1) ecological, e.g., climactic, geographical, and architectural aspects; 2) behavior settings, particular locations within which certain behaviors tend to be exhibited; 3) organizational – institutional properties of the situation; 4) characteristics of inhabitants, e.g., demographic variables of inhabitants; 5) perceived social climate, and 6) functional properties – response-consequence relationships.

Fredericksen (1972), on the other hand, suggests that environment classification should be based on the tendencies of situations to elicit similar behaviors. It is not clear that people behave sufficiently similarly to one another within a situation to permit utilization of this approach. Also, classification of environments by observed behavior does not allow for generalization of principles to other environments. The author's intent is not to dismiss this approach completely; it may be useful as a means of identifying similar environments. Behavior does not occur in a vacuum; the interactionist perspective clearly implies that the context of the behavior should be specified (note that a functional analysis of behavior does this). How best to specify the environment raises problems, however.

The second aspect of the fractionation problem is the grouping together of behavior units. Skinner (1953) proposes the concept of the response class, consisting of responses whose frequencies covary. Usually, however, workers in the field have defined response classes rationally rather than empirically. Aggressive acts are grouped together because they seem to go together; however, Castro (personal communication) found that verbal and nonverbal aggression covary positively in one situation and negatively in another. Thus, some rational groupings or empirical criteria may be inappropriate.

Price (1974) proposes cluster analysis of ratings of response appropriateness as a means for empirical categorization of responses. He presents a sample of this approach, the results of which are interesting but suggestive of some hazards. One of Price's responses is "talk," which does not cluster with any of the 14 other responses. Most likely, "talk" is interpreted very differently by different subjects; the interpretation of topic, wording, target for the verbalization, and situation may be very closely tied to ratings involving that verbalization. Waters (unpublished), for example, found that subjects rated the response "talk" as significantly more likely than the response "talk to a friend" (means were collapsed across seven different situations). Among Price's other responses were "mumble," "shout," and "argue," all of which are exemplars of the category "talk," and all of which appeared in different clusters.

Behaviors which have at least slight topographical differences must be grouped together, or else there will be too much information for psychologists to comprehend; however, the implications of different groupings must be researched rather than ignored.

In sum, assessing behavior is not the simple task it has been assumed to be. Interactionists are not the first to point out that behavior is a continuous interactive stream, but most laboratory research shows no recognition of this characteristic of behavior despite the long tradition of naturalistic observation in psychology.

Considerations In Instrument Development

If we are to obtain accurate measurement, we must develop accurate instruments. Space will not permit presentation of a complete methodology for instrument development; such methodology is presented elsewhere (see Wiggins, 1973; Goldfried & D'Zurilla, 1969). Rather, some of the steps common to most such models will be reviewed with an emphasis on specific considerations implied by interactionism.

The logical starting point is deciding what is to be measured. The bases for such a decision will depend largely on the context of the measurement. The behaviors and situations of interest in an elementary school will undoubtedly differ substantially from those in a psychiatric hospital. An environmental designer brought into a setting by someone else will often be expected to assess certain aspects of behavior. It should be recalled that the initial constructs of interest may not correspond to those employed in the final version of the instrument. For example, an initial construct might be "assertiveness," but further investigation may indicate that there is no unidimensional assertiveness factor; rather, "assertiveness" may be a summary term for a number of independent behaviors across many situations. Regardless of the context, one will have some initial ideas of constructs to be measured, and will be faced with the problem of determining which behaviors in which situations are exemplars of the constructs of interest.

In most cases, it will be impossible to include all items that are exemplars of a particular construct. Hence, it will usually be necessary to sample (not arbitrarily select) items representative of the construct. Four sources for such sampling are readily apparent. The first is direct naturalistic observation, preferably in an ethological style. It is hoped that no investigator would attempt to measure behaviors he/she has never seen – any description, recording, or summarization of behavior will contain less information than the actual events. A second source of information is the perception of others who have frequent contact with the population to be observed. These are people who, in most cases, have had more opportunity to observe the population than has the investigator. (We have found that ward attendants often have a wealth of information about the residents of their wards, and a concomitant lack of respect for the professionals who make the decisions on the basis of inadequate information.) A third source of samples is the population to be assessed. If assessing disruptive behavior in students, one should ask the students what behaviors they think disrupt the class or prevent them from working. We suspect that there is substantial overlap between the cognitive associations among behaviors and what might be established empirically as response classes. If people tend to construe two behaviors as accomplishing or meaning the same thing, then a person may well tend to do both in a given situation. The final source – previous psychological work and theory – may not always be available or useful; with most areas of human behavior, there is some relevant previous work.

An added consideration in the generation of items is the number of situations to which the measure is to be generalized. If an instrument is intended to assess behavior across more than one situation, then the items should take this into account. Observational codes should be designed to be equally applicable to all situations of interest, and instruments employing other methods should specify specific response-situation combinations. In many cases, it will be impossible to include all situations of interest; at such times, sampling from the population of situations is warranted.

Procedures for item selection are described elsewhere (see Wiggins, 1973), and will not be reviewed in detail here. One issue worth noting, however, arises when an instrument is designed to assess a construct across different situations. A decision must then be made: Are the same behaviors exemplars of the construct in all situations?

One approach is to group together behaviors whose frequencies covary within a situation; however, even if this worked, it would leave no basis for equating constructs across situations. Another method is to assess the situation-specific meanings of responses in particular situations. Whether these correspond to appropriate groupings is, of course, a difficult empirical question. No one method seems entirely satisfactory. Hence it is suggested that such construct groupings involving different situations be based on convergent validation. If several methods indicate the validity of such groupings, then it may be appropriate to combine the items. It is a common practice among behaviorists to group topographically different behaviors together on a rational basis; the need for empirical justification of such groupings has only occasionally been recognized (Kent & Foster, 1977).

It should be clear from the previous discussion that we lean toward a construct validation viewpoint. Construct validity is, for the purposes of this discussion, best characterized by its contrast with operationalism. An operational definition defines what is being measured as the result of the operations used to measure it (e.g., intelligence is the score obtained on an IQ test). A construct validity approach defines what is being measured as an underlying process or capability (e.g., intelligence is a capacity to process and integrate information), of which many measures may assess some aspect. Strict operationalism, hence, leaves little room for relationships among different measures of the same thing, while construct validity emphasizes an examination of relationships among the different measures. With a few exceptions (see Bechtoldt, 1959), we suspect that even the most rigorous behaviorists really do not believe that the operational definition truly is what is being measured. As one put it, "An operational definition in psychology just means a description of how we measure something." We have already made clear our stance concerning psychologists' arbitrary decisions on measurement, and this includes arbitrary operational definitions.

The strategies involved in construct validation approaches are clearly implied by an interactionist perspective, and are widely accepted by most workers in assessment. The only assessment devices for which the need for construct validation is not generally recognized are behavior observation codes. Kent & Foster (in press) argue that "The issue of construct validation becomes salient when a number of individual behaviors are grouped to provide an index of a general response class . . . "

A parting word on instrument development seems in order. An instrument developed for a particular population and set of situations may be wholly inapplicable to other populations and situations. Responses that are parts of constructs for one group may be irrelevant for other groups. Hence, if an instrument is to be widely used, its development should be based on a wide range of populations and situations, and its generalizability across these should be investigated (see Cronbach, Rajaratnam, & Gleser, 1963).

IMPLICATIONS FOR DATA COLLECTION

The above discussion is an attempt to present measurement considerations that are applicable to most data collection methods. Here, a few of the more method-specific considerations will be discussed. For the sake of brevity, the section will focus on two basic approaches — behavior observation and behavior report.

Observational data has been lionized by many researchers as the way to obtain objective data on what people do; however, as Kent & Foster (in press) point out, it is beset with a myriad of biases to validity and reliability. This does not mean that it is any worse as a method than other means of data collection. Interactionists have posed a few issues that users of behavior observation must consider.

Many have raised objections to "unidirectional causation" models in psychology (see Overton & Reese, 1973; Endler, 1975; Endler &

Magnusson, 1976). They argue that the organism affects and is affected by the environment (see Krasner & Ullmann, 1973), and that most research designs and measures do not take this into account. Many observational codes suffer from this problem, since they are designed to record only total frequencies of behaviors and not their sequential interactions. There are exceptions to this criticism. Patterson, Ray, & Shaw (1968) present a behavior code for family interactions which records the sequence of responses in a reciprocal causation format, Rausch (1965) records "interaction sequences" which provide the same kind of information.   It is true that certain (possibly crucial) information is lost in the recording of only response occurrence; however, as Endler & Magnusson (1976) point out, ". . . the methodology and technology to examine the nature of dynamic interaction have not been fully developed" (p. 13).

They also assert (quite rightly) that we are still searching for basic determinants of and relationships among behaviors, and that the unidirectional causation model is often adequate for this search. Further, at times (such as during some interventions), the primary measure of interest is behavior frequency. Hence, we concur with Endler & Magnusson in saying that at this point both approaches are useful, and that psychologists have neglected the reciprocal causation model.

However, if two responses covary, but their frequencies are widely disparate, is it more appropriate to sum their frequencies or to sum the standard scores of their frequencies? In making such decisions, it may be appropriate to consider the response cost, time required, and impact on the environment of the behaviors; otherwise, one might end up treating responses such as tearing down wall posters and tearing down walls as equivalent. In such pooling of responses, it is important to recall that such factors as impact on the environment may vary with the situation.

Kent & Foster (1977) point out that if an observation code is applied across different situations, the reliabilities may change with the settings.   This may happen as a consequence of changes in response frequencies, complexity of the situation, or even obscuration of vision due to greater density of people. These problems may make cross-situational comparisons difficult, and the possibility of their existence should be assessed.   Despite the potential biases, observational data may be a useful means of assessing current behavior. It may also be used in the study of environments by using Fredericksen's approach of classifying environments according to the behaviors they tend to elicit.

Behavior report approaches have the advantages of each of application, substantial face validity, and reasonable correlations with other measures (see Argyle & Little, 1972; Wiggins, 1973; Mischel, 1976). This suggests that people usually know (are aware of) their own behavior (and that of others around them), and usually verbalize accurately about their self-observations and reactions. There are, however, a few important factors which may influence such reports.

One is the acceptability or appropriateness of the response. People may be more inclined to exaggerate the likelihood of responses that are socially acceptable in a given situation, and to underestimate the likelihood of less desirable responses. This would make cross-situational and cross-response comparisons questionable. One means of checking the veridicality of self report is to obtain reports from others in the person's environment. Peer reports of behavior have been found to correlate with other measures as well (see Wiggins, 1973), and have the added advantage that reliability may be increased by increasing the number of peers sampled.

A variant of this approach is the peer- or self-prediction of behavior. This method has virtually the same advantages and weaknesses as behavior report methods. In some instances, peer prediction is more accurate than carefully developed, sophisticated psychological tests (see Wiggins, 1973).

Behavior report and behavior prediction methods can be very useful and efficient; however, they do not escape the methodological considerations of measurement. Biases must be tested for, particularly by comparing the results with those from other measures. In addition, the items should specify situation as well as response. Note, too, that the specificity of the item may affect the results. Waters (1976) found that response and situation specificity can affect estimates of likelihood for specific response-situation combinations. Hence, item specificity effects should be examined for the instrument.

Each method of measurement has some potential biases, including some that are yet to be discovered and, hence, cannot be controlled for. The best approach, therefore, is to use several methods for gathering data. If only one measure shows an effect, then the effect might be attributed to bias. If a number of measures, each with different biases, show an effect, then there is a stronger basis for concluding that the effect is truly present.

IMPLICATIONS FOR INTERVENTIONS

Although some workers in the field of psychological intervention (e.g., Goldfried & Davison, 1976) have proclaimed themselves interactionists, the mainstream interactionist literature has rarely confronted the issue of interventions. Hence, it is not clear what an interactionist intervention might be, nor whether such an approach would be appropriate at this time. Bowers (1973) attacks situationist models of behavior, but adds that "the situationist position has generated a great deal of needed change in therapeutic practices. It is not the practical utility of situationism that is here being criticized" (p. 308). Of course, the separation of assessment and intervention operations is more difficult to make in an environmental design approach than in some others – part of the goal of the field is to break down such distinctions. For example, an environmental design intervention might involve simply the introduction of a reactive measuring instrument. On the other hand, environmental design often involves a person-oriented intervention such as training people to design their own environments. On some occasions, environmental designers question the usefulness and ethical status of situationist interventions.

Still, interactionism implies at least two issues that environmental designers must confront. The first is the problem of nomothetic process assumptions, and the second is the role of cognition in behavior.

The term "nomothetic process" as used here refers to a general process (or effect) common to a number of individuals or populations. One of the broadest of such assumptions involves the law of effect. Some have assumed that a reinforcement process is crucial to learning across many infra-human and all human organisms; however, much of the research has utilized naive or low-level of functioning subjects in relatively simple situations; therefore, the justifiability of such a generalization may be questioned. It may be that contingency management has little effect on some people. O'Leary & Drabman (1971) point out that while group means may change, certain individuals seem unaffected by the introduction of a token economy. Additionally, as noted above, clinical and nonclinical populations may differ in responsiveness to situational stimuli.

Generally, the question of which intervention for which individual is an assessment issue, but it becomes an intervention issue when one is introducing group intervention. Since many environmental designers utilize group interventions, this may pose a serious problem.

We feel that interactionists' data contributes little specific information to this question. Interactionists have collected masses of data concerning patterns of responding across molarly defined situations, but have not examined whether specific molecular environmental differences might account for their interactions. Certainly, a heterogeneous sample may respond such that a group intervention is not feasible, but the amount of variation in a relatively homogeneous sample may show little enough variability to permit a group intervention. As Argyle & Little (1972) suggest, in some situations environmental variables may account for a great deal of behavioral variance.

To a large extent, the determination of adequacy of a group intervention is unexamined. Sarason, Smith & Diener (1975) argue that situation effects are typically small, but this is not the issue. Rather, the issue is if the "right" intervention is applied consistently to all members of a group, what is the magnitude of the effect? If environmental designers begin to do more careful assessment and intervention selection, and monitor their interventions to determine the consistency of application of the procedure, an answer to this question may be found.

The role of cognition in behavior is emphasized to a greater extent by interactional theorists than by many environmental designers. Does this mean that environmental designers are anachronisms − throwbacks to an earlier, more mechanistic era of psychology? The answer depends upon how "cognition" is defined, and of which environmental designers one speaks. All interventions are, in a sense, situationist, since all involve presenting a person with various situations. Cognitive often refers to those interventions that are construed as focusing on modification of hypothesized internal constructs called cognitions rather than on modification of the environment. One could similarly construe the most mechanistic reinforcement program as an attempt to modify cognitive expectations of response-consequence relationships; thus, cognitive may refer to an explanation as much as to the type of intervention. Cognitive may also refer to the degree to which the intervener utilizes the capacity of human beings to process and transmit information. For example, Krasner (1975; personal communication) contrasts two approaches to increasing the frequency of plural nouns – one may say "uh-huh" after each emission of a plural noun, or simply tell a subject "I would like you to say some plural nouns." Both methods work, but the latter saves a great deal of time and effort because it takes advantage of the person's capacity to process information.

IMPLICATIONS FOR RESEARCH

Despite the ambiguities surrounding the term "research" there are several considerations that seem appropriate here. In some ways, the juxtaposition of contemporary interactionism and environmental design is an intriguing one. Both are new fields formed by the integration of many previously existing streams of psychology and related areas. Environmental design's contribution might be seen as the attempt to integrate what we know about behavior-environment relationships, and to add to this body of knowledge. Contemporary interactionism's greatest contribution might be seen as pointing out how much we do not know about behavior.

We really do not know what behavior is, nor how best to characterize it, nor do we understand the relevant dimensions of environments for behavior. Our technology is so limited that most of the great complexity of behavior is lost before we look at our data, yet we do not know the consequences of this loss. A first step might be to apply our various data gathering methods, utilizing our various definitions of behavior, and examine the interrelationships among the measures and definitions. Similar approaches to situation measurement are also warranted. Until we discover how situations affect the processes that control behavior, we would do well to modify our research designs somewhat. Instead of arbitrarily selecting situations in which to place our subjects, we should sample from those situations that our subjects currently experience (see Brunswik, 1947). Instead of setting up analogue studies of the behavior influence process, we should study behavior change efforts when and where they occur in the real world (Waters & Graeff, 1977). In this way we can examine the generalizability of processes across situations (or assess probability rather than possibility, see Brunswik, 1947). We should include both person and situation variables in our designs, so as to ascertain their interrelationships (see Cronbach, 1957).

At the same time, however, environmental designers must keep in mind their reason for existence. Environmental design is an applied field and hence, must be bounded by the useful as well as the theoretically interesting. In a sense, interactionism and environmental design may be seen as representing Baer's (1977) two approaches to behavior-interactionism that often attempts to examine many variables contributing to behavior variance, while environmental design generally seeks to examine the most powerful. We believe that environmental design could benefit from a broadening of research designs to encompass more variables, but only if variables are retained for future study on the basis of power of effect and not simply because their effects are statistically significant.

CONCLUSION

These two integrative approaches to human behavior – environmental design and contemporary interactionism – share many common features. Several streams of influence are shared by both – most notably, behavioral psychology and environmental psychology. Many concepts of interactionism are reiterations of suggestions from these streams and, hence, many environmental designers are already "interactionists."

The principle implications of interactionism for environmental design seem to be in the area of assessment. The incorporation of both person and situation into assessment instruments and the careful investigation of different approaches to fractionation of the stream of behavior are paramount among these. It is less clear that interactionism has serious implications for interventions in environmental design. A general implication of interactionism is that we know very little about the determinants of behavior. The pattern of behavior across situations is apparently exceedingly complex and, at this point, no one has adequately described it, much less accounted for it. Of course, any self-respecting psychologist does not need to be told of the complexity of human behavior.

Environmental design has not been characterized as a strictly situationist approach, but its orientation is more situationist than is that of contemporary interactionism. One might well ask if there is too little of the person in environmental design. Wiggins (1973) expresses the view that situationism has served an important role as a corrective to the extremely person-oriented trait psychology. Bowers (1973) suggests that situationism is more a practical approach than a theoretically valid one. These views are not inconsistent with an environmental design approach. We hesitate to use labels such as "true" or "valid" in reference to any paradigm, including our own. We do believe, however, that if we work within a behavior influence paradigm, it will lead to positive consequences for us and for recipients of our services. Many of the implications of contemporary interactionism bring us closer to our own paradigm, to a further recognition of the interactional complexities of behavior, people and environments. To the extent that this is so, interactionism is a useful and important influence on environmental design.

NOTES

(1) Moos (1978: personal communication) argues that this consistency is less than others have suggested.

(2) Special thanks to Moos (1978: personal communication) for his help with this example.

5 Methods for Assessments of Environments

Richard C. Paradise and Ned L. Cooney

Assessment and evaluation are basic to the environmental design approach. We have been stressing the concept of the role of the participant-observer. Two elements are involved here: the "observer" part which is the more traditional method of assessment, and the newer question as to the methods of evaluation which derive from a concept of the participant-observer role. That is, what considerations come into the evaluation processes when the evaluation itself is considered to be part of the influence process?

This chapter focuses on the key issues of measurement and assessment of environments. Environmental influences on behavior must be not only identified but also quantified if we are to proceed in a systematic manner. The emphasis is on the evaluation of both people and environments and, particularly, the interaction between them in line with the theoretical orientation delineated in the previous chapter. The authors offer a series of criteria for the development of assessment methodology, including not only the traditional validity and reliability of the procedures but criteria of economy, immediacy, and simplicity.

Ed.

Measurement as a scientific behavior is of interest to us because we desire to make our own measurement methods as accurate and efficient as possible. The purpose of this chapter is to briefly review some of the more promising methodologies of measurement in the various fields which represent streams of influence in environmental design, and to describe the methods we have adapted most frequently.

FUNCTIONS OF ASSESSMENT

In psychology, measurement activity has been termed "assessment" probably because it has more often entailed qualitative classification than quantitative description. Assessment has served a number of functions in the science and technology of psychology. The most basic function is description and measurement of behavior (Ciminero, 1977; Craik, 1973; Goldfried and Sprafkin, 1974; Kanfer and Saslow, 1969; and Krasner and Ullmann, 1973). Many psychological studies and most environmental design efforts specify behaviors as major dependent variables in the narrow sense of observable activity. If behavior is taken in the broad sense to include domains such as verbal reports of subjective states, then all social science activities involve the measurement of behavior.

An historically significant function is prediction of behavior. Here, behavior is measured in one situation at one time to predict the probability (or other property) of some behavior in some other situation or at some other time. A classic example is Binet's development of the intelligence test to predict performance in classrooms. In this case, a child's perceptual-motor and verbal skills are measured in a standardized one adult — one child test situation to predict academic performance in school. A popular contemporary case is the selection of people for positions in organizations (Goldfried and Linehan, 1977; Wiggins, 1973).

With the advent of systematic application of psychological principles in behavior modification, two additional functions have been identified. Since a number of techniques were available to change the behavior of a client or trainee, assessment was used to select the most appropriate technique and to specify its parameters (Ciminero, 1977; Goldfried and Pomeranz, 1968; Goodkin, 1967; Kanfer and Saslow, 1969). Krasner and Ullmann (1973) discuss this function as follows:

> In either freely occurring naturalistic events or controlled experiments, enumeration (measurement) has the goal of altering the behavior of the psychologist or other consumer of information . . . we collect data (that is, measurements) to be able to make a decision about or alter our behavior toward other people. (P. 112)

An assessment of the behavior of a child might suggest a positive reinforcement procedure with parental praise as a reinforcer. To adequately fulfill this function, the assessment procedure should identify variables that influence the behavior of interest. In a discussion of clinical behavioral assessment, Goldfried and Linehan (1977) have asserted that:

> The primary goal has been to determine those variables maintaining any maladaptive behavior pattern and any client characteristics which have implications for both the selection and

implementation of the most appropriate behavior therapy procedure. (P. 16-17)

Another major function suggested by behavior modification is the evaluation of planned changes in the environment – the evaluation function (Ciminero, 1977). Cautela (1968) and Peterson (1968) implied that assessment was part and parcel of a functional analysis of behavior; that is, assessment included a planned change in the environmental influences and a measurement of the effects of those changes. Recently, this function has been clearly recognized (Ciminero, 1977; Dickson, 1975; Goldfried and Linehan, 1977; Krasner and Ullmann, 1973).

A fifth function of assessment, reactivity, is suggested by the recognition that the measurement procedure itself will affect the phenomenon being measured. Early in this century, the physicist Heisenberg found that the light required to observe the movements of a particle actually altered the speed and direction of the particle. He formulated the uncertainty principle to describe the limits of scientific knowledge – we can't be certain of how the particle would behave in the absence of measurement. Robert Rosenthal (1966) documented the psychological analogy – the behavior of experimental subjects was influenced by the measurement procedure. This has become known as "reactivity" to observation and some factors have studied (Kent and Foster, 1977). Recently, reactivity has begun to be used as a behavior change procedure. Nelson et al. (1978) found increases in "appropriate classroom verbalization" when the subjects observed their own behavior. Thus, the assessment procedure will operate as an environmental influence. If this is planned, it might be considered another function of assessment – the reactive function. However, the pursuit of the reactive function might conflict with other functions, most notably the evaluation function and the predictive function. If the only measure is obtrusive (potentially reactive), then the "pure" effect of the other planned environmental changes is indeterminate. The evaluation function may not be served. Similarly, the data from an obtrusive measurement procedure may not adequately represent the state of affairs when no measurement occurs. The predictive value might then be questioned. This issue of conflicting functions will be discussed in later parts of this chapter.

In the context of environmental design, assessment is likely to focus on two functions – identification of influences and evaluation of planned changes in the environment. However, the other functions may be pursued as well. A hypothetical example might illustrate this. Let us assume that an environmental design group is invited by a school administrator to work with teachers who would like to improve their students' academic progress. After the objectives have been formulated (see chap. 2), the first step would be an assessment of environmental influences on the students' academic behaviors – the identification function. This might include variables such as: the administrator's status and values; the teachers' values, and classroom behavior; the political, economic, and social organization of the school; the community and social support for education; and the physical design of the classrooms. The results of this assessment should suggest some strategies for further discussion and development. If the environmental design changes are to be evaluated, then the behaviors of interest would be measured before and after the changes were implemented. In this case, the students' academic performance would be measured, perhaps, by tests and observations of academic behaviors. A thorough evaluation might require measurement of the planned changes themselves. For example, if the strategy involved training the teachers in classroom management, then the teachers' classroom behavior might be observed.

Other functions of assessment could be called for by participants or by the two primary functions. If the students' academic performance is supposed to be related to employment and productivity after the school years, then the predictive function is requested. If the measurement of teachers' behavior is intended to make the teachers more aware of the ways in which they managed their classes, then the reactive function is suggested.

In summary, of the five functions of assessment – measurement, prediction, identification of influences, evaluation, and reactivity – the endeavor of environmental design directly requires identification and evaluation. The latter function usually involves basic measurement. Prediction and reactivity may be required by the specific goals of the participants.

CRITERIA FOR ASSESSMENT METHODS

The particular methods and instruments employed in the assessment process should fulfill certain basic criteria of psychological assessment. Most of these criteria apply to all of the functions, although each function also has its own criteria. These criteria serve as guides in the selection and development of methods and instruments for specific purposes.

Validity

The first criterion is a close correspondence or fit between theoretical concepts, the phenomena sampled, and the data produced. This is the validity of the method – the degree to which it does what it is supposed to do (Krasner and Ullmann, 1973). For example, if the teachers are concerned with measuring their students' creativity (the theoretical concept), then their observations of the students' drawing and writing (the behaviors measured) and the scores they assign (the data) should be clearly relevant to or at least empirically related to creativity. The validity of a measure is limited to its theoretical framework and specific purposes. A measure that is valid for identification of environmental influences would be invalid for the evaluation of personality changes. Assessment methods for identifying influences should be sensitive to and encompass a variety of variables, including cultural, organizational, interpersonal, educational, and architectural factors.

There are three traditional types of validity: content, construct, and criterion-related (Goldfried and Linehan, 1977; Krasner and Ullmann, 1973; Wiggins, 1973).

Content Validity

Content validity refers to the obvious relevance which the content of the instrument has to the theoretical variable that it purports to measure. A content-valid measure will produce observations which can be interpreted within the theoretical scheme being used. To fulfill the identification function of assessment for environmental design, an instrument should produce data on specified variables in an environment; for example, the ethical system, physical size and use of space, leadership behavior, and reinforcement system.

To fulfill the measurement function, an instrument should sample behavior that is relevant or representative of the class of behaviors of interest. For example, if a teacher were being trained in the use of positive reinforcement, several behaviors might be observed including praise, touching, and smiling, but approaching the student might be questionable since this could be done in a threatening manner. Content validity is usually established by the judgments of experts such as fellow professionals, clients, or significant others in the criterion situation (Goldfried and D'Zurilla, 1969; Krasner and Ullmann, 1973). If, however, the relationship between the behavior sampled and the theoretical concept is obvious to all, this face validity is often sufficient. There is some evidence that face-valid, direct measures are as good as, if not better than, indirect measures. (Krasner and Ullmann, 1973; Mischel, 1972)

Construct Validity

When the variable in question is inherently unobservable or there is some dispute among experts about its manifestations, the question of construct validity arises. A construct is a hypothetical entity which is theoretically related to other variables, some of which must be observable. Examples from environmental design might be social skill or open classroom. The construct validity of a measure, that is, its relevance to the construct can be established in at least three ways. First, the content of the measure can be logically derived from a theory. For example, Lewinsohn's theory on depression relates the social skill of the person to his elicitation of positive social reinforcement which is related to his mood. Therefore, any measure of the construct social skill should be related to the frequency of social reinforcement. A second way to establish construct validity is to demonstrate that groups which differ on the level of the construct according to another, content-valid, but available, measure also vary on the measure in question. For example, the construct validity of a laboratory measure of conversational skill could be established by correlation with naturalistic observation of the number and proportion of successful conversations.

A third procedure to establish construct validity is to show that an instrument is sensitive to treatment effects. If an intervention has significantly changed the output of a measurement procedure, we can be more sure that the procedure is related to the intervention and, barring alternative explanations, the relationship includes the construct. For example, Fawcett & Miller (1975) found that audience ratings of speaker performance increased after training in public speaking was given to community workers. This approach increases confidence in both the intervention and the assessment methods.

These procedures are not mutually exclusive, in fact, they complement one another. An excellent example is the Minkin et al. (1976) social validation procedure. In order to generate a measure of conversation skill, they observed female students talking with strangers in a simulated situation. They selected three behaviors that, from a theoretical and empirical standpoint, were related to conversational skill. Frequency counts of these behaviors were found to be correlated with global ratings of the girls' skill by significant others. This was evidence of content validity. Girls in a delinquency diversion program were found to have lower frequency counts of the specified behaviors.) This is a combination of the theoretical-empirical method (delinquent girls were assumed to have fewer social skills) and the contrasted group method of construct validation. After training on the identified behaviors, the behavior frequency counts increased as did the global ratings. This sensitivity to treatment lent construct validity to both the behavior observational code and the ratings.

Criterion-related Validity

Another kind of validity for method selection is criterion-related validity (Goldfried and Linehan, 1977; Krasner and Ullmann, 1973). This questions the relevance of the assessment results to the situation to which they are to be generalized. It is a sampling issue — does the subjects' behavior in the assessment situation represent their behavior in the situation for which a decision is being made? This has become an issue because of the emergence of evidence that behavior is influenced by the aspects of the assessment situation (Krasner and Ullmann, 1973). Examples are the Braginskys' (e.g. Braginsky and Braginsky, 1972) work on impression management by a broad range of psychiatric populations, Bernstein's (1973) findings that a "laboratory" setting induced lower fear scores than a "clinic" setting, and the extensive work on social desirability in self-report inventories. An assessment method will have maximal criterion-related validity if it is administered in the criterion situation. Goldfried and Linehan (1977) discuss this as follows:

> To the extent that the criterion situation and the test situation are one and the same, generalizability is not an issue, and questions of validity are thus, by definition meaningless. (P. 21)

If the method occurs in a situation substantially different than the criterion situation, e.g. filling out a questionnaire about the marital relationship alone in the therapist's office prior to an interview, criterion validity can be demonstrated by correlations between that measure and results of content-valid measures in the criterion situation.

The basic validity requirements for an assessment methodology are that it yields discriminating data (incremental validity) about the value of operationally-defined, theoretically relevant variables (content and construct validity) in settings which adequately represent or have empirical relationships to the situations to which the decision is being applied (criterion-related validity).

Reliability

Another set of requirements concerns the reliability of the assessment methodology. A reliable measure is consistent across items (internal consistency), occasions of measurement (test-retest reliability), and testers, e.g. raters or observers (interrater reliability) (Krasner and Ullmann, 1973). Cronbach and his colleagues have refined the concept of reliability into the notion that any measure has certain limits to the range to which the results may be generalized (Wiggins, 1973). For example, the selection and training of observers may have to be replicated in order to produce similar data. Data are generalizable to other items representing the concept, other times, and other testers to the extent that it has been shown that these do not significantly effect measurement results.

Environmental Design Criteria

In addition to these traditional requirements, there are some criteria mandated by the endeavor of Environmental Design (see Chap. 9). First, the assessment must be able to encompass the complex interplay of environmental influences. The interactions of a number of factors on each other and on the behavior of interest should be available to the assessor. Second, it must be feasible and economic (Krasner and Ullmann, 1973). The cost of the assessment should not be more than the cost of an incorrect decision. For example, if several teacher-training programs are available and the purpose of assessment is to choose between these, then the assessment should not cost more than the consequences of choosing the worst program. Beyond this, if assessment requires few resources, such as little time, it is more likely to be fully and continuously implemented. For example, an evaluative measure might come to serve as a quality control procedure. Third, since assessment is for the purpose of effecting the researcher's behavior and feedback is more effective when immediate, then rapid data analysis is desirable. Fourth, it should be possible to take measurements at many times in order to test hypotheses, including ones concerning interventions.

There are two additional concepts which guide our selection of assesssment methods. Webb, Campbell, Schwartz, & Sechrest (1966) pointed out that any single instrument is subject to some sources of invalidity and, thus, the data are open to alternative interpretations. Therefore, several should be used when possible to achieve a "triangulation" so that only the desired interpretation is plausible. Some measures might, for example, be unobtrusive to control for reactivity. The second concept is that particular methods are useful for a limited range of purposes and situations.

SURVEY OF ASSESSMENT METHODOLOGIES

There are a number of assessment methodologies available from psychology and related disciplines. Some of these fit well with the concepts and purposes of environmental design. A few of these will be briefly reviewed here in terms of their assumptions, the quality of data produced, their psychometric properties, and for what purposes they may be useful.

Traditional personality assessment has played a predominant role in clinical psychology. A variety of methods such as interviews, objective inventories, and projective tests are used to produce a qualitative description of the assessee's personality. The major assumption here is that there are identifiable traits of persons which impel behavior regardless of situational variations (Goldfried and Kent, 1972). A subsequent assumption is that the particular personality theory used for the selection and interpretation is valid (Goldfried and Kent, 1972). However, there is not sufficient evidence that any personality theory is generally valid (Goldfried and Kent, 1972; Krasner and Ullmann, 1973; Mischel, 1968). Furthermore, there is strong evidence that behavior is situationally specific (e.g. Endler and Hunt, 1969; Hartshorne and May, 1928; Lewin, Lippitt, and White, 1938; Liberman, 1964; Mischel, 1968; Moos, 1969). The type of data produced with traditional personality assessment is the existence and strength of theoretical constructs such as motives, needs, and drives. Although it is possible that this sort of data could be considered in planning environments for particular groups of persons (Moos, 1978), the environmental design orientation deemphasizes these on the theoretical and empirical grounds mentioned above.

Behavioral Assessment

In the past decade, there has been a surge in the development of behavioral assessment (Ciminero, 1977; Goldfried and Kent, 1972; Goldfried and Linehan, 1977; Kanfer and Saslow, 1969; Krasner and Ullmann, 1973; Wiggins, 1973). The focus in behavioral assessment is on specified behavior in a defined situation (Krasner and Ullmann, 1973). The behavior is described in terms of its topography, intensity, and perhaps duration and measured in terms of its frequency, intensity, or duration. The situation is defined in terms of the physical and social stimuli which precede or follow the behavior; for example, the sex of other persons, instructions given, and consequences such as getting into a treatment program. The central assumption of behavioral assessment is that behavior is a function of the environment (Ciminero, 1977; Goldfried and Kent, 1972). A methodological assumption is that the behavior assessed is a representative sample of the behavior designated. This is in contrast to the assumption of traditional personality assessment that the behavior assessed is a sign of a personality construct. The behavioral assumption is clearly less inferential and more directly testable (Goldfried and Kent, 1972).

Behavioral assessment is clearly tied to intervention in that determinants of the problem behavior may be identified (Goldfried and Pomeranz, 1968), continuous monitoring can serve as feedback for the evaluation of treatment efforts, and treatment effects further validate the measurement.

Within the field of behavioral assessment, there are a variety of methods including interview, behavior observation, and physiological measurement. Three books have recently appeared which review these in detail (Ciminero, Calhoun & Adams, 1977; Cone & Hawkins, 1977; and Hersen & Bellack, 1976). In general, the behavior observation and physiological measures have the most face validity, the behavior observation and a few physiological measures can be carried on in "natural" situations and so can have high criterion validity. But interviews are much less expensive and for some circumstances, like private therapy clients, can have a great deal of content validity. Behavior observation methodology is well suited to measurement and evaluation functions and will be treated in more detail below.

Environmental Assessment

A small group of assessment techniques focused on environments and environmental variables have been developed over the past decade. These methods, that vary on their assumptions, purposes, and validity, Craik (1973) has labeled environmental assessment.

Perhaps the earliest technique was the simple recording of objects in physical settings such as living rooms. Recently, this method has been extended to other settings, for example campgrounds (Shafer & Thompson, 1968). By using factor analysis, Laumann & House (1970) found that in living rooms there were dimensions of social class and style (modern-traditional). This technique is face-valid for descriptive purposes and, no doubt, highly reliable, however, its relevance to behavior is untested. Barker (see below) has integrated this method with behavior observation.

Another set of environmental assessment methods were designed to measure the "traits of places" by collecting impressions from people exposed to the environment. These techniques are analogous to the trait attribution approach in personality assessment (Craik, 1971). These methods rest on an assumption parallel to that of personality assess- ment – environments contain traits or qualities which impel behavior, in this case evaluative or descriptive responses. Another assumption was that the instrument, e.g. adjective checklists or rating scales, did not seriously bias the data. This latter assumption was called into question by differences between factor structures of different instruments (Craik, 1973; Danford and Willems, 1975). The overwhelming effect of such method variance was demonstrated in the Danford and Willems study. They obtained ratings on a building with an adjective rating scale from observers who either viewed slides, took a guided tour, or were only given the building's function ("a law school"). There were no differences among the groups — the subjects in the last group did not even have to see the building to replicate the ratings of the other observers. They concluded that:

> The validity of the large percentage of current and past research in environmental assessment that has employed simple, direct, subjective rating methods . . . must be called into question. (P. 512)

If subjective rating methods could be developed which are sensitive to differences between environments and the knowledge of raters, these could serve the evaluation and, perhaps, the reactive functions. For example, when the goals of an environmental design effort include increased satisfaction of participants, a subjective rating scale could be one measure of that.

Danford & Willems (1975) further suggest:

> Lest one become consumed by the frustration and apparent futility which characterizes so much of man-environment research today, . . . there remains yet one viable, relatively untested alternative — behavior . . . Numerous investigators from other fields have successfully employed behavioral approaches (particularly through observation programs) for determining the structure, content, patterning, and dynamics both of behavior and of its relation to environmental constructs. (P. 513)

Social Climate Scales

Moos (1974) and his colleagues (Insel & Moos, 1974; Moos & Houts, 1968; Moos & Humphrey, 1974; Moos & Trickett, 1974) have taken one step in that direction by asking inhabitants of social environments to report on typical behavior patterns of their environments. These patterns are assumed to reflect dimensions of the "social climate," a concept derived from Murray's interactionalist (need-press) theory (see chap. 4). Moos (1974) summarized the rationale as follows:

> The particular pattern of press in an environment creates a group atmosphere or social climate . . . . The theory is that social climates have effects on individual behavior by creating induced forces and possibly new needs, which in turn impel behavior in

particular directions that are shaped by these social climates...
(P. 2)

Moos' group has developed social climate scales for psychiatric wards, classrooms, work environments, families, university residences, and groups. These scales serve primarily descriptive functions, for example in program, institutional, or clinical evaluation. Each scale consists of about ten dimensions reflecting conceptually different aspects of the social climate of that environment. For example, the Classroom Environment Scale (Moos and Trickett, 1974) has dimensions of Involvement, Affiliation, Teacher Support, Task Orientation, Competition, Order and Organization, Rule Clarity, Teacher Control, and Innovation. The psychometric properties appear to be quite good: internal consistency, interrater reliability, and test-retest reliability are all adequate; and the scales have been shown to correlate well with other rating instruments and programmatic changes. However, there is little evidence of concurrent validity and conflicting evidence of predictive validity in terms of observed behavior of the inhabitants (Paradise, 1976).

The primary utility of these measures would seem to be in identification and evaluation. For example, if lack of interest by students is a problem, a social climate assessment might identify such influences as teacher's overcontrol, lack of affiliation, and lack of innovation. A reassessment after teacher training could evaluate the effects of training and the state of the climate for further changes.

Moos (1975) and his colleagues have reported that these scales can also be used to facilitate change in environments:

> Information about the social climate can be fed back to the participants in a social environment. The logic is that this kind of feedback will often motivate people in the environment to seek to change it . . . Presentation of social climate data leads to a detailed inquiry of the reasons certain data were obtained and a discussion of problems . . . Group meetings . . . can lead to positive interactions between members of social environments, to clarification of issues, and to increased discussion of values . . . This leads to basic changes in the relationships among members of the social milieu, that is, to a change in the social climate. (P. 35-36)

In other words, the social climate scales are well suited to the reactive function.

The social climate scale methodology has the advantages of being easy to administer and analyze, economic in time and expense, and face-valid. It produces quantitative data on a number of environmental variables. Unfortunately, the theoretical and empirical links between the dimensions measured and the members' behavior are not yet clearly established for the existing scales. The general method is promising, and the scales can contribute to an assessment package.

Behavior Setting Analysis

Barker (1968) described a rigorous methodology for environmental assessment which employed extensive behavioral observation in the natural environment. It involves the immediate recording of behavioral events by a passive observer. These observations are analyzed in terms of Barker's theory of ecological psychology. The theory identifies a basic environmental unit called the "behavior setting" which is generated independently of the observer and has obvious time-space boundaries. Behavior settings have two aspects: "standing behavior patterns" and the physical "milieu." These two aspects are mutually fit for each other – in Barker's terms they are synomorphic. The prototypical example is the classroom that exists independently of the observer and is bounded by walls and the school day. Standing behavior patterns of lecturing, listening, reading, sitting, and writing are synomorphic with milieu parts of blackboard, student's desks facing teacher, books, desk seats, writing surfaces, and implements. An entire community or institution can be analyzed in terms of the types and numbers of behavior settings.

Barker's central theoretical assumption appears to be that behavior and the environment are in perfect correspondence with one another. The two major methodological assumptions are that the settings and time periods observed are representative of all settings at all times, and that the observer does not drastically affect the environment or behavior. The results of behavior setting analysis are static, descriptive, and largely qualitative.

Since the observer takes on a passive onlooker role and views a number of typical activities, the assessment situation would be representative of the environment at other times. Thus, criterion-related validity is potentially high, depending on what the criterion is considered to be. The theoretical concepts appear to be sufficiently well-defined that reliability and content validity would be adequate, but we are unaware of any estimates of these. The procedure itself is expensive due to the large amounts of time required of observers well-trained in a complex theory. Although its assumptions are largely compatible with environmental design, its utility is hampered by the expense and the failure to identify a number of influences not immediately available to a passive observer. Behavior setting analysis might be most useful as a preliminary to a more complete analysis of a single setting and as a qualitative evaluation instrument.

PARTICIPANT OBSERVATION

Behavioral sciences related to environmental design, most notably sociology and anthropology, have developed assessment methods for large and complex social environments. One of these methods, participant observation, has proven quite useful for the preliminary goal of environmental design assessment – the identification of influences. Fry (1973) has defined participant observation as:

a method of collecting data in which the researcher, to some degree, takes on the role of a member of the group being observed and participates in the functioning of that group. (P. 274)

Glaser & Backer (1973) assert that:

participant observers study a process or environment by observing and experiencing it in depth . . . Data are collected by direct contact with the real life situations and by observing behaviors as they occur naturally. (P. 46)

The participant observer assumes a role in the environment, observes an extensive sample of the events and behaviors, participates in some of the activities, and converses with the members of the environment about past events, their perceptions of the environment and their feelings, attitudes, and values. Frequently, the participant observer will conduct formal interviewing, frequency counts, document analysis, and questionnaires (Katz, 1953; McCall & Simmons, 1969; Zelditch, 1962). For the present purpose, the term will be applied in the more restricted sense to denote a method in which a trained person immerses him/herself in an environment for an extended period of time, observes and participates in activities, and informally interviews the members.

The data generated by participant observation is an analytic description of an environment employing the concepts of a body of scientific theory (McCall & Simmons, 1969). Frequently, this method produces new concepts and hypotheses, particularly when an attempt is made to "understand behavior from the perspective of the observed" (Fry, 1973, p. 274). It has often been praised for providing rich and detailed information on influences and processes which are complex, subtle, or unavailable through other means (Glaser & Backer, 1973; Katz, 1953; McCall & Simmons, 1969; Zelditch, 1962).

Since this method can be utilized with a variety of theoretical viewpoints, the theoretical assumptions will vary. The central methodological assumption is that behavior is best studied in its environmental context. Another is that while the participant observer will undoubtedly affect the environment being studied, this impact can itself be influenced and assessed. This assumption is clearly articulated by Sullivan (1954) in his book on the psychiatric interview:

. . . the data of psychiatry arise only in participant observation. In other words, the psychiatrist cannot stand off to one side and apply his sense organs, however refined they may be by the use of apparatus, to noticing what someone does, without becoming personally involved in the operation. His principal instrument of observation is his self — his personality, _him_ as a person. The processes and the changes in processes that make up the data which can be subjected to scientific study occur, not in the subject person, nor in the observer, but in the situation which is created between the observer and his subject . . . There are no purely objective data in psychiatry, and there are no valid subjective data, because the material becomes scientifically usable only in the shape of a complex resultant – inference. (P. 3)

Rosenthal (1966, 1969) has thoroughly documented the existence of experimenter bias in the collection and analysis of data and experimenter effects on the behavior of subjects. More recently, O'Leary and Kent (1973) and Dubey, Kent, O'Leary, Broderick, and O'Leary (in press) have investigated the conditions under which these effects occur. The assumption of researcher participation is, then, empirically sound and theoretically consistent with environmental design.

Since participant observation has received little attention in psychology as an assessment methodology, yet appears promising for the identification of complex and subtle influences, the procedures and qualities of participant observation will be considered here in some detail. In order to illustrate aspects of this method, examples will be abstracted from some respected scientific works which employed this method. These include Gans' (1962) studies of an urban community – Boston's Italian West End; Liebow's investigation of black, male ghetto dwellers (1967); Fry's (1973) evaluation of a patient-run, drug-abuse treatment program; Glaser and Backer's (1973) consultation with a federal Concentrated Employment Program; and studies of mental hospitals by Goffman (1961); Levinson & Gallagher (1964); Perucci (1974); and Schwartz & Schwartz (1955).

There are several interdependent phases involved in conducting a participant observation study. First, the particular environment and topic to be studied and the theoretical framework to guide observation must be chosen. Second, the participant observer must enter the environment, define his/her role, develop sponsorships, incentives, and relationships with the members. Third, he exposes him/herself to activities and engages in conversations with the inhabitants of the environment. Fourth, he/she records significant observations, conversations, and reactions. Finally, the data is analyzed and interpreted.

Logically, the choice of the research topic may either precede or follow the selection of the particular situation in which it will be studied. When the topic is chosen first, it implies that the generality or validity of a theory or set of beliefs is being tested. For example, Gans (1967) wished to investigate the validity of scientific and popular literature concerning life in suburbia and so chose to study a newly constructed community, Levittown. When theory generation is the goal, the situation may be selected and entered without a clearly defined, specific topic. For example, Goffman (1961) examined a mental institution from several perspectives and constructed an explanation of the (mal)functioning of the institution with some novel concepts. In consultative or clinical situations, the participant observer may be invited into a setting and the topic selected mutually with the client. For example, Glaser & Backer (1973) were asked to evaluate a government employment program.

The theoretical framework which the participant observer brings to bear on the great amount of phenomena to which he/she will be exposed may be thought of as a variable of observer training and is revealed in the concepts around which findings are presented. Widely varying constructs are applied by different investigators. Gans (1967) asked for the expectations, attitudes, feelings, and participation of suburban residents; Goffman (1961) looked at the features, processes, moral climate, and model of interaction in a mental hospital; Liebow (1967) examined role behaviors; and Glaser & Backer (1973) described their impact in terms of "unassertiveness," "group participation and cohesiveness," "orientation contact," and "communication barriers."

Once the particular environment, topic, and theory have been selected, the participant observer must solve several problems related to entering the setting. One of the most important is the acquisition of a sponsor in the environment. A sponsor is a person who maintains a role in the group or organization and who is willing to introduce, explain, and defend the participant observer to fellow members. Goffman (1961) obtained the cooperation of an official high in the organizational structure. Liebow (1967) sought and gained the approval of an informal leader in the neighborhood. An alternative to acquiring a sponsor is the establishment of membership. Gans (1962, 1967) moved into the community, and Fry (1973) joined the treatment program as a patient.

The participant observer must define a role for him/herself or assume a role assigned by the environment. Usually this takes the form of stating his status as researcher; his future behavior of watching and talking to people; the information desired; and to what use the data will be put (Fry, 1973; McCall & Simmons, 1969). When researchers are forced to take on preestablished roles, they often find content restrictions on the types of information they can elicit (Fry, 1973; Riecken, 1956). Two roles that allow a good deal of latitude are "environmental designer" and "program evaluator" (Balaban, 1973; Glaser & Backer, 1973; see also chap. 8). These can emphasize collaboration on mutually agreed goals to provide incentive for cooperation and reduce evaluative anxiety.

There are two discriminable but related methods employed by the participant observer: informal interviewing of the inhabitants of the environment; and observation and/or participation in the activities of the environment. Both of these have aspects of sampling and mode, that is, which behaviors, activities, and members are observed or interviewed, and on what level.

Since the traditional random sampling method is usually not available to the participant observer due to "vagaries of the field relations," McCall & Simmons (1969) have characterized three procedures often used in such studies. The "quota sample" consists of a few persons or activities in each of a number of exhaustive categories. For example, Fry (1973) participated in activities appropriate to his status level in the five different status levels of a progressive release program. Although he could not observe or participate in all events, he was able to observe some events in all status levels. A "snowball sample" is obtained by following the leads suggested by information gathered in one activity or interview. Liebow's (1967) informant sample snowballed from a single acquaintance at a coffee shop, to a group drinking on a corner, to rooms and apartments of an enlarging circle of friends. None of the studies surveyed for the present work explicitly contained a "search for exceptions."

The mode of participant observation in activities may be conceptualized as a point on a continuum from "active participation" to "passive observation" (Schwartz & Schwartz, 1955). Gans (1967) specified three modes: total participant, researcher-participant, and total researcher. The participant observer selects one or more of these modes depending on the purpose and aspects of the environment; for example, size of the group and availability of a "scientific observer" role. Each mode generates different kinds of data, has different effects on the environment, and involves different risks.

These modes are ideal-types and, in most cases, researchers will use some combination of them throughout the study. Dean et al. (1967) noted that there is often a progression from passive observation to participation to interviewing. Fry (1973) used two observers: one as a total participant, the other as a researcher-participant. In environmental design, we often move from a primarily participant mode as influences, processes, and values are identified, to a primarily observer mode when changes are evaluated.

These ideal-types are also not pure. A total participant is continuously observing and a complete observer inevitably participates. These modes simply characterize segments of a continuum of active involvement in the behavioral stream.

The second method within participant observation to be considered here is the informal interviewing of inhabitants of the environment. There are several purposes in terms of the kind of information desired. The researcher may want information on previous or infrequent events or activities which cannot be observed such as high-level political meetings or sexual encounters (McCall & Simmons, 1969). In this case, the informant is acting as the observer's observer (Zelditch, 1962). Second, an inhabitant may convey information about established practices, rules, and statuses. Here the informant is a surrogate censustaker. Finally, the interviewer may ask for the inhabitant's feelings, motives, intentions, reactions and perceptions. The interviewee is termed a "respondent" in this case (McCall & Simmons, 1969).

There are a large number of considerations in selection of informants and the analysis of data gathered from them. Members of the various groups and people occupying various positions within the groups should be represented (Katz, 1953). Glaser and Backer (1973) interviewed program members at all levels from clients to top administrators. Those with different sources of information and motives for conveying it should be sampled (Katz, 1953; McCall, 1969). Dean et al. (1967) note that especially willing informants may be found among the frustrated; "habitues" or "fixtures"; subordinates; those who are "out" but "in the know"; and those who are naive as to what the interviewer represents. They find more sensitive informants among outsiders, rookies, the "nouveau statused" (those in transition within the hierarchy), and the unusually reflective or objective person. Informants will differ in their ability to report accurately and use vocabulary the interviewer will understand.

The recording of observations poses a difficult problem for the participant observer. Involvement in the ongoing behavior stream precludes any immediate recording for the more active modes. Mechanical recording devices would generate too much data over the usual course of a participant observation study and create a great deal of reactance. Note-taking during an event or interview will infringe on the observation of possibly significant events. The researcher's focus may shift during the study rendering previous records irrelevant (McCall & Simmons, 1969). The preferred method of data recording is note-taking in a log or journal after the event. This preserves the sequence and context of events over the course of the study, and eases the study of change within the environment, changing relations with members, and biases of the observer (McCall & Simmons, 1969). Later, these records may be indexed by topic and sorted to abstract observations on specific questions. Observations should be systematically recorded so that each research question is addressed each day.

Although one might suspect that recording after the event would subject the data to unacceptable inaccuracies and distortions, McCall & Simmons (1969) claim that:

> experience indicates that even a small amount of practice allows the researcher to recall in quite literal detail an astounding proportion of what he has witnessed. Periodic comparisons with tape recordings . . . typically reveal that the main outlines of the event or interview are correctly recalled, together with the detail of most segments, albeit with some reordering and total omission of some segments. (P. 74)

As an aid to memory and understanding, Schwartz & Schwartz (1955) suggest retrospective observation, in which the investigator imagines the situation, taking on the roles of others, and integrates his own perceptions with those of the participants.

The analysis and interpretation of the data collected in a participant observation study takes rather unique forms. McCall (1969) has characterized the definition of variables as the result of an inductive method of "theoretical interpretation of empirical incidents" as opposed to the deductive "validation of theoretical concepts" more familiar to psychologists. According to McCall (1969), the investigator starts with very general and poorly specified concepts. As descriptive accounts accumulate, the recorded data is sorted for similar content, and categories and hypotheses are tentatively formulated on the basis of common threads in the observations. The participant observer then "endeavors to sharpen his definition of the constructs" and apply the definitions to both accumulated and new observations. In this process, the indicators of the constructs and their relative weightings become more clearly specified.

Robinson (1951) labels the above procedure "analytic induction" and emphasizes that both the definition of the variable and the hypothesis undergo modification as more data is collected and analyzed. McCall (1969) states that this approach serves to establish the relevance of the indicators to the concept, since the concept grew out of the indicators, and confirms proposition relating concepts, since it is reformulated to do precisely that. He notes that it does not establish the equivalence of a given set of indicators with another set or the reliability of the classification of events.

If indicators and variables are adequately defined such that observations can be reliably classified, hypotheses may be tested in later phases of the study. Hypotheses concerning the distribution of a variable among the population or the association of two variables may be supported if the preponderance of cases fall into the proper cells of a contingency table (McCall, 1969). Barton & Lazarsfield (1955) suggest that where there are a few complex cases, they may be systematically compared, as in historical analysis. Geer (1964) recommends three ways in which hypotheses may be tested: search for negative cases; accumulation of positive cases; or predictions about the effects of foreseeably changed conditions.

In environmental design, we often employ structured behavioral observation as a more valid measure of concepts generated in the early phases. Hypotheses can be tested in a multiple-baseline experimental design when planned changes are implemented.

Measurement Properties of Participant Observation

Reliability is seldom measured in participant observation studies. McCall (1969) states that the equivalence of different indicators of a concept, the parallel of interitem reliability, is usually not established. Test-retest reliability is assumed on the basis that the participant observer usually spends sufficient time in the environment (on the order of months) for repeated observations in different contexts to reveal the sources of uncontrolled variation (Mensh & Henry, 1953). Interobserver reliability is seldom tested, and this is a serious deficiency. To the extent reliability is undetermined or uncontrolled, this would undermine the validity of any single participant observer procedure for the measurement of evaluation functions.

The validity of concepts and hypotheses arising from participant observation studies may be supported in one of at least two ways: the concepts or hypotheses may be applied to data from external sources; and/or other methods within the same study may be used, for example formal interviewing or document analysis. Goffman (1961) supported the validity of his concept of "mortification of the self" and the proposition that it was a feature of total institutions by citing descriptions of practices of institutions such as convents, prisons, and military training camps. Those excerpts clearly documented the presence of at least some of his indicators (e.g. "role dispossession" and "invasions of the territory of the self") in all of these other institutions. Other investigators may apply the concepts in new settings as another source of external validity. For example, Goffman's (1961) typology of inmate adaptation patterns (e.g. "withdrawal," "conversion," "playing it cool") was confirmed by Perucci's (1974) findings of the same patterns in another mental hospital a decade later.

Gans (1967) provides an example of internal validity checks with different methods. To confirm his proposition that suburbanites participate more in community and social activities than when they were in the city and were happier and less lonely, he had other researchers conduct formal interviews. Levinson & Gallagher (1964) developed a Role-Conception Inventory to obtain a quantitative assessment of patient attitudes as a test of hypotheses formulated in the participant observer phase. The validity of the results of a participant observation study must be established by one or both of these methods and is in question until then.

There are several limitations and problems associated with the participant observer method. Dean et al. (1967) pointed out that the data is gathered with nonstandard procedures and, therefore, cannot be treated with statistics, making it impossible to establish quantitative relationships. They find that the unique aspects of a situation or person may "inhibit attempts to define variables and specify relations." McCall & Simmons (1967) listed a number of problems: the strain of maintaining complex relationships with inhabitants; the lack of structure and uncertainties; the time-consuming and intellectually demanding task of writing up and organizing large amounts of notes; the difficulty of suppressing one's own feelings and habits; and the built over using others.

The advantages of the participant observer method include wide applicability, richness of data, flexibility, complexity of interpretation, efficiency, and potential for internal validity checks. It has been used successfully to investigate many aspects of a variety of environments. Hessler & Walters (1976) examined the link between social science research and public policy in consumer evaluation groups; Lynch (1975) studied the effects of staff member termination in a psychiatric hospital; Laslett & Warren (1975) analyzed organizational strategies for behavior change in dieting groups; and Hauser & Shapiro (1976) studied role relationships in faculty-student interactions.

This method puts the researcher in contact with a tremendous amount of phenomena from which observations can be drawn. It is both a rich source of concepts and hypotheses and a testing ground where more structured methods cannot be employed. The physical and social context of behavior is immediately available to the observer. Its longitudinal nature gives historical context and provides the opportunity to observe trends and isolate influential factors. From informants and self-observations, the participant observer has access to effective and cognitive responses.

The participant observer is able to be quite flexible in the application of the method. If the field is entered properly and relations well-established, he may work at various levels and with various groups. He/she can select particularly knowledgable, skilled, or insightful informants. He/she is able to shift between active participation, passive observation, and interviewing, depending on the perspective and kind of information desired. Data collection and interpretation are intertwined and mutually enriching processes. The focus and themes of the study may be changed; the variables, definitions, and hypotheses may be modified as data is collected.

The level of qualitative analysis may be quite complex. Since the restrictions of sampling and exact and consistent definition of variables of the usual statistical and measurement procedures are not always required, complex hypotheses may be examined in the light of empirical observations. Goffman's (1961) tracing of many of the problems of the mental hospital to the misapplication of the service model is a good example. Such hypotheses may be persuasively defended if credible attempts have been made to find negative cases or discredit rival hypotheses.

Participant observation has been considered efficient by some because it avoids misleading or meaningless questions; it places the most highly trained person in direct contact with the data; the most useful informants may be approached in a manner most likely to yield valid data; and it involves less labor and material expense than surveys.

Participant observation as practiced in the behavioral sciences traditionally concerned with the environmental context of behavior is probably best considered a powerful, but unreliable assessment method. Its power derives from the amount and variety of information to which the investigator is exposed; the ability to experience the effects of the phenomenon of interest; and the acceptibility of complex inter- pretation. Unreliability results from the biases and distortions in informants' statements and in the researchers' own observations. The power may best be used for the identification function in a particular environment and the theory-building stage of a scientific field. The emerging variables and hypotheses should be tested with more rigorous methods.

BEHAVIORAL OBSERVATION METHODS

At an advanced stage in the study of a research topic it is desirable to employ more reliable and precise environmental assessment methods than those of participant observation. Greater control over sources of bias is possible when the observer takes a passive role and focuses all of his attention and effort on behavior observation. Goldfried & Kent (1972) state that, "the least inferential approach to data collection is behavioral sampling of the individual's actual responses in naturalistic situations" (p. 412).

Paul Meehl (1954) has spoken of two stages in the scientific method, discovery and justification. In an inductive science, hard data is not necessary at the discovery stage but is critical at the justification stage. Reliable observation methods are required at the justification stage.

This is not meant to imply that behavior observation methods yield data free from distortion, but that more sources of bias can be controlled in a systematic behavior observation study. The choice of recording procedures will influence the character and quality of data they produce.

The first step in a behavior observation study is to decide what behaviors to observe. An experimenter may attempt to write down all observed responses in a narrative form. When environmental antecedents and consequences of responses are also recorded, this method provides an account of the actual stream of behavior (Barker, 1968). Problems associated with this method include high dross rate and the fact that the observer is directing much of his attention to the recording of data, thereby missing some of the subject's actual behavior. A more efficient and easier to quantify method of recording complex social behavior involves recording the occurrence of specific, operationally defined behaviors relevant to the study in a behavioral code (Lipinski & Nelson, 1974). These codes allow the observer to direct most of his attention to subjects' behavior and minimize his attention to the recording of behaviors. Some codes even allow the antecedents and consequences of responses to be recorded and, thus, preserve a quantitative account of the stream of behavior.

Kent & Foster (1977) discuss the question of validity of behavioral codes. They warn that the high face validity of these codes should not obscure more complex validity considerations. They outline a method which employs expert judges viewing criterion samples for determining on an a priori basis the validity of behavior observation codes.

Once one has developed an observation code, one faces the choice of how to sample the behavior to be recorded. In event sampling, a frequency count of events of a specified sort that occur within a given time interval is recorded. Another method is to record the occurrence or non-occurrence of an event within a number of small time intervals on a checklist. Time sampling is a variant of the checklist method where the observer records only during some time intervals, separated by pauses, so that observers can turn their attention to other matters.

Demonstration of high reliability is critical for clear interpretation of behavior observation data. The reliability criterion most commonly assessed in behavior observation studies is inter-observer agreement. The similarity of simultaneous judgments from pairs of observers provides a basis to make judgments about the objectivity of data and the amount of error variance. If observers report the same or similar frequency of selected behaviors over the same period of time, the reliability is considered high. For example, if one observer records 12 instances of sharing, nine periods of time in which solitary play occurred, two drawings completed, and one argument, while a second observer recorded 11 instances of sharing, nine periods of solitary play, two drawings, and one argument, reliability would be considered relatively high.

Reliability is usually checked by comparing the recorded raw data from two or more independent observers for the same time periods for the same subjects. For example, if a code is being used with time sampling, then for each interval the number of agreements on whether specific behaviors occurred would be counted. Quantitative estimates of reliability are calculated from these comparisons. For example, the number of agreements divided by the number of observations (agreements plus disagreements) yields an index which varies from 100 percent (perfect agreement) to 0 percent (perfect disagreement).

A number of factors have been found to affect reliability. The number of behavioral categories in the code is inversely related to reliability. There seems to be an upper limit of seven plus or minus two on the number of categories that can be reliably recorded at one time. Reliability is directly related to the specificity of the definition of the behavioral category. Global ratings of vaguely defined behaviors, e.g., aggression, are unlikely to be consistently scored. Usually, observation schedules go through a development of increasing specification of definitions.

Romanczyk et al. (1973) report that reliability measures were consistently and substantially inflated by the observer's knowledge that reliability was being assessed and by knowledge of which assessor was performing that task. Unmonitored data in their study was systematically biased such that the decreased reliability could not be accounted for by increased random error alone. In addition to the problem of decreased reliability on unmonitored observations, a phenomena labeled "observer drift" occurs whereby observers adjust their rating criteria as a function of the feedback they receive from other observers. This would introduce bias in data if different groups of observers observe different experimental conditions.

Unfortunately, assessments of reliability often occur under conditions that spuriously inflate the estimate. If the complexity of observed behavior varies systematically between reliability assessment and nonassessment sessions, the reliability estimates may be biased (Jones, Reid, and Patterson, 1975). For example, reliability of observations of the cooperative and competitive behaviors of one child is estimated when he is playing with one other child. But the observations for evaluation will occur when the child is working in a classroom group to organize an activity. Clearly, the decision about whether a particular act is cooperative or competitive is more difficult in the second situation and then the reliability is likely to be lower.

The implication of these findings is that reliability should be checked throughout the evaluation period, perhaps in a sampling fashion with the observers' being ignorant of precisely when it will occur. Reliability should be checked in the actual assessment situation, and by calibrating observers with specifiable training and experience (to control for observer drift).

Even with high reliability between observers, environmental influences can affect all of the observers. Robert Rosenthal (1966, 1969) pioneered the research on expectation bias in observational recording data. Rosenthal demonstrated that informing experimenters of predicted experimental findings results in biased recordings for tasks where the specificity of judgmental criteria was low.

More recent evidence suggests that when more specific codes are employed, observational recording data are not influenced by induced expectations alone. However, when an expectation is given to observers and contingent experimenter feedback regarding observational recordings is provided, a clear bias is obtained (O'Leary, Kent, & Kanowitz, 1975). The obvious implication is that all evaluative feedback regarding the experimental hypothesis should be withheld from observers. This also implies that investigators should not collect their own observational data, but should employ independent observers.

Over the past 25 years, social scientists have debated the extent of the influence of measurement procedures on the behavior of subjects. This debate remains unresolved as some investigators report substantial reactivity to observation while others report none (Kent & Foster, 1977). A habituation hypothesis has been postulated which states that, with time, a passive observer becomes a neutral stimulus in the situation. The extent of habituation to observers is also unresolved. Investigators who have found no reactivity problem with group data warn that there exist large individual differences in reaction to being observed (Moos 1968a; Dubey et al., in press).

Recently, investigators have begun to untangle specific factors that contribute to reactivity to observation, such as prior interactions between the observer and subjects (Surratt, Ulrich, & Hawkins, 1969; Mash & Hedley, 1975), characteristics of the environment (e.g., particular contingencies in effect), and obtrusiveness of the observer. For example, if the subject is aware of the predicted or desired behavior changes, and knows the observer or knows that the observations are likely to produce some desirable consequence, and knows whether the observer is recording at any particular time, there is likely to be a substantial reactive effect.

INTEGRATION OF ASSESSMENT
AND ENVIRONMENTAL DESIGN

Traditionally, social scientists have used assessment in an effort to test the validity and limits of theoretical propositions. More recently, assessment has been used to guide interventions such as behavior therapy or social programs. The environmental design orientation seeks to integrate theory, research, and practice throughout the behavior influence process. There are a number of advantages and a few methodological problems associated with this integration.

Assessment procedures require the clarification of theoretical concepts and test the limits of their applicability. For example, reliability checks, formal or informal, prevent "rubber sheet" concepts (which can be stretched to fit anything). Assessment may also spotlight a need for additional concepts and suggest hypotheses. The immediacy of the contact which the theoretician-researcher maintains with the phenomena of interest in participant observation facilitates these processes.

Not only does participation increase the scope of observations, but observation can increase the effectiveness of behavior change efforts. The more accurate we are in observing behavior, the more effective we will be in the long run (Krasner and Ullmann, 1973). Accurate observation improves our effectiveness by allowing us to make finer discriminations which lead to more accurate predictions regarding the consequences of change. In addition, through systematic observation we are more able to discriminate those consequences. This, in turn, controls our behavior by providing feedback on the adequacy of the change efforts.

When assessment is designed for the evaluation function, it becomes experimental research, and specific hypotheses emerging from a theoretical approach to practical goals are tested. The results will have implications for the validity and generality of the theory. Since the test is carried on in "natural" settings, there is greater confidence in generalizing the findings and methods to other natural settings (Tharp and Wetzel, 1969). The multiple baseline research design (Campbell & Stanley, 1963; Hersen & Barlow, 1976; Kazdin, 1973; Leitenberg, 1973) is particularly suited to environmental design studies. It avoids some ethical problems associated with control or reversal designs. In addition, the multiple baseline design with continuous data collection allows the change agent to feed results from the evaluation back into the behavior influence program. By sharing the results of his observations with his subjects, the environmental designer can provide immediate and specific feedback to those subjects.

In an Inner London Education Agency teacher training program, in which we collaborated, a teacher was using verbal reinforcement in one-to-one situations, but not in group situations. The trainer was able to illustrate his feedback to the teacher with the data. After the teacher's behavior changed, the trainer reinforced the new behavior by showing the teacher data reflecting that change. The teachers completed a form at the end of the course rating the value of in-classroom training and the disruptiveness of in-classroom program evaluation research. Most teachers rated the trainer visits as essential for the success of the training program and as never disruptive.

The integration of environmental assessment and behavior influence raises some fundamental methodological issues. If the environmental designer will be rewarded for reporting certain results, won't he "observe" behavior in accord with the desired results, like Rosenthal's (1966) experimenters? If the members of the environment are aware of the goals of the intervention, and know how they are being measured, aren't they likely to behave in accord with these goals, at least until the measurement period is over? The first is an instance of bias – a systematic distortion of the data. The consistency of the relationship between the actual phenomenon and the data is disrupted. This is a direct threat to the reliability and, thus, the validity of the assessment. There are several ways to combat bias. Reliability checks with observers who are motivated by consequences other than those which are likely to bias them are possible. Employing measures which require little interpretation or analysis lessens the probability of error, including biased error. Additional assessment procedures less subject to bias can serve as a check on potentially biased measures.

The second question raises the issue of reactivity. Reactivity threatens the evaluative function. Positive results of a planned change with obtrusive measurement may be due to the combination of the planned change and the measurement, not the planned change alone. This can be substantially answered by employing additional nonreactive measures and continuing these after the reactive measures are terminated. Hopkins & Conrad (1975) employed a second set of observers who were introduced and behaved so as to reduce any reactive effect. Reactivity also raises a sampling question related to criterion validity. The assessment situation may not represent the "criterion" situation, if the latter doesn't include assessment. The definition of the criterion situation is fundamentally a value decision. This would probably be decided by members of the environment. It is entirely possible that assessment would be part of the criterion situation. That is, assessment doesn't end, or at least, some measures of the assessment package continue. If these are having a reactive effect in the positive direction, all the better; they retain criterion and evaluative validity.

A multiple measures approach has been suggested at several points in this chapter. This could be employed both by implementing several of the methods described above and by devising additional measures pertinent to the specific purposes and the environment. For the classroom designed to enhance creativity, some possible measures are social climate scales, especially the Innovation dimension; behavior observation of free-play activities; ratings of variety in paintings and stories of children by other teachers, parents, administrators, and other children; standardized creativity tests; and ratings of use of materials introduced into the classroom. Webb et al. (1966) provide both the rationale for this approach and a number of sources for and illustrations of unobtrusive measures.

In spite of efforts to integrate theory, research, and practice, the functions may conflict and force a value decision. We encountered this in the ILEA teacher training study when we attempted to record behavior observations throughout a three-hour morning class. We found it impossible to simultaneously give feedback to the teachers and record data. As we were primarily interested in training, we did not compromise the training for the research. If, during an observation session, the teacher asked the observer for information or feedback, the observer would interrupt the formal observation and provide the necessary and timely consultation.

SUMMARY

There are four functions that assessment is likely to serve in the context of environmental design: identification of influences on behavior; measurement of behavior; evaluation; and reactivity. Criteria for the selection and development of methods include validity; reliability; economy; immediacy; and simplicity. A few of the more promising, available measurement methods are described below with the functions for which the methods are particularly suited; a multiple-measures approach is advocated.

Function	Methods
Identification	participant-observation; behavior-setting analysis; social climate scales
Measurement	behavior observation; unobtrusive measures
Evaluation	social climate scales; behavior observation and other measures in multiple-baseline research designs; subjective rating scales of environments
Reactivity	behavior observations; participant-observation as total participant; participation by members

The descriptions of these methods are intended to serve as examples or illustrations to encourage practitioners to develop new methods and instruments appropriate to their environments.

6 Environmental Design in Closed Institutions

Gary McClure

The next chapter represents a major key to understanding environmental design as the consequence of social, political, theoretical, philosophical, and architectural influences. The two settings in which environmental design, inadvertent and/or deliberate, has had major impact are: the mental institutions described in this chapter by McClure and the school settings described by M. Krasner in chapter 10.

McClure's careful placing of mental hospitals in their historical context illustrates a number of major points about professional healers as well as scientists and virtually every other professional. In each age, the professional believes that what he is doing is not only morally right but the ultimate in modernity. This "new view" contrasted to the antiquated, old-fashioned and erroneous procedures of the past. A second issue involves the professional controversies over power and control of the institutions involved. The struggle over the control of the mental hospital which McClure describes, has its analog in virtually every other field of science.

The design of the institution (both physical and social) is a function of the power conflict rather than any intrinsic merit. As one notes repeatedly in the history of any institutions or societies, events take on a life of their own determined by the vagaries of the influence process, and do not occur as even the best of planners would have hoped. As McClure points out, there is irony in the fact that moral treatment was, in part, destroyed by its own success. The same political and economic controversies are taking place in our current day over much the same issues, namely, control of the "institution." These controversies are frequently expressed over such key issues as who (which profession and/or which individuals within a given profession) should receive the mandate to design the environment of the institution and its inhabitants.

132

McClure emphasizes the consequences of "labeling," a major element in the influence process. All those engaged in environmental design utilize labels and metaphors. We must continually be alerted to the dangers of verification of our metaphors.

Ed.

<u>Primum non nocere</u>
first do no harm. (Leake, 1966)

This chapter addresses itself to the application of environmental design principles in institutional settings. It is not, however, intended as an empirical review of the various innovations and interventions that have been attempted in institutions generally; nor is it intended to provide a comprehensive evaluation of institutional practices. Rather, we shall attempt to provide a conceptual base for the linkage between the rapidly emerging discipline of environmental design and the various institutions which society has "discovered" (Rothman, 1971) and built in an effort to meet human needs over the years. In the limited space available, we shall examine the subtitles of the "behavior influence process" (Krasner & Ullmann, 1973) that have shaped both the form and function of contemporary institutions, particularly the mental hospital. In so doing, we shall trace briefly the history of institutions and their role in the societies they were designed to serve. We will then consider the major design influences of the last quarter century along with some of the legal aspects of institutional design. A concluding section will summarize some of the future directions in institutional environmental design.

As a starting point, it is necessary to consider the various criteria that define an institution and differentiate its members from society generally. An excellent account of such criteria is provided in the classic work by Goffman (1961). For present purposes we will limit ourselves to three basic questions or issues which are particularly germane to the functioning of institutions in the context of environmental design.

First, consider the demographic characteristics of the institution. We might ask the rather obvious question of who are its members. Are they "dependent groups" such as the poor, aged, or infirmed? Is their membership in the institution voluntary as in the case of the infirmed seeking relief; or is it involuntary involving instances of forced court committal? Are the members of the institution inhabitants due to an accident of birth, as in the blind, deaf, mentally retarded, or orphaned? Is the membership of the institution composed along lines of homogeneity or heterogeneity? The answers to these questions influence significantly the design of institutional environments.

Secondly, as we analyze the historical development of institutions we will want to consider the significance of the economic resource base supporting the institution. Is the facility the result of benevolent, private philanthropy of sectarian groups; or is it the result of nonsectarian support? Once established, is it financially self-supporting, or is it continually dependent on private philanthropy; or, alternatively, is it dependent on government via the process of taxation? If the latter, is the source of the taxing authority that of local, state, or federal agencies (or their international counterpart)? We shall see later that these issues have had profound effects on both the quality and quantity of institutional resources.

Finally, we may ask the critical question regarding the establishment, development, maintenance, and survival of any institution: Who really benefits from the existence of the institution itself? Ostensibly, the members of the institution are assumed to accrue primary benefit. Exceptions are the more obvious cases in which society has protected itself against the extremely violent behaviors of its members through the confinement and isolation of dangerous individuals. Even in these cases, however, society has purported to have as a parallel goal that of "changing" the person in ways that would rehabilitate him. Having done so, he could eventually profit from the institutional experience and function more normally as a productive member of society. We shall find this to be particularly true with respect to the establishment of early penitentiaries in America. Although service to the institutional member and society are not inherently incompatible, the behavioral objectives of the institutions have become increasingly obscure over the years.

Clearly, these and other issues are important to the understanding of environmental design as it relates to institutional settings. Equally clear is the fact that these influences operate in such subtle fashion as to often go unnoticed. We may note, for example, that even the name by which society refers to such settings is a rather remarkable summary index of the prevailing Zeitgeist. For instance, the State Care Act of 1890 was passed in New York and by legislative action the term "lunatic asylum" was changed to "hospital" reflecting the then changing attitudes and values regarding the inhabitants of such institutions. Similarly, as recently as 1974, the New York State legislature again changed the term, this time from "hospital" to "psychiatric center" providing what Commissioner Alan D. Miller called a more accurate reflection of the wide range of services provided by the institutions. In analogous fashion, "State Schools for the Retarded" became "Developmental Centers."

This chapter will attempt to show that changes such as these are not merely semantic exercises; rather they reflect the very subtle ways in which the behavior influence process has shaped and defined the "institution" as it has come to exist today. Through a better understanding of this process we will hopefully be able to address more intelligently the environmental design parameters that will shape the institutions of tomorrow.

ANCIENT INSTITUTIONAL ENVIRONMENTAL DESIGN

Turning now to our historical survey of institutional development, we find that the quotation at the beginning of this chapter was the guiding ethical principle among the Hippocratic physicians who functioned in the hospitals of Greco-Roman times. As with many facets of science, important contributions were provided by the ancient Egyptians which were later developed and expanded during the Greco-Roman period. Mental health appears to be no exception.

An excellent account of the design and structure of health care institutions during this period is provided by Leake (1927; 1930; 1966). Particularly germane for present purposes are those aspects of early health care having to do with the design of treatment environments. Although less archeological data are available regarding the architectural structure of the Egyptian health temples than for Greek temples, it is, nevertheless, clear that healing cults emanating from the Egyptian healer Imhotep coalesced to form the modern day counterpart of health centers. These centers served as focal points for the writing and dissemination of the remarkable medicinal procedures developed by the ancient Egyptian physicians. In terms of actual design, however, we do know considerably more about the emergence of the Greek health temples, particularly the splendid structures at Pergamon and Epidaurus (Leake, 1966). Treatment centers such as these were truly exquisite in design, both architecturally and aesthetically. The psychological effect of convalescing in such surroundings is considered to have been a major factor in the curative process. Indeed, perhaps the first person to recognize the importance of the relationship between the institutional design and therapeutic goals was the Roman architect Vitruvius during the reign of Augustus. He suggested that such environmental variables as noise, climate, and spatial surroundings be taken into account in the construction of health temples. Thus, temples were typically quite spacious with large open areas, gardens, and courtyards. They were set in a restful area with a comfortable climate.

The environmental concerns reflected in the structure and design of the early Greco-Roman health centers were enormously influential in shaping the form of institutional care for many centuries. While architectural form naturally reflected the changing cultural influences through the Middle Ages and the Renaissance, many of the design features remained remarkably stable across the millenia. For instance, the use of large, open spaces and rooms with high ceilings continued to be a basic design feature. Renaissance art makes it quite clear that the European hospitals were comfortable, spacious, well-staffed and well-furnished. There were exceptions, of course, such as Bethlehem Hospital, which was established in London in 1377. But generally it was not until the 1700s that we note the significant demise in the quality of both treatment and treatment environments with which we are so familiar. By then few hospitals in Europe could even approximate the humanistic treatment environment that was available to the ancient Egyptians and Greco-Romans 2,000 years earlier.

Indeed, the argument could be made that even today many of our hospitals would do well if they could but match the health-promoting aspects of these ancient institutional environments. It is very likely that confinement in many of our "modern" mental hospitals violates the basic right of a patient to a treatment environment that first does no harm (primum non nocere).

Many social, political, and economic factors played a significant role, then as they do today, in accounting for the deplorable institutional conditions which developed by the late 1700s. Two are particularly important, however, in the historical development of institutions.   First, organized religion was a potent influence which eventually led to the prevailing social value that the diseased were, in fact, receiving punishment for their sins. This being the case, society's responsibility for the care of the sick diminished. In fact, since the problem was viewed as one of religion, such persons were typically referred to the clergy for exorcism rather than to the physician for treatment. Deutsch (1949) has speculated that of the conservatively estimated 100,000 persons who were put to death as "witches" during the fifteenth, sixteenth, and seventeenth centuries, probably at least one third were mentally unsound. Thus, in the climate of ignorance and abuse, rational treatment for such persons was virtually nonexistent.

A second major contributing factor was the accelerating urbanization of an ever-increasing population, a problem that was later to be of profound importance in American institutional development. London, during the post-Renaissance period, is an excellent example of a city with an increasing population and limited resources.

EARLY AMERICAN INSTITUTIONAL
ENVIRONMENTAL DESIGN

Let us now focus our attention more specifically on the development of institutions in America, and attempt to identify the historical influences which contributed to the design of the large state institutions of the 1950s and 1960s, some of which had resident populations in excess of 10,000 patients. This is a far cry, indeed, from the early colonial period in our national development during which human needs were met by the family and local towns and villages. While it is unclear as to the quality of care received by the mentally ill under these conditions, Grob (1973) takes issue with the common view that such persons were singled out for unusual and inhumane treatment. He suggests that historians who have taken such a view, e.g., Deutsch, (1949), have accepted the social values and knowledge of the present and projected them on the past. In any event, it is clear that the early colonial period did demand a pioneer spirit and work ethic which placed an implicit responsibility upon each family for the care of its own members. The failure to establish benevolent facilities for the collective care of the less fortunate was probably due less to a prevailing social value than to the spartan living conditions of the period and to the scattered and rural demographic features of the colonies. To be sure, some abuses did occur, such as the witches of Salem, but these were surely in the minority. However, it is clear that, during the seventeenth and eighteenth centuries in colonial America, the situation did not demand nor precipitate a colony-wide social policy; the family provided the environment within which the needs of its deviant members were usually met.

As the colonies grew, the situation changed. As with Europe, urban areas grew rapidly, particularly the seaport cities. This accelerated growth, coupled with the concentration of such growth in areas like New York, Boston, and Philadelphia, resulted in demographic changes which precipitated what we would now call "social policy" regarding "dependent groups." The initial institution chosen as the vehicle to meet the needs of the various dependent groups was that of the almshouse. Like their European predecessors, the American almshouses were populated by an extremely heterogeneous clientele, including among others, the insane, the poor, the blind, the orphaned, the aged, and the infirmed. During this early period of social planning, it was apparent that a social community resource for diverse dependent groups was needed, and it was clear that there were sufficient numbers of afflicted persons when combined to populate such an almshouse and, thereby, justify its expense to the community. Thus, as Grob (1973) notes, the moral obligations and humanitarian concerns of the community could be met in an economical and efficient manner.

The important thing in the context of the present chapter is that the emergence of social policy regarding dependent groups, including the mentally ill, had virtually nothing to do with developments in the sciences or medicine; rather, the development of this basic institution, the almshouse, was the result of economic and social influences in the context of a young and growing nation. As a result, almshouses appeared in most of the major towns. Unfortunately, care in the almshouses of the United States was no better than that of their European counterparts. The pauper, the mentally ill, the aged, and others all lived within the same walls and received the same treatment, or, more accurately, nontreatment. Such institutions had not met the needs of dependent groups in England and were not likely to succeed in her colonies.

During the latter half of the eighteenth century circumstances began to change significantly as general hospitals began to appear throughout the colonies. Within the framework of behavior influence, it is noteworthy that the first general hospital established in America, Pennsylvania Hospital at Philadelphia, was the direct result of a complex interaction of religious and political influences. The founding of the hospital through the philanthropy of the Quakers was not just the result of urban needs, but was equally due to their diminishing influence in the political arena. No longer a dominant political power, the Society of Friends systematically focused their efforts on philanthropic activities. "In place of political power, they sought to influence society at large through private, voluntary, and nonsectarian organizations that embodied positive social purposes ordinarily within the responsibility of government" (Grob, 1973, p. 17; emphasis added). This first institution, founded in America as a general hospital for the treatment of the physically sick and mentally ill, was started through matching funds from the Pennsylvania Assembly and private philanthropy, largely Quaker. The effectiveness of this consortium is to be contrasted with other major cities, even Boston, that failed initially to generate the political and economic base necessary for such an undertaking.

The benevolence of the promoters of the Pennsylvania Hospital, such as Benjamin Franklin and Benjamin Rush, did not, unfortunately, influence the actual hospital environment and methods of care. Within the overall hospital, the insane were forced to live in basement cells approximately ten feet square. They were cold, dark, damp, and dreary – hardly an atmosphere designed to promote physical or mental health. Nevertheless, such an environment was touted as the most humane and benevolent care possibly available.

The present purpose, however, is not to document what we now perceive to be the inhumane treatment to which the afflicted were subjected; rather, it is to sharpen the focus on the truism that not only does society define what is abnormal behavior, but it also sets about to define and design an environment which will alter and modify that abnormal behavior according to the prevailing social values. "Treatment" then, proceeds within the limitations of the environment so designed. If this includes confinement in ten by ten foot cells with a bed of straw, as it did during the pre-Pinel period, treatment options are obviously limited. The situation worsens still further if such conditions are judged by "authoritative experts" to be offering the best possible care available. Add to this the sanction of the church through their financial support of such institutions, and it is no surprise that such conditions existed. Indeed, it would seem that society has had a propensity for accepting the judgment of the expert professional, e.g. physician and clergy, even if the treatment conditions run counter to common sense. In the later discussion on moral treatment, we will note the growing skepticism directed against the expert professional. William Tuke, a pioneer in the improvement of conditions for the mentally ill in England, was particularly unimpressed with the role of the physician and of medicine in caring for the mentally ill.

A second significant event in the historical development of institutions occurred with the establishment in 1770 of the Virginia Eastern Lunatic Asylum in Williamsburg, Virginia. This was the first institution ever established exclusively for the care of the insane. With the admission of the first patient, in September 1773, institutional care for the singular purpose of treating the mentally ill was inaugurated, and the care and treatment of such individuals would never again be the same.

The environmental influences affecting the development of this hospital are again important. Unlike the Pennsylvania Hospital, the facility at Williamsburg was supported entirely by state funds provided by the Virginia House of Burgesses without public philanthropy. Humanitarian concerns notwithstanding, its construction did not result from pressing human needs but, rather, was the result of a politically motivated governing elite who felt it their duty as enlightened elected officials to provide for the less fortunate (See Dain, 1971). This arrangement wherein a governing board operated a totally state funded institution was not to be duplicated until 1824, a half century later, with the establishment of the Eastern Lunatic Asylum at Lexington, Kentucky. Deutsch (1949) observes that no record regarding this early period of the hospital's existence is available. On the basis of inferences drawn by medical historians, it is speculated that traditional treatment methods were employed, including coercion, cell confinement, emetics, cathartics, and sedatives (Deutsch, 1949; Grob, 1973). In terms of the physical environment, Williamsburg Hospital's rural location provided it with spacious grounds. At the same time, its isolation from the mainstream of early urban American life probably prevented it from exercising a greater national influence on institutional care. It is also the case that it was a rather small facility having a capacity of only 30 beds. Thus, it did not materially contribute to the influence process affecting the design of hospital facilities generally.

Elsewhere, New York Hospital was established in January 1791 as a hospital for general disease (Earle, 1848). Originally financed by private donation, the almost completed structure was destroyed by fire, and the state legislature subsequently financed its reconstruction. As with the Pennsylvania Hospital, it likewise was a facility for a highly urban area, and met a variety of needs with the care of the mentally ill occupying a subordinate role. It, too, housed its lunatics in basement cells, while the physically ill received more appropriate quarters.

Where care for the mentally and physically ill coexisted in general hospitals, the former consistently occupied a lower priority in the allocation of funds and resources. Even these meager general hospital resources were scarce, however, and the insane typically continued to be lodged in almshouses, poor houses, and jails rather than in hospitals. It is this background of nontreatment, or maltreatment, against which the public reform movements of Pinel, Tuke, and others were subsequently to be directed. It is important to remember that care for the insane in hospitals was perceived as a tremendous improvement. However, the treatment provided the mentally ill in the better almshouses was equal to that provided by the average general hospital. The drive for the removal of the insane from jails and almshouses to hospitals was more significant in terms of its long-term social consequences than for improved care.

"Hospitals" were now established for "patients" in order for them to get "medical treatment" for their "diseased minds." This shift from the family's responsibility for the care of its aberrant members to the treatment of diseased sufferers by physicians gradually became de facto public policy during this period, first in England and then in the United States. To the writers' knowledge, the Act of 1774 regulating private madhouses in England (Jones, 1955) is the first legal basis for placing the care of the insane under the direct supervision and responsibility of the medical profession. The conflicts that have ensued over the two intervening centuries between medical or disease models of abnormal behavior versus psychological or environmental models probably has its legal origin in this Act. Certainly, it contributed significantly to the implicit assumption that the insane were suffering from a disease process of physical origin. This being the case, it logically followed that the physician was the expert resource person to whom one should turn for cure. Note the analogous nature of the relationship of the physician to the diseased insane with that of the clergy to the "possessed" insane of centuries earlier.

Again, in terms of environmental design, we note that the prevailing social values influence both the definition and the resolution of human problems. The very same behavior requiring exorcism by the priest now requires treatment by the physician. However, the then contemporary treatment by physicians was heroic in practice (Grob, 1973; Deutsch, 1949; Zilboorg, 1941). Even Benjamin Rush, the founder of American Psychiatry, promulgated practices and procedures ranging from his invention of the "tranquilizer chair" to cold water baths and numerous other methods of mechanical coercion. The design of such treatment environments was made legally and morally possible only because they were medical procedures dispensed under the supervision of physicians. It is not the purpose of this analysis simply to criticize the practices of restraint, coercion, blood-letting, purges, and other such treatments; it is our purpose, however, to note that such practices existed only because society accepted and reinforced them. Barbaric as some of these procedures seem to us now, we should keep in mind that procedures as grotesque as prefrontal lobotomies were performed in large numbers of patients as recently as the 1950s and "psychosurgery" remains a highly controversial medical procedure in the 1970s.

Little attention was given by the early hospital planners to the relationship between the physical design of the treatment environments and patient behavior. The potential importance of the rehabilitating influence and therapeutic significance of the early Greek health centers had been all but forgotten. Even the more recent structures of the Renaissance failed to influence therapeutically the design process. The large rooms, spacious grounds, gardens, solariums, and high staffing ratios of the seventeenth century hospitals were discarded (Leake, 1966). Although such facilities, even then, were directed largely toward the care of the physically sick rather than the insane, the psychological superiority of such environments for both groups can hardly be doubted. Yet, such considerations were seldom, if ever, considered in late colonial hospital construction. Indeed, Leake (1966) notes that, with the "recognition" of mental illness as a disease, both the construction and maintenance of general hospitals began to decline. This resulted in overcrowding, poor sanitation, and generally low quality care, a problem noted earlier. Late eighteenth century European hospitals, therefore, hardly provided an adequate model for the design of hospital environments in Colonial America.

THE EMERGENCE OF MORAL TREATMENT

It is in the context of this social milieu that two very significant reform figures emerged independently of each other, Phillip Pinel in France and William Tuke in England. We are all familiar with the events surrounding Pinel's removal of the chains confining the patients at Bicetre. Less widely known is the scholarly effort upon which Pinel based his views regarding insanity:

> . . . he delved deeply into the available literature on insanity, particularly the long-forgotten works by and about the ancient

Apostles of mild and kindly treatment – Asclepiades, Aretaens, Soranus, Caelium Aurelianus, and the rest. The conviction grew upon him that their precepts were sounder therapeutically . . . than the brutal methods everywhere prevalent in his day. (Deutsch, 1949, P. 89)

The influences that so greatly affected the behavior of Pinel and his followers can be traced directly to the ancient works of the Greeks and Romans. Thus, their influence on the development of moral treatment spans over 2,000 years of recorded history.

Pinel, as Grob (1973) notes, was an empiricist. Unlike most of his peer physicians, he readily evaluated treatment procedures on pragmatic grounds. Today he would probably be viewed as a proponent of treatment accountability and program evaluation. Pinel opposed most heroic procedures not simply on humanitarian grounds but because their effectiveness could not be empirically demonstrated. He similarly was not interested in abstract theorizing about such questions as the underlying cause of insanity. Pinel acknowledged multiple causation and focused his treatment efforts on the external manifestations of insanity and in developing treatment environments within which such problems could best be dealt.

William Tuke, unlike Pinel, was not a physician. He was a layman and devout Quaker. The influences affecting his behavior were interwoven with his role in the Society of Friends. Following the mysterious death of a Quaker woman at York Asylum in 1791 (Jones, 1955), Tuke proposed that the Society establish a facility for the insane to care for their fellow Quakers. In a manner prophetic of the name changes to come, he further proposed that such an institution be called a "Retreat" and, thereby, avoid the stigma of madhouse or asylum. This simple, but significant, act may be the first premeditated attempt to deal with the labeling problems in the design of treatment environments.

Such a retreat was seen by Tuke as a haven or a refuge for the troubled. Deutsch makes the important observation that the retreat sought to provide a ". . . family environment for the patient, as manifested by the noninstitutional aspect of the building and its surroundings" (Deutsch, 1949, p. 93). Patients were guests, not inmates. In contrast to other facilities of the time, the use of chains was not permitted, nor were most other heroic procedures. In fact, medicine in general occupied a decidedly subordinate role at the retreat (Jones, 1955) with the physician functioning primarily as a consultant in the treatment of the physically sick. The abolition of blood letting, for example, was a positive advance made by the retreat (Deutsch, 1949). In place of the more bizarre medical treatments, heavy reliance was placed on humane interaction among staff and patients, the use of exercise, and a variety of productive activities designed to occupy one's time and attention in a meaningful and therapeutic way. These included gardening, sewing, writing, knitting, and religious activities, among others (Jones, 1955).

Clearly, the environment of the retreat was designed purposely and systematically in such a way as to influence behavior in a very positive fashion. Its notable success was probably linked to many factors. It was small, housing only 30 patients. It was sectarian, serving only Quakers or those recommended by them. Thus, the prevailing social values of staff and clients were quite homogeneous. It is also true that the retreat was not burdened by having to provide for the insane poor, although it did provide a reduced rate for patients recommended by private Quaker donors or the Yearly Meetings. Clearly, however, the quality of care provided by the facility was limited to those who could afford it.

The model of treatment provided by the retreat was to influence considerably the development of moral treatment in America. Particularly, the influence of religion was much more in evidence among the institutions emanating from the retreat developed by Tuke. European institutions, influenced more by Pinel, minimized religion (Grob, 1973). We will note later that the influence of essentially protestant values on institutional values posed problems following the immigration wave of Irish catholics in the 1840s.

Thus, a summary description of the retreat in contemporary terms would picture a privately funded treatment facility serving a rather select group of middle class clients in an environment designed to promote the social and religious values of its founders and benefactors. A variety of medical and nonmedical procedures and activities was provided by a lay administration and a visiting physician in a pleasant, noncoercive, family-like atmosphere.

Moral Treatment in America

As we look at the development of moral treatment in America, we return to the difficult state of affairs described earlier at institutions like New York Hospital. This hospital is prototypical of institutions either built or reorganized during the early 1800s in order to provide moral treatment as espoused by Tuke and Pinel. It was by no means the only one, however. The Friends Asylum, for example, was established at Frankford, Pennsylvania, and was only the second institution in this country devoted exclusively to the care of the insane. Like the York Retreat, it was founded by and for private Quaker patients, although it became nonsectarian in 1834 (Deutsch, 1949). Space limitations preclude a review of the various facilities which emerged during this period. However, New York Hospital is typical, and an analysis of its development provides an excellent example of the many social, political, and economic influences that shaped the founding, development, and decline of an institution over a protracted time period.

As noted earlier, this facility had provided for the care of the insane in abysmal basement quarters since 1791. The situation became so bad that the New York State Legislature provided a grant to build a separate building on the same hospital grounds, and New York Lunatic Asylum opened in 1808. As this building, too, became hopelessly crowded, Thomas Eddy, Treasurer of New York Hospital and an active

Quaker, proposed in 1815 that a separate suburban institution be built and specifically administered according to a program of moral treatment as advocated at the York Retreat in England. The result was the establishment of the Bloomingdale Asylum which opened in 1821 after funds were solicited from the private sector and a $10,000 annuity was provided by New York State. A very interesting historical account of these early events is provided by Earle (1848), who served as one of the superintendents of the facility. He also provides a particularly illustrative outline of the principles of moral treatment during the early 1800s.

We shall consider this institution in detail for two reasons. First, although the demise of moral treatment during the second half of the nineteenth century is a matter of historical record, its therapeutic effectiveness and success can hardly be doubted. Indeed, Bockhoven (1972) calls moral treatment a forgotten success in the history of psychiatry. A consideration of the design of the treatment procedures and environment is, therefore, significant in its own right. Secondly, and perhaps more to our purpose, the thesis will be developed later in this chapter that contemporary efforts of broadly-based behavior modification programs are strikingly similar to the broadly-based intervention efforts of the moral treatment period. Both, in turn, may be seen as mainstreams in the development of environmental design.

Earle (1848) describes Bloomingdale sufficiently well to make clear that it was a pleasantly designed structure in both interior and exterior appearance. The three story main building was located on 50 acres overlooking the Hudson River on Bloomingdale Road (now Broadway). The grounds were well landscaped and included farmlands, ornamental shrubbery, grasslands, gardens, and a variety of trees. The institution housed its own natural water supply. The same was true for the heating plant which was fired by coal and provided air furnaces for the heating of all patient areas. Hot water was heated by steam for patient use and the facility included six bathing rooms. Each wing of each floor had its own water closet. In addition to the main building housing the patients, there was a farm center and barn, ice house, greenhouse, stables, carriage house, and conservatory.

In short, the physical environment was essentially a self-contained community serving an average daily census of about 63 patients during its opening year in 1821 to about 107 patients in 1844 when Earle was appointed Superintendent. The facility had an overall capacity of 150 beds, 75 male and 75 female. An institution with the environmental resources as described takes on particular significance only when we remind ourselves of the extreme deprivation and poor treatment patients were receiving at that time throughout the United States. It is also important to reemphasize that this institution and its particular treatment philosophy owed its very existence to Eddy's influence, which, in turn, was the direct result of his continuing dialogue with fellow Quakers in England at the York Retreat.

Moral treatment, in the words of Earle, had as its primary object the treating of

. . . patients, so far as their conditions will possibly permit, as if they were still in the enjoyment of the healthy exercise of their mental facilities . . . Nor is it less essential to extend to them the privilege, or the right, of as much liberty, as much freedom from personal restraint as is compatible with their safety, the safety of others, and the judicious administration of other branches of curative treatment. The courtesies of civilized and social life are not to be forgotten. (P. 26)

In many ways, the environment of this and other moral treatment communities sounds somewhat utopian in nature. Yet it is significant to realize that some of these very same points are those that would be obtainable 150 years later only through court action, e.g. right to the "least restrictive conditions necessary for treatment" (Wyatt versus Stickney, 1974). These early programs attempted to design an environment in which every person lived a full and productive day while concurrently effecting a restoration to "mental health." The means of accomplishing this quasi-utopian goal were varied, but several are particularly relevant.

Recreational exercise was an important element in the daily routine of all patients. A sound body promoted a sound mind. Every patient who was physically capable was provided outdoor exercise daily. Open spaces or "airing courts" were well designed with shady trees, flowers, and lawn chairs. Earle (1848) took issue with the argument that equally good exercise programs with less administrative difficulty could be had with open verandas guarded by latticework. "It appears to us that, to the minds of the patients, this must be more constantly suggestive of imprisonment, or confinement, than a large, well-shaded, cultivated court" (p. 30). It was this pervasive sensitivity to the design effects of interior and exterior environments on behavior that characterized the moral treatment institutions and set them apart from other contemporary institutions as well as those which would follow.

Other forms of exercise were also readily available for both sexes. Long walks with the attendants would range up to several miles. In warm weather, swimming and fishing were available. Carriage rides for up to eight patients at a time were regularly available from four to six times a day and traveled up to eight miles from the main house. Clearly, confinement was not oppressive in this treatment environment.

Instruction was also readily available. Earle himself conducted numerous lecture series on varied topics. In 1845 a more formal school for teaching basic subjects was founded. A library was established for the exclusive use of the patients, including five daily newspapers.

Amusement, or what we would now call recreational therapy, was also provided. The "games of grace" — backgammon, chess, checkers, and the like — were available continually within the house. Varied other activities were also available, including a bowling alley and the counterpart of football and baseball. One evening weekly, parties were held for the benefit of both sexes. Refreshments were provided for this social occasion and the ". . . parties differ but little from similar assemblies in private houses" (Earle, 1848, p. 35). Dances were held monthly. The cotillion was a festive occasion and was apparently the most prominent social event on the patient calendar.

Religion played an important part in early nineteenth century moral treatment in the United States. Bloomingdale was no exception, and by 1832 a chaplain was employed full time. However, it is interesting to note that, if a patient's illness was related to an inappropriate preoccupation with religion itself, attendance at religious services might be denied the patient. This appears to be one of the first written acknowledgments that religious conflicts could be a contributing cause of mental illness rather than religion being the basis of cure. In general, though, the influence of Christianity as a necessary adjunct to successful treatment was quite prevalent in the conduct of moral treatment in America. Quotes from ancient sources were everywhere apparent in the various institutions (Deutsch, 1949). Aeschylus' "Soft speech is to the distemper'd wrath, medicinal," and Solomon's "A soft answer turneth away wrath" were typical. David's treatment of Saul's melancholia through music is another common Biblical example.

The mainstay of moral treatment, especially for Earle, was that of manual labor. Labor was seen as a way of promoting sound and healthful sleep as well as a healthy body. This included farmwork, work the carpenter's shop, kitchen assignments, laundry chores, and general sewing to name but a few. Where possible, work within the institution was provided which correlated with a patient's preinstitutional vocational skills and postdischarge vocational expectations. There were those, however, who refused to work, particularly the more affluent patients. Significantly, no compulsory measures were taken to enforce work behavior, although it was no doubt socially expected and reinforced within the community. Nonetheless, Earle's frustration over his inability to elicit appropriate work habits from the more wealthy, paying patients at Bloomingdale contributed greatly to his dissatisfaction and subsequent resignation after only five years as superintendent (Bockhoven, 1972). In general, however, appropriate work habits were an integral part of most moral treatment programs.

In summary, if we were to characterize the basic philosophy upon which Moral Treatment rested, it would be simply that <u>clients were treated as if they were normal</u>. Restraint was used, but infrequently; and in the severe cases when it was used, its primary purpose was clearly to protect the patient from harming himself or others. It was not used as punishment.

Moral Treatment and Behavior Therapy

Before turning to an analysis of the demise of moral treatment in the latter half of the eighteenth century, let us consider briefly some of the inferences we might draw on the relationship between moral treatment and contemporary behavior modification. At first these two systems of care might be perceived as antithetical; moral treatment being the epitome of humanism and behavior modification being synonymous with a mechanistic view of man. In our opinion, the two in actuality are more in harmony than disharmony. Contrary to much popular opinion, moral treatment did not simply provide "tender loving care ad lib. Closer scrutiny shows that, to be sure, treatment was provided humanely; however, it is also the case that moral treatment communities provided extremely highly structured and well designed environments. Indeed, "The role of the superintendent was not fundamentally different from the role of the stern, authoritarian, yet loving and concerned father" (Grob, 1973, p. 168). Behavior was clearly "response contingent." It could be argued that much of its success was due probably to the fact that inappropriate behaviors, such as verbal abuse, were ignored (extinction) while appropriate behaviors were applauded and received ample social praise and attention from the staff and even the superintendent himself.

It is also true that most token economy programs design an environment in which client behavior is motivated by the same social and material reinforcers prevalent in early moral treatment programs. Anyone who has ever developed a token economy program in a state hospital likely knows the difficulty with which one is usually confronted when trying to obtain funds and resources for such reinforcers as refreshments, parties, dances, field trips, games, etc. Yet these very same reinforcers provided the foundation upon which most moral treatment programs rested.

As with moral treatment, behavior modification programs also treat the individual as if he were normal. For example, token economy programs are essentially a microcosm of the larger economic system of society in general of which they are but a part. The behavior of the individuals living within such an economy varies as a function of the same economic principles which govern the behavior of normal people operating within the natural environment (Winkler, 1971; Winkler and Krasner, 1971). The salient point is that in both moral treatment and behaviorally oriented programs, the environments are designed systematically such that behavior is response contingent.

Although punishment per se was not usually permitted in moral treatment programs, an examination of some of the control procedures is interesting. When punishment was used, one was to "punish disobedience preemptorily"; attendants were "never to threaten, but execute; offer no indignities" (Hall, 1829). Thus "Punishment, while necessary on occasion, was never arbitrary, capricious, cruel, or unjust" (Grob, 1973, p. 168). This is compatible with contemporary views of punishment; if punishment is to be used, it should be administered quickly following the inappropriate behavior. It should be dispensed firmly, but compassionately, in a clear and consistent manner. In other words, punishment, too, should be response contingent.

Moral treatment apparently also had its counterpart to the behavior therapy technique of "time out" (Leitenberg, 1965). If a patient were unruly, he was placed in a quiet room and denied the social company of others for a period of time. Similarly, the Virginia Western Lunatic Asylum employed what we would now call a flow system. When patients misbehaved they were "removed to a circle better adapted to their dispositions and habits. Such a system . . . induced patients to efforts of self-control and self-respect, for purposes of retaining their place or ascending still higher in the scale of distinction" (Grob, 1973, p. 229). It should be emphasized, however, that in both moral treatment and behavior therapy, punishment and/or time out were avoided in lieu of treatment efforts based on positive reinforcement principles.   Both systems are "designed environments" which humanely seek to influence behavior in positive ways in keeping with the socially accepted values of society and the patient. Where successful, such programs are able to put "the control of patient behavior in the hands of the patient" (Atthowe & Krasner, 1968, p. 42). It is our value judgment that this aspect of such programs may be their singularly most important contribution.

The Decline in Moral Treatment

Returning now to the institutions of the mid-nineteenth century, we note the rapid decline in the quality of institutional care for dependent groups including, importantly, those which were based on moral treatment principles. What accounts for the demise of institutions generally, and what accounts specifically for the end of an apparently successful treatment regime? Historians suggest a variety of reasons, all of which are interesting and important; but several are particularly significant in the context of environmental design.

First, the success of moral treatment may in itself have been its own undoing! While the actual "cure rate" for institutions, such as Bloomingdale and the Hartford Retreat, were a matter of controversy (Earle, 1887) it is clear that such institutions were perceived by the communities as the singularly appropriate vehicle for bringing about care and cure for the mentally ill. (Recall that psychiatry as a private practice was virtually nonexistent until about 1875.) It logically followed, therefore, that the appropriate treatment for insane persons was admission to an insane asylum. Reformers, particularly Dorothea Dix, crusaded throughout the country to get the insane who were inappropriately housed in jails, penitentiaries, and poor houses admitted to hospitals. Ironically, the net result of such reform was opposite to that which was intended. Hospitals, inundated by the influx of admissions from such facilities, now themselves deteriorated. Consequently, the quality of care actually received previously in the almshouses and jails was virtually comparable to that provided in hospitals. Functionally, only the name of the institution had changed, not the level of care.

Almost concurrently, another wave of admissions devastated the insane asylums. Fleeing famine and hardship, over 2 million immigrants came to the United States between 1830 and 1850. The majority were Irish Catholic. Most were unskilled and illiterate. Life in the urban slums and ghettos of New York, Philadelphia, and Boston was difficult. Jobs, where they existed at all, were low paying and often dangerous, e.g. tunnel construction and canal building. Add to this the customs and mores of an alien culture, plus the barriers of language differences, and one finds numerous behaviors judged aberrant or abnormal by the indigenous culture. Consequently, the foreign poor and insane quickly added to the rolls of the hospitals and poor houses in large numbers.

After admission, the problem only worsened, particularly for the Irish Catholics whose religious values differed sharply from the protestant-run hospitals.

It is also an interesting twist of fate that Pliney Earle, champion of moral treatment, was, in fact, a major contributing influence to its decline. He objected strongly to the prevailing practice of building what he perceived to be large and extravagant structures. These he thought only served to cover up the neglect of patients and their lack of treatment. In his judgment, the rationale for such construction was based on what he considered to be the fallacy of easy curability (Bockhoven, 1972). In other words, the well-known successes associated with moral treatment during the first quarter of the nineteenth century were used as the basis for building more (but larger) institutions. As a result, Earle sought to show, through a post-hoc analysis of treatment during this period, that the cure rate was a considerably lower percentage than was thought to be the case. His goal was to influence others to seek alternatives to the huge, expensive, and unwieldy institutions that were being built (Earle, 1887). The effect was the exact opposite. As Bockhoven (1972) and others (Caplan, 1964; Deutsch, 1949) note, the net effect was the beginning of an atmosphere of grave pessimism and termination of meaningful treatment throughout the country.

Exceptions existed, of course, but the general climate pervasive throughout the country was that insanity was an incurable disease. This view was further reinforced by continuing developments in medicine itself. Bayle's thesis, presented in 1826, that general paralysis was due to organic changes in the brain, stimulated much scientific research designed to identify the organic basis of other forms of mental illness (Zilboorg, 1941). Other breakthroughs heralded great advances in the physical sciences and fostered the adoption of mechanistic and organic approaches to all forms of mental illness. Gray (1885) was absolutely convinced that the manifestation of all forms of mental illness had an organic basis in the form of lesions in the brain. "The disordered mental state called insanity, is a symptom of disease of the brain, that is, a bodily disease; as much so as any other morbid state of the corporal system" (Gray, 1885, p. 1). More than any other single person, Gray was responsible for swinging the pendulum of treatment back to pre-Pinel views. It was but a matter of time, so the physicians thought, until the organic basis for the etiology of all mental diseases would be fully understood. Until such breakthroughs occurred and cures were discovered, there was obviously little that could be done for those afflicted by mental disease. Since they were incurable, the most that could be done for them was to provide a comfortable, custodial existence.

All of these factors combined to provide an atmosphere of therapeutic nihilism in which treatment was delivered with abject despair. A "disease model" of abnormal behavior was now fully established. Since insanity was due to an unknown disease process, it logically followed that recovery was not really possible. As Bockhoven (1972) points out, remission might occur, but in the absence of treating the underlying physical basis of disease, death was the only logical

course the illness could take. Obviously, therefore, patients could
be discharged as recovered, since discharge inevitably would resu
relapse. Bockhoven (1972) makes the very interesting observation tha

> The susceptibility of physicians to the dicta of the laborator
> rendered them peculiarly <u>harmful</u> as administrators with author-
> ity over the movements of people. The mentally ill might hav(
> fared better if mental hospitals had been under the direction o:
> <u>lay</u> superintendents with less respect for the findings of the
> laboratory science of the day. (P. 88; emphasis added)

It is, perhaps, significant that moral treatment centers were under
administration of lay superintendents during the period of time in wl
they are judged to have been the most successful and effective. Du
the period from its opening in 1821 until 1844, Bloomingdale,
instance, was operated by a lay superintendent and consulting physic.

If society were to believe Earle's argument that moral treatm
had not produced the high cure rates attributed to it, or if insanity w
indeed incurable, it followed in the minds of legislators that larger
more economical custodial facilities could better deal with the e
increasing hospital admission rates. While Earle was able to perpetu
his brand of moral treatment following his appointment as superint
dent at Northampton State Hospital in Massachusetts in 1864,
general effect of his critique on the curability of insanity disenfr
chized moral treatment throughout the country generally. Ear
influence on the rise and decline of moral treatment is paradoxical.

Another significant factor in the decline of moral treatment rela
to professional training. Moral treatment, like any other hun
endeavor, was primarily the result of strong-minded and influen^
leaders. Although we have focused largely on Bloomingdale, other mo
treatment programs developed concurrently under the charisma
leadership of persons like Dr. Eli Todd at the Retreat for the Insane
Hartford, Dr. Amariah Brigham at the State Lunatic Asylum at Uti
New York, Samuel B. Woodward at the State Lunatic Asylum
Worcester, Massachusetts, and many others. Through the assertiven(
of these individuals, moral treatment flourished in the institutions :
which they had personal responsibility. Even in the face of rising pati(
populations, these superintendents were generally successful in reta.
ing the essential features of moral treatment.

Unfortunately, however, a moral treatment leadership vacuu
developed with their deaths. This is somewhat contradictory inasmu
as they were among the 13 founding members of the Association
Medical Superintendents of American Institutions for the Insa
(AMSAII). This association, established October 16, 1844, was t
forerunner of the American Medico-Psychological Association, a
ultimately the American Psychiatric Association. This group al
established the <u>American Journal of Insanity</u>, which was the fir
English language periodical devoted exclusively to the treatment
mental illness. Both the Association and the Journal were primari
oriented toward solving the problems and difficulties confronted by i

members at their respective institutions. As a result, the Association was highly influential in affecting matters pertaining to institutional care, but was relatively unimportant in the development of the medical profession generally. Consequently, the early development of psychiatry cannot be separated from the institutions from within which it developed.

Until the mid-1870s, psychiatry was synonymous with institutional medicine, and it was the institution which shaped the professional values of this fledgling discipline during its early development. This resulted in a rather insular association of professionals divorced from their parent discipline. Their concerns were understandably self-serving and addressed pressing practical problems requiring immediate attention.   Thus, their activities focused on such problems as hospital construction, suicide prevention, rising census, non-professional personnel selection and training, and the causes and prevention of insanity (Hospital and Community Psychiatry, 1976, p. 464-65). Their efforts were to influence the hospital structures themselves more than the future administrators of these very same hospitals. Psychiatric training, where it existed, consisted of apprenticeship training. Each of the significant figures in moral treatment trained perhaps only one or two physicians in these principles. Since hospital construction and populations were increasing at a rapid rate, demand exceeded supply and the influence of those trained in the technique was quickly diluted. A failure to train an adequate number of replacements for the founding fathers of moral treatment may be seen as significantly influencing its decline.

OTHER VIEWS FOR TREATING THE MENTALLY ILL

Thomas Kirkbride: Physician/Designer

If moral treatment were to essentially disappear, what were to be the influences shaping the form of institutions during this period of pessimism regarding the curability of insanity? One of the most significant, if not the most important, influences on subsequent institutional functioning was the life and work of Dr. Thomas S. Kirkbride. His influence on the environmental design and construction of mental hospitals cannot be overemphasized, and we will consider his contributions in detail.

Kirkbride was superintendent of the Pennsylvania Hospital for the Insane in Philadelphia for 43 years. In 1847 he published an article entitled "Remarks on the Construction and Arrangements of Hospitals for the Insane" (Kirkbride, 1847) and in 1854 expanded his views into a book entitled On the Construction, Organization, and General Arrangements of Hospitals for the Insane (Kirkbride, 1854). In his own time, he was the recognized authority on hospital construction and traveled nationwide as a consultant in hospital design. In these two publications, Kirkbride set down basic hospital design criteria which were to form the basis of public policy regarding hospital design and construction during the next 50-75 years.

Chronologically, Kirkbride's career at Pennsylvania hospital began in 1840. Although by this time hospital enrollments were beginning to increase, moral treatment was still a very viable treatment environment and it greatly influenced Kirkbride's views regarding hospital construction. Hospitals should be built in pleasant country surroundings on no less than 100 acres, of which 30-50 should be used for the direct pleasure and benefit of the patients. The remainder was to be used for farming and gardening. Adequate provision for recreation and exercise should be available on the grounds. Kirkbride himself argued vigorously that no hospital should house more than 250 patients. In providing for the care of these 250 patients, he set forth basic design features which were intended to influence the behavior of its inhabitants in systematic and predictable ways. The central section, or building core, housed the physical plant support systems. These included the superintendent's quarters, the kitchen, storerooms, offices, chapel, and reception and visiting areas. The central core was flanked on either side by three receding wings. The wings were joined to one another and to the central administration building. Male patients were maintained in the three wings on one side of the building and female patients were maintained on the opposite side. In a curious departure from other moral treatment programs, Kirkbride advocated the separation of the sexes. While this has obvious administrative advantages, note that the design of such an environment has significant implications regarding the normalization of heterosexual interaction among patient populations.

Each three story wing ideally consisted of eight wards serving various diagnostic categories. Thus, a total of 16 wards each serving about 16 patients provided care for a population of about 250 patients, 125 male and 125 female. The most disturbed patients occupied the wards on the farthest receding wing, while the least disturbed occupied wards closest to the administration center. This indeed may be the origin of the phrase "back ward."

In Kirkbride's plan, each ward was essentially self-contained. In addition to the sleeping quarters, each ward had a dining room, bathroom, water closet, clothes room, and parlor. Private bedrooms, approximately nine by eleven feet, were provided most of the patients, although each ward also had a dormitory for four to six inmates (Kirkbride, 1854). Kirkbride gave close attention to detail, particularly size — corridors were to be at least 12 feet high and 12 feet wide, parlors were to be approximately 20 square feet, and bedrooms were to be approximately 100 square feet. (Interestingly, today many state and federal guidelines mandate a minimum of 100 square feet for a patient's bedroom.) He also gave painstaking detail regarding such diverse construction factors as the fire-proof characteristics of the building materials, the adequacy of the design of boiler and heating systems, and myriad other construction details.

This attention to detail earned him the respect of his colleagues and his architectural design principles were incorporated widely during the surge of hospital construction in the second half of the nineteenth century. With construction of the Alabama Hospital of the Insane in Tuscaloosa, Kirkbride's influence was fully established. Plans for this facility were prepared in 1852 under Kirkbride's direction by Sloan and Stuart, an architectural firm in Philadelphia. A fruitful collaborative relationship between Kirkbride and Samuel Sloan developed. They subsequently designed numerous other hospitals for the insane (Cooledge, 1963). At least 22 hospitals are probably the result of Kirkbride-Sloan efforts, and no fewer than 13 major hospitals are fully documented as Kirkbride-Sloan facilities (Cooledge, 1963). Clearly, whatever their empirical merit and therapeutic value, the hospitals of the period were, without doubt, greatly influenced by the treatment philosophy of Thomas Kirkbride.

Except for the segregation of the sexes, Kirkbride's 250 bed, self-contained, linear-model hospital was the embodiment of moral treatment. The design of the hospitals was functionally related to the behavior of the patients in the context of moral treatment. However, neither treatment philosophy nor hospital design could stave off the impending crisis as both treatment philosophy and design philosophy became increasingly corrupted by the demand for larger and larger hospitals to serve increasing patient populations in the most economic way possible. With the late 1800s and early 1900s, wings were added to wings, which were added to still other wings, producing huge, maze-like institutions where huge numbers of patients were essentially warehoused. Buffalo State Hospital, although avowedly built on Kirkbride's model, was almost a mile long (Bond, 1947).

The Cottage Plan

Other than the Kirkbride Plan, the intentional goal of influencing behavior through systematic environmental design was limited to but one other major effect during this period. The "cottage plan" spearheaded a movement which sought to alter dramatically the type of institutional care received by the insane. It emerged primarily as an attempt to discover alternatives to the large and overcrowded lunatic asylums and their rapidly deteriorating quality of care.

It was noted earlier that the Virginia Eastern Asylum was not particularly influential in national hospital design. However, James M. Galt, who became the institution's first medical superintendent in 1841, was extremely influential personally through his writings, particularly The Treatment of Insanity (Galt, 1846). He was especially familiar with the farm at St. Anne operated by the renowned French hospital at Bicetre (Galt, 1855). Galt objected to New England hospitals which ". . . appear mere prison houses, notwithstanding their many internal attributes . . . " As an alternative he suggested the design of an in-patient and after-care system which would have radically changed the existing institutional structure and philosophy. Galt advocated placing the more self-sufficient and dependable patients throughout the community. Chronic and less self-reliant patients could be housed as boarders with families in the immediately adjacent hospital communities. He argued that ". . . the insane, generally are susceptible of a much more extended liberty than they are now allowed" (Galt, 1855). Those requiring still greater attention, such as epileptics, could be housed in cottages on the grounds of the hospital. This graduated system of care, Galt believed, would provide better and more humane treatment while, at the same time, reducing construction and maintenance expenses associated with the larger, exclusively in-patient hospitals.

In principle, the program was very similar to the Gheel Model. Named after the farm community of Gheel, Belgium, this program had been popular for centuries. "In this system, the central institution was virtually eliminated for all but the most agitated or infirm lunatics, while other patients were boarded with village families and worked the land" (R.B. Caplan, 1969, p. 286). Unfortunately, rampant patient abuse and exploitation existed prior to midnineteenth century Belgium reforms. Earle had toured the area just prior to these reforms and, as a result, he vigorously opposed any adoption of the Gheel Model in America (Earle, 1851). Although Galt was one of the original 13 founders of the AMSAII, he was severely criticized by his peers for advocating such a plan.

Kirkbride was particularly incensed by the accusation that New England institutions were prison-like and denied adequate personal freedom. It is important to place this controversy in chronological perspective. The major points of the debate appeared in the American Journal of Insanity in 1855. Kirkbride's classic book on hospital design and construction had just recently appeared in 1854. The two positions could not have been more diametrically opposed in their design of optimal treatment environments. Kirkbride advocated environments designed to segregate the sexes, the classes, and the colors, and ultimately to segregate diagnostic categories. Except on behavioral criteria, e.g. degrees of violence, cottage plans typically made no such distinctions.

Although advocates argued the exact opposite, Earle and other critics contended that the cottage system was more expensive in the original cost of construction, continuing maintenance, and personnel requirements. From an environmental and economic perspective, it is interesting that the inordinate costs of heating individual buildings in cold areas was a major deterrent to their adoption (Grob, 1973). Such factors obviously have nothing to do with therapeutic considerations. Additionally, Earle (1868) was particularly concerned that the cottage-type hospital would create problems in patient surveillance for staff. In all such matters, the respected and influential hospital superintendents of the day viewed the cottage system as a significant step backward. Kirkbride, Earle, Ray, and others led the way in opposing the plan.

Although they believed the above arguments put forth in opposition to the Cottage Plan, an examination of history reveals that their motives were not without a self-serving basis. Their opposition was but a prelude to the violent arguments of the coming decades regarding the general issue of centralized versus decentralized care, a topic to be considered shortly. For the physicians of the AMSAII any treatment alternative that diminished their control, power, and influence regarding matters of insanity was a direct threat to be actively opposed, and this included acrimonious assaults on its dissident members from within if necessary. Predictably, differences of opinion within the psychiatric profession pitted the younger, less conservative, practitioners against the more prestigious and authoritative older members of the AMSAII, particularly Earle, Gray, Kirkbride, and Ray. After all, they were the expert authorities on insanity; they had formally set hospital standards since the founding of the organization; and they had borne the burden of treatment for decades. The political majority of the organization held steadfast to the insular views and argued ". . . that the authority of superintendents should not in any way be weakened" (Grob, 1973, p. 320). Most of the older superintendents, trained during an earlier age, persisted in their conviction that insanity was incurable and that moral treatment was the method of choice. The problem, they held, was one of ever-increasing hospital populations and inadequacy of resources. More hospitals were needed, not an alternative system.

At issue is not whether they were right or wrong. What is important is that this handful of professionals, through their assertive and charismatic leadership, were able to forestall the implementation of a treatment strategy for decades. Perhaps their greatest flaw in a pluralistic society was their stubborn refusal at least to experiment with and evaluate treatment alternatives based on values different from their own. However, moral treatment for them was functionally defined as treatment in hospital institutions and nowhere else. It would appear that they failed to appreciate the fact that moral treatment was a philosophical approach as well as a physical setting. We can only speculate as to the historical course moral treatment would have taken had these great leaders channeled their energies in the direction of designing noninstitutional moral treatment programs.

The position of the hospital administrators made their ultimate downfall inevitable. While theorizing about what cure rates could be with small, 250 bed hospitals, the reality of the situation rendered such positions pointless. Rising populations, declining discharge rates and the decline in hospital care were the facts. Gradually, public confidence in both hospitals and their administrators eroded. The problem became circular as the hospitals became overcrowded and treatment deteriorated. As treatment deteriorated, cure and discharge rates declined, and chronic patient backlogs increased, adding further to the overcrowding. As the number of incurables began to swell, these treatment facilities became the prima facie evidence supporting the criticism that institutional care itself was a failure. Since the superintendents committed to moral treatment had historically and consistently promoted the curability of mental illness, ". . . their inability to deliver on their promises, for whatever reasons, had seriously impaired their prestige and authority as preeminent spokesmen on this subject" (Grob, 1973, p. 323). In their own defense, Earle, Kirkbride, Ray and others argued vigorously that treatment failures were due to hopelessly large and unwieldy institutions which made it virtually impossible to provide moral treatment. For example, in the face of the pressures of reality the Association in 1866 had reluctantly modified its stand on hospital census and raised the number of patients in the "ideal size" mental hospital from 250 beds to 600 beds, although Kirkbride vigorously opposed this resolution.   The events of history, however, overtook individual practitioners.

The Association membership was recalcitrant in its views, and unwilling to change in the direction of relinquishing any of their power and control; such power and control was ultimately taken from them. Frederick Wines (1878) was one of the reformers to argue persuasively that the formation of social policy should not be exclusively the responsibility of medical superintendents. He strongly believed that since nonmedical issues were involved, nonmedical input should contribute to policy planning. At the same time, the Association fought the tendency of nonmedical governing boards to equate economic efficiency with institutional effectiveness. Therapeutic concerns should never be subordinated to economic exigencies. Yet, as Bockhoven (1972) notes, Earle's fiscal abilities as a superintendent were unfortunately the faculties most valued by the Commonwealth. At the same time, Wines and others argued that, realistically, legislative support would not be forthcoming sufficient to elevate the quality of care of the large, institutional, patient populations to a level that would adequately fund moral treatment environments. Wines concluded that " . . . the policy and principles advocated by the AMSAII were driving the chronic insane back to county jails and poorhouses . . ." (Grob, 1973, p. 324).

Alternatives to the large institutions were clearly needed, thought many, and the Cottage Plan was an idea whose time had come. Although major resistance to the Cottage Plan was provided by the Association, this system enjoyed substantial popular support as an alternative to conventional institutional care. Nowhere were the stakes higher in this controversy than in Worcester, Massachusetts. The aging Worcester State Lunatic Hospital was, by 1865, in great need of a new physical plant. Here was a timely opportunity to reorganize the hospital along alternative lines. More important was the fact that Massachusetts and New York were seen as the vangards of innovation and reform regarding dependent groups. As Massachusetts went so went the nation, so each side marshaled its maximum effort to have its opinions and positions prevail. The superintendent, Dr. Merrick Bemis, advocated the Gheel Plan. He was supported by Samuel Howe, Chairman of the State Board of Charities. The two had traveled widely in Europe and were impressed with the various features of the Gheel Plan. But, as noted earlier, Earle and the others were greatly opposed and the two camps were now enjoined in battle on an irreversible collision course.

Grob (1966) provides an excellent account of the subtle influence affecting the ensuing conflict. For present purposes, suffice it to report that Earle and his colleagues ultimately succeeded in scuttling the attempt to use the renovation at Worcester as a model of alternative care. The political success was a testament to their faith in institutions, but it was also the eventual epitaph of moral treatment which they had so vigorously tried to protect. Through their strength of leadership, facilities run by Earle, Ray, Kirkbride, and others would continue to provide at least marginally adequate care. Institutions in general would continue their rapid spiral of decay.

Since Massachusetts was a leader in matters of institutional care, it is almost a certainty that some form of the Gheel or cottage Plan would have seen wide adoption if the Worcester Hospital had been rebuilt along such lines. In spite of the Worcester failure, however, proponents of the cottage plan were not without some success. The plan was utilized more in the Midwest. Illinois State Hospital at Kankakee (Grob, 1973; 1966) was established in 1877 as a direct result of the cottage plan. The State Asylum at Kalamazoo, Michigan was established in 1885 as the first "farm colony" of the cottage plan.

Considered collectively, the cottage plan, the Gheel Plan, and the agricultural colony are all attempts at environmental design in which the insane are, at least marginally, viable members of the community. Fitze James, near Paris, for example, was an agricultural colony founded in 1847. It was totally removed geographically from the parent facility about three-quarters of a mile away. "All patients were provided with sufficient work; no coercion was practiced; and all interactable inmates were returned to the central facility" (Grob, 1973, p. 328). Grob quotes Howe as advocating the efficiency of the Gheel system on the basis of three major advantages.

> In the first place, it furnished employment for all patients in the company of sane persons. Secondly, the insane were provided with those "social and family relationships with sane persons" that nourished "unperverted sentiments and affections," and thus helped to restore "mental and moral balance." Finally, its managers gave the insane the greatest degree of personal freedom, which promoted mental health by emphasizing self-respect. (Grob, 1973, P. 329)

Bemis, as noted earlier, visited Gheel in 1868 and was impressed by the fact that patients living as boarders with members of the town "have a home, live in a family and are members of society, useless it may be, but still are identifiable as part of a community" (Bemis, 1868, cited in Grob, 1973, p. 330; emphasis added). After returning to the United States, Bemis advocated a decentralized hospital in contrast to the congregate Kirkbride structure.

The salient features of the so-called Cottage Plan makes it clear that they tended, in a large measure, to treat the patient as if he were normal in a philosophy reminiscent of early moral treatment. When the behavior of the patient could not be brought under control, as with for example, epileptics, retention at the parent or central facility was the practical alternative. But for the vast majority, care was provided in a manner prophetic of "family care" and "community care" that would not flourish in the United States for decades to come.

The failure of the cottage plan to be adopted on a widespread basis to a large extent cannot be separated from the political aspects of social reform. Rothman (1971) provides an unusually good account of the "discovery" of asylums during the Jacksonian era. He notes, further, that the institutions resulting from the reform movement of the period were developed not simply as the logical direction reform should take, but as the only direction it should take. "By describing the innovation as reform, they assume that the asylum was an inevitable and sure step in the progress of humanity. Ostensibly it was an obvious improvement not only over existing conditions, but over other possible alternatives" (Rothman, 1971, p. xiv; emphasis in original).

It was in the social climate of reform that early institutions were designed and developed. Their numbers swelled until every state had at least one, and sometimes several, insane asylums. As the population grew, so did the number of insane and the latter grew proportionately more rapidly than did the former. Demand always exceeded the supply of hospital beds. In an attempt to keep pace, communities built new hospitals and expanded old ones. Alternatives to hospitals were not seriously considered except for the cottage plan movement. By then the institutions had taken on a life of their own. Since institutions were the accepted solution to earlier social and psychiatric reform, it logically followed that the public simply needed to provide adequate financial support for more of the same. Yet by 1870, if not sooner, it was clear that the institution had not met the optimistic hopes of the reformers.

On Chronic Versus Acute Treatment

Many influences account for what Rothman (1971) calls the enduring nature of institutions. For our purposes, one of the earliest and most important is the effect of prevailing treatment attitudes regarding the differentiation between chronic and acute cases. This distinction, in turn, was to affect the controversy over congregate (Kirkbride Plan) versus noncongregate (cottage plan) approaches to mental illness.

Even at the moral treatment centers, the increase in chronic patients became apparent as the immigration wave of the 1830s began. By the time Earle left Bloomingdale in the 1840s, it had increasingly become a "dumping ground" and a place for custodial care. A general analysis of the increase in chronic patients is, in itself, interesting, but one of the most critical variables was the simple fact that the institutions began to lose more and more control over their own admission policies. The courts began to play an increasingly important role in commitment procedures (see Deutsch, 1949, Chapters 18 and 19). The legislatures became involved in legal definitions of insanity as well as the type of institutional care the insane would receive (e.g. Willard Act, New York, 1865). Additionally, a legalized exodus of the chronic insane from the jails and almshouses resulted directly from the reform actions of Dorothea Dix. Thus, superintendents found themselves inundated by admissions over which they had no control. The decay process had begun.

In spite of the deteriorating effects of such legalized and enforced admissions to state and quasi-state institutions, the treatment inadequacies in locally controlled poor houses, and their inherent vulnerability to abuse, had now been reduced. Whatever the difficulties of the insane asylums, they were, at the very least, hospitals. The care that was lacking at the local level in poor houses could, it was thought, be provided more therapeutically and economically at centralized state-level hospitals. "The shortcomings of community control of welfare, then, led inevitably to the assumption by the state of responsibility for dependent groups, including the care and treatment of the mentally ill" (Grob, 1973, p. 319).

But by the time the typical patient from the poor house went to the hospital, he had already reached a chronic state, having received little if any care and attention in years. The hope of quick recovery via centralized hospital care was short lived. Instead, chronicity accelerated. Between the exodus from the poor houses and the wave of immigrants, care in the centralized hospitals ultimately degenerated to the level of the decentralized almshouses from which the patients had come. No sooner had centralization occurred than it was clear that it would not, indeed it could not, work as then structured.

In response to the problem, one of the first solutions offered was the differentiation of patients as acute and chronic. The next step was to design and construct separate facilities for each. New York State is again an excellent case in point. In 1865 the Willard Act was passed providing for the care of the chronically insane at Willard Asylum and the acutely insane at Utica. The Binghamton State Asylum for the Chronic Insane was opened in 1881. One of the major consequences of the Willard Act was the inauguration of differential care since the daily cost per patient for the custodial care of the chronic was less than that for the active treatment of the acute. The cost of patient care was charged back to the county of residence. Thus, while supervising control of the facility was provided by the state, the county continued to bear the cost.

Willard Asylum alone was intended to house 1,500 chronic patients, a far cry from Kirkbride's ideal of 250 and almost three times the AMSAII standard of 600. Yet no sooner had Willard opened than it, too, became hopelessly overcrowded. Deutsch (1949) points out the untenable position faced by the Willard Asylum. The institution was mandated by law to accept chronic patients, and their inability to do so placed them in noncompliance with the law. In the face of this reality, counties were granted exemptions from the Willard Act and were permitted to provide for the care of the chronic locally. This they had wanted to do all along since they felt they could provide comparable care more cheaply than at the centralized state facility. The path had come full circle! Again, demand had exceeded supply. By 1871 (Deutsch, 1949), care for the chronic insane was again provided at the local level in almshouses in one-third of the counties of New York State.

In historical retrospect, this fiscal differential in chronic and acute care fueled the controversy surrounding congregate versus noncongregate models of care. Kirkbride, Earle, Ray, and others argued for centralized care for all patients, chronic and acute. Their conviction that a dual system of care was faulty provides a persuasive argument even today: Who was to say that the chronic could not benefit from intensive treatment? And by what and whose criteria did the acute patient make the transition from active acute treatment to the oblivion of custodial care at chronic facilities? More than any other issue, the question of centralization of care for all patients united the institution superintendents of the day.

Closely interwoven with the issue of physically centralized versus decentralized institutions was the issue of centralized versus decentralized administrative control. Until the mid-1800s public policy – good, bad, or indifferent – had been virtually nonexistent. Well and poorly run institutions alike enjoyed tremendous local autonomy, and this was precisely what the founders of the AMSAII had wanted. They argued that the solution to improving the poorly run facilities was not to diminish the power and decision making authority of the conscientious superintendents by placing them under regulatory governing boards. But the circularity of the problem became even more pronounced. As already noted, the directors were increasingly unable to cope with the rising patient population. They could not meet the needs of society through the institutions they directed, yet they continued to resist proposed alternatives; they argued for centralized institutions and yet were forced to return chronic patients to the local almshouses; they defined their role as expert professionals on matters of insanity, and yet were incapable of reaching a viable strategy with which to approach the problem.

Although variability existed among the states, in general it was clear by the late 1800s that the only solution consistent with the magnitude of the problem was the total state takeover of the care of the insane. The New York State Care Act of 1890 contained "the most sweeping legislative provisions in behalf of the insane ever enacted in the United States" (Deutsch, 1949, p. 262). Through the principle of total state care, the insane were once and for all removed from the poor houses. Whatever the quality of their care was to be, it would, hereafter, become largely the responsibility of state government supported by state taxes. With the focus of financial and political control shifting to the state, the influence of the local hospital superintendents rapidly diminished. No longer did the views of individuals such as Kirkbride or Earle prevail. In their place, nonprofessional governing boards, of one type or another depending on the state, supervised the delivery of services within the guidelines of state law and policy. The superintendent was to become essentially an instrument of the state with little local discretionary authority. The move toward centralized control had thus been accomplished in New York and was to follow quickly in other states.

There continued to be exceptions, however, as proponents of the cottage plan were persistent advocates. The most notable success associated with this plan was the system of care known as the Wisconsin Plan that was very influential in the midwest. Advocacy notwithstanding, however, even in the midwest the plan was not chosen as much as it was precipitated by local fiscal realities of the day. In other words, the design of treatment environments had nothing to do with the criteria of therapeutic effectiveness.

The debate raged between the advocates of congregate facilities based on the Kirkbride Plan versus the Wisconsin Plan (and its variants) well into the 1900s. No longer at issue, however, was the question of who had control over the care of the insane. It was clearly the state authorities.

An evaluation of the effectiveness of the respective views is not our purpose. It is relevant for us to be cognizant of the ways in which the design of the two environments affected behavior, or at least purported to affect behavior. In the decentralized county-state plan, the patient was physically based in cottages close to home, thereby assuring a more likely interpersonal interaction of the patient with friends and family. This curtailed the degree to which the patient became divorced from his local community. In contrast, patients geographically removed to centralized institutions were quickly cut off from their preinstitution-alization links with others.

Productive employment for the patient within the community was highly more likely in a decentralized facility. Employment in congregate facilities often served the economic needs of the institution as much, if not more than, it served the patient. Cottage plans accepted the reality that some people simply seemed to require a structured, supportive, and sheltered environment.

Attitudes toward the clients were markedly different in the two systems. In contemporary terms, we would contrast the different views as being correlated with medical versus psychological models of client-staff intervention. An excellent example of the distinction is provided by a comment from Deutsch's summary of a paper presented by Oscar Craig in 1891. ". . . state institution nearly always, and the county asylum very seldom, treats its mentally ill patients as sick persons, as in fact they are whether their illness is recent and curable or chronic and incurable" (Deutsch, 1949, p. 270). Thus, we see an early instance in which the design of the institutional environment determines whether inmates are to be treated as sick or not sick.

In a similar vein, it was argued that large state facilities were superior since, by sheer number of patients, they could provide a better opportunity for homogeneous grouping based on diagnostic classifications. Smaller facilities were an impediment to proper classification in the framework of a disease model. The bigger the hospital, the larger the number of wards; the larger the number of wards, the larger the number of labels which could be used to discriminate subtle differences in the disease process. In grouping the same labels together on the same ward, treatment and cure for the sickness could be provided more efficiently, particularly if science discovered the underlying cause of the disease designated by the label. Obviously, the behavioral choices and life-styles of the members were influenced by whether one was housed in a small or large institution. The design of each dramatically influenced the total life situation of both staff and inmates.

Although the Wisconsin Plan persisted in a few states, such decentralized state-county care plans were relatively uninfluential. In contrast, the prestige and influence of New York State and Massachusetts were pervasive as state after state emulated the New York system enacted by the Act of 1890. This system was to be the dominant influence on national policy for over half a century. Not until the passage of the Community Mental Health Center Construction Act of

1963 was there a really major shift in national policy regarding the general delivery of services for the mentally ill.

In the interim, state hospitals increased in number and expanded in population. Overcrowding continued as institutions grew and grew. Quality of life and quality of treatment continued to deteriorate as discoveries for the causes of mental illness failed to materialize, and mental illness continued to flourish unabated during the first half of this century.

THE PENITENTIARY

In the next section we shall examine the major contemporary influences which have continued to shape the environments of our mental hospitals during the last 25 years. Before turning to this point, however, let us very briefly consider one other major institution whose history is particularly germane in the context of Environmental Design – the penitentiary.

With the example of the penitentiary, we find one of the most deliberate and premeditated attempts to influence and control behavior through the mechanism of institutional design. An excellent account of the history of such facilities is provided in detail by Rothman (1971). For present purposes, only the most salient points specifically relating to Environmental Design can be considered. However, a full understanding of the "discovery" of penitentiaries cannot be separated from the very significant social attitudes toward crime during the late 1700s and early 1800s. For a more in-depth overview, the reader is referred to Rothman (1973). Sommer's (1974) discussion of "models and fads in prison design" is of particular contemporary interest.

Probably nowhere is there a more precise statement of the assumed effects of design on behavior than in two competing models of penitentiary construction during the nineteenth century as represented in New York and Pennsylvania. Each of these states advocated specific design features in the construction of penitentiaries with the avowed purpose of affecting specific behaviors. The superiority of one system over the other is less important than the recognition that here, perhaps for the first time, opposing public policies generated different design criteria to bring about behavior change in a target population of the general society. Now ". . . prison architecture and arrangement became the central concern of reformers of the period. Unlike their predecessors, they turned all their attention inward to the divisions of time and space within the institution. The layout of cells, the methods of labor, and the manner of eating and sleeping within the penitentiary were the crucial issues" (Rothman, 1971, p. 83).

In Pennsylvania, these concerns were translated into an organizational structure of separate care for individual inmates. This "Pennsylvania Model" provided the ultimate extreme in isolating the inmate from both society and other inmates. For the entire length of their sentence, inmates were isolated in solitary confinement. The blueprint of the environment was such that prisoners ate alone, worked alone, and slept alone in a single cell for the duration of their stay. This planned environment was predicated on the assumption that deviant behaviors had been learned in the context of a faulty upbringing. The vices learned during early life could only be undone through reeducation and rehabilitation in a well-ordered institution. Thus "the duty of the penitentiary was to separate the offender from all contact with corruption, both within and without its walls" (Rothman, 1971, p. 83; emphasis in original). Hence, the most complete isolation possible was the behavioral objective of the Pennsylvania system. The physical design of the institution produced an environment that precluded the contamination of one inmate by another.

In contrast the "Auburn Model," or congregate system, developed in New York. This arrangement also physically isolated the inmates at night, but during the day they labored together in the prison workshops and ate in common mess halls. Socialization and conversation, however, were not permitted for the same reasons espoused by the Pennsylvania Plan. In terms of environmental design, however, the main point is that architecturally the Pennsylvania and Auburn systems were markedly different. Both attempted to design environments compatible with the goals of the respective conflicting models. The Auburn Plan, by virtue of its congregate design, was cheaper to build and operate.   The Pennsylvania Plan, although admittedly more expensive, was defended as being more efficient in long-term rehabilitation effectiveness. Additionally, confinement in isolated cells permitted more individualized treatment of inmates. That is, "these arrangements would permit officials to treat prisoners as individuals, rewarding some with more frequent visitors and books for good behavior, depriving recalcitrant others of the privileges" (Rothman, 1971, p. 86; emphasis added). Designing a single cell, total living environment was also viewed as efficient in terms of surveillance since it would be unnecessary to transport inmates back and forth to common eating and exercise areas. In such total, self-contained, and isolated living conditions, "the prisoner began the process of reform . . ." in which his conscience would compel him "to reflect on the errors of his ways" and "after a period of total isolation, without companions, books, or tools, officials would allow the inmate to work in his cell . . . labor would not become an oppressive tool for punishment, but a welcome diversion, a delight, not a burden" (Rothman, 1971, p. 85-86). While the motives of the reformers were pure, note the similarity of such isolation procedures to the so-called brainwashing techniques of the Korean War period (Dean, 1954; Hebb, 1961; McClure, 1971). Both have in common the design of environments which systematically seek to influence behavior. The procedures are the same, only the goals and values are different. We will have more to say regarding this point later in our discussion of the START Program in Missouri.

The Auburn and Pennsylvania Plans generated a strong controversy over the years as advocates of the two camps sought to influence the future direction of penitentiary design. Today many of the issues surrounding the opposing views seem like pseudo-problems in the light of more recent court rulings regarding prisoner rights (e.g. Clonce vs

Richardson, 1974). The significance of the controversy in the development of environmental design in closed institutions is, nevertheless, important.

INSTITUTIONAL DESIGN IN 1950

As we examine the conditions of the institutional environments at the midpoint of the century, we find the "hospitalopolis" (Schultberg & Baker, 1969) reaching its zenith. By 1950, facilities serving New York City, for example, became huge. Pilgrim State Hospital, the largest in the world, had over 10,000 patients, and Central Islip State Hospital had over 7,000 patients. They were located within ten miles of one another on nearby Long Island. But the needs of the greater New York metropolitan area would only continue to escalate. Soon Pilgrim would have over 15,000 patients and Central Islip over 10,000.

An analysis of these huge institutions in the context of environmental design cannot be separated from the three major behavioral control strategies adopted by the institutions – psychosurgery, drug control, and behavior modification. It is with great practical and theoretical frustration that we find ourselves referring to these three social influences in the same sentence. Certainly it is our ethical belief and moral conviction that behavior modification is but one of many manifestations of a psychology of behavior influence (Krasner & Ullmann, 1973), with psychosurgery, hypnosis, sensory deprivation, and drugs being but a few of many other influences. Thus ". . . behavior modification refers to a very specific type of behavior influence" (Krasner and Ullmann, 1965, p. 2). However, this chapter is not the place to pursue this distinction further. Nor can the topic of ethics be dealt with generally. These problems are discussed elsewhere in this volume. It is necessary, however, to deal with the empirical fact that various procedures, including aversive control, have been subsumed under the generic term "behavior modification," particularly in institutional settings. It is also true that the courts have not usually discriminated among the various procedures whose end result is the modification of behavior, however accomplished (e.g. Knecht vs Gilman, 1973). Drug companies have added to the confusion even further with statements like "Prolixin Decanoate (R) . . . is a highly potent behavior modifier with a markedly extended duration of effect" (Squibb, 1977). It is equally important that the experimental foundation supporting the "appropriate" use of aversive procedures was derived from a literature generated largely by behavior therapists. Aversion Therapy and Behavior Disorders by Rachman and Teasdale (1969) is a case in point.

Unfortunately (depending on one's values), early and recent works have also continued to stress control as a salient aspect of behavior modification, even within the discipline. For example, Ulrich, Stachnik, and Mabry's Control of Human Behavior, Volume I (1966) and Volume II (1970) were influential publications. London's Behavior Control (1969) was significant in reducing behavior modification to a generic term meaning almost anything. Therefore, if we are to understand the design of environments in institutions during the last 25 years, it is necessary to place these social influences in historical and cultural context. After an examination of psychosurgery, drug control, and behavior modification, we will consider two topics in the contemporary design of institutional environments unrelated to treatment – the architectural influence of Humphry Osmond, and the effects of an administrative innovation in hospital organization called unitization.

On Drugs and Psychosurgery

Simply the magnitude of huge hospitals of the postwar period might alone have precipitated the necessity for noninstitutional alternatives except for the profound discovery of drug control and psychosurgery. While prefrontal lobotomies had been in vogue as a treatment for the more aberrant patients, its usage was limited compared to drug control. Psychiatric treatment by psychosurgery began in general use in 1935; approximately 5,000 such operations were performed during the next 15 years (K. Goldstein, 1950). Its popularity declined with the increase in the use of psychotropic drugs during the mid-1950s. However, such procedures are not without contemporary proponents (Mark & Ervin, 1970; Mark, 1974). Although the technique may be more sophisticated (e.g. laser beam surgery), the principle remains the same – the alteration of behavior via the destruction of brain cells.

It is, at the very least, questionable as to whether the large institutions of the 1950s and 1960s would have been able to maintain adequate administrative control over such large populations in the absence of drug control capability. It certainly is likely that in their absence psychosurgery and other coercive controls would have seen more, not less, usage. Let us consider briefly the influence of drugs on the design of institutional environments.

Although phenothiazines were synthesized by August Bernthesen in 1883, it was not until 1950 that chlorpromazine was synthesized by a French drug firm, Rhone-Poulence, and found to have a specific psychotropic effect. Rhone-Poulence marketed the drug in Europe in 1952 under the name Largactil (Swazey, 1974). Smith, Kline, and French patented the compound under the trade name Thorazine and began marketing it in the United States in 1954. Two million patients received the drug within eight months of its introduction in the United States. As with other innovations, New York again led the way. "In January, 1955, under the aegis of Henry Brill, M.D., assistant commissioner of mental hygiene, New York became the first state to adopt general use of chlorpromazine and reserpine in its public hospitals" (Hospital and Community Psychiatry, 1976, p. 505). Drug control of large masses of institutional patients had become a reality.

It is not our purpose to impune the motives of those who would use drugs as part of an ongoing active program of treatment intervention, particularly in private therapy where a patient is an active participant in the treatment process. Nor do we fail to recognize that drug therapy permitted the release and/or out-patient maintenance of large numbers of patients who otherwise would have been institutionalized. It is, nonetheless, an empirical fact that drugs have served a maintenance function in the custodial care of institutional populations. Although touted as a more humane alternative to such treatments as electro-shock, they still produced the proverbial "walking zombie." "The new tranquilizing drugs have introduced a new regime in the management of patients in mental hospitals. The drugs calm the patients without putting them to sleep. They are particularly effective in quieting elderly psychotics. . . " (Himwich, 1955, p. 3).

Drug therapy may have muted the profound deprivation inherent in the huge hospitals during the 1950s, but it equally served the needs of the institution and indirectly served to perpetuate their survival and very existence. Largely through the assistance of drugs, circumstances permitted the design of institutional environments which were inade-quate in almost every way possible. Equally important historically is the fact that the effectiveness of psychotropic drugs in ameliorating psychotic symptoms established more firmly than ever the viability of the medical model as the prevailing influence on institutional care and design. Their role historically in promoting the public and professional acceptance of mental illness as a disease is probably second in importance only to the identification of syphilis as a cause of general paralysis.

While drug therapy did make possible the treatment of many clients in noninstitutional settings, it was equally true and significant that those who remained institutionalized were extremely chronic or "treatment resistant" cases. A basic dichotomy arose between those patients having a good prognosis and maintained in public and/or private out-patient facilities, and those suffering from a less favorable prognosis and relegated to indefinite institutional care. Such institu-tional treatment was tantamount to drug therapy and custodial care. By the late 1950s and early 1960s it was extremely difficult to find a drug-free institutional patient.   Since drug therapy was by definition therapeutic, its use became an end in itself and indirectly contributed to the custodial design of institutions.

This is not to say that other treatment modalities were not available. Occupational therapy classes were initiated at Central Islip State Hospital as early as 1913. Art therapy was originated in England by Adrian Hill and introduced in this country by Margaret Naumbury in the 1940s (Hill, 1945). We note the documented use of music therapy in the early 1900s (van de Wall, 1924). Vocational rehabilitation therapy was established by Congressional action in 1920 and has been an active influence since (Anthony, 1976). Most of these activities are available at most progressive hospitals.

The key word in the above paragraph regarding the relationship of these disciplines to patients is the word "available." To argue that patients did not theoretically have available these services is question-able.   That all patients did not actually receive such services is a matter of statistical record. Ironically, the patients who needed broadly based attention the most typically got the least. That is, patients who were extremely regressed, assaultive, noisy, hallucinatory, delusional, etc. were the ones least likely to be referred for such services. Even if referred, they were unlikely to be tolerated in such programs since their behaviors were disruptive to program goals.

This does not mean that these disciplines were ineffective in contributing to the care of the limited number of patients they did serve. At issue is the circularity of the influence process in the design of treatment environments. When a patient behaves in ways that are troublesome or disruptive, this reinforces the staff's perception of the patient as severely ill, too sick in fact to be sent off the ward to the few programs that are available. If not provided active treatment, the patient remains on the ward and becomes even more troublesome and/or regressed. The accelerating regression proves further the point that the patient is truly ill and unable to profit from ancillary off-ward treatment programs. The patient is confined more and more to a closed ward.   If his on-ward behavior becomes disruptive enough, his medication regime is reevaluated. If his medication is high enough, his behavior will be controlled, but he is now not responsive to activities that are made available to him ad lib. The spiral continues. It is thus the case that one frequently observes the same "model" patients going to the same activities month after month, year after year. Meanwhile, the severely regressed and heavily sedated patient remains cloistered on the ward inasmuch as he is now a truly disturbed person.

At least part of the problem relates to the issue raised earlier regarding the question of who really benefits from the institutions. We, and probably many others, have observed programs within institutions which have themselves become social institutions. Thus, one sees programs which justify their existence and value by touting statistics based, for example, on numbers of patient-contacts − not patients contacted.   Such programs can demonstrate impressively high but misleading results. Fifty patient contacts per week per ward for ten patients is not the same as 50 different patients cared for ward-wide. That one cannot find in our institutions the same few patients engaged in the same few activities year after year while others are virtually ignored is a denial of reality. Bockhoven's conclusion that our institutions are largely custodial cannot seriously be questioned. "Over 99 percent of the mentally ill in America receive nothing more than custodial care of a low standard" (Bockhoven 1972, p. 112). The evidence is so obvious and overwhelming that even the courts have concurred as in the recent Willowbrook (New York) consent decree.

It is against this background that John F. Kennedy in 1963 called for a "bold new approach" in meeting the needs of the 1,500,000 mentally ill and retarded patients housed in state hospitals across the country: "Most of them are confined and compressed within antiquated, vastly overcrowded, chains of custodial state institutions" (Kennedy, 1963). In 1961 the Joint Commission on Mental Illness and Health issued a report entitled Action for Mental Health. This report, in conjunction with Presidential influence, ultimately resulted in the congressional legislation creating Community Mental Health Centers. The relationship of those centers to environmental design is discussed elsewhere in this volume (see chap. 7) and will not be considered here. It is important to point out, however, that through their foundation national attention was focused on the plight of institutions generally. As a result, they, too, benefited from increased federal funding, such as Hospital Improvement Program (HIP) grants (Lawson et al., 1971). It was in the framework of this "bold new approach" that innovative programs were implemented during the mid-1960s. Chronologically, it was also the case that institutional behaviorally based programs were being developed which could influence significantly the environmental design of institutions. It is to this topic that we now turn in our analysis of institutional environmental design.

Behavior Modification Programs

In spite of the pervasive influence of the medical model, modest accomplishments were being made in exploring psychological approaches to abnormal behavior. Numerous empirical studies had demonstrated very clearly that learning principles derived from the animal laboratory were applicable to the mentally ill in therapeutic settings (Ayllon & Michael, 1959; Fuller, 1949; Hutchinson & Azrin, 1961; Issac, Thomas & Goldiamond, 1960; and Lindsley, 1960). However, it was not until the introduction of such techniques on a ward-wide basis by Atthowe & Krasner (1968), Ayllon & Azrin (1965), and Schaefer & Martin (1966) that such procedures significantly influenced the design of environments in institutions.   An evaluation of the therapeutic effectiveness of such programs is not our intent. Rather, we will consider token economies as an example of "planned environments" (Krasner and Krasner, 1973) and their influence on the planning process.

While we need not review the technological aspects of token economies in detail, it is well that we consider the five basic features of such programs as enumerated by Krasner & Krasner (1973). The first essential characteristic of token economy programs is that of systematic observation. It is necessary to identify the specific behaviors of the patients for whom the program is intended and the consequences of those behaviors as they exist in the institutional environment. Next the designation of desirable versus undesirable behaviors must be determined. Only those behaviors recognized as desirable will be reinforced (e.g. making a bed, dressing oneself, etc.). The third element is to determine what objects or events that exist in the institutional environment may be considered valuable, "the good things in life" (Krasner, 1968) – those events which may be used as back-up reinforcers for each individual (e.g. trips, a favorite food, a pass, etc.). A fourth element is identification of the medium of exchange, an element which joins elements two and three. The token itself, whether a plastic disc, a stamp, or a check on a chart, stands for the reinforcing item to be earned. The comprehension of this element by the patient is essential to the success of the token economy program. It must be understood that the token itself represents buying power for desirable events or items, just as our system of payment with coins and bills represents our ability to purchase things within the outside society. It is then necessary to be aware of the fifth and final element, the exchange rules. Here the patient may see the actual value of the token as a unit of exchange. If these five basic elements are present in a well-designed and well-supervised program, token economies will result in predictable behaviors among the participants which are functionally related to the design components of the program.

That such token economy programs can work technologically in controlled settings can hardly be doubted. Since the publication of the Anna State results (Ayllon & Azrin, 1965), literally hundreds of successful token economy programs have been developed. Within only three years of the Ayllon & Azrin report, Krasner & Atthowe (1971) noted that 110 programs were underway in at least four countries. Clearly, token economy programs per se have been enormously successful. Considerably less convincing, however, are the data on the long-term positive influence of such programs on the design and planning of institutions themselves. All too often, token economy programs seem to be superimposed on an already existing structure for purposes which serve the needs and interests of the institution and of society, but not necessarily those of the patient. For example, it is often the case historically that token economies have been established and economically supported on the so-called chronic back wards.

Indeed, it is as if such programs were tolerated only because all other treatment modalities had been tried and had failed. It was in the atmosphere of "nothing to lose and everything to gain" that behavior modifiers, armed with their tokens, were permitted access to such wards. More often than not, however, such professionals have been employed as consultants to ply their technological skills in clearly circumscribed situations with little or no input into the overall design of the hospital-wide treatment environment. As such, token programs are too often seen functionally, if not theoretically, by administrators as a technique which can be applied in specific situations when and where necessary or needed. Importantly, therefore, token economy programs are frequently utilized as an isolated technique which may or may not reflect the prevailing attitudes and values of the staff and administrators toward mental illness per se. Token economy programs can themselves, under such conditions, become token treatment offered in the name of care (see Kazdin, 1977b).

Throughout this chapter it has been noted that the issue of who really benefits from the existence of the institution must be continually monitored. The present topic is no exception. If token economy programs are but part of a patient control strategy which simply makes it easier for the institution to exist peacefully, we should question the influences affecting overall institutional design. Just as Winett & Winkler (1972) were very critical of token programs used inappropriately to control questionable target behaviors in the public school classroom, we too should be alert to their misuse in institutional settings. Hence, if token programs are used in isolation to manage the behavior of persons who don't belong in an institution in the first place, they are clearly being misused in the design of human living environments. By so doing, we contribute to the perpetuation of an institution whose very basis of existence should be seriously reevaluated. Krasner (1976) has made the point quite forcefully:

> . . . to the extent that we were successful in developing a token economy program on a hospital ward, we were helping maintain a social institution, the mental hospital, that in its current form, was no longer desirable in our society. We decided that based on our own value system, we would not develop further token economy programs in mental hospitals. (P. 635)

The design and implementation of token economies can profoundly influence the environment, even the back wards of state hospitals. But their very effectiveness is precisely a source of ethical conflicts for the professional. Suffice it to point out that token economy programs "are no more than a facet of an approach to human behavior . . ." (Krasner & Krasner, 1973, p.351). If this one facet of the more broadly based environmental model is used out of context, it is no better, or no worse, than any other control procedure in the management of institutional masses. It is, perhaps, this unfortunate potential of abuse that has resulted in behavior modification techniques being viewed unfavorably as mind control techniques by laymen and professionals alike. London's (1969) work has been particularly influential in essentially equating "conditioning" with everything from psychosurgery to radioactive brain implants. All are seen as "tools of behavior control, the arsenal of modern psychology" (London, 1969). That such procedures can influence behavior is obvious, and in the context of closed institutions the issue is all the more critical. Token programs, if they operate isolated from a more broadly conceived system of environmental design and institutional-wide planning, could, in fact, be harmful, as Richards (1975) notes:

> It is even possible that token economies in mental hospitals are in the ironic position of being 'dangerous' — dangerous in the sense that, if they counteract the effects of institutionalization, they serve to support and justify a bad system when it would be preferable to adopt a new one. (P. 619)

It is likely that more and more professionals will become less and less willing to develop behavioral programs in the absence of a wider arena of influence in hospital design and planning generally. Certainly this issue is of critical importance in the training of environmental designers.

Well designed token economy programs supervised by competent professionals can exhibit a model living environment in keeping with the values of the designers. Effectiveness, at least in restricted environments such as hospital wards, can be demonstrated. However, such programs never operated in a social vacuum and the successful integration of the five elements of such programs as discussed above is subject to many influences. Typically, the more autonomous the environment, the greater the likelihood of achieving "stimulus control."

Federally funded demonstration projects, for example, are often exempt from the more confining rules and regulations of the overall institutional setting. The success of such programs under artificial conditions aptly shows the viability of the operant model under restricted conditions wherein adequate stimulus control is achieved. But the usual institutional setting does not often function in such a fashion.

As a result, behavioral programs often become diluted in their rigor and effectiveness in direct proportion to the degree of interaction between the program and the greater institutional culture. In short, unless autonomy is maintained, the program deteriorates. And if the program succeeds in remaining isolated and autonomous, its influence on the institution as a social system is minimal. Thus it is possible to find pockets of excellence on individual wards in hospitals that are otherwise abysmal. The problem is not one of technological capability, at least in limited settings. However, at a practical level, the operant model to date has had limitations in effectively dealing with entire institutional systems (Colman, 1975). If limited success can be attained on a single ward, why is it that this success does not have greater influence on the design of the entire institution? Why is it that these programs serve to help maintain the status quo of the institution rather than helping it evolve into some new, alternative form? Why is it that programs which are successful under the aegis of one designer go into a state of total collapse with a change of leadership? These and many similar questions are discussed fully by Coleman (1971; 1975). Two issues are critical, however, in the context of the present discussion.

First and foremost is our failure as behavior therapists to come to grips with the fact that institutions do not exist simply for the care of patients. Rather, the institution is a "self-perpetuating social system" (Krasner and Atthowe, 1971). In the past, we have not identified the target behavior, nor have we identified the reinforcers maintaining the target behaviors of the institution as a research subject. Nor have we been sufficiently sensitive to the role of the staff and administrators as independent variables. Only recently have we really begun to address the fact that we have been using the "right principles but wrong target" (Bornstein et al., 1975). This is not to say that we have not been painfully aware of some of the problems. Differential reinforcement of staff on a contingent basis is, for example, a goal all accountability-oriented program designers would welcome. Yet it is a fact that institutions are typically staffed by unionized civil servants who have negotiated salary structures through collective bargaining. As a result, local designers have no differential control over salary, time off, discipline, etc. Yet these are the very people who provide "direct patient care." Similarly, without exception, token economy programs stress the importance of staff training, but in New York, for example, a "Therapy Aide" need not even have a high school education, nor is there an adequate economic incentive that would foster paraprofessional training. As with other unions, seniority is the critical variable controlling the reinforcers.

Thus, token economy programs are frequently programmed with great rigor by extremely competent designers only to fail because of our inability to incorporate staff reinforcers into the program. Such difficulties led Colman to suggest ". . . that without stronger control over staff, behavior modification programs should not have been begun" (Colman, 1975, p. 417). Although this is probably true, it nonetheless begs the issue. How do we influence the economic and political process which in turn influences the system of staff reinforcers?

The second critical issue associated with the limited influence of operant approachers on institutional design has to do with the insular profile exhibited by the various disciplines. To the extent that behavior modification techniques and procedures are set apart and applied independently of other disciplines, they probably will be a long-term social failure. We teach students, for example, that the controlled environment of the Skinner Box sets the occasion for reinforcement by making certain behaviors more or less likely to occur. We appreciate the architectural design features of the Skinner Box but often fail to address problems arising from the interaction of operant behavior and the design of the Skinner Box in the natural environments, i.e. institutions. Indeed, it is as if many behavioral programs were developed in spite of architectural design considerations rather than in concert with and/or in response to such.

The situation is changing, however, as the catalyst for institutional change is seen more and more to be interdisciplinary cooperation. A number of disciplines are now coalescing to form a broadly based foundation for Environmental Design (as noted in chapter 1). Environmental Design as a body of knowledge and as an approach is, thus, seen to be the focus of institutional structure and function in the future. Token economy programs are but one of many facets of overall institutional design. Alone they probably only serve to help maintain a questionable institutional status quo; in concert with other disciplines they provide a planning vehicle for broadly based institutional change — structurally, functionally, and administratively.

Institutional Environmental Design and the Law

In considering the above group of procedures — psychosurgery, drug control, and behavior modification — from the standpoint of the judiciary, we find that, without exception, each has precipitated a variety of court rulings which in effect are attempts to control the controllers. Such legal rulings are very important as influences in the design of institutional treatment environments. While practitioners are being sued by patients demanding a "right to treatment" (Donaldson v. O'Connor, 1974; Wyatt v. Stickney, 1974), still others have sued to halt the treatment being provided (Clonce v. Richardson, 1974).

It is a mistake to assume that recent legal decisions affect only the more flagrant cases of maltreatment or malpractice. Rather, such rulings permeate almost every aspect of institutional design and treatment. The courts have increasingly determined who will be provided institutional care, the characteristics of the environment within which treatment will be accomplished, and the nature of the treatment provided therein.   Thus, "milieu therapy" (Cumming & Cumming, 1967) has been criticized when used as a veiled cover-up for custodial care (Morales v. Turman, 1974).   Group therapy is similarly judged insufficient treatment unless one has an individual treatment program as well (Donaldson v. Turman, 1974).   Inappropriate use of or indefinite maintenance on drugs, as has probably been the case in the past, has drawn the particular attention of the courts: "medication shall not be used as punishment, for the convenience of staff, as a substitute for a program, or in quantities that interfere with the patient's treatment program" (Wyatt v. Stickney, 1974; emphasis added). Thus drug therapy alone is now insufficient treatment. Aversive behavior control procedures have also been subjected to judicial review. Particularly questionable programs have drawn much public attention, such as the use of paralytic drugs at Vaccaville Prison in California (Mackey v. Procunier, 1973).

These types of court decisions involving the more controversial procedures are welcomed by most behavioral scientists as obviously being needed to curb the excesses of overzealous practitioners. However, equally important, but apparently less obvious to behavior modifiers, is the influence of these decisions on traditional programs, e.g. token economies. The Wyatt v. Stickney (1974) and Morales v. Turman (1974) decisions are particularly germane to token programs. Backup reinforcers that have been used historically in reputable programs are defined as rights by these two judgments. Thus, the manipulation of sleeping quarters, meals, television, etc., as in the Patton State (California) Program (Schaefer & Martin, 1966), could be duplicated today only with misgivings. While the Patton State project was an acceptable program (by our values), functionally it is lumped together with the same procedures employed by less acceptable programs (by our values) such as START (Special Training and Rehabilitative Treatment). Interestingly, the goals, principles, and procedures in START were essentially no different than those vigorously advocated by proponents of the Pennsylvania Penitentiary Model discussed earlier. Aversive and/or coercive control are obviously not new procedures developed by contemporary behaviorists. Only society's values have changed.

Values aside, the point is that the Clonce v. Richardson (1974) decision emanating from START equally affects the design of other planned environments. Certain basics — food, clothing, adequate bedding, visitation, and privacy, among others — are a right and not a privilege to be earned. Even more fundamental is the basic element of work in the token economy via which one earns privileges in the first place. Particularly as a result of Souder v. Brennan (1973) and Wyatt v. Stickney (1974), the variety of meaningful work opportunities available to patients or inmates has been severely curtailed. Consequently, a patient may earn tokens for therapeutic work tasks such as making one's bed, but specifically cannot perform any work task, therapeutic or not, if it involves institutional maintenance or operation. Further, if he volunteers for such work for pay, he must receive the minimum wage. (In our own experience, this has resulted in patients competing with union employees for jobs, thereby creating still further problems.) The fact that institutions have abused patients through enforced work is obvious and needs no comment. It should also be obvious, however, that blanket work restrictions inhibit the potentially therapeutic value of vocational skills training efforts which are often an integral part of token programs.

It is beyond the purpose of this chapter to deal with the potential long-term implications of various court rulings. Excellent discussions on the topic are provided elsewhere (Goldiamond, 1974; Martin, 1975; Schwitzgebel, 1971; Wexler, 1973). The above examples should make clear, however, that until very recently, "Behavior modifiers have for some time apparently had their collective head in the sand with respect to the public acceptability of their therapeutic practices" (Bornstein, et al., 1975, p. 64). This would seem to indicate that as professionals we have to date failed to heed Krasner's admonition that "It is the psychologist-researcher who should undertake the task of contact with the public rather than leaving it to the sensationalists and popularizers" (Krasner, 1964, p. 203). Consequently, scandalous practices and procedures, such as those revealed at Sunland Training Center in Florida (Whited & Kronlolz, 1972; Pothier, 1972), continue to represent for the public the nefarious lengths to which people will go in the name of behavior modification if unchecked. In terms of public opinion, it is a moot issue that the personnel and not the procedures were ultimately judged to be the source of abuse. Our practical concern is that public sentiment influences lawmakers, and lawmakers write state statutes governing the provision of psychological services, especially in institutions. Unless academic programs assume some responsibility for training clinicians in the context of broader social and environmental issues, it is quite likely that we shall produce behavior therapists who are competent and skillful practitioners, but who will have no place to ply their skills. Indeed, ". . . behavior modifiers seem to be busy constructing token economies unaware that legal developments may soon call for their demolition" (Wexler, 1973, p. 23).

Token economy programs are only the beginning. Other behavior modification programs, however virtuous in their intent, have themselves, or in conjunction with other control procedures, precipitated a variety of recent court rulings. In the context of Environmental Design, they cannot be ignored, nor should they be. The point is that "The behavior modifier, if he so desires, can step into the relatively untried role of changing social institutions, but to do so he must be trained appropriately . . ." (Krasner, 1969, p. 542; emphasis added).

Humphry Osmond

A consideration of Osmond's (1957, 1959, 1966) views are to be prefaced with the observation that such views are not being presented as superior design principles based on empirical evaluation. Indeed, as Osmond himself has noted, the "circular building" is only one of many design options available to the hospital planner. However, Osmond's collaborative work with the architect-planner Izumi is reminiscent of the Kirkbride-Sloan influence, and their work is the exact opposite of the "linear impartiality" of the Kirkbride era. Their views are illustrative of an alternative conceptualization of hospital design and complement our earlier discussion of the Kirkbride Plan.

Osmond's formulations are derived largely from the zoological studies of Hediger (1950, 1955). "The virtue of this method is that it starts with a careful inspection of the needs of the confined; for the mentally ill these needs can only be discovered by an analysis of the way in which they experience their surroundings and their own person" (Osmond, 1959, p. 29). For Osmond, such an analysis should address three major but overlapping areas of patient needs.

1) Institutions have a potential for exacerbating perceptual disturbances. By their very size, huge dayrooms and long corridors force changes in one's visual perception of his immediate environment. In comparison to previous home environments, one's perception of his "personal space" (Sommer, 1969) is dramatically altered with institutionalization. Similarly, architectural design can influence one's auditory sensations through "disturbing echos and auditory peculiarities" which can and should be eliminated by appropriate design. In the same way, institutionalization can promote disturbances in tactile perceptions through monotonous textures in clothing and surroundings. Coarse institutional "uniforms," smooth plastic covered furniture, ubiquitous marble floors, and room after room of smoothly surfaced plastered walls painted in monotonous "institutional green," have obviously contributed to institutional deprivation. (It is interesting to note that tablecloths, quality linen, and personal clothing were standard fare at the York Retreat discussed earlier.)

In the same vein, Osmond suggests that institutional design can influence one's olfactory senses with such basic things as the efficiency of the ventilation system in kitchens and toilets. In short, visual, perceptual, tactile, and olfactory "hallucinations" may be precipitated by the design features of the institution itself. There is certainly a dearth of studies in the sensory deprivation literature that argue for increased perceptual sensitivities in all modalities following isolation and/or deprivation (Zubek, 1969). It has been argued elsewhere (McClure, 1971) that sensory deprivation phenomena exist along a continuum from the extreme of solitary isolation and confinement to the "institutional deprivation" of hospitals and prisons. That confinement in institutions influences perceptual distortions, either by design or default, can hardly be doubted. A conscious attempt to minimize such influences is a major design component for Osmond.

2. Osmond's analysis of patient needs reveals a second major factor which psychiatric design can either foster or impede. This has to do with "changes in mood." Under stress, clients may or may not desire privacy or social interaction. The physical design of the environment may enforce or deny group interaction totally independently of the patient's transient needs or preferences. Clearly, institutional environments should permit "normal mood swings" as do home environments. Yet the opportunity for privacy has been virtually nonexistent in mental hospitals.

3. A third area of concern focuses on the way the institutional environment brings about what Osmond calls changes in thinking. Particularly in geriatric populations, a poorly designed environment can accelerate a decline in the clarity of the thinking processes associated with time, place, and other memory-related factors. Thus, the interior design of the institution should include such things as clocks, mirrors, personal lockers, clearly labeled rooms, etc.

In considering collectively these three major areas of patient needs, Osmond has developed design criteria based on what he refers to as sociofugality and sociopetality. The former is defined as ". . . a design which prevents or discourages the formation of stable human relationships . . . Sociopetality is that quality which encourages, fosters, and even enforces the development of stable personal relationships such as are found in small, face-to-face groups" (Osmond, 1959, p. 28).

When these design principles are applied to the huge hospitals of the 1950s, we find that they are usually sociofugal in nature. Long corridors flanked by massive dormitories and large dayrooms are not conducive to the establishment and maintenance of ordinary social relationships. In the natural community, patients ". . . don't sleep in groups of thirty and forty. They don't commonly eat in huge, garish restaurants or sit about with seventy or eighty . . ." patients in dayrooms (Osmond, 1957, p. 28).

Osmond and Izumi propose that their circular building design promotes sociopetality in institutional living. Although linear corridor construction is as much as 15 percent cheaper, they suggest that such buildings are sociofugal in nature and are counterproductive to the growth and retention of normal interpersonal relationships. Sociofugal structures may admittedly be more administratively and economically efficient, but they encourage social isolation, overcrowding, and monotony, while precluding patient privacy and impeding a definition of one's personal space and territoriality.

Osmond's position is predicated on the assumption that "structure will determine function unless function determines structure. The architect's task is to provide a structural expression of the functional requirements which have been communicated to him by his client" (1957, p. 23). In terms of Environmental Design, the "client" in the design of the state institution is obviously the state. Unlike other consumer/provider contracts, the confined mental patient historically has had no role in the design of the institution of which he is a major part. Rather, design goals have been articulated to the architect by the client, e.g. state government, whose design criteria has been motivated by political and economic factors. Little attention was given to therapeutic design criteria during the hospital boom of the first half of this century. Psychiatrists and psychologists seldom contributed to early design decisions. It has been as if the physical structure of the institution were a neutral factor in treatment, thereby making architectural planning a topic of concern only for bureaucrats trained in fiscal matters and their architectural counterparts. "Lowest bid construction" coupled with "volume purchasing" of monotonous interior furnishings produced the giant linear corridor hospitals discussed earlier.

Osmond's argument that hospital design should be determined on the basis of function is quite different from traditional bureaucratic thinking. For one thing, who and what defines function? Perhaps for the first time, the "who" includes the input of the behavioral scientist in a meaningful way; and the "what" defining function may be the behavior of the client. That this has not been the case to date hardly needs documentation. Institutions have interchanged highly different patient populations over the years in much the same way one interchanges inventory in a multipurpose warehouse. The same structure which has housed tubercular patients in one era, houses autistics today, and geriatric patients tomorrow. But the form and the structure remain transfixed in time.

Historically, it is difficult to separate the fiscal and political influences from the social and environmental influences of the atmosphere and subculture of the institution. After all, political decisions in the face of fiscal restraints produced the huge buildings of a 1,000 or more beds. These structures were obviously thought to be the most economical. A large centralized gymnasium was seen as more efficient than multiple smaller symnasiums in each building. The same was true of rehabilitation facilities, music centers, and services generally.

We see institutions which, by their very size, became large social systems themselves. These social systems struggled with the same issue of centralized versus decentralized control in much the same way the states had earlier. Institutions became subsystems of the larger state systems. As both systems grew, the state administration grew more detached from the scattered institutions, and the administrations of the institutions became more divorced from the direct care of patients in the large and scattered buildings throughout the hospital grounds. The superintendent had, in effect, become the political head of a small "city," sometimes exceeding a combined population of 20,000 patients and staff. History could not produce a model more extremely opposite of both Kirkbride the physician and Kirkbride the designer. No longer were diverse resources and services provided within the confines of a 250 bed self-contained and largely self-sufficient therapeutic community.

In contrast to such a centralized hospital organizational system, as described above, more recent innovation in the "administrative design" of the giant institutions is provided by the "unitized" reorganization of such facilities (Kiger, 1972; Schultzburg & Baker, 1969). Utilization ". . . divides the large hospitals into smaller treatment units which relate to specific geographic areas and are responsible for all the people in them who need care . . . Unitization . . . promotes more individual attention for patients in the hospital" (Rockefeller & Miller, 1970). Each unitized treatment center cares for approximately 300 to 500 in-patients utilizing "interdisciplinary treatment teams" physically based in the individual units, not in centralized departments. In principle, this organizational structure should provide for increased accountability and better patient care. In practice, it must be kept in mind that the care provided under the unitized model still occurs in the same physical environment of the same buildings by the same indigenous personnel.

In the context of environmental design, probably the most interesting aspect of unitization of state hospitals is not what the revised system does for chronic in-patients, but rather the effects of such procedures on the new acute admissions. With the rediscovery of community-based geographical catchment areas, increased attention has been focused on out-patient services and/or shorter length of stays when in-patient care is required. In effect, chronicity is impeded by making criteria for admission more stringent and by utilization and review analyses of average length of stays. Perhaps not so coincidentally is the fact that third party payment is most easily obtained during the early stages of acute care, with substantially less reimbursement for the custodial care of a chronic patient. We again see the interaction of economic and administrative factors with therapeutic concern. Most importantly, we find again the pendulum swinging away from the states in the direction of local community responsibility for mental health. This current trend is, of course, in tandem with the national community mental health care center movement as discussed in chapter 7.

With unitization we find an effort to dismantle the giant "hospital-opolis" (Schultsburg & Baker, 1969). Many of the huge impersonal buildings which represented a total corruption of the Kirkbride Plan are being remodeled. Partitions that were removed to make room for large dormitories are being replaced to provide private sleeping quarters. Peripheral wings that were added are being razed. Other entire Kirkbride type hospitals are scheduled for demolition as death rates exceed admission rates resulting in a general population decline of chronic patients, and as community based programs continue to contribute to the reduction in the need for in-patient hospitalization.

SUMMARY

Our historical analysis of institutional design shows that structures have most often been built according to what Caplan (1969) aptly describes as a "Maginot Line" approach. It is as if buildings were constructed to last permanently in much the same way as a medieval castle. In fact, the vigor of our past commitment to "hard architecture" (Sommer, 1974), has been inversely related to empirical data regarding the effects of architecture on behavior.

In the future, an empirically derived data base regarding the functional relationships between behavior and design is needed to reduce the degree of de facto design which has been so dominant in the past. While it may be a truism that design affects behavior, we have observed bureaucratic building policies that generally ignore this simple fact. At the same time, the empirical knowledge necessary to evaluate alternative design approaches has, for the most part, been lacking. Certainly, there is every reason to expect that continued research focusing on environmental design in institutional settings will contribute to a more intelligent planning process in the future design of such facilities.

Meanwhile, the failure of huge state hospital structures can, perhaps, best be viewed as an early evolutionary step in the design of environments which have attempted to meet human needs. If such is the case, we may view the Community Mental Health Center, or variants thereof, as a subsequent design effort in the evolutionary process. Their development will probably contribute greatly to the future decline in large hospital populations as they have already done in the past (Stewart et al., 1968). In the view of many, however, it is unclear as to whether or not such facilities can ever completely replace the traditional state hospital (Vail, 1966). Even if we assume the viability of the Community Mental Health Center model, significant Environmental Design questions still remain. Should such a facility, for example, be ". . . associated physically with a general hospital, a public health center, an educational and manpower complex, a multiservice welfare center, and so on?" (Caplan, 1969, p. 323). The point is that such design decisions continue to reflect indirectly our definition of service, i.e., treatment-oriented versus educationally-oriented models, to name but two.

While the empirical data base now being generated may or may not ultimately show the superiority of the Community Mental Health Center model, we cannot ignore the fact that institutions continue to exist not only as mental hospitals but also in the form of prisons, nursing homes, juvenile detention facilities, geriatric centers, etc. What, then, are some of the possible options which can be suggested in the context of environmental design.

One example of a promising tactic would be to adopt in institutional construction a design flexibility analogous to that of school construction based on "open education" models (Silberman, 1973). That is, the interior space of hospital structures could be designed to permit a flexible and changing pattern of usage by the inhabitants of the facility. Interior use of space could then be altered as a function of changing behavioral needs of clients and staff. Appropriate architectural design and construction could permit, for example, the inexpensive removal and replacement of moveable interior walls as space needs change across time.

Caplan (1969) also has suggested the use of less elaborate and less expensive prefabricated mobile building units for public service use. Such short-life structures could be moved about geographically to reflect the changing demographic characteristics and service needs of an area. Similarly, less expensive, but more pleasing interior furnishings could be replaced more frequently.

In essence, we are suggesting that change potential itself is an element of architectural design that should be programmed into institutional environmental design. Unfortunately, public structures are usually constructed in exactly the opposite manner. Although we are a "throw away society" in numerous respects, we seem to construct institutions as permanent and lasting monuments, literally, to their designers.   Such institutions are built to "last forever," they are generally rigid and inflexible in their use of space, and they are provided with long-lasting institutional furnishings. Efforts to change this state of affairs would seem to indicate a need for changing the behaviors of designers themselves – professionals, architects, the public provider, and the recipient client, among others. However, this is not an easy task. As Caplan (1969) has noted, even professionals place high value on job security and stability. These factors, in turn, are based on the security and stability of the institutions of which they are a part. The goal of "working oneself out of a job" may sound admirable clinically; but, in practice, the loss of professional job security has been a major problem in the phasing out of large public hospitals (Stewart, et al, 1968). Similarly, the threatened economic loss to communities associated with large institutions fosters the perpetuation and the permanency of facilities for social and political reasons, independent of client need or therapeutic value.

But whatever form and function institutional environmental design may take, it is unlikely that the environmental factors associated with institutional design will be ignored in the future as much as they have been in the past. In fact, the Joint Commission on the Accreditation of Hospitals has now established standards on matters relating to crowding, privacy, and the aesthetics of interior design. While there presently remains a vast discrepancy between such standards and actual institutional practices, it is encouraging to find that such environmental factors are at least beginning to be related to the criteria affecting the institutional accreditation process.

In arriving at a concluding descriptive summary of the contemporary state of affairs in institutional environmental design, we might best describe the situation as one of an emerging design awareness (Sommer, 1972). This chapter has attempted to further our awareness of present and future influences on the design process by examining in detail some of the historical influences of the past, from the ancient Greeks to modern times. Since the "value of any value is determined by still another value" (Krasner & Ullmann, 1973), our present concern has not been so much an evaluation of the design goals and outcomes as it has been a consideration of the factors influencing the means of arriving at the goal, "good" or "bad."

At the same time, there has been an implicit bias throughout the chapter that design awareness, past and present, is a good thing. Through such awareness, one is afforded a much greater opportunity of participating in the design of future environments. Within this framework, we can simultaneously seek to enhance the humanistic design qualities of institutions while remaining alert to inappropriate design features which might be counterproductive to the client's benefit. With such design awareness, all participants – consumer, advocate, and provider – might become participant observers (Sullivan, 1953; Krasner, 1973) in the design process. Roe (1959) notes that man alone is capable of contributing to the evolution of his own species through an awareness of himself and the world around him. Muller (1955) similarly observes that man is on the threshold of affecting his own evolution through an awareness of techniques of genetic control. And Huxley (1958) has fostered the view that psychosocial evolution is occurring and can be seen as an extension of biological evolution. Colman (1975) makes the point that behavior modification is linked to an evolutionary process. Indeed, man " . . . will now begin to think of how to change his own

behavioral   development   by   <u>designing   his   environment</u>   .   .   ."
(Colman, 1975, p. 412; emphasis in original).

These comments on global or macromolar environmental design are perhaps even more relevant for micromolar design settings, and nowhere is this design awareness more critical than in the relationship between behavior modification and institutional environmental design.

There is an increasing practical and philosophical awareness that specific behavior modification interventions are best conceptualized as but limited instances of a broader process of "behavior influence" (Krasner & Ullmann, 1965; 1973). As such, behavior modification is only one of many influence processes which affects the design of one's environment, either at an individual level or in the context of larger social institutions.

Thus, in addition to behavior modification, an understanding of several other specialty areas are now seen as vitally important if we are to understand more fully the complexity of human behavior as it occurs in its diverse physical settings. Such an interdisciplinary effort draws, therefore, on the resources of both the physical sciences, such as biology and genetics, and the social sciences in general. These disciplines are complemented by contributions from such widely different areas as architecture, law, ethics, ecology, cybernetics, environmental psychology,   and many others. Many disciplines are seen as contributing to the mainstream of a developing area of study that we may refer to as environmental design and one that is characterized by its pedagogical goal of training individuals to design their own environment in ways that are compatible with their own values (Krasner, 1975). Recent developments in psychology and other disciplines suggest that significant gains toward this goal are beginning to be realized. The knowledge derived from such efforts should be especially relevant and beneficial to the process of institutional environmental design.

7 Community Mental Health and Environmental Design*

Abraham M. Jeger

Having surveyed the role of "institutions" in the context of an environmental design framework, we now turn to a newer development in our society, the "community" as the locus of intervention for those deemed "treatment-worthy." Although each chapter in this volume is designed to link research and application in a wide range of fields, this chapter represents perhaps the broadest range of linkages. Virtually every discipline dealing with social and personal intervention procedures, e.g. psychology, psychiatry, social work, law, architecture, education, etc., is ensnarled one way or another with community mental health dealing as it does with social institutions such as the family, school, clinic, legal system, etc. Jeger demonstrates how treatment procedures and goals follow from the broad model of human nature which the practitioners (designers) may hold.

Ed.

When confronted with the task of writing on community mental health and environmental design, two possible approaches came to mind. One approach might attempt to answer the question, "How is community mental health a stream in environmental design?" or, "What does community mental health have to offer environmental design?" An alternative approach would attempt to answer the converse, "What can environmental design offer to community mental health?" The position taken here is that the two approaches are not mutually exclusive, a position which defines the purpose of this chapter.

This chapter proposes that the environmental design model, as developed in this volume, provide community mental health with both a conceptual framework and a data base for community interventions. In developing an environmental design approach to community mental health, the major strategy of this chapter is to review specific programs and point to several trends within the mental health fields that are especially compatible with an environmental design orientation. It will

*The author extends sincere thanks to Robert S. Slotnick for his useful comments on an earlier version of this chapter.

become apparent that many of these compatible trends are from the field of community mental health per se. Thus, this chapter accomplishes for community mental health what the entire volume does for environmental design — it integrates and systematizes an already "evolving" orientation and encourages its further development. Since the present chapter seeks to provide alternatives to current community mental health practice, the background and a critique of "traditional" community mental health need to be presented. This will serve to place the proposed model in historical perspective, a necessary task according to a basic environmental design premise — "new" concepts and movements cannot be understood apart from the social and historical context in which they develop.

BACKGROUND OF COMMUNITY MENTAL HEALTH

In his recent text on the field, Bloom (1977) delineated a series of ten characteristics that serve to identify the concept of community mental health as contrasted with traditional clinical practice. First, as opposed to institutional (i.e., mental hospital) practice, the community provides the practice setting. Second, rather than an individual patient, a total population or community is the target; hence, the term "catchment area" to define a given center's area of responsibility. A third feature concerns the type of service delivered, i.e., offering preventive services rather than just treatment. Continuity of care between the components of a comprehensive system of services constitutes the fourth dimension. The emphasis on indirect services, i.e., consultation, represents the fifth characteristic. A sixth characteristic lies in the area of clinical innovations — brief psychotherapy and crisis intervention. The emphasis on systematic planning for services by considering the demographics of a population, specifying unmet needs, and identifying "high risk" groups represents a seventh characteristic. Utilizing new personpower resources, especially nonprofessional mental health workers, constitutes the eighth dimension. The ninth dimension is defined in terms of the "community control" concept — consumers should play central roles in establishing service priorities and evaluating programs. Finally, the tenth characteristic identifies community mental health as seeking environmental causes of human distress, in contrast to traditional "intrapsychic" emphasis.

It should be indicated that the above listing is presented here to acquaint the reader with the "spirit" of community mental health. It does not imply the successful implementation of all these aspects in all centers. Insofar as the orientation of community mental health is concerned, the ten characteristics noted by Bloom can be seen as reflecting the best intentions of some of its leaders.

As to formal definitions of community mental health, suffice it to note that they run the gamut from a focus on individual treatment (though incorporating community resources for such service) to broader conceptualizations emphasizing prevention, normal growth, and community restructuring (Goldston, 1965). The best operational definition can be obtained by looking at the specific activities undertaken by agencies labeled "community mental health centers." We will be looking at these activities in the following pages against the historical evolution of community mental health centers.

Before proceeding, I wish to call attention to the close relationships between community mental health and the fields of community psychiatry, social psychiatry, clinical psychology, and community psychology. The specific relationships are discussed by Sarason (1974) and Zax & Specter (1974) and are only mentioned here to indicate the existence of several disciplines which influenced each other to varying degrees following World War II.

With the increased demand for psychiatric services during World War II the federal government was prompted into a new role in the mental health field.(1) With the passage of the National Mental Health Act in 1946, which led to the establishment of the National Institute of Mental Health, mental health was to become a target for public policy. The post-World War II era saw increased funds being channeled into psychiatric training as well as growth of the Veterans Administration hospital system.

A decade after the war, Congress passed the Mental Health Study Act (1955) which established the Joint Commission on Mental Illness and Health "to survey the resources and to make recommendations for combating mental illness in the United States." In Action for Mental Health, the final report of the Joint Commission (1961), the following was recommended: intensive care of acute mental illness in community-based clinics, each to serve a population of 50,000; improving care of chronic mental patients by reducing the size of state hospitals; developing after-care and rehabilitation services; and initiating consultation programs to community caregivers in order to educate the public and expand the mental health manpower. The Joint Commission suggested that the federal government bear the financial burden in supporting the recommended mental health programs.

The final report of the Joint Commission was studied extensively by governmental agencies. It led to President Kennedy's message to Congress on a national policy toward mental illness and mental retardation on February 3, 1963. In that historic address, marking the first time in history that a president presented his views on the topic, he called for a "bold new approach" to mental health problems. This approach was to focus on the prevention of mental illness rather than just treatment. For prevention to be achieved, the president called for "the general strengthening of our fundamental community, social welfare, and educational programs which can do much to eliminate or correct the harsh environmental conditions which often are associated with mental retardation and mental illness." This clearly represents a recognition of the broader social context in which human problems are developed and maintained.

The president went on to propose a "new type of health facility" — the "comprehensive community mental health center." He recommended that Congress authorize grants for the construction of such centers in local communities and that additional monies be provided to staff the centers. While he envisioned the community mental health centers as providing an alternative to institutionalization, the president also called for improving conditions in state mental hospitals through inservice training.

The Community Mental Health Centers Act (Public Law 88-164) was passed in October 1963, allocating construction funds, and an amendment followed in 1965 providing staffing grants. To be eligible for federal funding, centers were mandated to provide five "essential" services: inpatient; outpatient; partial hospitalization (i.e., day and night hospitals); emergency care (i.e., 24-hour crisis services); and consultation (i.e., indirect service) and community education (i.e., prevention). In order for a center to be considered "comprehensive" five additional services were required: diagnostic; rehabilitation; precare and aftercare; training; and research and evaluation.

The Community Mental Health Centers Amendments of 1975 (Public Law 94-63) redefined the notion of a comprehensive community mental health center from the five minimum/five optional services to a mandated set of 12 services. They include the five originally established as "essential" plus seven additional services: special services for children (diagnosis, treatment, liaison, and follow-up); special services for the elderly; preinstitutional screening and alternative treatment (as pertains to the courts and other public agencies); follow-up for persons discharged from state mental hospitals; transitional living facilities (i.e., halfway houses); alcoholism services (prevention, treatment and rehabilitation); and drug abuse services (prevention, treatment, and rehabilitation).(2) In addition to expanding the mandated number of services, the 1975 Amendments also obligated centers to allocate two percent of their operating budgets for program evaluation.

The reader will note that no formal definitions of "community," "mental health," and "community mental health" were offered. The reason being that these terms are best operationalized by the activities undertaken by specific agencies labeled "community mental health centers" to fulfill their mandate of delivering "mental health" services to their local "communities." Community generally was defined as constituting a targeted "catchment" area encompassing a population of 75,000-200,000 people. Thus, it was the legislation that defined and redefined community mental health practice. Some of the ramifications of this reality are explored in the following section.

Before delving into the problems that confronted community mental health centers it should be emphasized that the spirit of community mental health as a "movement" is currently being rekindled through President Carter's Commission on Mental Health (1978). The general "community" orientation to treatment and the call for focusing on prevention, both major aspects of community mental health, are said to characterize the so-called "third mental health revolution" (Bellak, 1964; Hobbs, 1964). Whereas the first revolution in mental health is identified with Pinel and the second with Freud, the "community" orientation is not associated with any single individual (Hobbs, 1964). Suffice it to note that when considered in a broader historical context, community mental health is best seen as representing "one of several 'evolutionary' phases of mental health ideology" (Golann & Eisdorfer, 1972, p. xi).

PROBLEMS OF "TRADITIONAL" COMMUNITY MENTAL HEALTH

Since its very inception, community mental health theory and practice has been subject to serious criticism from within and without the mental health fields. The most vigorous and comprehensive attack on the entire community mental health movement was leveled by Nader's study group report on the National Institute of Mental Health entitled The Madness Establishment (Chu & Trotter, 1974). Other critical views are reviewed by Bloom (1973, 1977) and Gottesfeld (1972). The purpose of this section is to discuss the major shortcomings of community mental health as a "bold, new approach." As is made apparent below, the problem areas considered are parallel to most of the ten identifying characteristics of community mental health that were cited earlier. An exposition of the limitations of current community mental health practice serves to identify the challenges that an environmental design model of community mental health will have to meet, if it is to provide a viable alternative.

Most of the criticism against community mental health can be seen as falling into either of two major categories. One challenges the basic goals of community by taking a stand against community treatment (see Bloom 1973, 1977 for a brief overview of such positions) and prevention. A second set of critical views accept the general intent of community mental health but point to the inability of current conceptions and intervention strategies to accomplish these goals. Since environmental design is congruent with the general spirit of community mental health, the concern here is with the latter type of issues.

The view taken here is that the major technical limitations of community mental health are tied to its underlying conceptual framework. Albee (1968) has shown that the model of human problems (e.g., medical, educational) determines the institutions that are developed, which in turn determine the nature of the personpower who will provide the service and the kind of service delivered. From the outset, community mental health centers relied on a "disease" model of human problems and were intended to be dominated by the medical profession. As President Kennedy (1963) stated, "We need a new health facility, one which will return mental health care to the 'mainstream of American medicine, and at the same time upgrade mental health services." Therein lies the inherent contradiction. As it turned out, relying on a medical model proved to be too narrow for a "bold, new approach" to treatment and prevention. Although Kennedy is not to be blamed for this orientation, his recommendation indeed reflects the "professional climate" during which the Community Mental Health Centers Act was passed.

What are some of the specific community mental health practices that resulted from adherence to a medical model? First, as noted by

Chu & Trotter (1974) and Snow & Newton (1976), with the exception of consultation/education, the five "essential" services clearly represent traditional services as derived from a one-to-one clinical (psychotherapy) model. A major consequence of the requirement for the specific five essential services is that often no more than these five were offered. By mandating the same "holy five" (Chu & Trotter, 1974) services across the board, no provisions were made for taking into account the unique needs of particular communities. As a result, populations which have traditionally been denied access to psychiatric care, i.e., the young, aged, poor, alcoholics, drug addicts, and ethnic minorities, continued to be excluded.(3) Related to this specification of mandated services is the specification of a "community" as the population residing within a geographically targeted "catchment" area. By cutting into existing "natural" communities (see Giordano & Giordano, 1976, and later section on ethnicity), not only were existing support systems damaged, but an impediment to voicing service needs was also accomplished. By delineating the required services, the public was offered what psychiatry was "good at." As Chu and Trotter (1974) put it, "Perhaps the most damaging consequence of the disease analogy is that it seriously impedes alternative and innovative service programs" (p. 56).

A major focus of criticism against community mental health concerns its relationships to the state mental hospitals (Chu & Trotter, 1974). Since a major goal of the community mental health centers program was to eventually supplant state hospitals, the fact that resident hospital populations declined (from 452,089 in 1966 to 308,024 in 1971) is cited as evidence for progress in this regard. However, other factors could have been responsible for the decline since community mental health centers cannot take credit for the drop in resident patients from 1955 (a peak of 558,922) to 1966 (452,089). The availability of tranquilizers to allow patients to be treated on an outpatient basis, increased alternative community facilities such as nursing homes and foster care, changes in administrative policies against long-term confinement, and the soaring costs of institutionalization are but some of the factors contributing to "deinstitutionalization" policies.

Granting that community mental health centers may have had a catalytic influence in the declining resident population, their primary effect should have been to reduce admissions to state hospitals by offering a community-based alternative. As Chu and Trotter (1974) noted, with the exception of specific catchment areas, overall admissions and readmissions to state hospitals increased consistently since the establishment of community mental health centers. The shorter stays combined with increased release of long-term patients still resulted in the reduced resident population cited above. To the extent that centers did not develop community support services to permit follow-up and "continuity of care" for discharged chronic state hospital patients, they contributed to the recidivism rates. Indeed many centers used the state hospital as "dumping grounds for the poor and chronically ill" (Chu & Trotter, p. 33). It follows that such practices would contribute to the strain in working relationships between the centers and state hospitals (see Wallis & Katf, 1972).

Issues surrounding deinstitutionalized mental hospital patients represent a major challenge to community mental health. In a provocatively titled paper, "Community Mental Health Myths and the Fate of Former Hospitalized Patients," Kirk and Therrien (1975) identified four myths pertaining to the impact of the community mental health center concept on chronically ill patients: the myths of rehabilitation, reintegration, continuity of care, and monetary savings. Although data pertaining to cost is less clear (see Bloom, 1977; Scull, 1976), the first three myths are difficult to question considering the "revolving door" admission patterns (with readmissions accounting for 64 percent of the 390,000 admissions in 1972) and the large-scale placement of former long-term chronic patients into unsupervised board and care homes that are more custodial in orientation than state hospitals (and deserving of the label "reinstitutionalization"). The state hospitals are being accused by local communities of "dumping" unprepared patients into unprepared communities with no provisions for follow-up services. To the extent that the public media portrays community mental health as being responsible for this dumping (e.g., Duffy, 1977; see also position statement by Jeger and Slotnick, 1978) unless centers direct their attention to the plight of discharged state hospital patients they stand to jeopardize support for the existing clinical and preventive services.

Turning to the only nontraditional service mandated, i.e., consultation as an indirect service and community education as prevention, extreme limitations were apparent. Statistical data available from the National Institute of Mental Health (NIMH) for an average week in January 1970 showed an average of only 6.6 percent of total staff time spent in consultation/education (Taube, 1971). More recent data (Bass, 1974) for February 1973 showed consultation/education services to account for 5.5 percent of total staff time. Of the 5.5 percent, case-oriented consultation received major time (47 percent, as compared with 22 percent for staff development, and 31 percent for program-oriented consultation).

The reason for the relatively low priority given to consultation/education by center staff is, according to Snow and Newton (1976), that it was not intended to be emphasized in the federal legislation despite President Kennedy's call for prevention. Based on an analysis of NIMH's description of the consultation/education service, Snow and Newton concluded that, for the most part, it was a mandate for extending the availability of direct (clinical) services, rather than changing social institutions. This, in turn, is explained by the domination of the community mental health centers program by the medical model, and a focus on indirect services aimed at social problems would represent "the greatest degree of change from a medical entity, in organizational structure and in ideology" (Snow & Newton, 1976, p. 582). This is in line with empirical data obtained by Mazade (1974) which indicates that the type of consultation offered (e.g., case-centered versus program-centered) is related to the organizational affiliation of community mental health centers. That is, case consultation was the likely focus in hospital-affiliated centers, whereas program-centered consultation was emphasized in autonomous, community-based centers.

The conceptual fallacy of viewing the prevention of human problems as a logical extension of the public health model in medicine was elaborated upon by Torrey (1974) in his provocatively titled book, The Death of Psychiatry. Briefly, Torrey has argued that translating broad social problems into disease terms in order to place them in the province of medicine represents the "psychiatrization of social problems," and doing so "makes it more difficult to find real solutions to them" (p. 105). An example of such gross distortion is reflected in Morowitz's (1978) suggestion that mental illness (specifically, depression) is a major cause of poverty and advocates medication and psychotherapy as strategies for dealing with the poor. For a sound conception of prevention to develop, a plea made by Reiff (1975) is deemed necessary — that we "move from the psychological study of social issues to the social study of psychological issues" (p. 194).

Another aspect of community mental health which has been the target of criticism involves the use of nonprofessional personpower. Whereas the incorporation of nonprofessional workers into the mental health system would appear to accomplish the dual purpose of meeting the mental health personpower shortage (e.g., Albee, 1959) as well as providing opportunities for indigenous people to develop human service careers (e.g., Pearl & Riessman, 1965), the emergence of such personnel into the traditionally, professional-dominated mental health arena resulted in unprecedented conflicts.

Chu and Trotter (1974) noted a resistance on the part of the professional community as evidenced by the late development of an organized training program for nonprofessionals within NIMH. It was not until 1971 that the New Careers Training Branch was established, despite the extensive evidence as to the efficacy of nonprofessionals as therapeutic change agents. In centers where nonprofessionals were accepted into the service delivery system, serious problems developed around issues of career advancement, salaries, the nature of their work, and relationships with professionals. According to Bloom (1977), "the most vexing problem regarding mental health personnel is the new type of worker — the so-called paraprofessional" (p. 222). Bloom went on to delineate several major problems involving nonprofessionals. One class of problems centers around their low salaries, low position in the hierarchy, and general lack of a career ladder or lattice. The other major problem, according to Bloom, is a developing "new segregation," whereby black nonprofessionals are assigned to serve black clients, and welfare mothers serve other welfare mothers, with the white professionals serving middle-class clients (see later section on ethnicity and mental health).

Professional-nonprofessional conflicts around such issues as decision making power, racial discrimination, and community control were seen as integral components of the crisis that resulted in the shutdown of the "model" Lincoln Community Mental Health Center in the Bronx Borough of New York City.(4) While the particular consequences surrounding the Lincoln experience may have been extreme, the root of the situation is still seen as reflecting the point made by Chu and Trotter (1974), that "the major difficulty in the development of paraprofessional careers is that they must be implemented within a hierarchical structure dominated by the medical profession" (p. 63).

Another area of difficulty concerned the mandate of citizen involvement in community mental health program planning. Lack of specific guidelines as to how to incorporate consumer input into a center's functioning resulted in an insignificant participation of community members. The discretionary policies adopted by the professional staff at each center generally limited consumer involvement. Rappaport (1977) has pointed out that although most efforts at influencing community control of mental health services were directed toward people in the lower socioeconomic classes, it may be a myth to assume that middle-class people are already having input. Where so-called "community advisory boards" did exist they were largely composed of "elite" citizens, as opposed to consumers.

Related to the issue of community participation is the notion of accountability and evaluation. The lack of an initial mandate for evaluating community mental health center programs represents a major criticism in this area. At a later point (in 1969), when one percent of the operating budget was to be appropriated for evaluation, Chu and Trotter (1974) attributed many difficulties to the fact that NIMH had contracted out the evaluative studies (as opposed to developing program evaluation units within the centers).

Equally disturbing in the realm of evaluation and accountability is that the information which was generated did not translate into programmatic changes within centers. The 1975 legislation which mandates community involvement in the evaluation process (see later section on program evaluation) represents the first systematic steps taken toward community accountability.

ENVIRONMENTAL DESIGN: TOWARDS A MODEL
FOR COMMUNITY MENTAL HEALTH

This section presents an environmental design alternative to the medical model of community mental health. This is not to imply that alternatives to the medical model have yet to be proposed; rather, the unique aspects of the environmental design framework are best contrasted with the dominant medical orientation. Since it was argued that the medical model is at the root of the criticism levied against community mental health, the focus of this section is to show how interventions derived from an environmental design conceptualization successfully meet these criticisms.

The strategy taken in this section is to consider eight major areas of community mental health within an environmental design framework: consultation, prevention, nonprofessional mental health workers, community treatment and "continuity of care," ethnicity and mental health, ethical issues, program evaluation, and training environmental designers for community mental health. In each of these areas examples of major programs and issues which reflect an environmental design orientation are reviewed and proposals for additional activities in line with an environmental design approach are proposed.

Before proceeding, an overview of the environmental design model is in order. Whereas Krasner (Chapter 1 of this volume) has presented the details of the environmental design perspective, the purpose here is to highlight the essential components of environmental design pertaining to this chapter. For this writer, environmental design is conceptualized as the applied wing of the "psychology of behavior influence" which was developed by Krasner and Ullmann (1973) in their volume entitled Behavior Influence and Personality. That is, environmental design represents the application of empirically derived "behavior-influence" procedures to the modification and design of environments (Jeger, 1975). The psychology of behavior influence, in turn, is defined as the merging of numerous diverse streams. These include: behavior modification; environmental psychology (Proshansky et al., 1970); social ecology (Moos & Insel, 1974); open education (Silberman, 1973); utopian planning; and ethics of large-scale social interventions.

The unique features of the orientation which are exemplified throughout this chapter include a rejection of the "disease" model of human problems, and a move away from the focus on pathology; a broadening of the mental health professional's role beyond the one-to-one psychotherapy model; and a merging of research, service, and training as integrated professional activities. The goal of environmental design interventions is to influence individuals in ways that the likelihood of their designing their own environments in accordance with their own values and goals is enhanced. With this overview, the interface of environmental design with the aforementioned eight major areas of community mental health are considered below.

Consultation and "Community Enhancement"

It will be recalled that a mandate of the Community Mental Health Centers Act was the "prevention" of "mental illness" in addition to the provision of community-based treatment. Attempts to fulfill this mandate became associated with the "consultation and community education" service – the only truly nontraditional component of the center program. On the surface, consultation as a strategy of indirect service delivery, and community education as a means of prevention are seemingly compatible with the notion of environmental design. However, in practice, only selected consultation efforts are in line with the model explicated in this volume.

First, it should be emphasized that the notion of "prevention" has no place in the environmental design model. Prevention is clearly a "medical" concept, and implies knowledge of the "causes" of specific "disease" entities. As was pointed out, this analogy to medicine is responsible for the shortcomings in the implementation of the consultation/education service. The aim of consultation/education within an environmental design framework is to influence training by community caregivers (i.e., parents, teachers, clergy) for increased behavioral skills/competencies/opportunities, and thereby increase the freedom of individuals. This resultant increase in behavioral options is more appropriately deemed as "community enhancement," as it seeks to promote strengths rather than prevent deficits. Finally, as was indicated in the previous section, the majority of consultation activities were geared to "cases" – assisting other professionals in delivering one-to-one clinical services. If so, what are some other types of consultation? Which are consultation activities that reflect aspects of the environmental design model?

Types of consultation

Recent years have witnessed a proliferation of consultation activities within the mental health fields, and, as evidenced by the entries in the Mannino et al. (1975) bibliography, consultation has emerged as a specialty in its own right. The classic typology of so-called "mental health consultation" was offered by one of the founders of the field, Gerald Caplan (1963, 1970). He delineated consultation activities into four major categories: 1) client-centered case consultation – where the focus is on helping the consultee deal with a particular case or client; 2) program-centered administrative consultation – whereby the major aim is to help the consultee in administering a treatment or prevention program; 3) consultee-centered case consultation – in which the primary goal is to assist the consultees through difficulties in working with clients in general; and 4) consultee-centered administrative consultation – with the goal of the consultant being to aid the consultee or consultee agency in planning, implementing, and maintaining mental health programs. Although the majority of consultation activities at community mental health centers were received by schools (Bass, 1974), numerous consultation efforts from within and without community mental health centers were directed to clergy (e.g., Dworkin, 1973), police (e.g., Bard & Berkowitz, 1967), and industry (e.g., Lepkin, 1975), among other groups/settings. Since Caplan's monumental work, additional taxonomies were developed by Bindman (1966), Hirschowitz (1973) and McClung & Stunden (1970). These were all based on problem and focus similar to Caplan's original categorization.

An alternative approach to classifying consultation models is based largely on the consultant's orientation. This is exemplified in the work of Woody and Woody (1971) who categorized consultation according to a process model, psychodynamic model, and behavioral model. In a similar vein, and in what represents the most recent and comprehensive attempt to relate the current status of the field, Dworkin and Dworkin (1975) presented a conceptual overview of four consultation models: consultee-centered, group process, social action, and ecological. They went on to describe each of these orientations along 10 dimensions. A brief summary of their analysis is offered here so that the reader can construe environmental design consultation against the background of the entire consultation field.

Consultee-centered consultation, associated primarily with the work of Caplan (1970), views the consultant as a professional expert, whose target population is another professional caregiver. The goals of consultation are to increase skills, knowledge, and objectivity.

The group-process model, largely identified with the work of Lippitt and his colleagues (1958), defines consultation as a relationship between a helper and a system or subsystem. The consultant serves as a participant observer and functions as a facilitator in bringing about organizational changes and mobilizing internal resources.

Social-action consultation, exemplified by the work of Alinsky (1969, 1972), characterizes the consultant's role as a community organizer and strategist. The target population is said to be indigenous community leaders, with the goal being to facilitate a transfer of power in order to meet basic human needs.

In the ecological model, which is reflected in the work of Kelly (1966, 1970), consultation is defined as a relationship between a professional team and an "ecosystem." The consultant serves as a team member, functioning as a planner and researcher with the goal of increasing the system's coping and adaptive mechanisms.

Within the field of consultation, that class of activities most directly compatible with the environmental design model has been labeled "behavioral consultation." The behavioral consultant as environmental designer may be defined as one who offers his/her knowledge of social learning principles and applications to a consultee or consultee system with the goal of intervening in a target client's environment to bring about behavioral changes in that client (Jeger, 1977). More often than not, the behavioral consultant as environmental designer will serve as a member of a team from the consultee institution during the course of developing, implementing, and evaluating a behavioral program (e.g., Jeger, 1977). The incorporation of an evaluation component is basic to the data-oriented behavioral approach. Also, behavioral consulting generally involves training others (i.e., such direct interventionists as teachers and child care staff) in the implementation of behavior change programs. Thus, while similarities with the "participant observer" and "researcher" aspects of the group process and ecological models do exist, behavioral consulting is unique in that it represents a merging of research, service, and training. As such it is prototypical of the environmental designer role. Some examples of specific projects follow.

In what is the earliest large-scale project employing behavioral consultation, Tharp and Wetzel (1969) trained "behavior analysts" (B.A.-level personnel) to serve as consultants to "mediators" (parents, teachers, and other school personnel) in the application of operant conditioning programs with "target" clients. Therein was created the so-called "triadic" model, with the professional psychologist supervising the consulting behavior analyst who trains the mediator, who functions as the direct behavior-change agent. The positive effects of the program were evident from improvements in specified target behaviors in clients, although such data as school achievement remained largely unaffected.

An extension of Tharp and Wetzel's (1969) work was reported by Keeley et al. (1973), who trained undergraduates to serve as behavioral consultants in a Head Start Classroom as well as play tutorial-modeling roles in homes. Positive supervisor reactions attested to the success of the program. In another project, subject to more rigorous evaluation,

Suinn (1974a) utilized undergraduates as behavioral consultants to Head Start programs, day care centers, and a speech clinic.

While the above projects are examples of client-centered case consultation, consultee-centered behavioral consultation has permeated the literature. For example, Meyers et al. (1975) employed a "multiple-baseline" design to demonstrate a functional relation between consultation and a reduction in negative teacher behavior. In a larger-scale project, as part of a community mental health center's consultation program, Gordon (1976) offered behavioral training to a group of elementary school teachers. Compared to controls, students in consultees' classes showed behavioral improvements on numerous targets, with a reduction in referrals to special services resulting. Program-centered behavioral consultation is reflected in the work of King et al. (1975) who attempted to reduce absenteeism in a predominantly Mexican-American school.

Perhaps the closest approximation of implementing the environmental designer role in the consultation and education service of a community mental health center is to be found at the Huntsville-Madison County (Alabama) Mental Health Center (Rinn, 1973; Turner & Goodson, 1972). The Center was awarded an NIMH grant to consider "the feasibility of employing an operant learning approach to all activities associated with a community mental health center" (Turner & Goodson, 1972). Specifically concerning the consultation/education unit, Rinn (1973) has stated its goals as developing mental health skills in such community caregivers as parents and welfare workers, and reducing the necessity for the Center to provide direct clinical services. He went on to define their tripartite system which was said to be comprised of consultation, education, and extension. That is, a continuum exists whereby Huntsville staff might first engage in client-centered or consultee-centered case consultation, then provide formal training in the principles and application of behavior modification to an agency's staff (e.g., teachers), and finally, "extension," which refers to the consultee-agency adopting or replicating a Huntsville program (e.g., conducting their own child management classes for parents).

In line with the data-oriented behavioral model, evaluations are built into the program design. This is largely accomplished by spelling out quantifiable goals for each of the three components on an annual basis. Agencies served by Huntsville's behavioral consultation unit have included schools, courts, and the church. (Additional features of the Huntsville Center are to be described in connection with the other subsections.)

Another community mental health center where behavior modification is being applied on a larger scale is at Oxnard, California. Liberman (1973) reported workshops for parents and behavioral consultation with teachers to prevent children's behavioral problems from becoming aggravated. (Other Oxnard programs are also cited in later subsections.) Similarly, as already indicated, Gordon (1976) of the Rutgers Community Mental Health Center (Piscataway, New Jersey) reported behavioral training workshops for teachers.

Issues in behavioral consultation

Since behavioral consultation is emerging as a strategy for modifying larger social units (classrooms, wards, institutions), behavior modifiers have become increasingly sensitive to the influences of the broader social system (e.g., Atthowe, 1973; Bornstein et al., 1975; Colman, 1971, 1975; Friedman et al., 1975; Geller, et al., 1975; Hersen, 1976; Jeger, 1977; Miran et al., 1974; Reppucci, 1977; Reppucci & Saunders, 1974; Richards, 1975). Although many of the issues are similar to those encountered in the course of implementing any innovative program, the fact that the program is behavioral and that it is carried out within a consultation context raises several unique concerns. The community mental health professional as environmental designer must be cognizant of these issues if he/she is to function effectively in such a capacity.

Although the unique concerns stemming from the "consultation" aspect of behavioral consultation are parallel to those in nonbehavioral consultation, they are considered together below in terms of the framework offered by Reppucci & Saunders (1974). In connection with their consultation to the Connecticut School for Boys, Reppucci and his colleagues from Yale (e.g., Reppucci, 1973; Wilkinson & Reppucci, 1973) converted the entire institution to one based on social-learning principles, 24-hour token economy cottages, and a community orientation. This long-term behavioral consultation effort provided the basis for what is, perhaps, the most systematic delineation of problems associated with developing behavioral programs in natural settings. Reppucci & Saunders (1974), in what is apt to become a classic paper, "The Social Psychology of Behavior Modification," spelled out eight major social systems variables that behavioral innovators must consider: 1) institutional constraints – i.e., competing reinforcers within the system which preclude making all reinforcers contingent upon positive behavior, strained communication channels, and turnovers in high level administrative staff; 2) external pressure – i.e., pressures from outside the institution resulting from say, a case of AWOL, which leads to an increased emphasis on maximum security; 3) language – specifically, problems associated with such derogatory labels as "behavior modification" (see recent paper by Woolfolk, Woolfolk, & Wilson, 1977); 4) two populations – i.e., problems centering around the fact that in natural settings it is the nonprofessional indigenous staff who carry out the behavioral programs, and constraints imposed by union regulations which prevent incorporating any differential rewards for staff who "perform" in a program; 5) limited resources – including shortages of back-up reinforcers, and limitations of time and manpower; 6) labeling – whereby indigenous staff object to the incorporation of certain ongoing activities into a contingency program due to their labels (i.e., "recreation," "educational trips"); 7) perceived inflexibility – similar to the previous problem, characterized by consultee's perception of behavior modifier's desire to include all aspects into a contingency program; and 8) compromise – a warning to behavior modifiers that they will have to compromise on behavioral methodology after contact with a setting (e.g., program contents or evaluation aspects).

While the above conceptualization was employed by Geller, Johnson, Hamlin & Kennedy (1975) in their analysis of a behavioral program in a correctional facility and by Jeger (1977) in an analysis of a behavioral consultation program to a psychiatric center, they each expounded somewhat on the Reppucci and Saunders (1974) scheme. Further, Reppucci (1977) himself added several categories to his initial framework. Due to the overlap in some of the points raised by these investigators only two additional social systems issues are presented here.

The first issue, one basic to the entire consultation field, centers around the "system entry" process. In light of the view that the institution is the client in consultation (e.g., Grossman & Quinlan, 1972; Katkin & Sibley, 1973), the point in the power structure at which entry is initiated has been a major concern for researchers and practitioners in the field (Caplan, 1970; Glidewell, 1959; Levine, 1973; Mann, 1972; Northman, 1976; Sarason et al, 1966; Schroeder & Miller, 1975). The critical aura associated with the entry phase in general is perhaps best captured by Northman's (1976) statement:

> The process of entry, while considerably less than half the fun, can appear to be something like ninety-eight percent of the work. One can be forgiven if goal substitution occurs and successful entry rather than program implementation or evaluation becomes an end in itself. (P. 2)

Although key features of the entry process (such as initial contact, obtaining sanctions, and establishing fees) vary according to the consultant's base institution (Lekisch, 1976) as well as the consultee's institution, it appears as though parallels do exist across settings and that a body of knowledge is developing in this area. For example, while it has long been suggested (Glidewell, 1959) that entry "at the top" is crucial, more often than not there are many "tops," and "sanctions at one administrative level do not automatically transfer to other levels" (Schroeder & Miller, 1975, p. 184). For example, programs were jeopardized when consultants did not become aware how high the "top" really was (e.g., Friedman et al., 1975) or when "middle" level staff were glossed over (e.g., Bolman et al., 1969). Reppucci (1977) has added that although support from staff at all levels is crucial for any innovation, it is "perhaps particularly so to a behavioral program in which consistency, immediacy, contingency, and clarity are so important" (p. 596). In connection with developing a behavioral program, Miron (1966) has cautioned that one must involve those who have "sabotage potential." Needless to say, that includes almost everyone. A potentially useful tool for behavioral consultants in particular is the Consultation Readiness Scale (CRS) recently developed by Cherniss (1978) to gauge the readiness of consultees to accept consultation.

Another aspect of the entry process which is derived from the literature on general consultation, but is especially relevant for behavioral consultation concerns the tendency of consultees to initially test the credibility of the consultant by confronting him/her with the most difficult "clinical" cases. The issue becomes one of the program or systems-centered consultant avoiding the trap of providing direct clinical services. For example, Rabiner et al. (1970) in a provocatively titled article, "Consultation or Direct Service?", showed how, at times, direct service was the prerequisite before consultation to administrative staff was possible. Grundle et al. (1973) described the entire consultation process as one in which "role shifts" from client-centered to consultee-centered to organization-centered are expected. Jeger (1977) added that since behavior modification is likely to be "oversold" in the eyes of many front-line staff, they may expect miracles with their most difficult clients. The behavioral consultant must be ready to meet such demands, and may have to reduce the mystical aura surrounding the techniques.

The second and final issue considered here concerns the potential of behavioral programs to persist following the consultant's departure. All too many innovations collapse when some key individual (s) depart from the scene (e.g., Miron, 1966). This is crucial if any long term effects are expected to result from a consultation effort. Ideally, the community mental health consultant as environmental designer should attempt to influence the development of a program which, though remaining after his/her departure, would be dynamic enough to adapt to the changing needs of the system as time goes on. Thus, the goal is not one of sustaining a program for its own sake.

On a national level, along these lines, the National Institute of Mental Health in collaboration with the Human Interaction Research Institute in Los Angeles has initiated a program of research designed to empirically determine the reasons for sustained innovations and develop a consultation model to enhance the likelihood for sustaining worthwhile changes in the human services. Clearly, this is a response to a critical gap in knowledge so necessary for the environmental designer role in community mental health.

Prevention and "Community Enhancement"

While the focus in the discussion on consultation clearly reflected an alternative to the traditional professional mental health role of providing direct clinical services, relatively few of the projects described were aimed at inducing large-scale changes in target populations who are community residents. Examples from the so-called fields of "prevention," which are in line with the environmental design model, are described herein to illustrate some emerging trends for even broader roles than those considered under behavioral consultation. While it will be recalled that the entire notion of prevention is incompatible with the theoretical underpinnings of environmental design, the purpose here is to highlight specific projects or activities carried out within a prevention context, but are in line with the proposed model for community mental health.

Caplan (1964) categorized prevention activities into three types: primary prevention – which seeks to eliminate the incidence of mental illness in a community; secondary prevention – aimed at curtailing the effects of already visible problems through early identification and intervention; and tertiary prevention – directed toward preventing the relapse or complication of already full-blown cases of mental illness. From these definitions, it is apparent how the notion of prevention is analogous to the concepts of public health, a medically-rooted specialty. Although (despite the labels) environmental design has a role in both secondary and tertiary prevention (as will become apparent at a later point), the emphasis here is on its role in primary prevention.

In a recent review, Munoz (1976) stated that "The primary prevention of psychological problems is becoming more than an article of faith" (p. 12). He described four "model studies" which incorporated fairly rigorous evaluation designs to document their primary preventative impact. They also reflect the definitional criteria adopted by Cowen (1973) – namely, that "Primary prevention activities are targeted impersonally to groups and communities; once individual distress is identified, intervention is other than primary" (p. 433). Thus, the efforts were at fostering resources and promoting strengths rather than being repairaive in orientation. Two of the studies, deemed most "unique" by the present writer, are summarized below.(5)

Heber and Garber (1975) conducted a 10-year longitudinal study aimed at preventing "cultural-familial mental retardation." Their efforts were directed at black, low-income mothers with IQ's below 75, and their newborn infants. An enrichment program aimed at infants was launched in a community-based center where infants spent five full days a week for 12 months a year up to age five. Paraprofessionals conducted training in perceptual/motor, cognitive/language, and social/emotional skills, and mothers were given training in child rearing skills as well as rehabilitation for employment. Compared to a control group, experimental infants were superior on Gessell norms, linguistic development, and IQ (i.e., E's at age 7 had an average IQ of 121 compared to 87 for controls). Experimental mothers fared better than controls in the area of employment (i.e., more were employed and their average weekly income was greater).

In another project, Maccoby and Farquhar (1975, 1976) taught behavioral skills in an attempt to prevent heart disease. Specifically, this study was designed to compare the effects of mass media training (radio and television) and mass media plus individual instruction to a high risk group on changes in smoking, exercise, and diet. Three comparable northern California communities (with populations ranging from 12,700 to 14,700) were assigned to either of the above conditions or a no prevention control group. Changes occurred in both experimental groups, with those in the individual instruction condition being greater. However, except for smoking reduction, by the end of the second year both experimental groups were roughly equivalent. Conducting the program on a community-wide level increased the likelihood of interpersonal social reinforcement for applying the concrete skills that were taught and is thus a major factor in the success of the program.

In a later paper on the above "three-community" study, McAlister (1976) suggested an interesting way of improving the results of media training without individual instruction. He recommended the formation of local viewing groups led informally by a volunteer peer counselor. He went on to speculate as to the future role for professional helpers implied by such a model — namely, media producers and community organizers (to develop self-help groups and recruit peer counselors).

Another media study largely compatible with the environmental design orientation was conducted by Mikulas (1976). In a pilot program of a "televised self-control clinic," seven one-hour shows were developed on such areas as behavioral goal setting, relaxation training, self-desensitization, contingency contracting, token systems, and thought stopping. The rationale for using television is based on its potential for the widespread dissemination of self-control information. It follows suggestions made by Risley, Clark, and Cataldo (1976) in connection with their development of a behavioral technology for the "normal" family. Further, the use of television as a medium is the logical step following the development of "nonprescription behavior therapies" (Rosen, 1976) consisting of written manuals designed to serve as self-help guides for specific problems (e.g., obesity, sexual dysfunction). Although of the written programs perhaps the most comprehensive is the recent book by Rathus and Nevid (1977), the most intriguing from the point of view of primary prevention is the manual by Alvord (1973) entitled, Home Token Economy: An Incentive Program for Children and Their Parents. Such large-scale interventions are a step in the direction of developing a "self-controlling community," the ultimate goal of a "behavioral-preventive approach to community mental health," as articulated by Meyers, Craighead, and Meyers (1974). Whereas community mental health was said to represent the "third mental health revolution" (Bellak, 1964) and behavior modification was dubbed the "fourth therapeutic revolution" (Levis, 1970), perhaps with a merger of the two we may be witnessing the development of a "fifth revolution" (Jeger, 1977).

Since the above programs, at most, represent an overlap between the "interpersonal action" and "social action" categories of primary prevention, as distinguished by Caplan (1964), some further articulation of environmental designers as social systems interventionists ("social action" category) is offered. As a modifier of social institutions, the environmental designer based in a community mental health center is in a unique position to influence school systems. A broader role for the behavioral consultant than that described previously would be to influence the development of "open classrooms" as alternative learning environments. Whereas previous works have discussed the relationship of open education to behavior modification (Madden, 1972; Winett, 1973) and more generally to environmental design (Krasner & Richards, 1976), suffice it to note that the purpose would not be exclusive adoption of this system over "traditional" classrooms, but rather the increase in options. Additional research is needed to empirically determine the resulting behaviors associated with open education and the kinds of students likely to profit most (e.g., Winett & Edwards, 1974). At this point, it can only be speculated that the open education environment is more conducive to the large-scale implementation of such innovations as children modifying teachers' behavior (Gray, Graubard, & Rosenberg, 1974) and the utilization of reinforcement to increase racial integration amongst first-graders (Hauserman, Walen, & Behling, 1973).

Utilizing the schools as targets through which to influence social change or primary prevention has a particular advantage since, by law, everyone goes through them. This point was used by Stickney (1968) in his argument that schools are our "natural" community mental health centers. It also lends support for recent proposals to influence the curriculum in order to incorporate courses in "pre-parent education" (Gabel, Haig-Friedman, Friedman, & Vietze, 1976) or "universal parenthood training" (Hawkins, 1974). Such courses could be made compulsory before obtaining a marriage license, or incentives could be offered to those attending. This is similar to the suggestion made by Lowman (1973) for offering premarital education to couples by assigning an interviewer to a Registrar of Deeds Office. To induce such changes, the community mental health professional as environmental designer will need to work closely with policymakers, legislators, school officials, community boards, etc., clearly placing him/her in the category of social activist.

An example of another social change activity deemed within the role of an environmental design community mental health worker lies in the area of employment. As Jones and Azrin (1973) put it:

Gainful employment is the single most reliable means for obtaining the fundamental benefits, privileges, and satisfactions available in our society. (P. 345)

They went on to conduct a behavioral analysis of job procurement and showed how a community-reinforcement procedure, consisting of a "reward" advertisement for anyone who provided information on a job opening which results in employment, led to 10 times as many job leads and eight times as many placements as a "no-reward" advertisement. Further, Azrin and his colleagues extended this social reinforcement view of the hiring process to the job-counseling situation and developed a behaviorally-oriented "job-finding club" (Azrin, Flores, & Kaplan, 1975).

In a similar vein, at the Community Psychology Action Center of the University of Illinois, social learning principles were applied in a training program for hard-core unemployed black men (O'Conner & Rappaport, 1970; Rappaport & O'Conner, 1973). In line with the "local" social change orientation of their center, when a state-wide job freeze was to preclude the hiring of program graduates against a previous agreement with the State Department of Mental Health, Rappaport and his colleagues created a social issue in the newspapers which resulted in the hiring of the men.

Finally, another suggestion for social action in the area of employment involves influencing legislators to modify existent laws concerning early retirement (Zax & Specter, 1974). At the time of this writing federal hearings are, in fact, being held in local communities. The influence of community mental health center staff in these efforts is unfortunately minimal or virtually nonexistent.

Thus, what was presented reflects some major examples of consultation and community enhancement activities that are compatible with the environmental design orientation. Suggestions for additional activities appear in a later section focusing on "future centers." The fact that most of the projects discussed in this section have not taken place in community mental health centers per se is consistent with the conclusions reached by both Carter & Cazares (1976) and Munoz (1976). In a review of the literature on consultation in community mental health, Carter & Cazares (1976) stated that:

> Although the provision of consultation-education services remains an integral component of the service elements of the community health center, it is questionable whether it has realized its goal of solving broad community problems through eliciting remedial and preventive forces in the social environment. (P. 5)

Similarly, in his review on primary prevention, Munoz (1976) stated that "most well-designed preventive work has not come from mental health centers" (p. 11). He did add, however, that "once preventive programs are tested for effectiveness, community mental health centers could be an appropriate avenue for dissemination" (p. 11), and suggested building incentives for such work into future funding. As already pointed out, in light of the domination of the centers by a medical model, it is not surprising that activities of the type discussed in this section do not constitute the norm. Some specific organizational factors that may be associated with prevention services within an environmental design model are discussed in the section on "future centers." At this point we turn to some of the more "traditional" features of the community mental health movement and discuss their relationships to environmental design.

Nonprofessional Mental Health Workers

It will be recalled that the increased utilization of nonprofessional manpower in mental health delivery systems was stated by Bloom (1977) as a key characteristic of community mental health. Even more so, the necessity for employing nonprofessionals in the human services is considered a major historical precursor to the passage of the community mental health center legislation. Specifically, Albee's (1959) book, Mental Health Manpower Trends, in which he projected serious manpower shortages confronting the mental health professions, is regarded as one of the most influential documents in terms of mental health legislation at the federal government level (Matarazzo, 1971).

Although nonprofessionals have been used in mental health settings long before Albee's (1959) statement, their functions were generally restricted to custodial tasks (e.g., attendants in mental institutions) or serving as "companions" (see Goodman, 1972 for a review of the latter). The shift in the utilization of nonprofessionals took place in the 1960s and was characterized by the changing roles of existing nonprofessional manpower (i.e., from attendant to psychiatric aide or therapy aide) as well as an increase in the numbers and kinds of people utilized for "rehabilitation" and "psychotherapeutic" roles (e.g., students, house-wives, and even clients). It was not long before the "nonprofessional revolution" (Sobey, 1970) permeated the university, with specialized two year curricula being designed to prepare students to serve in new "careers." The astronomical growth of these programs was documented by Young, True, and Packard (1976) who estimated that as of 1975, 15,000 people had graduated from 170 Associate Degree programs. Most of these programs are based on the first such program developed at Purdue University in 1965 (see Hadley, True, & Kepes, 1970) whose underlying philosophy was that of training a generalist.(6) Within psychology, the recent Vail (Colorado) Conference on professional training emphasized new roles for nonprofessionals at all levels (Korman, 1976).

It is apparent from the above that nonprofessionals have been used increasingly as primary interventionists in the delivery of psychological services. While it is still too soon to assess the large-scale impact of these workers in terms of their meeting the ever increasing demand for human services, it has become clear that their employment in community mental health centers has not been without conflicts. To reiterate the previously cited point made by Chu & Trotter (1974) in their critique of community mental health, the core obstacle to the development of sound paraprofessional careers within community mental health has been the medical domination of centers within a fairly traditional hierarchical structure. The purpose of this subsection, then, is to reconceptualize the nonprofessional revolution within an environmental design framework and point to several programs employ-ing nonprofessionals that are especially compatible with the environ-mental design orientation. It will be shown how this alternative orientation might meet some of the shortcomings of current parapro-fessional practice.

Before proceeding, some definitional aspects of "nonprofessional" need to be addressed. Goodman (1972) stated that "mental health work is headed for a tripartite stratification: professionals, paraprofessionals, and nonprofessionals" (p. 8). Nonprofessionals are said to be the least trained and they are supervised by professionals or paraprofessionals (who generally are defined as holding at least an A.A. Degree as a mental health generalist). For purposes of this chapter, such a distinction is not necessary and the terms are used interchangeably. Likewise, Schlosberg's (1967) distinction between volunteers and nonpro-fessionals is irrelevant from the point of view of this chapter. Perhaps the most compatible definition was offered by O'Leary & O'Leary (1972) who considered paraprofessionals those "who work beside or along with professional personnel, but who are not trained in all aspects of the profession or who do not have a professional degree" (p. 491). As such, it includes such personnel as psychiatric aides, teachers' aides, child care staff, parents, volunteers, and students, as well as nonprofessional consultants.

Considering the basic premise of environmental design – that human behavior problems are developed and maintained as a result of environmental antecedents and consequences, as opposed to being merely overt symptoms of some underlying "disease" (the medical model) – there follows a conclusion that "expert" professionals need not necessarily be the most effective helpers. Even more so, Tharp and Wetzel (1969) have stated that the behavioral model (a major stream in environmental design) will result in the "deprofessionalization of the helping enterprise." The reason being that "theories of disorders which view behavior largely as a function of the external social environment implicate nonprofessional involvement much more satisfactorily" (p. 14). This is not to imply that the behavioral model is the only alternative to the medical orientation. Clearly, the designers of the early paraprofessional program were not functioning within a disease orientation. However, in terms of the extension of nonprofessional staff to the medically-dominated community mental health center – with the implicit role demands that they serve as "junior professionals" (i.e., doing precisely the same things, such as psychotherapy) – role conflicts have and most likely will always abound.

The implied role for the nonprofessional environmental designer is that he/she not serve as a mirror image of the professional. Rather, a distinct role description is suggested, one that is inherently tied to a modified role for the community mental health professional as environmental designer. First, with a broadening of the professional's role to one of trainer, supervisor, consultant, facilitator, program designer, and evaluator, the way is paved for the paraprofessional to function as the primary direct service provider without inherent conflicts. Such a model for the delivery of direct services is exemplified in the behaviorally-oriented Huntsville (Alabama) Community Mental Health Center mentioned previously. Approximately 75 percent of the clinical staff have a B.A. Degree or less, and are cast in the role of direct caregivers. That is, they are responsible for providing clinical services in the various Center components (e.g., outpatient, aftercare) following extensive inservice training and continued supervision in the application of behavior modification techniques. Their effectiveness is attested by the evaluation data which showed that, during the second year since converting the Center to behaviorally-based treatment, 87 percent of outpatients reached their treatment goals in an average of 4.2 sessions (Bolin & Kivens, 1974).

Another factor built into the Huntsville program that makes it especially compatible with an environmental design orientation lies in its incentive-based performance system (Turner & Goodson, 1975). That is, behavioral principles are applied to staff along the same lines in which staff are expected to apply them to clients. In brief, staff salaries, promotions, and other reinforcers are contingent upon their adhering to agreed-upon duties that are developed by the supervisor against the employee's own base rate during the previous year. Based on these established goals, certain attainment levels are converted into points. It is of interest to add that client ratings of therapists at termination are built into the overall formula determining staff performance. The point system (token economy?) is coupled with mandated supervisor feedback. Thus, rather than seniority or academic credentials, competency is the primary factor in career advancement.

This employee motivational system, which its originators have labeled "Catch a Fellow Worker Doing Something Good Today" (Turner & Goodson, 1975), represents a clear recognition of the ubiquitous "behavior-influence" process underlying all human activity. More specifically, being cognizant of the environmental consequences under which employees operate, the administrators of the Huntsville program were able to manipulate these consequences to not only improve staff functioning but also enhance their job satisfaction (Krasner, 1974, Personal Communication). While employing positive reinforcement (social and material) to modify staff behavior follows from the empirical literature on training nonprofessional behavior modifiers (i.e., that trained aides will not perform in the absence of reinforcement; see Jeger, 1977), it is felt that the success of the Huntsville approach is in large measure due to a broader social system variable. That is, the more global environmental design facet pertaining to the employee motivation program is the comprehensive "accountability" orientation that permeates all Center activities. As such, not only are nonprofessional staff held accountable but also their supervisors, administrators, and so on up the line. Thus, the usual "double standard" which calls for evaluating bottom line employees while those at the top of the hierarchy remain largely "unaccountable" is virtually nonexistent at Huntsville.

Thus, the employee motivational, performance contracting system, coupled with the existence of differential role prescriptions for professional and nonprofessional staff (operationally defined, of course) reflect the unique aspects in Huntsville's use of nonprofessionals. It provides a viable alternative to common community mental health practice whereby professionals and nonprofessionals are assigned similar duties (i.e., individual psychotherapy with a caseload of 20 clients each) for differential salaries (despite instances of nonprofessionals being more effective and certainly no less effective; see Durlak, 1973). Although the long-term effects of the Huntsville model remain to be seen, it clearly represents a direction toward competency-based career advancement for paraprofessionals.

Another example of the use of nonprofessionals that is compatible with the proposed environmental designer role in community mental health comes from our work with students at Stony Brook. As stated by Krasner (see chap. 1) undergraduates are placed in various community settings and cast in the role of the participant observer. Groups of undergraduates functioning as a team in a given setting are supervised by graduate students in environmental design who, in turn, are supervised by a professional psychologist. Although in many cases these B.A.-track students were involved in direct client contact, the nature of their service was broader than the Huntsville B.A. level, direct interventionist. That is, even when functioning in a "clinical" setting, they did not engage in individual psychotherapy or even clinical "behavior" therapy.

The work of one team placed in a transitional facility of a state psychiatric center under the supervision of the present author (Jeger, McClure, & Krasner, 1976), illustrates how undergraduates played an integral part in the design of the environment. Specifically, they contributed to the overall community preparation effort by developing small group projects geared to training chronic psychiatric residents in social skills, academic survival skills, self-help (i.e., hot-line for discharged residents), and, in general, enhancing the "psychological sense of community" (Sarason, 1974) within the facility. Thus, their influence went beyond companionship or recreation, and even beyond individual counseling in a private setting. In some of the projects, students worked closely with the existing nonprofessional staff, thereby serving as trainers and role models in the conduct of such groups. Students gained experience not only in the application of behavior modification but also environmental psychology, training, program design, and evaluation. This role is seen as prototypical for a nonprofessional environmental designer, as it is deemed appropriate (with some variations) to other settings as well. Perhaps the B.A.-level designer could be trained to specialize in several major settings, community mental health centers being but one.

The hierarchical structure of our program allowed one professional to reach many more people than would otherwise have been possible. This is similar to the model for training, research, and manpower utilization in community psychology which Seidman & Rappaport (1974) have referred to as the "educational pyramid." It is likewise compatible with the "triadic" model for the application of behavior modification in natural settings outlined by Tharp & Wetzel (1969) and previously discussed in connection with behavioral consultation. It is further in line with Suinn's (1974a) program in which undergraduates were trained to serve as behavior modification consultants. Perhaps a unique feature of the environmental design role as it has been developing at Stony Brook centers around a relative lack of rigid definition or boundary. This inevitably resulted in a broad variety of activities relative to a more structured role of providing clinical consultation on specific behavioral problems. The contribution of the nonprofessional in a community mental health (or any human service) setting is likely to be a radiating one.

While space does not permit an extensive review of other paraprofessional functions that are in line with an environmental design view of community mental health, some recent trends and projected future directions are noted.

As previously indicated, the emergence of the nonprofessional revolution was reflected by the various kinds of people utilized in the helping process and the nature of their activities. Especially relevant to our notions of environmental design is the effects of helping on the nonprofessional helper. The phenomenon of "positive" attitudinal and behavioral changes said to result in nonprofessionals cast in a helping role has been termed by Riessman (1965) as the "helper-therapy principle." He went on to call for a "more explicit use of this principle in an organized manner" (p. 32).

Approximately a decade later, Fremouw and Feindler (1976) reviewed three streams of research on the helper principle. First, they pointed to a broad range of problems to which self-help groups have addressed themselves. These include Alcoholics Anonymous, Recovery Incorporated, Overeaters Anonymous, Smokers Anonymous, Divorcees Anonymous, Gamblers Anonymous, Parents of Youth in Trouble Anon, to name but a few. They called for systematic research to ascertain the salient therapeutic aspects of such programs as well as determine their cost-effectiveness. However, as they have noted, the antagonistic attitude toward professionals that is common among such groups has prevented their being subject to systematic investigation. Perhaps the necessary first step toward changing what is essentially an atmosphere of mutual antagonism took place with the recent conference on "Developing Effective Links Between Human Services Providers and the Mutual Help System" (Jones, 1977). As the title implies, the aim of the conference was to develop a spirit of cooperation between self-help activists and professionals.(7) More recently, Slotnick & Jeger (1979) developed the Long Island Self-Help Clearinghouse within the context of a self-help/professional collaborative model.

A second major area on the application of the helper principle as delineated by Fremouw and Feindler is peer tutoring. They cited research which shows positive educational gains in tutors as well as tutees in school settings. Additional examples come from the use of institutionalized retarded clients for training others in self-care skills. The notion of cross-age teaching in public school systems is very much in line with a major characteristic of open classrooms – a basic stream in environmental design. The involvement of retarded residents in the treatment process via "therapeutic pyramids" (Whalen & Henker, 1971) relied on the application of behavioral principles both in the training of the tutors and training contents, again a notion compatible with environmental design.

Finally, the third area exemplifying the use of the helper principle pointed to by Fremouw and Feindler is paraprofessional programs in general. These include such diverse nonprofessional workers as students and retired elderly. An interesting suggestion, from an environmental design viewpoint of community mental health, was noted by the authors. They proposed the development of "reciprocal helper" programs where people with complementary needs and resources would be brought together. For example, senior citizens could serve as advocates for retarded residents living in the community who, in turn, would provide assistance to the elderly.(8)

Fremouw & Harmatz (1975) developed what they call a "helper model" whereby they trained clients with specific behavioral problems (e.g., speech anxiety) to employ empirically-determined behavior modification procedures with other clients manifesting the same problem. Two unique features of this model stand out. First, rather than relying on "relationship" factors to elicit the desired change (as is the case in many self-help programs) specific behavioral skills are employed (Fremouw & Feindler, 1976). Second, the authors applied a rigorous experimental design to evaluate the impact of this model, including follow-up data as to the durability of resultant changes. In an extension of this paradigm, Jones, Fremouw, & Carples (1977) combined the helper model with "pyramiding" to train elementary school teachers in a classroom management "skill package." That is, after a group of teachers were trained, they each trained another group of teachers. Clearly, this represents a model for the geometric expansion of mental health manpower.

Another trend within the paraprofessional movement that merits separate attention is the increased use of parents as therapeutic agents for their own children. Although, as Guerney (1969) reminded us, Freud was the first to employ a parent in the treatment process (the 1909 case of Little Hans) and other psychoanalysts have also done so (see Guerney, 1969, pgs. 382-391 for a review), the widespread utilization of nonprofessionals as therapeutic agents followed from "the increased acceptance of treatment techniques which are relatively ahistorical and straightforward" (Guerney, 1969, p. 382; See also p. 1-6). This refers to the emergence of both Rogerian and Skinnerian techniques in particular, which are especially responsible for the expanding area of parent training.

Employing parents as behavior modifiers for their children is compatible with the environmental design orientation not only because it represents an expansion of the mental health manpower, but because parents are viewed as the natural social reinforcement agents in their child's environment. It is beyond the scope of this chapter to detail the varied situations in which parents were the primary change agents. Suffice it to note that in an extensive review, Johnson and Katz (1973) cited studies in which parents were used to modify antisocial behavior, speech dysfunctions, school phobias, and enuresis, among others. Although the studies varied in the comprehensiveness of their training, training contents, training methods, and the rigor with which outcomes were evaluated (Ford, 1975), the sophistication of the research in the area has increased to the point where a functional relation between parent behavioral training and child behavior change has been demonstrated unequivocally.

The use of behavioral parent training in community mental health centers is becoming more common. In what is perhaps one of the largest-scale applications, Rinn, Vernon, and Wise (1975) reported on a three-year program evaluation in which over 1,100 participated in "Positive Parent Training," the child management course offered at the Huntsville (Alabama) Community Mental Health Center. Of the extensive data gathered, perhaps most intriguing is the fact that, at follow-up, 84 percent reported not having sought additional treatment for their child. A manual based on this course entitled Positive Parenting has recently been published (Rinn and Markle, 1978).

Another community mental health center where parent behavioral training is offered is the Baton Rouge (Louisiana) Mental Health Center (Baenninger & Ulmer, 1975). An interesting finding in their program was that a large portion of the 164 families also trained another family in the procedures. Also, a major focus of several of the interventions was on doing school homework, clearly an important target behavior for preventing dropouts. The community mental health center of the Rutgers Medical School (Piscataway, New Jersey) represents another setting in which parent behavioral groups are conducted (Gordon, 1975; Lehrer, Gordon, and Leiblum, 1973).

Whereas the majority of the uses of paraprofessionals have been for treatment purposes, thereby expanding the mental health manpower, perhaps most intriguing in terms of future directions is their potential utility in nonpathology-oriented cases or for purposes of "enhancement." This is especially true with the utilization of parents, as indicated in the previous subsection concerning parent-implemented home token economies to increase behavioral alternatives in children. While enhancement-type interventions that were emphasized in the previous subsection were derived primarily from behavioral psychology, it should be noted that trends compatible with environmental design can be found from outside the behavioral stream as well. For example, Signell and her colleagues (Signell, 1975; Signell & Scott, 1973) developed a Parent-Child Communication Course based on Gordon's (1970) Parent Effectiveness Training as well as the theories of Carl Rogers and Virginia Satir. Essentially, parents receive six two-hr. group sessions geared toward developing competencies in respecting feelings, communication skills, and autonomy. The focus of the sessions is on experiential exercises. Parents are also taught to become instructors to train other instructors. Through this "spin off" model, Signell (1975) reported that over 2,000 parents were reached in the local community (San Mateo County, California).   As with many of the behavioral programs, the entire contents have been packaged for dissemination. With widespread adoption, this program has the potential of being a "mental health education model of primary prevention" which it was designed to become. Perhaps what is needed is an integrated behavioral/humanistic parent training package that lends itself to adoption by members of various income levels and ethnic groups.

To summarize, what was said in terms of nonprofessional manpower is that their increased use is called for by an environmental design orientation. Specific roles for paraprofessionals in line with an environmental design view of community mental health were discussed. It was indicated that the persistence of a medical domination in community mental health blocks the utilization of paraprofessionals to their fullest potential (even in a direct service context). Since the medical model has been "kicked around" a great deal in this chapter, it is appropriate to conclude this subsection with some recent empirical evidence in support of an alternative insofar as paraprofessionals are concerned.

Hurley and Tyler (1976) studied staff utilization in 10 community mental health center teams — six functioned primarily within a "medical, illness/clinical" (MIC) paradigm, and four within a "psychosocial, learning/community" (PSLC) paradigm. Of their findings, the most distinct differences emerged between the paraprofessionals on the two types of teams. The PSLC paraprofessionals had more flexible roles, rated themselves as having greater influence, reported greater team cohesiveness, and claimed greater satisfaction with work, supervision, and coworkers. As the authors concluded, merely introducing paraprofessionals into MIC systems is not sufficient to solve the personpower shortage in mental health. Since MIC systems are underutilizing their paraprofessional resources and are apparently alienating them, they are not likely to reach the indigenous community of which they are a part. Findings on MIC systems are in line with the results of a survey on paraprofessionals in community mental health centers conducted by Bartels and Tyler (1975). They found that, relative to all "problem" categories, the one mentioned most frequently was "difficulty working with professional staff" (e.g., lack of acceptance by professionals, tension, and conflict).

The environmental design model for paraprofessional utilization is analogous to the PSLC orientation which was found to be superior to the medical way of utilizing paraprofessionals. Thus, the Hurley and Tyler study lends support to the previously cited position of Chu and Trotter (1974) that the major impediment to the effective development of paraprofessional careers is the medical domination of community mental health centers. Evidence is also provided for Reiff's (1966) argument that meeting the mental health needs of the poor "is not primarily a problem of manpower but a problem of ideology" (p. 647). To Reiff, the ideological problem concerns endorsement of the medical model which is said to be at the root of the power struggle. The power struggle extends beyond interprofessional conflict, but also serves as a force to maintain existing institutional practices. Current institutional practices, in turn, prevent the utilization of new kinds of personpower since "effective" use of nonprofessionals (that they provide a true link between the professional and the poor underserved community) demands the creation of new professionals.

In conclusion, it is hoped that the environmental design orientation espoused in this volume will provide a framework for developing the new professionals that will permit effective utilization of paraprofessionals. Although the ideological struggle continues today, with no resolution in sight, it is felt that the intensity of the struggle has weakened as the medical model gives way to some development of alternatives.

Community Treatment and "Continuity of Care"

As previously stated, the development of community treatment programs as alternatives to state hospitals is a major mandate of community mental health centers. Issues pertaining to community services can be delineated into those involving two major target populations: clients who were never institutionalized – for whom alternatives to hospitalization are to be provided; and deinstitutionalization of hospitalized clients – particularly long-term residents of state hospitals. Since a critical theme common to both of these target groups is "continuity of care" (between hospital and community, and between various community services) this subsection was titled as such.

Relationships of environmental design to treatment in mental hospitals during various historical eras was already expounded upon by McClure (chapter 6, this volume). Suffice it to note that, although hospital-based behavioral programs (i.e., token economies – Atthowe & Krasner, 1968; Ayllon & Azrin, 1968) are most compatible with environmental design, the position taken here is that such programs have served to maintain the state mental hospital as an institution (see also, Jeger, 1977; Krasner, 1976; Richards, 1975). Although behavioral programs may be a necessary step in the deinstitutionalization process, a broader role for environmental designers in this regard would be that of institutional modifiers and designers of community-based alternative settings. Program descriptions that fall into the latter category are emphasized in this subsection.

As for nonchronic populations, "residential" treatment since the passage of the Community Mental Health Centers Act has moved increasingly in the direction of short-term stays. This was the case for general hospitals, V.A. hospitals, state hospitals, and especially community mental health centers. A recent critical review (Riessman, Rabkin, & Struening, 1977) found that, although a tendency for earlier reconstitution of patients subjected to brief hospitalization (3 to 60 days) relative to longer stays appeared, when considering the long-term effects, (1-2 year follow-ups) the groups were comparable. Thus, the authors suggested that aggressive aftercare might be a critical factor in maintaining clients in the community. Since this would appear to be particularly critical for short-stay clients, it is timely to reiterate that aftercare services were not one of the five "essential" services mandated by the original (1963) legislation. It was not until the list of essential services was expanded to 12 in the 1975 Amendments that follow-up of discharged clients and provision of transitional services became mandatory. The new legislation was largely a response to "revolving door" (e.g., Putten, 1977) characteristic of inpatient units; that is, although the resident population declined in mental hospitals (e.g., Bloom, 1973; Chu & Trotter, 1974) the number of admissions and readmissions were greatly increasing. This fact leaves open to speculation the value of even short-term hospitalization.

Concerning chronic populations or those institutionalized in state hospitals for uninterrupted periods of several years or more, the problems of community treatment were somewhat unique. This group was comprised of typical "back ward" residents who had lost basic skills necessary for independent living. Legislative mandates to deinstitutionalize and treat patients in the community resulted in the "dumping" of these chronic residents into various locales, largely unprepared (e.g., Scull, 1976). The places they were asked to reside in included many large hotels and "adult homes" whose populations of several hundred resembled mini-institutions (e.g., Bassuk and Gerson, 1978). Perhaps one of the critical examples of the consequences of such practice is in the city of Long Beach, New York, which is suing the State for large-scale dumping of chronic clients and requesting the closing of several adult homes. Again, an alternative is needed which would include community preparation of clients, adequate placement, and concerted follow-up — all within a coordinated "continuity of care" framework.

Before proceeding to relate some alternatives to traditional ward treatment that are in line with an environmental design viewpoint, it should be emphasized that successful deinstitutionalization of state hospitals is directly related to successful community mental health practice (short-term stays, community treatment, prevention, consultation/community education). In the eyes of the public, "community mental health" appears to be equated with community psychiatry which, in turn, is generally seen as synonymous with returning schizophrenics to the community (Jeger and Slotnick, 1978). For example, in a critique of New York State's deinstitutionalization policy in the Sunday New York Times, Duffy (1977), Chief of Nursing at Pilgrim State Hospital, stated that the "community mental health program is a Trojan horse." With professionals making such labeling "errors," how can the general public be blamed? Curiously enough, it was only months before the statement in the Times appeared that participants in the national symposium sponsored by the Kittay Scientific Foundation entitled "A Critical Appraisal of Community Psychiatry" felt "that the public should be disabused of the notion that the practice of 'dumping' former state hospital patients into communities unprepared to care for them is community mental health" (Warren, 1976, p. 10). The crucial link between the various issues (and programs) considered in this subsection is thus self-evident.

A conceptualization of alternatives

In a paper that has yet to receive the attention it merits, Ulmer & Franks (1973) proposed that "mental health" agencies be converted into "integrated, behavioral, social training programs." As an alternative to the current fragmented practice within a medical orientation, they outlined four social training levels that would be required for individuals with different levels of social competence, and that would enhance the continuity of training between these levels. Currently, the titles of the four settings corresponding to the increased competencies of clients are State and Community Mental (Psychiatric) Hospitals; Halfway Houses; Day Treatment Centers; and Outpatient Clinics. Clearly, these settings provide a continuum for a client's competence and levels of independence. Ulmer and Franks added that such integration would allow for a "scaffolding" upon which to build in staff training at different professional and paraprofessional levels as well as facilitate research and program evaluation activities.

Whereas Ulmer & Franks (1973) have presented the conceptual framework for this model, the purpose here is to cite specific programs within these levels that are in line with an environmental design approach (comparable to that of Ulmer and Franks) for developing alternatives to the hospitalization of acute psychiatric clients as well as deinstitutionalization of chronic patients. Although not all programs fit neatly into this four-way categorization, they are still discussed against this background.

In general, compatible programs vary in the scope with which supervision of clients is provided and whether the program is a residential one or not. Corresponding to the category of in-hospital programs, while it was already noted that token economy programs, which are indeed conceptualized as "planned environments" (Krasner & Krasner, 1973), may have been used to maintain mental hospitals in their existing form, they do have a viable role in connection with some recently emerging trends. For example, in terms of returning the institutionalized resident back to the community, a special "exit ward" based on behavioral principles was established at the Brockton (Massachusetts) V.A. Hospital (Avenie & Upper, 1976). By means of successive approximations, training was offered in three areas: self-maintenance skills (housekeeping, food preparation, clothing care, money management, and use of public transportation); social-interpersonal skills (group decision making and shifting their dependence from the hospital to the group); and work skills (a meaningful work assignment which they could maintain upon discharge). The transition from the hospital involved moving the group of trainees to an independent residence in the community.

A similar project exists at the Cleveland (Ohio) V.A. Hospital. Referred to as the "Behavior Development Program" (Taber, 1975), it aims to train residents who are scheduled for eventual community placement including such sheltered settings as foster homes). A similar program at Central Islip (New York) State Hospital operates within an educational model, whose origins are a "back ward" token economy (Jeger, McClure, & Krasner, 1976). Its purpose is to systematically prepare the institutionalized resident for community re-entry.

Perhaps a most ambitious attempt at bridging the gap between the institutional environment and natural community was developed by Fairweather and his colleagues (Fairweather et al., 1969; Fairweather et al., 1974). Following training in self-help, social, and vocational skills, an entire group of residents was discharged to form a cooperative "lodge" (a converted motel) whereby they jointly managed their own affairs. The lodge was not a halfway house or a transitional facility; as no live-in staff are available, supervision is phased out. Rather, it was an alternative to traditional discharge practices in which hospital residents are dispersed to different settings without a concern for lack of a social support group. The "psychological sense of community" (Sarason, 1974) that residents achieved while receiving training as a cohesive group was operating in the community facility. By means of offering janitorial and other custodial services to local customers, the lodge generated a profit of $52,000 in less than three years. Wage disbursement was the responsibility of lodge members, who allocated salaries based on a member's contribution.

Particularly intriguing about the lodge program, from an environmental design perspective, is that it was initiated as a social experiment. That is, following Fairweather's (1967) model for Experimental Social Innovation (ESI), which dictates that any new program be subjected to an experimental evaluation and utilize at least an existing program as a comparison group, the lodge was evaluated relative to a control group of patients who received traditional hospital treatment and outpatient after care. Following the closing of the lodge, nearly 80 percent of its members remained in the community, while less than 20 percent of controls did so. Further, almost 40 percent of lodge members were employed full-time, compared to less than 3 percent of the controls. From an environmental design standpoint, the Fairweather model is clearly a "social change" effort, especially when compared to the majority of token economy programs and other community preparation projects.(9) Despite its demonstrated utility, however, this approach was not immediately seized upon by hospitals. Through a special "innovation diffusion" grant from the National Institute of Mental Health, the entire lodge program has been packaged and attempts to disseminate the project to mental hospitals across the country are currently being made. Progress on lodge projects at various locations throughout the country is reported in the newly-created newsletter, Lodge Notes (Fergus, 1977).

In-hospital programs for non-institutionalized clients are found in the "model" behavioral community mental health center at Huntsville (Alabama). Behavioral training is totally individualized with no ward-wide token economy operating. An interesting and unique use of the "group" for such a population is evident at the Center. Goodson (1972) described a "group rounds" procedure as an alternative to the private practice model of individual doctor-patient rounds. That is, the entire staff and client groups meet jointly to operationalize goals, plan training, and share each other's charted progress. Continuity of care is ensured by incorporating staff from the Outpatient, Aftercare, and Day Treatment Services into the Inpatient Service, as well as by training family members of inpatients in behavior modification (Tarver & Turner, 1974).

The results of the Inpatient Service during its first year of operation were summarized by Goodson (1972). Of the 130 patients admitted, 80 percent of whom had a diagnosis of "psychosis" (diagnostic categories are employed only for administrative purposes and are not reflected in day-to-day work), the average length of stay was 18 days. Admissions to the state hospital from the catchment area were reduced by 47 percent and the jailing of mental patients was reduced by 21 percent. These data were, in turn, used to set objective goals for the following year (e.g., reducing length of stay, reducing recidivism).

An interesting experiment in the continuity of care was conducted at the Huntsville Mental Health Center (Rinn et al., 1974). Realizing difficulties in the traditional outpatient-centered aftercare (e.g., a high percentage of no-shows, failure to adhere to chemotherapy prescriptions), an alternative was introduced on an experimental basis – the Community Incentive Program (CIP). The same staff members who carried 20 client cases in office-centered treatment (OCT) engaged a comparable group of 20 clients in the CIP, which called for several unscheduled home visits to test for drug ingestion, monitoring of behavior modification programs, and administering of rewards. The CIP proved superior on all dependent measures: number of rehospitalized clients, days spent in inpatient and day treatment services, number of staff hours, and cost.

A nonhospital, residential alternative for adult "psychotics" that is compatible with environmental design is exemplified by Spruce House in Philadelphia (Henderson, 1971; Henderson & Scoles, 1970; Kelley & Henderson, 1971; Rutman, 1971). Spruce House was described as a "community-based operant learning environment" with programs for shaping work skills, development of appropriate social skills (through an intensive Interpersonal Relations Laboratory conducted daily), recreational activities, and instructional projects. A special "bridging system" is built in to transfer the acquired skills to the open community by rewarding job interviews and attendance at job training programs. When discharged to independent living, contact is maintained through membership in an Alumni Club (graduates of the program), thus allowing for continuity of care.

Originally conceived as an experiment, residents were randomly assigned to Spruce House, a General Hospital, or the State Hospital. At the end of an 18-month follow-up no significant differences between groups were apparent on such outcome variables as community tenure, rehospitalization, and employment (Rutman, 1971), although preliminary data appeared to favor Spruce House (Henderson & Scoles, 1970). On the positive side, the project demonstrated that a community-based residence was a viable alternative to psychiatric hospitalization for otherwise hospital bound clients.

Finally, another important facet of the Spruce House project, from an environmental design viewpoint, was addressed in a separate paper by Henderson (1969). Its focus was on "coexisting with the community" – overcoming community resistance to having potentially dangerous, mentally ill people in their midst. Despite court hearings and other obstructions, an effective program was launched, to the point of gaining community respect and acceptance. Thus, environmental designers must learn effective community relations procedures to shape "hospitality" (see Slotnick & Jeger, 1978).

Findings similar to those at Spruce House were reported for a nonbehavioral, relatively less structured program in the San Francisco Bay area – Soteria House (Mosher & Mann, 1979; Mosher, Mann, & Matthews, 1975). Relative to inpatient treatment in an active milieu/chemotherapy program in a community mental health center, the group of young, first-admission schizophrenics assigned to Soteria House fared similarly on most outcome measures at six-month and one-year follow-ups. However, a major difference favoring the community program was in perceived "psychosocial climate." That is, Soteria was perceived by its staff as being higher on relationship variables and lower on staff control, relative to the Center's staff perception of their wards. This further points to the viability of a community based program for this target population.

In another compatible program at the Mendota Mental Health Institute (Madison, Wisconsin), Stein & Test (1978) and Test & Stein (1975, 1976) found the "Training in Community Living Program," a total in-community effort (as opposed to residential or centralized setting) at training in coping skills to be a superior alternative to hospitalization. Again, beginning as a social experiment, patients seeking psychiatric hospitalization were randomly assigned either to short-term inpatient care or "community treatment" for a 14-month period. During the first year, subjects in the community program spent less time in the hospital and more time in independent (non-supervised) living, less time unemployed, indicated greater life satisfaction, showed reduced symptomatology, and reduced family burden (e.g., time missed from work, social life disruptions). The authors attribute the success of the program to the fact that it occurred in the natural environment, and suggest the extensive use of social learning principles for skill training. They recommend maintaining potential patients in their homes to avoid the stigma of hospitalization where they learn to adopt a "patient" role. Further, the use of a standard treatment site (i.e., "learning center") for higher functioning clients is recommended, while reserving in vivo training for those who are less likely to attend a centralized facility or for whom training does not generalize to the natural environment.

While the above program may be ideal, the majority of nonresidential programs for psychiatric clients, especially the chronically institutionalized, take place in day treatment centers (Luber, 1979). The widespread use of day treatment services is apparent from National Institute of Mental Health statistical data (Taube, 1973) which shows that, as of January 1972, there were over 118,000 persons treated in 989 programs, compared to less than 8,000 treated in 114 programs in 1963. The Community Mental Health Centers Act which mandated partial hospitalization as an essential service was, indeed, found to account for a large portion of the increase. However, programs also opened in state hospitals, V.A. hospitals, general hospitals, and free-standing clinics. Silverman & Val (1975) pointed to the particular importance of day treatment services due to their central position in the "continuity of service" network.

A day treatment program that is in line with an environmental design approach is the Oxnard (California) Day Treatment Center (Eckman, 1979; Liberman, 1973; Liberman et al., 1974; Liberman, King, & DeRisi, 1976). The entire programming at Oxnard operates around a Coupon Incentive System (token economy) and "educational" workshop model. Workshops are designed to develop social skills, self-management skills, and, in general, to promote a greater sense of autonomy. An interesting feature of the workshops is that they are conducted for eight week sessions, with two week intersession periods during which staff work on revising the curriculum. Further in line with this "school" model, tuition is charged for admission to workshops and credits (tokens) are earned commensurate with participation level. This reflects a unique merging of the behavioral and educational components of the program. Although based at the mental health center, DeRisi and Roberts (1975) reported hearing that clients told friends and relatives of their attendance at "classes" rather than going for treatment.

Many facets of the Oxnard program were subjected to rigorous evaluative studies. For example, Liberman et al. (1974) found significant increases in social participation following the introduction of the behavioral-educational workshop model at Oxnard, relative to another day treatment center. Also, pre- and post-observations showed Oxnard staff to have significantly increased the relative time spent in direct client contact. Using Goal Attainment Scaling as the evaluation tool, Austin et al. (1976) found greater attainment of therapeutic goals among Oxnard patients, relative to a comparable group at a "milieu therapy" day treatment program, with the Oxnard results being even more marked at a two year follow-up period.

The "continuity of care" process at Oxnard was reported on by Liberman (1973). Collaboration exists between the Oxnard Day Treatment Center and nearby Camarillo State Hospital which operates a behaviorally-oriented inpatient ward. Thus, patients may be sent to the Oxnard program while still returning evenings or weekends to the Camarillo ward. Staff of community-based board and care homes are trained in the application of behavioral techniques upon accepting an Oxnard client as a resident. Extensive use is made of contingency contracting as a vehicle for increasing the continuity of care with a multitude of more open community settings (schools, probation departments, etc.).

Presently, the Oxnard staff are engaged in a national dissemination of the Behavior Analysis and Modification (BAM) Project through a National Institute of Mental Health Innovation Diffusion Grant (similar to that for the Fairweather Lodge). The BAM Project encompasses a comprehensive set of behavioral packages applicable to community mental health centers. These include packages of the Day Treatment educational workshops, a Parent Survival Kit, Personal Effectiveness Training, and Contingency Contracting, among others (L.W. King, 1976).

Although it is not known how many community mental health centers are adopting the BAM package, some reports in the literature point to the increasing reliance upon social learning programs, at least in day treatment settings. Examples are to be found in the Partial Hospitalization Program of the University of Pittsburgh's Medical School (Luber & Hersen, 1976) and the Northeast Community Mental Health Center in Memphis, Tennessee (Sanders et al., 1976).

Finally, coming to the end of Ulmer and Franks' (1973) continuum (outpatient clinics for the more socially competent clients), suffice it to outline a direction for compatible environmental design interventions. First, environmental design reconceptualizes the traditional doctor-patient relationship in outpatient treatment to one of "teacher-trainee." This presupposes a more active role on the part of clients in learning skills to enhance their self-control and ability to influence their environment in accordance with their own values and goals. Available modalities include the broad-spectrum behavior therapies as well as other "behavior-influence" (Krasner & Ullmann, 1973) strategies such as group methods and social psychological techniques.

A particularly compatible set of principles that can provide the basis for environmentally oriented interventions by outpatient teams is to be found in the ever-growing field of crisis intervention (see Jeger, 1979; McGee, 1974). Specialized crisis intervention programs for numerous target populations have been developed (i.e., widows, divorced, suicidal). Such services are provided by means of treatment in outpatient units, on-site counseling at the crisis scene, telephone counseling, and ongoing mutual-aid groups. These functions are also relevant for meeting the emergency-service mandate for community mental health centers.

Appraisal and status

In conclusion, several points need to be made regarding community alternatives to hospitalization. First, it remains unclear whether the advent of community mental health centers helped to reduce admissions to state hospitals (see Windle & Scully, 1976), and to keep former state hospital residents in the community. Perhaps what is needed urgently is coordination between activities of state hospitals and community mental health centers, or as Wallis and Katf (1972) have put it, "The 50-Mile Bridge" needs to be crossed.

Concerning the deinstitutionalization of long-stay patients, the empirical basis for such policies (as they are being implemented) is still being questioned. For example, while such factors as the availability of phenothiazines to maintain clients in the community and the changing conceptions of institutional influences (e.g., Goffman, 1961) are generally used to support such policies, Scull (1976) has cogently argued that the recent impetus for the "decarceration of the mentally ill" is tied to the notion that "the availability of welfare programs has rendered the social control functions of incarcerating the mentally ill much less salient . . . other forms of social control have become equally functional" (p. 174). He considered the primary significance of the alternative arguments "to be their value as ideological camouflage" (p. 212).

Whatever the accurate rationale for the original policy turns out to be, the current state of affairs is best described by the recent conclusion reached in a 250-page report to the Congress of the United States by the Comptroller General (1977) entitled <u>Returning the Mentally Disabled to the Community: Government Needs to Do More</u>:

> Mentally disabled persons have been released from public institutions without (1) adequate community-based facilities and services being arranged for and (2) an effective management system to make sure that only those needing inpatient or residential care were placed in public institutions and that persons released were appropriately placed and received needed services. (P. 172)

It may very well be, as Gottesfeld (1976) concluded following his review of data on alternatives to hospitalization, "that funded programs for psychotics must be on a continual basis." (p. 9) and are needed indefinitely. It remains for future research to determine the relative efficacy of various community alternatives (e.g., foster care versus halfway houses; behavioral versus milieu day treatment programs).

While the search for nonhospital "utopias" has hardly begun, barriers to deinstitutionalization and pressures for maintaining the status quo of state hospitals abound (Jeger & Slotnick, 1978; Slotnick & Jeger, 1978; Slotnick, Jeger, & Cantor, 1978). Unless a viable alternative to hospitals can be found soon, the barriers will only strengthen. The position taken here is that endorsement of an environmental design viewpoint is a step in the direction of finding such an alternative. Some recent suggestions (e.g., Sheppard, 1977) as a reaction to findings of negative community attitudes toward the mentally ill (e.g., Fracchia et al., 1976) — professionals should be the first to change from their "disease" orientation which is responsible for their sharing the same negative attitudes — is consistent with an environmental design argument. The recent direction within NIMH and state department of mental health in establishing community support systems for discharged mental patients (see Stein, 1979; Turner & Shifrin, 1979) is highly compatible with environmental design. However, it is cautioned that professionals' adherence to the "mental illness" model may stand in the way of best intentions.

As a final note, it should be indicated that while this entire subsection focused on adult psychiatric clients, similar trends toward community alternatives are to be found for such populations/groups as children, mentally retarded, juvenile delinquents, adult offenders, drug addicts, alcoholics, and the elderly. These target groups are now incorporated (at least to some extent) into the domain of community mental health. A similar conceptualization to that offered by Ulmer and Franks (1973) for psychiatric clients would likewise be applicable for these populations. Many examples of programs for these groups that are in line with an environmental design viewpoint can be found in the recent volumes by Luber (1979) and Nietzel et al. (1977).

Ethnicity and Mental Health

In this day of ethnic awareness, any discussion of mental health would be incomplete without a consideration of the ethnic factor. This is particularly so when writing about environmental design which will be shown to have special implications for the delivery of community mental health services to ethnic minorities. The limited utility of traditional psychotherapy (e.g., psychoanalysis) to members of ethnic minority groups follows from similar observations to those on social class and psychotherapy.

E. Jones (1974) began his review of the empirical research on social class and psychotherapy by quoting Freud (1905/1953) who stated that for psychoanalysis "those patients who do not possess a reasonable degree of education and a fairly reliable character should be refused" (p. 263). It is, therefore, not at all surprising that lower class patients were more likely to receive such treatments as electroshock and tranquilizers, relative to middle and upper classes who received psychotherapy. Further, lower class patients were more likely to be diagnosed "psychotic," compared to middle class people who were more likely to be classified as normal or neurotic. Jones cited additional research which points to a relationship between social class and continuation in psychotherapy. That is, even when accepted, lower class patients were more likely to drop out. Similarly, blacks were more likely to drop out compared to whites.

In line with this research stream, Rabkin and Struening (1976) found differences in mental hospitalization rates between different ethnic and religious groups in New York City. Differences between blacks, Puerto Ricans, Jews, Italians, and Irish were in part attributed to differences in the socioeconomic status between these groups. This study reflects the more current trend which seeks to understand differences between ethnic groups, including white minorities, as opposed to just racial differences between blacks and whites.

Such a trend is especially evident in a recent large-scale study of minority group services provided by 17 community mental health centers in the Seattle (Washington) area (Sue, 1977). Differences between blacks, native Americans, Asian-Americans, Chicanos, and whites were found on such variables as utilization rates (blacks and native Americans were overrepresented, while Asian-Americans and Chicanos were underrepresented), diagnosis (blacks were more likely to be diagnosed as having a "personality disorder" and less likely to be considered in the category of "transient situational disorder," relative to whites; no differences between the other groups emerged), types of personnel seen (among other between-group differences, Asian-Americans and blacks were more likely to be treated by nonprofessionals when compared to whites, even when demographic variables were controlled for), types of services rendered (blacks were more often assigned to inpatient, relative to whites, with no differences emerging in the other groups), and premature termination (with each ethnic group having a significantly higher drop out rate, relative to whites). The latter finding was seen as especially disturbing, since termination was looked at following only one session. Thus, it appears as though community mental health centers have not been successful in being responsive to the mental health needs of minority groups that were already excluded from the mainstream of mental health services. It was suggested by the author that this may be partly attributed to cultural barriers that still exist between the middle class dominated centers and their target populations.

Some suggestions for improved community mental health services to minority groups were offered by Sue (1977). These include the training of mental health personnel to be sensitive to minority needs and hiring staff from the ethnic communities, developing specialized satellite centers in the heart of an ethnic neighborhood, and developing new therapeutic modalities that are geared to the members of diverse ethnic backgrounds. These suggestions also follow from a previous review of mental health services to Spanish-speaking/surnamed (SSS) populations by Padilla, Ruiz, and Alvarez (1975). They attributed the under-utilization of mental health services by the SSS groups to "discouraging institutional policies." These include such factors as inappropriate intake procedures, long waiting periods, inaccessibility due to geographic isolation, language barriers (lack of Spanish-speaking thera-pists), class-bound values (the 50-minute hour as the sole therapeutic intervention), and cultural values (professional misjudgment and mis-diagnosis associated with culturally accepted behaviors by ethnic minorities). Padilla et al. went on to offer some additional recommen-dations for improving community mental health services to the SSS groups. In addition to hiring community members who are bilingual and bicultural to serve as paraprofessionals, they emphasized the particular qualifications of faith healers and practitioners of folk medicine within these communities since they already have a fair degree of acceptance. Further, they suggested the incorporation of community representation in the administration of a center in order to enhance the center's acceptance within a community. Ultimately, it will be necessary to train more mental health professionals from SSS groups so that they will have a fairer representation in leadership positions. In order to enhance the accessibility of services, they suggested providing transportation services, child-care arrangements, and flexible operating hours, and advertising the availability of services in minority group media (e.g., Mexican radio stations).

While many of the above suggestions are compatible with an environmental design model for community mental health, some more unique contributions that follow from the model are indicated below. The failure of current community mental health centers to meet the needs of ethnic minorities is clearly predictable from an environmental design viewpoint. Perhaps most representative of an environmental design critique of current services is to be found in the following statement from Padilla et al. (1975):

> Mental health centers. . . are so overly committed to traditional models of health care delivery that they ignore other problems troubling the SSS that are of much greater severity. Occasionally centers and agencies offer chemotherapy with some variation of individual or group counseling to deal with emotional conflicts of an allegedly intrapsychic nature. These treatment services completely deny, of course, the bonafide problems of a "social" nature that are anxiety provoking, depressing, frustrating, enraging, debilitating, and potentially disruptive to adaptive psychological function. These problems include premature termi-nation of education among the young, elevated rates of arrest and incarceration, widespread abuse of alcohol and illegal drugs, and high rates of unemployment, to cite only the most obvious and destructive. (P. 900)

Thus, the limitations of a narrow medical model diverted the focus from the broader social context in which human problems are developed and maintained.

The above is in line with several critical points raised by Giordano and Giordano (1976) in a review of ethnicity and community mental health. They took the position that the limited impact of community mental health centers since 1963, especially as it pertains to ethnic groups, was due, among other reasons, to a focus on pathology which stood in the way of developing natural support and self-help systems, as well as the artificial notion of the catchment area that precluded servicing functional communities tied together by racial, ethnic, religious, or cultural bonds. These two factors are clearly intertwined since the "individualistic" nature of the intrapsychic model lacks a provision for considering the influence of the entire ecological sphere on individual behavior. The environmental design approach implies an emphasis on the promotion of positive, adaptive skills in an enhancement framework, as discussed in a previous subsection, rather than relying upon a curative, clinical orientation. Thus, environmental design calls for a true "community" alternative to the provision of services to ethnic minorities, rather than just providing modified psychotherapy services. The thrust of environmental design interventions, then, should be aimed at the modification of the social institutions which result in the conditions cited by Padilla et al. (1975), and are deemed to be at the root of their psychological well-being. This involves the utilization of community mental health personnel in roles of advocates to combat racial and ethnic discrimination by these institutions. Specifically, as suggested by Giordano and Giordano (1976), a concrete set of skills that need to be developed by mental health professionals centers around the mobilization of ethnic communities to form coalitions that might cut across several ethnic barriers to serve as advocates on their own behalf. The existing ties within an ethnic community can be exploited for such purposes. This follows from the notion that the problem is not one of mental illness, but is clearly social in nature.

Some interesting epidemiological data that bear on the use of a cohesive community stem from one of the alternative explanations for social class and schizophrenia relationships that was offered by Kohn (1973). The diagnostic biases discussed earlier notwithstanding, Kohn suggested that the greater incidence of schizophrenia among the lower classes is due, largely, to the high rates found for lower class members of specific ethnic groups residing in areas where other ethnic groups predominate. As an example he cited data from a study of Italian-Americans in Boston, who were found to have a high incidence of schizophrenia when living in predominantly non-Italian neighborhoods, while those living in Italian neighborhoods did not. This is consistent with some research cited by Padilla et al. (1975) on SSS members – the SSS subcultures contain built-in supports (e.g., the extended family) which protect their members from social breakdowns; and, with acculturation, the SSS will be subjected to increased emotional problems since their traditional social structure will be weakened.

Some unique applications of behavior-influence techniques to minority populations are beginning to provide a data base for environmental design interventions as they relate to community mental health services to ethnic groups. One example is to be found in the work of Miller and Miller (1970) who showed that offering tangible reinforcements to welfare recipient members of a self-help group markedly increased their attendance at meetings. Further, it appeared that attendance at these self-help meetings generalized to participation in other forms of self-help, including the increased use of tutors for their children. Thus, the large-scale use of reinforcement principles has the potential of increasing the prerequisite behaviors for poor people to take greater control in designing their environments.

Another example comes from a study by Hauserman, Walen, and Behling (1973), which was alluded to in an earlier subsection in connection with open education. In this study, the authors found that social and tangible reinforcement was instrumental in increasing social integration of black children in a predominantly white, first-grade classroom. The reinforced interactions in the lunchroom were found to generalize to interracial interaction in a free-play setting. The implication of this research is its large-scale applicability to inducing racial integration without first bringing about changes in attitude. Such activity is deemed to be within the role of the environmental designer based in a community mental health center's consultation unit.

In terms of clinical interventions with minority populations, the use of social learning principles likewise provides a viable alternative to traditional forms of verbal psychotherapy which were shown to be uniquely geared to YAVIS (young, attractive, verbal, intelligent, and successful) clients (Schofield, 1964). Although congruence between race and class of therapists and clients was found to enhance outcome (E. Jones, 1974), perhaps a unique aspect of the behavioral model with its emphasis on who is done (rather than who does it) lies in its potential to rely less on such congruence. By sensitizing influencers to the diversity of values associated with different cultures, it may not be necessary to attempt what is often impossible – matching therapists and clients on demographics. It is hoped that an environmental design contribution to community mental health services for ethnic groups will bring us a step closer to fulfilling Ullmann's (1977) vision for "behavioral community psychology":

> Much of our effort as a democratic group will be to make age, sex, race, and ethnicity irrelevant so that we can honestly focus on what people do and respond to them on the basis of their individual accomplishments rather than their demographic stereotypes. (P. xxiii)

In the course of striving for the above goal, however, it is clear that for behavioral skills training to be effective with ethnic groups, personnel from ethnic minorities at all professional levels may prove essential.

In his discussion of behavioral treatment with lower socioeconomic groups, Rappaport (1977) argued that:

> Although theoretically behavior modification requires the therapist to accept and understand the values and natural environment of his or her client, in practice this is not easy to achieve. Most behavior therapists, like traditional therapists, come from a middle class background. They are just as likely as other therapists to select goals and operate on a value system which seeks to make all people conform to middle class norms. (P. 88)

Rappaport cautioned that "both the goals and language of treatment need to make sense to the client in his or her own terms" (p. 88) if behavior therapists are to overcome the problems of relating to lower class persons encountered by traditional therapists.

Thus, the utility of minority personnel for conducting behavioral training is crucial just from the point of view of "communication." As emphasized by Yen (1976), in his discussion of behavioral treatments to minority groups, the use of minority "vocabulary" in such procedures as contracting and the production of parent training manuals in minority languages would be a major factor in dissemination, accessibility, and effectiveness. This is crucial considering the differential effectiveness of parent behavioral training with middle and low income groups. For example, in the behaviorally-oriented Huntsville (Alabama) Mental Health Center, the previously cited parent training program was found to be more effective with middle income clients – both in terms of goal attainment (93 percent versus 5 percent) and attendance rate (4.9 versus 3.1 sessions). White mothers and those with higher incomes were also more likely to profit from the previously cited behavioral parent training program at the Baton Rouge (Louisiana) Mental Health Center (Baenninger & Ulmer, 1975). An interesting practical suggestion for training lower-income parents in behavior modification is derived from Rose's (1974) project in which welfare parents were found to perform better when grouped with middle-class parents compared to those trained in a homogeneous group. The ethnic factor in parent behavioral training is especially crucial since parent training was a major strategy for community enhancement and the development of self-control.

Finally, although not emphasized in this subsection, the previous quotation from Ullmann (1977) necessitates at least some mention of women and community mental health services. A recent exposition of traditional psychotherapy's treatment of women can be found in Tennov's (1975) Psychotherapy: The Hazardous Cure. Briefly, Tennov traced the sexist image of women in the field of psychotherapy to the domination of Freudian theory which views women as inferior. Such biases prevail as a disproportionate number of women end up in client roles relative to therapist roles.

Although the concerns pertaining to behavioral treatment of ethnic groups also apply to women, Tennov (1975) pointed to the emerging behavioral approaches as a more promising alternative for mental health services for women. By relying on environmental explanations of human problems, behavioral therapies do not adhere to unvalidated sexist assumptions which stem from earlier intrapsychic theories. The compatibility of the behavioral viewpoint with a nonsexist orientation to women is also reflected in such recently initiated publications as the "Behaviorists for Social Action Journal" (Morrow, 1978) and "The Feminist/Behaviorist Newsletter" (Lewis, 1977). An example of a major area that pertains to the broader aspects of environmental design and follows from the merging of the feminist and behavioral streams is the study of sex-role development and change. Also compatible with environmental design is an interesting program by Davis (1977) in which she developed women's liberation groups as a primary prevention strategy. In conclusion, an environmental design model is beginning to provide a knowledge base from which alternative behavioral opportunities will be forthcoming to half the population.

Ethical Issues

Whereas attention has been increasingly directed to ethical considerations in psychotherapy as well as the general mental health field (e.g., Shore & Golann, 1973), and whereas the ethical concerns pertaining to the general field of environmental design have been discussed by Hutchison (chapter 2), the purpose of this subsection is to highlight some key ethical issues that are unique to the community mental health professional as environmental designer.

When moving beyond one-to-one clinical interventions to organizational and social change efforts, ethical concerns become especially critical. As Levine & Fasnacht (1974) have indicated, the "danger at this locus of intervention is that the errors we make will affect many people. Bad individual psychotherapy hurts one person; a bad token economy hurts an entire ward of people; bad social change hurts a countless multitude" (p. 13). Such ethical and/or legal issues as informed consent, confidentiality, invasion of privacy, the right to treatment, the right to refuse treatment, and the obligation to provide the least restrictive alternative, to name but some of the key areas of concern in individual and institutional behavior-change programs, are only more complicated in community practice. To a large extent, the behavioral consultant role proposed for the environmental designer in community mental health, which ultimately casts the professional as an institutional change agent, is at the root of a previously less complicated ethical dilemma. Jeger (1977) suggested that perhaps the major dilemma confronting a consultant is the question "Whose agent am I?"

To illustrate the above with an example, the following hypothetical situation is offered. A white, male consultant from a local, middle-class dominated community mental health center is called in by a white principal of a recently integrated ghetto school with implicit objectives of helping ease tensions which would allow all his white staff to maintain their jobs. Is the consultant the agent of the principal? the teachers? the "parent board"? the courts? the students? the mental health center? his/her profession? or his/her own agent? It is clear that the interests of those involved are at conflict and the environmental designer as consultant will have to choose sides since not everyone is likely to be satisfied. Are there times when consultation should not be undertaken at all? Certainly from an ethical standpoint, the issue raised by Cherniss (1976) in his discussion of "pre-entry" concerns in consultation – namely, that the "value congruence" between the consultant and the consultee system must be considered before making a decision to consult – is relevant here. Before offering a general ethical guideline that derives from the value system implied by an environmental design model, several additional factors that complicate the ethical dilemma are indicated.

Considering the basic "seeking-mode" style of service-delivery associated with the community mental health orientation (Rappaport & Chinsky, 1974), which is increasingly being reflected in the trend of mental health professionals offering consultation without waiting for an invitation (e.g., Miller, Pinkerton, & Hollister, 1970), the ethical questions become even more difficult to answer. The reality of increased contact with community caretakers as part of the consultation process led the respondents in Shore & Golann's (1969) survey of ethical problems in community mental health to indicate special confidentiality issues. Further, the increased reliance upon nonprofessionals as primary interventionists as well as consultants presents unique ethical problems. Due to the relatively short training periods, special care needs to be taken to insure that misapplications of behavior-influence techniques not take place. (Stein, 1975, raised the same question with professionals exposed to behavior modification techniques by means of short-term workshops.) Also, since environmental design represents a merging of service and research, special ethical issues arise from conducting research while offering community services. Examples of the latter include the ethics of employing control groups which do not receive the intervention. The position taken here is that we are obligated to our clients to employ control groups if we are to come closer to evaluating the relative impact of any service program. An additional concern regarding the increasing use of data banks and psychiatric case registers for community research, with special reference to the issue of privacy, was raised by Shore & Golann (1969). Finally, with recent emphasis on deinstitutionalization and the establishment of group homes and halfway houses in the community, strong resistance from residents appears to be the rule. The ethical/legal question here is, as Haywood (1976) put it, "What are the rights of individuals to say who will and will not live in their neighborhoods?" (p. 316)

The general ethical principle that is useful in guiding the community mental health professional as environmental designer is imbedded in the ultimate goal of environmental design as a movement — namely, to design communities that increase the likelihood for all individuals to plan their own environments in accordance with their own values and goals. By providing opportunities for people to influence their own environments we are enhancing their individual freedom. The only ethically sound interventions by mental health professionals are those that will increase their independence and autonomy, or as Skinner (1975) has stated in his paper on the ethics of helping, "one has most effectively helped others when one can stop helping them altogether" (p. 625). This notion is seen as compatible with the social reform theme that Hersch (1972) identified in community mental health — the notion of "community control." According to Hersch:

> Community control is a specific reflection of the larger social reform emphasis on the self-determination of people and on their control over the institutions that affect their lives. It had its origin in the "maximum feasible participation" concept of the

war on poverty, a concept which in many ways epitomized the
social reform spirit of the early 1960s. (P. 752)

In practice, as Hersch has stated, this involves employing members from
the consumer community on the policymaking board of a community
mental health service. Thus, the professional is an agent of his/her
constituency in line with the notion of the "professional as servant" (p.
751). It is, therefore, incumbent upon the environmental designer to
critically examine the likely consequences of his/her interventions upon
the freedom of his/her less powerful constituents before undertaking
any action.

The ethical stance espoused for environmental design is compatible
with the values of cultural relativity and diversity underlying Rappaport's (1977) ecological model of community psychology. His articulation of these values is particularly illuminating and is thus cited below.
He began by stating that all human service models are based on two
basic dimensions – an economic policy dimension and a cultural value
dimension. He then went on to distinguish between the conservative and
liberal positions within both of these dimensions:

> The conservative economic position favors individual respon-
> sibility as opposed to societal responsibility for economic
> welfare. The liberal economic position favors societal economic
> responsibility. With regard to cultural values, the liberal, while
> "tolerating" differences (e.g., one should not discriminate be-
> cause of them), seeks a unified society with one standard by
> which all people can be fairly judged. Each person has a right to
> private beliefs, but judgments of competence, and, therefore,
> employment and educational opportunity, must be based on the
> same standards for all. More important, the liberal tends to
> support a system in which the federal government helps everyone
> to adapt to the prevailing culture. . . . The conservative on the
> cultural value dimension is much more inclined to support
> diversity, believing one's own values are better, but differences
> among local communities, cultures, and people are a fact of life
> not to be tampered with by "big government". (Pp. 23-24)

The ecological model of community psychology proposed by Rappaport
is one that cuts across these two dimensions – a liberal economic
position and a conservative cultural position. This is summarized in
table 7.1.

Likewise, the liberal component of environmental design supports
federal provision of resources but has as its ultimate goal an
individualistic-conservative component which calls for individual and
local community determination of utilizing these resources rather than
imposing dominant middle-class values. Furthermore, since it is usually
the case that the poor lack the know-how of utilizing power due to a
prior history of not providing input, it becomes an ethical obligation of
the community mental health professional as environmental designer to
train his/her constituents for such activity. A promising direction for

Table 7.1. Dimensions of Human Services Models

	Economic	Cultural
Conservative	individual responsibility	supports diversity and differential community life styles
	no federal support of social welfare	no government tampering
Liberal	societal economic responsibility	seeks unified society with one standard
	supports social welfare programs	government should help people conform to prevailing culture

Source: Based on Rappaport, 1977.

such training can be derived from the behavioral stream of the environmental design model as exemplified by Briscoe, Hoffman, & Bailey (1975) who employed behavioral techniques in training members of a "community board" in problem solving.

Program Evaluation

Having emphasized the merging of research and service as a major aspect of the environmental design model — each intervention must also employ a built-in evaluation design — the purpose of this subsection is to consider the major types of evaluations and to highlight some of the key issues in the emerging field of mental health program evaluation. Although clinical researchers have long been concerned with the evaluation of psychotherapy (e.g., Bergin & Strupp, 1970; Eysenck, 1952, 1966; Meltzoff & Kornreich, 1970), program evaluation or evaluation research as a distinct specialty is said to be the outgrowth of the broader social and educational projects of the late 1960s and early 1970s (Glass, 1976). As funding and accrediting agencies increased their demands for accountability, the emphasis on evaluation permeated the mental health field. This emphasis is specifically reflected in community mental health centers, as the 1975 Amendments (Public Law 94-63) require federally funded centers to conduct program evaluation and obligates the allocation of two percent of operating funds for such purposes.

As is shown below, NIMH is actively engaged in developing guidelines to assist centers in implementing the foregoing program evaluation mandate. It will be recalled that issues pertaining to evaluation represented an area of criticism for the Nader group (Chu & Trotter, 1974). Specifically, NIMH's lack of an initial mandate for evaluation when the center program was launched, the later use of contract agencies to conduct evaluations (rather than require centers to carry them out for themselves), and the fact that the information generated was not translated into policy changes were among the major criticisms levied against NIMH. Thus, this shifting interest is clearly in line with the empirical accountability spirit of environmental design. To reiterate, the unique position of the environmental design model is that evaluation becomes an integral part of every service and intervention program, and that a constant flow of feedback derived from evaluative research be made available for purposes of implementing programmatic changes. That this latter aspect is gaining wide acceptance is reflected in the recent modification in the title of the journal, Evaluation (founded in 1972, and co-sponsored by NIMH) to Evaluation and Planned Change.

With the above as background, what are some of the common approaches derived from the field of program evaluation that pertain to the community mental health professional as environmental designer? Since there is no standardized way of categorizing the various approaches in the program evaluation area, the typology offered by McLean (1974) is adopted here to provide a framework for discussing the major issues.   Focusing on broadly-based mental health programs, McLean (1974) identified five major approaches to evaluation: program structure, program process, program outcome, cost analysis, and systems analysis.

Program structure

To McLean, the evaluation of program structure is seen as administrative evaluation, as its major concern is with the resources allocated to a program. It includes such data as staff-client ratios, the nature of the clientele, and characteristics of the physical facilities. In general, information derived from such evaluations are descriptive. Although not bearing directly on the effectiveness of a program, such data are especially useful to determine who is served and how much service is provided relative to the needs (Hammer, Landsberg, & Neigher, 1976).

Program process

Evaluation of program process is concerned with documenting what is going on during an entire intervention. It may consider such aspects as continuity of treatment and may incorporate analyses of case studies and treatment failures in search for what really happened. Ellsworth (1975b) pointed to the increased attention that is being paid to documenting what is done to clients in mental health settings, as peer review and quality control committees have developed to examine client records.   He cautioned against the emerging imbalance in the field — the focus on process monitoring at the expense of outcome evaluation — as it might lead to standardizing treatment practices without evidence of effectiveness. It should be added that many of the so-called process studies do shed some light on outcome by considering such variables as client satisfaction and even short-term indexes of effectiveness.

Program outcome

Outcome evaluation is considered by McLean (1974) "as the most fundamental and significant kind of evaluation data. It is the 'proof-in-the-pudding' of all mental health programs" (p. 90). Furthermore, R.R. Jones (1974) defined the entire field of program evaluation in terms of outcome assessment:

> For this writer, that part of social science research which has come to be known as evaluation has as its central concern the study of behavioral change: behavioral change that is public and hence observable, and behavioral change that is either directly or indirectly due to some form of programmatic manipulation . . . . Demonstrating that behavior has changed as a result of programmatic interventions serves as a major mandate for virtually all program evaluators and producing that behavioral change is the major mandate for all program planners and directors. (P. 1)

This statement of emphasis is very much in line with the environmental design position on the goals of interventions and criteria for the assessment of interventions — overt behavioral changes in target populations.

Issues pertaining to assessment are largely captured by McLean's (1974) statement: "The problem in outcome evaluation has been what to ask for, how to ask it, and when to ask it" (p. 90). While these same issues have plagued psychotherapy researchers they are even more complex when evaluating an entire mental health program, and especially when the program is of an indirect service type (e.g., consultation). Sources of data to assess changes have largely been directed toward client changes and measured by self-reports, staff ratings, ratings of significant others, or overt naturalistic behavior observations (with measures based on these sources not always correlating, Ellsworth, 1975a). Criteria have included symptom checklists, ratings of global functioning, changes in psychiatric traits, client satisfaction, or reduction of admissions to treatment facilities (McLean, 1974). Specifically focusing on outcome studies in mental hospitals, Erickson (1975) cited studies which employed hospital or community stays as outcome measures, while others looked at inhospital functioning, and still others emphasized follow-up measures of outcome. The demonstration of long-term impact represents the ultimate challenge of all mental health programs. It represents a particular challenge to behavioral interventions based on the operant conditioning model, as they were recently noted for the relative paucity of data pertaining to their long-term and/or generalization effects (Keeley, Shemberg, & Carbonell, 1976).

In terms of demonstrating long-term impact of a program, the timing dilemma inherent in evaluation that Wortman (1975) pointed to is worth noting. He stated that "The longer the period of evaluation, the more likely are systems feedback effects to alter and reduce its impact;

and the shorter the period, the less likely the program will have sufficient time to achieve its goals" (Wortman, 1975, p. 574). As is argued below, this points to the need for continuous assessment or at least measurement at several points in time.

Turning to research design, perhaps the key controversy centers around the utility of experimental designs. Clearly, from a methodological standpoint, a treatment/intervention versus control group design with pre- and postmeasures taken on both groups (i.e., a true experimental design, Campbell & Stanley, 1966) is seen as ideal. Despite difficulties in assigning clients to control groups in natural settings, leading behavioral scientists have advocated the experimental model in evaluating social programs. Prototypical of this approach is Fairweather's (1967, 1972) notion of "Experimental Social Innovation" mentioned in a previous subsection. To reiterate, he suggested designing innovations and scientifically evaluating their effectiveness by means of experimental comparisons with already existing programs. Although, as Thomander (1976) has noted, the problem of true random assignment still remains in such a model, the comparability of populations may be determined post hoc with unmatched factors to be accounted for statistically. Wortman (1975), in offering a psychological perspective on evaluation research, also advocated the classical experimental approach (although he incorporated aspects of nonexperimental evaluations in his model). This is also consistent with Campbell's (1969) notions of the "experimenting society," whereby an experimental methodology is recommended to evaluate social reform programs, and that the data serve to guide social policy.

On the other hand, Weiss & Rein (1970) pointed to the limitations of experimental designs in evaluating broad-aim social programs from both practical and conceptual perspectives. For example, a major drawback of the experimental model lies in its inability to shed light on negative findings. No between group mean differences allows for alternative interpretations to the apparent conclusion that the program had no positive impact. Unmeasured changes could have taken place, insensitive instruments could have been selected, or gains obtained by one segment of a population could have been cancelled by a relatively unaffected segment. Further, even in the case of positive findings, it is difficult to determine whether forces other than the program could be causing the effects due to the overwhelming number of uncontrolled factors. Also, the "Hawthorne Effect" associated with any new innovation becomes almost impossible to control in a field experiment, leaving placebo factors as a possible explanation in simple experimental versus control group designs (Erickson, 1975). The use of additional control groups is rarely possible in the field. Finally, group research which depicts the average client before and after an intervention may be of little relevance to front-line staff who deal with unique individuals (Thomander, 1976). Thus, such designs may meet with resistance from staff (Ellsworth, 1975a) and administrators who, in turn, would influence the nature of the data collected or even the entire operation of a program (Weiss & Rein, 1970).

Realizing the above limitations, alternatives to experimental designs propose evaluation models that are predicated on the view that action programs are a continuous, ongoing process. Rather than one-shot measures to assess outcome, the comprehensive feedback models which have been offered focus on a close monitoring of program process, incorporating historical and political analyses within a social systems framework (D'Augelli, 1976; Guttentag, 1971, 1973; Suchman, 1972; Weiss & Rein, 1970).

The flavor of these alternative evaluation models is best captured by the following statement from Weiss and Rein (1970):

> Evaluations of broad-aim programs should identify the forces which shaped the program, the nature of the opposition encountered, the reasons for success or failure, and the program's unanticipated consequences. Then, in addition, the research might decide whether or not anticipated changes occurred. The issue in the evaluation of broad-aim program is not "Does it work," but "What happened." (P. 103-4)

For the community mental health professional as environmental designer, the position taken here is that, wherever possible, experimental designs be employed, as they ultimately yield more convincing data regarding cause and effect relationships and the differential effectiveness of two or more programs – data which are necessary for empirically-rooted policies. However, realizing the limitations of experimental designs as well as the broader social context in which programs develop, process-type analyses are deemed essential if we are to arrive at an understanding of effects of the program and the social system on each other. (Jeger, 1977; Jeger & McClure, 1979a)

Before closing the discussion on outcome evaluation, two areas need to be considered. First, it will be recalled that client changes were deemed the major target in the assessment of outcome. While this is certainly the ultimate goal of environmental design interventions, in the case of such indirect service programs as consultation with community caregivers, training nonprofessionals, and community education, changes in consultees, trainees, and community residents are worthy goals in and of themselves even if they do not immediately translate into client changes (Jeger & McClure, 1979b). To take mental health consultation as an example, in their review of empirical studies on the outcome of consultation, Mannino and Shore (1975) identified three major targets of consultation or three levels at which outcome measures were obtained: consultees – changes in knowledge, skills, attitudes, etc. of the direct recipients of consultation: clients – behavioral and attitudinal changes in clients served by consultees; and system – changes in institutional structure or social environment. The latter measure is especially relevant from an environmental design point of view since it encompasses interventions directed toward changing systems. Measures of environmental change are again necessary for their own sake, as a modified environment in a desired direction would precede behavior change in individuals. Assessing changes at all three targets is clearly warranted, although to date only three studies on consultation obtained data on all three levels (Jeger, 1977; Keutzer et al., 1971; Schmuck, 1968). Further, what is clearly needed are environmental assessment procedures which are sensitive to environmental design interventions, and which are related to client outcome measures.

A promising direction in the field of environmental assessment, one that is especially compatible with our environmental design orientation, is to be found in the work of Moos (1974a) at the Stanford Laboratory of Social Ecology (see chapter 4). Briefly, Moos and his colleagues developed a series of "social climate" scales which conceptualize environments along nine or ten dimensions (subscales).

More recently, Kohn, Jeger, & Koretzky (1979) provided data to support a more parsimonious conceptualization of social ecological assessment. It is based on an empirically derived two-factor model of social environments (Support-Involvement versus Disinterest, and Order-Organization versus Disorder-Disorganization) which parallels Stern's (1970) research in educational and industrial settings in which he identified two classes of environmental "press" (anabolic and catabolic). A major advantage of the two-factor model lies in its potential to integrate the two key areas proposed by Cowen (1977) as "ideal candidates for primary prevention: the analysis and modification of social environments and competence building" (p. 6). That is, the two environmental dimensions appear to have parallels with the two-factor model of social competence (Interest-Participation versus Apathy-Withdrawal, and Cooperation-Compliance versus Anger-Defiance – Kohn, 1977; Kohn & Rosman, 1972; Koretzky, Kohn & Jeger, 1978) which have emerged with fair consistency over 50 years of personality research (Kohn, 1977; Peterson, 1961).

The above trends in environmental assessment were noted in order to emphasize their special compatibility with an environmental design model and to encourage their further development as program evaluation tools.

Cost analysis

To McLean (1974), the cost-effectiveness model is becoming more critical given the limited allocation of resources to most social service programs. The impact of a program must be assessed relative to its direct and indirect costs (loss of productivity, etc.). Within behavioral programs, some benefit-cost analyses are beginning to appear (e.g., token economy – Foreyt et al., 1975). Other aspects of mental health programs being subjected to cost-benefit analyses include the effects of psychotherapy versus medication (Karon & Vandenbos, 1975), the use of psychologists versus psychiatrists (Karon & Vandenbos, 1976) and professionals versus nonprofessional therapists (G.D. King, 1976). Clearly, cost analysis is not an alternative to the previous approaches but provides an additional focus.

Systems Analysis

As a model of program evaluation, McLean (1974) identified systems analysis as a macrolevel analysis of a fairly large region for policy purposes. His example from the mental health field is the utilization of cumulative psychiatric case registers for determining state-wide service needs. Extensive reports on the use of "needs assessment" techniques and strategies for conducting "needs assessment" studies for purposes of mental health planning are contained in Pharis (1976) and Siegel, Attkisson, and Cohn (1974). Systems analysis is used here in a broader context relative to its application in process and outcome analysis.

It needs to be emphasized that for large-scale data banks to be meaningful, they must rely on local information. Thus, it is imperative that some standardized data be collected from all centers. In addition to serving mental health planners, a promising feature of systems analysis lies in its potential to permit investigations of the many interacting factors related to outcome.

While the above was provided as an overview of five major evaluation approaches, with an emphasis on outcome evaluation, several additional issues which cut across all types of evaluation are highlighted here. The recent NIMH Guidelines (Windle, 1977) for implementing the program evaluation mandate contain many recommendations that are very compatible with the environmental design model. Among other suggestions, these guidelines (which are continuously being revised and updated based on new experiences) sensitize evaluators to the necessity for involving clinicians (i.e., direct service staff) in data collection and to offer them feedback based on information collected. Clearly, this will increase the likelihood of acceptability of findings and result in program changes. There is nothing more frustrating to evaluators than their data not being used to influence policy. Further, evaluation data are to be made available to catchment area citizens and discussed at a public forum. In addition, specific suggestions include evaluating the accessibility of services, looking at center effectiveness in reducing inappropriate institutionalizations, and at the "relative efficiency of direct and indirect services in achieving various center goals" (Windle, 1977, p. 7). An evaluation of the previous year's evaluation was also indicated.

As was mentioned in previous subsections, long before these NIMH mandates for evaluation, the behaviorally-oriented community mental health center in Huntsville (Alabama) was organized along evaluation lines (Bolin & Kivens, 1974). Their earliest annual reports (Turner & Goodson, 1971) constituted combined "Programs and Evaluations." It needs to be emphasized that the center-wide use of behavioral principles in treatment, prevention, and personnel management is viewed as a tool to realize the underlying objective of empiricism and accountability. As Goodson (1971), the Center's first director, had stated, behavior modification is seen as a "catalyst for evaluation." He further added that to dismiss the use of control groups in the evaluation of treatment approaches on ethical grounds (i.e., it withholds treatment from individuals who need it) is an example of being unaccountable, and that we "owe" it to our clientele to employ control groups. The latter point was reiterated by Haywood (1976) with even greater conviction. In response to those who claim that controlled research is "immoral," Haywood stated that they are implying "that since we are in possession of revealed truth, we must not deprive anyone of its benefits" adding that their "underlying assumption is that knowledge that is worthwhile comes about by revelation, rather than by systematic inquiry" (p. 314). It is hoped that the environmental design orientation will influence professionals and the public to dispel such attitudes.

In line with the Huntsville behavioral approach, researchers associated with the Behavioral Analysis and Modification (BAM) Project (another major effort at adopting behavior modification in community mental health centers) incorporated an evaluation of staff activities. In their paper, "Accountability Like Charity Begins at Home", King et al. (1974) described the application of goal attainment scaling to measure the accomplishments of their behavior modification project.

The final issues raised here pertain to increasing the utility of program evaluation in terms of program change as well as credibility of evaluative activities. Some of the guidelines offered by Zusman and Bissonette (1973) are worth noting. They cautioned against the emerging bandwagon approach to evaluation, arguing that "no evaluation at all is preferable to one conducted under pressure and in the spirit of an ill-conceived crusade" (p. 123).

They recommended that evaluations be conducted early in a program's history "before vested interests have solidified and organizational inertia has set in" (p. 123). Resistance to change would make the entire evaluation effort an exercise in futility regardless of how well designed it is. Further, they took the position that evaluations should not be conducted at all if they will not be carried out with "scientific accuracy." They cited Campbell and Erlebacher (1970) who stated that it is "fundamentally misleading to lend the prestige of science to any report in a situation where no scientific evaluation is possible." To the extent that the environmental designer role in a community mental health setting is likely to be one which merges research and service, this latter point is especially relevant. In fact, it can be said that sensitivity to the image of research and evaluation represents the environmental designer's "ethical" obligation as an agent of science.

CONCLUSION AND NEW DIRECTIONS

The present chapter offered an integration of community mental health and environmental design. On the one hand, the spirit of community mental health and many activities within community mental health were viewed as a stream of environmental design and thus contributing to the evolving environmental design model. On the other hand, the core of the chapter was devoted to explicating what should be viewed as a tentative conceptual framework for community mental health as derived from environmental design. This was accomplished by considering several major areas within community mental health and reviewing the practical applications implied by environmental design for each of the areas. The position taken was that environmental design is a necessary alternative to the medical model dominating community mental health, and that it meets the major criticisms directed against community mental health which were summarized at the outset of the chapter.

Barriers to Environmental Design

Since the implication throughout the chapter was that community mental health centers as currently operating could serve as a base for implementing the environmental designer role in any one of the intervention areas, several points from within a behavioral-systems framework (Harshbarger & Maley, 1974) need to be made about environmental design's viewpoint on the basic relation between the structure and function of centers. The major issue concerns the feasibility of carrying out the social change component of the environmental designer role that was subsumed under "consultation and community enhancement." It needs to be made explicit at this point that in a center dominated by the medical model, it is likely that attempting to carry out the environmental design role from a base in the consultation service is likely to turn out as an exercise in futility. Some evidence for this argument comes from a recent case study by Cherniss (1977) who analyzed some organizational variables which interfered with the development of a successful primary prevention program. Among other factors, one of the major reasons responsible for the failure of their program (which was blessed with a conducive ideology and available staff) was that "the existence of direct treatment commitments works against preventive programming" (p. 137) since increasing demands for direct service become the priority and draw away resources. Similarly, using funding arrangements as a focal point, Landsberg and Hammer (1977) suggested that strong reliance upon third-party reimbursement systems will cause centers to emphasize inpatient care (since this is most often reimbursable) and pay less attention to consultation and prevention activities.(10)

What are some systemic changes in community mental health centers that would accommodate a greater emphasis on prevention? Snow and Newton (1976) suggested an organizational structure whereby indirect services would gain greater credibility. They proposed a

> leadership triad with the director having skills in both psychotherapy and consultation superordinate to chiefs of direct and indirect service components. The director should be structurally equidistant from the two components; that is, the director should have no leadership role within either component so that he or she can mediate conflict and work to integrate the two task systems. (P. 593)

However, it is clear that such a hierarchical conception is hardly going to overcome the broader issues raised by Cherniss (1977) and Landsberg and Hammer (1977). In light of the institutional constraints that will apparently remain with us in the near future, the position taken here is that for a viable community mental health setting in which the broader environmental designer role can be practiced, the recommendation offered by Cherniss (1977) may need to be realized. Cherniss suggested that a "new, totally separate institution" be created whose sole mission would be to engage in primary prevention activities.(11) Ironically, Cherniss pointed to the medical delivery system as evidence for the viability of a separate institutional base for prevention:

> Although the medical care system in this country is a dubious model for community mental health, there is one feature we might do well to emulate in certain respects. In most instances, medical treatment and prevention are conducted within different institutional contexts. Public health departments were created in order to advance and coordinate preventive health programs. Such departments generally eschew direct service and devote all their energies to the cause of prevention. Over time, public health has developed a distinctive professional and institutional identity which now is recognized and supported by most communities. (P. 139)

A similar conclusion which called for the "structural segmentation" of treatment and prevention services was reached by Perlmutter (1974) based on an analysis of ideology, organizational theory, and professionalism in community mental health. It was recommended that consultation-education programs be designed to serve an entire city in order to have greater capacity to influence and collaborate with such institutions as employment services, education systems, etc. Although it is premature to spell out any workable model for implementing such a system, we conclude with some speculations as to how such an institution might be coordinated with local settings which may provide an ideal base from which environmental designers could operate in the interest of community enhancement. In lieu of such titles as "community mental health center" or "community prevention agency," such a setting may be called a "community resource center" without any implicit linkage to mental illness.

Some Fantasies About Future "Community Resource Centers"

It is envisioned that community resource centers could serve as headquarters for all activities conducted at the local community level with the explicit general goal of enhancing the capacities of community members to design their own environments (Jeger & Slotnick, 1980). Appropriate activities for environmental designers operating out of such a setting would include interventions directed toward modifying social institutions in ways that would increase the behavioral alternatives for individual community residents and thereby, enhance their freedom. Some examples of specific interventions are outlined here.

Several of the activities discussed in the previous subsections on "Consultation" and "Prevention" are particularly suited for such a setting. Interventions directed toward school systems might consist of influencing the adoption of "open classrooms" as an educational alternative and utilizing schools as bases to implement mandatory marital and parenthood training programs. Interventions pertaining to employment would include political action to influence the modification of mandatory retirement laws, while at the same time securing employment opportunities for young people entering the job market.

Another target system would be the media. For example, as MacLennan, Quinn, & Schroeder (1971) suggested, audiovisual experts can be trained "to be more sensitive to the community mental health implications of advertising or soap operas" (p. 24). In line with the center's orientation, rather than the mental health implications, it is the implications for behavioral alternatives that would be the focus. Utilizing the media to change such behaviors as racial and sexist discrimination as well as for disseminating behavioral self-control training programs and programs designed to enhance general personal happiness (e.g., Fordyce, 1977) represent additional environmental design activities.

Proposals for other interventions which are geared to a general enhancement of the quality of life are derived from the fields of environmental psychology, behavioral ecology, and behavioral community psychology. Examples include the encouragement of paper recycling (e.g., Geller, Chaffee, & Ingram, 1975), the prevention of shoplifting (e.g., McNees et al, 1976), energy conservation (Winett & Nietzel, 1975), finders' return of lost materials (e.g., Goldstein et al., 1976), the encouragement of such health behaviors as seeking dental care (e.g., Reiss, Piotrowski, & Bailey, 1976), and influencing the development of mutual-help networks in other areas of health and social functioning (e.g., Gartner & Riessman, 1977).

Finally, on an even broader level, possibilities for bringing to bear the utopian stream within environmental design to the planning of entire living environments provides the ultimate challenge for the environmental designer in a community resource center. Activities might range from participation in the design of operant-based experimental campus living units (e.g., Feallock & Miller, 1976) to urban design and "new town" planning. Concerning input from mental health professionals for designing new towns, a precedent exists in the case of Columbia, Maryland (see Lemkau, 1969). Continued involvement of mental health professionals in Columbia is reflected by the papers in Klein's (1978) recent volume entitled Psychology of the Planned Community: The New Town Experience.

Needless to say, the role of environmental designers in urban planning goes beyond recommending the number of psychiatric clinics needed. Some specific functions which may call for environmental design expertise run the gamut from planning day care settings and schools to senior citizen centers, recreational facilities, and housing design. Clearly, all these areas are integral to efforts directed at improving the overall quality of life (Flanagan, 1978). An empirical knowledge base from which input for these areas can be drawn is beginning to develop with the merging of the fields of environmental psychology and behavior modification (e.g., LeLaurin & Risley, 1972; Pierce, 1975; Pierce & Risley, 1974; Ribes, 1976). Planning for those people who will necessarily need to be removed from mainstream communities (people heretofore known as "psychiatric inpatients"), environmental design might call for a kind of retreat. The retreat would, in essence, be an engineered society similar to South Carolina's Village System, a residential community for inpatients built to resemble a small town in terms of social and physical design (Means & Ackerman, 1976).

Thus, the role of environmental designers in town planning involves participating in planning all phases of a city insofar as they influence the development of behavioral alternatives and contribute to the enhancement of a psychological sense of community (Sarason, 1974). As such, two guiding values that are central to the environmental design orientation need to be emphasized in reference to town planning. First, for environmental designers to participate in town planning from an ethical standpoint the planning process must be one that incorporates many pluralistic interests — i.e., numerous ethnic groups, political persuasions, religious denominations, and women. A mechanism must further be developed for insuring maximum input from citizens into the constant planning of change for the city. The second, related issue concerns incorporation of an evaluation process into the planning and functioning of the city. In addition to designing systematic data gathering systems in all components of the city, a plan for assessing the efficacy of the citizen input mechanism discussed above must be developed. This will make possible the "scientific" monitoring of the city.

In the context of his ecological model Kelly (1970) suggested some relevant longitudinal research designs to permit an evaluation of the extent to which citizens are involved in planning and implementing community change. He is particularly interested in looking at the diversity of citizen groups that participate in the community change process.

It is most appropriate to conclude this chapter by reiterating the basic value that should guide the work of environmental designers in the proposed community resource centers. To use the words of James Kelly (1970), "the goal for community development is to create opportunities for a community to plan for its own change" (p. 197).

NOTES

(1) It should not be assumed that community mental health is not tied to certain pre-World War II trends. The interested reader is referred to Rossi (1962) for a discussion of the prewar antecedents to community mental health.

(2) At the time of this writing, a House of Representatives bill is seeking to reduce to six the number of required services for a new center to phase in over its initial three years. They are: inpatient, emergency, outpatient, screening, follow-up, and consultation/education.

(3) It will be recalled that recent legislation was directed toward alleviating this shortcoming.

(4) For accounts of the entire background to the Lincoln incident the interested reader is referred to Kaplan and Roman (1973) and Roman (1973).

(5) The remaining two projects not reviewed here are the St. Louis program based on child rearing education to parents of school children (Glidewell, Gildea, & Kaufman, 1973) and the Philadelphia project based on interpersonal problem-solving training (Shure, Spivack, & Gordon, 1972; Shure & Spivack, 1975; Spivack & Shure, 1974). A similar program to the latter was reported on by University of Connecticut researchers (Allen, Chinsky, Larcen, Lochman, & Selinger, 1976).

(6) See Gartner (1975) for a directory of degree-granting programs for paraprofessionals in the human services.

(7) The increased professional interest in the self-help "movement" represents another positive direction. This is evidenced by the growing literature in the area (e.g., Caplan & Killilea, 1976; Gartner & Riessman, 1977), the initiation of a newsletter entitled Self-Help Reporter (Briggs, 1977), the development of a National Self-Help Clearinghouse at the CUNY Graduate Center, and the five self-help related symposia featured at the 1977 Annual Convention of the American Psychological Association. Also, in its final report, the President's Commission on Mental Health (April, 1978) emphasized mutual support systems as a major mental health resource.

(8) It should be noted that many aspects of the helper principle and self-help are also relevant to the previous subsection on prevention as they pertain to "community enhancement" through mutual aid.

(9) Another compatible project which has yet to receive comparable publicity and recognition was initiated at the Mendota State Hospital (Marx, Test, & Stein, 1973; Stein, Test, & Marx, 1975). Unlike most community preparation efforts that train patients in the hospital until they are "ready" for discharge, the Mendota Program took typically "non-ready" patients and immediately placed them in community settings, with staff available as resource persons. This group fared better on independent living and employment relative to an equivalent group trained at the hospital.

(10) Barriers to prevention are further apparent from the recent remarks

of former NIMH Director, Bertram Brown. He stated that prevention presents the "greatest danger of a cop-out in providing services" (APA, 1977, p. 1).

(11) Perhaps a first step in this direction is the recent proposal by Gerald Klerman, the new head of the Alcohol, Drug Abuse, and Mental Health Administration (ADAMHA) within HEW, for the addition of prevention to ADAMHA's triad of research, service, and training (APA, 1977, p. 1). Similarly, in its final report, the President's Commission on Mental Health (1978) called for a "primary" prevention center within NIMH.

8

Environmental Design in Action: The Training Program

William Hutchison,
R. Edward Harpin,
Judith Graeff, James M. Waters,
Julian D. Ford
and Leonard Krasner

In this chapter we describe an ongoing program in "environmental design" from which this volume itself has been given birth. The events to be described started in the fall of 1972. At that time Krasner initiated a "program in environmental design," within the broader framework of training in clinical psychology. Initially, a seminar format was the vehicle for training. The students worked in community settings as participant-observers. Then, primarily through the efforts of the students and the staff of the various settings in Stony Brook and London, the environmental design program described in this chapter grew and developed.

The focus here is on the major details and elements of the program; the roles of the participant observer and trainer, the team concept, the use of journals, specific exercises, descriptions of settings, and program evaluation. The aim is to convey an ongoing training process not a "finished" program. All elements in the program are designed for a process of continuing change and development. It is this process of continuity of change which we believe characterizes the model which we are presenting throughout the book.

Ed.

As a further stage in the development of the work of the "Environmental Design Team" at Stony Brook, two programs in environmental design have been set up, one at Stony Brook and the other in London, England. The primary purpose for setting up these two programs was to demonstrate and further develop the principles of behavior influence and environmental design in a context of training, research, and application.

The description of our interlinked programs to be presented in this chapter is not intended as a manual on how to set up and run a program, nor is it intended as the description of a finished product. We reject the approach of both cookbook and static programs. Rather, it is hoped that this chapter will serve both as an example of possible ways of applying environmental design principles in a training context and as a source of ideas to stimulate others involved in the behavior influence process.

The purpose of our programs is four-fold. First, we are training students in an environmental design approach to the behavior influence process. As expressed in chapter 1, we believe that the principles governing human behavior apply across a variety of situations and settings. Hence, we are not simply training future professionals for work in institutional settings, but are training individuals to function more effectively in any setting where the influencing of human behavior is an important factor.

Secondly, we are developing behavior influence procedures applicable in our training programs, the variety of institutional settings in which we work, and all of the other settings in which we influence human behavior, including our own behavior.

Thirdly, we are attempting to break down the distinctions among training, application or practice, and research. Examples of this process will be given throughout the chapter.

Finally, we are continuing to develop the principles and concepts within environmental design. If it has not already been made clear, it should be stated unequivocally now, that we are not working with a closed set of principles and a fully developed area of knowledge. On the contrary, we believe that we are only at a very early stage of a continually developing process.

BRIEF HISTORY

The two programs arose in connection with a graduate program in clinical psychology at Stony Brook. The orientation of that program is behavioral and, therefore, stresses the application of empirically derived principles to change the problem behavior of clients. Environmental design developed as an extension of those and other principles (see chap. 1) to a wider range of situations and settings.

The environmental design program began first at Stony Brook in 1972 with the undergraduate environmental design seminar – students attending the seminar were placed in open classrooms of local public schools. Placement settings were later expanded to include a psychiatric hospital, a food cooperative, schools for older children, and a crisis intervention hotline. The students were trained in (and aided in developing) the principles of the behavior influence process on location at their settings as well as in the undergraduate seminar. The following year a graduate seminar in environmental design was initiated in conjunction with the undergraduate course; various faculty members as well as graduate students attended or visited the seminar. A second program was set up in London two years later when funding became available. It was intended that the Stony Brook and London programs be closely linked, and have a mutual exchange of ideas and practices.

Why London?

Exposure to different cultures facilitates discrimination of functional relations in social systems and service delivery and decreases the likelihood of taking for granted the way in which things are done in a given setting. Furthermore, it is our observation that much of the social services system is more highly developed in London than in the United States. We feel that England represents a society which is much more planned than our own and, thus, serves as a useful example of one way in which the theory and practice of behavior influence can interact on a societal level. We also have observed more usage of an educational model in England than in the United States.

A program geographically removed from our home base gives those members of the team who run it a great deal of administrative independence; this increases the possibility of creative innovation. Another advantage of setting up our program in London is the enormous range of applications, settings, and problems located in the relatively small physical area of this giant metropolis. And last but not least, for this group anyway, London is a very enjoyable place in which to live and work.

THE TRAINING MODEL

How an Environmental Designer Might Approach Personnel Selection

In selecting students for placements in the settings available to our programs, we are looking not for a finished product, but for individuals with a basic repertoire of skills. We are guided by the environmental design model of human behavior which postulates that the likelihood of a person's success in a particular setting is dependent upon his having the necessary analytical and behavioral skills to meet the demands of that setting. Thus, our students are selected on the basis of having demonstrated already developed skills or the ability to respond to our training methods within a reasonable time period. We recognize that failure to respond to our methods may reflect a weakness in our methods; however, especially the London settings make such strong demands on student performance that basic skill deficits can lead to undesirable consequences.

A basic requirement for an undergraduate entering our program is that he have a general course background in psychology, including at least an introductory course in behavioral psychology. Students are not required to be psychology majors, though most are. To be accepted for the London program, the student should also have at least one semester's experience in the environmental design seminar at Stony Brook.

The students' participation in the seminar and in one of our placement settings on Long Island gives us the opportunity to observe and work with them. We particularly assess their ability to operate in a setting which differs markedly from a college campus, discriminate the impact their presence has on the behavior of the professionals and clients in the setting, and behave in a professional manner by taking on and dependably carrying out responsibilities related to the setting. We also look at how the students respond to the informal learning opportunities presented by the practical experiences. It is up to the students to design their own roles in the settings, select their goals for the semester, and utilize their supervisors to their best advantage. One of the most difficult adjustments for undergraduates is being presented with a flexible learning situation where they are responsible for selecting the means and priorities for learning. This aspect of the Stony Brook seminar gives the students a good sample of the challenges of London settings, and their supervisors a good sample of how the students react to this challenge. We also view their success in attempts to relate environmental design principles from the literature to the realities present in the setting as a major indicator of whether they will be able to utilize the London experience to its fullest. We look at the quality of the content and the clarity of their writing (the latter being a skill highly valued in Britain) and, when necessary, provide additional training in writing (note that whenever we provide training, we also assess response to that training). We also utilize a structured interview to assess their general knowledge of psychology (through use of a simple test), their financial means for the year abroad, their ability to adjust to a new living experience (using their adjustment to college as a measure), and their ability to handle a modicum of stress (through use of our interview session itself as a behavior sample).

Finally, we should note that we do not view the assessment as a one-way process. It is as important that the program be appropriate for the person as that the person be appropriate for the program. Hence, we provide the students with information concerning the program, opportunities (when possible) to speak with program graduates, and (through our Stony Brook program) a chance to sample environmental design briefly before committing themselves to a demanding full-time program.

General Training Model

A behavioral training model has had a strong influence on our methods (see chapter 9 and the section on exercises below).

Elements of the Program

The seminar

The core of both the Stony Brook and the London Programs is the seminar. These seminars consist of readings, discussions, exercises, and presentations by visitors on specific environmental design topics. Our seminars have focused on environmental design as an extension of behavior modification; the classroom as a planned environment; research as both an environmental design and a behavior influence; the token economy as a planned environment; economic principles as influences in the classroom, the mental hospital, and society; the architectural arrangement of space as an influence on behavior; the social role of behavior-change agents; the occupational career of an environmental designer; social and ethical implications of environmental design; the consequences of demography on planning environments; the design and function of community mental health centers; planned societies, utopias, or people designing their own environments; and civil liberties, social justice, and other worthy goals of environmental design. There is always too much to cover, but we try to direct the focus of the seminars to those variables which our experience and the immediate demands of the students' settings indicate are most important.

To further supplement the readings and discussions, other training procedures have been developed and utilized. We may use study guides to direct the readings and stimulate ideas. Current events which illustrate principles or problems we are attempting to convey are used as material for discussion. Theoretical topics are carefully related to practical applications in the various settings of the trainees. We encourage continual sharing of information among the seminar participants concerning each others settings. This sharing includes case presentations, discussion of developments in each of the settings, the evolving role of the student in the settings, and group trouble-shooting of problems encountered by students in their respective settings.

The participants responsible for a given day's seminar are encouraged to undertake careful planning of its structure in order to make it an optimal learning experience. In fact, the designing of seminars is used as another demonstration of environmental design in action.

Guests whose specialty areas are of particular interest to our group are frequently invited. Visitors have presented a wide range of topics: the incentive system in the new Chinese society; the philosophy of science as it relates to physics and psychology; law and human behavior; and ethics and decision making in behavior change. Most guests make single appearances, but some have developed ongoing links with our program and seminars, and add further dimensions to the process of learning and training.

Following the first year of the London program, we instituted a course in animal learning (mostly experimental analysis of behavior) in conjunction with the seminar. This provision has been for many years a part of some programs in applied behavior analysis, with the rationale that students should learn the basic concepts, principles, and procedures from behavior analysis in the context of basic experimental settings. The comparison between the students taking animal learning and those not taking it has supported our belief in the value of the course. The students become facile in using precise language and applying the appropriate concepts and principles to human situations, and they seem to be more likely to recognize the paradigms involved and to formulate appropriate interventions after taking this course.

Finally, we conceptualize our classes not as exhaustive surveys but as limited samples of the relevant material. We make explicit the need to utilize other sources of information in order to function adequately in a setting.

Setting placements and supervision of the participant-observers

Our students function in the role of participant observer (P.O.) (Krasner & Hutchison, 1974; Toscano, 1974; see also chap. 1) in the field settings where they work. Sullivan, in his Interpersonal Theory of Psychiatry (1953) as well as a number of authors in the field of sociology (McCall & Simmons 1969) discusses the notion of a participant-observer – a person who is both a participant in and an observer of the behavior influence process occurring between two or more individuals in a setting. Drawing from these and other authors and from our own experiences, we recognize the fallacy of the objective, non-influencing observer. We believe that it is impossible for one to be physically present in a setting without influencing the behavior of others in that setting. As a practical aside, many settings where people are involved in the purposeful influencing of human behavior will simply not accept the intrusion of a non-contributing observer.

A P.O. can actively test theories he has read about and developed from observations by carrying out planned influences. The P.O. gets the opportunity to practice new skills (including skills of intervention implementation) through exposure to many of the situations and problems of real life settings that might hamstring students newly arrived from training programs turning out "professionals" (cf., Reppucci & Saunders, 1974). Other programs often focus on the specific skills needed in order to pass the requirements for professional status and neglect the equally important area of how to implement these skills in an ongoing organization. Without the latter set of skills, the former may go to waste.

Another important aspect of the P.O. role is that the student learns to synthesize practice and research into a single course of ongoing activity. He is continually observing his own behavior, behavior of others in the setting, and how behavior is shaped by the various contingencies in operation. He is able to influence his role as practitioner and others' behavior through systematic manipulation of setting variables, and in his role as researcher can measure and evaluate the resulting changes. These measurements and evaluations prepare him for his future influencing strategies and so the process repeats itself. Ethical issues are of paramount importance in this process, as in all design procedures.

Thus far, the field settings have been chosen largely as a function of preferences of the trainers. There has been a range of settings including traditional clinical ones as well as so-called "normal" community settings. We have used open classrooms, an environmental design-oriented psychiatric ward of a mental hospital, a day center for the rehabilitation of former psychiatric patients, a pre-school day center, a child study center connected with an academic psychology department, a geriatric day center in transition to an assessment center, a training and research ward of a psychiatric hospital, experimental programs for retarded children, a neighborhood center, a youth center, a residential school for severely physically handicapped children, an educational alternative-to-prison program, a high school career placement center, and an open-space middle school.

Usually our P.O.s work with or under a permanent employee of the setting whom we refer to as the "setting director." Such a person generally knows more than the trainees about the setting and its population and, hence, can add to our training. We attempt to involve the setting director in training via several methods. One approach is to have them rate our students on the Environmental Design (EDSL). This directs attention to the specific behaviors we are attempting to train and often leads to discussion of specific strategies to be used, increasing the amount of training the setting directors do.

We are in the process of expanding the training role of setting directors further by giving them official appointments as external supervisors in our program. As the letter of appointment states:

> The main duty of this position is to train student interns from the program who participate in your setting, based on your special knowledge and skills. We enter into this collaborative arrangement with the students' continuous learning and development as our primary value, recognizing the necessity of, and many possibilities for, student involvement which contribute to the objectives for the setting. A supervisor from the program will also be involved in training the students in setting-related skills, and will collaborate with you in identifying goals, assessing student skills, and planning training strategies. We agree to consult with you concerning the suitability of prospective interns; to make the program supervisor frequently available; and to serve as a resource center providing information, personnel, materials, and contact with others with whom we are involved.

In addition we train our students in effective ways to ask for information, and encourage them to communicate regularly with setting directors.

The role of the trainer and teams: the hierarchy approach

Every P.O. in the environmental design program is assigned to work in one practicum placement as a member of a group numbering from two to six students. For example, six P.O.s might work in one elementary school setting, each placed in one of six classrooms available as placement settings. In the Stony Brook program, students work in settings one-half day per week as part of the seminar, while in London the students work three full days a week in their settings.

Each small group is coordinated by a trainer. The trainer is a person who has had more experience working in field settings and in behavioral theory and practice generally. To date, the trainers have been graduate students working toward M.A. or Ph.D degrees in clinical, community, or developmental psychology. Serving as program trainers has been an integral part of their own training as environmental designers.

The trainer's role includes the following duties: building the group into a team, serving as a liaison between the administrators and staff in the placement setting and the members of the Environmental Design Program; providing learning experiences for the P.O.s in the team; and serving as a self-trainer for himself. The role of the team has included the following: providing a supportive small-group milieu for P.O.s; serving as a medium for intensive skill training for P.O.s; and assisting P.O.s and trainers in troubleshooting problematic situations. Historically, these roles have evolved as a result of feedback from P.O.s, trainers, and placement setting staff. In keeping with the environmental design program's philosophy, there are no fixed "correct" procedures, but rather the continual development of methods that best fit the ever-changing goals and structures of both the environmental design program and the field placements, as well as the P.O.s and trainers.

A small group does not "automatically" become a team. Rather, the trainer must draw on ideas from group process research and theory (see Harpin, 1974) and interpersonal communication research and theory (e.g., Truax & Carkhuff, 1967; Watzlawick et al., 1967) as well as his own experience to design an environment that will promote cohesiveness, willingness to share feelings and needs, constructive as opposed to critical feedback, willingness to brainstorm and share information, and positive feedback for each member. Trainers often use such methods as modeling behaviors to promote these goals and to reinforce P.O.s for such behavior. They encourage P.O.s to answer their own and their peers' questions rather than assuming the role of authoritative expert; to explore alternative answers and actions rather than seeking a single solution to a question; to express their feelings openly, responding empathetically to expressions of feelings, rather than with criticism or unsolicited advice; to set up interactions with each other in which they can exchange and clarify ideas and values; to give sincere positive feedback for achievement and effort; to discuss group process as it has been occurring in their group; and to directly confront intra-group conflicts (i.e. effectively share feelings; problem solve) rather than ignoring them. The skills involved are similar to those involved in traditional clinical psychology.

The trainer has an equally important extra-group, political role in keeping in communication at all times with the staff and administrators at the placement setting. This function begins before the P.O.s enter their settings, when the trainer meets with those at the setting who will be working directly with P.O.s (e.g. teachers; nursing staff). In these meetings the goals and expectations of the administrators and staff for both P.O.s and the trainer are assessed (e.g. what days and times in the week the P.O.s will be in the setting; rules and policies, formal and informal, that P.O.s and trainers must observe; how P.O.s and trainers can and should assist the staff persons), the goals and expectations of the environmental design program for the P.O.s' learning experience and responsibilities are communicated, an informal contract that speaks to both of these groups' desires is agreed upon, and social amenities are exchanged (e.g. inviting placement personnel to visit the environmental design seminar; catching up on current events at the setting).

Following this, the trainer may arrange a meeting of the P.O. team and the administrators and staff members. This may involve a very brief introduction of the different people, a slide-show presentation describing the placement, or a group discussion in which staff members and P.O.s share their goals and expectations. In any case, the trainer must serve as facilitator, making sure that etiquette is observed and communications are clearly and accurately received.

For the remainder of a P.O.'s study in the placement (usually one academic year), the trainer maintains regular contact with both administrators and staff. His contacts with the administrator are carried out through formally scheduled progress-review meetings, brief chats as they meet in the hallway, and making himself readily available to offer consultation and to hear and remedy complaints. He regularly sees setting staff through visiting each classroom, ward, etc. where P.O.s are placed about once a week to chat with the supervising staff persons about goals, evaluations, complaints, and current events.

At the end of the year, it has been found useful to reconvene the entire group of P.O.s and staff persons (and sometimes others, if they have expressed a keen interest in the P.O.s' activities), to sum up and exchange feedback between and among staff and P.O.s. Here again, the trainer must serve as group facilitator, especially to ensure that every person gets some positive feedback for contributions made and that all questions are answered. It is also important for the trainer to end the meeting with a closing statement that expresses thanks to the staff persons and, usually, the hope that the placement can be continued in the next year. At this time, individual conferences with staff members may also be planned, based on requests from staff members or on the trainer's assessment that there may yet be unfinished business to complete.

Trainers offer many learning experiences to P.O.s in their teams. Initially, orientation is the primary concern, preparing the P.O.s to develop their own roles in the field settings via support, ideas from past years, ideas from didactic teachings from the seminar, and permission to go slowly in becoming more active participants. Also the trainer sensitizes P.O.s to crucial norms, expectations, and policies of the placement setting (e.g., how to dress, how to have staff and students or residents refer to you, importance of promptness); teaches basic communication skills including giving feedback (e.g. diplomacy in conveying observations, how to utilize rather than attack the other person's views or goals); forewarns P.O.s of critical incidents that are likely to occur (e.g., a staff member asking for feedback on something that you feel warrants negative feedback; a staff member asking you to do custodial or janitorial work; a fight between two pupils); and helps them to formulate and try out (via role-taking simulations) responses until they feel confident and comfortable with an effective reaction. Furthermore, the trainer helps each P.O. formulate at least tentative behavioral objectives which they can monitor during their placement experiences, in order to guarantee that each student will, indeed, learn and benefit from the practicum. He helps P.O.s to generate ideas about what to be looking and listening for in the setting as they are getting acquainted, and how to use the journal to record and integrate these observations with past experience and didactic learnings, so a data base is available for future actions.

Subsequently, trainers develop and implement learning experiences both in team meetings and in the placement settings. In team meetings, P.O.s and the trainer can share their observations and reactions to the setting, help one another to "make sense" of these data and to discuss interpretations of the observations. Other functions of the meetings involve troubleshooting and problem solving when one or more P.O.s (or the trainer) feels confronted by a dilemma; engaging in structured exercises (e.g., role play simulations with modeling and feedback) to learn and practice new skills and to experience different roles (e.g., the client role in therapy); and discussing ways to operationalize the ideas presented in didactic readings and seminars through new conceptualizations, more sophisticated observations, and/or active interventions in their placement settings. In these meetings, the trainer also plans and monitors coordinated activities developed by several P.O.s jointly in the field setting (e.g., running groups with students from several classrooms); and aids P.O.s in evaluating and modifying their initial behavioral objectives. At first, trainers have usually been rather directive in structuring learning experiences, providing modeling, and giving behavioral feedback to P.O.s. As P.O.s acquire experience in the team and in the field placements, trainers have found it useful to transfer the responsibility for decision making, implementation, and feedback evaluations to the P.O.s and to serve more and more as a facilitator rather than as a director. This encourages self- and peer-training, and enables P.O.s to contribute their own special expertise to amplify the team learning experience.

In the field placements, trainers inevitably begin by modeling effective communication and interaction skills for P.O.s as they coordinate the meetings between P.O.s and placement personnel. Once P.O.s begin to work in their specific placement settings, the regular visits by the trainer keep him in close contact with the supervising staff so that he can obtain direct feedback about the activity of the P.O. as well as support of the P.O. in initiating projects. In the setting, the trainer can provide direct on-line training for the P.O., observe the P.O. in his interactions with people and the physical environment, offer suggestions for alternative actions (e.g. observing the teacher as well as the students; ignoring rather than attending to disruptive behavior), give immediate behavioral feedback to the P.O. (i.e. praise and constructive negative feedback), model alternative actions directly, and generally chat with the P.O. about what he is observing and doing at that time. For example, when two students were learning to lead a role-play group of pensioners, they alternated between conducting the group and being a group participant receiving immediate feedback and suggestions from the supervisor.

When trainers visit a P.O.'s field setting, they do not usually attempt to present themselves as unobtrusive observers, but rather interact with the P.O., the staff persons, and the client population in a manner that is consistent with the behavioral and physical ecology of the specific setting (e.g., standing in a corner and whispering quietly with the P.O.; joining in with group activities that are ongoing in the setting; taking a walk with the P.O. and a student to see something of interest to the threesome; talking briefly with the teacher of ward staff and then joining the P.O. in his current activities; and so forth). The trainer's observations concerning the P.O., the setting, and the interaction of the two, also serve as valuable data for feedback and discussion in subsequent team meetings.

P.O.s may, with approval of the supervising staff, participate and observe in another P.O.'s setting. This provides opportunities for the "outsider" P.O. to see a different setting, to observe another P.O. at work, to observe the trainer at work, and to give feedback to the "home" P.O.

The trainer's final role is that of self-trainer, a role taken by all members of the Environmental Design Program that we have been attempting to develop and utilize. The trainer frequently and regularly solicits feedback, both positive and (perhaps more important) negative, from P.O.s and staff members at the field placement concerning their satisfaction with his performance in the role functions described above and their suggestions for improvements. It is not enough to just ask for negative feedback particularly with P.O.s, who are evaluated and graded in large part (even if almost always benevolently) by the trainer. The trainer must make certain the P.O.s do not feel that they will suffer if they comply with this request. One way to accomplish this is to specify very precisely to the P.O.s the bases for their evaluation, especially the behaviors (or lack thereof) that warrant each grade level. This is also an excellent way to facilitate self-monitoring and self-evaluation by the P.O.s. Another solution is to teach P.O.s how to give negative feedback in a constructive and nonthreatening way, and to demonstrate this by offering such feedback to P.O.s when appropriate. Perhaps most important, the trainer must be careful to reinforce rather than punish P.O.s for giving constructive negative feedback (e.g., by making a strong attempt to make the changes requested, and following through on promises).

P.O.s have several opportunities to acquire special skills (e.g., how to give feedback effectively) in the context of their team. Weekly team meetings are often devoted in part or entirely to role play simulations in which modeling and behavior rehearsal with feedback can be provided by the trainer and fellow P.O.s to teach skills that will help the P.O. to solve problems and carry out planned actions in the field setting. Trainers are encouraged to actively solicit requests from P.O.s concerning skills that they would like to learn. The trainer's visits to each P.O.'s field setting also offer many opportunities for modeling, prompting, and feedback from the trainer to the P.O. on any target skills.

Most team meetings focus largely on having the P.O.s and trainer review their experiences in the field placement in the past week, plan goals for the upcoming week, and troubleshoot actual or potential problems that have (or may in the future) interfered with the P.O.'s comfort, autonomy, and learning in the field setting. Systematic problem solving (D'Zurilla & Goldfried, 1971) is often used to structure such troubleshooting sessions. Trainers and P.O.s briefly discuss and formulate actions to deal with problematic situations when the trainer visits the P.O.'s field setting, especially in crises (e.g., a substitute teacher takes over unexpectedly and preempts the P.O.'s plans).

In addition to team meetings, trainers meet with P.O.s on an individual basis to provide one-to-one contact and supervision. The regular visit by the trainer to the P.O.'s field setting provides for direct individual interactions. Informal discussions during "breaks" in the seminar, and formal appointments (at least once a week in London) are another important means to this objective. Trainers can expect that many difficult issues may be raised in such interactions (e.g. giving negative feedback to the P.O. and developing constructive ways for positive change; personal conflicts that interfere with the P.O.'s ability to enjoy and learn from the program), but most are dealt with directly rather than ignored, again in direct continuity with clinical psychology.

The team is an important bridge for the P.O. between ideas presented in didactic readings and seminars and field placement experiences. Trainers have strongly encouraged P.O.s to draw on their didactic learnings when setting goals and methods for observations and interventions, and when generating and evaluating solutions in trouble-shooting sessions. This provides the P.O. with multiple opportunities to consolidate and operationalize his "textbook knowledge." It also models an important concept forcefully for the P.O.s: research, theory, and practice must be constantly integrated by the environmental designer.

The training hierarchy

The graduate student trainers are, in turn, supervised and trained by higher level graduate students as well as faculty members, who have the skills to facilitate the work of the trainers and the overall running of the program. These advanced skills include the implementation of training at all levels of our program; an environmental design theoretical perspective and practical orientation; mastery of the relevant content areas; personal familiarity with the placement settings and their personnel; and finally, interpersonal skills for dealing with students, setting personnel, and interactions between the two.

The intention of this hierarchical model of training and working is the efficient use of the expertise of all involved. We recognize that all skills are not needed at all levels and that trainees have useful skills to contribute. The model provides training at several levels, giving direct practice in the roles that students may later take as professionals in the field. This continuous training also serves to reduce the separation of training and application by demonstrating to students that continual learning and development are important, as opposed to stopping learning at a predetermined level of skill and never changing one's ways thereafter. Furthermore, the crisis in trained professional person power

(Albee, 1959) and the developing use of paraprofessionals (Jeger, 1975) in human services lend yet more support for the model of providing different levels of training, with different skills taught at each level. See Seidman and Rappaport (1974) for a good discussion of hierarchical models.

Journal as a self-training method

Each P.O. and trainer is required to keep a regular written record in the form of a journal of his observations, inferential interpretations, actions, plans, evaluations, and (as much as is felt acceptable by each individual) emotional reactions to field placement experiences. P.O.s are encouraged to write entries as soon as possible after a session in their field setting so as to minimize forgetting important facts and to maximize salience. The variety of forms that journals have taken is in itself an interesting phenomenon: free form prose without punctuation; highly structured essays; illustrative drawings (e.g., the floor-plan of an open space school that served as a field placement); thumbnail sketches of persons and their interrelationships in the field setting; outlined plans for action; and so forth. P.O.s are acquainted with the many options that are available to them for structuring their journals by reading through past P.O.s' and trainers' journals and also by brainstorming with their teams on ways in which they can personalize as well as optimize the value of their journals.

As the team progresses, the students' entries are also shaped by the specific feedback they get from trainers. It is worth noting that journal writing usually requires reinforcement of some kind to maintain it. Supervisors request and read their students' journals frequently and write numerous comments.

Ideally, the journal is more than a diary or a dull recounting of "what I did in my field placement this week," although such information is very useful to trainers in closely supervising their students. The basic core is, of course, the P.O.'s observations of events, behaviors, interactions, and environmental phenomena in and around the field placement. Requirements, limitations, and problems of different methodologies for systematic noninferential observation are discussed in the seminar and in team meetings (e.g., how and why to gain some measure of reliability and validity; reactivity; observer biases; and the necessity, but also limitation, of preselecting a restricted range of target phenomena for observation – See Johnson & Bolstad, 1973; Kent & Foster, 1977; Paradise & Cooney, chapter 5; and Weick, 1968).

P.O.s are encouraged to identify generalized targets for initial observations (e.g., descriptions of the physical characteristics, behavior, and interactions of staff members, administrators, students or residents, visitors, oneself, and any other participants in the setting; differences in the latter that covary with differences in the environmental setting, including room, area in the room, time of day, scheduled activity, and so forth). There is also a "Guide to Observation in the Classroom" (Krasner & Hutchison, 1973). This enables the P.O.s to get a coherent overall picture of the field setting, the people involved, and their roles in it, before they begin to focus in on more specific targets. Only the most basic precautions are recommended at this phase (e.g., noting whether observed phenomena occur in regular patterns or are one-time-only occurrences); and the P.O.'s attention is directed in large part to minimizing his obtrusiveness through establishing an accepted role in the setting.

During this initial adjustment and scanning phase, the journal serves as a valuable medium in which the P.O. (and the trainer) can summarize his/her observations. The act of writing affords the P.O. an opportunity to rethink his conclusions, look for questions that arise from the data, answer those questions by reanalyzing the data and/or by planning for future targets and methods for observation, and check out ideas and queries that have arisen in his readings and seminars. It also allows him to modify the notions presented in the didactic materials based on the observational data from the specific field setting (i.e., to operationalize abstractions in situation-specific patterns of events and interactions), plan future readings to answer theoretical or research questions that arise from the blend of experiential and didactic data, plan future activities and interventions in the field placement based on the data, and to evaluate the effects of his actions on the persons and physical environment of the field setting.

An important characteristic of the journal is that it is a written product of the students' experiences and thinking that can, in turn, serve as an effective stimulus to further analysis and reflection by the writer. This process can also increase "awareness" (i.e., ability to verbalize what is occurring). Issues that P.O.s have found worth pursuing in this way have included: What is (and what potentially could be) my role in this setting — what are the expectations that I and the persons in the field setting and my trainer have for me? How do the persons in the setting influence one another — verbally, nonverbally, directly, and indirectly? What are the roles of the staff members as designers of the field placement's environment — what do they do, what don't they do, how do they interact with one another within and between settings? How does the physical environment of the setting influence people's behavior — does it elicit, constrain, prevent, or facilitate? What are the primary influences from outside my particular field setting that have an impact on the people in that setting (e.g., school principals, hospital medical and administrative personnel, economic factors such as bond issues, school boards, civil rights advocates, institutional policies, political factors)? How is information communicated (or not communicated) in and around the setting? How are decisions made in the setting? What goals for change do the persons in the setting have, and what inertial forces will tend to keep the status quo in effect? How are the activities of the persons in the setting, especially students, integrated (or not) in a meaningful way? How can any positive outcomes resulting from my participation in this setting be maintained after I leave? What is this experience teaching me about myself — strengths and limitations, goals and interests, needs and fears?

The journal has also proven to be an excellent medium for systematic problem-solving, again following the model of D'Zurilla and

Goldfried (1971). The writers (students and trainers) can learn to respond to difficult situations they record by taking a "problem-solving orientation" rather than reacting emotionally or doing nothing. The written form of journals aids in formulating the problem operationally, "brainstorming" a number of possible solutions to the problem, carefully evaluating each solution and selecting the best one(s), and planning how to put the ideas into practice. This systematic approach has proven very useful in dealing with problem situations, and a written journal is a superb medium for doing it.

Thus, the journal is a medium for recording, rehashing, expanding, questioning, problem solving and brainstorming, evaluating, hypothesis formulation and testing, self-monitoring, planning, and integrating of didactic and experiential knowledge. In it, the P.O. can converse with himself in a self-teaching dialogue that allows the P.O. to greatly benefit from learning experiences without the often unavailable facilitation of an external teacher.

Recently, trainers and P.O.s have extended the scope of the journal to include two-way communication between the trainer and the P.O. using the model developed by Littky (1972). Most often, trainers have asked P.O.s to write journal entries shortly after each day in the field setting; they then read and write responses to the P.O.'s observations, hypotheses, inferences, plans, evaluations, and other reactions directly in the journal. Although this direct correspondence can place constraints on the P.O., trainers have tried to provide positive, constructive, and encouraging feedback and to explain to the P.O.s that the quality of thought and writing that goes into the journal will only enhance, and not detract from, the trainer's final evaluation of the P.O. The journal, thus, guarantees an accessible and open communication channel between trainer and P.O. in a modality (writing) that many P.O.s feel more comfortable with than direct face-to-face verbal conversation. It provides the trainer with regular samples of each P.O.'s conceptual work, thus affording many opportunities for the trainer to suggest new issues and directions that can facilitate the P.O.'s integrative learning. Finally, the two-way journal opens a relatively immediate feedback channel for both the trainer and P.O. that enables the trainer to contribute to and to keep in contact with the P.O.'s plans for action, and enables the P.O. to see how the trainer analyzes and evaluates issues, plans, and learning experiences. At the end of the year, the journal is an excellent tool for the P.O. and trainer to summarize their experience, as well as plan how to design the departure from the setting.

The journal has also served as a source of data for later use. All the journals over a two-year period were analyzed using a variation of the critical incidence technique (Flanagan, 1954) to establish the frequency of behaviors which occurred in settings (Toscano, 1974). The P.O.s frequently use their journals to reconstruct events and their earlier views when they write analytic papers. The journals also help trace the historical development of procedures and ideas, providing specific facts as well as a record of changing views of them.

Thus, in many ways, the journal is an important self-training device

– a method through which P.O.s can learn to continually teach themselves as they encounter learning experiences, planned and unplanned, in their work, and an instrument through which long-term maintenance of the skills and knowledge gained by the P.O. in the Environmental Design Program can be significantly enhanced. We have found the journal exceptionally useful, and at the time of this writing we are planning a research series to develop it further.

Exercises

We have found a number of specific training exercises particularly useful in conveying important behavior influence and environmental design principles to our students. A few representative exercises will be discussed here.

Role-playing (or micropractice).

Role playing is used for practicing difficult interpersonal situations which are encountered in work at the field settings. The model we have been using for micropractice follows that of Liberman, King, & DeRisi (1976), with self-control elements added by Harpin and Hutchison, (1976). The model was developed following the guidelines from research on specific skill training procedures (see Ford, chap. 9) and earlier models of microteaching (Cooper & Allen, 1970; Kansas Follow-through, 1972) and microcounseling (Ivey et al., 1968).

   The use of micropractice pervades the entire program, but space limitations prevent giving a full description here. A brief scenario follows: 1) the trainer sets up a role play situation which serves as an example of situations where the target skill should occur, selecting a scene that is salient and possible to role-play; 2) skilled behavior in "dry run" performance is reinforced by the leader and group members, and areas for improvement are suggested; 3) another person is chosen to model a higher level of the skill designated and the same scene is run again, with the leader cuing the student on the specific behaviors to observe; 4) the student "self-instructs" (i.e., repeats the description of desirable behavior correctly) and tries the situation again – he gets immediate reinforcement and sometimes receives whispered prompts or manual signals as the rerun takes place; 5) the student's improved performance is reinforced by the leader, group members, and by the student himself; 6) a homework assignment is given in which the student can practice the skill in a realistic situation outside the group.

Weekly topic-related exercises.

In connection with the seminars weekly topic-related exercises are utilized to reinforce the close interaction which we feel should exist between theory and practice. Examples of such exercises follow: We have asked students to write up an analysis of the influence of organization variables on behavior in one's setting, using references from the assigned readings to support the analysis. Students have designed (on paper) complete utopias or utopian human services organizations to be discussed in class. This exercise forces the students to examine their values and to defend their own positive examples against the critical analysis of their peers. As another example, we have had students carry out self-control projects based on the behavior modification and self-control literatures.

Co-loading the seminar.

The students select topics of particular individual interest and help develop and select readings and activities for that topic in collaboration with a trainer. In the seminar meeting, leadership may be traded back and forth between co-leaders, which provides modeling by the trainer and opportunities for ongoing coaching, cuing, feedback and labeling, and class feedback. At a later time, the student (or students together) will lead a seminar, with the trainer available for suggestions and precoaching. The "leader-for-a-day" may ask the other students what they would value in a seminar and related exercises (e.g., interesting, relevant readings; plenty of advance notice; stimulating exercises; specific group leading procedures; etc.). If a token economy is in force (see below), there may be differential points for quality of leadership (e.g., 25 for fair, 100 for good, 300 for excellent), which reinforces desired behavior and forces all to discriminate it. While the seminar is being led, trainers may provide ongoing feedback and coaching and may interrupt on occasion to discuss what is happening.

Ongoing token economy or simulated society (Krasner & Ullmann, 1973; Gamsen, 1971).

On several occasions, an ongoing token economy has been created in which all students participate. This requires an initial discussion of some issues (nature and properties of currency, basis of rules = political system, what behaviors to reinforce and change, etc.). Following the model of Martin (Krasner & Ullmann, 1973, p. 385), we suggest beginning with a dictatorship and only later yielding some control to the students, after they have learned how the economy influences their behavior. It is useful to make major and unusual changes in the economic system to make its influence more visible (e.g., major price and wage changes, regressive tax systems, etc.). This exercise demonstrates the technical details of economy, shows how tokens can influence behavior in predictable ways, puts economics in perspective with politics, and highlights the influence of nontoken sources of reinforcement.

Designing the training of others.

The students are given several chances to train other students in skills which they themselves have acquired, such as behavior shaping or group leading. They design the entire sequence for some of their classmates who need the skills. This gives the "trainers" more practice in a new situation that is very similar to situations they would encounter in a job where they might have to train others.

Doing research.

The students are required to do research exercises or projects in their settings and elsewhere using the methods covered in the seminar and readings. This provides practice with research methods but, just as important, sparks much discussion about the relevance and value of research of various kinds.

Site visits, conferences, outside projects

We take note of all available conferences, meetings, workshops, and training opportunities in the vicinities of our programs. Meetings expose students to ideas relevant to their interest, to professional behaviors they may need to acquire, and to specific professionals for further contact and discussion. Site visits to a number of centers by all or some of the students serve much the same purpose, and broaden the students' exposure to applications of environmental design ideas. The students have become involved in research, therapy, and training in several outside projects.

Workshops, receptions for others

We have held workshops and receptions in both Stony Brook and London. They serve several functions. They 1) give the P.O.s practice in setting up workshops, 2) convey information about the program and its orientation, 3) foster a sense of involvement in our program among setting people, 4) provide an opportunity for contact among people from various settings in order to share ideas, 5) provide ideas and training in specific skills to participants, and 6) improve relationships and provide a formal thank-you to setting people.

THE MODEL IN PRACTICE

Setting Up the Settings

There is a growing trend toward placing students from a variety of disciplines in applied placements in the community, and many settings have come to accept and encourage this practice. However, the P.O. role is not the same as many others, such as observer, experimenter, volunteer, or apprentice (nor is it the same in every setting). Therefore, in setting up a placement, one must clarify the role and negotiate the terms of the placement.

The P.O. is presented as a person acquiring skills who must have appropriate opportunities for acquiring them; with certain skills – conceptual and practical – not equivalent to many established roles in the setting (e.g., not a teacher-trainee); and willing to help in many ways, but hopefully in his areas of expertise (i.e., not a "volunteer"). We must negotiate a bargain which is reinforcing to people in the setting (see Hutchison & Harpin, 1974). This reinforcement can come from work done by the P.O., ideas and approaches brought in, contact with other settings connected with our program, enjoyment from working with and training enthusiastic young people, and invitations to participate in the seminar.

In the beginning in both Stony Brook and London, we worked with settings where we already had personal contacts. After successes in our first group of settings, new settings became much easier to acquire, so that we were even able to pick and choose among them. There is a vast range of possibilities for placements. The final choice is personal, influenced by the interests of the program leaders and P.O.s, available ideas and perceived possibilities for applications.

Activities in Field Settings

It is important to note that a P.O., unlike a student teacher, social worker trainee, volunteer, etc., does not go into a setting with a fixed role that he begins on day one and that remains essentially the same until the day he leaves. Rather, we negotiate with setting personnel an informal contract specifying a very simple outline of what the P.O. will do for the setting and what the setting will do for the P.O. This sort of agreement allows the P.O., and the setting, a great deal of flexibility in developing an optimal role over time through experience.

Very often our P.O.s have gone through a "break-in" period in their settings where, due to the undefined nature of their roles, they are given work that no one else at the setting wants to do. The trainers encourage the P.O.s to carry out these not-so-desirable chores in order to demonstrate that they are willing to work hard and contribute to the operation of the setting. This serves to dispel the notion that our students are ivory tower academics who have come only to observe and/or tell the setting personnel how they ought to run things. Furthermore, we feel that engaging in this preliminary work also serves the purpose of allowing the P.O. and the setting personnel a period of time for mutual adjustment to one another before the P.O. begins to actually initiate ideas and activities. It also gives the P.O. the opportunity to directly experience norms of the day-to-day operation of the setting that will hopefully root his future ideas and innovations in practical reality and allow him to share in the experiences of the setting staff so that cohesiveness is engendered.

Once the P.O. has adjusted to the setting and its personnel and vice versa, he is encouraged to begin to initiate ideas and activities which bring his specific environmental design/behavior influence skills into action. Some of the activities undertaken by P.O.s in their settings are discussed below.

We have had P.O.s doing systematic behavioral observation in school classrooms, psychiatric hospital wards, and other settings. This behavioral observation has generally been done in conjunction with a longer project such as a research study, helping a teacher to solve classroom problems, or in the role of a therapy aide monitoring the progress of a client.

P.O.s have served in the roles of teacher and therapist. For example, they have tutored normal and retarded children in academic skills, acted as primary therapists in behavior change programs for children, aided in the treatment of obsessive-compulsive and phobic patients in the hospital and in their homes, and designed interventions for elderly clients in an assessment center.

Another area where P.O.s have been active is in running skill training groups for a variety of clients in different settings. Examples of skills and populations include teaching social and practical skills to the elderly; training former psychiatric patients in job interviewing and interpersonal skills; and teaching social skills to individual psycho-therapy patients.

The students have increasingly become involved in designing and implementing their own research projects in their settings. These include research on the effects of and attitudes toward home versus hospital treatment of psychological problems; acquisition and mainten-ance of gesture language with retarded children; generalization of effects of a training program in behavioral teaching methods; effects of a training program in counseling skills for staff of a youth center; and comparison of modeling techniques in counselor training. In guiding the students, we attempt to foster the kind of integration of research, training, and service which characterizes our own program evaluation.

Another emerging area of involvement is staff training. Our students have trained counseling techniques to staff in a youth center, behavioral methods to teachers of retarded children, contingency management to staff of an assessment center for the elderly, research skills to hospital nurses, social skills training methods to social workers, and assertive group leading skills to the chairperson of the polarized board of directors of one of our settings.

The physical design of their settings and how design influences behavior have not escaped the attention of our P.O.s. For example, they have been involved in helping to plan the physical layout of the mobile components of a day care center and a mother-toddler club meeting area; and also in the layout and use of space in open classrooms. One P.O. initiated a very successful project, in conjunction with an open classroom teacher, which involved training sixth graders to design the physical layout of their classroom themselves.

Other examples of activities undertaken by various P.O.s include advising staff on the setting up and maintenance of a token economy; facilitating exchange of information and resources among different settings in a particular locality; bringing together two unfriendly groups occupying the same building; providing specific information about programs, procedures, ideas and readings relevant to a particular setting or setting problem; and finally, developing new procedures to enhance existing methods for solving problems or service delivery.

Problems Encountered

Our P.O.s have encountered some problems upon entering their field placements which we feel may be typical for persons entering a variety of such settings in a similar capacity. The lack of clearly defined role or status in the setting is a source of some confusion both to setting staff and to the P.O. What is he allowed to do or not to do? What are we allowed to ask him to do? What is he supposed to be doing here anyway? Is he evaluating us? Do we have to follow his suggestions? The P.O. might ask these same questions in the first person.

A second problem area is that the P.O. is usually inexperienced at trying to influence an organization directly and, therefore, often encounters difficulty in discovering the effective communication and decision making channels required to obtain resources and approvals for activities in a setting. In addition, conflicts are often generated when, after discovering the right channels and lines of communication, and obtaining approval for a project, a decision or promise is forgotten or revoked.

A third problem encountered is that since the role of the P.O. is both unique and undefined, the student often does not get reinforcement through the normal channels (salary, staff meetings, etc.) and early enthusiasm can rapidly wane. This problem is partially alleviated by direct, on-the-job reinforcement from the trainer (regular setting visits by the supervisor are crucial); and by the supervisor indirectly causing the P.O.'s work to be reinforced through drawing attention to his activities in the settings, at staff meetings, and seminars, and offering comments on his written work, etc.

A fourth problem involves competition with existing staff for available time and clients to pursue one's planned activities as well as competition for credit for innovations adopted by the setting. Fifth, we feel the P.O. must make a strong effort to avoid taking on the role of a regular employee in terms of becoming indispensable to the setting for the particular activities which he innovates and implements. We have seen too many well planned and executed projects immediately abandoned when the P.O. finishes his stay in the setting. We encourage and train P.O.s to become facilitators and consultants rather than being "doers" only. This is a further emphasis of the training aspect of the P.O.'s role in his setting.

Finally, but by no means last in importance, come the ethical problems. These include pressure from setting staff to support the system's status quo even when the P.O. feels his values are being compromised; going along with "medical model" approaches though he does not believe in their efficacy; being asked to administer I.Q. tests when he feels they are harmful to the client's interests; providing services to the overprivileged, and many others.

Many of the problems listed above are overcome through time and experience in the setting combined with the usually patient coaching of the trainers. Some problems however, particularly the ethical ones (see chap. 2), are never completely solved and provide a constant challenge to the P.O. (and provide many hours of animated discussion in seminars and supervisory meetings as well), that we feel is part of the learning and growing experience as well as a reflection of the ever-changing nature of both practices and values.

PROGRAM EVALUATION

A clear implication of the environmental design perspective is that the effects of any "intervention" should be assessed; clearly, this implication extends to the training program in London. Professional training is an important instance of behavior influence (see chap. 9), but has received less attention from program evaluation researchers than have other areas. The model described here is one of continual evaluation of an ongoing program, as opposed to a "one-shot" evaluation of particular training techniques.

There are a number of reasons why a continual evaluation seems preferable. Behavioral scientists have only begun to identify principles of behavior. Hence, the effect of a given training procedure is an empirical issue. It is even probable, given recent interactionist literature (Waters, chap. 4), that a given environment has different effects on different people; a training program that works for some may have to be modified for others. In addition, the evaluation can give feedback to the trainers, and thus serve as a contingency that shapes effective training methods. Ultimately, the trainers are accountable for their work, they must justify their enterprise else there seems to be no reason to have a training program. Accountability is a growing trend in many organizations (see chap. 2). A final reason for the continual evaluation is that the measures themselves can contribute to training. This idea is discussed more fully below, and accounts for the label we have attached to this model: Facilitative Evaluation Research.

Evaluation Model

The first steps in evaluating a training program are the same as those in planning training. One must first define the program's goals. This poses a problem for this program – namely, the skills necessary to a good environmental designer are not defined. (It is suggested that the same problem confronts most training programs, but is generally unrecognized; common sense and tradition rather than empirical evidence seem to dictate the set of skills taught to trainees in virtually all fields). A first approximation to a list of skills, the Environmental Design Skill List (EDSL, see fig. 8.1) has been generated. Some of the skills (e.g., "Can set up a token economy," "Can shape behavior using successive approximation") were derived from empirical literature. Others (e.g., "Can lead a group," "Can discuss effectively with others") seemed important to, or commonly used by, previous participant-observers. Many, however, reflected what are perhaps arbitrary biases about appropriate activities for an environmental designer (e.g., "Can identify and discuss clearly ethical issues. . .," "Can design and implement a process solution. . .," "Can utilize research literature appropriately . . ."). Some skills may prove irrelevant, others too vague; new literature or further experience may suggest new skills to be added to the list.

1. Can analyze the influences on an individual, including self, and test hypotheses about them (e.g., physical, social organizational, economic, and political influences; the effects of reinforcement; etc.).

2. Can generate alternative strategies for specific change in settings.

3. Can analyze and predict the probable consequences of alternative behaviors in a situation, including the more far reaching consequences on the larger system.

4. Can lead a group (discussion, role playing, skill training, etc.).

5. Can discuss effectively with others in a setting (director, staff, clientele, etc.) to negotiate goals, enlist aid, etc.

6. Can conduct individual interviews and counseling.

7. Can shape individual behavior using successive approximation.

8. Can design and implement skill training for individuals.

9. Can design and implement training programs for students (including peers), staff, and trainers of others.

10. Can design and implement procedures to train self (e.g., seek feedback from others, systematically observe own behavior, use self-control techniques, etc.).

11. Can design and implement a token economy.

12. Can identify and discuss clearly ethical issues involved in one's work.

13. Can maximize the chance of an innovation continuing after the active intervention.

14. Can design and implement a process for dealing with a goal (as contrasted with setting up a finished, pre-planned solution).

15. Can achieve acceptance for one's entry and continued role in a setting.

16. Can express ideas and plans in clear language without jargon except where appropriate, and understand ideas and plans from other orientations which prevail in the setting.

17. Can evaluate the results of an intervention or program.

18. Can locate and utilize appropriately the relevant literature in an area to develop and modify one's own practices.

19. Can work with others, especially in a team, so as to maximize each person's contribution (co-workers, setting directors, subordinates, etc.).

20. Can put ideas into practice, and can complete proposed projects.

21. Can design a viable new setting from scratch.

Fig. 8.1. Environmental design skill list (EDSL).

Hence, a major component of the research will involve evaluation of which skills are important to the role. One means of evaluating this question is examination of Incident Report Sheets (IRS), (Hutchison, Waters, & Graeff, 1976). The IRS is a behavior self report form on which trainees report experiences which contribute to their learning a particular skill. Since the majority of these experiences are instances of practicing the skill, the sheets provide estimates of the frequency of use of the various skills (preliminary analysis on this measure indicates that there are significant differences among frequencies of report of use of skills). Of course, this measure must be examined more molecularly, and in the light of further information, i.e., some skills may be unused because they are improperly learned rather than irrelevant; others may be rarely used, but crucial to an environmental designer's role on these rare occasions. Other comparisons will include correlations of ratings on specific skills with other measures, such as more global ratings of success in a setting. The issue of which skills to train must remain a continually reexamined empirical issue. Even if a valid list of skills were achieved, it seems likely, given the current rate of change of professional roles, that the list would be out of date within a few years.

The above discussion has dealt with the broader issue of which skills are useful without considering how a specific skill is measured. A substantial proportion of research time is devoted to the development of skill measures. Initially, an effort is made to analyze the skill into its component behaviors. This is done rationally, by consultation with "experts," and by examination of literature. In some cases, the analysis leads to the conclusion that the skill is multidimensional and should be separated into its component behaviors. Regardless, the analysis of the skill provides an aid to training, because it helps to identify which behaviors are to be trained.

In the design of a measure, several pragmatic factors must be considered: the measure should be inexpensive, easy to administer, and easy to score. Generally, the paper and pencil items possess substantial content validity, which Goldberg & Slovic (1967) found increases the likelihood of an item's validity across samples. Often, the measures approach the criterion behavior — a role-play of the skill assessed by a behavior observation code, in the case of training social skills; or a written simulation of the use of the skill (e.g., "generating alternative strategies for specific change in a setting"), which hopefully will provide the trainee with practice at the skill. It should be noted that, unlike in most research, every effort is made to maximize positive reactive effects; feedback is given when possible, and listing-tasks (e.g, "What are you doing or planning to do to achieve acceptance for your entry and role in your setting?") are used which draw attention to the necessity of performing skills. Reactive effects are "real" effects on human behavior, and should be utilized, particularly when research is planned as an ongoing part of the program (see Paradise & Cooney, chap. 5).

All measures are subjected to construct validation procedures (Cronbach & Meehl, 1955). Trainees themselves, all supervisors, and setting directors rate all trainees on a seven point scale for all of the EDSL skills. The IRS provides an estimate of the extent to which students are employing skills. The ratings, IRS data, and the measures may be examined by a multitrait multimethod matrix (Campbell & Fiske, 1959). The effect of training on a measure should also be apparent if the instrument is valid (Cronbach & Meehl, 1955).

There is a confounding of training effectiveness and instrument validity here; however, the reason for absence of effect on a measure may be elucidated by examination of other information. There are ratings by self and others which Wiggins (1973) concludes tend to possess some validity, self-reports of behavior on IRS sheets and in trainee's journals, and observations by supervisors. If there is evidence that a student is performing a skill well, but he/she obtains a low score on an instrument, the instrument is most likely inadequate. If the instrument and other measures correlate and agree in their assessment of minimal effect, then the training must be questioned. When evaluation is done by methods that are still being developed, obviously there will be interpretation problems. In most cases, however, a substantial amount of additional information is available to aid in this task.

The degree of experimental control is being assessed by a multiple baseline design. The prediction is that performance on a skill should increase more between measurements if the skill is taught between times of measurement than if it is not. Special attention must also be given to the reactive effects of the measures themselves — if an instrument is reactive, improvement should be observed on the instrument, and also on other measures of the skill. Some assessment of the reactive effects is also being obtained by use of control students who are not in the program. Another potential pitfall for the multiple baseline design is the possibility of learning experiences outside the program's training. The probability of such experiences is high, since supervisors encourage students to involve themselves in such activities. Once again, additional information may aid in interpretation of effects; for example, the IRS forms should indicate when students have had experience with a particular skill. If dramatic changes occur following particular experiences, comparable experiences might even be incorporated into the program. If changes are observed without such experience or training, the validity of the measure or the necessity for training might be questioned.

The use of the IRS forms in this context is notable, since it deviates substantially from conventional research use of a measure. The IRS is used as both predictor and criterion in training evaluation. It is a criterion because it provides information on frequence of use of a skill, and use of skills is an important goal of the program; it is a predictor because it provides information on the practice students receive at a skill, and it is assumed that practice is predictive of improvement. This dual usage of the measure is considered an appropriate and logical conclusion from the environmental design model. As a number of authors (e.g., Endler & Magnusson, 1976) have pointed out, most psychological research examines interactions among causes and their effects on a single variable. This can create an artificial distinction between independent and dependent variables; a more realistic view is a sequential reciprocal causation model in which each event is an effect of previous events and a cause of subsequent events. This is also highly consistent with the view of behavioral ecology, which assumes not only that the environment is an important determinant of behavior, but also that behavior is an important determinant of a person's environment.

It is important to emphasize that the research is an integral part of the training; the generalizability of results to training programs that utilize some of the training techniques without the research measures seems questionable. As suggested above, the evaluation model assumes that there will be no diminution of research commitment over time. The many uses for the research justify this continued time investment. The research measures can serve as part of the training procedure (if the designers are creative) providing feedback for modification of training techniques, aid in decisions concerning which skills to train, and even serve as a model of research for the trainees.

The several uses of the research relate to another way in which this model differs from more conventional research. Good conventional research often follows a sequential model. For instance, first a measure might be developed and validated; then the researcher utilizes the measure in an evaluation of some experimental treatment. Such a procedure may simplify interpretation of results, but is often impossible to use in evaluation research. By the time an appropriate instrument is validated, the skill which it measures might no longer be considered appropriate for the trainee's roles. The alternative utilized here is a hierarchical model wherein instrument development, skill usefulness validation, and training evaluation are conducted simultaneously. This makes interpretation difficult; it is generally necessary to examine additional measures in order to interpret a finding. Such ambiguity may make some researchers uncomfortable – some have hastened to point out that in this research it will be impossible to know for certain what is causing the observed effects. Obviously, any finding only adds incremental validity to a hypothesis – there are no unequivocal results in this or any other research. On the other hand, there is a difference between a reasonable and unreasonable interpretation of data. There are some experimental designs that add greater incremental validity than others. Within a research project such as this, most preliminary findings will probably be closer to being "suggestive" than "convincing"; only through subsequent research, on the basis of previous results, can reasonable demonstrations of effects be achieved.

Finally, it is worth noting that what might conventionally be dichotomized into "process" and "outcome" measures (or formative and summative evaluation) are not so labeled here. This distinction is not used because it is considered artificial. What are often referred to as "process measures" might as easily be labeled "interim outcome measures." Beyond this, it seems impossible to separate the processes by which behaviors are acquired from the performance of the behaviors (see the above discussion of the dual use of Incident Report Sheets). There is no time, save an arbitrary cut-off point, at which a final "outcome" is appropriately assessed. The trainees' performances throughout the course of the program and even in their future careers are all important. We carry out long-term follow-up, which seems as appropriate here as in any therapy program.

TRAINING IMPLICATIONS

The Behavioral Framework

We have found the behavioral approach, though primarily developed in the context of clinical psychology, to be very useful in conceptualizing and designing the training aspects of the program in environmental design (Ford, chap. 9). This is consistent with two important principles derived from the extensive research literature on behavior therapy – behavior therapy largely involves <u>training</u> clients in a number of specified skills in living; and the principles for influencing human behavior (and we definitely view training as an influence process) apply across a variety of situations including therapy, training, etc. It would be dramatically inconsistent of us not to apply our viewpoint to our own training program.

Of course, many other researchers and practitioners have utilized the behavioral approach in designing and evaluating training procedures. However, we feel that, in applying an environmental design conceptualization to our training program development, we are taking a broader and more "ecological" approach than that taken by the often narrow, technique-oriented behavioral training literature.

Relationship to Training Research

Empirical research investigating training methods has consistently supported several techniques and approaches as effective – modeling with discriminative cuing; behavior rehearsal with precise performance feedback delivered by multiple sources (e.g, fellow trianees, trainers, clients, or students); the provision of a supportive interpersonal milieu by and for trainees and trainers (e.g., through communicating warmly, empathetically, and genuinely, Truax, & Carkhuff, 1967); shaping skills by successive approximations; and interventions designed to maintain trainee performance after formal training has ended and trainees are working in the "natural environment" (e.g., contingency management programs, intermittent monitoring, and feedback from trainers).

Two other relevant research areas suggest further models and methods for training environmental designers. The self-control (or self-management) training techniques and approaches may facilitate self-training, enable the trainer to make optimal use of the training program's resources, and enhance post-training generalization and maintenance of the skills learned in training (Thoresen & Mahoney, 1974). The second area, problem-solving training (D'Zurilla & Goldfried, 1971), should enable environmental designers to effectively resolve the many problematic (and often unanticipated) situations which confront them in the "natural environment" and, thus, make the best use of their skills. Research within our program (Hutchison, 1976) comparing feedback and modeling for improving problem-solving skills showed that modeling produced greater immediate gains, but that these gains were lost a week later. Feedback by peers produced the greatest gains at follow-up.

Research in process as this chapter is being written is designed to provide a great deal of information about the effectiveness of the variety of techniques we use for training the skills on the EDSL. At present, we utilize several variations of the well-documented, behaviorally-oriented training methods to be found in the existing research literature. Modeling is provided through seminar discussions and simulations (role taking exercises), opportunities to observe fellow P.O.s in their placement settings (and often with cuing provided by an accompanying trainer), observing trainers as they demonstrate different approaches to situations that arise in the placement settings (e.g., through role play simulations and demonstrations in the training group); and through observing the staff at the placement settings as they work.

Behavior rehearsal with feedback is a key training procedure in most training team group meetings, especially in preparing for or rehashing problematic situations in the placement settings, with trainees and trainers offering feedback. The London program's practicum meetings similarly focus on this active procedure, and it is incorporated in the Stony Brook program's seminar. The placement settings themselves offer abundant opportunities for trying out new behaviors (e.g., working with individuals and groups of students or residents, teaching mini-lessons, providing feedback to staff members in different ways), with feedback provided (formally or informally) by the staff, students or residents, trainers, other trainees, and the trainee's own self evaluations. P.O.s are encouraged to gradually extend their role from that of observer to that of active participant and agent of intervention. Developing a role that fits the P.O. and the setting is a process based primarily in trying out ways of interacting, monitoring the feedback carefully, and attempting more effective ways of interacting.

The shaping-by-successive-approximations approach is evidenced in many ways in the Environmental Design Program. The desired performance is analyzed by breaking it down into specifiable, teachable components of behavior, and experiences are planned to build the student's current behavioral repertoire to the target criteria. Often this involves highly structured modeling, practice, feedback, and coaching (Ford, chap. 9). However, in general, we have attempted to build those important training elements directly into the program in ways which will be effective and likely to produce behavior which will generalize (i.e., come under control of the relevant stimuli in the "natural environment").

We are constantly testing our ideas and practices concerning what is needed to make a learning experience effective for a student at a given skill level. For example, most settings will naturally reinforce appropriate behavior in the situation of interacting with a setting director (i.e., the director smiles, makes comments, approves or denies requests, etc.), but the P.O. may require modeling, coaching, or supplementary reinforcement to build his repertoire and bring it under the control of the behavior of the director. Goldiamond (1974) and Liberman et al. (1975) provide excellent orientations to the shaping approach of using repertoire building procedures.

Self observation and development of behavioral awareness are important components of the shaping process. The use of journals by the P.O.s as well as continual cuing by trainers during the course of the program provide the student with a constant flow of information about what is being done and why. The goal is to increase the students' awareness of the behavior influence process and procedures, and to enhance their effectiveness in planning their own training environments.

Finally, generalization of skills from the classroom to the training setting have been provided for in several ways. First, techniques are taught, not as panaceas, but as potential tools for tackling problematic situations. Thus, P.O.s and trainers learn that it is more important to fully assess a situation and to plan actions that best fit that situation than to automatically apply fixed skills in a cookbook fashion. We encourage innovative modifications of the skills and principles learned in training (and the creation of completely new actions based on ideas gained through past didactic and applied experience and an assessment of the current setting) in order to handle each unique situation. A second general strategy to promote generalization and maintenance involves teaching students to be generalists rather than technicians. A wide range of ideas, from many fields and orientations of theory and research practice, is offered in the seminar to enhance P.O.s' and trainers' abilities to creatively formulate their own responses to problematic situations according to general principles. Particularly, P.O.s and trainers are taught to monitor the effects that their actions have – on themselves, on other people, on interactions, and on the physical environment – so that they can adjust their actions accordingly.

The opportunity for extensive practice in the placement settings, with modeling and feedback from the trainer, fellow P.O.s, staff, and students or residents, should greatly enhance generalization and maintenance as well. Trainers are encouraged to gradually give greater responsibility to the P.O.s for planning, implementing, and evaluating actions, to ensure that the skills learned can be utilized by the P.O. autonomously.

As with most training programs, the Environmental Design Program has no direct control over the kinds of environments in which P.O.s will work after they graduate. Therefore, direct environmental interventions (e.g., contingency management) cannot be used to increase generalization and maintenance, but must be replaced by teaching P.O.s and trainers to serve as self-trainers, to systematically plan their actions based on a wealth of general ideas and a thorough assessment of particular situations, and to monitor and evaluate their behaviors so as to constantly learn and improve. This is the key element in self-control and problem-solving training, and expresses a basic philosophy of our training program.

Continuing Development; Programs in Process

Research on training is new (Ford, chap. 9) and in the area of training trainers is even newer and sparser (Peck & Tucker, 1973). In light of this, it would be folly to present this training program model as a finished product. On the contrary, we have had to revise this chapter frequently as we adopted new methods based as it is on our own experience and research as well as that of others. The program should continue to develop, and will probably change enormously with time and experience. But as one model, it may have positive influence on others working in the same direction.

ETHICS

Hutchison (chap. 2) presented the model used for training ethics in the program. Skill training was examined as a proposed solution to many ethical dilemmas. The reasoning of its proponents is that there can be no objection to giving individuals additional skills, since available choice is increased in this way and no coercion is used. However, it is clear to us that there will still be many occasions for ethical issues. Many issues will arise in the activities of the trainees in settings, as examples above showed. But an important class of issues arises from training itself: What behaviors should we train (and avoid training?). Should we train students in skills of working for change within a system, from outside it, or in radical methods, as some advocate? Should we focus on changing individuals or on changing systems? Must we train only the most effective methods in order to gain ethical approval, as Davison and Stuart (1975) claim? What if our trainees disagree with our choices? As Hutchison concluded, a trainer cannot avoid responsibility by leaving choices of whether to learn or use skills to his trainees. In training the skills, one changes the relative response strengths and, thus, influences what the trainee's response will be. The key issue is the choice of behaviors to be trained. One value which influences our process of selection is research concerning the consequences of alternative behaviors. We recognize that our choices will be determined largely by the society in which we live, and will change over time. We make our personal choices and inescapably bear responsibility for them; this we must do with humility.

9 Training and Environmental Design
Julian D. Ford

This chapter presents a model of training as the key to environmental design. It represents training in a model (a way of looking at the world), and in techniques (how to bring about change and why, change for what purpose, goal, value, reinforcer). Perhaps this is the most "how to" chapter in the book. The design of environment also includes the design of people. Developing training programs to influence persons who are in positions to influence the environment is an important element in the conceptualization of environmental design.

The environmental design approach reconceptualizes the relationship between the giver and receiver of help, advice, and "therapy" from that of a biomedical restoration of a hypothesized preexisting state of health to that of a reciprocal interacting-training relationship in an educational context.

Ed.

This chapter will provide a critical overview to current theory and research on environmental design training. The roles that must be filled and the skills that must be possessed by a truly "complete" environmental designer will first be discussed, because these are the bases for the first major element in training program — the training objectives. The second central element in training — the curriculum — will next be considered by examining the environmental systems and scientific fields which are relevant for the environmental designer. Thirdly, issues and research concerning training methods will be reviewed, with a focus on areas in which substantive empirical research has been reported.

One ubiquitous theme will be frequently touched upon in all three sections. It is a philosophical/conceptual position of the writer's that there are no irrefutable standards for "Good" or "Bad"; thus, the important issues to be addressed and questions to be answered are not "who is best?" or "which way is optimal?" but rather, what are the different consequences of different actions done or beliefs held by different persons at different times and in different situations? The resultant emphasis on <u>functionalism</u> and <u>eclecticism</u> does not mean, however, that value issues will be overlooked. On the contrary, ethical issues will be constantly referred to in the chapter, but they will be analyzed from a relativistic and empirically-oriented perspective. We will ask: what is the potential range of possible training objectives in environmental design, and what is the importance of each different type of objective, rather than attempting to specify a fixed and limited set of training objectives that are "right" or "complete" for all trainers and trainees. Similarly, we will survey a variety of types of, and sources for, training curricula as a means to stimulate the reader to consider new topic areas and materials, rather than to tell the reader what is "correct" or "ideal." And we will examine the different outcomes that have been found to obtain when different training methods are used by different trainers with different types of trainees and for different training objectives, again to suggest a variety of possible methods that the reader can adapt to his/her own needs.

If the chapter has any major goal, it is to influence the reader to take on the perspective of a hypothesis tester where training (or any environmental design intervention) is concerned. The chapter is a resource, a source of ideas and new possibilities. It is up to the reader to translate these new ideas into terms that make sense for him/her and his/her role (e.g., student, social change agent, teacher) and environment (e.g., college, home, hospital, school), and into strategies for action (if the reader's goal is to bring about changes in those roles and/or environments). The reader also has the responsibility for evaluating the outcomes of such conceptual and action hypotheses, because what works for one person or in one setting may be very different from that for other people or environments.

In a word, the reader is invited to be an active participant while reading this chapter. Hopefully, we will stimulate questions rather than providing cookbook recipes. Answers to the many questions that we shall discuss will have to come from the reader's formulating and testing of hypotheses in his/her own life, although we will try to provide some hints in the form of an overview of the existing bodies of theory, problems, and data concerning the training of environmental designers.

With this framework in mind, let us turn first to a discussion of training objectives in environmental design.

TRAINING OBJECTIVES

While the term "environmental designer" certainly means many different things to different people (e.g., behavior modifier, architect, educator, community planner, interior decorator), a more generic definition will be provided so that the reader will not be nagged by the lingering question of, "Who is this who is being trained?" while reading the rest of the chapter. If you disagree with the definition, by all means develop a better one. We will consider an environmental designer to be a person who, when confronted with an environmental system that he/she wishes to change in some way, systematically utilizes principles from theory and research in the social and physical sciences and humanities and/or methods developed by the human service professions to develop comprehensive conceptualization hypotheses, integrated intervention strategies, and meaningful processes and outcome evaluations. In other words, an environmental designer is someone who attempts to produce social change of some sort using a scientific hypothesis-testing methodology. Fairweather (1972) and his colleagues (Fairweather, Tornatzky & Sanders, 1974) have provided a lucid description of the environmental designer role, based on their experimental social innovation model. Kelly (1970), in portraying the ideal community psychologist, has also captured several basic features of the environmental designer. Harpin and Ford (1974) have also depicted an environmental designer role for clinical psychologists.

A Hierarchical Role Model for Environmental Designers

Who can be an environmental designer? Virtually anyone — but training, to provide the person with certain key skills, is essential. Parents, classmates in elementary schools, inpatients in psychiatric hospitals, clinical psychologists, teachers, paraprofessional mental health staff-persons, psychiatrists, social workers, community planners, community psychologists, retarded persons, counselors, nurses, lawyers, economists, politicians, and many more, all have been trained — or could potentially be trained — to serve as environmental designers. There would seem to be four basic levels at which an environmental designer could function, depending on the nature and scope of his/her target objectives for social change.

First, an environmental designer could serve primarily as a self-regulator. This is a person who receives environmental design training in order to directly improve his/her own functioning or life situation or milieu (e.g., a client in an assertiveness training program, a student in school). For this person, the objective of training is to learn skills that will enable him/her to more effectively achieve his/her personal goals in his/her daily life. The types of skills that are most relevant for the self-regulator include observation (e.g., Krasner et al., 1977), problem solving (e.g., D'Zurilla & Goldfried, 1971), assertiveness (e.g., Rich & Schroeder, 1976), and self-monitoring and self-reinforcement (e.g., Thoresen & Mahoney, 1974).

Although many traditional socialization, rehabilitation, and self-improvement processes in our society (e.g., parenting, psychotherapy, education) can be structured as training in environmental design, this is not automatically the case. The following are value assumptions about the target objectives in training that seem to characterize an environmental design approach (cf. Ford & Hutchison, 1974b; Krasner & Krasner, 1973; Krasner & Ullmann, 1973).

Trainees are taught to function as autonomous environmental

designers. The goal of training is not simply to minimize deviance or to promote conformity to any belief system, but rather to teach trainees skills that will enable them to effectively control their own lives independently of the trainer's influence and guidance. While training can never be value-free, because the trainer always brings with him/her a personal belief system and cannot help but influence the trainee to adopt similar views — whether explicitly (through avowedly promoting these beliefs) or implicitly (through modeling and differentially attending to his/her own views) — the ultimate objective in environmental design training is to aid the trainee in acquiring self-regulation skills such that he/she can subsequently reevaluate all prior goals and beliefs and independently formulate his/her own objectives and views.

Trainers work with (rather than on) the trainee, seeking to widen (rather than constrict) the client's resources (e.g., ideas, behavioral options), and to increase (rather than restrict) the client's skills and capabilities. The goal is to broaden the trainee's universe of hypotheses and to make the trainee a more effective hypothesis tester in his/her own life, rather than to teach the trainee that certain things are "true" or "good" and other things are "false" or "bad." Trainees are treated as active participants in a collaborative teaching-learning process, not as passive recipients of expert healing or universal truths. And the emphasis is on learning effective ways to explore the consequences of different theories or beliefs and strategies for action (i.e., learning how to learn and be one's own teacher, cf. Dewey, 1934).

The second level for environmental design training involves the training of socialization agents whose primary goals are to facilitate the growth and development of other persons. We will label this kind of environmental designer a mediator (cf. Tharp & Wetzel, 1969). Parents, teachers, mental health paraprofessionals, children or adolescents who serve as change-agents for their peers, public health nurses, social workers, and many other persons are potential mediators. The objective of training for mediators is to teach skills that will enable them to train the persons for whom they are responsible to be effective self-regulators. Environmental design training for mediators might aim to teach parenting (e.g., Horowitz, 1976), classroom design and teaching (e.g., Krasner, 1976b), peer-teaching (e.g., Benassi & Larson, 1976), or ward counseling and management (e.g., Karlsruher, 1974) skills, among others. It is most important that persons in mediator roles not be trained simply as technicians; as with self-regulators, the goal in training mediators is to enable them to autonomously design, implement, and evaluate social influence strategies, and not to make them dependent on the trainer for guidance and direction.

Environmental designers may also be trained to serve as trainers. In a hierarchical fashion, environmental design trainers are persons who are responsible for training and supervising mediators. While the many types of human service professionals are all potential environmental design trainers (e.g., psychiatrists, lawyers, architects, community planners, psychologists, nurses, social workers, counselors), most are functioning primarily as "expert" mediators, providing direct care services to patients and consultees. Environmental design trainers are providers of indirect (e.g., community development, parent training, paraprofessional training) rather than direct (e.g., psychotherapy, ward management) services (cf. Snow & Newton, 1976), program-oriented rather than case-centered consultation (cf. Kaplan, 1970), experimental social innovation rather than traditional psychotherapeutic services (cf. Fairweather, 1972), and preventive or enhancement rather than remedial or curative (cf. Cowen, 1973; Kelly, Snowden & Munoz, 1977) interventions. The objective of training for environmental design trainers is to give them skills that will enable them to effectively diffuse their knowledge and their behavior influence techniques to mediators, and not simply to learn the behavior-change skills that are appropriate at the mediator level.

Finally, environmental design training can be geared to prepare trainees to serve at a fourth level, that of designer. Again following a hierarchical model, designers are responsible for the training and guidance of environmental design trainers. The designer must function as a theoretician, innovator, long-range policy planner, politically-astute social-influence agent, historian, methodologist, and consultant to trainers on technical and conceptual issues. They serve simultaneously as participant observers and external critics, balancing a direct involvement in ongoing environmental design interventions with a detachment from the moment-to-moment pressures that so often make it impossible to step back and take a much needed look at the "big picture" (i.e., the total systems context of the intervention). Designers are responsible not only for the preparation of trainers, but also for sparking paradigm shifts (cf. Kuhn, 1970), in which traditional goals and values and methods are reexamined from a new perspective. The writings of Argyris (1975), Keisler (1971), Krasner & Ullmann (1973), Mahoney (1976), and Pratt (1976) provide excellent recent examples of the inputs of social scientists who have taken on the role of designer.

Environmental designers can be trained at four hierarchical levels: self-regulator, mediator, trainer, and designer. The primary task for the latter three levels is the training of environmental designers at the next prior level. However, self-regulation skills are essential to all environmental designers, mediation skills are necessary for trainers and designers, and training skills are required for the designer role; environmental designers at each level in the hierarchy must be competent in the skills which they are teaching to their trainees, even though their major responsibilities will require other skills specific to their level in the hierarchy as well. If for no other reason, this is true because a central method of training is modeling, and a model must have competence in the skills he/she is demonstrating.

A hierarchical role structure has both heuristic and technological value (cf. Seidman & Rappaport, 1974). While, in reality, environmental designers will often have to take on the responsibilities included in more than one of the role levels, each level has a distinct scope and focus that is unique. If we fail to distinguish between all four role levels, we are likely to overlook important role functions of environmental designers (e.g., very little attention has, in the past, been paid to the training or role functions attributed to the designer level, although it is a pivotal role).

Similarly, the hierarchical model provides an efficient means for the diffusion of environmental design services. A relatively small number of designers can each train and supervise several environmental design trainers, who can, in turn, serve as facilitators for several self-regulators. For example, if each environmental designer can provide services for ten persons at the next lowest level in the hierarchy, then 1,000 self-regulators per each designer would be served. Whereas, if designers were instead trained only to fill the role of mediator, only 10 self-regulators could be served by each.

Skills for the Environmental Designer

While the specific skills that an environmental designer will need will be determined by the specific objectives that he/she has in his/her work and the level at which he/she is providing environmental design services, 13 basic types of skills are relevant for all environmental designers.

Observation Skills: The ability to accurately gather meaningful and complete information concerning all relevant aspects of a sociophysical context in which an environmental design intervention is to be implemented (e.g., Kent & Foster, 1977; Krasner & Hutchison, 1974; Webb et al., 1966).

Elicitation Skills: The ability to structure interpersonal interactions (e.g., interviews) or sociophysical environments (e.g., role play simulations, furniture arrangements) so as to elicit data that would not otherwise be observable (e.g., Ivey, 1971; Sommer, 1969).

Conceptualization Skills: The ability to develop and utilize cognitive information processing strategies (e.g., functional analysis, systems analysis, social learning models, ecological analysis) to screen, assimilate, organize, analyze, make available for planning, and memorize the data gathered through elicitation and observation methods (e.g., Bandura, 1969; Goldfried & Pomeranz, 1968; Harshbarger & Maley, 1974; Krasner & Ullmann, 1973; Willems, 1974).

Problem Solving Skills: The ability to systematically make decisions and plan strategies for action, so as to translate the conceptual scheme and the assessment data into practical interventions (e.g., D'Zurilla & Goldfried, 1971).

Facilitation Skills: The ability to redesign sociophysical environments so as to maximize the likelihood that one's behavior change objectives (which were established via problem solving) are achieved (e.g., discriminative cuing, the provision of necessary tools and material, contingency contracting, self-monitoring, modeling – Bandura, 1969; Krasner & Ullmann, 1973; Krasner & Krasner, 1973).

Consecution Skills: The ability to structure the sociophysical environment so that desired behavior changes are maintained (e.g., contingent reinforcement, response cost, or informational stimuli – Bandura, 1969; Leitenberg, 1976; Krasner & Ullmann, 1973).

Communication Skills: The ability to convey factual and effective messages with accuracy that will enhance other behavior influence (i.e., facilitation and consecution) interventions (e.g., assertive behavior; empathic, warm, and genuine communication; congruent verbal and nonverbal messages; persuasive communication – Bower & Bower, 1976; Chaiken & Eagly, 1976; Cialdini & Schroeder, 1976; Mitchell, Bozarth & Krauft, 1978; Watzlawick, Weakland & Fisch, 1974).

Self Control Skills: The ability to self-monitor, self-evaluate, self-cue, and self-reinforce, in order to regulate one's own actions (e.g., Thoresen & Mahoney, 1974).

Process Evaluation Skills: The ability to generate accurate and meaningful quality-control feedback (data), in order to monitor the effects and efficacy of ongoing behavior change interventions (e.g., Davidson, Clark & Hamerlynck, 1974; Harshbarger & Maley, 1974; Perloff, Perloff & Sussna, 1976; Schulberg, Sheldon & Baker, 1969).

Outcome Evaluation Skills: The ability to gather accurate, meaningful and comprehensive data concerning the multiple outcomes of a behavior change intervention (e.g., Ellis & Wilson, 1973; Guttentag & Snapper, 1974; Hamerlynck et al., 1974; Harshbarger & Maley, 1974; Schulberg et al., 1969; Willems, 1974).

Resource Allocation Skills: The ability to allocate a limited supply of resources (e.g., person-hours, dollars, time, equipment) so as to maximize the efficiency of all phases of an ongoing behavior change intervention (e.g., Harshbarger & Maley, 1974; Schulberg et al., 1969).

Coordination Skills: The ability to integrate multiple concurrent intervention programs or sub-programs (i.e., administrative or organizational development skills, e.g., Alderfer, 1977; Argyis, 1970; Lawrence & Lorsch, 1969).

Synthesis Skills: The ability to develop new theoretical paradigms and applied methodologies, and to adapt existing ones to the idiosyncracies of unique target populations, target objectives, and environmental contexts (e.g., experimental social innovation, the empirical-clinical methodology – Fairweather, 1972; Goldfried & Davison, 1976).

These 13 groupings represent the broad classes of skills that are necessary when an environmental designer seeks to bring about some planned social/behavior change. They roughly correspond to the six basic phases of an intervention program: assessment, goal formulation, intervention design, intervention, evaluation, and systems maintenance, with the addition of the last set of skills which enable the environmental designer to move beyond the scope of a single intervention and alter his/her entire conceptual and methodological framework (at the trainer or designer level) or to adapt past methods to the development of new interventions (at the self-regulator or mediator level). The specific skills or competencies within each of the thirteen classes of environmental design skills are virtually infinite in number and variety – limited only by the resources and imagination available to the environmental designer. The references cited for each skill type offer a few examples for the reader but are far from exhaustive.

Formulating Training Objectives

Every training program is a behavior change intervention requiring the six phases to which we just alluded. Therefore, before target objectives can be established, the trainer(s) must conduct a thorough assessment of several variables.

Goals Assessment: What are the goals of the persons, groups, and organizations that can exert an influence on the training program? For every training program, there are several "influential populations" (IPs) (Ford & Hutchison, 1974b) that are in a position to allocate or withhold key resources (e.g., active participation in the training process, money, knowledge and expertise, official sanctions, employment opportunities) contingent on the program's fulfillment of their objectives (e.g., meaningful training experiences, human services provided to the local community, adherence to legal and professional standards, cost efficiency, graduates with marketable skills). The major IPs are: trainees, trainers, administrators, community and consumer groups representing clients of the environmental designers who are being trained, representatives of the legal and professional establishments, and representatives of potential employers of graduates of the training program. Different methods will be more or less effective in soliciting goals from each IP (e.g., face-to-face interaction, survey questionnaires, consulting published legal and professional standards), but it is important to acquire an accurate and representative notion of the primary goals of each IP, and the relative importance that each IP assigns to each goal. Often it is wise to go beyond such data on current needs and project the probable future goals of the IPs, based on their current goals and the likely changes in their characteristics as groups (e.g., as the number of minority-group students grow, so too will the need for training in skills especially relevant to intervention in their varied cultural environments) and their sociophysical environments (e.g., the supply of psychotherapists in private practice and in academia is rapidly exceeding the demand for them, so training may be better geared to prepare trainees for more marketable roles).

Initial Goal Formulation: Based on these inputs from IPs, an initial and general set of target objectives for trainees (i.e., the role functions that they should be prepared to fulfill upon graduation) and trainers (i.e., the role functions that they will fulfill in providing training experiences for trainees and services to the community) must be established. Ford and Hutchison (1974b) and Guttentag and Snapper (1974) have outlined similar strategies for this task, based on cost-benefit analyses and utility scaling.

Needs Assessment: What skills or resources will the IPs need in order to achieve these broad goals, and what is their level of current competency in or supply of each? For trainees, this translates to an assessment of the skills and knowledge of environmental designers that they "bring with them" to the training program. For trainers, this means an assessment of their competencies as trainers, in terms of direct teaching and supervisory skills, and of environmental design skills which they can model for trainees. For the administrators, this involves an assessment of the current resources – money, personnel, facilities – available to the program.

For the other IPs, those who while not directly involved in the training process nevertheless regulate or consume the services of the environmental designers being trained, the needs assessment has a different significance. For these groups, it is necessary to determine what kinds of interventions will be necessary from an environmental designer in order to satisfy these IPs' goals (e.g., one-to-one versus milieu programs, therapy versus consultation, assessment versus behavior change, assertiveness training versus organizational development). That is, what should trainees be taught so that they can provide meaningful services to their future clients?

Once goals and needs have been assessed for all IPs, then specific training objectives can be defined. This second goal formulation phase requires the delineation of specific skills or competencies to be learned by trainees; specific learning experiences to be provided by trainers; and specific resources to be allocated by administrators. The details of administrative resource allocation are beyond the scope of this chapter, involving issues of economics, organizational management, and (hopefully) common sense. The questions involved in the provision of learning experiences form the subject matter for the next two major sections.

The first type of training objectives (i.e., trainee competencies) should ideally include skills from each of the 13 types of environmental design skills discussed above. The specific competencies that are optimal for any group of trainees or any individual trainee will depend upon the data obtained through the Needs Assessment, and on the role level for which the trainee(s) are being prepared. For example, both a teacher being trained for a mediator role and a clinical psychologist being trained for a designer role will need evaluation skills. However, while the psychologist/designer will probably need skills in formal psychometrics and sociometrics, the teacher/mediator would probably profit more from a working knowledge of the nontechnical basic principles of evaluation and from practical skill in the use of several specific evaluation tools.

Before moving on to discuss issues of the training curriculum, it is worth mentioning that training objectives will be more or less useful depending on the form in which they are cast. Behavioral objectives (cf. Mager, 1962) seem to work best, because they specify precisely who is to do what observable behavior(s) where and when, and how an observer or evaluator will be able to know when this has been accomplished (i.e., what will he/she see and hear the trainee doing; what permanent products, such as written reports, will result).

THE TRAINING CURRICULUM FOR ENVIRONMENTAL DESIGN

Once the goals for training have been established, they must be operationalized through the selection of content areas that will be covered and the curricular materials that will be utilized. These are the two major components in the training curriculum and we will discuss each in turn.

Content Areas in Environmental Design Training

One way of thinking of the content areas or topics that could be taught in environmental design training is to derive them from the distinctive kinds of environmental systems in which an environmental designer might be called upon to apply his/her skills. Thus, the topic areas would correspond to the special issues that arise for an environmental designer when he/she is intervening in each environmental system: the focal characteristics of the system (e.g., man-environment interactions, types of built structures, patterns of behaviors); variables to be considered when entering the system (e.g., chains of communication and influence); variables that merit special attention in assessment and interventions in that system (e.g., normative beliefs held by persons in the system, raging controversies, central patterns of interactions among persons in the system); and variables that will have significant effects on the permanence of the positive changes that were initiated by an environmental designer (e.g., the commitment of persons in the system to maintaining changes initiated by an outside change agent).

There are many prototypical environmental systems that are potential targets for environmental designers. These include schools, homes, hospitals, prisons, community governments, social service agencies, geriatric institutions, day-care centers, mental health agencies, clinics, welfare agencies, legal aide services, self-help groups, community planning boards, businesses, police departments, park and recreation services, planned parenthood centers, senior centers, youth centers, psychiatric hospitals, special education schools and classrooms, labor unions, and many more. Each setting poses special problems with which an environmental designer must be competent to deal and thus requires specialized training.

A second way to look at the content areas in training is to consider the types of variables that an environmental designer may be called upon to influence in his/her work in these settings (cf. Ford & Hutchison, 1974a). There are eleven main kinds of variables relevant for the environmental designer:

1. Geophysical (e.g., climate, terrain);

2. Architectural (e.g., room sizes and accessibility);

3. Spatial (e.g., territorial boundaries, personal space);

4. Interpersonal (e.g., person-to-person nonverbal communication);

5. Cognitive-Intrapersonal (e.g., beliefs and personal constructs);

6. Physiological-Intrapersonal (e.g., hormone levels, muscle tension);

7. Intrasocial-Sociopolitical (e.g., decision-making policies and ritualized interaction patterns within social groups);

8. Intersocial-Sociopolitical (e.g., decision-making policies and norms impinging on social groups from <u>outside</u> their boundaries);

9. Intrasocial-Economic (e.g., patterns of resource distribution <u>within</u> social groups);

10. Intersocial-Economic (e.g., patterns of resource distribution that affect social groups but which originate <u>outside</u> them); and

11. Education-Socialization (e.g., childraising patterns).

Each of these involves a multitude of specific variables which could be used by an environmental designer to effect changes in a setting. Different types of variables will often be differentially effective in interventions for different target objectives (e.g., interpersonal and intrapersonal variables are often the focus in psychotherapy with individual clients, while community development interventions require a focus on sociopolitical, economic, and educational variables) and in different settings (e.g., architectural and spatial interventions are often more effective than intrapersonal ones in psychiatric hospitals with chronic patients). Thus, an environmental designer should ideally be trained to deal with variables of several, if not all, types.

A third way of dealing with the content areas for training is to consider the types of skills which are relevant for an environmental designer. The 13 specific types of skills were described earlier. An entire seminar or even several courses could be devoted to teaching the many specific competencies that are involved in each of these classes of environmental design skills – the specific behaviors involved, the way each skill type can be applied to each of the types of variables which are relevant for an environmental designer, and the special considerations necessary when applying each skill type in different environmental settings.

There is no single "right" way to select and structure the topic areas to be covered in an environmental design training program; this is a decision which must be based on the specific training objectives of each individual program. However, our consideration of three ways to think about content areas in training suggests that a comprehensive training program must deal with most or all of the environmental design skill types and most or all of the types of variables which can be utilized by an environmental designer, as they apply to the specific target settings in which that program's trainees are being prepared to serve. As outlined in figure 9.1, there are as many as 143 potential content areas that can be dealt with in environmental design training to prepare trainees to serve as environmental designers in any specific type of setting.

Many scientific disciplines and professional fields offer multiple theoretical, empirical, and methodological perspectives that may be relevant for an environmental design training program, depending on its specific target objectives and the content areas it is designed to cover. Here again, it is the responsibility of the participants in each training

Target Setting: (e.g., elementary school; psychiatric hospital)

Classes of Variables

Classes of Skills	Geophysical	Architectural	Spatial	Interpersonal	Intrapersonal-Cognitive	Intrapersonal-Physiological	Intrasocial-Sociopolitical	Intersocial-Sociopolitical	Intrasocial-Economic	Intersocial-Economic	Educational Socialization
Observation											
Elicitaton											
Conceptualization											
Problem Solving											
Facilitation											
Consecution											
Communication											
Self Control											
Process Evaluation											
Outcome Evaluation											
Resource Allocation											
Coordination											
Synthesis											

Fig. 9.1. Content areas for environmental design training.

program to determine what kinds of information from what fields of study or service are most relevant for their particular program. To give the reader a feel for the diversity of potentially relevant fields, here is a brief sampler: ecology, physiology, sociology, environmental psychology, program evaluation, economics, law, behavior therapy, medicine, urban planning, community psychology, Rogerian psychotherapy, social psychology, political science, biofeedback, learning disabilities and special education, rehabilitation medicine, developmental psychology, ethics, "open" education, clinical psychology, human factors, psychiatry, social work, nursing, group dynamics, applied behavior analysis, organizational psychology, gestalt therapy, philosophy of science, human learning and memory, family therapy, psycholinguistics, epidemiology, communication theory, rational-emotive therapy, systems analysis, cybernetics, architectural design, and survey research.

In teaching each content area, it seems important to cover three separate, although interrelated, issues: theory, research, and practical applications. In other words, trainees are best equipped to function as environmental designers if they are aware of the major conceptual issues and variables, the empirical data bearing upon these issues and supporting different courses of action, and how to actually conduct an environmental design intervention in the context of that particular content area.

Curricular Materials in Environmental Design Training

The typical approach to training change agents involves the use of lectures, readings, and group discussions as the primary basis for the didactic or academic learning experiences. The range of curricular materials included varies, but generally they consist of selected books and journal articles, a few commercially manufactured films or slide-shows, and resource materials for brief demonstrations (e.g., samples of assessment instruments). While often useful, these do not begin to exhaust the universe of potential curricular materials.

Empirical research has consistently shown that curricular materials which involve the trainee as an active participant are more effective in teaching skills and concepts than materials that are oriented to passive learning activities (see the section on training methods, below; Ford, 1977, 1978; Hutchison, 1975a). Thus, programmed texts are more effective than prose texts, didactic lectures, or videotaped demonstrations in teaching both factual knowledge and behavioral skills to counseling students. Similarly, doing and then viewing videotaped rehearsals of counseling and teaching skills is superior to verbal lectures or textbook readings. And live or videotaped demonstrations (i.e., modeling) are more effective as teaching methods/materials than lectures or readings.

Teaching materials that engage the trainee as an active participant – and particularly those that provide opportunities for trainees to receive specific feedback on the outcome of their participations (see the training methods section, below) – are optimal. This is consistent with the philosophy and methods of the "open education" movement (cf. Krasner & Krasner, 1973; Silberman, 1973) and the extensive data-base of behavior modification (cf. Bandura, 1969; Krasner & Ullmann, 1973). The specific curricular materials to be used must depend upon the nature of the trainees, trainers, and target objectives of each training program, but the range of possibilities includes audiotaped demonstrations and exercises, values clarification materials, gestalt exercises, videotapes with which trainees can rehearse new skills and then view themselves and their peers, programmed texts, materials to be used by trainees in conducting self-change projects, and much more. The only limit on the types and efficacy of curricular materials is the level of creativity and energy of the trainers and trainees.

METHODS FOR ENVIRONMENTAL DESIGN TRAINING

The final question with which trainers of environmental designers must deal, once they have established their training objectives, content areas, and curricular materials, is that of what specific methods are to be used in operationalizing the training process. We will consider this question by discussing the types of training methods that are available to environmental design trainers, the issues that arise in research evaluations of training methods, and the results of existing empirical research concerning training methods. In so doing, our goal will be to suggest potentially useful strategies for environmental design training and for the evaluation of these training methods.

Types of Training Methods

A wide variety of training methods are available to environmental design trainers. These include specific training procedures and broader training programs which integrate several component procedures. Each major procedure and program may involve a variety of different components or parameters. We will consider several training procedures (instructions, modeling with cuing, performance feedback, behavior rehearsal, and contingency management) and four major programmatic approaches to training (microtraining, interpersonal process recall, integrated didactic-experiential training, and "traditional" training).

Instructions: verbal descriptions of the target behavior. Perhaps the most widely used method of training, and often the most direct and straightforward, instructions may be presented with several parametric variations: specificity (i.e., the precision and detail with which the verbal descriptions are given, varying from vague and global generalities to bit-by-bit task analyses); medium (i.e., written versus spoken); source (i.e., the power, status, expertise, attractiveness, and legitimacy of the person delivering the instructions); proximity to the trainee's performance of the target behavior (i.e., length of time between presentation of the instructions and the trainee's actual performance of the target behavior); and valence (i.e., the contingencies implicit or explicit in the message).

Modeling with Cuing: behavioral demonstration of the target behavior with salient signals to indicate exactly when it is occurring and whether it is a demonstration of correct or incorrect behavior. Modeling involves six components: the proximity to the trainee's actual performance of the target behavior; a message; a valence; a model; a medium; and cuing. The proximity component is the same as for instructions. The message may vary in terms of specificity (i.e., the detail with which the target behavior is demonstrated), whether both correct and incorrect behavior, or only one, are shown, the type of target behavior (i.e., a specific response versus a series of interrelated responses), and the environmental context (i.e., the type of scene used as a background for the demonstration, e.g., a real therapy office versus a lecture hall versus a blank screen). The valence in modeling depends upon whether the model is depicted as receiving positive, negative, or no consequences as a result of demonstrating the target behavior (i.e., whether the target behavior is depicted as effective or ineffective). The characteristics of the model, as with those of the source in the case of instructions, may also be widely varied with potentially significant effects on training (e.g., sex, age, status, familiarity to viewers). Several media have been used to present modeling demonstrations including videotape, audiotape, live role playing, live in a real interaction (e.g., an actual consultation session), or written descriptions. It should be noted that written modeling is not the same as written instructions; the former involves showing by example, while the latter consists of verbal directions (e.g., the difference between the actual dialogue versus the stage instructions in a play). Finally, the cuing may point out only correct or incorrect behavioral examples, or it may point to both and, thus, help the trainee to distinguish between the two (i.e., discrimination training); and the cues may be presented via several different media (e.g., spoken words, visual signals, or audible signals).

Performance Feedback: the presentation of information to the trainee, after he/she has attempted to perform the target behavior, concerning the nature of the trainee's performance. Feedback involves a proximity level, a message, a valence, a source, and a medium. Feedback may be presented immediately after the trainee has performed the target behavior, or not until after the trainee has completed an entire training exercise, or a delay (which may vary in length) has passed after the training exercise. The message may be a simple "right" or "wrong," or it may include an informational component (e.g., detailed analyses of the trainee's performance and comparisons with the ideal performance of the target behavior) in addition to the evaluative part. At the most basic level, the message may simply be a replay (e.g., on videotape) of the trainee's behavior, with neither evaluative nor informational cues. Feedback may include explicit response-contingent reinforcement (e.g., social praise) or punishment, or it may have no explicit valence. Supervisors, peers (i.e., fellow trainees), clients, or the trainee him/herself may present the feedback, and the personal characteristics of these various sources may be varied as well (e.g., sex, attractiveness, expertise, status). Finally, the potential media for feedback include videotape replays, audiotape replays, visual or audio signals (e.g., a green light to indicate "right" and a red light to indicate "wrong"), written or spoken evaluations, and numerical or verbal information.

Behavioral Rehearsal: the opportunity to practice the target behavior. Behavior rehearsal is a widely, although rarely systematically used training technique (e.g., "practice makes perfect"). The nature of the behavior rehearsal method will vary depending upon the setting (analogue versus real-life), the response mode (actual target behavior versus a scaled-down analogue), the valence (the results of performing the target behavior for the trainee), the temporal proximity of the rehearsal to the time when the trainee must perform the target behavior in situ, whether or not (and what kind of) feedback is given subsequent to the practice session, and whether or not the trainer prompts or coaches the trainee so as to help him/her to perform the target behavior appropriately.

Contingency Management: the systematic presentation or withholding of reinforcers or aversive stimuli contingent upon the trainee's performance of the target behavior. Several different behavioral contingencies can be used to increase trainees' competencies in meeting the training objectives: positive reinforcement, negative reinforcement, response cost, punishment, and so forth. The consequences provided as reinforcers or aversive stimuli may be social, monetary, or material (e.g., attention versus money versus food), they may be intrinsic or extrinsic (cf. Ford & Foster, 1976), and they may be on a variety of schedules (e.g., fixed interval versus variable ratio versus continuous). The characteristics of the source who provides the consequences, the temporal proximity of the consequences to the time when the target behavior was performed, and whether or not informational feedback is also provided may also be varied. Finally, the contingency may be explicitly contracted between the trainer and the trainee, or it may be determined solely by the trainer (or trainee) and administered without being explicitly stated.

Thus, even these "basic" methods of training are indeed rather complex, involving as they do a wide variety of potential parametric variations in several basic components: the message, the source, the medium, the setting, the valence, and the degree of temporal proximity to the trainee's in situ performance of the target behavior. Each separate method, alone, gives the trainer a great deal to think about when he/she is designing a training strategy. However, the separate methods must also be integrated into a coherent and comprehensive training program. At this point, the trainer must consider not only how to operationalize each basic training method that he/she wishes to use, but also how to sequence the separate training techniques so that they form an integrated program. We will now consider the four most widely utilized and thoroughly researched approaches to establishing a complete training program for environmental designers.

Microtraining (MT) incorporates behavioral rehearsal, performance feedback, contingent reinforcement, modeling with cuing, and programmed texts in the following training sequence: trainees videotape brief

behavior rehearsal role-play simulations; read programmed texts describing the target skills; view models who demonstrate, either live or on
videotape, the target skills and provide specific cues identifying these
behaviors; view the videotape which they originally made, receiving
performance-specific informational feedback and contingent social
reinforcement from their trainers. The supervisor and trainee then take
turns performing the target skills while role playing with each other,
alternating modeling by the trainer with rehearsal by the trainee, and
with the supervisor prompting the trainee and giving detailed immediate
feedback; trainees videotape a second role-play simulation, and repeat
the prior steps until they have demonstrated competency in the target
behavior (Ivey, 1971; McKnight, 1969). The basic principle applied in MT
is that of shaping by successive approximations – gradually and
systematically assisting the trainee to increasingly meet and master the
behavioral requirements of the target skills. Several similar training
packages have been developed in this model: assertiveness training
(Rich & Schroeder, 1976); personal effectiveness training (Liberman,
King & DeRisi, 1976); and structured learning training (Goldstein, 1974).

Interpersonal Process Recall (IPR) is in many respects similar to MT
but adds a few important twists. IPR integrates modeling with cuing,
behavior rehearsal, and performance feedback so as to shape trainee's
skills by successive approximations in the following sequence: videotaped modeling with extensive discriminative cuing; role-play behavior
rehearsal of the target skills, with prompting and performance feedback
from both supervisors and peers; practice in rating model therapists,
using a systematic behavior observation code, with discriminative
feedback; conducting and videotaping a series of real (but scaled-down)
therapy sessions; viewing the videotapes, while the supervisor provides
performance feedback and prompts the trainee to recall his/her
feelings, plans, and other internal reactions from the session; observing
the client as he/she views the videotaped session and is prompted (by
the trainer) to recall his/her thoughts and feelings from the session;
conducting a similar "recall session," but with another trainee's client;
and jointly conducting a "recall session" with the trainer and one's own
client, while the trainer gradually phases out his/her active participation and allows the trainee to take responsibility. IPR, thus, provides
the trainee with multiple sources of feedback, and several scaled down
opportunities to rehearse the target skills with real clients (Kagan,
1973).

Integrated Didactic-Experiential Training (IDET) has evolved as the
primary approach to training Rogerian therapists, although it is
applicable to the training of other types of environmental designers.
IDET merges extensive instructions, modeling with cuing, discrimination
training, behavior rehearsal, and performance feedback in the following
training sequence: lectures and readings; modeling, through listening to
audiotaped therapy sessions by experienced therapists; practice in
rating these model therapists, using a systematic behavior observation
code, with feedback on accuracy provided by trainers; in a group with
fellow trainees, verbally rehearsing target behaviors in response to
audiotaped statements made by real clients, with modeling by peers and

feedback from the trainer; role-play behavior rehearsal of the target behavior, and audiotaping this so as to receive performance feedback from the trainer; rehearsing the target skills in one-shot interviews with clients, and receiving feedback from peers and the trainer as well as self-evaluating one's own performance; and continuing to receive performance feedback in this fashion while conducting ongoing therapy cases with clients. IDET also relies on the approach of shaping by successive approximations and adds in a final stage, not included in MT or IPR, that is designed to help trainees maintain their levels of competency after the intensive initial training is completed. IDET also requires that trainers consistently provide a supportive interpersonal milieu in addition to carrying out their skill training functions, and gives trainees the opportunity to participate in a supportive "quasi group therapy" to further enhance the training milieu (Truax & Carkhuff, 1967).

Traditional Training is an approach that is not nearly as clearly defined or consistently applied as MT, IPR, or IDET. However, most training programs for social scientists and human service professionals have adopted a model that involves the following basic components: lectures; seminars; readings; films; gradual experience in interacting with clients; and supervisory sessions that typically require the trainee to "describe the session," after which the trainer provides some form of feedback or instructions. Training programs that fit the "traditional" model are less oriented to providing systematic skill training than are MT, IPR, and IDET, relying more on the discretion of the trainer and the diligence of the trainee than on an explicitly structured and experientially-focused program.

As the reader can see, the three systematic training programs provide virtually the same basic sequence of skill-training learning experiences for trainees:

1. Detailed instructions (e.g., programmed texts).

2. Modeling with cuing of both positive and negative examples of the target behavior, that includes responses to a variety of different client behaviors.

3. Discrimination training, through practice in rating sample audio- or videotapes and extensive feedback on accuracy.

4. Behavior rehearsal in scaled down (e.g., role play simulations) contexts which nevertheless offer a variety of client behaviors, with coaching by the trainer. The prompting is gradually phased out as the trainee increasingly acquires competency.

5. Detailed and immediate performance feedback is provided by the trainer, with contingent social reinforcement as well. The immediate feedback and social reinforcement are gradually phased out as the trainee increasingly acquires competency.

6. Detailed but delayed performance feedback is provided by viewing videotapes of one's own rehearsals, listening to the evaluations of the trainer and peers, and self-evaluating. Contingent social reinforcement is provided as well.

7. In vivo practice in scaled down interviews (e.g., the trainee is instructed to simply get to know the client while practicing utilizing the target skills) with real clients in which the trainer serves as a co-consultant. The supervisor thus provides coaching, modeling, and immediate performance feedback, but gradually phases these out as the trainee increasingly demonstrates competence.

8. As in 6, detailed but delayed feedback is provided by self-evaluation and peer and trainer evaluations of videotaped sessions with these clients.

9. Continued in vivo practice is provided in the context of (autonomously) conducting ongoing interventions with clients, and through continued feedback from reviewing videotaped sessions in group supervisory sessions.

10. A supportive milieu for trainees and trainers.

Before moving on to discuss the issues involved in conducting research evaluations of training methods, one application of the contingency management method which has not been discussed merits mention. Often continued supervisory sessions are logistically impossible, and thus an alternative means for assuring the maintenance of trainee skills must be developed. The research literature on methods for training paraprofessional change agents suggests such a method: trainers systematically monitor the trainee's behavior on an intermittent "time sampling" basis, and then implement a combined, positive reinforcement (e.g., trainees earn bonus pay for performing the target behavior appropriately) and response cost (e.g., trainees lose the opportunity to advance to a higher pay bracket if they fail to perform the target behavior appropriately) program. While the mechanisms for monitoring and consecuting trainees' behavior must be carefully designed so as to not pose ethical problems (e.g., avoiding systems that are, in and of themselves, aversive to the trainees), and the reinforcers utilized must be carefully chosen (ideally, ones that are intrinsic to the target behavior rather than extrinsic), this contingency management approach offers a practical alternative for maintaining the trainees' new skills after intensive training has ended.

Given that several potential methods for training environmental designers exist, we must next ask whether any of them have been empirically evaluated, and what the results of such research can tell us in terms of the kinds of outcomes associated with these methods, and their relative effectiveness levels compared to one another. Before reviewing the literature that reports the results of the research evaluations of training methods, we must first, however, consider several issues that arise in such research. Two types of issues merit our special attention: the methodological rigor of the research evaluating training methods and the external validity of these research investigations.

Methodological Rigor: Evaluative Criteria

The methodological quality of a research study which evaluates training methods depends on the extent to which certain criteria are fulfilled: the power of the research design; the reliability of the dependent variable(s); and the validity of the dependent variable(s).

Research design

In experimental empirical investigations, the research design must isolate the independent variables (training methods, in our case) that are being examined, while controlling for any extraneous confounding factors, such that there is a high probability that any changes measured in the dependent variables have been produced by the independent variables alone (cf. Campbell & Stanley, 1963). Between-subjects control group designs in which subjects (trainees, in our case) are randomly assigned to experimental and control conditions, and two within-subjects designs, the multiple baseline and reversal designs, in which each subject serves as his/her own control fulfill these requirements. In both cases, the control condition(s) must be selected carefully so as to rule out the effects of potential causal variables other than the training method(s) being investigated: a no-training control condition rules out the effects of general life events and random changes; a placebo-control condition (e.g., an unsystematic discussion group which covers the same topics as in the systematic training group) additionally rules out the effects of exposure to the target skills and situations, contact with a trainer and other trainees (if training is done in a group), and (if the condition is well designed) the trainees' expectancies that they will improve on the target skill(s).

The between-subjects strategy provides trainers with information as to the relative cost-effectiveness of the training method across groups of trainees but does not, alone, demonstrate that the training method was effective for all trainees, nor does it tell trainers for which types of trainees the method is most effective. The within-subjects approach, in contrast, shows whether or not training has been effective for each trainee, but does not demonstrate that the training methods can be generalized to other trainees nor whether they are cost-effective compared to alternative methods. It would seem that a combination of these two research designs is optimal for demonstrating which training methods are cost-effective and generalizable, and which ones trainees tend to gain most from (and conversely, for which trainees a different training approach is necessary).

Correlational and uncontrolled case study approaches may often yield valuable preliminary data that will lead to the design and subsequent experimental evaluation of training methods. However, such nonexperimental research designs cannot be used to make strong inferences about the effects and effectiveness of training methods.

Data reliability

Two basic kinds of dependent variables have been used in the research on training methods: (a) ratings or behavioral frequency-counts made by persons who observe the trainee performing the target behavior; and (b) trainees' written self-evaluations and clients' evaluations, usually on multi-item questionnaires. Different, although similar, reliability precautions hold for these two approaches.

For observer ratings, reliability must be demonstrated in terms of both the agreement between independent observers and the stability of each observer's ratings over time (cf. Kent & Foster, 1977). The most precise measures of interobserver agreement are rarely used in the training research literature, where, unfortunately, product-moment correlations (for ordinal ratings) or percent agreement (for frequency counts) are the most typical statistics — intraclass correlations and measures of percent agreement which control for the effects of chance agreements are preferable. Stability data are typically presented in the form of test-retest correlations.

For data provided by self-evaluations or client evaluations on written questionnaires, there is only one "rater," so internal consistency (e.g, split-hold reliability) must be demonstrated. As with the observational data, stability over time is also essential.

Data validity

There are four interrelated criteria to be met when the validity of a dependent variable is being evaluated: content validity (do the rating categories or questionnaire items provide a representative sample of the target skills being measured?); concurrent validity (do the obtained data correlate well with data from different measures of the same or similar skills?); predictive validity (are the obtained data correlated with trainees' abilities to actually produce changes in their clients' behavior, or with some other measure of post-training "success"?); and discriminant validity (do the obtained data correlate poorly with those from other measures of other dissimilar skills?). Taken together, these criteria provide evidence for the construct validity of the dependent variable (the extent to which it measures the construct(s) that it is intended to measure) (Campbell & Fiske, 1959; Cronbach & Meehl, 1955).

When we discuss the results of the research literature in which training methods have been evaluated, we will need to take a close look at the extent to which these methodological criteria have been fulfilled. As can be seen, it is essential that training investigations permit strong causal inferences to be made about the specific effects that the training method(s) have on the specific target behaviors being taught. They must also tell us to what extent these effects will vary with different types of trainees and trainers, target behavior, and training settings.

Criteria for External Validity

External validity signifies the extent to which the findings of a research investigation can be generalized beyond the specific context of that particular study. If the conclusions cannot be applied except in a very restricted context, the investigation will have limited value to other trainers and training programs. The characteristics of trainees and trainers, independent variables (i.e., training methods), and dependent variables, and the durability of the findings over post-training time periods are the major determinants of external validity in research investigations which evaluate training methods.

Ideally, research on training methods is done with the actual trainers and trainees in environmental design training programs (e.g., experienced trainers and graduate-level trainees in a clinical psychology training program). When this is not the case (e.g., with graduate students serving briefly as trainers, with undergraduate research subjects as trainees), the results cannot be definitely said to hold for real ongoing training programs.

Similarly, the training methods used as independent variables would ideally be ones that are representative of the training interventions which would take place in real ongoing training programs. Results obtained with relatively brief training methods (e.g., 1-2 hours) cannot be generalized to the case of longer and more extensive training interventions. Nor can the findings of a training study which is set in a research lab be generalized to apply to training interventions that have more real-life settings (e.g., classrooms, practicum settings).

Thirdly, the dependent variable(s) must be representative samples of the target behaviors. The settings (time and place) used to measure the dependent variable must be comparable to those in which trainees will actually be performing the target behavior once they are functioning as environmental designers (e.g., data from a role-play simulation in a classroom cannot be directly generalized to apply to a real consultation with real clients). Similarly, the responses measured must be comparable to behaviors that the trainees will be called upon to produce as environmental designers (e.g., results concerning the training of a single response such as "open end lead statements" cannot be assumed to hold when a more complex skill repertoire such as "effective communication" is the target).

Lastly, it is essential to monitor the extent to which the impact of the training methods persists after the training intervention has been terminated. If the changes in trainees' competencies that are produced as the result of a training procedure or program dissipate significantly when trainees have graduated, then the value of that procedure or program is called into question. Ideally, training methods would produce long-term rather than merely transient changes in the trainees' skills. If they fail to do so, then trainers and researchers must seriously consider how they might either be redesigned so as to have durable effects and/or supplemented by special "maintenance" interventions.

These external validity criteria must be adhered to if the research evaluations of training methods are to have utility for other trainers and training programs. Along with the methodological criteria, they provide a strong and stringent basis for assessing the overall quality of training research investigations. So, with these guidelines in mind, we turn now to a review of the findings of the empirical research concerning methods of training.

Research Evaluating Training Methods: An Assessment

In reviewing the research evaluations of training methods, we will discuss eight topics: the types of trainees and trainers; the types of target objectives; an assessment of the methodological rigor; an assessment of the external validity; results concerning the overall efficacy of different training methods; results concerning the efficacy of different training methods for different types of trainees; results concerning the efficacy of different training methods for different types of training objectives; and an integrative summary, in which the implications for future training and research on training are considered.

Types of trainees and trainers

Several groups of persons have been involved in training research as trainees: medical residents, post-MA clinical psychology graduate students, and pre-MA counseling psychology and guidance counseling students (Ford, 1977); teachers and student teachers (Hutchison, 1975a); mental health paraprofessionals (Balch & Solomon, 1976; Jeger, 1975a); parents (cf. Ford, 1975; O'Dell, 1975); schoolchildren serving as change agents for their peers (cf. Benassi & Larson, 1976); and assertiveness training clients (cf. Rich & Schroeder, 1976). The reader is referred to the review papers cited for more detailed descriptions of the research in each area.

Trainees have come in all shapes and sizes. Ages have ranged from first-graders to adults of all ages. Both males and females have been trainees. A wide range of socioeconomic statuses (SES) have characterized the training literature as a whole, although relatively few individual studies have reported dealing with persons of several SES levels. Most trainees have been Caucasian, although this is often not reported at all. Trainees have included non-, para-, and professionals, with the latter ranging from students to experienced change agents. Some trainees have been described as being treated for a psychological dysfunction at the same time they were receiving training. (These were all in the non-professional group.)

Trainers have usually been experienced training supervisors or practicing counseling, clinical, or community psychologists, psychiatrists, social workers, psychiatric nurses, or teachers. Occasionally, the trainers have been advanced graduate students under the supervision of experienced trainers.

Types of target objectives

Trainees have almost always been described as being trained to serve either as self-regulators or mediators, rather than as trainers or designers. The specific roles for which they have been trained include behavior managers, ward or classroom managers, tutors, therapists, teachers, or effective interpersonal interactants. They have been taught primarily observation, elicitation, consecution, communication, and (less often) conceptualization skills. Usually, these skills have been described as discrete behaviors (e.g., reflective restatements, instructional probes, contingent praise, open-end leads, administering "time out," empathic communication, or behavior observation), although a few have been phrased as comprehensive skill repertoires which integrate several separate behaviors (e.g., "consultation," "tutoring," or "indirect teaching"). Trainees have been prepared to serve as mediators for children, adolescents, and adults who have been variously labeled as "emotionally disturbed," "oppositional," "mentally retarded," "juvenile delinquent," "learning disabled," "enuretic," "psychotic," "deaf," "hyperactive," "brain injured," "interpersonally anxious," "phobic," "autistic," and "normal."

Assessment of methodological rigor

In terms of research design, most published research on training has involved controlled experimental designs, primarily between-subjects control group procedures. Typically, a no training control condition has been utilized, and, much less often, researchers have provided placebo-control conditions to control for the effects of contact with trainers and a training program and for trainees' expectancies. Within-subjects designs have been used less often, primarily by studies in which parents or peers were trained as change agents. Only rarely were within-subject or correlational designs merged with between-subject designs to provide data on the differential effects of training methods that accrue with different types of trainees, trainers, or training objectives. In general, basic criteria for adequate research design were met by most research investigations on training. The results of these studies will be reported only for those which did provide acceptable experimental designs.

Several behavior observation codes were developed to systematically assess trainees' skill acquisition (Truax-Carkhuff Accurate Empathy Scale, Counselor Verbal Response Scale, Microcounseling Behaviors Scale, Stanford Appraisal Guide), and equally often researchers simply devised their own specific operational definitions for observers to use in scoring the behaviors being learned by trainees. Interobserver agreement was usually demonstrated in training studies, but most often with rather lenient statistics (e.g., product-moment correlation rather than intra-class correlation) and without any mention of whether or not certain key procedural precautions were taken to assure the meaningfulness of such reliability rates (e.g., guarding against observer drift or bias). Stability over time of these measures was almost never verified.

Several written tests of skill were also developed to assess trainee gains (Michigan State Affective Sensitivity Scale, Carkhuff Discrimination Indexes, Porter Counselor Skills Test). Neither inter-scorer agreement nor internal consistency have been well demonstrated by such measures, nor has stability over time.

Several questionnaire measures have also been developed to assess the clients' evaluations of the trainees (Barrett-Lennard Relationship Inventory, Counselor Effectiveness Scale, Tuckman Teacher Feedback Form). These instruments have generally been shown to be internally consistent and stable over time.

Reliability ranges from strong to very poor in studies evaluating training methods; however, the overall reliability of most measures used in most such investigations was adequate.

Concerning validity, most of the measures of trainee skill acquisition have excellent content validity, involving items or categories that are clearly operationally defined and which appear to comprise a representative and complete sample of the kinds of responses or competencies they are intended to measure. However, concurrent validity has been investigated only for two instruments: Patterson's (1976) observation code, and Gardner's (1972) Trainee Proficiency Scale. Similarly, predictive validity has been well established for only one measure (i.e., the Barrett-Lennard Relationship Inventory, cf. Gurman, 1978), although scattered studies have appeared in the research literature to demonstrate that improvements in trainees' behaviors are associated with parallel changes in their clients' or students' behaviors (e.g., increased teaching skill leads to improved achievement test scores or classroom behavior by the teacher/trainee's students). Replication of these investigations will provide strong evidence for the predictive validity of the variables that have been used to assess trainee skill acquisition. Finally, discriminant validity has never been reported to be investigated for any measure used in the training research literatures.

It must be concluded that the construct validity of the instruments used to assess the efficacy of training methods is not at all strong. We must, therefore, be cautious in appraising the results of these investigations, always remembering that replication with better validated measures is a prerequisite for truly conclusive results.

Assessment of external validity

We shall now examine the degree of realism or representativeness that characterizes the studies concerned with evaluations of training methods. The trainees and trainers have usually been representative of the populations of therapists, teachers, mental health paraprofessionals, parents, and peer change agents to whom the results of these studies might be applied in future training programs. There are two exceptions: undergraduate research subjects have served as trainees and graduate students have served as trainers in several therapist training investigations, thus decreasing our confidence in these studies; graduate students have served as trainers in several other studies, thus making the results from these evaluations directly applicable to novice trainers but not to more experienced ones.

Training methods were usually either brief applications of single techniques (e.g., modeling), or integrated but still relatively brief (e.g., 2-75 hours) packages of training procedures (e.g., MT, IPR, IDET). The effects of the broader programmatic context in which these interventions were set (e.g, differential impacts of different types of total training programs) were seldom mentioned and never systematically evaluated. The question of how to blend several training techniques or packages into a total training program remains a crucial, but unanswered, issue for further research.

Dependent variables were typically measures of discrete skills, rather than of complete skill repertoires. Here, too, the question of how to provide training interventions so that trainees will acquire complete skill repertoires (and not just useless collections of isolated skills) will require future research.

In addition, the dependent variables were usually analogue in nature (e.g., written skill tests, when the target behaviors were verbal and nonverbal interpersonal skills; role-play simulations; or brief therapy interviews) and/or measured in a restricted sample of environmental contexts (e.g., only at the family dinner hour and in the dining room, when the target objective was changed throughout the day and in all home settings; only one of several therapy interviews). Before these measures can be used with confidence, we must have empirical evidence that they produce data that are generalizable to complete and real contexts; in most cases, this has not been evaluated, and when it has the results cast doubt on the external validity of these analogue or restricted sample methods (cf. Ford, 1977b).

Finally, long-term, followup data have been reported only rarely by training investigators, and almost never for time periods as long as six months after the end of formal training. When the permanence of training outcomes has been investigated, the typical finding is that skills dissipate rapidly unless bolstered by systematic maintenance interventions (e.g., prompts, feedback, and contingent rewards). This underscores the importance of post-training maintenance interventions, and requires that we view all results from the research literature on training methods as holding only for the short term, unless long-term maintenance was explicitly programmed.

Overall efficacy of different training methods

With these methodological and external validity limitations in mind, and remembering that all results apply only to the types of trainees and target objectives which have characterized training investigations up to the present, we turn now to an appraisal of the empirical support that has been produced for the major methods of training.

Instructions are usually found to be insufficient by themselves to produce skill acquisition or maintenance in trainees. However, instructions do enhance modeling, behavior rehearsal, and performance feedback, if provided during or before, but not after, these other interventions, and more so with complex skills rather than simple and readily discriminable ones. Specific instructions have been shown to be more effective than global and vague ones.

Modeling has been found to be more effective than instructions, videotaped or verbal feedback, lectures or readings for aiding trainees in acquiring new skills. Modeling is significantly enhanced by instructions, cuing, feedback, discrimination training, and behavior rehearsal. Videotape modeling is as effective as live demonstration, and either specific responses or complex response chains can be presented with equal effect. Modeling alone is not effective in improving or maintaining skills which the trainee has already acquired.

Behavior rehearsal and performance feedback have been shown to be more effective than instructions or modeling, for aiding trainees in consolidating or improving skills which they have already acquired at a rudimentary level. It is enhanced by modeling, instructions, or social reinforcement, and seems to work best when moderate performance standards are used initially and then gradually replaced by more demanding criteria. A variety of parametric refinements have been empirically delineated for performance feedback. Verbal feedback is preferable to videotape self-confrontation, and a combination is optimal. Performance-specific feedback is more effective than that which is global or effect-oriented although, again, a combination is optimal. Feedback is most effective when it is immediate rather than delayed, unless the latter is bolstered by videotape self-confrontation or faded-in gradually. Concerning the message conveyed, feedback is most effective when it is based on improvement rather than absolute competency level, when it cues the trainee to observe mistakes as well as confirming positive behaviors, and when it is accurate rather than "sugar coated." Feedback is most effective when administered on a variable, rather than fixed or continuous, schedule. Finally, peers, clients (or pupils), and trainers all provide equally valuable feedback, although supervisor feedback seems optimal at the very beginning of training (when precise and skill-focused feedback is most important). Performance feedback during training has, however, not been found to be effective in maintaining trainees' skills after the formal training has ended.

Behavior rehearsal and coaching (prompting) have seldom been investigated separately from performance feedback, so their effects as independent training interventions are not known. They do significantly enhance modeling and instruction, and have been shown to be more effective than instructions alone. External coaching (i.e., prompting by a trainer to cue the trainee to emit a target behavior) has been found to be more effective than self-produced prompts. For behavior rehearsal, spaced practice has been found to be somewhat preferable to massed practice, while vicarious versus live (or covert versus overt) practice has been found to have an equivalent effect (although this will probably vary with the type of trainee and target objective). Continued post-training prompting does seem to provide for effective maintenance of trainee skills (compared to no maintenance intervention at all), and is particularly effective in this regard when paired with performance feedback.

Contingency management has only rarely been evaluated as a specific technique in formal training programs. It has, however, been shown to effectively motivate trainees to attend classes and to do their homework, as well as to enhance modeling or feedback. When used as a maintenance intervention, contingency management seems to be the single most effective technique, and it is significantly enhanced by prompting and feedback.

Thus far, the results suggest that these separate training methods can be effective on a one-at-a-time basis, but that their impacts are greatly increased when they are combined with one another. Thus, it will not be surprising to find that the systematic training packages which have been developed are highly effective in aiding trainees to both acquire and perfect environmental design skills.

Microtraining and similar programs used in assertiveness and personal effectiveness training have been several times shown to be significantly more effective than any single training technique, any traditional training program of comparable length, or any placebo control condition. Microcounseling, a variant of MT, has also been shown to be equally or more effective than IDET. Clearly, MT approaches to training have been proven effective as means to facilitate short-term skill acquisition and development.

Similarly, integrated didactic-experiential training has received consistent, well-replicated validation as a method for producing short-term skill acquisition and improvement. It, too, has been shown to be more effective in this respect than any single training technique, any traditional training program, or any placebo control condition. It is also clear that both the skill-training and affective-support components of IDET add to its efficacy, although the skill-training portions seem to be more powerful than the affective-support portions.

Interpersonal process recall has been less extensively and less conclusively validated than the MT or IDET approaches, but it, too, has been shown to be significantly more effective in facilitating short-term skill acquisition and development than either comparable traditional training programs or no training control conditions.

In contrast, evaluations of traditional approaches to training have rarely employed sophisticated research designs, more often relying on case study reports of nonequivalent control group designs. The few relatively well-executed studies have provided, at best, equivocal evidence for the efficacy of traditional approaches, and they have been consistently found less effective than MT, IDET, or IPR.

We can conclude, therefore, that several training packages have been developed which have strong track records for the teaching of relatively discrete skills in relatively brief time periods. Further parametric research is certainly merited, both to examine the effects of different combinations and sequences of the individual training techniques within these packages and to further clarify the effects of variations in the basic parameters of those individual techniques. This optimistic conclusion must be tempered by an awareness of the fact that trainers are only beginning to develop effective means for assuring that trainees will continue to properly utilize the skills learned in formal training once such training has ended; this is perhaps the most critical area for future research on training methods. In addition to the data which supports the use of prompts, feedback, and contingency management as maintenance interventions, several other approaches are suggested (and require empirical evaluation) by unreplicated training studies and other related areas of research and theory: gradually fade out all external cues, prompts, feedback, and reinforcement as trainees acquire increasing competency so that trainees' performances will come under the control of self-produced and natural cues and contingencies (i.e., skills will be maintained if and because "they work"); in line with the previous suggestion, research is needed to determine if trainees cease to emit behaviors which were learned in training because they develop alternatives that are more effective ways to influence their clients or to control their own lives than the skills learned in training − if so, perhaps training objectives need to be restructured; systematic cognitive training (e.g., Mahoney, 1974) may enhance skill maintenance (e.g., teach trainees ways to self-cue and self-evaluate themselves systematically); teaching skills for coping with the stress that may interfere with performance of the skills learned in training in real life. The strategy of giving trainees responsibility for conducting real-life interventions (which necessitate the use of skills learned in training) has been found to enhance trainee's performances more than instructions and feedback; and, allowing trainees to tailor the specific ways in which they perform the target behaviors may facilitate the incorporation of these skills into trainees' repertoires.

For both formal training and maintenance interventions, the reader is encouraged to regard the data and descriptions of training methods presented here as a source of hypotheses, and not as definitive evidence that certain training methods are the "right" ones. Every trainer must use his/her own ingenuity to develop his/her own training methods, and then must empirically evaluate the outcome of his/her training program, rather than assuming that any method(s) can be applied without planning and evaluation. These data suggest that certain training methods are likely to be more effective than others, but this is only a statement of probability and not certainty. For that reason, we need to consider carefully the meager evidence concerning the differential efficacy of different training interventions when used with different types of trainees, trainers, and training objectives.

Efficacy of Specific Training Methods with Specific
Types of Trainees and Trainers

Theoretically, different training interventions will be differentially effective with different types of trainees and trainers (cf. Ford, 1977b). The personal characteristics of trainees and trainers which might interact with type of training method include, among others, demographics (age, sex, race, SES, and education level), experience and baseline performance level in the skills being taught, cognitive styles, and goals for training and career. Trainee-trainer complementarity in these respects, and their perceptions of one another (friendliness, expertise, status, attractiveness, and similarity) are also potential factors.

Training should be optimized by matching trainees and trainers with the methods best suited to them. For example, modeling and discrimination training may be unnecessary or even aversive for experienced trainees, but essential for novice trainees. Or trainees who perceive their trainer as understanding and friendly might learn more in training which emphasized confrontive performance feedback than would trainees who view their trainer as detached and impersonal. The question is, what guidelines do the data offer us?

Concerning the interaction of trainee characteristics and type of training method, trainees who at baseline show low levels of competence in the skills being taught require lengthier training; less experienced trainees profit from supervisor as well as self-evaluative feedback, where more experienced trainees do just as well with only self-evaluation; low SES trainees, or trainees with relatively little formal education, benefit more from training that emphasizes modeling and behavior rehearsal and feedback than that which involves readings and group discussion. It has also been found that mixed SES trainee groups are as, or more, effective when compared to groups with only high or only low SES trainees, and that when two persons are involved (e.g., parents), it is more effective to train both than only one. Thus, the guidelines are consistent with "common sense," but they only begin to "scratch the surface" in terms of all the potential trainee-method interactions which merit empirical investigation.

The research results concerning the interaction of type of trainer and type of training method are virtually nonexistent. We know only that trainers who are more behaviorally empathic and supportive tend to be more effective in administering IDET than those who are colder and more restrictive. The multiplicity of other personal characteristics and other training methods have not been evaluated.

Worse yet, there is no research at all concerning the differential impacts of different training methods with dyads of trainer and trainee who have different levels of complementarity or different perceptions of one another. There are also no empirical data concerning the effects of trainee-trainer dyads with different levels of complementarity or types of mutual person-perceptions with any single training method. Research from several areas, especially on modeling and observational learning (e.g., Bandura, 1969) and on attributional processes (e.g., Mischel, 1973) strongly suggest that this is an important area for future training research.

In view of these findings, it should not be surprising that all attempts at empirically identifying criteria for selecting trainees who will be most successful in training programs have met with almost total failure (cf. Ford, 1977b; Jeger, 1975). Not one of the many trainee selection criteria that are traditionally used by professional and paraprofessional change-agent training programs (e.g., academic record; scores on standardized tests of attitudinal and personality variables) has ever been consistently found to be predictive of success in training. However, it must be remembered that these results apply almost entirely to the selection of trainees for traditional training programs and with measures of outcome that were of questionable reliability and validity (e.g., single ratings by a trainer). It seems reasonable to expect that better predictive relationships could be delineated for more innovative training programs (e.g., MT, IPT, IDET), if more reliable and valid measures of training outcome were employed (and multiple rather than single measures) and if different types of potential predictors were examined (e.g., trainees' baseline competency levels in the skills being taught in the program, as measured in actual behavior samples; measures of self-perception and cognitive style). Initial evidence in favor of this position is provided by Suinn (1974), who found that trainees' baseline skill levels (as measured in behavioral simulations) contributed significantly to the prediction of their post-training competence (as measured by ratings of trainers and field supervisors), in a behaviorally-oriented (e.g., involving modeling, behavior rehearsal, performance feedback) paraprofessional training program.

SUMMARY

In evaluating the research on methods of training, we have seen that a wide variety of types of trainees has been successfully trained to fill several kinds of environmental design roles — although they have generally been taught only a limited number of environmental design skills and have been prepared to function primarily as self-regulators or mediators and not as trainers or designers. This suggests that future research is needed to evaluate different methods for training a wider variety of skills to environmental designers of all levels (e.g., training parents in facilitative communication skills as well as teaching them behavior modification observation and consecution skills), and especially for the training of trainers and designers.

We have also found that several innovative training methods and packages have been developed and rather extensively empirically evaluated. These training interventions offer viable alternatives to the more traditional didactic-academic training approaches which can be used and evaluated by trainers in their own training programs. However, it is also true that essential, but very complex, questions in two areas have only begun to be answered by the training research literatures: What are the optimal parametric variations in the many components of each training method (e.g., the source, message, medium, valence, and scheduling of presentation)? And what are the optimal matchings of training methods with type of (a) trainees and trainers, and (b) training objectives? We can suggest a general sequence of types of training methods for different stages in a training program, but more detailed recommendations can only be surmised.

Clearly, the research on training methods can take many important and exciting directions in the future. In addition to those just mentioned, it will also be important to essentially break new ground in several areas: evaluation of total training programs and the effects of different types of total programs on the efficacy of the more restricted training interventions; evaluation of the efficacy of different training methods for teaching trainees complete skill repertoires; and development of methods within formal training programs which will improve long-term skill maintenance. Until the issues in these areas have been empirically addressed by training researchers, it is doubly important for trainers who are administering environmental design training programs to develop their own hypotheses as to what types of methods and what program structure will be most effective for them and their trainees and to continuously evaluate and improve the training interventions that they use.

10 Environmental Design in the Classroom

Miriam Krasner

The previous chapter included the classroom teacher among those who were both trainees and trainers in environmental design. In the next chapter, an elementary schoolteacher describes the classroom as a planned environment. As indicated earlier, the two major institutions in our society most illustrative of environmental design (both "good" and "bad") are the mental hospital and the classroom. It is in the classroom that some of the most exciting and innovative applications of environmental design are being developed.

The material in this chapter is prototypical of the environmental design process. This includes the designer's (in this case the teacher's) concept of his/her role as a planner and as a source of values, the designer as a continual self-trainer. In effect, the teacher is a participant-observer with all of the implications that concept has come to mean thus far in the book.

We have been contending that there are value decisions and implications in every aspect of the environmental designer's role. In the next chapter, Krasner demonstrates this in her presentation of "an open education" philosophy and its implications for the design process.

A concept which has been only peripherally touched upon thus far is that of the "consumer" of environmental design. As a consumer, where does the teacher obtain the exposure to the philosophy and techniques of designing environments? Our calculated intuition is that many experienced teachers would see their own classroom work as highly compatible with environmental design concepts.

Ed.

302

Of the various settings in which the environmental design approach can be utilized, it is the classroom that will have the greatest impact on American society. It would seem obvious that the education of subsequent generations is the key to influencing future adult behavior. Nietzel et al. (1977) point out that, "Behavioral research in school and child-care settings is the most developed area in terms of quantity of studies, methodological sophistication, and procedures and variables investigated" (p. 5). No attempt will be made to review these research studies since comprehensive and critical reviews already exist (O'Leary & O'Leary, 1977). Instead, this chapter on the classroom will concentrate on studies and illustrations of open and informal education emphasizing the linkage of these studies within the context of environmental design. Since this chapter is written by a third grade elementary schoolteacher who has worked closely with the environmental design team and especially with the editor of this book (Krasner & Krasner, 1973), it offers the point of view of a consumer and participant-observer of environmental design.

The roots of our view of education lie in both the field of psychology and the field of education. We emphasize the personal because our views represent the result of the mutual interaction of an open education teacher with a purveyor of applied psychology whose professional roots are in clinical/behavioral psychology. We believe that the merger of these concepts and fields are not idiosyncratic but rather reflect an important aspect of the educational scene in the United States in the late 1970s. Clearly, we cannot cover, nor would we want to, all of the ramifications of investigators and scholars in education and psychology. From our theoretical perspective, to do a thorough job in developing a concept of linking education and psychology in terms of environmental design, we should cover the historical, economic, social, political, and religious context in which the school system functions, and this we at least point out as necessary, if we do not cover it comprehensively.

Our intended audience for this chapter consists of fellow consumers of environmental design, the individual schoolteacher, the psychologist who functions as a practitioner and/or a trainer in schools and other social systems, the paraprofessional who helps design and mold the social environment, and the parent who, like all of us, must have a better understanding of the mutual influence between schools and children, parents, and community. The roles of each of the participants in the school system — the child, the teacher, the parent, the administrator, the psychologist, the paraprofessional — are all subtly evolving, changing, and mutually influencing. It is to this process of ongoing change, its philosophical, psychological, and social implications, that we address ourselves.

THEORY IN THE CLASSROOM

Virtually every theory of human behavior offered by philosophers or psychologists has had its impact on the classroom. In the current century, this has been particularly true of the theories of Dewey, Freud, Peztalozzi, Piaget, Thorndike, Watson, Skinner, Rogers, and Erikson. The nature of the relationship between psychologists and educators has been a continually changing and mutually interactive one.

The prevalent, and by now almost traditional, view is that psychology, as a science, is basic to education as an applied profession. This point of view was clearly expressed by the psychologist Baldwin in 1895 and with little variation has remained unchanged to the present time:

> The second great education function of psychology is this: it should mould and inform educational theory by affording a view of mind and body in their united growth and mutual dependence. Education is a process of the development under most favorable conditions of full personality, and psychology is the science which aims to determine the nature of such personality in its varied stages of growth, and the conditions under which its full development may be most healthfully and sturdily nourished. One of the first duties of psychology, therefore, is to criticize systems of education, to point out "the better way" in education everywhere, and to take no rest until the better way is everywhere adopted. (p. 381)

It should be clear at this point that the environmental design approach, whether it be in a mental hospital or in the classroom, does not accept a fundamental dichotomy between psychology and education, between research and application, or between theory and practice. The concept of the teacher as environmental designer has also been influenced by theories of behavior and the next section will detail three broad theories of "human nature" which have influenced this approach.

HISTORICAL STREAMS

First of all, as other aspects of environmental design in other chapters, our model must be placed within a historical context. A historical analysis is not intended as a demonstration of scholarly skill but is, itself, an integral part of a theoretical model. A major part of the theory of environmental design is that historical antecedents, paradigms, beliefs, and/or myths are major influences on the current behavior of the teacher. We will focus on three of these streams of influence.

The Behavioral Stream

Among the early influencers in the behavioral stream was Edward L. Thorndike. It is of interest to note that Thorndike had never even heard the word "psychology" until he took a required course in it in 1893 at Wesleyan University. He was also influenced by taking a course with

William James at Harvard in 1897 when he switched from literature to psychology as his major (a switch similar to one later made by another behaviorist, B.F. Skinner). Out of his doctoral dissertation came the law of effect.

Much of Thorndike's subsequent work influenced both the behavioral stream in psychology and the applications of psychology in the classroom. His studies on learning produced considerable material useful for theories of instruction. In Principles of Teaching (1906) he offered illustrations on the topics of attention, reasoning, feeling, and moral training. He also dealt with the design and choice of teaching materials, the organization of instruction, the ways of adjusting to individual differences in the classroom, and the methodology of judging student progress. It was through his efforts that research in psychology became the basis for classroom application; in effect, Thorndike carried into practice the linkage between psychology and education which Baldwin advocated.

Cremin (1961) summarizes Thorndike's influences by indicating that

. . . no aspect of public-school teaching during the first quarter of the twentieth century remained unaffected by his influence. . . . Ultimately, Thorndike's goal was a comprehensive science of pedagogy in which all education could be based. His faith in quantified methods was unbounded, and he was quoted ad nauseam to the effect that everything that exists exists in quantity and can be measured. Beginning with the notion that the methods of education could be vastly improved by science, he came slowly to the conviction that the aims, too, might well be scientifically determined. (P. 114)

We have started with Thorndike rather than with more current behavioral influencers such as Skinner to emphasize that the relationship between psychological theories of behavior and the classroom is certainly not new or restricted to recent times. With only slight paraphrasing, Thorndike's linkage of learning and instructional theory to the planned environment of the classroom would still apply today. The more current "behavioral" influences can be traced to Skinner and to other investigators working with operant methodology and those influenced by it (O'Leary & O'Leary, 1977).

Many of the developments in education involving the classroom in the last decade have been influenced by this behavioral stream including the teaching machine, programmed learning, computer-assisted instruction, behavioral objectives, behavior modification in the classroom, token economy, competency-based teacher education, accountability, contracts, peer teaching, and microteaching. Are all of these part of "environmental design in the classroom?" They can be and, as such, the teacher must be skillful in the use of these techniques and concepts, but by no means do these behavioral influenced developments exhaust the desired training repertoire of the planner of classroom environments.

Perhaps the most important of the behavioral techniques in their implications for environmental design are operant conditioning, modeling, and the application of reinforcement and training principles in the form of token economies. This latter procedure, token economy, as eventually applied in classrooms and hospitals derives from the behavior modification streams of operant conditioning and utopian planning (Atthowe & Krasner, 1968; Ayllon & Azrin, 1968; Skinner, 1948).

Within the behavioral approach, there have been linkages with open education. Yawkey and Jones, who have been utilizing standard behavior modification procedures in classrooms, reason that, "One type of classroom setting in which the reinforcing event of teacher attention is most likely to be operative is the open education classroom or open space settings . . . suggested by recent developments in some English infant schools" (1974, pp. 321-22). They offer seven major characteristics of these classes which would apply to both approaches: lack of interior partitions; learning by manipulation of objects; individual learning style; learning centers; teacher and children both contributing; importance of interest and expression; and total evaluation.

Progressive Stream

A second stream of influence on environmental design in the classroom is that of American "progressive" education. Cremin's (1961) classic book The Transformation of the School, traces the influence of progressivism in American education. Cremin offered the following four elements in progressive education:

> First, it meant broadening the program and function of the school to include direct concern for health, vocation, and the quality of family and community life. Second, it meant applying in the classroom the pedagogical principles derived from new scientific research in psychology and the social sciences. Third, it meant tailoring instruction more and more to the different kinds and classes of children who were being brought within the purview of the school. Finally, Progressivism implied the radical faith that culture could be democratized without being vulgarized, the faith that everyone could share not only in the benefits of the new sciences but in the pursuit of the arts as well. (p. vii, ix)

All four of these elements have affected the environmental design approach. The most influential individual, towering above all others in the progressive stream, is John Dewey (1859-1954). His theories were mediated by his voluminous writings, his specific ideas on the nature and function of education, his personal contacts with almost every leading educator of the twentieth century, and the kinds of procedures carried out at his lab school.

Dewey's contributions are legion both in terms of his actual influence and the misattributions to him. One could cite here Dewey's notions of "school as a community," "training for democratic living," and the "teacher as a social change agent" (Dewey, 1915). The following statement from Dewey is one of the best and most subtle of statements of the philosophy of the classroom as a planned environment (quoted in Dworkin, 1959, p. 24). "The teacher is not in the school to impose certain ideas or to form certain habits in the child, but is there as a member of the community to select the influences which shall affect the child and to assist him in properly responding to these influences."

John Dewey was born in Burlington, Vermont in 1859. He received his doctorate from Johns Hopkins University in 1884 and went on to teach at the University of Michigan until 1894. He then accepted a professorship at the University of Chicago. Dewey was attracted to Chicago because education there was in one department with philosophy and psychology. It was at Chicago that he established his experimental lab school. About that time, he also wrote, The School and Society (1899) and developed his pragmatic approach to the theory of mind and his instrumentalist theory of logic. In 1896 he published a paper, "The Reflex Arc Concept in Psychology" which has had a significant impact on developments in psychology in America.

Dewey resigned his professorship at Chicago in 1904 because of his dissatisfaction with the university administration's actions toward his lab school. He accepted a position at Columbia University as a professor of philosophy with teaching responsibilities in Teachers College as well. In 1929 he retired from teaching. During the 1930s, he produced some of his most ambitious philosophical writings.

Dewey's early thinking was shaped by Hegel's dialectical philosophy. He had been raised in the New England Puritan tradition which emphasized the sharp dualism between mind and body. For Dewey, Hegel's dialectic provided the explanation for the interaction between mind and body and eliminated the dualism which he was unable to accept.

The aim of Dewey's work was to encourage the application of scientific method and critical thinking to moral and social beliefs and practices. To him, it seemed that the primary obstacle to this was the idea that theory and ideas are positive entities, logically deried and not subject to empirical test. This idea was supported both by a long tradition in Western thinking and by the discipline of philosophy itself. The complement to this notion is that practical experience is not suitable for the realm of critical thinking and control. Therefore, Dewey's primary concern was the development of a logical system which would tie together theory and practice (like mind and body) into a unified whole.

For Dewey, modern science was a perfect example of the interplay and unity of theory and practice. Ideas are the "mind's" response to problematic situations and guide the further observations to be made of the situation. The observations (the direct experience with the situation), in turn, shape new ideas concerning the problem. Thus, Dewey postulates a kind of dialectical process whereby direct experience leads to ideas which, in turn, guide further direct experiences. Either one without the other is only a half-attempt at handling a problem situation.

Throughout his career, Dewey stressed the idea that the goal of education was to teach students the skills and attitudes necessary to the development of their ability to solve problems. Consequently, he felt that school curricula should not, as they traditionally have done, emphasize the learning of facts and fixed ideas, but rather should stress the learning of a method for obtaining facts for oneself and reasoning out ones own ideas about the world. This educational philosophy went along with Dewey's rejection of absolutes supported only by tradition in any area of endeavor and his emphasis upon open-mindedness as the most important attitude for a critical thinker to cultivate.

Progressive education, as influenced by Dewey, attempted to reform the traditional education in which the teacher lectured and the students copied, learned by heart, and recited. Students sat at desks which were fastened to the floor and required permission to speak or even move. Dewey stressed the importance of the individual child progressing at his own pace, the importance of the child developing interest in the subject matter and, most important of all, that the child learn by doing, and by direct contact with people, places, and things.

Dewey's strong belief in the desirability of a liberal democratic social order influenced the broad nature of classroom structure emphasizing greater freedom, informality, and activity on the part of the child who would be able to gather materials from many sources and who would work in small groups with other children. This involved training the student to live in and contribute to a democratic society.

It is with great reluctance that we do not go further into the influences of Dewey. When we talk about environmental design in the classroom, virtually every comment in this chapter has been anticipated somewhere in Dewey's writings. This same point can probably be made about much of the material presented throughout this book.

We will devote no more than passing comment to the educational social reformers of the 1950s and 1960s (Cremin, 1970). Some of these reformers (e.g., Silberman) will be mentioned in the next section when we discuss influencers in open education.

Open Education

Another important stream in the development of environmental design concepts is open education which was influenced by the earlier progressive movement but also had some independent roots, particularly in some aspects of British primary education. Krasner and Krasner (1973) offer a conceptual linkage between the concept of open education and planned environments such as token economies. In the open classroom, the teacher uses her experiences and ingenuity in planning or designing 25 individual environments. In the training program described in Chapter 8, the open classroom has served as the most useful kind of environment in which students can observe and apply environmental design principles. The open approach is in process of development, and people in training can both observe a process and influence it. Further, open education as a process closely links the notion of desirability of achieving valued social behavior as well as competency and skill with designing the learning environment to achieve these valued objectives. More and more, the teacher realized that he or she must talk in terms of goals and purposes for every design or feature that is put into the environment. Put another way, the teacher carries out a "functional analysis of behavior" in planning a classroom environment.

A major source of influence has been a few key educators who had visited and been impressed with the British Infant School following the publication of the Plowden report (1967) which described the exciting new developments of open education in British schools. For example, Lillian Weber visited England in 1965 and came back with enthusiasm for the approach she viewed. In 1970, Vincent Rogers published an anthology of essays by leading British primary educators after he, too, visited the British primary schools.

Another source of introduction of open education has been state educational departments, particularly in Vermont and North Dakota. These states introduced open education in many of their schools soon after the Plowden Report. Still another and similar related influence is the impact of nonprofit groups such as the Education Development Center in Newton, Massachusetts. It operated as the EDC Follow Through Program which involved over 100 classrooms in 10 different cities. They planned for continuing growth of schools, not merely as a blind imitation of the British Infant School. A major source of influence and innovation in open education has been The Workshop Center for Open Education at City University of New York, directed by Lillian Weber, and its newsletter, Notes, edited by Ruth Dropkin.

Thus open education, as it developed in the United States in the 1960s and 1970s, was influenced both by the progressive movement and the enthusiastic reports on the British primary schools by educators and journalists (Featherstone, 1971; Holt 1967; Plowden, 1967; Rogers, 1970; Silberman, 1973). The major elements as it developed in this country are the integrated day, individualized instruction, and the systematic design of the usage of people and space.

The concept of the integrated day encompasses a total environment in which there is a blurring of distinctions between subject matter and between inside and outside the classroom. In effect, the integrated day involves having available in the classroom environment a wide variety of stimuli and learning conditions which make the learning situation interesting, exciting, meaningful, and reinforcing to the child.

Open education is clearly designed to maximize the likelihood of each individual child learning at his/her own pace with measurement of learning using the individual's own base rate as yardstick. In effect, the teacher is designing the individual learning environment for each of the children in her class.

One of the major misunderstandings and criticisms of open education is that an open classroom lacks structure. On the contrary, the open classroom is carefully structured by the teacher with a wide range of environmental materials (often inexpensive materials found in most environments such as water, sand, and common household utensils) designed for specific stimulation of individual children. Recognition of the structure involved in the open classroom, with its strong behavioral components, is expressed by the following comment by Drucker, 1972:

The English open classroom, now widely copied in this country, usually is considered cognitive and child-centered. It is. But, it is also one of the first rigorous applications of behaviorism to large numbers of human learners. The child does indeed learn his or her way there. He programs himself also according to a strict behaviorist scheme. What he is working (or playing) on is determined by the tools, playthings, and experiences offered. Reinforcements and rewards are built in at every step. Above all, the school predetermines the norms of achievement as rigorously as a scientist lays them down for a rat in a maze. And the child does not move on to the next level until he attains and retains the norm.

Many of the writers on open education wisely restrict their definitions to descriptions of the behavior of the participants, the teachers and the children. For example, in their introduction to a comprehensive sourcebook on open education, Nyquist and Howes (1972) describe the children in an open education classroom working ". . .at their own individual initiative" in a variety of activity areas. They freely talk and move about in classrooms and corridors ". . .as they work, their teacher moves among them helping, suggesting, questioning, observing, commenting, evaluating, encouraging, comforting, and when needed, ordering. The teacher plays a key role by knowing each child thoroughly and guiding his development as a unique and complex individual." (P. 1)

Perhaps most importantly, they describe the teacher functioning as "an independently responsible professional, one who creates the learning environment of the classroom and guides the children's activities in the light of his or her strongest interest and abilities, while at the same time cultivating each child's development to the full with expert professional insight" (p. 3).

Environmental-Ecological Stream

A major focus among the investigators in the environmental-ecological stream has been on the impact and utilization of physical space in the classroom. The critique of space utilization in open education by key contributors to the environmental stream, Ittelson, Proshansky, and Rivlin (1974) indicates

. . .not all open schools use their space to the best advantage. Staff leadership would seem to be a critical factor here, for it is not environments that teach but a combination of teachers interacting with students and stimulating materials. Environments can support improved learning approaches. In a real sense, teachers and students must learn to utilize their environments in the interests of their goals, both immediate and long-range. This is a skill in itself and may require a new kind of training for environmental awareness. Given the open plan, it may prove to be that the freedom here actually does foster the child's ability to realize his capacities. At this point, we simply do not know. What appears to be needed now is a closer study of the variety of activities that take place, and how the particular physical setting facilitates or hinders the participants, both teacher and pupil, in reaching their goals. When this is known, the architect/designer can step forward with more confidence than is now the case. (Pp. 381-82)

The environmental-ecological stream derives from environmental psychology (Craik, 1973; Moos & Insel, 1974; Proshansky et al., 1970; Sommer, 1969) and ecological psychology (Barker, 1968) (see chapters 1 and 3). Although not synonymous, both of these fields are concerned with the influence of physical settings on behavior. As Roger Barker puts it, "We found, in short, that we could predict some aspects of children's behavior more adequately from knowledge of the behavior characteristics of the drugstores, arithmetic classes, and basketball games they inhabited than from knowledge of the behavior tendencies of particular children" (p. 4).

Sarason (1971), in discussing the culture of the school, places considerable emphasis on the ecological approach and the concept of behavior settings as presented by Barker, particularly in his book with Gump (Big School, Small School, 1964). The work on ecology seems thus far to be concentrated in high schools, but the open education approach offers the ideal setting for integration of social ecology in any classroom.

It should be pointed out that this environmental stream has roots which go back at least to Kurt Lewin (1944) who coined the term psychological ecology which was viewed as the intersection of the individual's life space and his social and physical environment. Lewin's research set the basis for subsequent emphasis on the study of settings in which behavior occurs as exemplified by Barker's work.

Again we turn to Ittelson et al. (1974) for a summary description of the impact of an ecological system.

A well-fitting physical system, however, is essential to human functioning on all levels; the important thing is that it should itself be "adaptive" to the behaviors it supports. In this sense, the "open" environment is that which permits the maximum realization of intended behaviors on the part of the user rather than, let us say, the designer or architect. (P. 347)

THE IMPACT OF PHYSICAL SETTINGS

The point reiterated over and over again by those who identify themselves with open education is that open education is a philosophical approach which may be aided by open space but is not dependent upon it. As Proshansky and Wolfe (1974) express it, "The physical design of space cannot, by itself, create a successful open learning situation. If practitioners do not have a clear understanding of their position, the physical space, in actuality, can inhibit or interfere with the teachers' goals." As they point out, ". . .the over-riding theme of matching physical space to educational philosophy is relevant to any educational setting."

We should note that the design and arrangement of space functions in several ways to implement the goals and purposes of the teacher as designer. First, there is a symbolic communication of expectancies. For example, in our classroom, the teacher's desk is off on the side of the room. It is a repository of materials, products of the children which they expect the teacher to react to or do something further with. In effect, the teacher's desk has been restructured to symbolize a resource center consistent with the role of the teacher as a resource person.

Secondly, the use of space and furniture must, of course, be carefully designed to facilitate the kinds of behavior which the teacher desires.   For example, materials are placed in areas in which anticipated activities will take place: pencils, crayons, and scissors call for and elicit behaviors such as drawing, cutting, writing, etc.; placement of books and soft cushion pillows elicit reading behavior; balancing scales, bead frames, abacus and math activity cards should elicit behavior involving number concepts. Individual carrels offer opportunities for privacy.

A third way in which the design of space utilization is used to achieve teacher goals involves the communication of the principles of environmental design itself. For example, placing a round table in part of a classroom, in contrast to individual desks, results in interactive and cooperative behavior. Discussion of this activity results in the students themselves verbalizing awareness of the difference in their behavior resulting from the furniture arrangement. Students also become aware of the fact that there is a relationship between furniture arrangement (e.g. five chairs around a round table) and population density for a particular activity. The availability of individual closed areas, the carrels, communicates the importance given to the concept of privacy. We deliberately use space so that the students themselves learn the principles and philosophy of designing environments. They learn that design is not based on an authoritarian decision by the teacher but that they themselves can influence the design process.

Proshansky and Wolfe, (1974) offer one of the few practical discussions and illustrations of ways in which the classroom can be designed, linking open education philosophy with practical application. They emphasize the process of design and refuse to offer easy recipes.

Another investigator, Richard Chase, identifies his research within an environmental design context. His approach may be succinctly summarized by the title of one of his papers, "Information ecology and the design of learning environments" (1974). Chase focuses on designing the relationship between people and information in their environment. He describes a series of exercises in a course on environmental analysis which illustrate his approach. He uses concepts such as "the economics of information exchange involving large classes of college students teaching each other."

> . . .in all the exercises, our proposal objective was to show how the information available to members of a group can be vastly increased by appropriate redesign of the communication systems used by the group. We were trying to show how opportunities for learning can be significantly increased by selecting, organizing, formating, and making accessible information that has relevance to the interests of a group. (P. 284)

Chase's work represents an approach virtually unique in his combination of ecology and communication as an influence.

THE OPEN WING

The "open corridor" program, with which the author has been involved as a teacher since 1970, has been described earlier in the context of "open education" (Krasner & Krasner, 1973; Krasner & Richards, 1976). The program will be discussed within the context of environmental design. The theoretical influences on the author in helping initiate the program included a combination of readings, courses, and other exposures to open education, behavior modification, and environmental psychology.

It is important to stress some features of environmental design frequently ignored in reports on open education. These include the role of school administration, the selection of pupils, the planning of space, the reporting to parents and children, the relations with parents and community, the relationships among the teachers themselves, and the role of the teacher as an environmental planner. In addition, our program has included the beginnings of a program of systematic evaluation.

This program developed in the early 1970s at a time when there were major upheavals and unrest in the entire field of education (Silberman, 1970). Alternative programs were developing in many schools influenced by new ideas and slogans such as open education, free schools, behavior modification, computer-assisted instruction, individualized instruction, and many others.

We, the five teachers initiating the program, applied the label "open corridor" to our program. It was influenced by the many cross currents of ideas of the time; but in its specifics, it was indigenous to our own school and our own individual backgrounds. The school itself in which this program developed is a 1000 pupil, suburban school. Our particular program involves five classrooms (K through 4th Grade). Physically, five standard classrooms and the corridor upon which they bordered were involved. The school itself is a standard one-story building.

The most important feature in setting up an open classroom is that it represents an approach to student and classroom which cannot be imposed upon the teacher. However she becomes exposed to the approach – via formal training, reading, watching others, workshops, or evolving on to it over a number of years – the teacher must make her own decision that this approach is comfortable for her.

The teachers involved in this project had been working together for several years. Each in her own way had been evolving in her conceptions from viewing a classroom in the traditional manner to that of a more open nature. The influences on the teachers were partly that of reading, discussions with each other, the encouragement of the principal, and feedback from the classroom environment as change developed.

For a year before the initiation of the program, we discussed plans for it. We were tired of the old structure, although each of us ran an open classroom of sorts. We decided we should get together and we had many hours of talking to each other about how we look at life, how we look at children, and then we slowly developed the idea for an open corridor. The function of the teaching team, in addition to all other things, is similar to traditional group therapy in which members support and encourage each other, share similar experiences, and understand and sympathize with each other to an extent greater than that of a principal or spouse.

Silberman (1970) complained about joylessness of students in American education. It is clear that lack of joy to a large extent may emanate from the teacher, although it is mutually interactive, a process in which teacher and student each depresses and dejoys the other. In the open classroom, inevitably, the teachers spontaneously demonstrate their joy of teaching. This is both a reflection of and influence on the children.

Starting an open corridor was like frosting the cake. Each of us had been evolving an open program individually. Now it was like coming together in a corporation. The program exposed the children to a broader world. It would be hard to prove, but our guess is that individual open programs should first develop and then merge into an open wing; to go directly from traditional to open corridor might be disastrous. Environmental planning, like individual shaping, must be done small bits at a time.

A major element is the relationship of the program to the school administration. This goes beyond mere cooperation and passive support. The administration must be convinced about the potentialities of the approach and actively support it in terms of its own participation – support with supplies and, particularly support in relation to the remainder of the school community not involved in the program. The administrator's enthusiasm or his concerns are quickly communicated to others – the teachers, the students, the parents – and this increases the likelihood of the success or failure of the program. In our program, we were grateful for the active support of the administrator of our school, E. Michael Helmintoller.

The eventual success of any program depends to a very large extent on the way in which a program is initially set up. The major element in the preparation for the program is the contact with the community. Several meetings were set up with the parents the year previous to the initiation of the program to present the plans. The children could enter the program only if the parent committed the child's participation for a full year. The parents were so enthusiastic that they volunteered double the number of children that could be accommodated. The resolution of this dilemma was to select the students by lottery. The president of the Parent Teachers Organization picked the names out of a hat, and these were the children selected.

As an example of integrating the contribution of parents to meet the design purposes of the teacher, there is the manner in which we utilized one father who was trained as a social planner. He expressed a desire to contribute to the educational process of the classroom. After discussion with the parent, which revealed his interest in the planning of new towns, the author indicated that she would like a project in which all of the students could participate in the design and planning process. The parent came up with a plan of presenting a general problem of designing a town to the children and asking them to plan on paper the specifics of running a town including buildings for living, shopping, school, transportation, banking, police, fire, and City Hall.

As one illustration of utilizing environmental design in an open classroom, the development of the human behavior lab in our open wing (Krasner et al., 1977) is cited. This human behavior lab represents a translation of environmental design principles to the training of young children to observe and influence their own environment. In effect, the lab is a prototype of the entire program demonstrating that even quite young children can learn to design their own environments so as to elicit positive responses from adults and peers.

The particular skill areas covered include self-observation and observation of others in the group, in the classroom, outside the classroom, and at home; teaching a mini-lesson to other children in their class; and finally taking over the teaching of the next group of children in the lab. The children were taught to observe behavior as well as its consequences, especially in social interaction situations. Specific devices and techniques used included mirrors and tape recorders for self-observation; self-monitoring, modeling, role-playing, social rein-forcement, and games (revived or invented) to illustrate points (e.g., "gossip" to illustrate distortion in giving and receiving information).

The effect on the behavior of the four children in the group and on the other children in the class was assessed by questionnaires to the teachers and parents and taped interviews with the children. Outcomes achieved with this group of children included improved social skills and group functioning for all the children, improved status of at least one low-status child within the classroom, skill in teaching other children, and an understanding of "psychology."

Another illustration of environmental design in an open classroom is the student planning his or her own "ideal" classroom to be described in the next chapter.

THE SHOREHAM MIDDLE SCHOOL

The open corridor program which has been very briefly described illustrates environmental design in a limited alternative program within a school in which the majority of classrooms are considered traditional. A program in which a school institution is totally involved in environmental design is described by its originator and principal, Dr. Dennis Littky (1973) who was trained as a behavioral psychologist. This school, located in Shoreham, New York, may well be the most innovative use of designed environment in a school setting since Dewey's Lab School.

It is of interest to note that the basic premises followed by the Shoreham school were adopted from the Vermont State Education Department, thus linking with the progressive and open education streams of influence:

1. A student must be accepted as a person.

2. Education should be based upon the individual's strong inherent desire to learn and to make sense of his environment.

3. Education should strive to maintain the individuality and originality of the learner.

4. Emphasis should be upon a child's own way of learning.

5. The teacher's role must be that of a partner and a guide in the learning process.

6. We must seek to individualize our expectations of a person's progress as we strive to individualize the learning experiences of each person.

7. The environment within which students are encouraged to learn must be greatly expanded.

8. The arts should become an integral part of the day.

9. The affective, as well as the cognitive, domain must be worked with.

10. Real tasks (work) must begin to appear in the school day.

11. School should be life and comparable with reality.

THE TEACHER AS ENVIRONMENTAL DESIGNER

We will conclude this chapter by returning to a view of the classroom from a consumer of environmental design, the teacher. The author believes that there are eight major elements in her role as a teacher – learning facilitator – which link her role with the concept of environmental design.

These principles are certainly consistent with the environmental design approach to the classroom which we have been describing throughout this chapter.

1. The teacher as a planner of environment: The teacher states her objectives in behavioral terms so as to achieve specific behavioral objectives with each individual student. This is an operational way of defining and evaluating "individualized instruction," a key concept. As an environmental planner, the teacher must systematically utilize her own behavior, that of other adults in and out of the classroom, and the physical environment to influence the learning process in each individual child.

2. The teacher as a source of values and as a socially responsible individual: The teacher is sufficiently aware of her own values (personal preferences) so that she can distinguish between value issues and objective questions and so that she can recognize ways in which she can help her students recognize that values enter into virtually every learning situation.

3. The teacher as a continual self-trainer: The teacher keeps a journal as a useful source of self-observation and utilizes reactions from peers, principal, and students as a source of feedback to change her behavior. She makes use of community resources such as teacher centers, college courses, and workshops to improve her teaching skills.

4. The teacher as participant observer: All of the elements of the participant observer role apply to the teacher herself, who observes and records pupil behavior, the relationship between environmental stimuli and pupil behavior and, most important for a participant observer, observes and records the relationship between her own behavior and that of the pupils. In effect, participant observation is a continuous, ongoing process. The concept of teacher as participant observer may well be the key to understanding and undertaking environmental design in the classroom.

5. The training of students in techniques of observation and self-observation: An important skill which should be developed in students is that of being able to accurately observe their social and physical environment. An equally important related skill is that of the student being able to self-observe in terms of physical, affective, and behavioral responses. The Human Behavior Lab is a technique of developing this skill in children.

6. The application of specific behavior influence skills in classroom to achieve behavioral objectives in children. Using such an approach, a teacher is able to select appropriate positive reinforcers from the natural environment, she utilizes positive feedback, especially praise, to enhance specific pupil skills. Contracts are developed with the students that are both individualized and interactive. Other specific techniques include modeling of behavior (films, video tapes, and self-modeling) and group techniques (group dynamics, small group leadership, and role-playing) to accomplish the individualized behavioral objectives.

7. The design of physical environments as learning environments. The teacher utilizes spatial arrangement of furniture and materials ("stuff" to use the "open ed" vernacular) so as to achieve individual behavioral objectives. A multitude of media, including films, tape recorders, cameras, and phonographs are used in creating specific learning environment areas in science, social science, math, language arts, arts, and music. An important element here is the teacher's ability to use time as well as space in designing learning environments.

8. The teacher as a resource administrator. The environmental design teacher utilizes the appropriate classroom, school, and community resources as necessary. These include peers, administrators, guidance people, school psychologists, consultants, university resources, teacher centers, books, etc. to achieve her objectives and as a backup to enhance the effectiveness of her procedures.

Book Binding As Environmental Design

We have developed a number of procedures which derive from our model of the teacher. This is illustrated with an example which has proven to be exciting and stimulating to the children in my third-grade class and to myself. The classroom has been designed with one area designated as a publishing company. The children write, illustrate, bind, publish, and distribute their own individual books. Not only does this activity represent a creative integration of reading, writing, and the language arts, but it also demonstrates a planned use of space to achieve specific behavioral objectives of the teacher as an environmental designer.

The concept of a book publishing company developed almost naturally from our emphasis on the importance of writing by young children. A major element in the curriculum has been journal keeping. The children were writing in every conceivable form: short stories, reports, and poems. Why not put them in book form? A love of books has always been important in my classroom. For an adult to see his/her own creation in the form of a completed book is an enormous sense of accomplishment. For a child, it is even more so and should be a source of initial imprint for lifelong self-confidence. The next element in the publishing company was the actual operation of binding a book. Herein is involved a skill that can be readily learned by a teacher and then taught to children.

The publishing company becomes real to the individual child with the labeling of his/her finished book as the product of Open Wing Press, Stony Brook, New York, 1977. An area of the classroom is designed as a center for the publishing company with space for displaying books and technology of the book production. Finally, as with all published books, the library's Dewey decimal classification system is applied to the spine of the book by the author (adding additional study skills to the child's experience).

It should be noted in this day of universal budget crunches that the cost involved in this kind of publishing company is inexpensive. Almost all the materials (except for the tape) are readily available in schools with perhaps the aid of a bit of scrounging. The publishing company serves as a means of integrating the teaching of writing, reading, and study skills. Equally important, the teacher as environmental designer is able to combine the various learning modalities and concepts (classroom space, learning by doing, reinforcing consequences, basic skills, sense of accomplishment and joy of learning).

The general principles which have led to a publishing company in the classroom can, of course, be applied to the development of other creative ventures in the classroom. As a designer of the classroom environment, I have become alerted to the importance of the use of space (in effect, the children and I together create the built environment in which we learn); the importance of "learning by doing" (the time-honored hands-on method); the need to incorporate as many learning modalities into a single task as possible; incorporating the behavioral principle of immediate reinforcing consequences to what the child does; the importance of development of skills in the basics —

reading, writing, and mathematics; and, most important, that skills follow motivation, love of learning, and a sense of enjoyment.

11 Designing an "Ideal" Classroom
Dries van Wagenberg

The next chapter offers an illustration of an environmental design project developed within the context of the training program described in chapter 9. The project described was developed in the "open wing" classroom of Miriam Krasner described in the previous chapter.

van Wagenberg traces the influences on himself as environmental designer from the field of psychology with emphasis on the research of the Gestalt group which is quite consistent with orientation described throughout the book.

Ed.

INTRODUCTION TO A TECHNOLOGY FOR INTERMEDIATE ENVIRONMENTAL DESIGN

Intermediate environmental design technology is a new development within environmental design. It is an attempt to adapt to techniques of environmental design for use in small groups with emphasis on the fact that all members participate in the decision making process about innovations in their own environment. Intermediate Environmental Design Technology (IDET) has its philosophical roots within the work of Dewey (1915), Habraken (1972), Schumacher (1973), Turner (1976), and Ward (1975). Many of its techniques, however, are modified versions of those developed in environmental design and other related fields.

INFLUENCES ON THE DEVELOPMENT OF THE TECHNOLOGY
FOR INTERMEDIATE ENVIRONMENTAL DESIGN

Gestalt Psychology

The Gestalt psychologists objected to the simplistic approach of earlier psychologists like Pavlov and Ebbinghaus. They argued that a human being is not confronted with one stimulus at a time, but with patterns of stimuli at the same time or specific chains of stimuli over a time period. A human being does not break up these patterns or chains of stimuli into single units, but seems to process many stimuli at the same time, as an entity or over time. As such, the Gestalt approach focused on the environment. Gestalt psychologists confronted subjects with complex stimulus situations and had the subjects respond verbally to them. Gestalt psychologists discovered the importance of the context of the stimulus and its influence on the meaning of the stimulus itself.

The Gestalt psychologist Kurt Lewin became one of the founders of the environmental orientation within psychology. Much of the research done by Lewin and his students can be considered environmental psychology or sometimes even environmental design. Morton Deutch (1969) wrote about Kurt Lewin:

> He believed that the attempt to bring about change in a process is the most fruitful way to investigate it; that the important social-psychological phenomena can be studied experimentally; that the scientist should have a social conscience and should be active in making the world a better place to live in; and that a good theory is valuable for social action as well as for science. (P. 478)

Lewin's topological field theory was very useful to analyze real life situations and to plan for social action. Lewin, Lippitt & White (1939) conducted a lab study, in which the researchers created three different "social climates" and observed the development of aggressive behavior in the three different groups. Lewin and his students found that the group with democratic leadership style generated the least aggression and was far more productive. This study inspired many social scientists to study differences in leadership styles.

Festinger, Schachter & Back (1950) studied the development of relations within a student housing project and Deutch and Collins (1951) looked at the formation of relationships between black and white families in two different low-cost apartment complexes. In the last two studies the researchers considered the differences between the physical environments (the independent variable), and considered the variation in relationships (the dependent variable), that was measured by interviewing the families involved. These studies are among the first attempts to evaluate the impact of architecture on human behavior.

Two features seem to be present in the studies done by Lewin or his students, and both are important for an intermediate environmental designer: 1) The change in the field setting is always made in a systematic way, or a clear difference between the settings in study is indicated and documented. 2) The results are measured and evaluated in a systematic way. Many of the studies are idealistic in character and Lewin always stressed the involvement of all participants in the change process.

Roger Barker, one of Lewin's first students in the United States, developed a different approach to the study of human behavior. Not satisfied with the fact that Lewin "limited psychology to an encapsulated system of purely psychological constructs", Barker (1976) tried to deal directly with the nonpsychological environment in order to explain human behavior. Barker's contribution to environmental psychology is impressive. Important concepts developed by Barker and his students are: behavior setting, behavior episode, and undermanning of settings. Barker brought much of his research together in his book, Ecological Psychology: Concepts and methods for studying the environment of human behavior (1968). (See chapters 1 and 3, this volume.)

According to Lewin's theory, the participants in a setting acquire a certain understanding of their environment and what it does for them. At a certain time and place, an individual has a certain understanding of his environment and is able to identify certain forces at work. This knowledge and the forces at work determine the life space of the individual. His action will be the result of the forces at work and his understanding of the situation. A successful action will reinforce his understanding and an unsuccessful action will alter his understanding. Lewin was one of the first researchers who tried to analyze and classify the different systems at work in the environment of a human being. His theory seems to be a good basis for intermediate environmental design, especially because the theory also deals with interactions of the individual with other individuals. Lewin's theory does not deal, however, with the differences between experimenting with one's own environment and being instructed to change and then experiencing the consequences of the change. For an intermediate environmental designer it is, however, that the user himself is designing his environment.

Architectural Psychology

In the early 1960s, another environmental-oriented field developed within psychology. In general, it was labeled "Architectural Psychology," but sometimes it was called environmental psychology. Calvin W. Taylor (1974), a pioneer in architectural psychology, notes:

> Man's interactions and interrelations with natural environments and with existing constructed environments must be better understood, so that the future environments will be as well designed as possible for man and his purposes. Architects design environments for people and psychologists study the reactions of the people to environments. So the public tells us that architectural psychology should have occurred "from the beginning." (P. 2)

Among others, Cohen & Filipczak (1971) and Studer (1973) have made extensive contributions to the development of a more holistic approach to design of new environments. Two projects done by Cohen, Filipczak & Bis (1967) and Lent, Leblanc & Spradlin (1967) are good examples of this approach.

Taylor (1976) reported at the EDRA Symposium in Vancouver that there are now programs in architectural psychology in eight major universities. Unfortunately, traditional architecture has been of little help in the development of environmental design. Traditionally, buildings are evaluated on the basis of cost benefit calculations and their esthetic appearance. Architectural psychology made environmental designers aware of the influence of building on human behavior and, therefore, should help the users to plan these influences according to their own wishes.

The environmental designer traditionally has taken the role of an expert and collaborated with the management of the organization he is planning for. As such, environmental design experts have trained teachers, managers, prison guards, psychiatric aides and administrators in the use of, for example, operant principles and helped them to make any changes in their institutions. Some of those changes have affected clients or workers within the organizations, in their opinion, in a very negative way. The newly learned techniques were only used to solve the problem of the staff without considering the implications for those whose behavior had to be modified. To avoid this situation, we argue for the role of the I.E.D. who is always planning his work in such a way that the users have the ultimate say over the design process.

Intermediate Technology

The publications of Habraken (1972), Schumacher (1973), Turner & Fichter (1972), and Ward (1973), have revived the interest in the impact of large scale organizations on the quality of life. Several major ecological catastrophes have made people aware of the fact that large organizations sometimes create more problems than they solve. Schumacher, for example, pointed out that large bureaucracies of rich countries are catering expensive technology to poor countries which, as a result, become even more poor and dependent of these rich countries. Schumacher's work has greatly stimulated the development of what he called technology. This is a type of technology that can be characterized by its simpleness, the fact that it is inexpensive, and that it can be used on the spot by an experienced layman. Intermediate technology is ecologically oriented and adapted to the culture in which it is used. So far, it has only developed for use in the Third World.

Habraken, Turner, Fichter and Ward have done a similar thing for mass housing. They have documented the destructive influence of large governmental organizations on the housing of low-income families and have, subsequently, developed techniques to help families to plan and build their own houses and neighborhoods. These intermediate planning techniques are very useful for an I.E.D. expert and should be incorporated in his work. He will strive with his group for simplicity and ecological-oriented solutions, and try to incorporate cultural variables.

Learning By Doing

As early as 1916, Dewey made us aware that we see the world according to our own experiences and that we learn by doing. Dewey's work implies that a person who has never created a new thing will not be able to see the beauty of the creation process that surrounds him.

One of the first scientists to experimentally study the influence of behavior on perception was Ames of the Hanover Institute for Associated Research (1915). Ames combined his ingenious experiments and the philosophical theory of transactions developed by Dewey and Bently (1949) into his theory of transactional functionalism. Although transactional functionalism is usually considered to be a theory of perception, there is no reason not to consider it also an environmental theory. Transactional functionalism maintains that what we perceive is the result of assumptions we have learned to make while we are acting on our environment. One of Ames' experiments explains quite well his transactional functionalism. Suppose you are looking into a room through a small hole. The room appears to be quite normal, but in reality it is distorted. The distortions cannot be seen because you are looking into the room from a particular angle. We infer that the room is rectangular, that all the windows have the same dimensions, and that all the walls are equally high. From the point that we are looking these assumptions are not disqualified, except that we see a human face moving from one window to the other and this face appears much larger in the first window than in the second. This, of course, is bugging us and it makes us wonder, but the experience is not strong enough to abandon our assumptions. What is required to make us abandon our previous assumptions? Floyd Allport (1955) gave us an interesting discription of what is required:

> The solution of the problem brings into focus the important principle of _action_. Let us try to _act_ with some reference to the room by hitting a spot on the rear wall with a ball, or by tracing the border of that wall with a wand. At first we make many errors. But with practice we find that we can succeed and can gradually learn more about the true spatial properties of the room. We come now to a very important point. As this overt exploration proceeds, something very significant happens to our perception of the room. Its appearance gradually changes, and we come to see it more nearly as it is — that is, as a room that is disturbed in certain ways. (Pp. 277-78, emphasis in original)

Operant Psychology

Operant psychology added another important feature to the model of an organism interacting with its environment. It concentrated on the consequences of behavior and how the consequences had an influence on that behavior. Staddon and Simmelhag's (1971) evolutionary model is one of the more current explanations of the influence of consequences on contingent behavior or on instrumental behavior. Staddon and Simmelhag put forward two principles to explain behavior: 1) The principles of variation of behavior (analogous to Mendalian genetics), and 2) the principles of reinforcement.

In Staddon and Simmelhag's model the organism will display the variety of behavior appropriate for that environment, and reinforcement which is contingent on a particular behavior "locks up" that behavior in time, so that the appropriate behavior is displayed at the right time in relation to a change in the environment. They key peck just before the reinforcement not only operates the food hopper, but is also the most important behavior just before eating. The result is high probability for a key peck period prior to food. Within the environment, the experimenter has set up a feedback loop for the operant "pecking." The behavior has a consequence and this results in a change of the environment, e.g. the availability of food for 3 seconds.

Premack's theory (1965, 1971) of reinforcement fits very well into Staddon and Simmelhag's theory. Suppose we disconnect the environmental system "peck gives food" and food would be a permanent part of the environment. Now we would find certain probabilities for the display of a great variety of behaviors. Later in the experimental situation, one behavior is made contingent on another. Now, eating is only possible if pecking or some other behavior is done at the appropriate rate or time. The new environmental system establishes a functional relationship between two behaviors, and the organism reacts to the situation with a different probability of the different behaviors possible in the new environment. This environmental system is what Skinner has called a "schedule." Many different systems and their effects on the behavior of a variety of organisms have been investigated. The intermediate environmental designer should be aware of the environmental system and explain its influences on human behavior to the future users of the system. During the design process, the creation of new systems has to be considered and lead to a more satisfactory environment for the users.

Ethology

The model proposed by Staddon and Simmelhag can also be used to analyze some of the experiments done by Tinbergen (1951), who showed how digger wasps use environmental cues to locate the entrance of their nests. The experimental design used in this study is as follows. The experimenter studied the digger wasps in the field. Their behavior was considered to be stable and to repeat itself in time. Tinbergen placed some pine cones around the entrance of the nest. The digger wasps got used to the cones after some time. Tinbergen took away the cones while the digger wasp was looking for food. When it returned, it landed right in the middle of the circle of cones, which were set apart from the entrance of the nest. We may consider the environment of the digger wasp far more complex than the Skinner box, but nevertheless stable. Tinbergen changed the location of the pine cones and this altered the nest locating behavior and all the other behaviors for a while. We may consider this as a disturbance of the environment. Tinbergen did not connect or disconnect an environmental system as Premack did, but changed the spatial arrangement of several environmental stimuli and observed the new distribution of behaviors of the wasp. He observed that the digger wasp went to the wrong spot, but later discovered the entrance of his nest. So methodologically, the experiments of Tinbergen and Premack are similar, but the environments of the organism to be studied and the environment variables, which are manipulated, are different.

An intermediate designer is always dealing with a field situation and, for that reason, he can learn a lot from the ethologist. He works in already existing environments, which are more similar to those studied by ethologists than the ones studied by operant psychologists. As we mentioned earlier, the role of an intermediate environmental designer is to assist participants of the setting to design their own environment and to experiment with it, and not as an operant psychologist who controls an environment without any input by the user and studies the results of the changes made by the researcher.

Finally, we would like to mention an experiment done by Baum (1974). He introduced a feedback system to the pigeons in his attic (field situation) and studied their matching behavior. This study shows how operant principles can be applied in a field setting. For an intermediate environmental designer, it is important, however, to make first an analysis with the other participants of their environment and the impact on their behavior. Experimental operant methods can be useful for that purpose.

ENVIRONMENTAL SYSTEMS: A WAY TO LOOK AT THE ENVIRONMENTS

An individual is living in an environment that can be seen as a collection of many different systems. He interacts daily with these systems and learns to make assumptions about them. In our opinion, the nature of these systems can be instrumental, spatial, social, biological, and climatological.

The human being is acting on these systems and his actions make the system respond. The responses of the systems provide him with opportunities for other behaviors. The influence of a system is sometimes experienced directly or as a modification of an adverse influence. For example, in the case of an individual walking under the roof of a shopping center when it is raining, the roof (a spatial system) is protecting that person against the rain (an adverse influence), and permitting that person to continue to shop.

Some systems provide a desirable change in the environment, others respond in an undesirable way and, therefore, should be avoided. The operation of these systems costs time, and this factor has to be considered in combination with the pay off of a particular system.

A human being will distribute his time over as many systems as he is able to control. We assume that an individual is constantly trying to create a utopian environment, which is free from adverse events and provides immediate opportunities for as many different rewarding behaviors as possible. This is similar to Premack's notion of a free choice situation. In reality, environmental systems are not stable, however, and their character changes all the time. Some have to be created and maintained continuously. The interaction between environmental systems and individuals will formulate certain assumptions related to the stability of the environment, which will make the individual act as if the systems will never change. The stability will last until one of the structures of the system is changed. The changed environment will lead eventually to a new set of assumptions.

Certain conditions are so important for survival of the individual, that they have to be maintained all the time. For example, the body temperature has to stay at 37 degrees Celsius and the individual is constantly acting on his environment to keep his body temperature constant. In such case, the individual is functioning as a controller with a set point counteracting all disturbances in his environment. In regard to other conditions, a person is not constantly acting on his environment, but only for certain periods during the day. For example, people only eat at certain times during the day. In such cases, it is difficult to say that the individual controls the environmental system. We will use the term "operate," to identify these actions. As we mentioned earlier, the environment of an individual can be better understood by classifying the environmental systems in 5 broad categories.

Instrumental Systems

Mankind has created an enormous amount of instrumental systems during the last 150 years. Furniture, tools, and machines are all instrumental systems. Machines fill more and more the human environment. The house is more and more a workshop, the kitchen a cooking laboratory. Different types of furniture are especially designed for sleeping, writing, eating, or talking. We use so many kinds of tools that we can hardly keep track of them. Architects design environments with many different systems clustered together (a setting), which usually facilitates certain behaviors. Think, for example, about a factory. We spend considerable time operating all these systems, and conservative estimates maintain that we spent at least 80 percent of our time in a man-made environment. Individuals are not only operating the systems, they also have to maintain them, and this demands time and energy. Operant psychology has given us an understanding of the influence of several instrumental systems on behavior.

Spatial Systems

A human being spends much of his time traveling from one environment to another. Travel behavior has a drastic influence on the environment of an individual. Traveling changes his environment and creates new opportunities for behavior. Many times, environmental systems are clustered together and linked by a transportation network.

As far as spacial behavior is concerned, we can position the different systems in space and study the displacement of individuals. It is interesting to note here that the matching law might apply here too. Roads, canals, rivers, and paths are all spatial environmental systems.

Social Systems

The most important and complex systems in the individual's environment are, however, other human beings. An individual is nearly always socializing. He is educated by his parents and the community. His behavior is shaped into a cultural pattern and constantly monitored by individuals in his environment. The child has to learn what is appropriate and what is not, when he will be rewarded and when he will be punished. Finally, we should mention that many environmental systems are built to protect man against man and to shape him into certain interactions. We think, for example, about rules and laws.

Biological Systems

Many conditions needed for the survival of mankind are the result of plant and animal life. Humans cannot eat or breathe without plants and animals in their environment. However, for western man, the time he is interacting with nature for survival has decreased drastically. Many people no longer grow their own food or hunt to supply their family with meat. Instead, food is purchased in stores and prepared at home. Besides for food, individuals have used animals as a source of materials to make clothes, to help them to hunt, and to assist with physical labor. But even these interactions have disappeared nearly completely for most people. We may conclude that only farmers spend their time in dealing with environmental biological systems to produce food and other resources, while most people spend very little time interacting with nature directly with such an objective in mind.

Climatological Systems

The battle against the climate is a continuous one. The body is constantly regulating its temperature. Humans don't like cold, snow, rain, or extremely high temperatures. To deal with these fluctuations, mankind has created buildings, climatological systems, clothes, and conditioned cabins for transportation. The battle is a continuous one because an individual can only counteract against changes in the weather, but does not control the climate itself.

I would like to conclude the explanation of the environmental classification system by noting that most human beings take the environmental system for granted and, in general, do not try to evaluate its effectiveness nor try to map it carefully. Environmental design cannot take place, however, without a critical analysis of the existing environmental systems and the desire to improve the effectiveness of certain systems or to change their effect. An individual has a set of assumptions that reflect the regularities of the systems he has experienced. For that reason, change will always be a painful and difficult process, because the participant not only has to abandon a system that was functioning somewhat, but also has to change his assumptions about his environment. The participant has to learn to operate the new design systems, and this takes time. Just after the change, the individual is less effective in operating the change system and that usually affects the ongoing operations of other systems. As a result, the time after the change is sometimes rather hectic and painful until the new system is understood completely and functions well.

INTERMEDIATE ENVIRONMENTAL DESIGN TECHNIQUES

An Appropriate Setting

Intermediate environmental design can be successful only in settings which are willing to change. The participants should like working in small groups and being involved in the creation of their new environment. It is extremely important for environmental designers to enter an organization in the appropriate way. First, they should establish an administrative contact that will allow them to enter the organization. They can start with a short presentation outlining the background, skills, philosophy of the intermediate environmental designers, and the idea of "learning by doing." Groups or individuals interested in such a project then sign up for a separate interview as a next step, and, finally, an appropriate number of groups is selected.

Intermediate Environmental Design Teams

Intermediate environmental designers are better off working in teams of two. This creates a situation in which one can be actively involved in working with the group while the other is able to observe the interaction, and vice versa. The team approach facilitates learning and creativity, and prevents frustration.

As soon as the group is functioning, members can form teams to lead the group and evaluate their group leading skills. The intermediate environmental designers and the participants form a community which has an objective innovation of the environment of the participants.

Decision making is democratic, and the group as a whole has the ultimate say about the decision. This is extremely important as an intermediate environmental design principle and a necessary condition for a good, functioning community.

Formation Of An Intermediate Environmental Design Seminar

To create your own environment is a very unusual thing. Participants in different intermediate environmental design projects need each other for encouragement, advice, role play, and feedback. Therefore, the I.E.D. team should set a time for participants of different groups to meet on a regular basis to learn from each other.

Participant Observer

The concept of the participant observer is crucial in intermediate environmental design. By taking the role of a participant observer, the intermediate environmental designer becomes part of the community and this allows the members of that community to have an influence on its behavior.

The intermediate environmental designer brings in his knowledge about the process for change, goal settings, observations, experimental design, group discussions, brainstorming, behavior influence, and examples of social organizational structures, rules, and physical environments and contacts with other groups. This task is to train the participants in the use of these techniques while they work on a real change in their environment.

Intermediate Environmental Design Circle

The intermediate environmental design circle is developed to structure the process of change in time. The I.E.D. circle helps the participants plan for the different steps and, while going through the circle, the participants learn to plan, to reconstruct, and to evaluate their environment. Finally, the intermediate environmental designer has to evaluate the impact of the experience on the behavior of the participants in terms of their continued use of similar processes for change. This can be done with the help of a follow up.

Analysis of the setting environment

The following techniques are useful for the analysis of an environment.

1. Make a floor plan of the setting. Which places are reinforcing for the different participants?

2. List all the activities on little pieces of paper, and put them

on an appropriate place on the floor plan. Which activities are reinforcing and which are adversive? What are bottlenecks?

3. Every 15 minutes, a participant lists what he is doing and with whom. He has to do this for several days. What was nice and what was not very reinforcing?

4. Make a sociogram to assess the social environment. Whom do you like and whom not?

5. Make behavioral observations in the settings. Rotate until all participants have had a chance to make these observations. Try to identify consequences of the behavior of the different individuals.

6. Make observations of the traffic flow.

7. Measure the temperature, hours of sunlight, and humidity in the setting.

The analysis of the setting will change everybody's assumptions about the setting. The experimenting observers are in the same positions as the person in Ames' experiment with the distorted room. Because they are now able to observe their environment from many different angles, the participants start to change their assumptions. This will help them to set new goals and to plan for change.

Goal setting and measurement; baseline observations

A good way to set a goal is to ask the participants to formulate individually their long-term goals. A good question to ask is: How should the setting function and what should it look like one year from now? In a group discussion, the participants now should pick three or more goals they all can agree on. If the long-term goals are set, short-term goals can be formulated. They should be formulated in behavioral terms that will help to construct an adequate measurement scale. The participants should select a moderate goal if it is the first time they are trying to make changes.

The designer can suggest appropriate experimental design like a control group design, A.B.A.B. design, or multiple baseline design to evaluate the impact of the changes. The circular character of the I.E.D. circle in itself leads to a multiple baseline. When the measurement scale is developed baseline observations should be taken. All participants can be involved in this on a rotation basis. Reliability checks are important.

Planning for change; alternatives; model of human behavior

Now that the participants in the setting have started to understand their environment and have set a few goals for change, they have to find a way to accomplish these goals. A good way to approach this process is to have all the participants brainstorm. Before the real brainstorming starts, however, it is a good idea to test the group on ability to react positively and to avoid negative comments. If necessary, the group should be trained in appropriate behavior to facilitate creativity.   The ideas can be translated into activities and the previously developed labels can be rearranged in the floor plan. They can be clustered in different patterns according to certain conditions which are desired.   For example, quiet activities can be clustered together and separated from activities which don't need a silent atmosphere. New rules can be made and training for appropriate new behaviors can be set up.   The group can, for example, think about temporary token economy to train each other in new interaction behaviors. Different traffic routes can be studied while working on the floor plan. A scale model will facilitate the brainstorming about changes in the physical environment.   Planning for change is a slow process and, between meetings, participants should try to test with simple means the ideas they have proposed.   In general, trips to other settings as well as reading about other settings are useful during this part of the process.

The designer should help the participants to generate alternatives to their plans and to investigate the consequences of the changes they are proposing. Simulation games may help to predict behavioral conse- quences. At the end of this stage, the group should select several plans to be implemented.

Planning for reconstruction

The group should first work on a timetable to organize the reconstruc- tion.   Role play and dry runs have to be scheduled to prepare the participants for an effective change in social behavior. Social skills training is an example of such a technique. If the group is planning to change the physical environment, materials should be ordered, special- ists contracted, and materials prepared for their use. If the group decides to build new furniture for the setting, they should organize an assembly line. In a design process for the construction of a building, this stage would be equivalent to the activity of the contractor who is making the preparations, according to the blueprints of the architect, to start the building.

Reconstruction

The I.E.D. team should be present during the reconstruction and help wherever they are needed.

Evaluation of the changed environment

After the reconstruction, the setting usually needs time to readjust to the new situation. After a couple of weeks, however, all participants have readjusted to the new situation. This is the time to repeat the baseline observations. Again it is important to have the participants do some of the observation and they should work out the results on a daily basis. The participants are usually very curious to know if the new environment is actually "better."

Evaluation of the intermediate environmental design circle as a process for change

The I.E.D. team is responsible for the process of change and, therefore, should try to evaluate the effects of the process itself. This can be done in several ways. The I.E.D. team can do a follow-up study to see if the participants in the setting have continued to plan for change. The team could start off with observations in the setting and record all changes they have noticed since they left. With these changes in mind, they can interview the participants and find out more about the process of change used by the participants. The I.E.D. team also could repeat once more the baseline observations they have done earlier to evaluate new changes.

DESIGNING AN "IDEAL" CLASSROOM

Mario G. Salvadori has worked with seventh grade students of a junior high school in Harlem and taught them via "learning by doing" all the basic principles underlying architectural structures. His students have built bridges, domes, and frames and they have become very involved and enthusiastic about the study of the built environment (Salvadori, 1977). In 1970, The Group for Environmental Education, Inc. published Book Seven: Our Man-Made Environment, a study guide for young children. Ward and Tyson (1973) offered a useful resource book for teachers who wanted to expand their classrooms into the community. The project and the books show that the man-made environment can be a continuous source of inspiration for education. The immediate environment offers the teacher a natural structure to teach the basic skills. Language and mathematics can be integrated in the study of the existing environment and in planning and design for change.

As for the training of children in the planned usage of space itself, there is a paucity of studies in which children themselves are educated to plan their living space. When architectural ideas are brought into the classrooms, they usually are remedial in nature and require an adult (the teacher or an expert) to do the actual designing of the space.

An intriguing question for architects, teachers, and psychologists has been "At what age are youngsters able to conceptualize a plan for a new environment?" Young children play with all kinds of blocks. They build fantasies and play for hours with their creations, often encouraged by adults. As they grow older, however, their interest in building is less likely to be inforced, and their attention becomes focused on other subjects. Unfortunately, the natural desire of the child to build is rarely used in education. Children usually do not learn anything about architecture and town planning in school or at home. As a result, as adults they know little about the architecture and planning of their environment. Nevertheless, they will spend nearly their whole lives in a man-made environment. In recent years, a small, but growing, number of architects in the western world (Frogen, 1976; Habraken, 1972; Kroll, 1976; Spille, 1975; and Van Wagenberg, 1976) have tried to interest tenants and other users of buildings to participate in the design process.

Future users can become actively involved in the planning and design of new structures. The architects, however, often encounter a fundamental problem when they work with the future users. The user often has many exciting ideas but knows neither how to communicate nor how to develop them. Further, the architect was not trained to simplify his proposals to basic concepts which the user can understand. The participating user often feels incompetent to make basic design decisions. As an architect, the senior author encountered these problems several times and came to the conclusion that, if designing wasn't taught at school at an elementary level, participation of the future user in the design process always would be a difficult and time consuming activity. Thus, it was important to determine if children could learn to design a new environment, and to develop a procedure for such training. In the "open education" approach (Weber, 1971) teachers tried to systematically utilize the "natural" interests of the child, which are the result of daily experiences, as an integral part of the education process. As indicated earlier, construction is one of the things a young child likes to do. Teachers working in an open education setting as environmental designers try to use this interest of children in building as an integral part of the learning process.

"Learning by doing" is an often cited phrase in publications about open education. With this in mind, an architect (the author) and an elementary school teacher (Miriam Krasner) planned a design project for a group of six students of the teacher's third grade class at the North Country Elementary School, Stony Brook, New York (see chapter 10.) A special corner in the classroom was set aside where the students and the architect could work. Finished drawings could be hung against a nearby wall, and the materials involved in the project such as cardboard, paper, scissors, and glue were also stored in this corner. Meetings of the group were held every week for one semester for approximately one and a half hours in the "design studio." All the students were considered as partners and were referred to as fellow architects.

During the first session, the objectives were explained to the students and the different design techniques were described. After that, meetings usually started with a short introduction. Then the children began to work alone or in teams of two. They were encouraged and coached by the architect with short remarks and funny stories. The meetings ended with a group discussion and a preview of the following week. During the discussion the group focused on everyone's production and tried to look for both the good and the less successful solutions in the different designs. To express positive feelings about some of the good aspects of the designs was a major activity.

The students were very excited about designing their ideal classroom. The first step was to analyze the existing classroom by building a scale model of the room as it then existed. The fellow architects soon understood what had to be done. One of them came up with the bright suggestion to use the square black and white tiles on the floor as a grid to make a floor plan. They counted the tiles and made corresponding squares on their quarter-inch black and white graph paper. They discovered the concept of "scale" and started to build their model. To make the walls, the students had to measure the height and width of the wall and had to draw it in scale on a piece of cardboard. Then they determined the position and measurements of doors, windows, paintings, and equipment against the walls and drew pictures of these elements on the cardboard walls. The architect then cut the windows and doors according to their drawings.

After the floors and walls were finished, tables, cupboards, and chairs were constructed. While doing this, each student learned about the measurements of furniture and how these are related to his or her own body. One student built a fine replica of the refrigerator.

After the analysis of the physical environment in terms of measurements, colors, ornaments, and equipment, the actual activities taking place in the classroom were analyzed. The students made a floor plan and started to indicate who was doing what in the classroom. They discovered areas which didn't change, like the reading area, and areas which were used in many different ways. The experience they obtained during these first few sessions was to be of later assistance in the design of the ideal classroom.

A period of brainstorming and sketching began. Each student had to make a floor plan for his ideal classroom. At the end of the session everybody explained his design to the group. One student, Peter, previously had destroyed his work immediately after he had finished it. The group asked him to save his drawings this time and spontaneous applause rewarded his description of his efforts. During this session two students worked with Tom Baker, a headmaster from England who was visiting the school. Baker made a match program out of the design task by emphasizing proportions, scale, and volumes.

When it was announced that at the next meeting everybody had to design different floor plans, the students protested loudly. It was difficult to convince them that a good architect develops many alternative plans before he decides what he wants to build. The next session was used to develop these alternative floor plans and many interesting new ideas appeared.

In order to influence the students to conceptualize their classroom as a part of a whole school, wooden blocks and old cans were introduced to help them build a model of their own school building. The students constructed different shapes with the blocks and cans and made sketches of the different constructions. Everybody had to submit his favorite floor plan and the two best were to be selected by group vote. But before the vote, each floor plan was built in a professional scale model (developed at S.U.N.Y. at Stony Brook). This helped the students to judge and conceptualize each other's floor plan. After the vote, the students started to build the two winning designs in cardboard.

The winning project was a classroom in the shape of a circle which was divided into six sections. Each section had to be used for a specific activity. It is interesting to   note that this architect introduced a special area for visitors.

The second best was a classroom which was heavily oriented towards the outside. This architect designed big bay windows to bring the room as close as possible to the nature outside. A third design was an attempt to change the organization of the classroom. The architect proposed to build smaller classrooms to improve the quality of the program. He designed a classroom for eight to ten students and one student teacher as a coach.

The election itself was a difficult operation. At first, everybody wanted to win. But when it was made clear that the losers were not bad architects, everybody agreed to help in the evaluation of the designs. It was emphasized that the group was working as a team and not as competing individuals. A period of hard work began. The students cooperated in building the two winning designs out of cardboard. The supervisor did the cutting, but all the other work was done by the students. Two models of an ideal classroom and one model of a futuristic school were completed. The students landscaped a garden for the school building.

The project was finished with a meeting in which the whole class (n = 29) participated. Before the final meeting took place, all the students in the class had made a floor plan of their own room at home. For the final meeting they designed their ideal room in which they would like to live and to sleep. Sitting in a circle, the students worked for one and a half hours on this task. At the end of this last session each student presented his design to the other students, and the students frequently applauded each other.

The effects of the training on the behavior of the students were evaluated in three different ways. First, two architects were requested to review all the floor plans the students in the whole class had made. The architects did not know which students were trained and which were not. Both architects are experienced teachers in the Technical University Eindhoven (The Netherlands) and have reviewed the architectural designs of many students for several years. They were asked to determine the skillfulness with which the floor plans were made. Both reviewers were allowed to give their own dimensions to the question: "How skillful is this designer?"

The 24 designs were ordered according to the obtained scores and the Mann Whitney U test was used to test for a difference between the ranking of the trained group ($n=6$; H_0, $\alpha \leqslant 0.01$; one tailed) and the ranking of the control group ($n=18$). According to the scores of architect A, the difference between the two groups was significant at the 0.01 level (architect A; obtained $U=16$; $p(U \leqslant 19)=0.01$.) The rankings according to the scores of architect B for the two groups were significantly different at the 0.001 level (architect B; obtained $U=9.5$; $p(U \leqslant 10) =0.001$.)

It may be concluded that the trained group designed better floor plans than the control group. The results also show that the trained students were able to utilize their newly learned skills to solve a new problem. Neither group had ever worked on a design for a bedroom or a livingroom, nevertheless the trained group did significantly better on this task.

We also computed the Kendall rank correlation for the scores of the two architects. We found $\gamma = 0.59$ (n=24) . If we test the significance of $\gamma = 0.59$ under the Ho, the scores of architect A and B are not correlated; we find $p < .00003$. We may conclude that the rankings of both architects are interrelated. Both architects were looking for design skills developed by the students. It is likely that instructing reviewers about the specific skills to look for would result in a higher correlation between the ranking of different reviewers.

In the second evaluation it was hypothesized that a "trained" student would draw more <u>elements</u> in his floor plan. An element involves separate units like doors, a wall, or chairs, which taken together comprise a floor plan. It should also follow that a "trained" student would draw more of the <u>basic elements</u> in the floor plan of his or her bedroom than a student who had not been trained. The following elements are considered to be basic for a floor plan of a bedroom: walls, windows, entrance, chair or bench, bed, desk or table, closet, light fixture, and a bathroom or washstand.

The Mann Whitney U test was used to test for a difference between the average number of elements and of <u>basic elements</u> placed by the students of the two groups in their floor plans. Ho (no difference; $\alpha \leqslant 0.01$; one tailed). The results confirmed both hypotheses. (Obtained U=13 all <u>elements</u> included; U=12.5 <u>basic elements</u> included; $p(U \leqslant 19 = 0.01)$. The "trained" group drew both more <u>elements</u> and more <u>basic elements</u>. The training had given them a broader repertoire of elements to consider and gave them a feeling for the basic elements to place in a floor plan of a bedroom.

The third evaluation involves the analysis of stories written by the students. A few days after the final meeting of the architecture group, the teacher asked her students to write a story with the title "The whys of my ideal bedroom." Sixteen students wrote stories. A content analysis of the stories showed that the students very frequently used the words bed and T.V. (in seven of the sixteen stories). They also used the words desk and corner frequently (in five of the sixteen stories). A corner was often used to place a piece of furniture.

We will quote two stories to give the reader an idea of the quality of the stories which the students wrote. The first story was written by Tom, a "trained" student, and the second by Jackie, who was not trained. Both students drew floor plans which were ranked very high by both architects. Tom's floor plan ranked as 20 and 21, 24 being the rank for the best design. Jackie's floor plan was ranked as 21 and 20.

Tom's story:

> I put the bed there because I wanted to. The bed is a bunk for me and my brother. I put the bookcase near the bed so I can grab a book. All my clothes are near me so I can get them easily. The t.v. is facing the bed so I can watch t.v. in bed. I want it there so I can get to it quicker. I put my desk near a window so I have light when I work. It is the same with the research table. I have

chairs so I can sit down. I have a storage space for scissors, pencils, etc. and other things I put in there are my toys (darts, pivot pool). I also put some in the toychest and in the closet. I can practice jumps, flips, turns, spins, etc. and I have a little place to hide for when I play hide and seek, and I have lots of room to walk around." (Story from Tom, third grade student, trained group)

Jackie's story:

Why did I put a candy store in my bedroom? Because then I could just have control and push the candy store button and eat whatever kind of candy I want. Instead of going through the halls and my mother telling me not to eat any candy. Why did I put a pingpong table in my room? Well it is almost the same as the candy store. I put it in my room because of going through the halls and going downstairs. Why did I put little claws? For my homework because I hate homework." (Story from Jackie, third grade, not trained)

Tom gave a much more detailed rationale for his decisions than did Jackie. During the design process of the ideal classroom, the implications of the different proposed floor plans were discussed many times. Tom picked up many of the rationales which he learned and used to defend his floor plan for his ideal bedroom.

It is possible to teach third grade students in the necessary skills to design a new environment. They are able to utilize the new learned skills to solve different problems. The reviewers of the floor plans made us aware of the necessity to train the students for a longer period in the use of proportions and scale. They also recommended training the students to work with colors and to give them a feeling for a possible use of different levels in a design. Third graders can be trained as environmental designers. They are very interested in their environment and love to learn more about it. They will work very intensely and will become involved in the change process.

Environmental design and open education come together when students learn the basic skills which are necessary to make decisions concerning change in their own environment. Their classroom should be a starting point for studies in math, language, sciences and social sciences. The knowledge and skills obtained from studies of small scale environments could be extended to study, design and change of the larger school environment. This would prepare students for life and help them to take responsibility for the improvement of the environment they have to live and work in. Students trained in such a school environment would be ideal partners in the design process of their home, street, neighborhood, community, school, hospital, town hall, and work environment.

12 Environmental Design in Alternative Societies: Children's Village

Leonidas Castro-Camacho

Children's Village represents a fascinating example of a program influenced by the general environmental design orientation. As detailed as the chapter is on the development of this particular "community" it still is only an introduction to the growing field of endeavor in which the planning of a "community" is the intervention procedure used to solve individual and/or societal problems. Eventually, there should be a spate of reports evaluating and comparing such programs.

In viewing the planning and development involved in Children's Village as prototypical of the environmental design approach, we particularly note two aspects of the program: the involvement of the recipients of the design (in this case the children and youths) in the planning process, and the clear implication throughout that the designing of the environments is an ongoing process rather than the designing of a complete entity called Utopia.

Ed.

The concept of environmental design, as shown in previous chapters, has several important implications for the analysis and modification of human behavior. By changing the immediate focus of interest from behavioral events to environmental variables, there is a shift in emphasis from the identification of behavior problems and the development of procedures for their modification to an emphasis on the analysis and design of environmental influences on human behavior at

* I am indebted to the citizens and members of Children's Village and to its Director, Father Javier de Nicolo, who kindly provided information and suggestions for the preparation of the present chapter. I thank William Hutchison and Claire De Zubiria for helpful comments in the elaboration of the manuscript.

large. This implies not only a broadening of targets of intervention but also different approaches in applied programs. It is a further departure from the medical model in terms of reconceptualization of influence processes – a movement which was initiated by behaviorists but is now, paradoxically, resisted in some respects by them. Another dimension of this new approach is its emphasis on social intervention and design of communities rather than just the behavior of individuals.

The present chapter represents an attempt to integrate many of the concepts dealt with in other parts of the book around the framework of an existing environmental design program, an experimental community for children and adolescents. Although interest in the design of communities and societies is now new, many formulations have been either literary or fictitious, and few systematic attempts have been made to utilize scientific principles in the process of developing and planning communities. One of the most influential works in initiating concrete attempts was Walden Two (Skinner, 1948). Although this book was still "fiction," it opened the possibility, at least in theory, of incorporating principles derived from the experimental analysis of behavior to the design and planning of microsocial systems.

The first attempt to make Walden Two real was made in 1967 by a group of eight persons who had been influenced by Skinner's formulation. The Twin-Oaks Community (Kinkade, 1973a, 1973b) represented an alternative way of life and, to a certain extent, an experiment in environmental design. Its main characteristic was its purported reliance on Walden Two after which it was designed.

A second attempt to incorporate principles of behavior analysis in community design was made by a behavioral psychologist, Roger Ulrich, in Kalamazoo, Michigan (Ulrich, 1973, 1974, 1975). In 1968, he and a group of students initiated a project in environmental design and early education. Learning Village was a pre-elementary program for children from the age of two months to two and a half years with the goal of enhancing an adequate behavior repertoire through a favorable physical and social environment. The success of this initial attempt led them two years later to expand the scope of experimental living to a community for adults. Lake Village had to overcome a great number of difficulties before it became relatively stable. However, this represents a clear illustration of the nature of difficulties involved in the development of a community. Ulrich expressed this some years later:

> The problems of just financing Lake Village are tremendous. Then there are interpersonal problems. Although it may be possible to quantify and analyze these problems, I don't have the time and I don't know who does. Lake Village is not Walden Two, just as Twin-Oaks is not Walden Two. There is no Walden Two nor will there ever be. . . .This is not to say that the principles of behavior aren't working. It is simply saying that there is no Frazier who understands totally what is happening or who is in total control, and has predicted or quantified ahead of time what's happening. (Ulrich, 1974b, p. 5, emphasis in original)

This conclusion illustrates the high degree of complexity involved in the development of experimental communities. Although Ulrich is not arguing against the feasibility of such projects, he does indicate the limitations of systematic analyses within this context.

A third illustration of attempts to systematically apply behavioral principles to community living is represented by the Achievement Place project in Kansas (Phillips et al., 1972). Unlike the two previous examples, which were more concerned with the development of an alternative way of life, this program has a mainly remedial objective aimed at reeducating a group of predelinquent, problematic youths. Although it was not designed as a commune, aspects of community life and socialization through behavioral methods are especially relevant to this chapter's analysis. Achievement Place is similar to Children's Village described in this chapter. The main vehicle of change is through design of social and motivational environments, and the community is organized around a structure of small groups of youths led by trained teaching parents. Although its efficacy has been repeatedly demonstrated (e.g. Fixsen & Wolf) through carefully designed experiments and the model is extending throughout the United States, the program is still problem oriented and does not claim to offer alternatives to education.

Children's Village, our focus of interest in this chapter, has several resemblances to the above mentioned programs. However, it also shows certain unique characteristics which make it a very relevant example of the environmental design approach.

First, the program is being implemented in Bogota, Colombia, thus providing an opportunity to analyze the role of an environmental design program in the process of a nation's development. Since environmental design is concerned with social influences at large, this description will offer some illustrations about the way in which planned influence is designed – although not entirely achieved – in Children's Village.

A second fundamental feature of this program is its user. Children's Village has been designed to provide an alternative mode of education for children living in the streets of Bogota. They have abandoned or been abandoned from their homes since their early years and have lived in the streets exposed to an extremely hostile and demanding environment. They have engaged in petty robberies, thefts, and other antisocial activities resulting in further rejection by society. In summary, they constitute a unique example of very flexible and adaptive – although not accepted – behavior, given the very special environmental conditions to which they have been exposed.

This chapter will show an alternative way of designing environments and the role of social systems in the production of this problem, as well as the social responsibility of the environmental designer for implementing effective methods for the influence and change of social systems. Therefore, the focus will not be the behavior which has been labeled abnormal or antisocial but, rather, the modification of the social matrix which led to that kind of behavior.

Children's Village represents an attempt to design a total environment, a small community. It demonstrates the usefulness of integrating all possible elements of the environmental complex in a unified and coherent program. Integrated design of the physical environment – the social structure, environmental contingencies, the economic variables, and the political systems – results in a small-scale experiment in social systems, an experiment which may have implications for the society at large. This integrative feature of environmental design should be emphasized since it is one of the main loci of difference from previous approaches.

One of the most valuable characteristics of this program is its continuous emphasis on experimentation and change. This design did not follow a preconceived outline about the way environmental programs should be carried out, according to specific theories or individuals. There are no definite answers in that respect, and restriction to specific models may interfere with the possibility of developing new trends and ideas. This does not mean that the usefulness of other approaches has been ignored. In fact, several authors (such as Makarenko, Piaget, Skinner, Freire, Lewin, St. John Bosco, Mounier, and others) have had definite influence in the design; and procedures derived from social psychology, behavior modification, open education, and other areas have been incorporated into the program. Therefore, one of the main keys for the success of the design is its continuous reliance on empirical facts as criteria for implementing specific procedures.

As a necessary consequence of the latter, the environmental design program is a continually changing process rather than an end product, static system. This dynamic characteristic should be emphasized since it represents a further innovation over previous approaches. We could conceive of environmental design as a process of designed change, although the final result toward which the system is moving may be uncertain (at the preliminary stages of the design). To some extent, the environment determines the direction of change.

This particular program is not problem oriented with respect to individuals. Unlike other approaches concerned with the modification of specific problematic behaviors, the present approach is concerned with offering an alternative way of education which may influence the process of social change. A problem such as children living in the streets is a social, environmental problem rather than an individual one, e.g., predelinquent or disturbed children. Therefore, the solution should be formulated in environmental and not individual terms, although the latter may change as a consequence of redesign of environment.

Finally, behavior influence in this program is based on "positive" not "aversive" procedures. Therefore, participants of the program stay because they find the new environment more attractive than their current options and not because they anticipate negative consequences if they choose not to stay. This has a very important implication in terms of the design of an environment which is highly reinforcing for its individual users.

ORGANIZATION OF THE CHAPTER

Considering the broad context is crucial in any attempt to redesign an environment. Therefore, the description starts by presenting a general view of some historical, social, political, and cultural influences that resulted in the social phenomenon of children living in the streets. This will serve as a general framework within which the environmental design will be developed. A detailed description of current environmental influences and behavioral characteristics of the children will be offered in the subsequent section. After considering social and individual elements of the current situation, the focus will be on the description of the program.

For purposes of clarity, the program will be presented in a longitudinal way with emphasis on selected aspects in each stage. We will cover the period from the time the child is first exposed to a new environment until he is incorporated into the social system. This approach facilitates the analysis of sequential changes in the program as well as relationships between diverse stages and among several environmental interventions within the same stage. Some of the ethical and social implications of this approach will be discussed, not to provide straightforward answers but to highlight the social responsibility inherent in an environmental design program.

ENVIRONMENTAL DESIGN AND SOCIAL CONTEXT

One of the most fundamental but most easily neglected steps in the process of environmental design is the careful consideration of the different sources of influence from the general environment which give rise to a specific social phenomenon. This will always be a relevant factor, irrespective of the scope of a particular program – from the design of a controlled environment for an individual, to the careful planning of a classroom environment to improve learning conditions, to the design of a community or a political system. There will always be an "outside" or broader environment within which the specific design will be functioning – a psychiatric hospital, a school district, or a nation. Environmental design does not operate in a social vacuum; and to the extent that social, political, and economic variables are overlooked, the implemented design will be likely to be simplistic, if not irrelevant to the required needs.

In the case of Children's Village, social, political, and economic variables become especially relevant. They provide bases for understanding the confluence of these different factors resulting in the children leaving their homes and living in the streets and the current variables maintaining that state of existence.

History Of A Social Problem: "Gaminism"

Gamin is the colloquial label assigned by society to children living in the streets. The social phenomenon of about 5,000 of these children living in the streets of Bogota and other cities of Colombia can be traced back to the beginnings of this century, even though the dimensions of the problem have increased in the last decades. The determinants of this situation represent a complex net of confluent factors: sociological, demographic, economical, political, and cultural. Although a detailed analysis of them is beyond the scope of this chapter, at the risk of oversimplifying, some of the more salient factors will be outlined.

Migration from rural areas to the main cities has been repeatedly pointed out as one of the main causes of gaminism (Granados, 1974). This process has been increasing and is, in turn, related to political and economical variables. From the former perspective, political violence in the rural areas of Colombia that reached its critical point in the late 1940s and early 1950s (Guzman et al., 1962) led many peasant families to migrate to urban areas looking for safety and protection. Colombia, like many other developing countries, is characterized by a marked imbalance between rural and urban development. Progress in technology, culture, education, and general improvement of living conditions are mostly confined to urban areas. The rural counterpart has been bypassed. Advocates in communication media and transportation have presented the "advantages" and greater comforts of the city to the country person. This, however, is a mere illusion since most migrants are lacking in the necessary skills to perform many kinds of jobs in the city, most of their previous experience being largely confined to agriculture.

The imbalance existing between urbanization and industrialization has resulted in a high rate of unemployment. This, added to cultural characteristics and lack of birth control, produces a situation conducive to the phenomenon of children living in the streets. Migrants usually have to live as aggregates in the urban complex, forming what has been called "misery belts" around the city in conditions of overcrowding and misery; a house originally built for five persons is actually sheltering up to ten families with an average of seven members per family (Granados, 1974). Incidence of delinquency is very high in these ghettos providing many modeling opportunities for young children. From their early years, they learn delinquency pays off both in terms of economics and with respect to power positions within the social group. A high incidence of alcoholism among the parents and the resultant abuse and violence eventually leads to children abandoning home and parents or, in many cases, being thrown out by parents or stepparents. In a sociological study about children in the streets in Bogota, Granados (1974) reports that only seven percent of their parents had been born in the city, although approximately 50 percent of them were residents of Bogota. The average number of siblings of these children is six and about 60 percent of their parents are separated. Almost 60 percent of the interviewed children reported that the reasons for leaving their homes were physical abuse and violence.

This brief account of the development of gaminism as a social problem clearly indicates the role of the social system at large in the appearance of the problem. It also points to the fact that, although attempts may be addressed to remediate individual elements of the problem, the core causes can only be attacked through large-scale changes in the sociopolitical system.

Environment And Behavior Of The Gamin

After considering some of the determinants of "gaminism" as a social phenomenon our next step in the environmental design process is to analyze its individual dimension. We will examine current environmental influences, activities, and behavior of children in the streets as well as the process through which society came to label them with the contemptuous term of "gamin."

When a child leaves home, he may turn to his peers in the streets who may invite him to join the gallada, a group of about seven to ten children who spend most of their time together. The gallada functions as the primary social group providing protection and organization of activities such as planning and execution of small robberies. The group is headed by a chief who is usually the oldest and strongest. At night, they sleep in a group called camada to warm each other and protect themselves from other groups. Activities are generally unstructured and, to a large extent, depending on immediate conditions and contingencies. Frequent behaviors include begging, trash salvaging, singing at theater doors or in buses, and engaging in petty theft, pickpocketing, purse-snatching, stealing windshield wipers, brake lights, or radios from cars – which are sold later for money. The children are usually seen riding through the city hanging from the backs of trolley buses or simply playing around in parks or alleys. Gutierrez (1967) describes them in the following terms:

> The gamins are characterized by rebellious behavior, and seem to have defeated the capacity of Colombian society and the state to keep them within the boundaries of established norms. These homeless children live in the streets, constantly harrassing the police and annoying the public. They sleep in public areas, and walk around half-naked and filthy. They beg, singing at theater exits, and offer to perform small jobs such as guarding cars in parking areas or shining shoes, as well as trying to sell lottery tickets or newspapers. Rather than appealing to the public's generosity, they rely on annoyance, and their attitude is aggressive and defying. (P. 9, translated from Spanish)

In general, their behavior could be characterized as generally aggressive, violent, and immediatist; they live for the moment, unconcerned about eating the following day. Many of them use marijuana and sniff gasoline on a regular basis. They spend most of their time in commercial areas of the city and "hot areas" frequented by delinquents and prostitutes.

From a traditional perspective, this behavior could easily be labeled as abnormal, maladaptive, antisocial, or predelinquent. However, taken in its environmental and social context, it is clearly the product of the prevailing environmental conditions. Furthermore, it is an example of highly adaptive behavior in an extremely adverse environment. Otherwise, survival would not be possible. Our approach was that these are not abnormal children; the abnormality lies in the environment. Their behavior is maintained both by primary needs to survive and by social contingencies from the peer group. The conceptualization of their behavior not only as normal but as adaptive has very important consequences in terms of available alternatives. Nevertheless, saying that this behavior is adaptive at an individual level does not necessarily mean that it is desirable at a social level. That implies that the rehabilitation or remedial approach is irrelevant and misleading and that any intervention should be addressed to the environmental influence. This has not always been the case, and in the next section some of the previous approaches in this direction will be discussed.

Previous Approaches And Proposed Solutions

Proposed solutions to the problem of children living in the streets have ranged from highly individualized modes of treatment derived from the medical model to large-scale social changes proposed by some political radicals. Each proposed alternative assumes a different model about the nature and origins of the phenomenon and, therefore, to a certain extent, this section is dealing with different conceptualizations of gaminism.

The first approach to the problem of gaminism is based on the medical model which views these children's behavior as abnormal and produced by a basic personality disorder (Ballesteros, 1968; Beltran, 1970). According to the proponents of this theory, this disturbance is rooted in the early years of life, or even before. These children have been rejected, and economical and family tensions produce an extremely high level of stress in the pregnant mother which may have irreversible consequences in later development of the child's personality. One implication of this is that the child will never be normal. Furthermore, as soon as the infant is born, he will perceive the feelings of rejection by his parents. Therefore, besides organic damage caused by birth traumas, malnutrition, and poor prenatal conditions, abnormalities in personality development will likely be present. Beltran (1969), for example, characterizes the phenomenon of gaminism in terms of a basic trilogy. First, the mental pathology of these children in which the intrapsychic conflict is dominant; second, pathology of the family plays a fundamental role in the development of his personality; and third, deficits in the educational system complete the causal structure of the problem. According to this author, children in the streets are the product of social segregation and rejection, and they are at a disadvantage because of mental deficiency, chronic brain damage, or severe neurotic conflicts. They spend their early years of life in abnormal homes which show a greater incidence of disorders affecting family stability. At a certain point in their development, they suffer an

existential crisis with severe regression characterized by a confrontation between ego forces and their subjective world resulting in their
values being dominated by the primary process and their structure by
the pleasure principle.

This conceptualization in terms of abnormality led to an intervention consistent with the theory. The child should solve his basic conflict
through psychotherapy. Therefore, some of the state programs relied
heavily on the provision of individual psychotherapy in institutions in
care of these children. Nevertheless, despite the fact that a considerable amount of time, professional effort for psychodiagnosis and
psychotherapy, and money were invested, results were clearly disap-
pointing both from an individual and social point of view. To some
extent, this conclusion may be extended to other nonpsychoanalytic
individual approaches.

A second approach, and the most common, is what could be termed,
the rehabilitation approach. The very term "rehabilitation" clearly
relates it to the first approach since rehabilitation implies abnormality.
Unlike the previous model, however, abnormality does not have an
intrapsychic connotation but a legal one. These children are, therefore,
considered predelinquents needing rehabilitation, ideally in an institutional setting. Most of the existing institutions have a correctional goal,
serving the functions of reception, observation, and rehabilitation.
They are sponsored by the state or by private foundations. According to
Granados' data, there are currently 23 institutions in Bogota with the
primary goal of treatment and rehabilitation. Interestingly, only 8.7
percent of them accept children on a voluntary basis; most of them
admit children referred by juvenile courts or the police which means
that staying in the institution is mandatory. These settings may host up
to 3,000 children; in 1973, 2,500 children were confined. Most of them
offer food, bed, educational, medical, and psychiatric services. However, there are several limitations which restrict the influence and
effectiveness of these settings. There is a lack of coordination among
the different programs and poorly defined objectives in most of them.
Without definition of long-term goals or planning of transition of the
child to the "outside" world, any efficacy they may have is not reflected
in life outside the institution. Finally, concentrating on the individual's
problem without taking into account the social dimensions of the
situation makes this kind of intervention superficial and socially
ineffective.

A third alternative is the extreme opposite of the previous one; i.e.,
concern for the social dimension at large with little regard for the
individual aspects of the children. According to proponents of this
approach, if children in the streets are the product of an inadequate
social system, then the system must be radically changed. Furthermore,
any attempt to improve the condition of the children would be seen as
instrumental in maintaining the system.

This approach is the most congruent with an environmental design
perspective. However, there are important differences in degree of
emphasis placed on both the immediate dimensions of the problem and
the individual needs of the youths, as well as in the level of

intervention.   In the next section we will concentrate on a more detailed description of the program.

A CASE HISTORY IN ENVIRONMENTAL DESIGN

Historical Background And General Overview

The original idea and the fundamental elements of the design and development of Children's Village to a great extent are due to its Director, Father Javier de Nicolo. In order to trace the origins of the program, therefore, we will discuss some antecedents of its main influencer.

Father de Nicolo, a Salesian priest, has been actively involved in educational projects with youths and children for several years. In 1965, he and a group of colleagues organized a study group to critically evaluate formal education. They soon became aware of the need to go beyond theoretical analyses, and to undertake concrete projects in order to offer a feasible alternative to the inadequacies of traditional systems. In 1968, he became Chaplain of one of the juvenile prisons in Bogota which had a very high population of children from the streets. There he became repeatedly frustrated in his attempts to influence these youths through talks and other methods of interaction. The atmosphere in the prison was aggressive and violent, and behavior was controlled only by anticipation of punishment. He soon realized that his action was completely futile and in such an environment, without a radical change in environmental conditions, nothing could be achieved. Therefore, with the cooperation of a psychologist and the director of the prison, he began to attempt new methods of intervention. Their first attempt was to change the environment of a group of boys for a limited time. Since this was impractical in the prison setting, they organized a three-day picnic to a summer house out of town for a group of 33 boys. They gave them new clothes and programmed several activities (lectures, discussions, and recreation) in a nonthreatening atmosphere. The outcome of the experience was impressive. The same youths who displayed aggressive and violent behavior in the prison were now participating in the discussions and actively cooperating with the group in different activities.

The sharp difference in behavioral patterns in the same youths across different situations convinced Father de Nicolo about the role of environmental influences and the external determinants of behavior. He then decided to work directly with children in the streets rather than continuing in the prison setting. He repeated this experience with several groups of children and started to develop the idea of a designed environment, establishing a dormitory facility that he called Liberia to accommodate a small group of children. He still wanted to pursue his more ambitious idea of a large-scale, designed environment, and after several failures to get cooperation by state agencies, he decided to initiate a program on his own. However, in 1970 he received a formal offer from the Institute of Social Welfare, an official agency of the local government within the District of Bogota, to organize a program for the protection of abandoned children. They gave him carte blanche in organizational and administrative matters and financial aid from the lottery of Bogota and the telephone company.

The first stage of the program was initiated through the opening of three main locations: Bosconia – dormitories and main living facility, strategically located in a highly dense area in the city; Chibchala – the workshops located in a residential area in the south end; and, La Arcadia – the school, located in an adapted farm in a rural area near the city. These three locations and their corresponding activities comprised the first stage of the program. Children and youth, aged six to seventeen years were admitted on a voluntary basis with Bosconia as their home base while alternating school and workshop activities every other day. In the meanwhile, the physical setting for the second stage, a small village especially designed for the purpose of the community, was being built in the National Park of La Florida, near Bogota. Children's Village was inaugurated and opened for service in 1974 when the first group of youths who had completed the first stage of personalization in Bosconia, moved to La Florida to begin their formal training in social structure and community living.

The third and last stage of the program is Suamox – an industrial village currently being planned and expected to develop in the very near future. After completion, this village will provide qualified technical training to the youths who have completed the two previous stages. A detailed description will be offered at the end of this chapter.

Following this brief, historical introduction and general outline of the longitudinal organization of the program, some administrative aspects and human resources available should be clarified. As described above, although this program is administratively dependent upon the Department of Social Welfare of the City of Bogota, its internal organization and design is autonomous. The Board of Directors includes the Mayor of the City of Bogota, the Secretary of Health, the Director of the Department of Social Welfare, the Director of the Children's Village Program, and two representatives of the city council. The internal organization of the program integrates administrative and technical elements. The General Director, Father de Nicolo, is in charge of the general organization and coordination of the program. As will be explained later in the chapter, administrative staff includes skilled professionals as well as community youths – depending on the degree of expertise required for the position. Decision making processes involve the participation of directors, staff, the children, and members of technical committees.

The staff is composed of directors, who are each assigned to different settings within the community, and educators, whose roles are those of primary mediators. There are two kinds of educators: interns and externs. The interns live in different settings within the community and there is usually one per dormitory. They are in continuous contact with the youths, teaching during the day at school and at night coordinating meetings and organizing activities in the living areas.

Extern educators are in charge of teaching activities in the regular day schedule. Some of them work at the school and some are instructors at the workshop. Several religious communities collaborate in the program as well. Their role is equally important since they also function as mediators. They are in charge of the coordination of service personnel, kitchen, and laundry, making their contact with youths continuous. Some of them are in charge of preschool levels and perform other educational activities. Additional staff oversee kitchen, garden, general maintenance, and security, and drive buses.

In terms of other human resources, the program counts on professional and technical advice from several sources. The technical advisory committee is a multidisciplinary team of professionals in the fields of psychology (including the author), sociology, education, economics, and related areas, who provide advice on assessment and intervention procedures. In the health area, medical and dental care are provided by qualified professionals. Finally, the program is assisted on technical aspects of workshop functioning and instruction by the National Service of Apprenticeship, SENA, which is the national agency in charge of providing technical and professional training in Colombia.

First Exposure To An Alternative Environment

One of the more basic and preliminary questions of the environmental designer is how to introduce an individual to a new environment. The conditions under which children in the streets are living and some basic features of the design, such as the voluntary entrance and permanence in the setting, make this problem especially difficult. On the other hand, most of the environmental interventions in further stages will be built upon this initial one — thus requiring even more careful design than this first introduction. One of the basic premises of the design is to offer an environment which is more attractive for the child than the one he is currently experiencing in contrast to the traditional method of institutional confinement. The goal of this first contact derives directly from that premise. Expose the children to the rewarding characteristics of the new environment and let him contrast both environments before he makes a choice. There are two specific steps involved in this process: first, to make him aware of the existence of an alternative environment, and second, to have him actually experience some of its contingencies.

Night visits to the camadas

One of the methods used to acquaint the children with the program is to visit them in their camadas. It will be remembered that the strategic physical location of some of the settings facilitates introduction to this program, especially considering that information spreads very easily among these children. However, as a more direct approach, a group of children and educators often go out late in the evening and establish contact with camadas. It should be pointed out that since they have been part of, or are very familiar with, that subculture, they can communicate easily on the children's own terms. This practice is known in the program as Operation Friendship which accurately describes the goal of the visits. To some extent, this is an initial exposure to the kind of social interaction which prevails in the different settings of the program.

The role of picnics

We already described, in the history of the project, the initial role of picnics as a form of microenvironmental design. Closely related to the role of the night visits, picnics serve the fundamental function of exposing the children to new and rewarding environments. Usually, during one of the visits to the camadas, it is announced that there will be a trip to one of the nearby towns with warmer weather where there will be swimming, playing with other children etc. They depart on a bus in the morning, spend the day in a summer house, swim and play, and return in the evening. It should be pointed out that children in the streets are not normally exposed to these kinds of activities and, therefore, this initial exposure plays an important function. Through the night visits and picnics, the children learn about the program and some of its activities.

The day care club

These methods present certain restricted elements of social environment and activities to the children. To some extent they take some elements of the environment to where the children are. The day care club, however, is a physical location which implies that the children are coming to the new environment where they are exposed not only to its physical elements but also to a broader range of activities. The club is located next to Bosconia in the center of the city. This is a relatively small space but includes playgrounds and sufficient space for the services provided. The club is open during the day and any child in the street has access to it. It may accommodate about 100 children per day. Besides recreational facilities, the following services are offered without any cost: medical service, dentistry, haircutting, laundry, and food. Furthermore, the children may take a warm bath; a luxury unavailable to them in the streets.

The function of this club is very important. First, it is easily accessible to the children of the streets due to its urban locale. It achieves the goal of exposing the children to some rewarding properties of the environment that had been unknown to them and fulfills certain needs such as medical and dental care. Second, it serves the function of introduction to Bosconia, the main living place of the program. Third, contact is established with leaders of galladas and other children so that night visits can be facilitated and the range of influence increased. The children begin to view the program as a positive experience. Interaction with children who are already participating in the program also serves as a very useful source of information. Finally, it facilitates the process of knowing potential applicants in advance.

We have reviewed some of the resources used to introduce a new environment to potential users. Emphasis has been placed on exposure to different elements of the new environment, many of which are rewarding. Methods of persuasion are overtly avoided and, on the contrary, the alternative of applying for admission is presented as a difficult one where one has to strive in order to be accepted. This represents a mechanism of introducing the new alternative through positive, not aversive, contingencies; a clear departure from more traditional methods of institutionalization. The continuous contrast between two environments — the streets and the designed environment — is a further element in the process of choice. To a great extent, this is also a process of natural self-selection and screening of future applicants.

Designing Transition Environments: Stage Of Personalization

One of the most challenging and fundamental steps in the process of design of an environment is the planning of the first transition to a new environmental complex. To a large extent, the success or failure of the program will be dependent on careful implementation during the transitional stage. The larger the extent to which the physical, social, or any other environmental element is redesigned, the more difficult the transition will be. This, therefore, calls for a careful programming of the change to maximize the likelihood of success of the design.

As may be expected, where physical and built environments, social structure, activities, and many other subtle elements of the environmental complex are modified, only a carefully designed transition environment will allow the success of further stages. This concept of transition environment merits further analysis since it pervades most stages of the program. We have already pointed out the importance of considering environmental design as a process of planned change, which implies that all elements and stages of the design constitute transition environments, within the continuous process of change. This applies not only to physical elements but to every single aspect of the environmental context. A transition environment, therefore, involves a gradual, stepwise process of fading into a new context. It keeps many of the structural and functional characteristics of the old environment, especially those associated with its reinforcing value, and introduces new changes associated with positive consequences as well.

Through this process of gradual implementation of environmental change, along with clearly specified contingencies analogous to the process of shaping of behavior, the new environment acquires positive valence and maximizes the likelihood of influence. To some extent, this may represent an extension to a more complex level of the findings in the animal laboratory about errorless learning in stimulus control (Terrace, 1966). In other words, by programming gradual changes in the environment, we may prevent the occurrence of "errors" in the new condition and, therefore, maximize the probability of influence. This process will be thoroughly illustrated in several descriptions.

This first stage also has the fundamental goal of enhancing personalization. Once the child enters the program, he will find new resources for effectively controlling his physical and social environment. A physical space under his control and a token account to his name are the new elements in his immediate environment. Moreover, he will have his role in the group and his social behavior will take on a new dimension. Communal behavior will begin to be facilitated and shaped, not only through the social structure of the community, but also through formal activities and contingencies which will be in effect during the rest of his stay in the program. A final goal is adequate training in academic and labor skills which will constitute the basis upon which his social influence will have a major effect in further stages so that when he eventually returns to the "outside society," he will be able to meet the challenge.

The process of entrance has several important characteristics which should be noted. Once the initial contact with the child has been established and he has been exposed to certain dimensions of the experiment, and after he has contrasted these new aspects with his environment in the streets, he may choose to request admission to the program. As mentioned earlier, this is presented as a difficult target which requires effort to attain. There are no specified requirements for admission beyond the necessary condition that the applicant is, in fact, a child living in the street. Once he is admitted, he is assigned to an already formed group of children who have some experience in the program. As will be explained later, this is a very important resource, facilitating learning through social imitation. However, after one month's participation in the program, the child is usually asked to leave! He is, therefore, going back to the streets after having had some experience in the program. This procedure has very important implications since it is related to the role of contrasting two environments in environmental choice. It is assumed that one of the most effective ways to assess an environment is through a process of contrast with other environments. Only after the child has had experience in the streets, the program, and in the streets again, and has established a clear comparison of both environments is he admitted to the program on a permanent basis. Usually a small percentage of the children who are asked to leave remain in the streets while most of them request to be admitted once more. This is also a very effective way of screening through environmental procedures. Since it is very difficult to identify good predictors on an a priori basis with these children, this self-selection procedure has clear advantages for future outcome.

Fading Into A New Physical Environment: Maintaining Openness

The fundamental influence of physical and architectural environment on human behavior has started to gain recognition in recent years, among both behavioral scientists and architects (Canter, 1970; Canter & Lee, 1974; Hall, 1959, 1966; Moos & Insel, 1974; Proshansky et al., 1976; Sommer, 1969; Wohlwill & Carson, 1972). Since a close analysis of the diversity of ways in which built environments affect human behavior has been the topic of a previous chapter (Pomeranz, ch. 3), we shall focus on two dimensions of architectural design in the present section: first, the role of architecture in the establishment of transition environments; and second, the main relationships between specific physical settings and programmed activities during this first stage.

One of the essential requirements for the establishment of transition environments is a carefully detailed analysis of the prevailing environmental conditions of the future users, its more salient elements, and the possible aspects which may remain unchanged without interfering with the goals of the initial stage. In viewing some of these features in the environment of children in the streets, several elements may be pointed out. First, the environment is essentially urban and the child is used to the overstimulation of the city – crowding, noise, pollution, etc. Second, the child is living in an open environment. There is no physical location which he can identify with as his own and he is used to changing continuously his points of reference within the city, as prevailing conditions may require. Third, he is continuously moving throughout the city and a considerable amount of his daily life is spent in traveling from one end to the other in the city. Therefore, on the basis of these unique characteristics, the first stage of the program tends to provide a smooth transition to the physical environment. In order to maintain some of the more salient features of the child's environment, the program is not located in a single place but rather has several locations in various parts of the city. The children are, therefore, in a continuous state of mobility since they use all the locations.

In summary, the first stage of the program illustrates the concept of transition environment which was described above. Urban characteristics within the environment are maintained by the localization of the settings. Mobility and openness, which were very salient in the original environment, are also conserved through the distribution of dormitories, school, and workshops in different geographical locations. This provides the additional advantage of relating specific physical settings with certain activities which may provide a more effective control of physical environment on behavior. Next, this latter point will be expanded, providing a more detailed description of the main settings.

Bosconia, the main living setting, is an old four-story building, formerly a convent and later adapted and expanded to house about 250 children. The first floor includes space for administrative offices, service areas, kitchen, sports fields for soccer and basketball, a comfortable indoor room for games and TV, dining rooms with tables for seven children at each, and a bank where many transactions of the internal economy of the community take place. Upper floors include eight dormitories, each hosting approximately 30 children, bathrooms and showers. The library and the cooperative are housed on the third floor. It will be remembered that the day care club is located adjacent to Bosconia (Bello, 1973).

Liberia and Camarin are also dormitories located in different points in the city accommodating approximately 30 children each. Besides living facilities, they also include recreation areas and dining rooms. Children entering the program are usually assigned to these settings.

Chibchala represents the labor environment of the first stage. This is a two-story building providing space for workshops in each of the six areas of training. The first floor includes space for administrative offices and mechanics, ornamentation, soldering, and woodwork, while the second floor accommodates workshops for technical drawing, electricity, and painting, as well as the pre-apprenticeship laboratory. Sports fields and indoor recreational areas are also provided in this setting as well as a small dormitory for 30 children, kitchen, dining room, and service areas.

La Arcadia represents the school environment at the first stage and also the children's first introduction to a life within a rural setting and so prepares them for the final transition to the totally rural environment of the following stage at La Florida. Its location is in consonance with the open and self-active system which characterizes academic education at La Arcadia. This is a large farm adapted for the purposes of the program. The main house includes administrative and faculty offices, recreational space for indoor games, TV room, dining room, kitchen, and a dormitory housing about 30 children. Eleven classrooms are located in a prefabricated structure near the main house, each with a capacity to accommodate eight to twelve children. Space for special cultural activities, theater, and music are also available as well as sports fields, gardens, and panoramic surroundings.

This concludes descriptions of the physical settings within the first stage of the program. Our emphasis has been on the molar influence of the environment, mostly relating the transition of physical environments to specific activities. Most of the settings have been adapted for program purposes and none were especially designed or built for the community. Many details of the molecular environments were omitted since we will concentrate on these aspects in the description of the experimental community which was especially built for the purposes of the program. However, this first stage represents an illustration of the manner in which already-existing resources may be incorporated and integrated into the design of a new and total environment.

Fading Into A New Social Environment: Shaping Communitarian
Behavior And First Steps Toward Self-Government

Even though physical and architectural environment have a definite influence on human behavior, they are interrelated and, to a large extent, dependent on the impact of other environmental variables. As a physical framework, built environments may facilitate and maximize, or interfere with, the influence of other elements in the environment. Among these, the design and impact of the social environment are central in the present program. One of the most innovative and valuable contributions of this project is its integration of social structure within the general process of education. Along these lines, three main resources used in this stage to achieve the above-mentioned goals will be described: the social organization and structure of the community, the role of programmed activities as a vehicle for communication and social skills training, and the importance of the diverse administrative jobs and positions as a process of training in increasing responsibilities.

We have illustrated the point that physical features of the environment of children in the streets before entering the program should be carefully studied in order to design a physical transitional environment. To the same extent, one should study the social characteristics and organization of the children in the streets in designing an adequate transition to a new social environment. From the account of the social organization of children provided at the beginning of the chapter, several salient features may be pointed out. A structured social organization does exist in the streets, as shown by the existence of relatively permanent groups, the galladas, with highly specific goals and activities. Secondly, there are power structures based mostly on aggression and dominance. Thirdly, there is an implicit and strict set of norms which regulate relationships within and between groups, such as the "law of silence" which prohibits giving information about peers when interrogated by authorities. Violation of norms may have very serious consequences such as physical punishment or expulsion from the group. In a transition environment, therefore, many of these salient elements of the social organization in the streets which have a clear and specific adaptive value will be maintained in the program. Many of the goals will be reformulated, however.

The social structure of the gallada will consequently be maintained in the program in the form of a clan, a group of 15 children all sharing the same dormitory and all participating in the main social activity, the night meeting. This group constitutes the basic social unit of the community and the cornerstone of self-government in later stages. Every two clans living in a dormitory comprise a tribe. Since the role of the clan is essential in the design-at-large, several of its functions will be reviewed in more detail.

The clan is the main vehicle for socialization and integration to community life. There are several ways through which the group serves this function. First, as a social context it provides information about behavioral patterns expected in a given situation. This may be illustrated by the initial integration of the child into the program. A group of new children is not assigned to the same physical location because they would not get a clear discriminative content concerning expected behavior. Instead, each new child is assigned to an already existing group which has lived for some time in the program and which, therefore, offers continuous cues about behaviors, conditions, and consequences. Second, and closely related, the group may serve as a model through which subtle elements of new behavioral patterns may be effectively learned. Models have the dual function of instigating alternative ways of behavior and being an indirect source of contingencies through vicarious processes. The same conditions which influenced their behavior in the streets are now used to modify certain behavioral patterns in the new environment. In the same manner that they learned to control the environment in the streets through aggression and theft, best exemplified by the chief o the gallada, they now learn that these behaviors are no longer effective. They can see the cooperative and community-oriented behavior of the chief of the clan and of many members of the group. While the first two functions of the group are related to the acquisition of new behavioral patterns, the group as a source of peer reinforcement serves the function of maintenance of already acquired responses. It should also be pointed out that peer reinforcement is one of the main factors maintaining their behavior in the streets, and it continues exerting the same influence in the program.

Besides the implications inherent to the group structure, per se, the design and programming of social activities may increase considerably the reach of influence within the clan. The night meeting represents such an activity. Every night after dinner, members of each clan get together under the coordination of the chief and talk about different events of the day, personal problems, etc. Through this meeting, several important goals are attained. First, it serves as a vehicle for communication and problem-solving of personal and group conflicts. It also constitutes a training experience in communication and social skills. It was mentioned before that these children exhibit an overall aggressive style of verbal and nonverbal communication. Through continuous feedback from the educator, who usually attends meetings, and from other members of the group who model and role-play, communication patterns are gradually modified towards a more productive and socially acceptable style. Secondly, discussions at the night meeting are one of the main resources to reflect community-oriented values and to provide training experience in social organization and influence necessary for the stage of self-government. Some of the activities of the night meeting, such as distribution of responsibilities for maintenance and household matters, election of the chief of the clan and evaluation of his performance, problem solving and decision making in relation to individual or community affairs, and continuous monitoring of each member's behavior and change provide the basis upon which self-government will develop.

A further resource used to provide training in social influence and community behavior is the role of jobs and positions in the community. As will be described later, self-government requires a complex organization in which several members of the community have important responsibilities in terms of both organization and decision making. Therefore, beginning with the first stage of the program, a proliferation of "bureaucracy" is implemented. That is, many roles or positions involving diverse degrees of responsibility are created offering the opportunity to acquire the skills necessary for active participation in designing their environment.

Another important function of this organizational structure is that it offers incentives since most of the criteria for election are specified in behavioral terms. Consequently, the motivational nature of the system may have important effects in accelerating the process of change. The chief of the clan, for example, is a highly valued position which implies both modeling and social facilitation functions. The youth occupying this position is in charge of the internal organization of the group in terms of activities and coordination of night meetings as well as monitoring behaviors of members of the group and supervising maintenance duties. There are also several other managers in charge of facilitating the functioning of the program in areas such as dormitories, school, sports, workshops, etc. The dormitory manager is responsible for assigning and evaluating specific jobs for maintenance of the physical setting. The classroom manager is in charge of making instructional materials available, taking care of the physical rearrangement of the furniture as activities change, and so forth. Similar functions in terms of tools and materials are assigned to the manager of workshops. Other jobs include security and vigilance, giving information and guiding tours for visitors, cleaning common areas, gardening, etc. In every instance, prestige and value are usually associated with the degree of community service involved.

Designing a school environment: La Arcadia

The role of academic training is central in the present program, not only because it will be required for returning to live in society, but also because it is an integral part of the global educational process which will increase the range of influence on the social system. Nevertheless, in consonance with the goals and premises of the program, the school methods represent a clear departure from traditional methods in several senses.

First, the educational system at La Arcadia is characterized by being open. From a physical perspective, it is not accidental that the school is located in a rural area where many natural resources may be integrated into the learning process. The classroom, therefore, is not a restricted area for learning, but only one of many settings which may be used in the educational process. Field experiences and learning from the natural environment are advocated while the role of the teacher, rather than that of the traditional lecturer or provider of knowledge, is more that of a resource person who facilitates the active process of learning by the child. A second feature is the prevailing emphasis on learning by doing as one of the main principles of the educational experience, although it may be clear by now that this principle is not restricted to the school but underlies almost every activity in the program. As a necessary implication of this principle, the children use the surrounding environment, not strictly the classroom, as a laboratory. Biology and natural sciences are learned in the field, and notions of zoology are acquired by working with living animals. The educational process transcends the classroom space and time boundaries and becomes integrated with many experiences in daily life.

A third characteristic is the incorporation of the child's value system and conceptual universe in every aspect of the learning experience. Examples used in reading or writing are taken from the child's reality and not artificially drawn from textbooks. Fourth, the learning process at La Arcadia is integrated in contrast to teaching concepts as if they were independent entities. In teaching geometry, for example, the concept of the earth globe may be introduced and parallels and meridians explained which may lead to talking about the geographical situation of the country, history, and political organization, etc. (Bello, 1973). This approach has several advantages in training the child to establish continuous relationships among different learning experiences.

Finally, as an example of the tendency we have shown in several areas of the program to use positive rather than negative or aversive forms of influence, there is an explicit attempt to make the school environment a highly rewarding and "fun" experience. This has several implications for the methods used. The content of the curriculum has immediate relevance, if possible, so that the boys can apply what they have learned in their daily living. The traditional system of grades is eliminated and replaced by a self-paced, programmed model in which each child is responsible for his own unit and is able to monitor progress on a continuous basis. Unnecessary competition is eliminated and when comparisons are established, they are based not on the progress of other children, but rather in relation to previous performance of the same child.

In summary, the school system at La Arcadia is a reflection and extension of many of the principles working in other areas of the environmental design. The self-active system incorporates principles derived from a diversity of sources such as open education, programmed instruction, active learning, and others, and adapts them to the needs of the particular situation. As in other areas in the program, the school is evolving, and the system is undergoing continuous modifications.

Designing a labor environment: Chibchala

The heavy emphasis on physical work as a learning experience is one of the most important innovations of this program over traditional educational models. Its purpose transcends integration of training in labor skills as an essential element of the educational experience. School and labor activities are, therefore, closely interrelated and equally represented since all children and youths in the program spend every other day in each of these settings. As at school, learning by doing at workshops is a basic principle, and a positive, rewarding environment tends to prevail in all work activities. "Work as play" is one of the slogans at Chibchala which means that work should not only be accomplished but also enjoyed.

One function of this activity is to offer an experience in a labor environment and an exposure to the different elements of work as necessary to live in society. This is the first exposure to a way of life which is an alternative to the one experienced previously in the streets. The labor environment at Chibchala tends to be as realistic as possible, including even a salary (tokens of the internal economic system) for the amount and quality of work accomplished which may be used for basic needs and privileges. Through this means, the children are expected not only to learn the adaptive value of work but also to value it as a satisfying experience. This is a means of personal expression through creativity, also a way to appreciate the immediate use of their products in the community.

Besides experiencing work as an alternative way of subsisting, they are getting training in specific skills which serve as the basis for the more formal training and production in the third stage, at Suamox. Other activities inherent to work are also learned — group interaction and cooperation, task completion, self-control and self-discipline, continuous monitoring of work accomplished, personal responsibility, keeping schedules, and other pertinent chores which are of high, adaptive value outside in society.

A second, broad goal of work activities is training in community behavior and values. The youths realize that the product of their work is reflected in the benefit of the community in concrete ways. Most furniture used in Children's Village has been designed and built in the workshop which constitutes a clear demonstration of participation in community life.

The first exposure to a labor environment is made in the pre-apprenticeship laboratory where most children, lacking knowledge of work settings, experience manual work as play and creativity. There they are also introduced to some tools and materials and possible choices of work among the available alternatives. Although they have free choice, once a choice is made they are not allowed to change their area of concentration until the term is completed. After this initial phase, each youth works in one of the following areas: mechanics, electricity, ornamentation, soldering, technical drawing, woodwork, or printing. These were selected on the basis of their usefulness for specialized training at Suamox and the existing demands in the industrial world outside the community. A group of 15 children work in each area under an instructor with professional expertise in the specific field. Although they cannot make products for use outside the community because of administration and legalities, they do produce items such as beds, lockers, doors, tables, chairs, seats, blackboards, lamps, and other products found to be useful in different settings of the program.

Designing a motivational environment: The Florin

It has been repeatedly pointed out that a positive, rewarding environ-ment in all settings and activities should be the main means for maintaining youths in the program, overriding the value of alternatives. We will concentrate on some specific procedures which are being presented in order to illustrate some of the resources used to increase the positive value of this environment.

Social reinforcement plays a role in every activity of the program. Adults working in the program — educators, instructors, and staff — attempt to give continuous feedback and encouragement. However, sources of reinforcement are not limited to educators but, more importantly, also include peers. Some of these influences have already been considered in the context of social organization. The role of positions and jobs has also been mentioned as an important motivational element since it implies a greater amount and frequency of social reinforcement provided by the community in the form of leadership or "social prestige." A further motivational resource is what is known in the community as the "method of impact." The method is used when a positive event occurs in the community life, such as the election of a new mayor at Children's Village, or a negative event, such as a group of children dropping out. In order to emphasize these events, the routine of the whole community is interrupted and special activities, according to the nature of the event, are programmed. There is a salient mobilization of children and the environment clearly indicates the occurrence of a special event.

Although the wide variety of motivational resources outlined above are used in the program, we will concentrate here on the analysis of the internal economic system as a motivational factor.

Florin is the name of the internal currency used throughout the program. It may be one of the most useful but potentially counter-productive means, depending on the design of its implementation. The system was originally designed and implemented in the format of a token economy where points were delivered or withdrawn, according to specific behavioral targets, across all settings of the program: work-shop, classroom, dorm, bus, etc. However, it was later restricted to workshop and work-related behaviors. In its original format, the token economy presented enormous practical difficulties for implementation because the points, or florins, represented a real monetary value whose back-up was the budget from external sources of financial support. On the other hand, there was an increasing resistance by different participants of the program, including children and youths, because of the implications of rewarding behaviors which would not be maintained by the same contingencies in the real world.

Since generalization to the environmental conditions prevailing outside of the program is a basic necessity, it was decided to establish a system resembling as much as possible the natural environment. Therefore, the florin is currently being given at the workshop only, although it may be used in all settings of the program. Usually an average of 44 florins per day are available on the basis of work performance, completion of assigned work, quality, and social behavior and cooperation at that particular setting. At the end of each session, the instructor, in conjunction with the child, evaluates the child's performance and assigns the corresponding amount of florins. These are recorded in the individual card of each child as well as a report form which will be sent to the bank for the payment of the florins. Objectivity and clear specification of behavior targets are emphasized and carefully planned. Every week, the earned amount of points is reported to the bank which will reset the balance in florins in each child's account. At the end of each month, each child may exchange the points earned for the corresponding amount of florins which are specially designed bills in denominations of 1, 5, 10, 20, and 50. A certain percentage of florins, the "free florin," may be exchanged for real money and spent outside the community. This percentage may vary according to each boy, or to the number of activities scheduled outside the program in a given month.

Besides the obvious function of maintenance of labor behavior at the workshop and of incorporating the economic element to the work environment, the florin serves other very important functions in the program. First, it represents a system of acquired rights. One of the main disadvantages of the traditional institutional, or welfare, setting is that its paternalistic nature promotes mendacity and begging because of the availability of "free" services and benefits. Self-esteem and dignity in the users is thereby lost, since they perceive themselves as the recipients of charity. The florin system rejects this inhumane conception and introduces the concept of acquired rights which restores the feeling of self-esteem and dignity to the users. According to this, a fixed amount of florins is charged for the basic services of the program, housing and food, on a montly basis. If a boy does not earn enough florins to pay for these basics (which is very rare), he cannot stay any longer since it implies that his contributions to the community are less than what he is getting from it.

A second important role of the florin is that of facilitating communal behavior. Just as the economic system may promote competency and individual values and behavior, it may be used to enhance an opposite set of values. The Village utilizes a system of contributions to the community, analogous to taxes in the outside society. This means that the contribution to the community increases as the amount of florins earned increases. However, the child who makes larger contributions is entitled to the respect of his peers and the community at large. His name is written in the Golden Book of the Community and he is proclaimed to other members as a model of participation and interest in the community. His likelihood of being elected to important positions is, therefore, increased. Instead of interfering with the reinforcing value of the florin as a kind of response cost, the system of contribution to the community becomes a source of social reinforcement and recognition.

Another strategy used to increase the value of the florin is what has been called Factor C, C representing community. This is a group contingency whereby the purchasing value of the florin fluctuates as a function of overall behavior of members of the community. Therefore, if some negative behavior occurred, such as a fight, it would automatically be reflected in a devaluation of the florin. Positive events such as elections, new admissions, or improvement in social behavior, would be reflected in an increase in the purchasing value of the florin. Weekly fluctuations of the economy are published on the board at the different settings as well as the reasons for these fluctuations.

The florin may also serve a useful function of training in economic skills which will facilitate later functioning in the natural environment. For this purpose, most of the possible uses of florins as purchasing resources are facilitated in the program through the existence of the cooperative. This is a store where the children and youths can buy a variety of objects such as personal goods, soap, toothpaste, shoes, clothes, toys, games, etc. The value of this learning resource includes experiencing the purchasing value of money, the relative value of different objects, establishment of priorities, and self-control. Training in delayed consequences is a further by-product of this experience and the bank plays a fundamental role in this respect. Each boy has his own bank account where he can save "real money" – or florins – for later use. Finally, in spite of its restrictions to workshop activities, the florin may serve as an indirect way of assessment of community and social behavior.

Designing a leisure environment

Leisure time and activities also constitute an integral part of the designed environment both as a further educational resource and as a vehicle for personal development. Leisure may take many forms in the program including cultural activities, theater and music, recreation, sports, picnics and excursions, military exercises, and visits to the city.

Early exposure to the arts and cultural events is considered a high priority within the activities of the program. Dramatic arts and theater are especially favored since, besides their learning value, they facilitate personal expression and creativity which play a central role in the educational goals of the environment. Therefore, the boys participate in all steps of production: the writing of the script, rehearsals, choreography, costumes, and the final presentation on stage. Themes of scripts are often related to their life in the program in contrast to their previous life in the streets, serving conversely as a powerful source of influence on their values and behavior. Theater presentations are special events in community life, and all members attend and comment on the play. On certain occasions, people from the "outside" are also invited. Music is another frequent artistic endeavor and is formally taught for children who have shown special aptitude and interest. The youths have their own band and play for special community events.

Recreation and sports fill a high percentage of leisure time. Indoor games and TV are also provided in most settings, although sports represent the main recreational daily activity. Soccer, basketball, and volleyball are often enjoyed, and special championships, both within the program and with several schools of the city, are frequently organized. Social behavior and appropriate interaction are especially emphasized in all sport activities. Other physical activities include gymnastics and military games. Finally, during vacation periods, picnics and excursions to several places in the country are organized, not only as recreational experiences but as a learning opportunity outside of the physical setting. In addition, children are allowed to spend certain days in the city, usually on weekends, where they find their own recreation such as movies, walks, and activities of personal preference.

Designing An Experimental Community: Stage Of Socialization

The last section dealt mostly with the design of transition environments and the description and analysis of the first stage, emphasizing personalization as its main goal. We will now focus on an experiment in social systems which constitutes the main feature of the second stage of the designed environment. This does not mean that the stages are independent or unrelated, but rather, they represent consecutive loci of emphasis along the same continuum of planned change. That is, the same principles outlined in the introductory remarks hold in all the stages of the program, although the particular environment may be designed in such a way as to favor certain areas at different points in the process. For example, most of the activities described in the first stage, such as school and workshop, will still be in force. However, the social structure will be enhanced through a physical environment especially designed for that purpose, and a system of self-government will be instituted in order to make the already existing social structure more functional and salient. This second stage represents another dimension of environmental design which illustrates not only the integration and interrelation of several environmental elements, but also the continuity of the process of change.

In addition to the previously described goals of the first stage, socialization becomes the focus of action at Children's Village. This is not new, of course, since we have already examined the role of a designed social environment at Bosconia. What is new is that through the possibility of actively participating in the design and operation of a social system, this stage is providing valuable training in environmental design. The implications of this system for the later role of youths as behavioral influencers and social change agents constitute the long-term goal.

La Florida, the second stage of the program, is an experimental community which tends to be more independent and self-centered, both physically and functionally, than the other stages. The first phase at Bosconia was more integrated into the society because of its transitional nature, and the third stage at Suamox will also need to be in close contact with the community. This is like a parenthesis in the designed environment in which intensive training in social systems will be provided to enhance the long-term reach of influence.

In order to become a citizen of La Florida, the applicant must fulfill certain requirements in addition to having gone through the first stage at Bosconia. Citizens should be at least 13 years old and know how to read and write; they must have attended at least three community workshops (besides academic and workshop training) and have been outstanding members of the clan in terms of community-oriented values and behavior, cooperation, and group participation. Citizenship, granted after the applicant has spent a probation period in the Village, implies rights such as having access to physical facilities and services; to vote and be elected; to hold legislative, judiciary, or executive positions in the government; to participate and vote in the General Assembly; and to represent the community in cultural, social, civic, or sports events before the society at large. It also implies duties to fulfill and respect the Constitution, show respect for the community and its members, and participate in scheduled activities and in the process of government.

We will now concentrate on the description and analysis of two main innovations: first, the specific relationship between built environments and purposes of the design; and second, social structure and system of government in the community. The establishment of relationships between these two aspects will be clearly outlined as an example of the integrative nature of environmental design.

Built environment in relation to community structure

La Florida is a small village located in a rural area approximately 20 miles from Bogota, surrounded by a national park from which it derives its name. Unlike previously described physical settings, this was entirely designed and built for the purposes of the program so that it is a good illustration of how a built environment may be integrated in the design of a total environment. Emphasis is placed on the relationship between geographical, molar, and molecular elements of the environment and purposes and activities of this stage.

To reiterate the special characteristics of the first stage, a smooth transition to the new designed environment was facilitated by using settings that were located in the city, except for the school that was located out of the city to prepare the transition to this stage. On the assumption of success for this first arrangement, other priorities are established and consequent changes in the physical environment should follow. If we assume that attention to the social process within the community will be more likely in the absence of interfering social distractors, then physical isolation from other communities would seem ideal. Location of the community in a rural area should encourage a sense of autonomy and internal cohesion, hence facilitating the influence of the social structure and environment.

In terms of the organization of physical structures within the Village, most of the buildings are located in a circular arrangement surrounding a main plaza in the center. The 32 houses are distributed in groups of four, forming eight residential settings. This arrangement provides a degree of independence from the rest of the Village, although the areas are at the same time closely related through the plaza, the center of confluence of the built structure. The auditorium, administrative offices, governmental offices, bank and cooperative, post office, sound control, and reception area are all located in the main plaza, while the school and the cabildo, or Village Hall, are located on the side. Sports fields are behind the buildings. This starwise organization has several advantages. First, it facilitates the confluence of activities and provides a place for meetings in one specific location in the center, enhancing communication and interaction among members of the community living in different locations. To some extent, the distribution of the environment discourages isolation of groups and tends to direct activities toward interaction among groups. Second, it provides visual access to the whole setting from many different points in the Village which also facilitates participation in different community activities, since ongoing activities can be easily seen. Third, the architectural arrangement offers settings fostering interaction among youths in small, primary groups – e.g., the house and settings encourage interaction among members of different primary groups. The latter include informal settings like open spaces, plaza, and sports fields and structured settings such as the multiple room and the Village Hall. Finally, as in the previous stage, a clear relationship between physical location and activity tends to be preserved so that the architectural environment's controlling properties are enhanced.

Molecular-built environments, on the other hand, play a fundamental role in providing the framework within which most of the social organization takes place. The organization of living areas in small houses rather than in large dormitories or buildings is an essential requirement for enhancing the role of the primary group as the cornerstone and main functional unit of the community. The architectural design of the house, therefore, will have a great influence on the internal structure of such primary groups. Each of the three-story brick houses constitutes the living unit for a group of 15 youths. As pointed out earlier, furniture is made in the workshops while internal decoration is each group's responsibility. The first floor includes the living room, which is the main space for social interaction, including the night meetings and informal gatherings. The dining room, also located on the first floor, represents an important innovation over the previous stage in which the boys ate in large dining rooms. The experience of eating together as a group not only facilitates cohesiveness and group identity, but it also avoids the sense of anonymity involved in massive dining rooms. Meals are prepared in a central kitchen for the whole community and carried to each house in small cars by members of the civic service. Bathrooms are also located on the first floor. Second and third floors are dormitories, each one accommodating seven or eight youths. One interesting feature is the lack of walls within the house which tends to set up the conditions for social interaction at almost any time. Lack of privacy should be understood in the context of previous history and sociocultural variables previously discussed.

Since group cohesiveness, independent from the rest of the community, is not considered desirable for the purposes of the program, two resources of the physical environment have been planned to foster between-groups interaction. First, the organization of houses in groups of four forms a clearly defined neighborhood, and second, there is a special house at the end of each row which serves as a common recreational setting where indoor games and social gatherings among members of the neighborhood take place. Communication among inhabitants of different houses, therefore, is enhanced through the organization of activities in this common area of interaction. The central cafeteria, where the youths may have snacks and other meals at different times of the day, also serves a similar function.

In addition to living areas, academic settings such as classrooms and a library are also available in the Village. Community gathering meetings, on the other hand, are concentrated in two main places. The multiple room, located on the main plaza, is an auditorium-like structure with stage and balconies which, as indicated by its name, serves multiple functions such as group presentations, theater, concerts, church, voting place, and any other activity which involves the participation of a large group of citizens. The second community place is of great importance since it represents the seat of self-government, the Cabildo, or Village Hall. This is a circular, straw-roofed structure, reminiscent of the pre-Colombian temples built by the Indians. The Council of Chiefs, the representatives of the community, hold their regular meetings sitting in a circle of chairs identical to the ones used in the Congress of Colombia. Observers and visitors are usually seated in the outside rows of the circle. This setting is restricted to legislative or judiciary events.

We will not give detailed descriptions of other physical facilities; it suffices to mention the availability of space to be used by government executives such as the mayor and secretaries, justice officials, administrative and directive staff, professionals, health service personnel, and educators. Well-equipped, central kitchen, laundry, and other service areas are also available.

So far we have concentrated on the description of built environment of the Village as an important source of influence. An analysis was made of the role of geographical location, molar and general organization of buildings in the Village, and molecular environments and specific settings such as houses and community areas providing a physical framework setting up the occasion for social structure and processes. However, environmental design goes beyond designing and building physical structures, just as environment is not restricted to architectural elements. Our approach represents an integration of physical, educational, social, motivational, political, and other elements of the environment. So here, we will consider social organization as a vehicle for change.

Self-government: youths designing their own environment

The innovation at this stage involves changes in the function of the already existing social structure in the design of the environment. The training of environmental designers can be an effective means of educating for change and training social change agents. That is, users and participants of the environment will have an active role in its modification. If it is true that a great part of human behavior is a function of environmental contingencies, it is also true that the individual is not a passive puppet subject to capricious manipulations of environment, but rather an active agent capable of influencing the environment which, in turn, will influence him/her. To the extent that an individual is continuously changing (designing) the environment, he is attaining behavioral changes and exerting more control over the environment. The focus, then, will be on self-government as a way of training in environmental design, emphasizing both the social organization, which will make possible the design of change, and the implementation of change, per se.

Self-government as decision-making training

Social organization plays a major role in the decision-making process. Since other functions were described previously, we will concentrate only on those related to the facilitation of decision making.

The tribe is the basic social unit of the community and the basis of self-government. It is a group of 15 youths living in the same house and with many of the functions and activities of the clan, its former equivalent. Members of each tribe elect a representative to the community called the Chief of Tribe, subject to confirmation by the Council of Chiefs and the Secretary of Government. The Chief serves a fixed term of at least one month with the possibility of reelection. The youth elected to this position is in charge of both the internal coordination of the group and representation to the Council of Chiefs. He presents to the Council any new ideas raised in the night meetings or proposals of individual members to study changes in the program, and he keeps each group informed of ongoing discussions in the representative board.   The Council of Chiefs, the organ of representation in the community, is composed of 32 Chiefs of Tribes. Weekly sessions at the Cabildo are chaired by a president who is a member of the council elected for a three-month period with the possibility of one reelection. The president is in charge of encouraging and coordinating participation by all members as well as inaugurating the mayor of the Village. The vice-president, elected for the same term, replaces the president in his temporary absences. The secretary, also elected by the Council, is in charge of keeping the minutes of each session, filing, and correspondence.

One function of this unit is to study projects of legislation, activities, or other changes related to community life which are not contrary to the Constitution; and to enact the corresponding legislation. Proposals may be presented by any tribe through its Chief or by the Council of Government through the mayor or any of the secretaries. A second function is to call for a General Assembly (see below), to inform citizens about new legislation, and to call for general elections. A third function is to call any of the members of the Council of Chiefs to public hearings, when necessary, and to confirm the appointment of new Chiefs of Tribe with the consultation of the secretary of government.

The General Assembly is the highest authority of the community composed of all citizens of the Village and may be called to session by the Council of Chiefs or by the mayor. Its principle function is to elaborate the Constitution or to approve constitutional amendments. Decisions at this level are taken by a two-third vote of the attending citizenry.

Although this system is still in its initial stages (the first Constitution was enacted in 1976), it may be pointed out that the system represents a training experience not only in the establishment of norms which regulate a social system, but what is more important, in undertaking continuous changes in the system. This is a learning experience in political systems that is expected to show its influence on society when the training program is completed. Although the initial system has several resemblances to a democratic political system, changes and evolution are expected to occur.

Self-government as training in social influence and leadership.

Although training in decision making and social systems is a necessary ingredient of the educational environment, other essential elements are the acquisition of specific skills of behavior influence and leadership, and the design of an appropriate environment to facilitate the learning process. Some of these means, such as group activities and social skills training, are used on a small group basis. However, self-government represents a useful mechanism of social skills training at a more general level of influence, such as communication of a program in government to a large group of youths or to the whole community.

Elections for executive and judiciary positions are held every year at Children's Village. This constitutes the main event of the year in the community and all activities are interrupted to facilitate the process of electoral campaigns. Although the specific process of election is still developing (the first election was held in 1975), it retains many of the features of the democratic system. Candidates are usually proposed by their own tribe on the basis of general behavior, interest in the community, and specific qualifications for the proposed position. After a preselection process in conventions by the General Assembly, usually two or three candidates develop their electoral campaigns until the election day. The campaigns include talks to several groups of the community, discussion sessions about topics of interest to the community regarding plans of government, presentations on closed circuit TV, etc. It should be emphasized that participation of all members of the community in the electoral process is continuously facilitated and programmed. Election day is a special day of joy for the community, and several social and recreational activities are scheduled. Each citizen deposits his vote in a closed box and, at the close of the day, votes are counted under public scrutiny. The inauguration of the elected members of the Council of Government takes place in a special ceremony attended by the entire community and by representatives of the government of Bogota.

The educational value of the elections as an experience in behavior and social influence can hardly be overemphasized. On the one hand, it is a way of keeping the attention of the whole community on the process of change and continuous redesign of environment. It also represents a skill training experience in leadership and organization that should eventually influence the broader, outside community.

Self-government as a training experience in implementing change.

Another important element of the training of environmental designers is training in operative and procedural aspects involved in the functioning of any social system. This is achieved through the tenure of several positions in the government of the Village. It should be pointed out that most of the youths have been exposed to this experience since their entrance to the program, through a long process of increasing responsibilities in different administrative positions. The Council of Government of the Village is made up of the following positions:

The mayor is the central coordinator of the community and is in charge of the practical implementation of the decisions made by the Council of Chiefs with the cooperation of three secretaries. Since he has been relieved from his usual duties at the community (as have the other elected members of the Council of Government), he is expected to devote all his time and energy to the functioning of the community. At a formal level, the mayor is the official representative of the community to society at large and attends official events on behalf of the citizens of the Village. He is in charge of inaugurating the other members of the Council of Government.

The secretary of government is in charge of the organization of the Civic Service, a special force in the community composed of a group of citizens appointed on a rotation basis for a fixed term. Their duties are to take care of the physical settings of the Village, to coordinate internal information through a news board, to distribute meals to the houses, to maintain cleanliness in all public areas, and to give information and guide visitors through the Village. The secretary of government's second function is to organize the elections by appointing an electoral board and coordinating all the electoral processes. He approves appointments for Chiefs of Tribe and replaces the mayor in his temporary absences.

The secretary of education is in charge of organization and coordination of cultural and sports events as well as the improvement of learning conditions at school and in the library. He appoints citizens for the positions of classroom manager and librarian to facilitate the availability of educational resources and material in the corresponding setting. Organization and care of recreation activities are also his responsibility.

The secretary of budget has, as his responsibility, the organization of the internal economy of the Village. He must coordinate the functioning of the bank, cooperative, and cafeteria by appointing members of the community to develop the manager function in each of these settings. He informs the community about fluctuations in the economy and reasons for those fluctuations, and regulates the system of taxes for contributing to the community. He must also coordinate the financial aspects of recreational activities and present a monthly report to the Council of Chiefs about the financial state of the community.

One of the most important training functions of this Council of Government is in enhancing responsibility toward the community at large. This, not power, is considered the main characteristic of these positions.

Self-government as training in community self-regulatory systems.

One mechanism necessary for the survival of a social system is some kind of regulatory of judicial system which establishes consequences for violations of norms dictated by the community. Usually when any breach against the community occurs, the first unit to study the case is the tribe. Under the coordination of the Chief, members hear the defendant, consider the specific circumstances, and either admonish him or proceed with a formal trial.

The judicial system is chaired by the judge, a youth who is elected by the General Assembly for a one-year term. When informed of the case by the Chief of the respective tribe, the judge initiates the judicial process. He appoints a jury of five citizens selected from the most senior and outstanding members of the community, presides over and coordinates the trial, determines the sentence according to the judgment of the jury, and informs the Council of Chiefs of the outcome. The range of consequences that can be imposed by the judge, according to the current Constitution, are verbal or written public admonition, prevention of participation in community service activities for a fixed term, suspension of some constitutional rights for a fixed term, suspension of all constitutional rights for a fixed term, removal from any position held, if any, and finally, loss of citizenship – which implies expulsion from the community.

Another member of the judicial system is the defender of the Constitution, or prosecutor, who is also appointed by the General Assembly. The defender of the citizen, on the other hand, is in charge of pointing out the extenuating circumstances and serving as a defense attorney.

The judicial system at Children's Village represents a mechanism of control within, but more importantly, by the community; that is, an opportunity to develop and implement procedures with the participation of all citizens.

We have reviewed some dimensions in which the structure of self-government constitutes a training experience in social influence. Along the transition features pervading other areas of the environment, this is the end point of a continuum of control: from a clearly determined external control in the initial stage of the program to participation in the direction of change at this stage. However, one could now ask about the limitations of self-government. In fact, this represents a rather longer-term goal than what the literal meaning of "self-government" may imply. This end point in the continuum is, in turn, a departure point for the evolution of the system. The fundamental implication is that this evolving system is a designed implementing change through continuous experimentation. Although the direction of self-government is as yet undetermined, at least it may constitute the first step toward "utopia."

Future Trends: Suamox, Toward A Production Stage

Suamox, the industrial community, represents the third and last stage of the designed environment. Although it is not yet functioning, its physical locations are already built and most of the design has been planned, which means that this project will start working in the very near future. Characteristically, many of the features present in the previous two stages will still be present in this one, although the main emphasis will be on the implementation of the new transition back to society. Planning here will maximize the likelihood of success of the outcome achieved previously and set up the initial basis for active intervention by, or aimed at, the youth in the social system.

Although continuous contact with society has been maintained throughout the program, this last transition represents a very difficult step, not only in terms of the youth's incorporation into society, but also from the viewpoint of society's reluctance to accept him. This is due, in part, to the previous history of the youth as a child of the streets and, in part, to the general difficulty of entering the production system in a society with a high rate of unemployment. If this problem is not faced and concrete solutions planned, there is a high probability of wasting the efforts and achievements so far attained.

Considering this critical difficulty in transition, there are two main approaches in this phase which tend to address the two basic dimensions of the problem. Active involvement by members of the "outside society" will be overtly encouraged and promoted, although this implies the necessity of making some changes in administrative and organizational structures. For example, one important difference from the rest of the program is that Suamox is not financially or administratively dependent on the state. Rather, its organization and financial support depends entirely on a private foundation composed of members of the Bosconia-La Florida program, members of industry and business in the external community, and a group of qualified professionals in several fields. Although this industrial stage will be initially supported by state and private grants, it is expected eventually to be self-supporting on the basis of its production. The role of industrialists and business persons, however, will go beyond financial and technical assistance. They are potential employers of youths graduating from the program, and furthermore, they may become capitalistic partners of small businesses that the youths may eventually develop. They also play an important role in opening new places of employment and facilitating the hiring of these youths in the industrial areas.

At this stage, the program will also count on the technical assistance of the SENA, which was already described, and of a group of highly qualified professionals with experience in training labor skills. In summary, the active involvement of relevant members of the industrial community in the development and functioning of this stage, as well as their role as facilitators preparing the social system to receive graduates from the program, is expected to be a highly effective resource to facilitate a successful transition.

Nevertheless, the above strategy will not be sufficient, unless the youths are highly qualified and trained in specific skills. This constitutes a basic goal in this stage and also requires a thorough familiarization with all aspects of organization and running a business. Thorough training should encourage independence and broaden the range of alternatives available to the young men when they leave Suamox. It should be pointed out that this community represents an initial source of financial support and employment for the youth since they get a monthly salary for work accomplished as with Chibchala.

This final stage marks the beginning of their active involvement and influence as change agents in their prior early environment. It is hoped that they will start applying their skills in eradicating hovels where their relatives are living and building living areas while initiating communitary business in poor areas of the city.

Suamox is an industrial village built in an area of over 25 acres in Bogota. Like La Florida, it has been especially designed and built for the purpose of this particular stage, i.e., industrial production. Therefore, the most important locations are the plants and workshops designed at six different structures for the six areas of production included in the program: machine-tools, woodwork, metalwork, construction, graphic arts, and electricity-electronics. Areas for meetings and seminars and for technical drawing are also available. Living areas are provided by 24 houses, similar to those already described at La Florida, and recreational settings including a large auditorium, social club, and sportsfield. The industrial village may host approximately 800 youths, although only 500 will be using these facilities in the initial stages of development.

Youths entering this last stage should have completed the two previous ones. Their ages will range between 14 and 18 years, and they are required to have completed academic courses at least at the elementary level, as well as to have experienced workshops at Chibchala. Finally, they will take aptitude tests to determine their specific area of training.

Training has been programmed to have a duration of two years, distributed in four terms. The first two terms will be devoted to training basic skills in the elected area through a combination of theory and practice at the workshop. The working day would consist of four hours spent in classrooms and four in workshops. In the machine-tool workshop, for example, the trainees will learn the operation and maintenance of a diversity of industrial machines; woodwork includes the operation and production of wood elements involved in construction, furniture, etc.; metalwork is related to training in assembly, soldering, etc.; while construction's emphasis is on prefabrication and plumbing. The graphic arts workshop involves training in printing, bookbinding, and related areas. The electricity-electronics area will eventually prepare them for jobs as radio/TV technicians and train them in the maintenance, installation, and repair of electrical equipment. Theoretical courses will be offered in the areas of mathematics, technical drawing, science, human relations and communication, business administration, and technology.

The planned curriculum is aimed at training not only in specific labor skills but also other techniques which should facilitate the independent organization of industries. Advanced skills will be especially emphasized during the last two terms when the trainees will start working on contracts and actual orders from real customers within the community. During the last term, the trainee will be supervising and training first-year students and will be involved in practical aspects of business administration such as cost evaluation, calculation of budgets, contract writing, etc.

In summary, to the same extent that the impact of the designed environment depended on the careful design of the initial transition stage at Bosconia, the long-term effects of the environmental outcome will depend on this last transition to the environment from which the youths initially come. The strengthening of links with the outside community should increase employment opportunities for the graduate and, in general, will make the social system receptive to the once-rejected youths. At the same time, technical qualifications in labor skills, selected to have an impact on the development within the community, along with experience in management and administration will provide the necessary autonomy for the youths to participate effectively in the process of social change.

With this hope for the future, we come to the conclusion of our description of an ongoing program in environmental design. And while the last and final stage seems the end of a cycle of planned change initiated when the first contact with children of the streets was made, it is also the beginning of a more basic process of influence and redesign of an environment that produced these children. This influence will be a crucial test for the adequacy of the present program and, hopefully, a testimony to the future of the inhabitants of Children's Village.

13 Environmental Design in Alternative Societies: The People's Republic of China
Charles Hoffman

It may seem unusual to have a chapter on China, written by an economist, in a book on environmental design focusing on the research and application of certain psychological and architectural theories. Yet, virtually every aspect of the situation in China described by Hoffmann has its analog in the other chapters in this book.

We will only point out a few of the obvious linkages. For example, the orientation to life described as "scientific-experimental"; the continuous problem solving approach; the linkage of theory and practice in everyday living; explicit statements as to the value system toward which the system is working; education and training as a constant ongoing process; the general use of modeling as an influence technique in every aspect of life; education as an "open door" process between school and community; a systematic incentive system (not too dissimilar from the token economy of Walden Two); the belief in the process of change as a way of life; and the emphasis throughout every aspect of society on the application of scientific research. In many ways, schools in the United States serve our society the same way that schools in China serve theirs, namely, in both there is a prototype of the outside social order which is brought into the school.

Ed.

Training individuals means rearranging environments to help them to change – to be able to vote Republican, to be aware of pine trees' aroma, to learn how to catch abalone, to address a large gathering, to persuade a tax examiner to modify an assessment downward, to taste and enjoy food long considered repulsive, to buy less beef and more fowl, to give up smoking – by adding to knowledge and understanding, heightening consciousness, replacing old values, learning new and discarding old behaviors. Whether such behavior modification occurs through conscious design or not, it is constantly occurring in the process of acculturation that we all experience throughout our lives. It involves, both actively and passively, dealing with interrelated small and large social systems, their goals, values, policies and the institutional arrangements set up for goal-value-policy achievement, the sum total of these social systems within a country, its culture, and how perennial cultural imperatives and lesser needs are met. This macroenvironment must be seen as affecting significantly the behavior of individuals carrying out their roles in more narrowly defined environments that reflect in themselves the broad cultural process and its value elements. In this chapter, we focus on one of these larger social systems, its institutional structures, and their relevance for changing individual behavior.

In any social system, whether it be authoritarian or democratic, the questions of change for what purposes, decided by whom, and how are critical ones since the kinds and directions of change and the power or influence over the decision process affect vitally the options individuals have for self-realization through control of material and human resources and the social processes which shape the utilization of those resources. Getting people to use energy resources more efficiently involves more than retraining them narrowly through raising prices for coal, gas, oil, and electricity. For old, deeply ingrained behaviors to be modified involves a variety of changes affecting feelings and attitudes about what a "comfortable" house temperature is, giving up the spontaneous use of one's car when the urge to buy a chocolate bar three miles away (at a cost of 17 cents a mile or more) surfaces, and paying careful attention to house lights being left on and refrigerator cooling levels being too high.

The study of formal and informal, conscious and unconscious training processes in their cultural context reveals how social processes condition individuals directly and indirectly. Though random factors are always involved, the success or failure of a new product (hoola hoop, Edsel), new living arrangements (condominiums), and new entertainment styles (country music) is the result of complex forces. Such forces are transmitted through existing or newly created organizational modes aimed at changing present arrangements and behaviors. These changes are effected in line with the change promoters' value objectives, a reward system galvanizing the necessary material and human resources, and imagined or real gratification with the change on the part of the users whose values, life styles, and feelings are expected to be realized in the change. Consumers, producers, and others are thus constantly being trained and retrained in modern society, whatever its political and social bent, and no matter at what rate change is taking place.

As individuals in society are persistently subject to change — to training and retraining — resistances act as inhibiting forces. The continuities of the past — old attitudes, feelings, behaviors, institutions — act as barriers to the pressure for change, and often either frustrate the change or reshape it into something other than its designer's envisioned.   Such resistances arise from varied vested interests, whether psychological or material. They are often loudly proclaimed but, just as often, unspoken for tactical reasons or because of a lack of awareness. Continuities of the past frequently are utilized subtly in the decision processes that determine direction, speed, and quality of change. In most contemporary societies, even in the face of major unsettling and polarizing problems that cry out for significant social and individual change, the processes that determine what changes are to occur, for what purposes, and how are not easily identified and understood.

In surveying China's (Maoist) model for achieving a Communist future during the period before Mao's death in 1976, we are dealing with a case of revolutionary environmental design in a very different cultural setting. To the extent that our survey reveals how human behavioral change is geared to newly devised social mechanisms and controls, it should help us to understand, in extreme form, how values, needs, and institutional mechanisms are interrelated, and how training proceeds formally and informally in a planned, rapidly changing society. The stark differences in ideology and culture are useful: attempting to change drastically from an undeveloped, agrarian-feudalistic to a modern, revolutionary-industrialized society demands clear societal training (or acculturation) programs that relate means (new institutions and values) and ultimate ends (ideological goals and values) in operational ways. Since the modernization process throughout the world has followed converging cultural paths (similar economic mechanisms and communications networks, role models with particular cultural touches), the Chinese attempt to achieve modernization in a new value and institutional configuration, perforce, puts our known values and mechanisms in sharp contrast with their design. Thus, Chinese diagnoses and training prescriptions for social environments different from ours confront us with one way of designing new environments that deal with perennial modern issues: elitism, specialization, bureaucracy, ecological deterioration, mass education, urban sprawl, adequate health care, self-realization, centralization of power, inequality, integrity of leadership, and participatory governance. Exposure to the Chinese experiment may force us to review the ways by which our culture conditions or trains us to look at and deal with such problems. The resistances that the Chinese face to the new systems they attempt to establish highlight for us the persistent conditioning processes of inherited environments; successful Chinese organization of new relationships and behaviors clarifies how the dead hand of the past may be effectively or partially numbed.

The leaders of the Chinese Communist Party (CCP) under Mao were committed to transforming the social system they inherited and the varied behaviors of the people acting out new and old roles. They approached their revolutionary task — transforming a feudalistic-capitalistic society into a socialist one and developing the conditions essential for communism to emerge — with a Marxist-Leninist view that individuals' consciousness is a reflection of their class situation and their functional political, social, and economic relations dictated by the exigencies of the social system. In other words, people think and behave according to the way the social process conditions them. Mao Tse-tung saw China, unlike many other countries, as "poor and blank" in a capitalist world and, hence, the opportunity for radical change was wide open.

The opportunity for achieving a radical transformation in the social system and the attitudes, thoughts, and behaviors of people was not seen by CCP leaders as without major obstacles. As Marxist-Leninists, they were well aware of the heavy baggage of the past: centuries-old institutions and vested interest; village customs and relationships little changed in a millennium; folk myths, superstitions and fears reflecting this age-old, primitive, rural environment and still molding the thought and being of over 80 percent of the Chinese nation (750 million people live in the countryside today) and affecting significantly, the lives and well-being of the 150 million who populated the cities and their environs. For Mao and his followers, changing such an environment into a socialist society was not something to be achieved by correct wishes and designs alone, but rather required clear ideological and organizational objectives, an understanding of the workings of China's major institutions and their differential susceptibility to change, insight into the thought processes and deep personal interests of different classes in society (particularly the peasants), and many other critical elements in the social system. The continuities of the past – the present social system and its heritage – had to be confronted imaginatively, isolating those elements that needed to be under constant attack and surveillance (e.g. landlord property holdings) from those (such as traditional mutual aid groups) that could be used to advantage in the process of molding new, socialist mechanisms and institutions (such as rural communes).

In meeting head-on the crucial issue of changing important environments and human behaviors continuously, China's leaders at various levels were committed to employing Marxist dialectics in "using the past to serve the present," in borrowing and adapting advanced capitalist technology, and in pioneering in social areas yet uncharted. Thus, the cultural remnants of China's past (classical literature, philosophy, and art, as well as archeological finds) were used to reinforce the people's sense of cultural accomplishment and of outrage at the exploitive projects of past rulers and ruling classes. Such a critical framework for viewing the social process (through Marxist bifocals) was the basic context in which all the people were to be trained and retrained in the new thinking and working processes of emergent socialism. Changing the Chinese people's thought processes and behaviors meant, for CCP leaders using the dialectic (class analysis) technique, experimentally changing as many aspects of the work and living environments ("the material conditions of living") as possible, with particular environmental elements (the means of production and their social relationships) demanding immediate modification. The changing of the old as well as the fashioning of the new are processes that formally and informally involve people at all levels in a training process that is an integral part of the new environment. All actors- workers, peasants, military personnel, students, residents, technicians, and supervisors were expected to be participant observers who could discuss the problems, try to implement changes, review the results, prescribe again, implement again, and so on as environments changed, presumably in line with ideological objectives and the exigencies of resistance from continuing environments (the continuity of past conditions and attitudes).

The ideological commitment of the CCP to the revolutionary modernization of China was unequivocal in Marxist-Leninist terms. From the point of view of environmental design, we must analyze that commitment and the process of revolutionary modernization in terms of what values and behaviors are to be realized, the kinds of environments expected to generate the desired modernization process and for what purposes, and who decides what direction and pace the process is to take. Since the environment from which revolutionary transformation was to issue forth included many values, attitudes, institutions, and class differences which stood in the way of desired goals, a grand training process discouraging certain old ways and introducing and reinforcing socialist new ways had been set in motion.

The ultimate goal of revolutionary modernization was a classless communist society of equality, community, and social solidarity. Such a society cannot be mandated or achieved in short order, but can only arise over time as succeeding phases of social organization evolve following certain laws of social development – capitalism, various phases of socialism, and then communism. Communism, therefore, is only possible when the "material conditions" of existence (environment) have reached a certain level and quality which shape and reinforce institutions and behaviors that are collectivist and egalitarian. In such an environment, individualistic, elitist, and exploitive institutions and behaviors would be as typical as collectivist, egalitarian, and nonexploitive are in contemporary capitalist societies. Socialist society would be a transitional environment containing yet discouraging, the old ways while cultivating and nurturing the new.

The basic economic environment of communism would be nonexploitive. For the CCP and other Marxist-Leninists, this means a society in which production and distribution would be for use rather than for profitable exchange. The means of production – factories, farms, railroads, and mines – would be socially owned and controlled, and human and social relationships on the job would be consonant with the needs of the people involved. Commodity production – producing for a market in response to price and profit – would be superseded by production on a planned basis according to the determined overall needs of the nation. The fruits of such a process would be distributed to people ultimately according to the communist principle of remuneration – work input according to ability, income payment according to need.

The egalitarian bent of this ideology calls for the elimination of prominent economic and social inequalities inherited from capitalist as well as socialist societies. The Chinese Marxists maintained that communism could only function in an environment without the "three gaps": disparities between town and country, workers and peasants, and mental and physical labor. The social environments and opportunities in all parts of the country had to be similar (educational, recreational, cultural, occupational, and political) if communist behavior was to be fostered and extended. Furthermore, on-the-job environments had to be similar in terms of general working conditions, input in decisions, and welfare benefits. Finally, the sharp dichotomy between intellectual and physical work with its bureaucratic and elitist implications had to be replaced by the sharing of physical labor where necessary and providing intellectual labor roles of some sort for all. The mystique of expertness (bureaucracy) had to be contained.

The commitment to eliminate economic and social inequalities also included the eradication of discrimination between the sexes. The heritage of female infanticide, binding girls' feet, child brides, subservience to a husband and his family, and the like reflected an environment especially exploitive of women. Mao's goals of cultivating the conditions necessary for communism explicitly embodied the integration of women, who "hold up half the sky," as active and equal members throughout the work force, in the party, in government, and in the family.

The dictatorship of the proletariat was considered an imperative aspect of socialism as it evolved from capitalism, and attempted to transform continuing "bourgeois" institutions (the old environment) into new "socialist" forms. The class struggle that has dominated history was not to be allowed to slacken under socialism and the dictatorship of the proletariat. Rather, it was to be intensified since not only do capitalists and "bourgeois rights" still exist (e.g. differential wage scales, commodity market exchange) but bourgeois attitudes and values are perpetuated among all people and, thus, there is constant danger of return to capitalism in various forms.

This environment or social system that China's revolutionary leaders under Mao were committed to mold over time was expected to generate and internalize a set of collectivist values and attitudes and to cultivate proletarian behavior patterns. These exemplary communist values and behaviors were expected to arise in the process of China's advance from capitalism to "people's democracy" through several phases of socialism and, finally, into a social system whose "material conditions" would strongly reinforce communist awareness and activism. We catalog these expected values and behaviors to juxtapose alongside the institutional mechanisms and training processes which were designed to move China's social system in the desired direction.

The primary values of a nonexploitive, egalitarian communism required a more detailed and integrated preference structure consonant with those values and covering major aspects of life. This structure had to define the individual in relation to the group, the means by which self-realization properly occurs, and the instruments by which decisions about life's chances are made. In effect, these values had to answer the questions for what, by whom, and how was environmental design − a communist society for China − to be implemented.

At the head of the value structure stood the community. The slogan, "Serve the People," embodied the value of "social interest first; individual interest second." All endeavors were geared to social service. The primacy of the communal interest meant that the individual's self-realization could properly occur only within a social context. Thus, cooperation rather than individual competition was emphasized. The slogan, "friendship first, competition second," broadcast widely in sports events, expressed this value set: the social and cooperative were primary, the individual and competitive were secondary. It was through such a collectivist ethos that the material needs of people could best be met and individual talent put to optimum use.

Beyond the concept of "serving the people" was the value of self-reliance for China as a whole, and for all social, economic, and political units throughout the country. As in the case of the primary commitment to the community, the commitment to self-reliance was not absolute. Each unit relied on itself first; when necessary it received cooperative support. Thus, self-reliance was not complete self-sufficiency or autarky but, rather, an emphasis on units actively taking the initiative on all major matters over which they exercise control and respon- sibility. Even where external assistance occurred, as it frequently did, the initiating unit maintained its leadership role. This value was important in generating and reinforcing self-confidence in a peasantry long put down, and in developing competent decentralized agencies for carrying out varied social tasks.

A closely related value was the "mass line": the requirement that the masses – organized groups of people (peasants, workers, youth) – be involved actively in all affairs, that government and Party organizations be supervised from above as well as below (the masses), and that the masses be brought into decision making, problem solving, day-to-day management. Marxist and Maoist ideology imputed a major creative role to the masses: the revolution should be by and for these masses. Mass involvement in group study and discussion of varied problems was a means of upward transmission of mass sentiment, as well as development of different kinds of social and technical expertise. The call to mass action was a corollary of the responsibility of everyone to be generalists as well as specialists. The development of the mass line was a counterweight to the often intimidating authority of the technical specialist (bureaucrat) who usually has the last word on technical matters in his/her specialty.

A Marxist value of overriding importance for modernization and effective execution of serving the people through self-reliance and mass movements was the scientific-experimental approach to all life, physical as well as social. The Marxist world view of dialectical materialism and its social corollary, historical materialism, demanded a scientific outlook and provided this philosophical framework for dealing with all problems. Harnessing nature and nurture in the service of socialist development called for a continual problem solving mechanism that would relate means and ends in an experimental way.

The CCP leaders under Mao stressed a scientific approach which was heavily empirical without rejecting scientific tradition and theoretical accumulation. The scientific-experimental approach was to "link theory and practice" dialectically. This meant avoiding reliance on theory alone (dogmatism) or taking practice or experience as the only authority (empiricism). Rather, the ideal combination was one in which the two would support one another.

What values, attitudes, and behaviors were required in the govern-ance of this dictatorship of the proletariat striving to design new environments leading to communism? The Marxist-Leninist principle guiding governance is "democratic centralism" which calls for dialec-tical involvement of all constituents in the process of decision making in party units. The concept, democratic centralism, involves the polar terms, "freedom" and "discipline," which are to be joined in dealing with all questions that have to be resolved at any one or a combination of the hierarchic levels within the party. "Freedom" denotes the area of choices open to each party constituency considering a particular question, and "discipline" means the limits within which decisions can or may be made.

Marxist and Maoist doctrine mandates that all party issues are to be thoroughly and openly thrashed out before any final decision is made. Even salient strategic decisions usually made at the party center are required to be discussed at all party levels with feedback from grass-root units up the party communications line. Party policies must be acceptable to "the masses"; any attempt to force such policies on particular constituencies is considered "commandism" and is anathema to the ideological dogma. When discussion of policy issues is concluded, final decision is made by majority vote at the particular party level up to the center. Once the policy is so decided upon, democratic centralism mandates cohesion by all (minority and majority) unless the policy is changed at a later date by the same process.

In the dynamics of democratic centralism there is a functional dichotomy on policy roles between the higher echelons and the lower level units in the party. The party center and the leadership in each of China's 29 administrative units were responsible for broad strategic and ideological issues, while the party operating units below the administra-tive levels down to the basic grass roots level had tactical autonomy in the carrying out of party directives. There was an important feedback process up and down the hierarchy so that the sense of particular policies could be changed as perceptions on the results of first implementation attempts were registered. If mass reaction was strongly negative, basic level party leaders could modify or ignore party directives; strong positive mass reaction could occasion a revised, more optimistic version of the policy.

The exemplary qualities of human behavior expected of communists by CCP leaders were clearly and widely broadcast throughout China under Mao for all to see, hear, and emulate. Chinese cultural tradition has for millennia used role models explicitly, both positively and negatively, to project images of correct behaviors for masses, gentry, nobility – people in all statuses and functions. Party leaders quite explicitly identified, explained, functionally, and celebrated the signal importance of positive role models in real life and theatrical perfor-mances (opera, ballet, drama) and held negative role models and their behaviors up to derision so all knew what was correct and wrong behavior.

Ideal communist behavior carries out the values and attitudes discussed above. The ideal communist person embodies the revolutionary proletarian ethos in his/her behavior and demonstrates many collectivist values spontaneously since they are deeply ingrained after a lengthy period of reinforced correct daily practice.

Such behavior exhibits, throughout, a strong commitment to collectivist work and life style. In whatever area of living or working, the ideal communist's attitude toward any issue or problem is to seek a collective format for resolving it. An active leadership role in galvanizing and helping others to struggle cooperatively carries with it the obligation both to lead and when appropriate to be led. One's selfless investment in the community is expected to engender both a self-awareness of one's own worth as well as a realization that that worth is embodied in the group's primacy. Thus, confident, self-asserting, initiating behavior is expected to be combined with humility and acceptance of the need to achieve group consensus rather than succeeding in having one's own way through use of one's official status.

The individual's attitude toward and execution of work is another touchstone of his/her genuine proletarian quality. Devotion to work on the job as well as in the community for its intrinsic value and need in furthering the interests of all the people is expected of communist activists. Every one of these individuals is exhorted to be "Red and Expert" in that order; that is, to link proper collectivist thought, attitudes and behavior with thorough expertness in a particular skill, occupation, or profession. That expertise, though, is to be complemented with ready willingness to work in any project requiring one's input, and to become a generalist keenly aware of the relation of narrower work issues to the overall problems of a farm, factory, mine, office, etc. In approaching any work task, the exemplary proletarian activist is to be scientific-experimental in considering the problems, set of approaches and solutions, and the human organizational means of dealing with them. Theory — scientific models and Marxian dialectics — is to be utilized along with the informed practice of all involved to confront any problem from controlling insects that threaten crops to resolving questions of high energy physics.

The cultivation and motivation of more and more such persons carrying the banner of communist activism was an essential Maoist requirement if the social process was to succeed in achieving communism. Strong leaders were to teach people how to make decisions, shape policies and implant them collectively. Since the CCP followed the Marxist materialist notion that thought, attitudes, and behaviors are a function of the "material conditions" one lives in (the social environment), the conditioning, training, and educating of the Chinese people to approximate the ideal of communist behavior depended heavily on setting up and developing fresh environments — new institutions, mechanisms, and processes for carrying out the day-to-day needs of the society. We look now, therefore, at several salient aspects of Maoist Chinese life to see what their principal characteristics were, how they conditioned and trained people to become exemplary proletarians, who got involved and how in the designing and implementing of the new environments.

To a degree, education and training were a constant process for all people in China inculcating revolutionary values as well as the skills and techniques essential for modern living, making people "red and expert." And since the cultural revolution that process emphasized revolutionary values more deeply and widely. At the same time, the school and training environments have been modified in critical ways consonant with the Maoist vision of training for communism. Formal education and training were to "serve the people" and their needs rather than be ladders to successful careers and elitist achievement. Programs were reduced in duration, combined with practical work, opened up to outside groups and organizations ("open door education"), and made available more readily to people with peasant and worker backgrounds. All schools were made subject to oversight by local peasant or worker representatives as well as by representatives of internal constituencies until the post-Mao period.

Primary and middle (high) schools were made available to almost all Chinese children and were reshaped in the form of the new model. Lower and upper middle schools were telescoped reducing their programs by about a year and making young people available for work at a younger age. Graduates of middle schools did not go directly to colleges or universities, but first had to spend at least two years at work on communes, in factories, or in the military services before being eligible for higher education. Millions of middle school graduates were sent to the countryside each year to contribute to its development, to apply skills already acquired, and to learn new ones relevant to the problems and tasks of the communes.

"Serve the People" was a goal and value projected and reinforced starting in preschool institutions and carried on more widely and formally as children climbed the education ladder. In preschool and kindergarten settings, the content of any formal schooling was interlarded heavily with stories about serving collective interests, and positive role models of workers and peasants were paraded before the children. This "book learning" was supplemented in two ways: live role models visited from local factories and communes, and the children were involved in productive activity related to a local factory or commune (e.g. making bottle tops or other small items usable in the factory or commune). In primary schools, the curriculum encompassed the usual array of academic subjects (including foreign languages such as English or Russian), but also required the linking of theory with practice in several ways: formal courses were given in mechanics, electronics, modeling, etc. where students collectively made items used in the economy; regular links with factories and communes were forged with student groups spending time in those environments; and student groups were also responsible for cultivation of farm produce and repair and maintenance at the school. The "serving of the people" in such an environment also nurtured values of self-reliance, collective work style, the dignity and importance of labor, group decision making, significance of science and experimentation, and the primacy of the collective interest.

The colleges and universities were even more drastically changed after the cultural revolution to conform more closely to revolutionary ideals and goals — education for workers and peasants, not mainly for children of intellectuals; curriculum in the service of the collective, not for the advancing of individual careers. Admissions, curriculum, and governance were all vitally affected.

The new admissions policy greatly increased working class membership in the student body. Middle school graduates could apply for admission after two years of work. Their applications were sent to higher education institutions if their co-workers and supervisors on the job recommended them as diligent, competent, imbued with proper class attitudes, and having demonstrated collectivist work style. They were then expected to return from college to advance the commune's or plant's operations. Their qualifications were reviewed competitively by university personnel as to proper outlook and academic competence (were they "Red and Expert"?) and ultimately a fraction of the applicants were admitted. (After Mao's death, modifications in these new educational procedures were widely effected.)

Curriculum changes were forged in several dimensions: overall courses of study were reduced in duration, course content was reworked, applied work was expanded including participation in physical labor, veteran workers and peasants were utilized in instruction, university and college course activity was opened to problem solving for outside community groups, collaborative work by students (even in examinations) was encouraged. Thus, higher education programs were set up to train students as well as outside citizens in collective behaviors necessary to modernize China rapidly.

The applied aspects of new curricula moved in several directions. Principal among these has been the direct linkage between school and the community (factory, commune, office) and its problems. Internally, this has meant setting up actual factories and farms in the universities and colleges. Such activities are run by workers and peasants as well as by students and instructors and become integral parts of the curriculum. For example, Tsinghua University in Peking, China's outstanding polytechnical institution, has its own factory operations which include various advanced machine tool sections in which science and engineering principles and problems are dealt with in direct applied course projects. Universities also use external resources in the application of course theory to practice. Students and faculty take their theoretical learning to specific plants and communes in the field in response either to their own questions of application of theory or to the requests of factories and farms confronted with operational problems. In similar ways universities and their inhabitants are open to the pressing problems of the broad community.

The governance of colleges and universities still follows the usual hierarchic structure, but important cultural revolution innovations were added under Mao. The revolutionary committee was responsible for day-to-day operations, and its chairman and vice chairmen were the administrators of the institution. The committee had representation from the various constituencies (faculty, students, staff) and its chairman was often a party secretary. (At Peking University, for example, it was a vice chairman, (Chou Pei-yuan) an outstanding physicist, who was the guiding faculty presence. At the various departmental levels, analogous political representation and interaction took place. In addition to the oversight of the local party committee, there was a local worker or peasant group (depending on location) which reviewed and provided input for institutional policies and practices.

Though the primacy of the collective interest was unequivocally set forth in all matters including choice of major academic interest, there was room for individual preference in selecting a field of study. The extent of such choice was a function of one's demonstrated competence in a field, one's credentials in proper attitude and behavior, and the particular demand for people in that field. The earlier an individual demonstrated attitudinal and technical qualification in the educational sphere, the greater his/her professional training options. Similarly, in professional placement, individual preference was greater or less depending on degree of qualification and the need of the collective to locate skilled technicians and professionals in particular economic sectors at specific sites. University graduates or any work force members were not allocated via wage and salary differentials in a labor market, but by assignment.

Completing the usual academic structure were the research institutes under the Academy of Sciences, the Academy of Medical Sciences, and the Academy of Agricultural Sciences. Though China's universities carried on research as part of their curricula, the principal basic and applied research was the responsibility of special institutes. They, too, were modified after the cultural revolution with greater emphasis on applied problems and the encouragement of open research in which scientists' responsibilities went beyond their own particular research projects.

The several academies were reorganized after the cultural revolution to effect these new ideas. Those institutes which mainly dealt with applied scientific research were decentralized by being put under the administrative jurisdiction of the provinces in which their work was most relevant and where direct contact with operating units was more easily effected. Institutes dealing with fundamental research (high energy physics) remained in the structure of the appropriate academy. All institutes were required to cultivate and expand open research so that each scientist would have to devote a significant part of his/her time to community research activity. Such activity would involve particular scientific problems of a community, hospital, farm, factory, mine, etc. which needed the expertise of scientists to inform their collective solution. (After Mao's death such activities were minimized.)

Beyond the conventional educational structure just sketched, the Chinese leaders fashioned other formal institutions and arrangements for training and educating the Chinese people in the skills and attitudes of revolutionary modernization. These facilities were mostly new and provided varied opportunities to the millions of workers and peasants past school age. Though the emphasis was on technical training, cultural education was not neglected.

The "spare-time" educational mechanisms offered a wide range of subjects to working people enabling them to overcome illiteracy, to acquire academic and cultural knowledge, and to become trained in specific occupational skills. Such spare-time schools offered courses at convenient hours and places and played a major role in reducing Chinese illiteracy from 85 per cent to about 20 per cent and in developing a wide range of skills among workers and peasants. These schools operated in key sites: plants, mines, communes, and offices. They were run under varied auspices: trade unions, management, and other mass organizations.

The recently designed facilities for training and education were set up to maximize the opportunity for training individuals who then contributed to multiple positive effects in production units. The factories and farms in schools have already been noted. They had counterparts – schools in factories and communes. Many factories had "July 21 Colleges" which offered complete curricula for workers to take on a full-time basis. The linking of theory and practice was readily achieved and aimed at providing very useful, telescoped course sessions. Completion of the curriculum gave workers some general plus a specifically defined technical education (in draftsmanship, mechanics, electrical engineering, etc.), the values of which could be shared with co-workers on the shift and provided a basis for intelligent participation in factory decision making and technical problem solving.

In the countryside, the "May 7 Colleges" were analogs to the "July 21 Colleges" in factories. The May 7 schools were designed for peasants. They were not limited to a particular commune but covered a wide agricultural area; communes sent selected members for full-time study in agricultural sciences. These peasants were supported by their commune and returned to it when their course of study was completed. Their skill improvement and education were explicitly to advance their ability to "serve the people" and such gains were expected when they rejoined their work units.

In addition to these formal training operations, there were less formal modes for training and education. A couple of examples should suffice to convey the commitment of Maoist China to educational opportunity. Many communities had scientific exchange centers where a permanent staff provided facilities and know-how available to individuals and groups desiring specific technical information to deal with a particular problem. Another means of training was through technical exchange emulation campaigns in which groups of workers or peasants from a particular plant or commune visited other such units to demonstrate a specific set of operations, to respond to questions, and to work with the observing group to implement and adapt the operations to the specific needs of the host factory or commune.

In all of these training and education situations, several principles were explicitly enunciated and reinforced: 1) the course of study was to serve the community rather than advancing an individual's career; 2) the educational facility itself linked theory and practice; 3) the curriculum and its implementation stressed proper work attitudes as well as technical expertise; 4) the training institution or mechanism was structured for governance through representation and mass involvement; and 5) the institutions were expected to rely heavily on their own resources in carrying out their mission – self-reliance. Both the new institutions conceived during the cultural revolution and the modified old institutions provided a new environment for training and educating China's people, young and old, in revolutionary modernization. Thus, the overall system – rewards, aspirations, evaluations, costs, expectations, obligations, curriculum, management, and so on – was greatly modified in line with clearly identified revolutionary values and goals. But important attitudinal and value elements of the old environment still exist and are expected to continue to exist. In this changing educational situation, new behaviors and values were anticipated. Their approximation to what CCP leaders aimed at depends on the extent to which the social environment is modified by the will of the leaders and the led – the extent to which "class struggle," to use the jargon of the party, is successfully waged.

In the revolutionary drive toward communism, motivation commanded prime consideration. The deep-seated heritage of personal profit and income maximization was viewed as a powerful negative continuity that had to be transformed over time into a prevailing ethos of communist behavior – each person working to the best of his/her ability and recompensed according to need. This principle of distribution operated throughout society with cooperative elements and performance standards internalized and the propensity to accumulate personal material things diminished and sublimated in the progress of the community.

Significant as proletarian motivation is to the successful achievement of communism, Mao and his party followers emphasized the need to move cautiously and deliberately in the direction of a work incentive system consonant with evolving communist values and institutions. They explicitly recognized the ingrained sense of personal interest in the old incentive mechanisms at the same time as new collectivist incentive modes were experimented with and assimilated. This means proceeding toward collectivist mechanisms and modes in answer to the question: If not the old, material, extrinsic rewards for work well done or coercion in shaping new collective forms, then what kind of system will fulfill ideological objectives and meet human needs?

In reshaping the work incentive system, Chinese policymakers under Mao attempted, after much groping, slowly to introduce new, "socialist" modes as the old, "bourgeois" mechanisms were deemphasized and partially retracted. The process was less a substitution of "socialist" analogs for "bourgeois" mechanisms than a qualitative change in the work environment that included modifying "bourgeois" mechanisms with "socialist" elements.

One way of looking at the CCP's incentive policy is to consider incentives as dichotomous, having external or extrinsic and internal or intrinsic aspects. The inherited incentive system was mainly extrinsic, that is, rewards (wages, bonuses, commendations, etc.) were directly linked to performance units (output) and were both material (money or goods) and nonmaterial (token awards) and usually based on the individual's output but external to the work process itself. The communist motivation objective (socially motivated performance with reward according to need) implies internalized motivational dynamics with intrinsic incentives in which the rewards are inherent in the work process and its results – satisfaction from a job well done, gratification in working collectively toward joint goals, and contentment with the realization of group planned objectives – at the same time as material needs are reasonably adequately taken care of and raise no problems. In the transition from the old incentive system the work environment has to be changed with extrinsic mechanisms being retained but modified with collective elements at the same time as processes strengthening intrinsic motivation are invented, tested, and implemented over wider work areas. In other words, the old incentive environment was not to be junked, but transformed gradually as intrinsic motivation was cultivated and extrinsic motivation downplayed, the pace of transformation being a function of the degree and quality of acceptance of the new modes and their efficacy in sustaining adequate levels of performance.

If we look at the incentive system Mao and the CCP shaped, some significant changes in the work environment become apparent. The old, extrinsic mechanisms were still generally in operation. In factories and communes, graduated pay scales according to skill and output expectations prevailed. Workers were paid usually in eight grades, from least to highest skilled, the maximum grade about three times that of the minimum. Peasants were also paid in a parallel scaled manner, though the range and number of grades was narrower and the multiple of maximum to minimum was usually less than three to one. In both work environments, though, the earlier (1950s) versions of extrinsic incentive mechanisms were considerably modified. First, in the late 1950s, many incentive devices were linked to groups rather than individuals. Since the cultural revolution, piece-work pay rates in which individual and group output was directly and proportionally linked with pay (e.g. five cents pay for each weed uprooted) as an extrinsic mechanism par excellence were all but eliminated in industrial plants and were cut back widely in communes. Bonuses similarly were abolished as were various mechanisms which related pay directly with output. In addition, many competitive, extrinsic, nonmaterial awards were eliminated and others retracted as perpetuators of individualistic work styles inimical to socialist development.

Other extrinsic material incentives also were cut back sharply or eliminated. Pay scales for all supervisory, technical, and professional personnel were telescoped from the top levels down. The highest paid leaders in government, party, and industry had their salaries scaled down to almost half their former maximum levels. Top managers in factories and communes experienced similar reductions as well as elimination of certain material perquisites. Material awards for inventions, technical improvements, and innovations which followed a generous graduated scale according to the value of such contributions during the 1950s and early 1960s were also eliminated.

At the same time as extrinsic incentive mechanisms were pared down and made less prominent motivators, a diverse set of new elements cultivating intrinsic motivation were introduced into the work environments of workers and peasants. Aimed at developing a new collectivist work style for organizing, planning, training, coordinating, and managing personnel as well as stimulating enthusiasm for work through heightening work satisfaction and responsibility, the production process and its surroundings in many factories, communes, mines, etc. were modified according to Maoist conceptions. One salient condition underpinning the cultivation of intrinsic incentives was the provision of meeting, on a very modest level, the basic material needs of all — minimum availability of food, clothing, shelter, health care, education, recreation, and cultural resources. The roles of workers or peasants, vis-a-vis one another and technical and supervisory personnel, were developed in new ways at the same time as the experts' roles and status were linked more closely with workers or peasants, as the work situation defined.

In factories and on farms, workers and peasants were involved in day-to-day decision making indirectly and directly. As elected members of the revolutionary committee that ran every social or economic unit, workers or peasants were involved in the overseeing of the production process for their constituencies. Selected workers or peasants were periodically given managerial positions for a specified term and brought their experience and outlook to bear at top levels. Their presence there probably made more open the administering of the unit and served as training both for managerial positions and informed leadership of workers' or peasants' participation in management.

Such worker or peasant involvement in plant or commune management was limited to small numbers, but other "new" mechanisms were devised that involved larger numbers and could expand to include a large majority of the unit's work force. One mechanism was the three-in-one combination of workers or peasants (technicians) and cadres (supervisory personnel) which was used for a variety of continuing or ad hoc problems: technical improvements, new product design, cost reduction, maintenance and repair emergencies, safety, innovation, rule modification. Instead of relying, as in most countries, on a particular technical or supervisory person (bureaucrat) to handle problems in his/her specialty, the Chinese used the three-in-one combination to draw on collective experience and to cultivate a proletarian work style. One means of involving workers continually in plant decision processes was a special three-in-one combination — the factory economic management group — which was organized for the plant, its shops, and its work units and utilized about a third of the plant's workers together with cadres and technicians in all phases of management. This included: welfare and workers' living conditions, technology and production, finance, safety, and political and ideological education.

Another collective form in which workers participated by the hundreds in plant administration and management of some factories was the veteran workers' advisory group. This group was utilized in appropriate subgroups that attended all important party committee meetings and sessions on major questions affecting plant operations and executed investigative and technical tasks assigned to them. Still another collective form was the organization of production groups, basic producing units of about 50 workers. Each group had production and trade union leaders (cadres) plus five workers elected by their peers to assure worker participation in all decisions affecting the group. The trade union in any plant was another instrument for worker input and influence. Specific functions − safety, welfare, and social insurance − were carried out, but other issues and grievances were aired through the trade union.

Workers and peasants also had an impact on, and were involved in, the management of their work environments. Mass movements, encompassing most of the workers or peasants in a unit, were employed widely to deal with a variety of issues of a general nature and lent themselves to inputs based on the work experiences of the masses − lowering costs, changing rules and regulations, raising productivity, etc. Mass meetings to discuss and heighten worker or peasant awareness of the importance of an issue were often followed by subgroups taking on specific implementation objectives. Mass criticism sessions were also frequently held in which the poor policies of leaders or the shortcomings of some workers or peasants were aired and rectification programs defined. Mass emulation movements were frequently employed to heighten workers' labor enthusiasm and performance.

Workers and peasants were also afforded other opportunities in their work situations to play diverse roles in the diurnal factory and farm processes that consumed major portions of people's waking hours, influenced their overall behavior, and allowed them to be more than cogs in a relentless impersonal production mechanism. Such opportunities ran a broad range and functioned within as well as outside the labor site, making those workers and peasants who seized the opportunities active citizens of a ramifying social polity. On the work site, workers and peasants were exhorted to take initiatives in criticizing cadres and technicians when their policies and performance did not meet socially expected standards. In its simplest form, criticism was institutionalized through wall newspapers (da zi bao) put up throughout factories and communes. This mode was one of the means by which individuals and groups could call to task those who carried out policies ineptly, did not carry them out, violated standards of responsibility, acted arbitrarily or arrogantly, etc. The wall newspaper criticism could in itself lead to rectification, or set in motion other criticism mechanisms (trade union grievance process, party committee discussion, mass criticism meeting, and so forth) that all cadres and technicians had to face. The process of worker and peasant criticism of working conditions, production issues, social welfare (safety, illness, education e.g.) and other aspects of the work environment contributed to the individual's sense of participation and involvement in influencing important processes.

Workers and peasants also engaged in special functions that expanded the range of participation. They were called on or decided to undertake investigations of their or other work places, they might have been commissioned or initiated literary efforts about their or another factory's or commune's history; and they might have been encouraged to paint pictures of the work activities surrounding them. In all such endeavors their opportunities to influence their own and other work environments affected their attitudes and behaviors on the job.

Another role that stimulated positive worker-peasant work attitudes was teaching. July 21 colleges in factories and May 7 colleges in rural agricultural areas drew upon selected workers and peasants to teach skills and understanding accumulated over the years. Groups of workers and peasants also played roles in the oversight of schools and higher educational institutions. The administration of such institutions since the Cultural Revolution has formally included "worker propaganda teams" and other popular control teams and committees.

Thus, the workers' and peasants' sense of participation in a variety of work-related as well as civic functions that shape the particular environments has further heightened and affected their attitudes and behaviors on the job. To the extent that these diverse activities reinforce the new values of the revolution and fulfill personal needs for satisfaction on the job, they intensify intrinsic motivation. A work environment that is satisfying, that takes into account wants and needs of its constituency, that affords that constituency avenues for influencing its management, and that has means for resolving conflicts is expected to generate positive attitudes and high morale which should translate into higher productivity.

Clearly, the roles that workers and peasants play on the job are significant elements in the work environment. But equally important are those of cadres and technicians – the bureaucracy. In fact, the problem of bureaucracy and its containment and control are perennial and crucial in all cultures and have reached a critical state today throughout the modern world. In the PRC, Mao tagged the satisfactory resolution of the bureaucracy issue as being imperative if communism were to be realized. Two aspects of bureaucracy in China concern us, though in effect the issue reduces to whether the bureaucracy will be in charge of or in the service of society and the people. The two aspects we consider are: how, in Mao's scheme, Chinese bureaucrats were to be integrated into the work environment so as to enhance intrinsic motivation; and how the authority of these bureaucrats was to be radically modified without vitiating their necessary contributions.

The three-in-one combinations in industrial plants and on farms are microcosms of the kinds of roles expected of the three constituencies in society as a whole. By CCP doctrine, in order for such groups to work effectively each constituency had to "serve the people," and workers and peasants were accorded increasing authority and responsibility. This outcome required demystification of expertness without undermining its need and use, improved technical competence (specifically and generally) of workers and peasants, and a collectivist style of cooperative problem solving for all, but especially for technical and managerial staff.

In factories and on communes, important changes were implemented after the cultural revolution so far as cadres (supervisory and technical staff) were concerned. These changes have to be seen as complementing the modifications in workers' and peasants' work roles and working conditions with the goal of enhancing intrinsic motivation by heightening the excitement, challenge, and fulfillment of work and the environment in which it is carried out.

One way of integrating cadres into a collectivist work style was by requiring them to engage in physical labor on a scheduled basis. Such a mandate called for regular involvement of cadres on specific work shifts or teams at the steel hearth or in the rice paddies. As many as 100 such physical labor days in a year were standard for many cadres depending on the particular work contexts. (Of course, some cadres tried with varying degrees of success to get out of such requirements or to make them token or counterfeit experiences. Their degree of success or failure was frequently determined by the activism of the workers or peasants in putting criticism and other political mechanisms into operation.) This participation in labor by cadres was expected to enhance technical and political efficacy, diminish their arrogance, display them to the masses as fallible human beings, develop proletarian work style, and so on.

Participation by cadres in physical toil was also an element in another new institution – the May 7 Cadre School. Such schools were located in the countryside throughout the PRC and all cadres (except very old, ailing, and certain exempt ones) were expected to attend them on a rotating basis for about six months every several years. At these schools, cadres participated in physical labor on site (running the school's farms, kitchen, dorms) and at nearby communes at regular intervals. In addition, the cadres were supposed to be "re-educated" by the peasants on the communes. (This means learning about and helping to improve the peasants' life, work, welfare and being subject to criticism at mass meetings and in other situations.) A final element in the May 7 Cadre School's "curriculum" was study (individually and in groups) of Marxism-Leninism – reading classic works, the thoughts of Mao, and current political tracts and documents – and discussion of its application to the problems of China's development of socialism and communism.

Back on the communes and in the factories cadres were expected to be criticized functionally (i.e. as the production process and its feedback system unfolded) as well as when there were major errors in judgment and failures to achieve production goals that the collective work group (workers or peasants and technical and supervisory cadres) had agreed upon in earlier mass and smaller group sessions. The on-site criticisms to which cadres were subject supplemented the oversight and criticism that higher level and local officials in the party and government structure carried out. At work, criticism came from several sources: individual or group wall newspapers (da zi bao), general and special mass criticism meetings, factory or commune party or revolu-tionary committee action, trade union branch sessions, work groups (workers' or peasants' advisory groups, three-in-one combinations, technical production groups), and other units. This developing criticism mode was expected to condition cadres to take account of the masses and their work and living needs as well as to share problems and unexpected outcomes with them. Cadres at the work level were thus cognizant of hierarchic as well as popular accountability and could only ignore pressing rank and file issues if the masses were docile and other higher responsible officials similarly insensitive.

Cadres' status was also modified materially to conform to more egalitarian and less relatively lavish standards of living so that the deemphasis on material incentives for workers and peasants would not become a one-sided, class differentiation. In effect, higher level cadres suffered major reductions in their incomes and perquisites after the cultural revolution, reducing the income and level of living gaps between the highest paid cadres and the average worker and peasant. One measure of this leveling can be seen in salaries. In 1965, before the cultural revolution, Chairman Mao and other high party and government leaders received monthly salaries 10 to 13 times the average worker's monthly pay; after 1968 this gap was reduced to less than seven to one.

In factories and communes the reduction in cadres' pay was telescoped following examples set by national leaders. The highest paid person in factories received five to six times the average worker's wages in 1965; in 1968 his or her salary was between two and a half and three and a half times that of the average worker. But in numerous industrial plants, the person with the top pay was not even a cadre but a veteran worker. In even more factories, the highest pay did not go to the person in charge but to some other cadre (engineer, physician e.g.), reflecting the deemphasis on material incentive. For example, in one Shanghai factory, the manager received the same pay he had been getting as a skilled worker before being promoted. In communes, similar reductions in cadres' pay have also occurred.

Perhaps even more important in putting cadres in a more equal relation to workers and peasants was the elimination or cut back in perquisites along with the raising of standards of exemplary behavior for cadres. Before 1966 cadres, according to their hierarchic position, often received special treatment in diverse ways that translated into income equivalents and extra opportunities. Being put at the top of the housing mailing list; receiving better, larger housing accommodations; using factory or commune vehicles for personal purposes; obtaining special privileges and rations; placing offspring in special schools for cadres' children – these and other privileges not only raised the living levels of cadres but also set them apart further from workers and peasants rather than eliminating the gap between mental and manual labor. A new class was emerging. After the cultural revolution, however, this development was reversed. The revolutionization of education, outlined above, eliminated special (elitist) schools and drastically changed admissions procedures reducing probabilities of special treatment.   In general, cadres' perquisites were formally eliminated and these leaders were expected to set examples in their behavior and life style with the austere quality of Chairman Mao's life projected as a model. Proletarian leaders, who could be required to reverse roles and become workers or peasants periodically or for protracted periods, were expected to "serve the people" better and become models of collectivist work style if their work environment eliminated or reduced drastically opportunities for special privilege.

Another salient value (objective) in the CCP's design for an emergent communist society was the cultivation and spread of self-reliance. This key operational concept had significance for diverse other objectives: popular control of factories and farms implied technically and politically competent constituencies ("creativity of the masses"); containment of authoritarian bureaucrats likewise required capable masses; rapid economic development and modernization could be facilitated if imports could be kept to a minimum by a versatile work force that adapted modern technologies to particular Chinese conditions; correlatively, a self-reliant work force learned more skills faster and thus contributed to a more rapid growth and adaptation of new technology; development of self-reliance throughout China helped to speed up the movement of human and material resources in the location of new industries and living communities; and so on.

The social and economic development of the PRC was predicated on self-reliance and was, at least partially, reflected in all aspects of life. We look at the shaping of a few new or the remolding of several old social and economic environments with a view to how both the objectives of self-reliance and other principal values (reducing the gaps between town and country, and workers and peasants contributing to the Third World's development) were expected to emerge.

The commune — the basic political, social, and economic organizational unit — was a new environment (dating from 1958) which emerged from the grass roots of old and rapidly changing relationships of work, governance, and family. After the family, the commune was the fundamental social system that ministered to all needs of China's roughly 750 million peasants and their families and that connected them in various ways with the rest of rural and urban China. Functionally, the commune was a multifaceted environment covering the area of the old administrative village that was expected self-reliantly to carry on various economic (not just agricultural) activities essential to people's livelihood, governmental and administrative operations, education up to the high school level, military defense through a people's militia, health care ministration and public health functions, as well as cultural and recreational activities.   This meant that communes were expected to meet their own needs mainly through their own efforts. (In emergencies relief from outside sources was clearly acceptable and rapidly forthcoming as was the relief in the wake of devastating earthquakes in north China in the summer of 1976.) To the extent that they did more than meet basic needs, they benefited from the sale of excess output beyond the commune in exchange for goods and services from the outside.

The organization of the commune aimed at facilitating realization of primary needs with considerable dependence on internal resources to achieve collectively agreed upon ends and means. Obligation to the rest of Chinese society was embodied in the planned commitments of deliveries of food grains and other produce. The reciprocal of this tie to the outside was the ability to call upon outside expertise to join with commune personnel to deal with technical production and other problems. But essentially, each commune (there were over 50,000) was expected to be self-sufficient in providing its own food and other basic product and service needs; such self-sufficiency to expand as the commune developed its own capabilities and facilities.

The commune had three formal operational levels with a fourth informal basic unit – the family. At the hierarchic peak was the commune itself which mainly administered a diversity of activities affecting the lives of thousands of members. (On average, a commune had about 14,000 population but the range was wide, going from several hundred in sparsely populated areas to over 60,000 in some sections of the country.) The commune had considerable operational autonomy in the way it used its resources. It was, however, limited on basic items such as grain, by the national plan, its quota grain commitments being subject to mutual agreement. Operationally, the commune was responsible for commune-wide activities (high school, coal mines, food processing, finance, purchase-sales, hydroelectric power, hospital, and so on).

The next lower operational level was the production brigade (covering the old natural village) of which there were usually about ten on each commune. Like the commune, the brigade's operational functions were limited to activities that broadly covered the population in its jurisdiction (swine, fish, timber production; health stations; primary and lower middle schools; credit co-ops; brigage-wide construction).

At the basic living level of the commune was the production team which generated the commune's major production activity, usually food (grains, vegetables, livestock, dairy products) though certain communes specialized in industrial crops (cotton, wool, flax). The production team touched on the lives of all commune members day-in and day-out and it was there that the individual's and family's share of the output (their income) was determined within the team's governance structure and that the principle of self-reliance must meet the test of practical operation. The operationalization of the principle was expected to be carried out in a wide variety of activities: applied science to control grain strains, insects, fungi, water, sanitation; primary health care through "barefoot doctors" (paramedic, peasant, production team members), public health units, preventive medical indoctrination; organized projects to expand the team's productive capacities (through its capital accumulation funds); and many others.

The commune's management placed responsibilities throughout the structure. The commune itself was subject to the managerial and governance oversight of local, district, county, provincial and central authorities (party and government) and had representation in those structures. Within itself, at the commune and brigade levels, it was managed by its own administrative and party committees. The revolutionary committee ran the commune on a day-to-day basis, while the party committee (a kind of policy board of directors) oversaw implementation of policies and conformity to party principles. Both committees were elected by their respective constituencies and each selected its head.   At the brigade level, there was the same dual organizational set up; while at the team level, there was only one administrator – the team leader, selected by the members (with party concurrence). The team's member congress was made up of all voting members in the team and the brigade's congress was the same, encompassing all team members in the brigade. The commune's "people's congress" was a representative body selected by the member congresses. Thus, there was a ready network for upward and downward communication and decision making with basic strategic decisions being made, after considerable discussion and feedback, at higher levels and with a wide variety of tactical and local-strategic decisions being made in the commune. In such local decisions, it was expected that implementation would be financed by the units themselves with possibilities of consortium funding where the project cut across units (communes, counties, districts, provinces). Major qualifications to this were: 1) the young high school graduates sent to the countryside each year represented an important additional labor resource; and 2) the transfer of other resources from richer areas (in the entire country as well as within communes) to poorer areas was a significant supplementary flow. In either of these situations, however, the utilization and deployment plans for the resources were determined primarily by the local units who were expected to be self-reliant in the execution and follow-up to the plans.

The principle of self-reliance was promoted in other environments. One important such activity we have already looked at is the factory. There, self-reliance was fostered in several policies. Though factories usually were specialized (steel, machine tools, electrical machinery) they were expected to bè versatile enough to improvise and expand their expertise. When supply bottlenecks arose or repair services were necessary, and waiting for the usual external sources to deliver caused delays, many workers and cadres initiated their own solutions: they made necessary materials, recycled factory wastes and discards, machined essential tools, and serviced broken down machinery. This spirit of self-reliance, highly publicized in the media, often assumed heroic proportions – for example, the manufacture from scratch for the first time in China of a sophisticated bore machine by a three-in-one combination to save the foreign exchange required for its importation. Self-reliance was also encouraged in other directions. Many factories had their own vegetable plots, orchards, animals, and used the products instead of purchasing them. Factories also cultivated self-reliance through campaigns promoting preventive medicine, do-it-yourself recreational and cultural projects, writing, painting and sculpturing, and so forth. The party believed that nurturing activist roles in all areas of living sowed the seeds of the communist society of the future.

The system of cooperative health care in several major areas of the nation was also founded on notions of, and depended on, self-reliance. On communes and in local neighborhoods, such systems have been developed. We look at the commune health care mechanisms to get an impression of what kind of environments were intended to provide for developing adequate health services and a population self-reliant in the building and maintenance of such services.

Though Chairman Mao's mandate to the health professions and the Ministry of Health in 1965 clearly demanded that those establishments redirect many of their human and material resources to serve the people in the countryside where medical care was minimal and inadequate, he stressed that health care must be developed by the masses in a self-reliant mode if it were to be successful and advance revolutionary values. The systems developed emphasized relying on local financing and training, use of indigenous (traditional) as well as modern medical practice, expansion of ages-old herbal and other folk medicinal vegetation, wide public training in simple health care, and preventive medicine.

The implementation of an environment conducive to these objectives has been executed within the commune structure (as the street and neighborhood organizational structure in the cities). At the base, the production team, where almost all ailments and illnesses originate, the barefoot doctor, a peasant trained by doctors as a paramedic (there are several millions throughout the country) ministers to the health needs of fellow peasants. Most ailments and illnesses are handled by the barefoot doctors who also are responsible generally for checking standards of public health, sanitation, and dissemination of birth control material. Those ailments and illnesses not resolved at the team level are dealt with at the brigade health stations and clinics if possible, where more complete facilities with trained personnel are found. Some cases have to be sent on to the commune hospital – gynecological-obstetric, gastrointestinal, and emergency surgery – for treatment. For the relatively few cases that present complications not readily resolved by doctors at the commune hospital, the county or nearby city hospitals are used.

The financing of this comprehensive health care system comes principally from within the commune. Each commune member pays a nominal annual fee (about $1 or $2) as well as nominal fees on treatment (25-75 cents). In addition, the welfare funds of the teams, brigades, and communes are tapped to meet medical expenses. (Where individuals are too needy to pay, fees are waived.) The parallel public health and sanitation structures are financed as are any other commune activity. Outside resources – visiting doctors, training programs, mobile medical facilities – are provided by county, city, provincial agencies. Some of this is paid for by the communes but, inevitably, there are some costs which are subsidized. The integrated environment of the commune absorbs many health care activities into its structure, and education and propaganda for disease prevention, good health practice, and other aspects of public health are readily combined with other important campaigns to heighten and reinforce exemplary attitudes and behavior.

The quality of self-reliance is widely broadcast in China, and its reiteration and reinforcement are very consciously projected in many aspects of living; one means of its propagation and reinforcement is through "export" to Third World countries receiving economic aid from the PRC. Since the middle 1950s, China has provided grants and loans, often including technical assistance, to countries in Africa, Asia, Latin America, the Near East, and even Europe (Albania and Malta). This assistance has become relatively substantial for a poor country such as China, exceeding $3 billion in the years since 1970, and has made an important impact directly and indirectly on Third World countries.

In terms of self-reliance, such aid has affected the Chinese themselves as well as the recipients of aid by exporting some elements of the domestic environment. For the Chinese personnel administering technical and financial assistance in the recipient nations, their service abroad has not become a junket to high living. Rather, they have been expected to assist their hosts to learn the technical processes of industrialization-modernization in collaboration with their Chinese guests. Those guests live in the same conditions as their host counterparts and share in the hardships, problems, and successes of the particular aid project.   No special perquisites or payments are distributed. The Chinese workers and technicians are called upon to teach their hosts how to master the exported technology and adapt it to the indigenous conditions of the country as Chinese cadres, workers, and technicians are expected to do in the reverse situations at home. These envoys of China's revolution are also expected to learn from their hosts and the new work situations. The construction of the Tanzam railway through the rugged mountainous and jungle terrain of Tanzania and Zambia in eastern Africa was one such aid venture involving thousands of Chinese in the process of foreign assistance, in which the Chinese experience was a reinforcement of the patterns of self-reliance propagated at home and the notions of solidarity with other peoples of the world.

As for the host country and its receiving personnel, they are treated to the lesson of self-reliance Chinese style. In the Chinese view, the strengthening of the host country's economy and the development of a more skilled and confident work force is expected to help that country to resist penetration and dominance by foreign powers. To the extent that autonomy is reinforced among Third World countries, not only can they meet their own problems more effectively and build confidence further, but politically, as a group, their joint power and influence should grow and become a counterbalancing force to that of the Soviet Union and the United States. China's internal autonomy would be enhanced in a world of more rather than less equal power.

In our presentation of the various environments the Chinese designed under Mao to achieve important attitudinal and behavioral changes, we have dealt with the positive changes desired and achieved. But dysfunction or negative results not only occur, the Chinese expect them to occur and have built into their environments mechanisms to deal with them. For those who are considered the "enemy" and by repeated violation of social norms and law indicate that they are "bad elements" and do not wish to conform, several kinds of penal institutions exist. Convicted hardened criminals and dangerous counterrevolutionaries are sent to traditional-type prisons, usually for indeterminate terms, where they are involved in work tasks and may by exemplary behavior be released. Unlike United States and Soviet prisons, in such prisons inmates and staff are organized into the same small groups and all activities revolve around these groups. (Capital punishment exists for the most serious crimes.) Group tasks are organized collectively and group and individual criticism is one mode used to inculcate and reinforce revolutionary values. For lesser criminal acts, a variety of reform units house the convicted persons while they are being rehabilitated.

For "the people," a variety of modes is employed to deal with violations of norms and law. Deviant behavior on the job and in the different parts of the community is considered a responsibility of the group and calls for group response. Where the individual's behavior is acknowledged by him/her to be asocial, the group is expected to assist the individual to modify his/her behavior. If the individual denies the undesirability of certain behavior and resists group suasion, sanctions may be undertaken. (Of course, minor deviant behaviors are often ignored and the nonconformist often continues such behavior with impunity.)

The gamut of social intervention runs a range of formal and informal modes. The informal modes are used mainly at the basic community level when a worker violates required practice, a child steals, or a couple has a violent conflict. The group intervenes, usually with criticism sessions. If the transgression is responsibly admitted, the group works with the individual to overcome the negative conditions and behavior. If the individual resists, informal assistance is sought from the next group level (trade union or party branch in a factory, street committee in a neighborhood). Such social involvement and pressure within the basic work or living unit ordinarily contains most nonconforming behavior. Where it does not, and successive informal interventions are also unsuccessful, if the violation is serious enough, the individual may be recommended to be "re-educated through labor" — sent to work stints in the countryside where the individual has the opportunity to rectify his/her behavior in organized groups.

When informal approaches to deviance are unsuccessful, and the violations are serious enough (clear-cut violations of the law), then formal judicial proceedings are undertaken before local courts. (The court is usually a group of several judges including worker or peasant representation.) Conviction yields various sentences up to imprisonment. Imprisonment in traditional walled prisons is for the most extreme crimes. Less severe infractions may require "reform through labor," a more severe form of "reeducation through labor," in work battalions sent to the countryside. The reformees are restricted in their movement and carry out onerous work tasks of economic construction. Organized in groups, they are expected to demonstrate an acceptance and development of proper behavior in order to return to their communities. The notion that the right kind of environment, including proper group functioning, is a reinforcer of "correct" behavior is an important ideological principle that is expected to inform and shape the rehabilitative process.

While it is too early to assess the Chinese results in any but the most tentative way, the Chinese have demonstrated the ability to change mass attitudes and behaviors through mass campaigns in line with a generally sketched plan for modernizing Chinese society. In place of the disunited, humiliated giant of a nation subject to the predatory encroachments of world industrial powers, the leaders of the CCP have been able, despite the burdens of the Korean War and their own periodic ideological traumas, to shape a united country and to begin the modernization process at a high sustained rate of growth. This process has also developed in the Chinese people a strong sense of purpose and community. The Chinese experience thus far bears out the environmental design principle that changed behaviors follow changed environments.

Whatever our evaluation of the costs and benefits of the PRC's changed environments – evaluations which perforce come from a quite different social environment which generates and sustains its own set of attitudes, behaviors, and values – certain results in China seem relevant to our earlier questions of environmental design for what and who decides. Mao insisted on a concern for the lowliest peasants and workers having their conditions improved, not just through mandates from the central authorities but through a process of popular involvement, experimentation, modification, and finally, where appropriate, acceptance. Where that sequence did not result in acceptance, retreat, rather than dictation, was required, followed by searching out the reasons for non-acceptance and then going back to persuade the people.

For optimum environmental design, therefore, it appears that there must be a link between for what and who decides. Designing environments must be socially experimental with the inhabitants of the proposed environments participating actively. This does not rule out the expert. There must be a mutual involvement and exchange to come up with a viable first-approximation environment which has to change as its inhabitants test its livability, modifying it as conditions dictate.

Another major perennial problem that the Chinese experience highlights is the braking effect of the continuities of the past. Even in a revolutionary society where the momentum for change is so great, the dead hand of the past may be a major hurdle to implementing newly designed environments. One generalization that the Chinese experience backs up is that change can often be most effectively brought about if selected continuities of the past are utilized positively in designing the change (e.g. building agricultural cooperatives on old Chinese mutual aid institutions). The Chinese put it this way: "let the past serve the present."

As for training and retraining people, the Chinese have had to face formidable barriers transforming a mostly illiterate peasant population into a modernizing nation learning radically new skills, attitudes, behaviors, and values. Effective training and retraining depends on strong motivation and efficacious training modes. Since designing and implementing new environments is an experimental activity, it can never just be the implementation of blueprints thought out by a small group. It must combine both principles and practice. If the designed environment is being built for its inhabitants and they are vitally involved, motivation can be optimum. If the implementation continues to involve them in modes that combine principles of environmental design applied experimentally on new environments subject to modification as the applications are tested, the modes (themselves subject to experimental modification) should approach the norm of effectiveness.

The barriers to effective environmental design of social systems more responsive to popular needs and wants are forbidding. But there is really no other way to go if a democratic solution to the perennial questions of providing for self-realization in a bureaucratically explosive and frustrating world is to be achieved.

14 Environmental Design in Practice: Implementation Process and Personal Experience
Robin Christopher Winkler

Throughout each chapter in this volume the emphasis has been on the broader implications of the particular topic and linkages with all other aspects of the environmental design approach. Yet we feel that if there is any one chapter basic to understanding all the others, it is Winkler's discussion of his own experiences as an environmental designer. Indeed, he aptly demonstrates the importance of the role of the "participant" in the model of the designer as "participant observer." His observations, although personal, speak for all of us would-be environmental designers.

Ed.

A common experience of recent university graduates from professional training courses is that what they have learned has little to do with what they have to do on the job. The result, frequently, is that whatever new concepts and idealism are there at the outset are beaten down by the apparently impossible task of implementing (in the face of enormous opposition) what seem eminently reasonable ideas. The "real world" seems impossibly complex, alien and byzantine. What seemed so sensible and simple in the literature seems hopelessly naive and complex when it comes to implementation.

There are many reasons for these discrepancies. Programs, when reported, are usually presented as completed entities and in their most favorable light. The fears, fights, uncertainties, mistakes, and confusion that are involved in every human venture, let alone one of social change, are swept under the carpet as irrelevant or somehow 'unclean' and inappropriate. Frequently, the people who read and teach have not themselves been active participants in establishing programs and, therefore, accept the available written reports as viable descriptions of what is important to know.

The majority of reports of environmental design projects appear to be based on a false understanding of the nature of what has occurred.

Creating change is a continually emerging process. The process does not begin and end with the reaching of some established, clearly definable, steady state. For every program reported, in this fashion, there are many more that were attempted but collapsed. The program that is reported is always based on extensive groundwork which was crucial to its very existence but is almost never reported. By the time a program is finally reported, it has often collapsed or is nothing like it was when reported.

Environmental design is not simply a matter of procedure or technique. A fundamental process in environmental design is creating the circumstances where a procedure can actually be used, and can continue to be used. By far, the most energy and time goes into this process, yet it is the least discussed in the literature.

There can, of course, be no substitute for learning the realities of implementing principles of environmental design by actually trying to implement them. Nevertheless, accounts of experiences in implementing environmental design and what has been learned from the experience may prevent first attempts at implementation from being the last. Much of what follows is little more than "horse sense" and "common humanity" but, unfortunately, horse sense and common humanity are not given high priority in the halls of academe.

Sarason (1972) has, perhaps more than most, drawn recent attention to the processes of implementing environmental design programs. His term, the creation of settings, is particularly appropriate in that it goes beyond formally defined "programs" and is more sensitive to the emergent process of developing new settings. As Sarason points out, although settings vary enormously, there are consistent themes that can be found in attempts to make changes in them. These commonalities have formed the basis of a number of valuable analyses of the process of creating settings or of implementing environmental design (Alinsky, 1971; Collarelli & Siegel, 1966; Goldenberg, 1971; Graziano, 1974; Levine & Levine, 1970). Similar conclusions can be arrived at from experiences in a variety of settings and from action inside or outside institutional structures.

This account is based primarily on work inside psychiatric institutions and is, therefore, most relevant to the creation of settings inside existing institutional structures. Research reports arising from this work (e.g. Battalio, et al., 1973; Winkler, 1970) are typically inappropriate descriptions of the settings involved: chronic wards of state psychiatric institutions in Sydney (Gladesville) and New York (Central Islip). Richards (1975) has written a more sensitive account of the political realities of the token economy part of the New York program. Both the Sydney and New York programs were behaviorally oriented and involved token economies. The latter program was designed and run jointly by Leonard Krasner and the author.

The following analysis of the creation of settings is organized in two parts: 1) Sequential stages in the implementation process; common experiences in the creation of settings can form the basis of broad principles in creating settings. However, it is naive and inappropriate to suggest implementation is simply a matter of technique. 2) The experience of people involved in creating settings; the decision to undertake the role of an agent of change is an intensely personal one. The role requires fundamental commitment and is frequently not taken up or is allowed to slip away because of failure to come to grips with the personal realities it entails. Similarly, failure to understand the experience and perspective of colleagues inevitably results in failure in creating settings. Accounts of private, personal experience are as crucial to the understanding of setting creation as are chronicles of events.

STAGES IN THE IMPLEMENTATION PROCESS

There are never very clearly defined stages in the implementation process of any program. However, there are certain themes which can, to a certain extent, be arranged in sequence, with full recognition that these themes may be relevant at any stage. These are preliminary analysis; developmental groundwork; establishment and maintenance; and passing on and dissemination. The latter two stages are better seen as four but have been collapsed for economy of presentation.

Preliminary Analysis

The analysis one makes from the outset about the nature of the enterprise being undertaken is crucial to what will follow. A frequent error is often made from the outset which can pervade all that follows. Goldenberg (1971) states it clearly in his account of the development of a residential youth center:

> If there was anything we had learned (and learned well) from our involvement in different organizations, it was that one could be certain of only one thing: There would always be problems. The problems would vary in content and intensity, but they would always be there, always pose some present or potential danger to the organization, and always threaten the goals of the setting and the welfare of its people. To say that one could always count on the existence of problems seems to be little more than a glimpse of the obvious. Our past experiences, however, had left us with a residue of unhappy examples of just how rarely this apparent truism is taken seriously enough to be translated into, or lead to the development of, the kinds of organizational vehicles that might enable a setting to deal with its problems in nonself-defeating ways. To be aware – however dimly, perhaps even unconsciously – of the inevitability of problems is one thing; to anticipate their occurrence and to plan or devise internal mechanisms for handling them is quite another. . . . (italics added).

Failure to understand that there must be problems is a fundamental cause in the frustration and defeat of so many attempts to create settings.

It is, therefore, essential to attempt to have at least a rudimentary analysis of where problems might arise and what they might be. This analysis can then guide decisions about whether to do anything at all, where in a system is the most likely place to begin, and what general strategy is appropriate.

Ultimately, however, this analysis emerges from deeply held assumptions about personal and social politics. Creating change is an inherently political process. It must involve concepts of power and powerlessness, conflict and consensus, and means and ends. It is deeply rooted in values and ideology. The process of implementing programs continually forces decisions about basic political issues. Unless, from the outset, the environmental designer has some notion of who he is and what he believes in, he will be buffeted about from pillar to post. At the same time, an analysis that precludes learning by praxis and putting self and beliefs at risk will also produce failure.

At the more superficial level, consideration needs to be given to defining the arena of action and the power balances in it. Creating change always involves a network of people and structures. Each of those people and structures have some degree of power and interest, each a different degree, and each will be in consensus and conflict on different matters. Inevitably, some will support a change, some will oppose it, and some will be disinterested. From the outset, an appreciation of the inevitability of conflict and apathy is essential. Change is always resisted and generally resisted most by people who have most to lose. These people frequently have the most power in the situation to be changed. Analysis of who is likely to be most threatened, who has most to gain, and the relative power of these groups can be used to sketch out where and when different problems are likely to arise.

This preliminary analysis is necessary to guide decisions about whether to work inside or outside a system, and which part of a system is likely to be the most fruitful in which to begin. Such decisions are crucial to the future course of events. For example, inside a given system, such as a psychiatric institution, various administrators may be possible supporters. Association with one administrator may be unfortunate if he leaves, loses power, or is disliked by other important people. Another person or group may offer support but may be unable to provide it when needed. There may be areas where few existing groups have an interest where it is more possible to go it alone.

As well as making a preliminary analysis of the arena in which a setting is to be created, the environmental designer must make an analysis of the impact of creating the setting on his/her own personal life.

Usually, an environmental design program is not the only work the designer wishes or is obliged to do. Inevitably, less time and energy is available for other interests. The designer needs to make decisions ahead of time about what other commitments may have to go, and communicate to relevant others that they can expect less of him/her over the forthcoming period.

This type of preparation cannot be made without a consideration of the intensity and length of commitment the proposed program is likely to involve (Reppucci, 1973). It is not uncommon for projects to fail because the project attempted took more time or commitment than those who planned it could or wanted to give. Biting off more than one can chew can occur because of overzealous idealism, naive estimates of the difficulties involved, a desire to start too big, a lack of humility about one's energy and time reserves, expecting too much of people, being seduced by administrators (or desperates) into areas where angels have feared to tread — a myriad of reasons. On the other hand, frequently, designers find doing what others consider impossible a major challenge. Indeed, there is always someone who says the easiest change is impossible. Generally, however, one is not likely to be wrong by assuming the worst, so that one can be pleasantly surprised and joyful if less commitment required must be continually revised. At the very early stage of deciding whether or not to start, information from people who have tried similar ventures and/or know the arena in which the changes are proposed is crucial.

Depending on the size of the project, extensive informal discussions may be needed before deciding whether a project should be even seriously considered, let alone started. Some art may be required in floating ideas and estimating support without being seen to have begun a project. It might be argued that no preparation for a project should begin until one is sure the project will succeed, but this can amount to a counsel of no experimentation. Rarely is it possible to know in advance what will succeed or fail.

On the other hand, a history of attempts that did not meet expectations saps morale and produces resistance to subsequent proposals. Individuals and groups can acquire reputations for sapping morale in this way. For example, university people are frequently highly suspect when approaching other organizations, because, in the past, university people have come in for a short period, served their own purposes, and left with no feedback. They leave behind hopes that have been raised and dashed, resentment about being used, and distrust about grand ideas which involve more work for all but the proposers and whose effects are forgotten in the longer time perspective of the organization. In psychiatric institutions, it is almost a part of normal routine for university people to come in for a few months, have residents and staff running about all over the place, leave with little more than a formal "thank you," and go on to publish a report of what seems to be a beautiful and effective program. Meanwhile, back in the institution, cynicism grows a step stronger, as the residents go back to their usual behavior, life returns to "normal," and the staff ready themselves for the next hot-shot to tell them (tactfully) they don't know what they are doing and why don't they give this a try.

This process must be recognized in advance and respected by prospective designers. Analysis of what they can and will give and what others can and will give must precede the first steps of implementation, and be revised throughout. Generally, the more accurate that analysis and the more it is communicated as understanding, the more chances of success the program has. The more time and energy the designer gives, the more he might expect those he works with to give, while understanding that he might have more freedom to give and different motivation than those with whom he works. The designer who is seen to give primarily because of career aspirations or some external demand is not likely to command giving from those who do not share those aspirations. Similarly, the designer who e.g., has a high salary, no problems with child care and job security has to understand that colleagues on low salaries, who have constant child care problems and are afraid of losing their jobs may have greater limits on how much they can work for change.

Developmental Groundwork

The period of preparation before program establishment is crucial. Indeed, in cases where a program is usually effective once established e.g., with token economies, the crucial determinant of the program's success is whether it is allowed to exist in the first place.

The period of development prior to establishment sets a clear stamp on the ensuing program once it is established, a stamp which may be extremely difficult to alter. For example, often choices can be made about staff. Staff, once accepted or rejected, shape all that follows and may be difficult to move at a later date. Expectancies established in the development stages are crucial in shaping others' concepts of the program's success or failure and what may or may not be demanded of it. Opportunities offered by initial supporters, keen to show they are on-side, may never be offered again. Potential opposition, if not removed or countered during the development phase, may sabotage the program beyond repair once it is established. Indeed, the signal to begin a program depends on the obtaining of initial support and an assessment of no impossible opposition.

A fundamental process in this development phase is, of course, making sure the resources needed for the program can be defined and are available. The resources may be financial support, staff, space, or time allowances, but whatever they may be, as Sarason (1972) points out, the designer almost always expects more resources than are forthcoming. Inappropriate expectancies over resources inevitably are frustrating and morale sapping. On the other hand, a judiciously timed success in obtaining resources not previously forthcoming can be a great morale booster. In the development phase of one token economy, the author was offered by an administrator, wishing to demonstrate the power of his support, a number of staff lockers. Staff were then asked by the author to make a shopping list of resources with the expected result that staff lockers would be included, as they had been frequently requested in the past. The administrator was able to demonstrate his power in the institution by obtaining some lockers and the author was able to suggest his power to enlist powerful support to get results in the bureaucracy where other staff had been unsuccessful. Cautious under-statement of this success suggested working with the author might be worthwhile.

A common experience, however, is that programs often do not proceed beyond the development phase because the designers wait for full resources to appear before starting. Generally, resources are scarce and difficult to obtain. Experience would suggest that a start might be made by stretching available resources rather than waiting for full support. Often, initial successes are sufficient to produce further gains which may create sufficient enthusiasm to sustain a program without the need for large-scale funding. One can argue that careful planning, energy, and enthusiasm coming from a committed group are more important than funding. For example, a radical psychiatric patients' collective, the Pala Society (after Huxley's The Island), formed in Sydney, and after nine months of weekly meetings, a detailed grant proposal was prepared for an alternative, collectively run "asylum." The preparation of the grant proposal directed considerable energy and coalesced a trusting, open group of people who, with support from friends, found their own houses and moved in to establish the first Pala Society house. The grant proposal, although submitted, was almost forgotten, and its later rejection was greeted with some relief because of its potential threat to the independence and radical concept of the, by then, Pala houses (Kenny & Cox, 1976).

The formation of a working team in the development phase is crucial and well-recognized. In the Pala project, the nine months before the first house saw the emergence, from weekly meetings of 15-40 people per night, of a stable core group, who through regular open interaction, working together and a common purpose, had worked through sufficient trust exercises to make their subsequent move into the first Pala house a success. In psychiatric institutions, a stable, well trained, cohesive, and motivated staff, if it can be developed, almost ensures the success of a forthcoming planned therapeutic environment. Rarely, however, is this achieved, and if it is, it needs constant care if it is to continue.

Trust exercises may take a number of forms. For example, shortly after joining a chronic ward of a psychiatric institution, the author once found himself faced with two residents fighting in a courtyard. Looking around, he saw the staff, who were present a few seconds ago, had disappeared. With barely concealed trepidation, he dealt with the fight and looked around again. The staff who had disappeared were there, watching how the professional with all the grand ideas was dealing with the nitty gritty realities of their world. In another ward program, the author's loyalties were put to the test on numerous occasions – Where would his office be? on the ward or with "the other" unit administrators? How would he handle internal ward staff conflicts and unit rule violations? by frank discussion in the ward or by reference to outside authorities? How far can he be pushed? Is he another of these professionals who can be easily twisted around the fingers of the old hands who know professionals want to win their support? If he says something, does he mean it? Can he be trusted in a crisis? How does he deal with the well-known troublemakers who can be relied upon to put anyone through their paces? Why does he want to go through all this aggravation? Is he just using us for his own ends or does he really care? How long will he be around? Will he give up easily? Can we wait him out? and a host of other questions, which are never fully answered in the minds of those involved, but which need some preliminary answers before a program can begin.

Establishment and Maintenance

Although an environmental design program may slowly develop in relatively unnoticed stages, most programs usually can be defined as having a particular starting point, at which groundwork is turned into visible reality. Two key factors at this point are expectations and procedural clarity.

It is important that those involved in a program do not have expectations which are too high or too low. Care needs to be taken to lower expectancies of those who are overenthusiastic or overoptimistic about what is likely to be achieved. Too high an expectation increases the probability of later frustration and disappointment. On the other hand, sour pessimism, rationalized as being realistic, needs to be dealt with, using such arguments as: let's try it for an experimental period, then we can revise it; let's proceed step by step, reviewing all the time; some people will change, some won't, but we can't tell who in advance. Discussion among those involved about what might be expected and what might be regarded as initial effects is essential, particularly when the hold-outs find themselves in the minority. Acceptance of a certain amount of pessimism may be important, as long as this does not unduly dampen the enthusiasm of others. One of the major processes at this stage is often the enthusiasm of a core group or leader whose energy carries people over their hesitancy. Such enthusiasm, which cannot be manufactured, can override "real, rational" problems that a non-enthusiast may insist on solving before starting. Realistic optimism seems to be the trick.

In the first days and weeks of a program, clearly defined procedures are needed to reduce the inevitable confusion and anxiety that change brings. Formulation of procedures in association with those who are to use them can reduce initial resistance and later teething problems. Written, detailed procedures displayed or communicated effectively prior to the starting point provide a focus for rehearsal and discussion, which can reduce teething problems. Close, rather more pedantic than usual, supervision of the details of these procedures at the points at which they are implemented is crucial during this period. Without close, point of contact involvement at this stage, misunderstandings can become institutionalized, resentment about remoteness can arise, and appropriate revisions may not be made or made too late.

A balance needs to be struck at this stage between recognizing obvious errors and making too many changes during early confusion. Clear decision making procedures which are genuinely accessible to all involved, and which are effective, are crucial to prevent enthusiasm being turned into a flurry of ad hoc, poorly communicated and, perhaps, inconsistent decisions being taken by all concerned. If a decision is made at this early stage, it is especially important that it be followed through into practice, and be seen to have been followed through, so that those involved can have faith that involvement in decision making is meaningful and not a waste of time. Accordingly, early decisions are best kept simple, few in number and restricted to those most likely to achieve definable, visible results, which are, nevertheless, relevant to the needs of those involved.

Positive feedback about results achieved is also crucial in the early stages of a program. Previously stated short-term goals can be examined, and data from all relevant sources used to indicate that continued involvement is likely to pay off. Feedback needs to be given judiciously. Frequently, the most minor changes may be felt significant, particularly if they run counter to previously stated expectancies. Graphs, behavioral observation, or other hard data may be disregarded or doubted, if unaccompanied by examples relevant to the evaluation framework of those involved. Too "naive" a belief that progress has been achieved leads to a weakening of support among those reserving judgment. Understatement, when results speak for themselves, may be far more effective than glossy rapture. An image of success, however, is invaluable, and wide communication to key people of realistically reported results which can forestall possible unfounded criticism is extremely important.

Those involved in a successful program should not necessarily expect people will react favorably to hearing their work has been successful. Success can produce negative reactions in those working in similar arenas who have not been successful or who once tried and failed. Failure to recognize this process, and failure to acknowledge the role of fate and special circumstances, frequently sow the seeds of later program failure.

A final point that is often overlooked is that initial enthusiasm can never last. Three to four months after the initial rush of enthusiasm, the pace settles down. What was once tight, becomes sloppy. What was once exciting, becomes routine. This period should be anticipated and new inputs planned to go into effect at that time. They may take the form of a major revision, a new subset of programs, or a new resource input held back for introduction at this time.

Once a program becomes established and taken for granted, a new set of processes takes over. The preprogram period is forgotten. What was once only an indulgent hope has become a boring fact of life, ripe for criticism. New people come in who did not know the setting before, assume that the changes fought for always existed, and pressure for more. The people who were once the new guard become the old hands who resist new pressures. The people who thrive on initiating change and the excitement of newness move on, and those who prefer maintaining a system move in. In a sense, it is a sign of success that such things happen, but it can also be the end of growth.

Passing On and Dissemination

The passing on of programs does not receive a great deal of attention. Starting is always more involved than passing something on. But insufficient attention to the need for passing on a program and problems involved in achieving this, frequently lead to short-term gains that wither away to be forgotten. The people who are effective change agents often make poor administrators of the status quo, even if they themselves have helped create that status quo. It may be that some prefer a program to die with their departure rather than have it be seen as independent of them. Often, a key person or group's departure is used as an opportunity for others to kill off a program when it is most vulnerable. Or the space cleared may simply become 'overgrown' again due to inertia during a leadership hiatus.

Atthowe (1973) has commented that the persistence of behavior change over time and settings has received insufficient attention in the behavior change literature. The problems of passing programs on and persistence in behavior change are closely related. Rarely is it the case that one person or group can remain effective for a long time over a variety of settings. Without care in passing programs on, the program ceases to operate after a certain time, not necessarily due to lack of knowledge about the basic behavioral principles required, but because the principles are simply no longer maintained in practice through a continuing program.

A similar point applies to generality across settings. A great deal of energy, resources, and time may be devoted to establishing a new environment for one setting, with the result that energy, resources, and time are so depleted that too little is left for the sequence of new programs that are needed to produce behavior change across new settings.

It is essential, therefore, to plan well ahead when and how a given program will be passed on as well as what sequence of programs in new settings are necessary. For example, at Central Islip, from the outset, the overall program included 1) a token economy, 2) community preparation unit, 3) follow-up community support, and 4) a self-supporting living community in the larger community (Fairweather et al., 1969). It was, therefore, necessary to pace the using up of energy, resources, and time for these tasks. Core group staff who trained on the first program produced a leader who took charge of that program, while the leader of the core group moved on to establish the second. The second program, once established, could be run by a leader produced from its core group, thus freeing the initial figures to expand into the third program, and so on. A key component in this sequencing is that early efforts are made to ensure that positions, personnel, and resources will be available when needed at later stages.

The importance of passing the program on to either new personnel in the same setting or to new settings needs to be communicated clearly to those controlling necessary resources from the very outset of the initial phases of the overall program. At each stage in a sequence, new personnel are best introduced before old personnel leave, so that continuity is ensured. However, care must be taken not to undermine the independence and initiative of new figures by too close an indoctrination in the 'old' ways.

If a program of environmental design has been successfully implemented and shown to be effective according to definable criteria, there is still a final stage, that of dissemination. Demonstration programs, even if long lasting, can only be demonstrations that under a unique, often quite advantageous, set of conditions, certain changes can be made with certain effects. This in no way indicates the program will be broadly adopted in other conditions or, if more broadly adopted in other conditions, it will have similar effects. The dissemination of social innovations is itself a major process. As Fairweather and his colleagues (1974) have argued, the process of implementing environmental design should include dissemination programs to encourage widespread adoption and evaluation of programs shown to be successful in the initial setting. Their research is a major contribution to both the research and practice of dissemination of social innovations.

PERSONAL EXPERIENCE IN SETTING CREATION

The Experience of the Environmental Designer

Creating change is a difficult, involved, and stressful experience. This is frequently perceived by those asking themselves whether they wish to enter that role and often results in a decision to reject the role because of the personal cost. The cost may be the risk and stress, the energy required, the size of the opposition, or, perhaps more fundamentally, what the role can do to your personal life. It has been my own experience, for example, that potential change agents, be they in university classes or activist groups, will often not make a sustained commitment to struggle for change because of the fear of what it can do to you as a person.

This concern is tied up with the mode of being in the world that is thought of as required for a committed agent of change. Life is thought to become a never ending grind of meetings, manipulations, basic hack-work, frustration, disappointment, power plays, plotting, anger, recrimination, duplicity, confrontation, futility, and despair. Is there never any opportunity, it is asked, for quiet slow time with friends and family, feelings of peace with oneself and the world, warmth and honesty, love and caring, gentle understanding, and general enjoyment of life? The tension between these different modes of being — active, struggling agent and quiet, joyful reflector — is one that is at the center of decisions to both enter the role of social change agent and to maintain that role once entered. The tension between turning into oneself and turning out to the environment is, I suspect, experienced by every environmental designer and demands some consideration. Much of the bringing together of Eastern and Western philosophies deals with these tensions at a broader level and this conjunction is of immediate relevance to the experience of being an environmental designer.

There are many processes in the implementation of environmental design that force the people involved to turn away from their own experience. Foremost is the misleading view that environmental design, because it is concerned with external environments, demands all energy to be turned to that environment outside the person who is the designer.

This view is continually reinforced in meetings, structures, and relationships, all of which are directed towards events "in the world." Purposes and goals become paramount. There is never enough time. One response to a demand produces more demands. A group expectancy can develop in which those who respond to demands are perceived to be almost inhuman in their capacity to respond. Fatigue, fear, and uncertainty, already taboo topics, become almost unacceptable weaknesses.

Frequently, however, enthusiasm, feelings of achievement and meaningful purpose, and even naivete are sufficient to put aside the problems of these demands. The business of social change can provide fundamental personal meaning as well as great pleasure and excitement. There is a great satisfaction to be derived from trying to integrate ideas and action, at both an intellectual and personal level. Crises and difficult problems can become the very stuff of life to the extent that their absence is boring. There is a great deal of intense experience to be treasured in group struggle towards a goal, in confrontation, in despair, and in joy over losses and gains. It is not a dull life.

Unfortunately, however, the positive side of the experience of being a committed environmental designer, once stated, has a definite Richard Nixon, puritan ring to it. There is a need to attend to the preservation of personal happiness in acting as a social change agent which, somehow, avoids the puritan work ethic (albeit for what seem more noble than usual ends) and which avoids the old, work hard-play hard view. A balance between personal happiness and changing conditions must, it seems, be struck, if a long commitment to action for changing conditions is to be made. Self-destruction in the course of action would seem to be eventually counterproductive in seeking the original goal. However, personal comfort, peace, and joy can be very seductive, particularly when phrased in acceptable social change language, in weakening the commitment needed in implementing designs for environments.

In a sense, these are trite statements. But they do not receive serious discussion in environmental design courses and many of the casualties in environmental design (and designers) are related to the failure to genuinely respond to these issues.

The Experience of Participants

The preceding account of implementation processes in environmental design has been viewed primarily from the perspective of the change agent, facilitator, or leader. Inevitably, this perspective is limited. A large number of people, in widely differing roles, are all involved in the process of implementing any environmental design program. Each has his or her own perspective. Failure to perceive and understand these different perspectives among participants in, and facilitators of, change seriously weakens the chances of successful implementation.

With this in mind, during the implementation of the programs at Central Islip in 1970-1971, the author (the primary facilitator) and another key participant (a nurse on the token economy ward) kept independent, regular diaries during the development, establishment, and maintenance phases of the token economy program. After the author had left the hospital and university to return to Australia, key figures in all stages of the Central Islip program were interviewed by a graduate student who had spent an internship on the program, but was no longer working there. Among those interviewed were patients, an attendant, nurses, the unit psychiatrist, and the administrator in charge of the unit.

The following brief selections from this wealth of material illustrate far more clearly than general statements some of the realities of implementing environmental design programs. The selections are taken from the ward nurse's diary and deal with the period shortly before and after the introductions of tokens in the token economy. Although they cover events associated with implementing a token economy in a chronic ward of a large state psychiatric institution, the social processes depicted have considerable setting generality. Names and places have been changed. Roles of participants are noted. The author's involvement made reading the nurse's diary at times stressful, and at times gratifying. Hopefully, both types of selection have been included here.

Excerpts from diary kept by Ward Nurse

May 27, 1970

Rather quiet day, no big skirmishes as far as ward 130 is concerned. Enthusiasm regarding recording has dwindled but that is to be expected. Meg's (attendant) patients finally got to go out in the yard now that the weather has cleared. I am still having problems with Bobby (attendant) in this area. She always has a million and one excuses! We finally received a refrigerator and display case. Some girls, including myself, were disappointed with the display case. Ward charge meeting consisted mainly of specific instructions to charge duties. Charges listened passively but appeared annoyed. They are looking for answers but answers that we cannot always give. Very frustrating. Having many problems with Gaynor (charge attendant) on 140. She refused to go to the oxygen therapy class I held. She will be counselled by Irene (Chief Nurse of Unit) over this. She is continually making snide comments to me, I am really angry! However, the other girls on the ward are suddenly supporting me. Thank God!

June 10

Today was the opening of the token economy, it was hectic, exciting and it went very well. Patients are catching on to the idea quite fast. Most know what tokens can buy, and what you must do for one. Some patients don't feel that they get enough for each token. It's quite interesting. The ward was put on smoking restriction, for some patients. Flicking ashes on the floor and not cleaning them up. Most smokers are quite upset over the restriction, especially M. and P.

(residents). M. posted a sign that patients should be on strike and not work until they were allowed to smoke. Amazing! Had a long talk with Robbie and found out his immediate plans for the ward. I am really looking forward to all that will be happening. I feel that we are really doing something, I am sure that the girls feel the same. Satisfaction and success in their work is something these girls rarely have ever had. I think now we see results the entire ward will be different. I feel very much a part of it now.

June 14, Sunday

Today was hectic, Dr. W. (unit psychiatrist) was on the rampage re medical problems on 130. I think he is really upset over the token economy and the change he has to cope with rather than medical problems. I guess we will really have to play up to him. The girls of 130 were confused and irritable today. They do not feel that Robbie is giving them enough support. I think they were just nervous about being on their own. However, there does seem to be a few inconsistencies in what they have been told. I always feel lost after my two days off. I hope everything clears up tomorrow. Sunday is always a mess. The girls always make a big issue over nothing. I was not able to get them to settle down and look at things in proper perspective.

June 16, Tuesday

Robbie and I talked about the happenings on Sunday. He gave me some good suggestions on how to handle Sundays. Talks are very encouraging for me. He is very supportive. I wish I could be the same for him. He really needs support.

June 18, Thursday

We had ward meeting on 130 today. Robbie was unbelievable. He told all the girls what they were doing wrong and made it seem as if he were complimenting them. I never heard anyone chew anyone out in such a soft voice and with a calm manner. It was great! Dr. W. finally transferred H. (resident) to 126. He will probably get her back in a few days. It's such a shame.

June 22, Monday

Today was an interesting day filled with meetings and intrigue. I met with Dick and Steve (graduate students) in the morning. They are great guys who are genuinely interested in our program. I think we will work well together. While I was meeting with Dick and Steve, Robbie was meeting with Dr. G. (Assistant Director, Hospital) and other big shots re community preparation program. Robbie returned quite excited. (Well, as excited as Robbie gets). He told us that we have a good chance of getting what we want. In the afternoon G.F. and crew and Mr. B. came to our IDT staff meeting. The meeting went very well and I was getting more excited every second. However, on the tour, G. baulked at the fact that two patients on 130 were not wearing shoes! Plus he must have thought he was on ward 110 because he asked what happened to the pictures! At this point Dr. G.'s mood changed and he disappeared. Irene, Robbie and I were afraid he might turn to male Unit. We can't allow him to do it. Dr. G. likes pretty pictures so we are starting a beautify the wards campaign. Also Robbie has to get a crash program on 130 about wearing shoes. All for Dr. G.! Dr. G. wants a show place for the men from Albany (Head Office, State). He has to impress them! Either us or the male side will be the lucky ones. Bob says that Dr. G. is trying for a position in Albany. It really annoys me that patients have to be pawns in their political chess games. Oh well, as long as our patients get a program they need in order to get out of this dammed place, I guess Dr. G.'s motives are unimportant.

June 25, Thursday

I was quite upset with Robbie's actions today. Irene had a conference with Dr. W. and finally got him on our side concerning community preparation. I was quite excited about this. I told Robbie and he said he wanted to have a conference with Irene and I. At this conference he became very angry because he was not included when Irene talked to Dr. W. At the same time, I could not understand why he was angry. I thought he would be happy that Irene got Dr. W.'s backing. He seemed to be upset because he worked so hard in making community preparation something more than words and now he is afraid he will lose control. I really was disappointed in him. All I could think of was shades of Dr. G. and shades of Irene! I still don't completely understand. I feel that we all knew and wanted essentially the same things, for our patients from the community preparation programme. If Robbie was completely honest with Irene about his plans, and she was as enthusiastic as he, then he should be able to trust her to at least talk to Dr. W. about running it. As I see it now he doesn't trust us or give us any credit with respect to the planning of the programme. He wants complete control and probably he'd do a fantastic job, but I doubt if he will ever get complete control. Maybe I am misinterpreting his anger. I hope so because I hate to be disillusioned.

July 5, Sunday

Nice quiet Sunday with no major catastrophies on 130. I opened the store in the morning, which is amazing. I took over the charge as much as possible. Had a long talk with Irene. She is becoming quite discouraged over everything in general. She feels that she, in a way, is being pushed out of the role by Robbie. She doesn't think he is doing it purposely but the fact that Dr. G. only talks to Robbie, it takes away some duties of Irene. If Dr. G. thinks the rest of the staff are a bunch of yo yo's and he only communicates with Robbie, then what is going to happen to the unit when Robbie leaves?

July 8, Wednesday

Rather exciting day. Irene became very upset at the end of the day. She called Dr. G. to get permission (for Community preparation) to go out of uniform. G. became very angry and slammed the phone in her ear! I don't believe that man. Irene was ready to ask for a transfer. I felt very sorry for her and I hope it works out. She is afriad Robbie will be angry and that she ruined Anne's chances. Dick wanted to ask Dr. G. but Irene thought it was her job. I agree with Irene, I think it will work out. Good news I got my head nurse's item.

July 9, Thursday

Irene called Minnie (G's secretary). Minnie said G. has been very uptight and right before Irene called yesterday, he had had a fight with somebody. She told Irene not to be upset, he just took it out on her. I guess men at the top get angry too. Irene felt much better after that conversation. Had a long talk with Gaynor. She is very discouraged. She doesn't feel that token economy is successful. She thinks many changes should be made. Also the patients are in control rather than the attendants. She is also discouraged because she doesn't feel included. Robbie doesn't meet with her anymore. She doesn't feel in charge. She and I decided to corner Robbie as soon as he gets back to talk all this out.

July 13, Monday

Received quite an education today in the games people play. Had a long talk with Robbie about the unit and he says G. has been pressuring him to take over the whole unit. I was surprised he told me this, however, I was even more surprised when I found out that he told Irene this. Irene is really running scared. She isn't thinking straight. She stated at lunch time that she was thinking of confronting G. because G. was impressed by honesty. I did not agree at all. I don't think G. has ever been honest or respects anyone who is honest and open. I am really afriad and thought that Irene would be making a terrible mistake if she approached G. honestly and openly. In the evening I found out that Irene told Robbie of the plans and he discouraged her. I was glad to hear she changed her mind. However, she said that Robbie also told her that G. thinks she is a fool. I can't understand why Robbie told her that. I don't know if he is trying to help her, or if he thinks this conflict will render her totally helpless. Maybe he wants this "either or effect." If Irene could only accept this situation and accept Robbie and work with him. She is so hung up. Somehow I think it is more than team that she is afraid of losing. I think she is afriad of losing her own power. Maybe she doesn't even realize this herself. I think she sees Robbie as a threat to her rather than to the team. Personally, I think that we can work effectively as a team with Robbie. I think Robbie is controlling only when he has to be. Every team needs a leader and Robbie is a good one. I said this to Irene, but she says Robbie has been forced on us as a leader and a leader has to evolve, even though Robbie would most likely have evolved as the leader. That is a lot of words. Irene is really confused, I don't know if her confusion is causing her to contradict herself or if it is because she doesn't really trust me and thinks I may take everything back to Robbie. I really don't understand. I can empathize with Irene because in some ways I am a lot like her. I don't know what I would do in her situation. I can't help but wonder if besides weeding out staff on 130 if Robbie has plans for weeding out the staff on the professional level.

September 10, Thursday

Dr. G. on the unit today. He was quite impressed with everything except 130. I was sick! When he walked on to the ward Gaynor, L. and C. (attendants) were sitting around the table pushed in front of the store room door eating peanuts and reading the paper. Lying on the floor in full view was I. First thing out of G.'s mouth was "what does Dr. Winkler plan to do about patients lying on the floor. I can't bring the commissioner up here with patients lying on the floor." I was really sick. I tried to play it cool by describing the activity program we have planned. G. was still looking for pictures on the wall. Did state that the mood was 100% better. J. (Charge Attendant) handled him beautifully on 125. She is a real charmer. I don't think he even noticed the bench across the door way. How I wish we could have Jenny on 130.

NOTE

(1) The decision by the charge attendant to restrict residents' smoking "privileges" on the very day the tokens were first introduced reflected her fears about loss of control and was an unusually clear example of forthright resistance, in that it was certain to produce hostility among the residents of the ward. Two years later, when one of the more outspoken ex-residents on the ward, who was particularly disliked by the charge, was interviewed, she specifically recalled this incident:

> Interviewer: From your point of view, what kind of mistakes do you think people have made setting up the token economy, setting up community preparation?
> F: Well, smoking restrictions. I was one of the first ones who was allowed to have matches. But I was beaten up by (another resident). I had to return them by the allotted time, had to return them to the smoking tables (!). You're supposed to return them, but some of the girls didn't return them. . . and I fell over a pail and hit my head and got all wet. . .because I tried to return the matches. . . .

These smoking restrictions were defined by the charge as her territory and were rationalized on the grounds that the ward was messy from cigarette ash. The author's initial approach was to try to work with the charge, on the grounds that it would be too disruptive to do otherwise.   After six months, it became clear that the cost of this approach for the residents, staff, program and author was too high, and every attempt had to be made to transfer her. This unpleasant task was eventually achieved. The dilemma of working inside institutional structures was very clear in this case. A compromise with the existing personnel (structures) would have been the humanitarian thing to do, from the charge's point of view, but in so doing, the author would have been forced to condone the damage she was doing to people. By compromising, it is so easy to become part of what is inherently a destructive system. Who is changing whom?

Appendix

In this section we are listing the names and addresses of Newsletters and other informal communications from organizations and individuals involved in environmental design. Just as the more formal means of communication between individuals in this field has grown, such as journals, books and organizations, the informal newsletter has more than kept pace. In many instances, today's newsletter will become tomorrow's journal.

Advance

> Advance is the publication of the Association for the Advance-ment of Psychology, Suite 400, 1200 17th Street N.W., Washing-ton, DC 20036. In reporting government actions relevant to psychologists, it provides useful information and commentary about current and future regulations and funding of many areas of interest to us (human experimentation, all federal funding of training and research, national health insurance, social services provisions, education, etc.).

Alternative futures

> Alternative Futures, is an interdisciplinary journal of utopian studies, started publication in 1978. It includes articles on utopian literature and thought, communitarianism and social experiment, utopian/dystopian science fiction, and future inquiries which are non-technical in nature. A former newsletter on thought and literature, Utopus Discovered (1975-77), edited by Kenneth M. Roemer, emerged as the News Center of this journal. It is published by Human Dimensions Center, Rensselaer Polytechnic Institute, Troy, New York, 12181. Merritt Abrash of R.P.I., and Alexandra Aldridge of the University of Michigan are coeditors.

American journal of community psychology

American Journal of Community Psychology publishes original
articles on program evaluation, social analysis, and innovative
professional roles; critical reviews; and descriptions of collaborative development of community-based services and programs.
Published by Plenum Press in association with Division 27
(Community Psychology). Write Plenum Publishing Corp., 227 W.
17th St., New York, NY 10011.

Analytic review of utopias and utopianism

Wayne Wheeler, Editor
Institute for Icarian Investigations
P.O. Box 31161
Omaha, NE 68131

APA division 28 newsletter

Travis Thompson, Editor
Box 392 Mayo
University of Minnesota
Minneapolis, MN 55455

AP-LS newsletter of the american psychology-law society

Richard Izzett
Newsletter Editor
APLS
209 Burnett Hall
University of Nebraska-Lincoln
Lincoln, NE 68588

APT word-the association for precision teaching

Mrs. Nancy Brown
APT Word
163A North Harvey
Oak Park, IL 60302

Association for behavior analysis (ABA)

ABA publishes two regular publications: ABA Newsletter and The
Behavior Analyst. The Newsletter Editor is R. Wayne Fuqua,
Department of Psychology, Western Michigan University, Kala-
mazoo, Michigan 49008. The official journal of ABA, The
Behavior Analyst, is edited by W. Scott Wood, Department of
Psychology, Drake University, Des Moines, Iowa 50311.

Association for man-environment relations (ASMER)

ASMER seeks to advance understanding of the functional interaction between the environment and human biological, psychological, and social activities by (a) providing mechanisms through which interdisciplinary discussions of problems in this area may take place and (b) disseminating information to policymakers that will provide more meaningful resolution and handling of person-environment problems. ASMER, P.O. Box 57, Orangeburg, New York 10962

Barefoot behavior modification

Barefoot Behavior Modification is a quarterly journal published by the Manitoba Behaviour Therapy Association. The cost to nonmembers is $5. Write Carolyne Chick, Secretary, MBMA, St. Paul's College, University of Manitoba, Winnepeg, Manitoba, Canada.

Behavior influence newsletter

Leonard Krasner, Editor
Psychology Department
SUNY at Stony Brook
Stony Brook, NY 11794

Behaviour modification

Behaviour Modification is a newsletter published about 4 times a year, "providing information about operant conditioning and related fields." Articles are directed at applied professionals, covering a wide range of applications, behaviors, situations, and settings, particularly in the U.K. Also included is information about training opportunities, jobs, events, books, and films. Cost is 1 pound for 3 issues, 1 pound 50 pence overseas, for personal subscriptions. Previous issues of the newsletter (since 1972) provide a very good overview of behavior modification in the U.K., but unfortunately many back issues are no longer available. Write Behaviour Modification, Psychology Department, Moss Side Hospital, School Lane, Maghull, Liverpool L31 1BD U.K.

The behavior therapist

Michael F. Cataldo, Editor
Association for Advancement of Behavior Therapy
420 Lexington Avenue
New York, NY 10017

Behavior today

> Behavior Today
> 2814 Pennsylvania Avenue
> N.W. Washington, DC 20007

Behavioral employment blurb

> Behavioral Employment Blurb will provide information on places
> to look for jobs, ads about jobs to fill, summaries of existing
> articles on the topic, and articles on careers and graduate school.
> It will cost $2 for 5 issues, which will come out irregularly as
> information is accumulated. Write Gerald Mertens, Psychology
> Department, St. Cloud State University, St. Cloud, MN 56301.

Behavioral engineering

> Behavioral Engineering is a "practical journal dealing with
> behavioral treatment techniques using instrumentation." Pub-
> lished quarterly for $4 per year, $5 outside North America, by
> Farrall Instruments, P.O. Box 1473, Grand Island, NE 68801.

Behavioral newsletter

> Behavioral Newsletter is "a non-profit venture with the objective
> of offering a means of communication to behavioral people in the
> Midwest . . . .I see the newsletter as specifically oriented
> towards the Experimental and Applied Analyses of Behavior, with
> a general interest in all behavioral research and applications."
> Write Jerry Mertens, Psychology Department, St. Cloud State
> University, St. Cloud, MN 56301.

The behavioral voice

> The Behavioral Voice is "a newsletter by students, for students of
> behavior modification and applied behavior analysis." It is
> published three times a year by the students of the Center for
> Human Development at Drake University. Write: Editors, The
> Behavioral Voice, Center for Human Development, Drake Uni-
> versity, Des Moines, IA 50311.

Behaviorally speaking

> Society of Behaviorists
> P.O. Box 171
> Dayton, OH 45459

Behaviorists for social action journal

> Behaviorists for Social Action
> Special Interest Group of MABA
> Attn: Elizabeth de la Ossa, Corresponding Secretary
> Psychology Department
> Western Michigan University
> Kalamazoo, MI 49008

Bioethics digest

> The growth and recognition of the importance of ethical and moral issues in the behavior influence process is attested to by a new digest service, Bioethics Digest (Information Planning Associates, 2 Research Court, Rockville, MD 20850 . . . a hefty $48 a year for 12 issues). The Digest will publish 200 abstracts from 3,000 articles, books, and monographs each month dealing with such subjects as behavior control, death and dying, human experimentation, genetics research, medical technology, population control, and health care delivery. It will also publish full length articles on recent developments in bioethics by "experts" in the field.

Boston behavior therapy interest group newsletter

> Tim O'Farrell, Editor
> Psychology Services
> VA Hospital
> 940 Belmont Street
> Brockton, MA 02400

The Boulder behaviorist

> The Boulder Behaviorist was brought to our attention by Sue Maloney, its editor. It is published at the Boulder River School & Hospital, Boulder, MT 59632.

A brief guide to newsletters in early childhood education

> A Brief Guide to Newsletters in Early Childhood Education was compiled by Janet Fagan Allgaier for the ERIC Clearinghouse on Early Childhood Education. It is available from the College of Education Curriculum Lab, University of Illinois, 1210 W. Springfield Avenue, Urbana, IL 61801 for 30¢.

Bulletin of division 6

> Bulletin of Division 6 (Experimental Analysis of Behavior) of the Federacion Colombiana de Psicologia, is a Spanish-language newsletter in its second year, looks good to us. Write to Roberto Kopec, Editor, Apartado Aereo 91212, Bogota, Colombia.

The CHEIRON newsletter-international society for the history of behavioral and social sciences

The International Society for the History of Behavioral and Social Sciences (CHEIRON) is an organization involved in the history of behavioral sciences, with a membership of 300 from 14 academic disciplines. Their newsletter is edited by Elizabeth Goodman, 115 West Royal Drive, De Kalb, IL 60115. The growing involvement of psychologists in evaluating historical processes emphasizes the importance of the historical context in understanding current influences on the behavior of behavioral scientists.

Child behavior therapy

Cyril M. Franks, Editor
Graduate School of Applied and
    Professional Psychology
Busch Campus, Rutgers University
New Brunswick, NJ 08903

Childhood city newsletter

Environmental Psychology Program
Graduate School of the City University
    of New York
33 West 42nd Street
New York, NY 10036

Classroom interaction newsletter

School of Ed.
American University
Washington, DC 20016

Classroom Interaction Newsletter was begun a dozen years ago by Ned Flanders and Anita Simon. Its new editors are Myra & David Sadker. $7.00 for two years $9.00 for overseas.

The clinical psychologist

Jerome H. Resnick, Editor
Department of Psychology
652 Weiss Hall
Temple University
Philadelphia, PA 19122

Cognitive-behavior modification newsletter

Cognitive-Behavior Modification Newsletter is a newsletter

appearing "once and perhaps twice a year . . . .to facilitate communication about cognitive behavior modification (CBM) among research-practitioners." Editor Donald Meichenbaum, Psychology Department, University of Waterloo, Waterloo, Ontario N2L 3Gl, Canada.

Community mental health review

Community Mental Health Review is a new newsletter with 6 issues a year, each containing a major review article and 75 to 100 annotations. Harry Gottesfeld is editor, Haworth Press, 149 Fifth Avenue, New York, NY.

Consequated behavioral news

The Consequated Behavioral News (edited by Jerry Mertens, Psychology Department, St. Cloud University, St. Cloud MN 56301) offers a unique method of interaction with its readers. It offers working papers written by readers as a basis for feedback and interaction from other readers. Only those who respond to earlier papers continue to receive it.

Division 25 recorder

Michael F. Cataldo, Editor
Division 25 Recorder
Department of Behavioral Psychology
John F. Kennedy Institute
707 North Broadway
Baltimore, MD 21205

Division of community psychology newsletter

Meg Gerard, Editor
Psychology Dept.
University of Kansas
Lawrence, Kansas 66045

Edcentric

Edcentric
P.O. Box 10085
Eugene, OR 97401

Edcentric is "a smorgasbord of iconoclastic articles and useful resources" and an ". . .analysis of both the conventional schooling system and the movement for educational change." $6 for 6 issues/year.

EDC (educational development center) news

> EDC (Educational Development Center) News is a newsletter for communication of EDC with their "friends: the teachers, administrators, parents, and students who share our intention of making schools a better place for everybody." The excellent work done through EDC comes under the categories of international and open education, media, social studies, science, and math. Write E.D.C., 55 Chapel Street, Newton, MA 02160. Also at that address are their Information Center and Distribution Center.

EDRA design research news

> EDRA Design Research News is published four or five times a year by the Environmental Design Research Association which promotes basic and applied research on the human-made environment and natural environment. A state-of-the-art conference is held each year.

> Willo P. White, Editor
> L'Enfant Plaza Station
> P.O. Box 23129
> Washington, DC 20024

Ekistics-habitat, The U.N. conference on human settlements

> Ekistics
> Page Farm Road
> Lincoln, MA 01773

Environmental history newsletter

> Dr. John Opie
> Department of History
> Duquesne University
> Pittsburgh, PA 15219

Environmental management

> Dr. Robert S. DeSanto, Editor
> Environmental Management
> 972 New London Turnpike
> Glastonbury, CT 06033

Environmental psychology and non-verbal behavior

> Environmental Psychology and Non-Verbal Behavior is a new journal for $4.95 per year (introductory price) for 2 issues a year. Editor: Randolph Lee, Department of Psychology, Trinity College, Hartford, CT 06106.

European association of behavior therapy newsletter

> This is a new newsletter published by the EABT, which is a loosely affiliated group of national B.T. associates and institutes, with only a few individual members. Newsletter is sent to these associations rather than to individuals, and may be copied and distributed by them. The newsletter gives a strong feel for the growth and enthusiasm of behavior therapists in all parts of Europe. Editor: Sten Ronnberg, Department of Education, Stockholm University, S-104 05 Stockholm 50, Sweden.

European journal of behavioural analysis and modification

> European Journal of Behavioural Analysis and Modification is a new journal. Write Editorial Secretary Mrs. M.E. Wengle, 8000 Muchen 81, Titurelstrasse 5, West Germany.

Evaluation

> Program Evaluation Resource Center
> 501 South Park Avenue
> Minneapolis, MN 55415

Evaluation (journal)

> NIMH & Program
> Evaluation Resource Center
> 501 South Park Ave.
> Minneapolis, Minnesota 55415

Evaluation quarterly

> Sage Publications
> 275 S. Beverly Dr.
> Beverly Hills, CA 90212

The feminist/behaviorist newsletter

> Judy Lewis, Editor
> Psychology Department
> Marietta College
> Marietta, Ohio

Forum for behavior technology

> Forum for Behavior Technology is a newsletter published quarterly or semi-annually for 50¢ a copy. "We hope Forum will promote communication among those engaged in the delivery of human services within a behavioral framework." They plan to cover "treatment methods, evaluation and recording procedures,

announcements of workshops and training opportunities, a training package exchange for unpublished programs, reviews of
published articles, reviews of books and films, invited articles,
classified ads listing positions available and situations wanted, as
well as materials which may be purchased." Write Forum, Box
4792, Overland Park, KS 66204.

The gerontologist

Gerontological Society
#1 Dupont Circle
Washington, D.C. 20036

Group for the use of psychology in history newsletter

Charles B. Strozier
History Program
Sangamon State University
Shepherd Road
Springfield, Illinois 62708

Growth alternatives

Center for Growth Alternatives
1785 Mass. Ave.
N.W.
Washington, D.C. 20036

The Hastings center report

Hastings Center Report
360 Broadway
Hastings-on-Hudson, NY 10706

Health planning

Plus Publications, Inc.
Dept. B
2314 Penn. Ave., N.W.
Washington, D.C. 20007

Hospital and community psychiatry

Hospital and Community Psychiatry is an interdisciplinary
journal published by the American Psychiatric Association. Write
Editor, Hospital and Community Psychiatry, 1700   18th Street
N.W., Washington, DC 20009.

Human behavior

Curriculum project for secondary schools

John K. Bare
Carleton College
Northfield, Minnesota 55057

Human ecology

Andrew P. Vayda, Editor
Plenum Press
227 West 18 St.
New York, NY 10060

Human ecology and world development

Anthony Vann & Paul Rogers, Editors
Plenum Pub. Corp.
227 W. 17 St.
New York, NY 10011

Human factors society

The Human Factors Society focuses on human factors in systems development and technology advancement. Membership: psychologists, engineers, physiologists, and other interested scientists.

Human factors society
P.O. Box 1369
Santa Monica, California 90406
Executive Assistant: Marian Knowles

Human services monograph series

For improving the management of human services,
SHARE, P.O. Box 2309
Rockville, MD. 20852

Humanities perspectives on technology

Stephen H. Cutcliff
Maginnes Hall #9
Lehigh University
Bethlehem, PA 18015

The individualized learning letter

The Individualized Learning Letter
67 East Shore Road
Huntington, NY 11743

Information

>Information is "intended to provide the educational community with information about current research activities and the results of N.I.E. projects." It is the quarterly journal of the National Institute of Education, Dept. of H.E.W., Washington, DC 20208.

Innovations

>Innovations, an experimental magazine published three times yearly, presents problems and techniques for planned change in the mental health field. It is free from American Institutes for Research, Box 1113, Palo Alto, CA 94302.

Insights

>Insights
>Center for Teaching and Learning
>Corwin Hall
>University of North Dakota
>Grand Forks, N.D. 58202

I.E.

>I.E. is the monthly French-language bulletin of the Institut de L'Environnement. It includes information on European conferences, exhibits, and publications relating to the built environment. Write Institut de L'Environnement, 14-20 Rue Erasme, 75005 Paris, France.

ISR newsletter

>The institute for Social Research, University of Michigan, publishes the quarterly ISR Newsletter, available free. It reports on Institute research findings, other reports of interest, and publications. Write I.S.R., 426 Thompson St., P.O. Box 1248, Ann Arbor, MI 48106

Journal of behavioral education

>Journal of Behavioral Education, is "a journal for disseminating the results of applying the principles and techniques of behavior theory to classroom settings. In particular. . .those children for whom the existing system has proven inadequate for progress." Published quarterly by the Special Education Program, College of Education, University of Vermont, and Office of Federal Programs, State Dept. of Education.

Journal of behavioral medicine

W. Doyle Gentry, Editor
Duke University Medical Center
Durham, North Carolina

Journal of community health

Journal of Community Health is a new quarterly by the
Association of Teachers of Preventive Medicine, containing
articles, case histories, and book reviews on health care delivery
and prevention of illness. Individual rate, $9.95 per year. Write
Human Sciences Press, 72 Fifth Ave., New York, NY 10011.

Journal of community psychology

Clinical Psychology Publishing Company
Brandon, VT

Journal of moral education

Journal of Moral Education is edited by Derek Wright, Psychology Dept., University, Leicester LE1 7RH England.

Journal of open education

Journal of Open Education is published three times a year at a
cost of $8.50 per year. "While not neglecting the broader issues
in education, the primary focus is on practical 'how to' articles
for use by others." There is a regular Resources section with
information about organizations and services. Write Institute of
Open Education, Antioch Graduate Center, 133 Mt. Auburn St.,
Cambridge, MA 02138.

The journal of organizational behavior management

The Journal of Organizational Behavior Management (Suite 1-P,
3300 N.W. Expressway, Atlanta, Georgia 30341... $41. a year)
links organizational behavior and behavior modification in attempting to "bridge the gap" between the behavioral research
and management in business, industry, and government.

Journal of personalized instruction

Journal of Personalized Instruction, a journal containing research, case studies, theoretical and methodological papers,
review articles, abstracts, technical notes, and an annotated
listing of all articles recently published in other journals. Write
Journal of Personalized Instruction, Room 29, Loyola Hall,
Georgetown University, Washington, DC 20057.

The journal of world education

> The Journal of World Education (edited by George Nicklin, 3 Harbor Hill Drive, Huntington, New York 11743) is oriented to promote intercommunication among educational institutions and individuals working toward a global view in education creating a worldwide system of education and promoting research relating to world education.

Law and human behavior

> Law and Human Behavior, a journal edited by Bruce Sales, Law-Psychology Program, 209 Burnett Hall, University of Nebraska, Lincoln, Nebraska 60588 (published by Plenum, New York, $20. a year) publishes articles linking the legal process and the legal system with all aspects of human behavior.

Leaves of twin oaks

> Leaves of Twin Oaks
> Twin Oaks Community
> Louisa, Virginia 23093

Man-environment systems

> ASMER, Inc.
> P.O. Box 57
> Orangeburg, NY 10962

MANAS

> MANAS is "a journal of independent inquiry, concerned with study of the principles which move world society on its present course, and with search for contrasting principles – that may be capable of supporting intelligent idealism under the conditions of life in the 20th century. MANAS is concerned, therefore, with philosophy and with practical psychology." The journal is $5 a year from MANAS Publishing Co., P.O. Box 32112, El Soreno Station, Los Angeles, CA 90032.

The mental health law project

> Mental Health Law Project
> Suite 300
> 1220 Nineteenth Street, NW
> Washington, DC 20036

Mental health scope

> Resources News Service, Inc.
> P.O. Box 28596
> Washington, DC 20005

National association of environmental professionals

NEPA
1815 N. Ft. Meyer Drive
Suite 408
Arlington, VA 22209

National institute of child health and human development

Dr. Jonathan T. Lanman, Director
Center for Research for Mothers & Children
NICHHD
Room C-703
Landow Building
Bethesda, MD 20014

National institute of environmental health sciences

Extramural program
NIEHS
P.O. Box 12233
Research Triangle Park,
North Carolina 27709

New ways

New Ways, a new publication, "reports on innovative theory and practice in the fields of creativity and the arts, alternative strategies, special education, and the arts and therapy." It is published by Educational Arts Association and the Advisory for Open Education, P.O. Box 158, Cambridge, MA 02140 six times a year for $6 a year.

New Zealand society for behaviour therapy

L.S. Leland, Jr.
Psychology Dept.
University of Otago
Box 56
Dunedin, New Zealand

Newsletter on science, technology, and human values

Newsletter on Science, Technology, and Human Values (Aiken Computational Lab 231, Harvard University, Cambridge, Mass. 02138 . . . $6 for four issues each year) is designed to serve as a resource guide for research and teaching which focuses on the ethical and social dimensions of sciences and technology.

Newsletter zum verhalterstraining bei Lehrern, eltern, und erziehern

Newsletter zum Verhalterstraining bei Lehrern, Eltern, und Erziehern is a new German-language newsletter assembled by the "Munchner Gruppe" and managed by Walter Spiess, a former member of our Environmental Design Group. The newsletter is concerned in the broadest sense with training of teachers, parents, and students, and is open to participation by all. For the present it is sent free, courtesy of the Social Psychology Section of the Max Planck Institute. Write Walter Spiess, Wissenschaftl. Begleitung an der Grundschule II, 8 Munchen 45, Heinrich-Baum-Weg 10, W. Germany.

Outlook

Outlook, the magazine of the Mountain View Center for Environmental Education, serves preschool and elementary school teachers, teachers of day care centers, and future teachers. "By this term (environmental education) we mean education through fuller use of all the environments in which children live – physical, social, natural, and the environments of books, ideas, and history."   Write Mountain View Center for Environmental Education, University of Colorado, 1511 University Ave., Boulder, CO 80302. Cost is $6 a year (3 pounds in U.K.) for 4 issues/year.

Pacesetter

Pacesetter presents a behaviorally-oriented approach in correctional agencies. It is published bimonthly by The Rehabilitation Research Foundation, Alabama Industrial School, P.O. Box 3587, Montgomery, AL 36109.

The personalized system of instruction newsletter

Center for Personalized Instruction
Georgetown University
Washington, DC 20057

Perspectives in environment and behavior

Perspectives in Environment and Behavior is a new annual review series from Plenum Press (see above) to be edited by Irwin Altman and Joachim Wohlwill. (Item from Environment and Behavior Task Force Newsletter).

Policy publication review

Published bi-monthly by:

IPC Science and Technology Press, Ltd.
32 High Street
Guildford, Surrey GU1 3EN England

"Selected current listings of primary source publications for industrial and government executives, policymakers, planners, researchers, educationalists, . . .Contains reports, surveys, reviews, special studies issued by various countries."

Population and environmental psychology newsletter (Division 34, American Psychological Association)

Toni Falbo, Editor
Dept. of Educational Psychology
University of Texas at Austin
Austin, Texas 78712

Population center foundation

Initiatives in Population
P.O. Box 2065
Makati Commercial Center
Makati, Rizal, Philippines 3117

The psycho-history review

There are three organizations represented by newsletters which illustrate a growing development in the behavior influence process, increasing awareness of the effect of the ideology (belief system about basic human nature) of the historian of the "facts" of history. The Psycho-History Review (Sangamon State University, Brookens 493, Springfield, Illinois 62708) is the newsletter for the Group for the Use of Psychology in History, affiliated with the American Historical Association. The approach to history by the members of this group is clearly psychoanalytical and each of the articles in the Newsletter clearly reflects this orientation. The approach of the psycho-historian initiated by Lipton and Erickson has become a major influence in the history field and illustrates the possibilities of deriving a methodology of historical interpretation from a theory of human behavior.

School applications of learning theory (SALT)

In the education area, we take note of several kinds of publications. SALT is back! School Applications of Learning Theory has been revived by Dan Hursh, Department of Educational Psychology, West Virginia University, Morgantown, West Virginia 26506. SALT, which is really a combination newsletter and journal, is oriented toward people involved with behavioral analysis in educational settings. It should continue to represent an important communication link between those involved in the influence process in the classroom.

Self-help reporter

Naomi Curtis, Editor
National Self-Help Clearinghouse
CUNY Graduate Center
33 W. 42nd St.
New York, N.Y. 10036

Social ecology network

The Social Ecology Network is an interest group in social ecology to bring together those working in the area of environmental assessment. Contact Dr. Abraham M. Jeger or Dr. Robert S. Slotnick Dept. of Behavioral Sciences, New York Institute of Technology, Old Westbury, N.Y. 11568

Sex roles, a journal of research

Plenum Publishing Corp.
227 West 17th St.
New York, NY 10011

Social impact assessment

Social Impact Assessment is a newsletter published in conjunction with ongoing monthly meetings of a special interest group at NSF in Washington. Objectives are identifying and analyzing critical areas of concern within executive agencies and legislative process with regard to social impact; and demonstrating the urgency and utility of social research and social knowledge in relation to the executive and legislative process. Contact C.P. Wolf, City University of New York, New York, N.Y.

Society for the behavioral analyses of culture newsletter

The newsletter of the Society for the Behavioral Analyses of Culture (Steve Hayes, Department of Psychology, University of North Carolina, Greensboro, N.C.). The newsletter is new, although the society is not. They have been sponsoring conferences on behavioral technology in higher education and are now turning to other topics within the purview of the society's title. The members of the current small group are all behavior analysts and have expressed intentions to keep that criterion for membership, although one proposed activity is interaction with other relevant disciplines (e.g., anthropology, economics, political science).

Society for social studies of science-4S

> 4S
> Department of Sociology
> Southern Illinois University
> Carbondale, Illinois 62901

Sociological practice newsletter

> Sociological Practice Newsletter is intended to link practicing
> sociologists, encouraging readers to send descriptions of their
> projects and ideas to the editors. Contact Donald Gelfand &
> Bernard Phillips, Dept. of Sociology, Boston University, Boston,
> MA 02215.

State-of-the-art of socio-physical technology

> State-of-the-Art of Socio-Physical Technology. Write Editor
> Andrew Euston, Urban Design Program Officer at H.U.D., 451 7th
> Street S.W. Washington, DC 20410.

The subterranean sociology newsletter (vol. 9 in 1976)

> Editor: Marcello Truzzi
> Dept. of Sociology
> Eastern Michigan University
> Ypsilanti, Michigan 48197

> The Subterranean Sociology Newsletter is "published twice a year
> at strange intervals. . . .seeks to promote Truth, Beauty, Justice,
> and jollies for all." $3.00/year. It contains submitted satirical
> articles, notices, editorial rantings, book reviews ("notes"), and
> lists of published materials of interest in irregular sources.

Urban anthropology

> Jack R. Rollwagen, editor
> Plenum Publishing Corp.
> 227 W. 17th St.
> New York, NY 10011

Utopus discovered (See Alternative Futures)

> Kenneth M. Roemer
> Department of English
> UT Arlington
> Arlington, TX 76019

Work performance

> 2921 N.E. 28th St. (Suite 103)
> Lighthouse Point, FL 33064
>
> Behavioral management in the workplace is the subject of <u>Work Performance</u>, published 12 times a year for $24.

The worm runners digest

> James V. McConnell, Editor
> Mental Health Research Institute
> The University of Michigan
> Ann Arbor, Michigan 48109

For a comprehensive list of organizations in the multidisciplinary field of environment and behavior see White, (1979)

Bibliography

Abelson, R., and Nielsen, K. History of ethics. In The encyclopedia of ethics, P. Edwards, ed. vol. 3. New York: Macmillan/Free Press, 1967, pp. 81-117.

Albee, G.W. Mental health manpower trends. New York: Basic Books, 1959.

_____. Conceptual models and manpower requirements in psychology. American Psychologist 23 (1968): 317-320.

Alderfer, C.P. Organization development. Annual Review of Psychology 28 (1977): 197-223.

Alinsky, S. Reveille for radicals. New York: Vintage Books, 1969.

_____. Rules for radicals. New York: Random House, 1972.

Allen, G.J.; Chinsky, J.M.; Larcen, S.W.; Lochman, J.E.; and Selinger, H.E. Community psychology and the schools: A behaviorally oriented multi-level preventive approach. Potomac, Md.: Erlbaum,1976.

Allport, F.H. Theories of perception and the concept of structure. New York: Wiley, 1955.

Altman, I. Territorial behavior in humans: An analysis of the concept. In Spatial behavior of older people, L. Pastalan and D.H. Carson, eds. Ann Arbor: University of Michigan-Wayne State University Press, 1970, pp. 1-24.

_____. Some perspectives on the study of man-environment phenomena. Representative research in social psychology 4 (1973): 109-126.

_____. Privacy: A conceptual analysis. In Privacy, S.M. Margulis, ed. Milwaukee, Wis.: Environmental Design research, 1974, pp. 3-28.

_____. The environment and social behavior: privacy, space, territory, crowding. San Francisco, Calif.: Brooks/Cole, 1975.

_____, and Wohlwill, J.F. Human behavior and environment, vol. 3. New York: Plenum, 1978.

Alumbaugh, R.V. Another "malleus maleficurum?" American Psychologist 27 (1972): 897-899.

Alvord, J.R. Home token economy: An incentive program for parents and their children. Champaign, Ill.: Research Press, 1973

American Heritage Dictionary, W. Morris, ed. New York: Houghton Mifflin, 1969.

American Psychological Association (APA) Ad Hoc Committee on Ethical Standards in Psychological Research. Ethical principles in the conduct of research with human participants. Washington, D.C.: American Psychological Association, 1973.

_____. Prevention is Keynote at ADAMHA chief's debut. American Psychological Association Monitor (December, 1977): 1.

Ames, A., Jr. Visual perception and the rotating trapezoidal window. Psychological Monographs 65 (1951): no. 324.

Anthony, W.A. Principles of psychiatric rehabilitation. Amherst, Mass.: Human Resource Development Press, 1976.

Argyle, M. Social Interaction. New York: Alherton, 1969.

_____, and Little, B.R. Do personality traits apply to social behavior? Journal for the Theory of Social Behavior 2 (1972): 1-35.

Argyis, C. Intervention theory and method. Reading, Mass.: Addison-Wesley, 1970.

_____. Dangers in applying results from experimental social psychology. American Psychologist 30 (1975): 469-485.

Arkowitz, H.; Lichtenstein, E.; McGovern, K.; and Hines, P. Behavioral assessment and social competence in males. Behavior Therapy 6 (1975): 3-13.

Asher, J. Sociobiology: Behavior from a genes point of view. American Psychological Association Monitor 6 (1975): 4-5.

Astin, A.W. The college environment. Washington, D.C.: American Council on Education, 1968.

Atthowe, J.M., Jr. Token economies come of age. Behavior Therapy, 4 (1973): 646-654.

_____. Legal and ehtical accountability in everyday practice. Behavioral Engineering 3 (1975): 35-38.

_____, and Krasner, L. A preliminary report on the application of contingent reinforcement procedures (token economy on a "chronic" psychiatric ward). Journal of Abnormal Psychology 73 (1968): 37-43.

Austin, N.K.; Liberman, R.P.; King, L.W.; and DeRisi, W.J. A comparative evaluation of two day hospitals: Goal attainment scaling of behavior therapy vs. milieu therapy. Journal of Nervous and Mental Disease 163 (1976): 253-262.

Aveni, C.A., and Upper, D. Training psychiatric patients for community living. Paper presented at the meeting of the American Psychological Association, Washington, D.C., September, 1976.

Ayllon, T. and Azrin, N.H. The measurement and reinforcement of behavior of psychotics. Journal of the Experimental Analysis of Behavior 8 (1965): 357-383.

_____. The token economy: A motivational system for therapy and rehabilitation. New York: Appleton-Century-Crofts, 1968.

_____, and Michael, J. The psychiatric nurse as a behavioral engineer. Journal of the Experimental Analysis of Behavior 2 (1959): 323-334.

Azrin, N.H. Ethical issues in behavior modification. Paper presented at Eastern Psychological Association Convention, New York, April, 1975.

_____. President's message. Association for the Advancement of Behavior Therapy Newsletter 3 (1976): 1-6.

_____; Flores, T.; and Kaplan, S.J. Job finding club: a group-assisted program for obtaining employment. Behavior Research and Therapy 13 (1975): 17-27.

Baenninger, L.P., and Ulmer, L.I. A workable behavior modification program for parents and children in a community mental health center based upon Wahler's and Ora's work. Paper presented at the Meeting of the Association for Advancement of Behavior Therapy, San Francisco, December 1975.

Baer, D.M. A note on the absence of a Santa Claus in any known ecosystem: A rejoinder to Willems. Journal of Applied Behavior Analysis 7 (1974): 167-170.

_____. Perhaps it would be better not to do everything. Journal of Applied Behavior Analysis 10 (1977): 167-172.

Balaban, R.M., The contribution of participant observation to the study of process in program evaluation. International Journal of Mental Health 2 (1973): 59-70.

Balch, P., and Solomon, R. The training of paraprofessional as behavior modifiers: A review. American Journal of Community Psychology 4 (1976): 167-180.

Baldwin, J.M. Mental development in the child and the race: Methods and processes. New York: Macmillan, 1895.

Ballesteros, G. Psicopatologia del gamin bogotano. Revista de Psicologia (Bogota) 13 (1968): 149-160.

Bandura, A. Principles of behavior modification. New York: Holt, Rinehart and Winston, 1969.

_____. Modeling theory. In Psychology of learning systems, models, and theories, W.S. Sahakian, ed. Chicago: Markham, 1970.

_____. Behavior theory and the models of man. American Psychologist 29 (1974): 859-869.

_____. Self-reinforcement: Theoretical and methodological considerations. Behaviorism 4 (1976): 135-155.

_____. Social learning theory. Englewood Cliffs, N.J.: Prentice-Hall, 1977.

Bard, M., and Berkowitz, B. Training police as specialists in family crisis intervention: A Community psychology action program. Community Mental Health Journal 3 (1967): 315-317.

Barker, R.G. Ecology and motivation. In Nebraska symposium on motivation, M. Jones, ed. vol. 8. Lincoln: University of Nebraska Press, 1960.

_____. On the nature of the environment. Journal of Social Issues 19 (1963): 17-38.

_____. Explorations in ecological psychology. American Psychologist 20 (1965): 1-14.

_____. Ecological psychology: Concepts and methods for studying the environment of human behavior, Stanford, Calif.: Stanford University Press, 1968.

_____. On the nature of the environment. In Environmental psychology: people and their physical settings, H. Proshansky, W.H. Ittelson, and L.G. Rivlin, eds. New York: Holt, Rinehart and Winston, 1976, p. 12.

_____. The stream of behavior. New York: Appleton-Century-Crofts, 1963.

_____, and Gump, P. Big school, small school: High school size and student behavior. Stanford, Calif.: Stanford University Press, 1964.

_____, and Schoggen, P. Qualities of community life. San Francisco, Calif.: Jossey-Bass, 1973, pp. xii, 562.

Barry, H.; Child, I.; and Bacon, M. Relation of child rearing to subsistence economy. American anthropologist 61 (1959): 51-64.

Bartels, B.D., and Tyler, J.D. Paraprofessionals in the community mental health center. Professional Psychology 6 (1975): 442-452.

Barton, A.H., and Lazarsfeld, P.F. Some functions of qualitative analysis in social research. Frankfurter Beitrage zur Sociologie, 1, (1955): 321-361.

Bass, R.D. Consultation and education services: Federally funded community mental health centers, 1973, Statistical Note 108. Rockville, Md.: National Institute of Mental Health, 1974.

Bassuk, E.L., and Gerson, S. Deinstitutionalization and mental health services. Scientific American 238 (1978): 46-53.

Bates, M. The human environment. Theory into practice 13 (December 1974): 354-357.

Battalio, R.C.; Kagel, J.H.; Winkler, R.C.; Fisher, E.B.; Basmann, R.L. An experimental investigation of consumer behavior in a controlled environment. Journal of Consumer Research 1 (1974): 52-66.

Battalio, R.C.; Fisher, E.B.; Kagel, J.H.; Basmann, R.L.; Winkler, R.C.; and Krasner, L. A test of consumer demand theory using observations of individual consumer purchases. Western Economic Journal 11 (1973): 411-428.

_____ An experimental investigation of consumer behavior in a controlled environment. Journal of Consumer Research 1 (1974): 52-66.

Baum, A., and Davis, G. Spatial and social aspects of crowding perception. Environment and behavior, in press.

Baum, A., and Valins, S. Architecture and social behavior: Psychological studies of social density. Hillsdale, N.J.: Lawrence Erlbaum Associates, 1977.

Baum, W. The correlation-based law of effect. Journal of the Experimental Analysis of Behavior 20 (1973): 135-153.

Baum, W.M. Choice in free ranging wild pigeons. Science 185 (1974): 78-79.

_____ and Rachlin, H.C. Choice as time allocation. Journal of the Experimental Analysis of Behavior 12 (1969): 861-874.

Bechtel, R.B. Human movement and architecture. Trans-Action 4 (1967): 53-56.

_____. Human movement and architecture. In Environmental psychology: Man and his physical setting, H.M. Proshansky, W.H. Ittelson, and L.G. Rivlin, eds. New York: Holt, Rinehart and Winston, 1970, pp. 642-658.

Bechtoldt, H.R. Construct validity: A critique. American Psychologist 14 (1959): 619-628.

Begelman, D.A. Ethical and legal issues of behavior modification. In Progress in behavior modification vol. 1, M. Hersen, R. Eisler, and P. Miller, eds. New York: Academic Press, 1975.

_____. Response to Day's paper. In Behavior modification and ethics J. Krapfl and E. Vargas, eds. Kalamazoo, Mich.: Behaviordelia, 1977.

Behavior Analysis and Modification Newsletter. BAM Project, 840 West Fifth St., Oxnard, Calif. 93030.

Bellak, L. Community psychiatry: The third psychiatric revolution. In Handbook of community psychiatry and community mental health L. Bellak, ed. New York: Grune and Stratton, 1964, pp. 1-11.

Bello Diaz, G. Un ensayo de autoeducacion de ninos marginados: "Gamines": Estudio de caso del programa Bosconia-La Florida, Proyecto de educacion no formal. Educacion Hoy 3 (1973): 1-19.

Beltran Cortes, L.M. La metamorfosis del "chino de la calle." Bogota: Temas Colombianos, 1970.

Bem, D.J., and Allen, A. On predicting some of the people some of the time. Psychological Review 81 (1974): 506-520.

Bem, S.L. Sex-role adaptability: One consequence of psychological androgyny. Journal of Personality and Social Psychology 31 (1975): 634-643.

Benassi, V.A. and Larson, K.M. Modification of family interaction with the child as the behavior-change agent. In Behavior modification and families, E.J. Mash, L.A. Hamerlynck, and L.C. Handy, eds. New York: Brunner/Mazel, 1976.

Bennett, F.H. Is behavior modification a major menace to patients' rights? American Psychologist 31 (1976): 894.

Bennett, G. Yundong: Mass campaigns in Chinese Communist leadership. Berkeley: Center for Chinese Studies, University of California, 1976.

Bergin, A.E., and Strupp, H.H. New directions in psychotherapy research. Journal of Abnormal Psychology 76 (1970): 13-26.

Bernstein, D.A. Behavioral fear assessment: Anxiety or artifact? In Issues and Trends in Behavior Therapy H. Adams and I.P. Unikel, eds. Springfield, Ill.: Charles C. Thomas, 1973.

Bigelow, G.E.; Emurian, H.H.; and Brady, J.V. A programmed environment for the experimental analysis of individual and small group behavior. In Experimentation in controlled environment, C.G. Miles, ed. Ontario: Addiction Research Foundation, 1975, pp. 133-144.

Bindman, A.J. The clinical psychologist as a mental health consultant. In Progress in clinical psychology, E.L. Abt & B.F. Riess, eds. New York: Grune and Stratton, 1966.

Birdwhistell, R.L. Kinesics and context. Philadelphia: University of Pennsylvania Press, 1970.

Bloom, B.L. Community mental health: A historical and critical analysis. Morristown, N.J.: General Learning Press, 1973.

_____. Community mental health: A general introduction. Monterey, Calif.: Brooks/Cole, 1977.

Bockhoven, J. Moral treatment in community mental health. New York: Springer, 1972.

Bolin, D.C., and Kivens, L. Evaluation in a community mental health center: Huntsville, Alabama. Evaluation 2 (1974): 26-35.

Bolman, W.M.; Halleck, S.L.; Rice, D.G.; and Ryan, M.L. An unintended side effect in a community psychiatric program. Archives of General Psychiatry 20 (1969): 508-513.

Bond, E.D. Dr. Kirkbride and his mental hospital. Philadelphia: J.B. Lippincott, 1947.

Boring, E.G. Current trends in psychology. Psychological Bulletin 45 (1948): 75-84.

Bornstein, P.; Bugge, I.; and Davol, G. Good principle, wrong target — An extension of "Token economies come of age." Behavior Therapy 6 (1975): 63-67.

Bower, S., and Bower, G. Assert yourself. Reading, Mass.: Addison-Wesley, 1976.

Bowers, K.S., Situations in psychology: A critique. Psychological Review 80 (1973): 307-336.

Brady, J.V.; Bigelow, G., Emurian, H.; and Williams, D.M. Design of a programmed environment for the experimental analysis of social behavior. In Man-environment interactions: Evaluations and applications D.H. Carson, ed. Environmental Design Research Association, 1974.

Braginsky, D.D., and Braginsky, B.M. The intelligent behavior of mental retardates: A study of their manipulation of intelligence test scores. Journal of Personality 40 (1972): 558-563.

Brandt, R.B. Ethical theory. Englewood Cliffs, N.J.: Prentice-Hall, 1959.

Briggs, H.C. ed. Self-help reporter. Newsletter published by the National Self-Help Clearinghouse, Graduate School and University Center. New York: City University of New York, 1977.

Brigham, A. The moral treatment of insanity. American Journal of Insanity 4 (1847): 1-15.

Briscoe, R.V.; Hoffman, D.B.; and Bailey, J.S. Behavioral community psychology: Training a community board to problem solve. Journal of Applied Behavior Analysis 8 (1975): 157-168.

Brown, B.S.; Wienckowski, L.A.; and Stolz, S.B. Behavior modification: Perspective on a current issue. Washington, D.C.: NIMH, HEW Publication (ADM) 1975, pp. 75-202.

Brunswick, E. Systematic and representative design of psychological experiments. Berkeley: University of California Press, 1947.

Bry, P. Discussion of Knapp's paper. In Behavior modification and ethics J. Krapfl and E. Vargas, eds. Kalamazoo, Mich.: Behaviordelia, 1977.

Buckout, R. Pollution and the psychologist: A call to action. In Environment and the social sciences: Perspectives and applications, J.F. Wohlwill and D.H. Carson, eds. Washington, D.C.: American Psychological Association, 1972, pp. 75-86.

Burgess, R.L., and Bushell, D. Behavioral sociology: The experimental analysis of social process. New York: Columbia University Press, 1969.

Burgess, R.L.; Clark, R.N.; and Hendee, J.C. An experimental analysis of anti-litter procedures. Journal of Applied Behavior Analysis 4 (1971): 71-75.

Calhoun, J.B. Population density and social pathology. Scientific American 206 (1962): 130-148.

_____. What sort of box? Man-Environment Systems 3 (1973): 1-28.

Callenbach, E. Ecotopia. Berkeley: Banyan Tree Books, 1975.

Campbell, D.T. The informant in quantitive research. American Journal of Sociology 60 (1955): 339-342.

_____. Blind variation and selective retention in creative thought as in other knowledge processes. Psychological Review 67 (1960): 380-400.

_____. Variation and selective retention in socio-cultural evolution. In Social change in developing areas H.R. Barringer, G.I. Blanksten, and R.W. Mack, eds. Cambridge, Mass.: Schenkman, 1965.

_____. Reforms as experiments. American Psychologist 24 (1969): 409-429.

_____. The experimenting society. Paper presented at APA (Distinguished Scientific Award) Convention, 1970.

_____. Methods for the experimenting society evaluation research paper series. Evanston, Ill.: Northwestern University Press, 1971.

_____. Onthe genetics of altruism and the counter-hedonic components in human culture. Journal of Social Issues 28(1972): 21-37.

_____. "Downward causation" in hierarchically organized biological systems. In Studies in the philosophy of biology T. Dobzhansky and F.J. Ayala, eds. London: MacMillan, 1974a.

_____. Evolutionary epistomology. In The philosophy of Karl Popper, vol. 14, I and II: The library of living philosophers P.A. Schilp, ed. La Salle, Ill.: Open Court Publishers, 1974b.

_____. Unjustified variation and selective retention in scientific discovery. In Studies in the philosophy of biology. T. Dobzhansky and F.J. Ayala, eds. London: MacMillan, 1974c.

_____. On the conflicts between biological and social evolution and between psychology and moral tradition (Presidential address to APA). American Psychologist 30 (1975): 1103-1126.

_____, and Erlebacher, A. How regression artifacts in quasi-experimental evaluations can mistakenly make compensatory education look' harmful. In The disadvantaged child vol. 3. Compensatory education: A national debate, J. Hellmuth, ed. New York: Brunner/Mazel, 1970.

_____, and Fiske, D.W. Convergent and discriminant validation by the multitrait-multimethod matrix. Psychological Bulletin 56 (1959): 81-105.

_____, and Ross, H.L. Connecticut crackdown on speeding: time-series data in quasi-experimental analysis. Law and Society Review 8 (1968): 33-53.

_____, and Stanley, J.C. Experimental and quasi-experimental designs for research. Chicago: Rand-McNally, 1963.

Canter, D.V. Architectural psychology. Proceedings of the conference at Dalandhui University, Strathclyde, 1969. London: RIBA, 1970.

_____, and Lee, T. Psychology and the built environment. London: Architectural Press, 1974.

Caplan, G. Types of mental health consultation. American Journal of Orthopsychiatry 33 (1963): 470-481.

_____. Principles of preventive psychiatry. New York: Basic Books, 1964.

_____. The theory and practice of mental health consultation. New York: Basic Books, 1970.

_____, and Killilea, M. eds. Support systems and mutual help: Multidisciplinary explorations. New York: Grune and Stratton, 1976.

Caplan, R.B. Psychiatry and the community in nineteenth century America. New York: Basic Books, 1969.

Carson, D.H. ed. Man-environment interactions: Evaluations and applications vols. 1-12. (Proceedings of the Fifth International Environmental Design research Association Conference. Washington, D.C.: Environmental Design Research association, 1974.

Carson, R. Silent spring. Boston: Houghton Mifflin, 1962.

Carter, B.D., and Cazares, P.R. Consultation in community mental health. Community Mental Health Review 1 (1976): 5-13.

Catania, A.C. Concurrent operants. In Operant behavior: Areas of research and application, W.K. Honig, ed. Englewood-Cliffs, N.J.: Prentice-Hall, 1966.

_____. Freedom and knowledge: An experimental analysis of preference in pigeons. Journal of the Experimental Analysis of Behavior 24 (1975a): 89-106.

_____. Pigeons' preference for free choice over forced choice: Controls for information, variety, and number of stimuli. Paper presented at EPA, New York, N.Y., April 3-5, 1975b.

_____. A behaviorist view of freedom. Paper presented at American Psychological Association Convention, Washington, D.C., September, 1976a.

_____. Truth and consequences: The role of instruction and contingencies in the shaping of human behavior. Paper presented at the Association for the Advancement of Behavior Therapy Convention, New York, N.Y., December 1976b.

Cautela, J.R. Behavior therapy and the need for behavioral assessment. Psychotherapy: Theory, Research, and Practice. 5 (1968): 175-179.

Chaiken, S., and Eagly, A.H. Communication modality as a determinant of message persuasiveness and message comprehensivility. Journal of Personality and Social Psychology 34 (1976): 605-614.

Chapman, A.H. Harry Stack Sullivan: the man and his work. New York: G.P. Putnam's Sons, 1976.

Chase, R.A. Information ecology and the design of learning environments. In Alternative learning environments: Emerging trends in environmental design and education, G. Coates, ed. Stroudsburg, Pa.: Dowden, Hutchinson and Ross, 1974.

_____. Human behavior and environmental design: The design of learning environments. In Human learning capacity in neurobiological perspective, P.C. Ritterbush and K.H. Pribram, eds. New York: Plenum Press, in press.

Chase, R.A.; Williams, D.M.; Welcher, D.W.; Fisher, J.J., III; and Gfeller, S.E. Design of learning environments for infants. In Man-environment interactions: Evaluations and applications, D.H. Carson, ed. Washington, D.C.: Environmental Design Research Association, 1974.

Chase, R.A.; Williams, D.M.; and Fisher, J.J., III. Exercises in the design of learning environments. In Control of human behavior: In education, vol. 3 R. Ulrich, T. Stachnik, and J. Mabry, eds. Chicago: Scott, Foresman, 1974.

Cherniss, C. Pre-entry issues in consultation. American Journal of Community Psychology 4 (1976): 13-24.

_____. Creating new consultation programs in community mental health centers: Analysis of a case study. Community Mental Health Journal 13 (1977): 133-141.

_____. The consultation readiness scale: An attempt to improve consultation practice. American Journal of Community Psychology 6 (1978): 15-21.

Chu, F., and Trotter, S. The madness establishment. New York: Grossman, 1974.

Cialdini, R.B. and Schroeder, D.A. Increasing compliance by legitimizing paltry contributions: When even a penny helps. Journal of Personality and Social Psychology 34 (1976): 599-604.

Ciminero, A.R. Behavioral assessment: An overview. In Handbook of Behavioral Assessment, A.R. Ciminero, K. Calhoun, and H. Adams, eds. New York: Wiley, 1977.

_____, Calhoun, K., and Adams, H., eds. Handbook of Behavioral Assessment. New York: Wiley, 1977.

Clark, R.N.; Burgess, R.L.; and Hendee, C. The development of anti-litter behavior in a forest campground. Journal of Applied Behavior Analysis (1972): 5, 1-5.

Cohen, H.L. Educational therapy: The design of learning environments. In Research in psychotherapy, vol. 3, J.M. Shlien, ed. Washington, D.C.: American Psychological Association, 1968, pp. 21-53.

_____. Symposium of the interface between environmental design and applied behavior analysis, EDRA 7, Vancouver, 1976.

Cohen, H.L., and Filipczak, T. A new learning environment, San Francisco: Jossey-Bass, 1971.

Cohen, H.L., Filipczak, T., and Bis, T. Case I. A study of contingencies applicable to special education. Educational Facility Press, I.B.R., 1967.

Colman, A.D. The planned environment in psychiatric treatment: A manual for ward design. Springfield, Ill.: Charles C. Thomas, 1971.

_____. Environmental design: Realities and delusions. In Applications of behavior modification, T. Thompson & W.J. Dochens, eds. New York: Academic Press, 1975, pp. 409-423.

Cone, J.D., and Hawkins, R.P., eds. Behavioral assessment: New directions in clinical psychology. New York: Brunner-Mazel, 1977.

Cone, J.D., and Hayes, S.C. The submerged discipline of environmentally relevant psychology. Psychological Bulletin, in press.

Cook, S.W.; Kimble, G.A.; Hicks, L.H.; McGuire, W.J.; Schoggen, P.H.; and Smith, M.B. Proposed ethical principles submitted to the APA membership for criticism and modification (by the) Ad Hoc Committee on Ethical Standards in Psychological Research, American Psychological Association Monitor 2 (1971): 9-28.

Cooledge, H.N., Jr. Samuel Sloan (1815-1884), architect. Ph.D. diss., University of Pennsylvania Mich.
Cooney, N. Participant-observation in the environmental design program. Unpublished manuscript, SUNY at Stony Brook, 1977.
Cooper, J.M., and Allen, D.W. Microteaching: History and present status. Final report, Research project # OEC 0-8-080490-2706 (010). United States Office of Education, Washington, D.C. 1970. ERIC Clearinghouse No. ED 036 471.
Cowen, E.L. Social and community interventions. Annual Review of Psychology 24 (1973): 423-472.
_____. Baby steps toward primary prevention. American Journal of Community Psychology 5 (1977): 1-22.
Craik, K.H. The comprehension of the everyday physical environment. Journal of the American Institute of Planners 34 (1968): 29-37.
_____. Environmental Psychology. In New directions in psychology, vol. 4., R. Brown et al., eds. New York: Holt, Rinehart and Winston, 1970a, pp. 1-121.
_____. The environmental dispositions of environmental decision-makers. Annals of the American Academy of Political and Social Science 389 (May 1970b): 87-94.
_____. The assessment of places, In Advances in Psychological Assessment, Vol. 2, McReynolds, P., ed. Palo Alto, Calif.: Science and Behavior Books, 1971.
_____. Environmental psychology. Annual Review of Psychology 24 (1973): 403-422.
_____. The personality research paradigm in environmental psychology. Paper presented at Clark University Conference, 1975.
Craik, K.H., and Zube, E.H., eds. Perceiving environmental quality. New York: Plenum Press, 1976.
Cremin, L.A. The transformation of the school. New York: Alfred A. Knopf, 1961.
Cronbach, L.J. The two disciplines of scientific psychology. American Psychologist 12 (1957): 671-684.
_____, and Meehl, P.E. Construct validity in psychological tests. Psychological Bulletin 52 (1955): 281-302.
_____, Rajaratnam, N., and Gleser, G.C. Theory of generalizability: A liberation of reliability theory. British Journal of Statistical Psychology 16 (1963): 137-163.
Dain, N. Disordered minds: The first century of Eastern State Hospital in Williamsburg, Virginia, 1766-1866. Williamsburg: Williamsburg Foundation, 1971.
Danford, S., and Willems, E.P. Subjective responses to architectural displays: A question of validity. Environment and behavior 7 (1975): 486-515.
D'Augelli, J.F. Evaluation process: A model. Paper presented at the meeting of the American Psychological Association, Washington, D.C., September, 1976.
Davidson, P.O.; Clark, F.W.; and Hamerlynck, L.A., eds. Evaluation of behavioral programs in community, residential and school settings. Champaign, Ill.: Research Press, 1974.

Davis, M.S. Women's liberation groups as a primary preventive mental health strategy. Community Mental Health Journal 13 (1977): 219-228.

Davidson, G.C., and Stuart, R.B. Statement on behavior modification from the AABT. Letter dated March 14, 1974, New York City.

_____. Behavior Therapy and civil liberties. American Psychiatrist 30 (1975): 755-763.

Davison, M.C., and Temple, W. Preference for fixed-internal terminal links in a three-day concurrent chain schedule. Journal of Experimental Applied Behavior 22 (1974): 11-19.

Day, W. Ethical philosophy and the thought of B.F. Skinner. In Behavior modification and ethics, J. Krapfl and E. Vargas, eds. Kalamazoo, Mich.: Behaviordelia, 1977.

Dean, J.P.; Eichhorn, R.L. and Dean, L.R. Observation and interviewing. In An introduction to social research, 2nd ed., Doby, J.T., ed. New York: Appleton-Century-Crofts, 1967.

Dean, N.F. General Dean's story. New York: Viking Press, 1954.

Department of Health, Education, and Welfare. The institutional guide to HEW policy on protection of human subjects. Washington, D.C.: DHEW # (NIH) 1971, pp. 72-107.

DeRisi, W.J., and Roberts, J. Day treatment: A re-orientation and discovery. Paper presented at the meeting of the American Psychological Association, Chicago, September, 1975.

Desor, J.A. Toward a psychological theory of crowding. Journal of Personality and Social Psychology 21 (1972): 79-83.

Deutsch, A. The mentally ill in America. New York: Columbia University Press, 1949.

Deutch, M. Field theory in social psychology. In Handbook of social psychology, vol. 1, 2nd ed. G. Lindsey and E. Aronson, eds. Reading Mass.: Addison-Wesley, 1969, p. 478.

_____, and Collins, M.E. Interracial housing: A psychological evaluation of a social experiment. Minneapolis: University of Minnesota Press, 1951.

de Villiers, P. Choice in concurrent schedules and a quantitative formulation of the law of effect. In Handbook of operant behavior, W.K. Honig and J.E.R. Staddon, eds. Englewood-Cliffs, N.J.: Prentice-Hall, 1977, pp. 233-287.

Dewey, J. The school and society. Chicago: University of Chicago Press, 1899.

_____. The school and society. Chicago: University of Chicago Press, 1915.

_____. Democracy and education. New York: Macmillan, 1916.

_____. Experience and education. New York: Macmillan, 1963.

Dewey, T., and Bentley, A.F. Knowing and the known, Boston: Beacon Press, 1949.

Dickson, C.R. Role of assessment in behavior therapy. In Advances in psychological assessment, vol. 3, P. McReynolds, ed. San Francisco: Jossey-Bass, 1975.

Dollard, J., and Miller, N.E. Personality and psychotherapy: An analysis in terms of learning, thinking, and culture. New York: McGraw-Hill, 1950.

Drucker, P.F. School around the bend. Psychology Today 6 (June 1972): 49-51, 86-89.

Dubey, D.R.; Kent, R.N.; O'Leary, S.G.; Broderick, J.E.; and O'Leary, K.D. Reactions of children and teachers to classroom observers: A series of controlled investigations. Behavior Therapy, in press.

Dubos, R. The human environment. Science Journal 5A(4) (1969): 75-80.

Duffy, B. Cruel plans for the mentally ill. New York Times, Sunday, January 2, 1977.

Durlak, J.A. Myths concerning the nonprofessional therapist. Professional Psychology 4 (1973): 300-304.

Dworkin, E.P. The implementation and evaluation of clergy and interagency mental health consultations programs. Proceedings of the 81st Annual Convention of the APA, Montreal, Canada, 1973, pp. 981-982.

Dworkin, A.L., and Dworkin, E.P. A conceptual overview of selected consultation models. American Journal of Community Psychology 3 (1975): 151-159.

D'Zurilla, T.J., and Goldfried, M.R. Problem solving and behavior modification. Journal of Abnormal Psychology 78 (1971): 107-126.

Earle, P. The Bloomingdale asylum. New York: Egbert, Hovey, and King, 1848.

_____. Historical sketch of the institutions for the insane in the United States of America. In New York Academy of Medicine, Transactions, L, part L, 9-13 (published 1851).

_____. Prospective provision for the insane. American Journal of Insanity (July 1868): 51-65.

_____. The curability of insanity: A series of studies. Philadelphia: J.B. Lippincott, 1887.

Eckman, T.A., Jr. Behavioral approaches to partical hospitalization. In Partial hospitalization: A current perspective, R.F. Luber, ed. New York: Plenum Press, 1979.

Edwards, P., ed. Encyclopedia of philosophy. New York: Macmillan/Free Press, 1967.

Edwards, W. Social utilities. Engineering Economist 19 (Summer symposium series, VI, 1971).

Ekehammer, B. Interactionism in personality from a historical perspective. Psychological Bulletin 81 (1974): 1026-1048.

_____, and Magnusson, D.A. A method to study stressful situations. Journal of Personality and Social Psychology 27 (1973): 176-179.

Ellis, R.H., and Wilson, N.C. Evaluating treatment effectiveness using a goal-oriented automated progress note. Evaluation. Monograph 1, 1973.

Ellsworth, R.B. Consumer feedback in measuring the effectiveness of mental health programs. In Handbook of evaluation research, vol. 2 M. Guttentag and E.L. Struening, eds. Beverly Hills, Calif.: Sage, 1975a.

_____. A developing imbalance in the evaluation of mental health programs. Paper presented at the meeting of American Psychological Association, Chicago, September, 1975b.

Emurian, H.H.; Emurian, C.S.; Bigelow, G.E.; and Brady, J.V. The effects of a cooperation contingency on behavior in a continuous three-person environment. Journal of the Experimental Analysis of Behavior 25 (1976): 293-302.

Endler, N.S. Conformity as a function of different reinforcement schedules. Journal of Personality and Social Psychology 7 (1966a): 175-180.

_____. Estimating variance components from mean squares for random and mixed effects analysis of variance models. Perceptual and Motor Skills 22 (1966b): 559-570.

_____. The case for person-situation interactions. Canadian Psychological Review 16 (1975): 12-21.

_____, and Hunt, J.McV. Generalizability of contributions for sources of variance in the S-R Inventories of Anxiousness. Journal of Personality, 1969, 37, 1-24.

_____, and Magnusson, D. Personality and person by situation interactions. In Interactional psychology and personality, Endler and Magnusson, eds. Washington: Hemisphere Publishing, 1976, pp. 1-25.

Environmental Education Act of 1970 (Public Law 91-516).

Erickson, R.C. Outcome studies in mental hospitals: A review. Psychological Bulletin 82 (1975): 519-540.

Esser, A.H., ed. Behavior and environment: The use of space by animals and man. New York: Plenum, 1971.

Esser, A.H.; Chamberlain, A.S.; Chapple, E.D.; and Kline, N.S. Territoriality of patients on a research ward. In Recent Advances in Biological Psychiatry, J. Wortis, ed. 7 (1965): 36-44.

_____, and Deutsch, R.D. Environment and mental health: An annotated bibliography. Man-environment systems 5 (1975): 333-348.

_____, and Greenbie, B.B., eds. Design for communality and privacy. New York: Plenum, 1978.

Eysenck, H.J. The effects of psychotherapy: An evaluation. Journal of Consulting Psychology 16 (1952): 319-324.

_____. Behavior therapy and the neuroses. London: Pergamon Press, 1960.

_____. The effects of psychotherapy. New York: International Science Press, 1966.

_____, ed. Experiments in behavior therapy. New York: Pergamon Press, 1964.

Fairweather, G.W. Methods for experimental social innovation. New York: Wiley, 1967.

_____. Social change: The challenge to survival. Morristown, N.J.: General Learning Press, 1972.

_____; Sanders, D.H.; Cressler, D.L.; and Maynard, H. Community life for the mentally ill: An alternative to institutional care. Chicago: Aldine, 1969.

_____; Sanders, H.H.; and Tornatzky, L.G. Creating change in mental health organizations. Elmsford, N.Y.: Pergamon Press, 1974.

Fawcett, S., and Miller, L. Training public-speaking behavior: An experimental analysis and social validation. Journal of Applied Behavior Analysis 8 (1975): 125-135.

Feallock, R., and Miller, L.K. The design and evaluation of a worksharing system for experimental group living. Journal of Applied Behavior Analysis 9 (1976): 277-288.

Featherstone, J. Schools where children learn. New York: Liveright, 1971.

Fergus, E. Lodge Notes: MSU-NIMH Innovation Diffusion Project. Psychology Department, Michigan State University, 1977.

Festinger, L.; Schachter, S.; and Back, K. Social pressures in informal groups: A study of human factors in housing. New York: Harper, 1950.

Findley, J.D. Programmed environments for the experimental analysis of human behavior. In Operant behavior: Areas of research and application, W.K. Honig, ed. New York: Appleton-Century-Crofts, 1966, pp. 827-848.

Fisher, E.B., Jr.; Winkler, R.C.; Krasner, L.; Kagel, J.; Battalio, R.C.; and Basmann, R.L. Economic perspectives in behavior therapy: Complex interdependencies in token economies. Behavior Therapy 9 (1978): 391-403.

Flanagan, J.C. The critical incident technique. Psychological Bulletin (1954): 51 327-358.

_____. A research approach to improving our quality of life. American Psychologist 33 (1978): 138-147.

Ford, J.D. Behavioral approaches to training parents as change-agents: Review and analysis. State University of New York at Stony Brook, 1975.

_____. Training in clinical psychology: A reappraisal based on recent empirical evidence. Clinical Psychologist 3 (1977): 14-16.

_____. Research on training counselors and clinicians: Review and analysis. Review of Educational Research, 1978, in press.

Ford, J.D., and Hutchison, W.R. New strategies for self management within behavior modification. Paper presented at the Drake University Professional Issues in Behavior Analysis Conference, Des Moines, Iowa, 1974a.

_____. Elements of an effective and responsive training program for community-based psychologists. Paper presented at the City University of New York Psychology in Action Conference, New York, 1974b.

Fordyce, M.W. Development of a program to increase personal happiness. Journal of Counseling Psychology 24 (1977): 511-521.

Foreyt, J.P.; Rockwood, C.E.; Davis, J.C.; Desvousges, W.H.; and Hollingsworth, R. Benefit-cost analysis of a token economy program. Professional Psychology 6 (1975): 26-33.

Foster, S.L. The environmental context of reinforcement: Clinical implications of the matching law. State University of New York at Stony Brook, 1976.

Fracchia, J.; Canale, D.; Cambria, E.R.; Ruest, E.; and Sheppard, C. Public views of ex-mental patients: A note on perceived dangerousness and unpredictability. Psychological Reports 38 (1976): 495-498.

Frank, J.D. Persuasion and healing. Baltimore, Md.: Johns Hopkins University Press, 1961 (1973, rev. ed.).

Frankena, W. Ethics. Englewood Cliffs, N.J.: Prentice-Hall, 1973.

Fredericksen, N., Toward a taxonomy of situations. American Psychologist 27 (1972): 14-123. Reprinted in R.H. Moos and P.M. Ingels, eds. Issues in social ecology: Human miliens. Palo Alto, Calif.: National Press, 1974, 29-44.

Freedman, J.L. The effects of crowding on human performance and social behavior. Columbia University, 1972.

_____. Crowding and behavior. New York: Viking Press, 1975.

_____; Klevonsky, S.; and Ehrlich, P.R. The effect of crowding on human task performance. Journal of Applied Social Psychology 1 (1971): 7-25.

Freedman, H. Mental health and the environment. British Journal of Psychiatry. 132 (1978): 113-124.

Fremouw, W.J., and Feindler, E. The "helper principle" revisited: Toward a cost-effective model of service delivery. Paper presented at the meeting of the Southeastern Psychological Association, New Orleans, April, 1976.

Fremouw, W.J., and Harmatz, M.G. A helper model for behavioral treatment of speech anxiety. Journal of Consulting and Clinical Psychology 43 (1975): 652-660.

Friedman, P. Legal regulation of applied behavior analysis in mental institutions and prisons. Arizona Law Review 17 (1975): 39-104.

Friedman, R.M.; Filipczak, J.; and Reese, S.C. Problems in initiating, implementing, and evaluating a large-scale behavioral program in the public schools. Paper presented at the meeting of the Association for the Advancement of Behavior Therapy, San Francisco, December, 1975.

Friedmann, A.; Zimring, C.; and Zube, E. Environmental design evaluation. New York: Plenum, 1978.

Fry, L.T. Participant observation and program evaluation. Journal of Health and Social Behavior 14 (1973): 274-278.

Fuller, P.R. Operant conditioning of a vegetative human organism. American Journal of Psychology 62 (1949): 587-590.

Gabel, H.; Haig-Friedman, D.; Friedman, S.; and Vietze, P. Pre-parent education: Proposals and prospects. Journal of Community Psychology 4 (1976): 403-405.

Galbraith, J.K. The new industrial state. Boston: Houghton Mifflin, 1967.

Galt, J.M. The treatment of insanity. New York: Harper and Brothers, 1846.

_____. The farm of St. Anne. American Journal of Insanity (January 1855): 352-357.

Gambrill, E.D. Behavior modification: Handbook of assessment, intervention, and evaluation, San Francisco: Jossey-Bass, 1977.

Gamson, W.A. Simsoc: Establishing social order in a simulated society. Simulation and games 2 (1971): 287-305.

Gans, H.J. The urban villagers. New York: Free Press, 1962.

Garcia, J. and Koelling, R.A. Relations of cue to consequences in avoidance learning. Psychonomic science 4 (1966): 123-124.

Gardner, J.M. Selection of nonprofessionals for behavior modification programs. American Journal of Mental Deficiency 76 (1972): 680-685.

Gartner, A., ed. College programs for paraprofessionals. A directory of degree-granting programs in the human services. New York: Human Sciences Press, 1975.

Gartner, A., and Riessman, F. Self help in the human services. San Francisco: Jossey-Bass, 1977.

Geer, B. First days in the field. In Sociologists at work, P. Hammond, ed. New York: Basic Books, 1964.

Geller, E.S. Prompting anti-litter behaviors. Proceedings of the Eighty-First Annual Convention of the APA 8 (1973): 901-902.

_____. Increasing desired waste disposals with instructions. Man-Environment Systems (March 1975): 125-128.

_____, Chaffee, J.L. and Ingram, R.E. Promoting paper recycling on a university campus. Journal of Environmental Systems 5 (1975): 39-57.

_____; Farris, J.; and Post, D. Prompting a consumer behavior for pollution control. Journal of Applied Behavior Analysis 6 (1973): 367-376.

_____; Johnson, D.F.; Hamlin, P.H.; and Kennedy, T.D. Behavior modification and corrections: Are they compatible? Paper presented at the Seventh Annual Southern California Conference on Behavior Modification, October, 1975.

Gelwicks, L.E. Design can brainwash the chronic care patient. The Modern Hospital 102 (3) (1964): 106-111.

_____. Best function needs right environment. The Modern Hospital 106 (3) (1966): 93-97, 172.

Giordano, J., and Giordano, G.P. Ethnicity and community mental health: A review of the literature. Community Mental Health Review 1 (1976): 4-14.

Glaser, E.M., & Backer, T.E., A clinical approach to program evaluation. Evaluation, 1972, 1, 54-59.

Glass, G.U.; Tiao, G.C.; and Maguire, T.O. Analysis of data on the 1900 revision of German divorce laws as a time-series quasi-experiment. Law and Society Review 4 (1971): 539-62.

Glass, G.V., ed. Evaluation studies review annual. Beverly Hills, Calif. Sage, 1976.

Glidewell, J.C. The entry problem in consultation. Journal of Social Issues 15 (1959): 51-59.

_____; Gildea, C.L.; and Kaufman, M.K. The preventive and therapeutic effects of two school mental health programs. American Journal of Community Psychology 1 (1973): 295-329.

Goffman, E. Asylums. Garden City, N.Y.: Anchor Books, 1961.

_____. Behavior in public gatherings: Notes on the social organization of gatherings. New York: Free Press, 1963.

_____. Interaction ritual. New York: Doubleday, 1967.

_____. Relations in public. New York, Basic Books, 1971.

Golann, S.E., and Eisdorfer, C., eds., Handbook of community mental health. New York: Appleton-Century-Crofts, 1972.

Goldberg, L.R., and Slovic, P. Importance of test item content: An analysis of a corollary of the deviation hypothesis. Journal of Counseling Psychology 14 (1967): 462-472.

Goldfried, M.R., and Davision, G.C. Clinical behavior therapy. New York: Holt, Rinehart and Winston, 1976.

Goldfried, M.R., and D'Zurilla, T.J. A behavioral-analytic method for assessing competence. In Current topics in clinical and community psychology, vol. 1, C.D. Spielberger, ed. New York: Academic Press, 1969.

Goldfried, M.R., and Kent, R.N. Traditional versus behavioral personality assessment: A comparison of methodological and theoretical assumptions. Psychological Bulletin 77 (1972): 409-420.

Goldfried, M.R., and Linehan, M.M. Basic issues in behavioral assessment. In Handbook of Behavioral Assessment, A.R. Ciminero, K. Calhoun, and H. Adams, eds. New York: Wiley, 1977.

_____, and Pomeranz, K.M. Role of assessment in behavior modification. Psychological Reports 23 (1968): 75-87.

_____, and Sprafkin, J.N. Behavioral Personality Assessment. Morristown, N.J.: General Learning Press, 1974.

Goldiamond, I. Justified and unjustified alarm over behavior control. In Behavior disorders: Perspectives and trends, O. Milton, ed. Philadelphia: Lippincott, 1965.

_____. Toward a constructional approach to social problems. Behaviorism 2 (1974): 1-80.

_____. Singling out behavior modification for legal regulation: Some effects on patient care, psychotherapy, and research, in general. Arizona Law Review 17 (1975): 105-126.

_____. Singling out self-administered behavior therapies for professional overview. American Psychologist 31 (1976): 142-147.

_____. President's message. MABA Newsletter 2 (1978): 1-2.

_____; Dyrud, J.; and Miller, M. Practice as research in professional psychology. Canadian Psychologist 6a (1965): 110-128.

Golding, S.L. Flies in the ointment: Methodological problems in the analysis of the percentage of variance due to persons and situations. Psychological Bulletin 82 (1975): 278-288.

Goldsmith, J.B., and McFall, P.M. Development and evaluation of an interpersonal skill-training program for psychiatric inpatients. Journal of Abnormal Psychology 84 (1975): 51-58.

Goldstein, A.P. Structured learning therapy. New York: Academic Press, 1974.

Goldstein, A.S. The insanity defense. New Haven: Yale University Press, 1967.

Goldstein, K. Prefrontal lobotomy: analysis and warning. Scientific American, 1950, offprint.

Goldstein, R.S.; Minkin, B.L.; Minkin, N.; and Baer, D.M. Finders keepers?: An analysis of free found ads in community newspapers. Paper presented at the meeting of the American Psychological Association, Washington, D.C., September, 1976.

Goldston, S.E., ed. Concepts of community psychiatry: A framework for training. (DHEW PHS Publication No. 1319). Washington, D.C.: U.S. Government Printing Office, 1965.

Goodkin, R. Some neglected issues in the literature on behavior therapy. Psychological Reports 20 (1967): 415-20.

Goodman, G. Companionship therapy, San Francisco: Jossey-Bass, 1972.

Goodson, W.H. In and out − A behaviorally oriented inpatient service. Huntsville-Madison County Mental Health Center, Huntsville, Alabama, 1972.

_____. Behavior modification − A catalyst for evaluation. Paper presented to the Fourth Annual Behavior Modification Institute, Tuscaloosa, Alabama, May, 1971.

Gordon, S.B. Training teachers in behavior modification: Responsive teaching vs. a control group. Paper presented at the meeting of the American Psychological Association, Washington, D.C., September, 1976.

Gottesfeld, H. Alternatives to psychiatric hospitalization. Community Mental Health Review 1 (1976): 4-10.

_____, ed. The critical issues of community mental health. New York: Behavioral Publications, 1972.

Gove, W.R.; Galle, O.R.; McCarthy, J.D.; and Hughes, M. Living circumstances and social pathology: The effect of population density, over crowding, and isolation on suicide, homicide, and alcoholism. Working paper. Madison, Wis.: Center for Demography and Ecology, 1975, pp. 75-133.

Granados Tellez, M.F. Gamines. Bogota: Tercer Mundo, 1974.

Graves, R. The greek myths, volume 2. London: Penguin, 1955.

Gray, F.; Graubard, P.S.; and Rosenberg, H. Little brother is changing you. Psychology Today (March, 1974): pp. 42-46.

Gray, J.P. Insanity: it's frequency and some of its preventable causes. American Journal of Insanity 42 (1885): 1-45.

Greenberg, J. I never promised you a rose garden. New York: New American Library, 1964.

Griffitt, W., and Veitch, R. Hot and crowded: Influences of population density and temperature on interpersonal affective behavior. Journal of Personality and Social Psychology 17 (1971): 92-98.

Grob, G.N. The state and the mentally ill: A history of Worchester state hospital in Massachusetts, 1830-1920. Chapel Hill: University of North Carolina Press, 1966.

_____. Mental institutions in America: Social policy to 1875. New York: Free Press, 1973.

Grossman, F.K., and Quinlan, D. Mental health consultation to community settings: A case study of a failure to achieve goals. In Handbook of Community Mental Health, S.E. Golann and C. Eisdorfer, eds. New York: Appleton-Century-Crofts, 1972, pp. 617-640.

Grundle, T.; Emiley, S.; and Webb, D. Entry credentialization and role change in consultation to a consultation program in a school system. Journal of Community Psychology 1 (1973): 383-386.

Guerney, B.G. Psychotherapeutic agents: New roles for non-professionals, parents and teachers. New York: Holt, Rinehart and Winston, 1969.

Gurman, A.S. The patient's perception of the therapeutic relationship. In The therapist's contribution to effective psychotherapy: An empirical assessment, A.S. Gurman and A.M. Razin, eds. Elmsford, N.Y.: Pergamon Press, 1978.

Gutierrez, J. Infancia en la miseria. Bogota: Tercer Mundo, 1967.

Gutman, R. People and buildings. New York: Basic Books, 1972.

Guttentag, M. Models and methods in evaluation research. Journal for the Theory of Social Behavior 1 (1971): 75-95.

_____. Subjectivity and its use in evaluation research. Evaluation 1 (1973): 60-75.

_____, and Snapper, K. Plans, evaluations, and decision. Evaluation 2 (1974): 58-64, 73-74.

Guzman, G.; Fals Borda, O; and Umana Luna, E. La violencia en Colombia. Bogota: Tercer Mundo, 1962.

Habraken, N.J. Supports: An alternative to mass housing. London: Architectural Press, 1972.

Hadley, J.M.; True, J.E.; and Kepes, S.Y. An experiment in the education of pre-professional mental health workers: The Purdue program. Community Mental Health Journal 6 (1970): 40-50.

Hall, E.T. The hidden dimension. New York: Doubleday, 1966.

_____. The silent language. New York: Doubleday, 1959.

Hall, M.C. Responsive parent training: Helping parents help themselves and other parents – A behaviorally based assessment, intervention, and evaluation program. Symposium presented at the meeting of the Association for Advancement of Behavior Therapy, Atlanta, Georgia, December, 1977.

Hall, P.G. The world cities. New York: McGraw-Hill, 1966.

_____. London 2000. New York: Praeger, 1969.

Halle, L.J. Out of chaos, Boston: Houghton Mifflin, 1977.

Hamblin, R.L., and Kunkel, J.H., eds. Behavioral theory in sociology: essays in honor of George C. Homans, New Brunswick, N.J.: Transaction Books, 1977.

Hammer, R.; Landsberg, G.; and Neigher, W., eds. Program evaluation in community mental health centers. N.Y.: D and O Press, 1976.

Hargreaves, W.A.; Attkisson, C.C.; and Sorenson, J.E., eds. Resource materials for community mental health program evaluation, 2nd ed. Rockville, Md.: National Institute of Mental Health, 1977.

Harpin, R.E. A review of the development of group behavior therapy: From verbal conditioning to its place in a modern ecological view of behavior change. State University of New York at Stony Brook, 1974.

Harpin, R.E., and Ford, J.D. The psychologist as designer of sociophysical environments. Paper presented at the City University of New York Psychology in Action Conference, New York, 1974.

Harpin, R.E., and Hutchison, W.R. Self-control package: For use with personal effectiveness training. Maudsley Hospital, London, 1976.

Harshbarger, D., and Maley, R.F., eds. Behavior analysis and systems analysis: An integrative approach to mental health programs. Kalamazoo, Mich.: Behaviordelia, 1974.

Hartshorne, H., and May, M.A. Studies in deceit. New York: Macmillan, 1928.

Hauser, P.M., and Duncan, O.D., eds. The study of population. Chicago: University of Chicago Press, 1959.

Hauser, S.T., and Shapiro, R.L. An approach to the analysis of faculty-student interactions in small groups. Human Relations 29 (1976): 819-832.

Hauserman, N.; Walen, S.R.; and Behling, M. Reinforced racial integration in the first grade: A study in generalization. Journal of Applied Behavior Analysis 6 (1973): 193-200.

Hawkins, R.P. Universal parenthood training: A proposal for preventive mental health. In Control of human behavior, vol. 3: Applications in Education. R.E. Ulrich, T. Stachnik, and J. Mabry, eds. Glenview, Ill.: Scott, Foresman, 1974.

_____. Who decided that was the problem? Two stages of responsibility for applied behavior analysts. In Issues in evaluating behavior modification, W.S. Wood, ed. Champaign, Ill.: Research Press, 1975.

Hayes, S.C.; Johnson V.S.; and Cone, J.D. The marked item technique: A practical procedure for litter control. Journal of Applied Behavior Analysis 8 (1975): 381-386.

Haywood, H.C. The ethics of doing research and of not doing it. American Journal of Mental Deficiency 81 (1976): 311-317.

Hebb, D.O. Introduction. Cognitive and physiological effects of perceptual isolation. In Sensory Deprivation, Solomon, Kubzansky, Leiderman, Mendelson, Trumball, and Wexler, eds. Cambridge, Mass.: Harvard University Press, 1965, pp. 6-8.

Heber, R., and Garber, H. The Milwaukee project: A study of the use of family intervention to prevent cultural-familial mental retardation. In The exceptional infant: Assessment and intervention, B.Z. Friedlander, G.M. Sterritt, and G.E. Kirk, eds. New York: Brunner/-Mazel, 1975.

Heimstra, N.W., and McFarling, L.H. Environmental psychology. Monterey, Calif.: Brooks/Cole, 1974.

Henderson, J.D. Coexisting with the community, Paper presented at the meeting of the American Psychological Association, Washington, D.C. September 1969.

_____. A community-based operant learning environment. I: Overview. In Advances in Behavior Therapy, R.D. Rubin, H. Fensterheim, A.A. Lazarus, and C.M. Franks, eds. New York: Academic Press, 1971, pp. 233-237.

_____, and Scoles, P.E., Jr. Conditioning techniques in a community-based operant environment for psychotic men. Behavior Therapy 1 (1970): 245-251.

Herrnstein, R.J. Relative and absolute strength of response as a function of frequency of reinforcement. Journal of the Experimental Analysis of Behavior 4 (1961): 267-272.

_____. Onthe law of effect. Journal of the Experimental Analysis of Behavior 13 (1970): 243-266.

_____. The evolution of behaviorism. American Psychologist 32 (1977a): 593-603.

_____. Doing what comes naturally: A reply to Professor Skinner. American Psychologist 32 (1977b): 1013-1016.

Herrnstein, R.J., and Loveland, D.H. Matching in a network. Journal of Experimental Applied Behavior 26 (1976): 143-153.

Hersch, C. Social history, mental health, and community control. American Psychologist 27 (1972): 749-754.

Hersen, M. Token economies in institutional settings. Journal of Nervous and Mental Disease 162 (1976): 206-211.

Hersen, M., and Barlow, D.H. Single case experimental designs: Strategies for studying behavior change. Elmsford, N.Y.: Pergamon Press, 1976.

Hersen, M., and Bellack, A.S. Behavioral assessment: A practical handbook. Elmsford, N.Y.: Pergamon Press, 1976.

Hessler, R.M., and Walters, M.J. Consumer evaluation research: Implications for methodology, social policy, and the role of the sociologist. Sociological Quarterly 17 (1976): 74-89.

Hill, A. Art versus illness. London: Allen and Unwin, 1945.

Himwich, H.E. The new psychiatric drugs. Scientific American, 1955, offprint.

Hirschowitz, R.G. Mental health consultation: The state of the art. Psychiatric Quarterly 47 (1973): 495-508.

Hobbs, N. Mental health's third revolution. American Journal of Orthopsychiatry 34 (1964): 822-833.

Hoffmann, C. The Chinese worker. Albany: State University of New York Press, 1974.

_____. Work incentives and social control. In Social control and deviance in contemporary China, A. Wilson, R. Wilson, and S. Greenblatt, eds. New York: Praeger, 1977.

Holland, J.G. Behavior modification for prisoners, patients, and other people as a prescription for the planned society. Paper presented at EPA, Philadelphia, April, 1974.

_____. Are behavioral principles for revolutionaries? Behavior Modification (1974): 195-208.

Holland, T. Organizational structure and institutional care. Journal of Health and Social Behavior 14 (1973): 218-225.

Hollinger, D.A.T.S. Kuhn's theory of science and its implications for history. American Historical Review 78 (1973): 370-393.

Holt, J. How children learn. New York: Pitman, 1967.

Homans, G.C. The sociological relevance of behaviorism. In Behavioral Sociology, R.L. Burgess, and D. Bushell, Jr., eds. New York: Columbia University Press, 1969.

_____. Social behavior: Its elementary forms, 2nd ed. New York: Harcourt, Brace, Jovanovich, 1974.

Hopkins, B.L., and Conard, R.J. Putting it all together: Super school. In Teaching special children, N.G. Haring and R.L. Schiefelbusch, eds. New York: McGraw-Hill, 1975.

Horowitz, F.D. New directions for parenting. In Behavior modification and families, E.J. Mash, L.A. Hamerlynck, and L.C. Handy, eds. New York: Brunner/Mazel, 1976.

Hu,S.M., and Seifman, E., eds. Toward a new world outlook: A documentary history of education in the People's Republic of China. 1949-1976. New York: AMS Press.

Huesler, C. The gilded asylum. In The participant observer, G. Jacobs, ed. New York: George Braziller, 1970.

Huntington, E. Civilization and climate. New Haven: Yale University Press, 1911.

Hurley, D.J., Jr., and Tyler, F.B. Relationship between systems' mental health paradigm and personpower utilization. Paper presented at the meeting of the Eastern Psychological Association, New York, April, 1976.

Hursh, D.E. The interface between environmental design and applied behavior analysis. Paper presented annual meeting, Environmental Design Research Association, Vancouver, 1976.

Hutchinson, R., and Azrin, N. Conditioning of mental-hospital patients to fixed-ratio schedules of reinforcement. Journal of Experimental Analysis of Behavior 4 (1961): 87-95.

Hutchison, W.R. Behavioral methods in teacher training. State University of New York at Stony Brook, New York, 1975a.

_____. Ethics: A non-traditional reformulation with no easy answers. Paper presented at EPA, New York, April 3-5, 1975b.

_____. Measurement and systematic training of creative problem solving skills. Ph.D. diss., State University of New York at Stony Brook, 1976. Dissertation Abstracts International, 37(11), 5832-B, order no. 77-10,736.

_____. A behavioristic approach to preserving civil rights: Discussion of Wood's paper. In Behavior modification and ethics, J. Krapfl and E. Vargas, eds. Kalamazoo, Mich.: Behaviordelia, 1977.

_____, and Harpin, R.E. The best-planned programs of mice and men. Paper presented at the Psychology in Action Conference, City University of New York, October, 1974.

_____, Waters, J.M., and Graeff, J.A. The incident report sheet and guidelines for the IRS. State University of New York at Stony Brook, 1977.

Insel, P.M., and Moos, R.H. Work Environment Scale. Palo Alto, Calif.: Consulting Psychologists Press, 1974.

Isaacs, W.; Thomas, J.; and Goldiamond, I. Applications of operant conditioning to reinstate verbal behavior in psychotics. Journal of Speech and Hearing Disorders 25 (1960): 8-12.

Ittelson, W.H.; Proshansky, H.M.; Rivlin, L.G.; and Winkel, G.H. An introduction to environmental psychology. New York: Holt, Rinehart and Winston, 1974.

Ivey, A.E. Microcounseling. Springfield, Ill.: C.C. Thomas, 1971.

Ivey, A.E.; Normington, C.J.; Miller, C.D.; Morrill, W.H., and Haase, R.F. Microcounseling and attending behavior: An approach to prepracticum counselor training. Journal of Counseling Psychology, Monograph Supplement 15 (5, part 2), (1968): 1-12.

Janes, R.W. A note on phases of the community role of the participant-observer. American Sociological Review 26 (1961): 446-450.

Jeger, A.M. Training nonprofessional behavior-change agents: A review of the literature. State University of New York at Stony Brook, 1975a.

_____. Behavior modification and community psychology. Paper presented at the meeting of the Eastern Psychological Association, New York, April, 1975b.

_____. The effects of a behavioral consultation program on consultees, clients, and the social environment. Diss. State University of New York at Stony Brook, 1977. Dissertation Abstracts International 38, 1405B, University Microfilms No. 77-20, 019.

_____. Behavior theories and their application. In Suicide: Theories and clinical aspects, L.D. Hankoff, ed. Littleton, Mass.: PSG Publishing, 1979.

Jeger, A.M., and McClure, G. Evaluation of a behavioral consultation program: Changes in consultees, clients, and the social environment. Paper presented at the meeting of the Eastern Psychological Association, Philadelphia, April, 1979a.

_____. The attitudinal effects of undergraduate behavioral training. Teaching of Psychology, 1979b, in press.

Jeger, A.M., McClure, G., and Krasner, L. A predoctoral community psychology internship: Implementing the environmental designer role. Paper presented at the meeting of the American Psychological Association, Washington, D.C., September, 1976.

Jeger, A.M., and Slotnick, R.S. Position paper: Community mental health and the media – Practical implications. New York Institute of Technology, Old Westbury, 1978.

Jeger, A.M., and Slotnick, R.S. Community mental health: A behavioral-ecological perspective. New York: Plenum Press, 1980, in preparation.

Johnson, C.A., and Katz, R.C. Using parents as change agents for their children: A review. Journal of Child Psychology and Psychiatry 14 (1973): 181-200.

Johnson, S.M., and Bolstad, D.D. Methodological issues in naturalistic observation: Some problems and solutions for field research. In Behavior change: Methodology, concepts, and practice, L.A. Hamerlynck, L.C. Handy, and E.J. Mash, eds. Champaign, Ill.: Research Press, 1973, pp. 7-67.

Johnson, S.M., and Lobitz, G.K. Parental manipulation of child behavior in home observations. Journal of Applied Behavior Analysis 7 (1974): 23-32.

Johnston, J. Is there a right to punish? In Behavior modification and ethics, J. Krapfl and E. Vargas, eds. Kalamazoo, Mich.: Behaviordelia, 1977.

Joint Commission on Mental Illness and Mental Health. Action for mental health. New York: Basic Books, 1961.

Jones, E. Social class and psychotherapy: A critical review of research. Psychiatry 37 (1974): 307-320.

Jones, F.; Fremouw, W.J.; and Carples, S. Pyramid training of elementary school teachers to use a classroom management "skills package." Journal of Applied Behavior Analysis, 10, (1977): 239-253.

Jones, J. Self-help activists talk of joining forces. American Psychological Association Monitor 8, (August, 1977): 1;12.

Jones, K. Lunacy, law, and conscience: 1744-1845: The social history of the care of the insane. London: Routledge and Kegan Paul, 1955.

_____. Mental health and social policy: 1845-1959. London: Routledge and Kegan Paul, 1960.

Jones, M.C. A laboratory study of fear: The case of Peter. Pedagogical Seminary and Journal of Genetic Psychology 31 (1924): 308-315.

Jones, R.J., and Azrin, N.H. An experimental application of a social reinforcement approach to the problem of job finding. Journal of Applied Behavior Analysis 6 (1973): 345-353.

Jones, R.R. Design and analysis problems in program evaluation. In Evaluation of behavioral programs in community, residential, and school settings, P.O. Davidson, F.W. Clark, and L.A. Hamerlynck, eds. Champaign, Ill.: Research Press, 1974, pp. 1-31.

Jones, R.R.; Reid, J.B.; and Patterson, G.R. Naturalistic observation in clinical assessment. In Advances in psychological assessment, vol. 3, P. McReynolds ed. San Francisco: Jossey-Bass, 1975.

Kagan, N. Can technology help us toward reliability in influencing human interaction? Educational Technology 13, (1973): 44-51.

Kagel, J.H. Token economies and experimental economics. Journal of Political Economy 80, (1972): 779-785.

Kagel, J.H.; Battalio, R.C.; Winkler, R.C.; Fisher, E.B.; Miles, C.G.; Basmann, R.L.; and Krasner, L. Income, consumption and saving in controlled environments: Further economic analysis. In Experimentation in controlled environments, C.G. Miles, ed. Ontario: Addiction Research Foundation, 1975, pp. 71-88.

Kagel, J.H., and Winkler, R.C. Behavioral economics: Areas of cooperative research between economics and applied behavior analysis. Journal of Applied Behavior Analysis 5 (1972): 335-342.

Kahn, R.L., and Mann, F. Developing research partnerships. Journal of Social Issues 8 (1952): 4-10.

Kanfer, F.H., and Phillips, J.S. A survey of current behavior therapies and a proposal for classification. In Behavior therapy: Appraisal and status. C.M. Franks, ed. New York: McGraw-Hill, 1969, pp. 445-475.

_____. Learning foundations of behavior therapy. New York: Wiley, 1970.

Kanfer, F.H., and Saslow, G. Behavioral Diagnosis. In Behavior therapy: Appraisal and status, C.M. Franks, ed. New York: McGraw-Hill, 1969.

Kansas Follow-Through Program. Training procedures. Section in Workshop Manual, Follow-Through Program, Midwest Regional Center, Lawrence, Kansas: University of Kansas, Department of Human Development, 1972.

Kantor, J.R. Principles of psychology. New York: Knopf, 1924.

_____. The scientific evolution of psychology. Chicago: Principia Press, 1963.

_____ . Behaviorism in the history of psychology. Psychological Record 18 (1968): 151-166.

Kaplan, S. The challenge of environmental psychology: A proposal for a new functionalism, American Psychologist 27 (February, 1972): 140-143.

Kaplan, S.R., and Roman, M. The organization and delivery of mental health services in the ghetto: The Lincoln Hospital experience. New York: Praeger, 1973.

Karlsruher, A. The non-professional as a psychotherapeutic agent: A review. American Journal of Community Psychology 2 (1974): 61-77.

Karnow, S. Mao and China. New York: Viking, 1972.

Karon, B.P., and Vandenbos, G.R. Treatment costs of psychotherapy as compared to medication for schizophrenia. Professional Psychology 6 (1975): 293-298.

_____ . Cost/benefit analysis: Psychologist versus psychiatrist for schizophrenics. Professional Psychology 7 (1976): 107-111.

Kasmar, J.V. The development of a usable lexicon of environmental descriptors. Environment and Behavior 2 (1970): 153-169.

Katkin, E.S., and Sibley, R.F. Psychological consultation at Attica State Prison: Post-hoc reflections on some precursors to a disaster. In The helping professions in the world of action, I.I. Goldenberg, ed. Lexington, Mass.: Lexington Books, 1973, pp. 165-194.

Katz, D. Field studies. In Research methods in the behavioral sciences, L. Festinger, and D. Katz, eds. New York: Holt, Rinehart and Winston, 1953.

Kaye, S.M. Psychology in relation to design: An overview. Canadian Psychological Review 16 (April 1975): 104-110.

Kazdin, A.E. Methodological and assessment consideration in evaluating reinforcement programs in applied settings. Journal of Applied Behavior Analysis 6 (1973): 517-531.

_____ . Extensions of reinforcement techniques to socially and environmentally relevant behaviors. In Progress in behavior modification, M. Hersen, R. Eisler, and P. Miller, eds. New York: Academic Press, 1977a.

_____ . The token economy: A review and an evaluation. New York: Plenum Press, 1977b.

Keeley, S.M.; Shemberg, K.M.; and Carbonell, J. Operant clinical intervention: Behavior management or beyond? Where are the data? Behavior Therapy 7 (1976): 292-305.

Keeley, S.M.; Shemberg, K.M.; and Ferber, H. The training and use of undergraduates as behavior analysts in the consultative process. Professional Psychology 4 (1973): 59-63.

Kelley, K.M., and Henderson, J.D. A community-based operant learning environment II: Systems and procedures. In Advances in behavior therapy, R.D. Rubin, H. Fensterheim, A.A. Lazarus, and C.M. Franks, eds. New York: Academic Press, 1971, pp. 239-250.

Kelly, J.G. Ecological constraints on mental health services. American Psychologist 21 (1966): 535-539.

_____. The quest for valid preventive interventions. In Current topics in clinical and community psychology, vol. 2, C.D. Spielberger, ed. New York: Academic Press, 1970.

_____. Qualities for the community psychologist. American Psychologist 26 (1971): 897-903.

Kelly, J.G.; Snowden, L.R.; and Munoz, R.F. Social and community interventions. Annual Review of Psychology 28 (1977): 323-361.

Kelman, H.C. A time to speak: On human values and social research. San Francisco: Jossey-Bass, 1968.

_____. Manipulation of human behavior: An ethical dilemma for the social scientist. Journal of Social Issues 21 (1965): 31-46.

Kennedy, J.F. Message from the president of the United States relative to mental illness and mental retardation (Eighty-eighth Congress, first session, U.S. House of Representatives Document No. 58). Reprinted in American Journal of Psychiatry 120 (1964): 729-737.

Keutzer, C.S.; Fosmire, F.R.; Diller, R.; and Smith, M.D. Laboratory training in a new social system: Evaluation of a consulting relationship with a high school faculty. Journal of Applied Behavioral Science 7 (1974): 493-501.

Kent, R.N., and Foster, S.L. Direct observational procedures: Methodological Issues in naturalistic settings. In Handbook of behavioral assessment, A.R. Ciminero, K.S. Calhoun, and H.E. Adams, eds. New York: Wiley-Interscience, 1977.

Kessen, W., ed. Childhood in China. New Haven: Yale University Press, 1975.

Kiesler, D.J. Experimental designs in psychotherapy research. In Handbook of psychotherapy and behavior change: An empirical analysis, A.E. Bergin and S.L. Garfield, eds. New York: Wiley, 1971.

Kiger, R. Adopting the unit plan. Hospital and Community Psychiatry 23 (1972): 23-27.

King, G.D. Evaluation of training programs. Paper presented at the meeting of the American Psychological Association, Washington, D.C., September, 1976.

King, L.W.; Austin, N.K.; Liberman, R.P.; and DeRisi, W.J. Accountability like charity begins at home. Evaluation 2 (1974): 75-77.

King, L.W.; Cotler, S.B.; and Patterson, K. Behavior modification consultation in a Mexican-American school: A case study. American Journal of Community Psychology 3 (1975): 229-235.

Kinkade, K. A Walden two experiment. Psychology Today 6 (1973): 35-42.

_____. A Walden two experiment: The first five years of Twin Oaks community. New York: William Morrow, 1973.

Kiresuk, T.J. Goal attainment scaling at a county mental health center. Evaluation (1973) monograph 1.

Kirk, S.A., and Therrien, M.E. Community mental health myths and the fate of former hospitalized patients. Psychiatry 38 (1975): 209-217.

Kirkbride, T. Remarks on the construction and arrangements of hospitals for the insane. American Journal of the Medical Sciences (1847): 40-56.

Kirkbride, T. On the construction, organization, and general arrangement of hospitals for the insane. Philadelphia: Lindsay and Blakiston, 1854.

Knapp, M.L. Nonverbal communication in human interaction, 2nd ed. New York: Holt, Rinehart and Winston, 1978.

Kohlenberg, R.J. A behavioral analysis of peaking in residential electrical energy consumers. Presented at APA Annual Convention, September 1974.

Kohlenberg, R.J., and Phillips, T. Reinforcement and rate of litter depositing. Journal of Applied Behavior Analysis 6 (1973): 391-396.

Kohlenberg, R.J.; Phillips, T.; and Proctor, A. A behavioral analysis of peaking in residential electrical energy consumers. Paper presented at the American Psychological Association meeting, Montreal, 1973.

Kohn, M.L. Social class and schizophrenia: A critical review and a reformulation. Schizophrenia Bulletin, 1973, 7, 60-78.

Kohn, M. Social competence, symptoms, and underachievement in childhood: A longitudinal perspective. Washington, D.C.: Winston-Wiley, 1977.

Kohn, M.; Jeger, A.M.; and Koretzky, M.B. Social ecological assessment of environments: Toward a two-factor model. American Journal of Community Psychology (1979), in press.

Kohn, M., and Rosman, B.L. A social competence scale and symptom checklist for the preschool child: Factor dimensions, their cross-instrument generality, and longitudinal persistence. Developmental Psychology 6 (1972): 430-444.

Koretzky, M.B.; Kohn, M.; and Jeger, A.M. Cross-situational consistency among problem adolescents: An application of the two-factor model. Journal of Personality and Social Psychology (1978), in press.

Korman, M., ed. Levels and patterns of professional training in psychology. Washington, D.C.: American Psychological Association, 1976.

Kozol, J. Death at an early age. New York: Houghton Mifflin, 1967.

Krantz, D. On Weddings. In Ecological perspectives in behavior analysis, A. Rogers-Warren and S. Warren, eds. Baltimore, Md.: University Park Press, 1977.

Krapfl, J.E. Accountability for behavioral engineers. In Issues in evaluating behavior modification, W.S. Wood, ed. Champaign, Ill.: Research Press, 1975.

Krapfl, J.E., Noah, J.C. and Maley, R.F. The nature of behavioral systems analysis. Paper presented, Association for the Advancement of Behavior Therapy, San Francisco, December 1975.

Krapfl, J.E., and Vargas, E.A. Behaviorism and ethics. Kalamazoo, Mich.: Behaviordelia, 1977.

Krasner, L. Behavior control and social responsibility. American Psychologist 17 (1962): 199-204.

_____. The behavioral scientist and social responsibility: No place to hide. Journal of Social Issues 21 (1965): 9-30.

_____. Assessment of token economy programmes in psychiatric hospitals. In Learning theory and psychotherapy, R. Porter, ed. London: Churchill, 1968.

_____. Behavior modification – Values and training: The perspective of a psychologist. In Behavior therapy, appraisal and status, Cyril M. Franks, ed. New York: McGraw-Hill, 1969, pp. 537-566.

_____. Behavior therapy. In Annual review of psychology, vol. 22. P.H. Mussen, ed. Palo Alto, Calif.: Annual Reviews, 1971, pp. 483-532.

_____. What are the variables necessary for training environmental designers? Paper presented at the Alcoholism and Drug Addiction Research Foundation on Controlled Environment Research and Its Potential Relevance to the Study of Problems of Behavioral Economics and Social Policy, Toronto, October 16, 1973.

_____. Behavior modification: Ethical issues and future trends. In Handbook of behavior modification and behavior therapy, H. Leitenberg, ed. Englewood Cliffs, N.J.: Prentice-Hall, 1976a.

_____. The classroom as a planned environment. Educational Researcher, 1976b, 5, 9-14.

_____. The future and the past in the behaviorism-humanism dialogue. American Psychologist 33 (1978): 799-804.

Krasner, L., and Atthowe, J.M. The token economy as a rehabilitative procedure in a mental hospital setting. In Behavioral intervention in human problems, H.C. Rickard, ed. Elmsford, N.Y.: Pergamon Press, 1971, pp. 311-334.

Krasner, L.; Ford, J.D.; Harpin, R.E.; and Krasner, M. The human behavior lab as an environmental design procedure. Education (1977), in press.

Krasner, L., and Hutchison, W.R. Guide to observation in the classroom. State University of New York at Stony Brook, 1973.

_____. Helping people change by designing environments. State University of New York at Stony Brook, 1974.

Krasner, L., and Krasner, M. Token economies and other planned environments. In Behavior modification in education, C.E. Thoresen, ed. National Society for the Study of Education, 72nd Yearbook. Chicago: University of Chicago Press, 1973.

Krasner, L., and Richards, C. Issues in open education and environmental design. Psychology in the schools 13 (1976): 77-81.

Krasner, L., and Ullmann, L.P. Behavior influence and personality: The social matrix of human action. New York: Holt, Rinehart and Winston, 1973.

Krasner, L. and Ullmann, L.P., eds. Research in behavior modification: New developments and implications. New York: Holt, Rinehart and Winston, 1965.

Krasner, M. The teacher as environmental designer: How to create a publishing company in your classroom. Paper presented at the Environmental Design Conference in London, April 1977.

Kroll, L. Meme et Fachiste a Wolnive, Universite de horwain Bruselles, Technique et Architecture 311 (1976): 38-46.

Kuhn, T.S., The structure of scientific revolutions, 2nd ed. Chicago, Illinois: University of Chicago Press, 1970.

Landsberg, G., and Hammer, R. Possible programmatic consequences of community mental health center funding arrangements: Illustrations based on inpatient utilization data. Community Mental Health Journal 13 (1977): 63-67.

Lang, J.; Burnette, C.; Moleski, W.; and Vachon, D., eds. Designing for human behavior: Architecture and the behavioral sciences. Strouds-burg, Pa: Dowden, Hutchison, and Ross, 1974.

Langton, S., ed. Citizen participation in America: Essays on the state of the art. Lexington, Mass.: Lexington Books, 1978.

Laslett, B., and Warren, C.A. Losing weight: The organizational promotion of behavior change. Social Problems 23 (1975): 69-80.

Laumann, E.O., and House, J.S. Living room styles and social attributes: The patterning of material artifacts in a modern urban community. Social Science Research 54 (1970): 321-342.

Lawrence, P.R., and Lorsch, J.W. Developing organizations: Diagnosis and action. Reading, Mass,: Addison-Wesley, 1969.

Lawson, R.B.; Greene, R.T.; Richardson, J.S.; McClure, G.; and Pading, R.J. Token economy program in a maximum security correctional hospital. Journal of Nervous and Mental Disease 152 (1971): 199-205.

Leake, C.D. Percivil's medical ethics. Baltimore, Md.: 1927.

_____. Roman architectural hygiene. Annals Medical History n.s. 2 (1930): 135-163.

_____. Beauty was the best medicine in hospital care of ancient times. Modern Hospital 106 (March 1969): 94-97, 172.

Lehrer, P.M.; Gordon, S.B.; and Leiblum, S. Parent groups in behavior modification: Training or therapy? Paper presented at the meeting of the American Psychological Association, Montreal, August, 1973.

Leitenberg, H. Is time-out from positive reinforcement an aversive event? A review of the experimental evidence. Psychological Bulletin 64 (1965): 428-441.

_____. The use of single-case methodology in psychotherapy research. Journal of Abnormal Psychology 82 (1973): 87-101.

Leitenberg, H., ed. Handbook of behavior modification and behavior therapy. New York: Appleton-Century-Crofts, 1976.

Lekisch, H.A. Consultants' contexts, priorities, and courses of action in long-term consultation. Paper presented at the meeting of the American Psychological Association, Washington, D.C., September, 1976.

LeLaurin, K., and Risley, T.R. The organization of day-care environ-ments: "Zone" versus "man-to-man" staff assignments. Journal of Applied Behavior Analysis 5 (1972): 225-232.

Lemkau, P.V. The planning project for Columbia. In Mental health and the community: Problems, programs, and strategies, M.F. Shore and F.V. Mannino, eds. New York: Behavioral Publications, 1969.

Lent, T.R.; Leblanc, T.; and Spradlin, T.E. Designing a rehabilitative culture for moderately retarded, adolescent girls. Parsons Research Center, Working paper # 174, 1967.

Lepkin, M. A program of industrial consultation by a community mental health center. Community Mental Health Journal 11 (1975): 74-81.

Lerup, L. Building the unfinished. Beverly Hills: Sage Publications, 1977.

Levi, L. A synopsis of ecology and psychiatry: Some theoretical psychosomatic considerations, review of some studies and discussion of preventive aspects. Reports from the Laboratory for Clinical Stress Research, Stockholm, November 1972, p. 17.

Levi, L., and Anderson, L. Psychosocial Stress: Population, environment, and quality of life. New York: Spectrum, 1975.

Levine, D. The dangers of social action. In Behavior analysis and systems analysis: An integrative approach to mental health programs, D. Harshbarger and R.F. Maley, eds. Kalamazoo, Mich.: Behaviordelia, 1974.

Levine, F.M., and Fasnacht, G. Token rewards may lead to token learning. American Psychologist 29 (1974): 816-820.

Levine, M. Some postulates of practice in community psychology and their implications for training. In Community psychology: Perspectives in training and research. I. Iscoe, and C.D. Spieldberger, eds. New York: Appleton-Century-Crofts, 1970.

_____. Problems of entry in light of some postulates of practice in community psychology. In The helping professions in a world of action, I.I. Goldenberg, ed. Lexington, Mass.: Lexington Books, 1973.

Levinson, D.J., and Gallagher, E.B. Patienthood in the mental hospital. Boston: Houghton Mifflin, 1964.

Levis, D.J. Learning approaches to therapeutic behavior change. Chicago: Aldine, 1970.

Lewin, K.; Lippitt, R.; and White, R. Patterns of aggressive behavior in experimentally created "social climates". Journal of Social Psychology 10 (1939): 271-299.

Lewinsohn, P.M., and Shaffer, M. Use of home observations as an integral part of the treatment of depression: Preliminary report and case studies. Journal of Consulting and Clinical Psychology 37 (1971): 87-94.

Lewis, J. Feminist/Behaviorist Newsletter. Psychology Department, Marietta College, Marietta, Ohio, 1977.

Liberman, R.P. An experimental study of the placebo response under three different situations of pain. Journal of Psychiatric Research 2 (1964): 233-246.

_____. Applying behavioral techniques in a community mental health center. In Advances in Behavior Therapy, R.D. Rubin, J.P. Brady, and J.D. Henderson, eds. New York: Academic Press, 1973.

Liberman, R.P.; DeRisi, W.J.; King, L.W.; Eckman, T.A.; and Wood, D.D. Behavioral measurement in a community mental health center. In Evaluation of behavioral programs in community, residential, and school settings, P.O. Davidson, F.W. Clark, and L.A. Hamerlynck, eds. Champaign, Ill.: Research Press, 1974.

Liberman, R.P.; King, L.W.; and DeRisi, W. Behavior analysis and therapy in community mental health. In Handbook of behavior modification and behavior therapy, H. Leitenberg, ed. Englewood Cliffs, N.J.: Prentice-Hall,1976.

Liberman, R.P.; King, L.W.; DeRisi, W.J.; and McCann, M. Personal effectiveness: Guiding people to assert themselves and improve their social skills. Champaign, Ill.: Research Press, 1975.

Liebow, E. Tally's corner. Boston: Little, Brown, 1967.

Lindsley, O. Characteristics of the behavior of chronic psychotics as revealed by free-operant conditioning methods. Diseases of the Nervous System 21 (1960): 66-78.

Lipinski, D.P., and Nelson, R. Problems in the use of naturalistic observation as a means of behavioral assessment. Behavior Therapy 5 (1974): 341-351.

Lippitt, R.; Watson, J.; and Westley, B. The dynamics of planned change. New York: Harcourt, Brace and World, 1958.

Loch, L., and French, T.R.P. Overcoming resistance to change, Human Relations 1 (1948): 512-532.

London, P. The modes and morals of psychotherapy. New York: Holt, Rinehart and Winston, 1964.

_____. Behavior control. New York: Harper and Row, 1969.

Loo, C. Important issues in researching the effects of crowdings on humans. Representative Research in Social Psychology 4 (1973): 219-226.

Lowman, J. Development and evaluation of a premarital education program. Proceedings of the Eighty-first Annual Convention of the American Psychological Association. Washington, D.C.: American Psychological Association, 1973.

Luber, R.F., ed. Partial hospitalization: A current perspective. New York: Plenum Press, 1979.

Luber, R.F., and Hersen, M. A systematic behavioral approach to partial hospitalization programming: Implications and applications. Corrective and Social Psychiatry and Journal of Behavior Technology, Methods, and Therapy 22 (1976): 33-37.

Lyman, S.M., and Scott, M.B. Territoriality: A neglected sociological dimension. Social Problems 15 (1967): 236-249.

Lynch, V.J. Staff member termination in the milieu setting. Journal of the National Association of Private Psychiatric Hospitals 7 (1975): 24-29.

Maccoby, N., and Farquhar, J.W. Communication for health: Unselling heart disease. Journal of Communication 25 (1975): 114-126.

_____. Bringing the California health report up to date. Journal of Communications 26 (1976): 56-57.

MacLennan, B.W.; Quinn, R.D.; and Schroeder, D. The scope of community mental health consultation and education. Rockville, Md.: National Institute of Mental Health, 1971.

Madden, P.C. Skinner and the open classroom. School Review (November, 1972): 100-107.

Mahoney, M.J. Cognition and behavior modification. Cambridge, Mass.: Ballinger, 1974.

_____. The scientist as subject: The psychological imperative. Cambridge, Mass,: Ballinger, 1976.

Maley, R.F., and Hayes, S.C. Coercion and control: Ethical and legal issues. In Behavior modification and ethics, J. Krapfl and E. Vargas, eds. Kalamazoo, Mich.: Behaviordelia, 1977.

Maloney, M.P.; Ward, M.P.; and Braucht, G.N. A revised scale for the measurement of ecological attitudes and knowledge. American Psychologist 30 (1975): 787-790.

Mann, P.A. Accessibility and organizational power in the entry phase of mental health consultation. Journal of Consulting and Clinical Psychology 38 (1972): 315-318.

Mann, T. The Magic Mountain. New York: Knopf, 1953.

Mannino, F.V.; MacLennan, B.W.; and Shore, M.F. The practice of mental health consultation. Rockville: National Institute of Mental Health, 1975.

Mannino, F.V., and Shore, M.F. The effects of consultation. American Journal of Community Psychology 3 (1975): 1-21.

Mark, V.H. A psychosurgeon's case for psychosurgery. Psychology Today (July 1974): 8.

Mark, V.H., and Ervin, F. Violence and the brain. New York: Harper and Row, 1970.

Marler, L., A study of anti-litter messages. Journal of Environmental Education 3 (1970): 52-53.

Marsden, H.M. Crowding and animal behavior. In Environment and the social sciences, J.F. Wohlwill and D.H. Carson, eds. Washington, D.C.: American Psychological Association, 1972, pp. 5-14.

Marston, A.L. Behavior ecology emerges from behavior modification: Side-steps toward a non-special profession. Paper presented at annual meeting, American Psychological Association, San Francisco, September, 1977.

Martin, R. Legal challenges to behavior modification. Champaign, Ill.: Research Press, 1975.

Mash, E.J., and Hedley, J. Effect of observer as a function of prior history of social interaction. Perceptual and Motor Skills 40 (1975): 659-669.

Matarazzo, J.D. The interview. In Handbook of clinical psychology, B. Wolman, ed. New York: McGraw-Hill, 1965.

_____. Some national developments in the utilization of nontraditional mental health manpower. American Psychologist 26 (1971): 363-372.

Maurois, G. Des Marelles I et II, Environment and Comportement. 4. Rue du Dahoney. 75011. Paris, 1975.

Marx, A.J.; Test, M.A.; and Stein, L.I. Extra hospital management of severe mental illness. Archives of General Psychiatry, 29 (1973): 505-511.

Mazade, N.A. Consultation and education practice and organizational structure in ten community mental health centers. Hospital and Community Psychiatry 25 (1974): 673-675.

McAlister, A. Television as a medium for delivering behavior therapy: A pilot study of a televised smoking cessation program. Paper presented at the meeting of the Association for the Advancement of Behavior Therapy, New York, December, 1976.

McCall, G.J. The problem of indicators in participant-observation research. In Issues in participant observation, G.J. McCall and J.L. Simmons, eds. Reading, Mass.: Addison-Wesley, 1969, pp. 230-237.

McCall, G.J., and Simmons, J.L., eds. Issues in participant observation. Reading, Mass.: Addison-Wesley, 1969.

McClung, F., and Stunden, A. Mental health consultation to programs for children. Chevy Chase, Md: National Institute of Mental Health, 1970.

McClure, G. Behavioral and physiological responding under conditions of sensory deprivation as a function of deprivation interval and age. Ph.D. diss., University of Vermont, Burlington, Vermont, 1971.

McDonald, J. Strategy in poker, business, and war. New York: Norton, 1950.

McEvay, J., and Dietz, T., eds. Handbook for environmental planning. New York: Wiley, 1977.

McGee, R.K. Crisis intervention in the community. Baltimore, Md.: University Park Press, 1974.

McGinnies, E. Social behavior: A functional analysis. New York: Houghton Mifflin, 1970.

McKeown, T. The modern rise of population. New York: Academic Press, 1976.

McKnight, P.C. Microteaching in teacher training: A review of the research. In The social psychology of teaching, A. Morrison and D. McIntyre, eds. Baltimore: Penguin Press, 1969.

McLean, P.D. Evaluating community-based psychiatric services. In Evaluation of behavioral programs in community, residential, and school settings. P.O. Davidson, F.W. Clark, and L.A. Hamerlynck, eds. Champaign, Ill.: Research Press, 1974. Pp. 83-102.

McNees, M.P.; Egli, D.S.; Marshall, R.S.; Schnelle, J.F.; and Risley, T.R. Shoplifting prevention: Providing information through signs. Journal of Applied Behavior Analysis, 9 (1976): 399-405.

Meadows, D.H.; Meadows, D.L.; Randers, J.; and Behrens, W.W. The limits to growth. New York: Universe Books, 1972.

Means, G.C., and Ackerman, R.E. South Carolina's village system. Hospital and Community Psychiatry 27 (1976): 789-792.

Meehl, P.E. Clinical versus statistical prediction: A theoretical analysis and a review of the evidence. Minneapolis, Minn: University of Minnesota Press, 1954.

Meltzoff, J., and Kornreich, M. Research in psychotherapy. New York: Atherton, 1970.

Mehrabian, A., and Russell, J.A. An approach to environmental psychology. Cambridge: Massachusetts Institute of Technology Press, 1974.

Mensch, I.N., and Henry, J. Direct observation and psychological tests in anthropological field work. American Anthropologist 58 (1953): 461-480.

Mercer, C. Living In Cities. Psychology and the Urban Environment, 1975.

Meyer, A., Collected papers of Adolf Meyer, 4 vols. Baltimore, Md.: Johns Hopkins Press, 1948-1952.

Meyers, A.W.; Craighead, W.E.; and Meyers, H.H. A behavioral-preventive approach to community mental health. American Journal of Community Psychology 2 (1974): 275-285.

Meyers, J.L. Fundamentals of experimental design. Boston: Allyn and Bacon, 1973.

Meyers, J., Friedman, M.P., and Gaughen, E.J. The effects of consultee centered consultation on teacher behavior. Psychology in the Schools 12 (1975): 288-295.

Michael, J. Deferred consequences and the ethics of a behavioral ethic. In Behavior modification and ethics, J. Krapfl and E. Vargas, eds. Kalamazoo, Mich.: Behaviordelia, 1977.

Michaels, J.W. On the relation between human ecology and behavioral social psychology. Social Forces 52 (1974): 313-321.

Michelson, W. Man and his urban environment. Reading, Mass.: Addison-Wesley, 1970.

Michelson, W., ed. Behavioral research methods in environmental design. Stroudsburg, Pa.: Dowden, Hutchinson and Ross, 1975.

Mikulas, W.L. A televised self-control clinic. Behavior Therapy 7 (1976): 564-566.

Milgram, S. The experience of living in cities. Science 167 (1970): 1461-68.

Mill, J.S. Utilitarianism. London: 1861.

Miller, F.T.; Pinkerton, R.S.; and Hollister, W.G. An "action-facilitation" entry pattern of mental health consultation. Professional Psychology 2 (1970): 359-362.

Miller, H.L., Jr. Matching-based hedonic scaling in the pigeon. Journal of Applied Behavior 25 (1976): 335-347.

Miller, L.K., and Miller, D.L. Reinforcing self-help group activities of welfare recipients. Journal of Applied Behavior Analysis 3 (1970): 57-64.

Miller, S.M. The participant observer and "over-rapport." American Sociological Review 17 (1952): 97-99.

Minkin, N.; Braukman, C.; Minkin, L.; Timbers, G.; Timbers, B.; Fixsen, P.; Phillips, E.; and Wolf, M. The social validation and training of conversational skills. Journal of Applied Behavior Analysis 9 (1976): 127-140.

Minnesota Guidelines for Behavior Modification Programs. State of Minnesota: Department of Public Works, 1972.

Miran, M.; Lehrer, P.M.; Koehler, R.; and Miran, E. What happens when deviant behavior begins to change? The relevance of a social systems approach for behavioral programs with adolescents. Journal of Community Psychology 2 (1974): 370-375.

Miron, N.B. Behavior shaping and group nursing with severely retarded patients. In Reinforcement theory in psychological treatment: A symposium. J. Fisher and R. Harris, eds. Research monograph no. 8. Sacramento: California Department of Mental Hygiene 1966, pp. 1-14.

Mischel, W. Personality and assessment. New York: Wiley, 1968.

_____. Direct versus indirect personality assessment: Evidence and implications. Journal of Consulting and Clinical Psychology 38 (1972): 319-324.

_____. Toward a cognitive social learning reconceptualization of personality. Psychological Review 80 (1973): 252-283.

_____. Introduction to personality. New York: Holt, Rinehart and Winston, 1976.

Mischel, W.; Zeiss, R.; and Zeiss, A.R. Internal-external control and persistence: Validation and implications of the Stanford preschool internal-external scale. Journal of Personality and Social Psychology 29 (1974): 268-278.

Mitchell, K.M. An ecological orientation to the helping process. Rehabilitation Research and Practice Review 1 (1970): 9-17.

Mitchell, K.M.; Bozarth, J.D.; and Krauft, C.C. A reappraisal of the effectiveness of accurate empathy, non-possessive warmth, and genuineness. In The therapist's contribution to effective psychotherapy: An empirical assessment, A.S. Gurman and A.M. Razin, eds. Elmsford, N.Y.: Pergamon Press, 1978.

Moore, G.E. Ethics. London: 1912.

Moos, R.H. The assessment of the social climates of correctional institutions. Journal of Research in Crime and Delinquency 5 (1968a): 174-88.

_____. Behavioral effects of being observed: Reactions to a wireless radio transmitter. Journal of Consulting and Clinical Psychology 32 (1968b): 383-388.

_____. Situational analysis of a therapeutic community milieu. Journal of Abnormal Psychology 73 (1968c): 49-61.

_____. Sources of variance in responses to questionnaires and in behavior. Journal of Abnormal Psychology 7 (1969): 405-412.

_____. Differential effects of psychiatric ward settings on patient change. Journal of Nervous and Mental Diseases 5 (1970): 316-321.

_____. Assessment of the psychosocial environments of community-oriented psychiatric treatment programs. Journal of Abnormal Psychology 79 (1972): 9-18.

_____. Conceptualizations of human environments. American Psychologist 28 (1973a): 652-665.

_____. The family environment inventory. Palo Alto, Calif.: Social Ecological Laboratory, Department of Psychiatry, Stanford University, 1973b.

_____. Changing the social milieus of psychiatric treatment settings. Journal of Applied Behavioral Science (1973c).

_____. Evaluating treatment environments: A social ecological approach. New York: Wiley, 1973d.

_____. Evaluating treatment environments: A social ecological approach. New York: Wiley, 1974a.

_____. Ward atmosphere scale manual. Palo Alto, Calif.: Consulting Psychologists Press, 1974b.

_____. Systems for the assessment and classification of human environments. In Issues in social ecology: Human milieus, R.H. Moos and P. Insel, eds. Palo Alto, Calif.: National Press, 1974c, pp. 5-28.

_____. Evaluating correctional and community settings. New York: Wiley, 1975.

_____. The human context. New York: Wiley, 1976a.

_____. Evaluating and changing community settings. American Journal of Community Psychology 4 (1976b): 313-326.

_____. Conceptualizations of human environments. In Environmental psychology: People and their physical settings, 2nd ed., H.M. Proshansky, W.H. Ittelson, and L.G. Rivlin, eds. New York: Holt, Rinehart and Winston, 1976c, pp. 37-51.

Moos, R.H., and Browstein, R. Environment and utopia. New York: Plenum Press, 1977.

Moos, R.H., and Houts, P. Assessment of the social atmosphere of psychiatric wards. Journal of Abnormal Psychology, 73 (1968) 595-604.

Moos, R.H., and Humphrey, B. Group environment scale, Palo Alto, Calif.: Consulting Psychologist Press, 1974.

Moos, R.H., and Insel, P., eds. Issues in social ecology: Human milieus. Palo Alto, Calif.: National Press Books, 1974.

Moos, R.H., and Trickett, E. The classroom environment scale manual. Palo Alto, Calif.: Consulting Psychologists Press, 1974.

Morowitz, D.A. Chronic emotional depression's role in poverty. New York Times, Sunday, February 19, 1978, section IV.

Morris, N. The future of imprisonment. Chicago: University of Chicago Press, 1974.

Morrow, J.E., ed. Behaviorists for social action journal. Sacramento: California State University, 1978.

Mosher, L.R.; Menn, A.; and Matthews, S.M. Soteria: Evaluation of a home based treatment for schizophrenia. American Journal of Orthopsychiatry 45 (1975): 455-467.

Mosher, L.R., and Menn, A. Soteria: An alternative to hospitalization for schizophrenia. In Alternatives to acute hospitalization, H.R. Lamb, ed. San Francisco: Jossey-Bass, 1979.

Mowrer, O.H. Apparatus for the study and treatment of enuresis. American Journal of Psychology 51 (1938): 163-66.

Mowrer, O.H., and Mowrer, W.M. Enuresis — A method for its study and treatment. American Journal of Orthopsychiatry 8 (1938): 436-459.

Munoz, R.F. The primary prevention of psychological problems. Community Mental Health Review 1 (1976): 5-15.

Murray, H.A. Explorations in personality. New York: Oxford University Press, 1938.

Myers, K.; Hale, C.S.; Mykytowycz, R.; and Hughes, R.L. The effects of varying density and space on sociality and health in animals. In Behavior and environment, A.H. Esser, ed. New York: Plenum Press, 1971, pp. 148-187.

Navarick, D.J., and Fantino, E. Stochastic transitivity and unidimensional behavior theories, Psychological Review 81 (1974): 426-441.

Neigher, W.; Hammer, R.J.; and Landsberg, G., eds. Emerging developments in mental health program evaluation. New York: Argold Press, 1977.

Nelson, R.O.; Lipinski, D.P.; and Boykin, R.A. The effects of self-recorder's training and the obtrusiveness of the self-recording device on the accuracy and reactivity of self-monitoring, Behavior Therapy 9 (1978): 200-208.

Nietzel, M.T.; Winett, R.A.; MacDonald, M.; and Davidson, W.S. Behavioral approaches to community psychology. Elmsford, N.Y.: Pergamon Press, 1977.

Nordquist, V.M. The modification of a child's enuresis: Some response-response relationships. Journal of Applied Behavior Analysis 4 (1971): 241-247.

Northman, J.E. Innovative programming in school mental health: Search for a methodology. Paper presented at the meeting of the Eastern Psychological Association, New York, April, 1976.

Nyquist, E.B., and Hawes, G.R., eds. Open education, New York: Bantam, 1972.

O'Connor, R.D., and Rappaport, J. Application of social learning principles to the training of ghetto blacks. American Psychologist 25 (1970): 659-661.

O'Dell, S. Training parents in behavior modification: A review. Psychological Bulletin 81 (1974): 418-433.

Odum, E.P. The emergence of ecology as a new integrative discipline. Science 195 (1977): 1289-1292.

Oksenberg, M. Methods of communication within the Chinese bureaucracy. China Quarterly 57 (1974): 1-3.

O'Leary, K.D., and Drabman, R. Token reinforcement programs in the classroom: A review. Psychological Bulletin 75 (1971): 379-398.

O'Leary, K.D., and Kent, R.N. Sources of bias in observational recording. Paper presented at American Psychological Association annual convention, September 1973.

O'Leary, K.D.; Kent, R.N.; and Kanowitz, J. Shaping data collection congruent with experimental hypotheses. Journal of Applied Behavior Analysis 8 (1975): 43-51.

O'Leary, K.D., and O'Leary, S.G. Classroom management: The successful use of Behavior Modification, 2nd ed. Elmsford, N.Y.: Pergamon Press, 1977.

O'Leary, K.D., and Wilson, G.T. Behavior Therapy. Englewood Cliffs, N.J.: Prentice-Hall, 1976.

Orleans, L. Every fifth child: The population of China. Stanford, Calif.: Stanford University Press, 1972.

Osgood, C.E.; Suci, G.T.; and Tannenbaum, P.H. The measurement of meaning. Urbana: University of Illinois Press, 1957.

Osmond, H. Function as the basis of psychiatric ward design. Mental Hospitals 8 (1957): 23-39.

_____. The historical and sociological development of mental hospitals. In Psychiatric Architecture, Goshen, C., ed. Washington, D.C.: American Psychiatric Association, 1959.

_____. Design must meet patient's human needs. Modern Hospital 106 (1966): 98-100.

Overton, W.R., and Reese, H.W. Models of development: Methodological implications. In Life span developmental psychology: Methodological issues, J.R. Nesselroade and H.W. Reese, eds. New York: Academic Press, 1973.

Padilla, A.M.; Ruiz, R.A.; and Alvarez, R. Community mental health services for the Spanish-speaking/surnamed population. American Psychologist 30 (1975): 892-905.

Page, C.W. John S. Butler: The man and his hospital methods. American Journal of Insanity 57 (1901): 477-499.

Paradise, R. Psychometric properties of social climate scales for psychiatric wards. State University of New York at Stony Brook, 1976.

Park, R. Human communities: The city and human ecology. New York: Free Press, 1952.

————. Human ecology. In Studies in human ecology, G. Theodorson, ed. Evanston, Ill.: Row Peterson, 1961.

Parsons, H.M. The bedroom. Human factors 14 (1972): 421-450.

Patterson, G.R. Stimulus control in natural settings. In Determinants and origins of aggressive behavior. V. de W.T. Hartrup and W. Hartrup, eds. The Hague: Mouton Press, 1974.

————. The aggressive child: Victim and architect of a coercive system. In Behavior modification and families, E.J. Mash, L.A. Hamerlynck, and L.C. Handy, eds. New York: Brunner/Mazel, 1976.

Patterson, G.R.; Ray, R.S.; and Shaw, D.A. Manual for coding of family interactions. Eugene: Oregon Research Institute, 1968.

Paul, G.L. Insight versus desensitization in psychotherapy two years after termination. Journal of Consulting Psychology 31 (1967): 333-348.

Pavlov, I.P. Lectures on conditioned reflexes, W.H. Gantt, trans. New York: International Publishers, 1928.

Pearl, A., and Riessman, F. New careers for the poor. New York: Free Press, 1965.

Peck, R.F., and Tucker, J.A. Research on teacher education: State of the art, 1971. In Second handbook of research on teaching, R.M.W. Travers, ed. Chicago: Rand McNally, 1973.

Perlmutter, F. Prevention and treatment: A strategy for survival. Community Mental Health Journal 10 (1974): 276-281.

Perloff, R.; Perloff, E.; and Sussna, E. Program evaluation. Annual Review of Psychology 27 (1976): 569-594.

Perucci, R. Circle of madness. Englewood Cliffs, N.J.: Prentice-Hall, 1974.

Peterson, D.R. Behavior problems of middle childhood. Journal of Consulting Psychology 25 (1961): 205-209.

————. The clinical study of social behavior. New York: Appleton-Century-Crofts, 1968.

Pharis, D.B. The use of needs assessment techniques in mental health planning. Community Mental Health Review 1 (1976): 5-11.

Phillips, E.L.; Phillips, E.A.; Fixsen, M.L.; and Wolf, M.M. The teaching family handbook. Lawrence: University of Kansas, 1972.

Pierce, C.H. Recreation for the elderly: Activity participation at a senior citizen center. Gerontologist 15 (1975): 202-205.

Pierce, C.H., and Risley, T.R. Recreation as a reinforcer: Increasing membership and decreasing disruptions in an urban recreation center. Journal of Applied Behavior Analysis 7 (1974): 403-411.

Plowden, L. Children and the primary schools. A report of the Central Advisory Council for Education (England), vol. 1. New York: British Information Service, 1967.

Porteous, J.D. Environment and behavior: Planning and everyday urban life. Reading, Mass.: Addison-Wesley, 1977.

Pothier, R. Experts say Sunland abused good method. Miami Herald, April 7, 1972.

Pratt, L. Family structure and effective health behavior. Boston: Houghton-Mifflin, 1976.

Preiser, W.F.E., ed. Environmental design research: vol. 2, Symposia and workshops. Proc. Fourth International Environment Design Research Association Conference. Stroudsburg, Pa.: Dowden, Hutchinson, and Ross, 1973.

Premack, D. Reinforcement theory. In Nebraska Symposium on Motivation, 1965, D. Levine, ed. Lincoln: University of Nebraska Press, 1965.

_____. Catching up with common sense or two sides of a generalization: Reinforcement and punishment. In The nature of reinforcement, R. Glaser, ed. New York: Academic Press, 1971.

Price, R.H. The taxonomic classification of behaviors and situations and the problem of behavior-environment congruence. Human Relations 27 (1974): 567-585.

Price, R.H., and Bouffard, G.L. Behavioral appropriateness and situational constraint as dimensions of social behavior. Journal of Personality and Social Psychology 30 (1974): 570-585.

Proshansky, H.M. Methodology in environmental psychology: Problems and issues. Human Factors 14 (October 1972): 451-460.

_____. The environmental crisis in human dignity. Journal of Social Issues 29 (1975): 1-20.

_____. Environmental psychology and the real world. American Psychologist 31 (1976): 303-310.

Proshansky, H.M.; Ittelson, W.H.; and Rivlin, L.G., eds. Environmental psychology, New York: Holt, Rinehart and Winston, 1970.

_____. Environmental psychology: People and their physical settings, 2nd ed. New York: Holt, Rinehart and Winston, 1976.

Putten, T.V. The rising hospitalization rate of psychiatric patients. Paper presented at the meeting of the American Psychiatric Association, Toronto, May, 1977.

Rabiner, C.H.; Silverberg, S.; Galvin, J.W.; and Hankoff, L.D. Consultation or direct service? American Journal of Psychiatry 126 (1970): 1321-1325.

Rabkin, J.G., and Struening, E.L. Ethnicity, social class, and mental illness. New York: Institute on Group Identity and Mental Health, American Jewish Committee, 1976.

Rachlin, H. Self-control. Behaviorism 2 (1974): 94-107.

Rachlin, H.; Green, L.; Kagel, J.H.; and Battalio, R.C., Economic demand theory and psychological studies of choice. In The Psychology of Learning and Motivation, vol. 10, G.H. Bowen, ed. New York: Academic Press, 1976.

Rachman, S., and Teasdale, J. Aversion therapy and behavior disorders: An analysis. Coral Gables, Florida: University of Miami Press, 1969.

Rapoport, A. Symbolism and environmental design. International Journal of Symbology (April 1970): 1-9.

Rappaport, J. Community psychology: Values, research, and action. New York: Holt, Rinehart and Winston, 1977.

Rappaport, J., and Chinsky, J.M. Models for delivery of service from a historical and conceptual perspective. Professional Psychology 5 (1974): 42-50.
Rappaport, J., and O'Connor, R.D. The psychological center in a psychology department. Professional Psychology 4 (1973): 92-98.
Rathus, S.A., and Nevid, J.A. Behavior therapy: Strategies for solving problems in living. New York: Doubleday, 1977.
Rausch, H.L. Interaction sequences. Journal of Personality and Social Psychology 2 (1965): 487-499.
Rausch, H.L.; Dittmann, A.T.; and Taylor, T.J. Person, setting, and change in social interaction. Human Relations 12 (1959): 361-378.
Rausch, H.L.; Farbman, I.; and Llewellyn, L.G. Person, setting, and change in social interaction: II a normal control study. Human Relations 13 (1960): 305-332.
Reiff, R. Mental health manpower and institutional change. American Psychologist 21 (1966): 540-548.
_____. Of cabbages and kings. American Journal of Community Psychology 3 (1975): 187-196.
Reisman, J.M. History of clinical psychology, New York: Irvington Publishers, 1975.
Reiss, M.L.; Piotrowski, W.D.; and Bailey, J.S. Behavioral community psychology: Encouraging low-income parents to seek dental care for their children. Journal of Applied Behavior Analysis 9 (1976): 387-397.
Reppucci, N.D. The social psychology of institutional change: General principles for intervention. American Journal of Community Psychology 1 (1973): 330-341.
_____. Implementation issues for the behavior modifier as institutional change agent. Behavior Therapy 8 (1977): 594-605.
Reppucci, N.D., and Saunders, J.T. The social psychology of behavior modification: Problems of implementation in natural settings. American Psychologist 29 (1974): 649-660.
Ribes, E. A behavioral methodology for housing and urban design. Paper presented at the Inter-American Conference on Behavior Modification in the Community, Winnipeg, Manitoba, July, 1976.
Rich, A.R., and Schroeder, H.E. Research issues in assertiveness training. Psychological Bulletin 83 (1976): 1081-1096.
Richards, C.S. The politics of a token economy. Psychological Reports 36 (1975): 615-621.
Riecken, H.W. The unidentified interviewer. American Journal of Sociology 62 (1956): 210-212.
Riessman, C.K.; Rabkin, J.B.; and Struening, E.L. Brief versus standard psychiatric hospitalization: A critical review of the literature. Community Mental Health Review 2 (1977): 1-10.
Riessman, F. The "helper" therapy principle. Social Work 10 (1965): 27-32.
Rimm, D., and Masters, J. Behavior Therapy: Techniques and empirical findings. New York: Academic Press, 1974.
Rinn, R.C. Consultation and education services: A model for community intervention. Paper presented at the meeting of the Southeastern Psychological Association, New Orleans, April, 1973.

Rinn, R.C.; Bailey, A.; Tapp, L.; and Howard, J. A comparison of aftercare programs. International Journal of Mental Health, 3 (1974): 153-159.

Rinn, R.C., and Markle, A. Positive parenting. Cambridge, Mass.: Research Media, 1978.

Rinn, R.C.; Vernon, J.C.; and Wise, M.J. Training parents of behavioral-ly-disordered children in groups: A three years' program evaluation. Behavior Therapy 6 (1975): 378-387.

Riskin, C. Maoism and motivation: Work incentives in China. In China's uninterrupted revolution, V. Nee, and J. Peck, eds. New York: Pantheon Books, 1975.

Risley, T.R.; Clark, H.B.; and Cataldo, M.F. Behavioral technology for the normal middle-class family. In Behavior Modification and families, E.J. Mash, L.A. Hamerlynck, and L.C. Handy, eds. New York: Bruner/Mazel, 1976.

Robinson, W.S. The logical structure of analytic induction. American Sociological Review 16 (1951): 812-818.

Rockefeller, N.A., and Miller, A.D. New York State Department of Mental Hygiene, 1970 Annual Report.

Rogers, C.R. The use of electrically recorded interviews in improving psychotherapeutic technique. American Journal Orthopsychiatry 12 (1942a): 429-435.

_____. Counseling and psychotherapy: Newer concepts in practice, Boston: Houghton Mifflin, 1942b.

_____. In retrospect: Forty-six years. American Psychology 29 (1974): 115-123.

Rogers, V.R. Teaching in the British primary school, New York: Macmillan, 1970.

Rogers-Warren, A., and Warren, S., eds. Ecological perspectives in behavior analysis, Baltimore, Md.: University Park Press, 1977.

Roman, M. Community control and the community mental health center: A view from the Lincoln Bridge. In Community mental health: Social action and reaction, B. Denner, and R.H. Price, eds. New York: Holt, Rinehart and Winston, 1973.

Romanczyk, R.G.; Kent, R.N.; Diament, C.; and O'Leary, K.D. Measuring the reliability of observational data: A reactive process. Journal of Applied Behavior Analysis, 6 (1973): 175-184.

Rose, S.D. Group training of parents as behavior modifiers. Social Work 19 (1974): 156-162.

Rosen, G.M. The development and use of nonprescription behavior therapies. American Psychologist 31 (1976): 139-141.

Rosenthal, R. Experimenter effects in behavior research. New York: Appleton-Century-Crofts, 1966.

_____. Interpersonal expectations: Effects of the experimenter's hypotheses. In Artifact in behavioral research, R. Rosenthal and R.C. Rosnow, eds. New York: Academic Press, 1969.

Ross, H.L.; Campbell, D.T.; and Glass, G.M. Determining the social effects of a legal reform: The British "breathalyzer" crackdown of 1967. American Behavioral Scientist 13 (1970): 493-509.

Rossi, A.M. Some pre-World War II antecedents of community mental health theory and practice. Mental Hygiene 46 (1962): 78-98.

Rothman, D.J. The discovery of the asylum: Social order and disorder in the new republic. Boston: Little, Brown, 1971.

Rothman, J. Planning and organizing for social change: Action principles from social science research. New York: Columbia University Press, 1974.

Rothman, J.; Erlich, J.L.; and Teresa, J.G. Promoting innovation and change in organizations and communities. New York: Wiley, 1976.

Rotter, J.B. Generalized expectancies for internal vs. external control of reinforcement. Psychological Monographs 80 (1966): 609.

Russett, B., et. al. World handbook of political and social indicators. New Haven: Yale University Press, 1964.

Rutman, I.D. Preventing chronicity: A study of three alternatives (Final Report Summary). Philadelphia: Horizon House, 1971.

Ryan, W., Blaming the victim. New York: Vintage, 1971.

Sahlins, M. The use and abuse of biology: An anthropological critique of sociobiology, Ann Arbor, Mich.: University of Michigan Press, 1976.

Sajwaj, T.; Twardosz, S.; and Burke, M. Side effects of extinction procedures in a remedial preschool. Journal of Applied Behavior Analysis 5 (1972): 163-175.

Salvadori, M.G. Architectural structures: A teacher's manual for upper elementary and junior high students, 1977, in press.

Sanders, S.H.; Williamson, D.; Akey, R.; and Hollis, P. Advancement to independent living: A model behavioral program for the intermediate care of adults with behavioral and emotional problems. Journal of Community Psychology 4 (1976): 275-282.

Sarason, I.G.; Smith, R.E.; and Diener, F., Personality research: Components of variance attributable to the person and the situation. Journal of Personality and Social Psychology 32 (1975): 199-204.

Sarason, S.B. The culture of the school and the problem of change. Boston: Allyn and Bacon, 1971.

_____. The creation of settings and the future societies. San Francisco: Jossey-Bass, 1972.

_____. The psychological sense of community: Prospects for a community psychology. San Francisco: Jossey-Bass, 1974.

_____. The nature of problem solving in social action. American Psychologist 33 (1978): 370-380.

Sarason, S.B.; Levine, M.; Goldenberg, I.I.; Cherlin, D.L.; and Bennett, E.M. Psychology in community settings: Clinical, educational, vocational, and social aspects. New York: Wiley, 1966.

Schaefer, H., and Martin, P. Behavioral therapy for "apathy" of hospitalized schizophrenics. Psychological Reports 19 (1966): 1147-1158.

Schauer, F. Discussion of Maly and Hayes' paper. In Behavior modification and ethics, J. Krapfl and E. Vargas, eds. Kalamazoo, Mich.: Behaviordelia, 1977.

Schlosberg, N.K. Subprofessionals: To be or not to be. Counselor Education and Supervision 6 (1967): 108-113.

Schmuck, R.A. Helping teachers improve classroom group processes. Journal of Applied Behavioral Science 4 (1968): 401-435.

Schnaitter, R. Ethical choice in a behavioral framework. In Behavior modification and ethics, J. Krapfl and E. Vargas, eds. Kalamazoo, Mich.: Behaviordelia, 1977.

Schnelle, J.F.; Kirchner, R.E.; McNees, M.P.; and Lawler, J.M. Social evaluation of two police patrolling strategies. Journal of Applied Behavior Analysis 8 (1975): 353-365.

Schnelle, J.F., and Lee, F.J. A quasi-experimental retrospective evaluative evaluation of a prior policy change. Journal of Applied Behavior Analysis 7 (1974): 483-496.

Schnore, L.F. Population theories and social change, working Paper 72-13, rev. Madison: Center for Demography and Ecology, February, 1975.

Schofield, W. The psychologist as a health professional. Professional Psychology 7 (February 1976): 5-8.

_____. Psychotherapy: The purchase of friendship. Englewood Cliffs, N.J.: Prentice-Hall, 1964.

Schroeder, C.S., and Miller, F.T. Entry patterns and strategies in consultation. Professional Psychology (1975): 6, 182-186.

Schulberg, H.C., and Baker, F. Unitization: decentralizing the mental hospitalopolis. International Journal of Psychiatry 7 (1969): 213-223.

Schulberg, H.C.; Sheldon, A.; and Baker, F., eds. Program evaluation in the health fields. New York: Behavioral Publications, 1969.

Schumacher, E.F. Small is beautiful: Economics as if people mattered, New York: Harper, 1973.

Schurmann, R. Ideology and organization in communist China, 2nd enlarged ed. Berkeley: University of California Press, 1965.

Schuster, R., and Rachlin, H. Indifference between punishment and free shock: Evidence for the negative law of effect. Journal of Experimental Analysis of Behavior 11 (1968): 777-785.

Schwartz, M.S., and Schwartz, C.G., Problems in participant observation. American Journal of Sociology 60 (1955): 348-354.

Schwitzgebel, R.K. Development and legal regulation of coercive behavior modification techniques with offenders. Publication no. 2067 Chevy Chase, Md: Public Health Service, 1971.

Schwitzgebel, R.K. A contractual model for the protection of the rights of institutionalized mental patients. American Psychologist 30 (1975): 815-820.

_____. Treatment contracts and ethical self-determination, 1975, in press.

Schwitzgebel, R.K., and Kolb, D.A. Changing human behavior: Principles of planned intervention. New York: McGraw-Hill, 1974.

Scull, A.T. The decarceration of the mentally ill: A critical view. Politics and Society 6 (1976): 123-172.

Seidel, V.W., and Seidel, R. Serve the people. New York: Josiah Macy Jr. Foundation, 1974.

Seidman, E., and Rappaport, J. The educational pyramid: A paradigm for research, training, and manpower utilization in community psychology. American Journal of Community Psychology 2 (1974): 119-130.

Self, P. Introduction: New towns in the modern world. In New towns: The British experience, H. Evans, ed. Wiley, 1972.

Seligman, M.P. On the generality of the laws of learning. Psychological Review 77 (1970): 406-418.

Sells, S. Dimensions of stimulus situations which account for behavior variance. In Stimulus determinants of behavior, Sells, S., ed. New York: Ronald Press, 1963.

Shafer, E.L., Jr., and Thompson, R.C. Models that describe use of Adirondack campgrounds. Forest Science 14 (1968): 383-391.

Shaw, M. Ethical implication of a behavioral approach. In Behavior modification in social work, D. John, P. Hardiker, M. Yelloby, and M. Shaw, eds. London: Wiley, 1972.

Sheppard, C. Stigmatized groups: An assessment of community and counselor perceptions and their relation to social planning and change. Symposium presented at the meeting of the Eastern Psychological Association, Boston, Mass., April, 1977.

Shore, M.F., and Golann, S.E. Problems of ethics in community mental health: A survey of community psychologists. Community Mental Health Journal 5 (1969): 452-459.

Shore, M.F., and Golann, S.E., eds. Current ethical issues in mental health (NIMH Monograph, DHEW Publication No. HSM 73-9029). Washington, D.C.: U.S. Government Printing Office, 1973.

Shure, M.B., and Spivack, G. A preventive mental health program for young "inner city" children: The second (kindergarten) year. Paper presented at the meeting of the American Psychological Association, Chicago, 1975.

Shure, M.B.; Spivack, G.; and Gordon, R. Problem-solving thinking: A preventive mental health program for preschool children. Reading World 11 (1972): 259-273.

Shute, C. Aristotle's interactionism and its transformations by some 20th century writers. Psychological Record 23 (1973): 283-293.

Siegel, L.M.; Attkisson, C.C.; and Cohn, A.M. eds. Mental health needs assessment strategies and techniques. Rockville, Md.: National Institute of Mental Health, 1974.

Signell, K.A., and Scott, P.A. Parent-child communication course (PCC): Instructors' manual. Berkeley, Calif.: Wright Institute, 1973.

Silberman, C.E. Crisis in the classroom: The remaking of American education. New York: Random House, 1970.

_____. The open classroom reader. New York: Vintage, 1973.

Silverman, W.H., and Val, E. Day Hospital in the context of a community mental health program. Community Mental Health Journal 11 (1975): 82-90.

Simmel, G. The sociology of Georg Simmel. New York: Free Press, 1950.

Sinclair, I. Hostels for probationers. London: Her Majesty's Stationery Office, 1971.

Skeels, H., Adult status of children with contrasting early life experiences: A follow-up study. Monograph of the Society for Research in Child Development 31 (1966).

Skinner, B.F. The concept of reflex in the description of behavior. Journal of General Psychology 5 (1931): 427-458.

_____. The behavior of organisms: An experimental analysis. New York: Appleton-Century-Crofts, 1938.

_____. Walden Two. New York: Macmillan, 1948.

_____. Science and human behavior. New York: MacMillan, 1953.

_____. Verbal behavior. New York: Appleton-Century-Crofts, 1957.

_____. The phylogency and ontogeny of behavior. Science 153 (1966): 1205-1213.

_____. Contingencies of reinforcement. New York: Appleton-Century-Crofts, 1969.

_____. Beyond freedom and dignity. New York: Knopf, 1971.

_____. About behaviorism. New York: Knopf, 1974.

_____. The ethics of helping people. Criminal Law Bulletin 11 (1975): 623-636.

_____. Herrnstein and the evolution of behaviorism. American Psychologist 32 (1977): 1006-1012.

Slotnick, R.S., and Jeger, A.M. Barriers to deinstitutionalization: Social systems influences on environmental design interventions. Paper presented at the meeting of the American Psychological Association, Toronto, Canada, August, 1978.

Slotnick, R.S., and Jeger, A.M. Promoting natural support systems: Experiences from the Long Island Self-Help Clearinghouse. Conversation Hour/Resource Session, Special Meeting at the Eastern Psychological Association, Philadelphia, April, 1979.

Slotnick, R.S.; Jeger, A.M.; and Cantor, A. The interface between organization and community: Behavioral-systems strategies for organizational managers. Paper presented at the meeting of the Association for the Advancement of Behavior Therapy, Chicago, November, 1978.

Smith, A. The wealth of nations. London: 1776.

Snyder, W.U. Some investigation of relationship in psychotherapy. In Research in psychotherapy, E.A. Rubinstein and M.B. Parloff, eds. Washington, D.C.: American Psychological Association, 1959, pp. 247-259.

Snow, D.L., and Newton, P.M. Task, social structure, and social process in the community mental health center movement. American Psychologist 31 (1976): 582-594.

Sobey, F. The nonprofessional revolution in mental health. New York: Columbia University Press, 1970.

Sommer, R. Studies in Personal Space, Sociometry 22 (1959): 247-260.

_____. Leadership and group geography, Sociometry 24 (1961): 99-110.

_____. The distance for comfortable conversation: A further study. Sociometry 25 (1962): 111-116.

_____. The Ecology of Privacy. Library Quarterly 36 (1966): 234-248.

_____. Small group ecology. Psychological Bulletin 67 (1967): 145-152.

_____. Personal space: The behavioral basis for design. Englewood Cliffs, N.J.: Prentice-Hall, 1969.

_____. Design awareness. San Francisco: Holt, Rinehart and Winston, 1972.

_____. Tight Spaces: Hard architecture and how to humanize it. Englewood Cliffs, N.J.: Prentice-Hall, 1974.

Spille, R. Mieter planen mit. Rowohlt Taschenbuch Verlag GmbH Reinbeck bei Hamburg, 1975.

Spivack, G., and Shure, M.B. Social adjustment of young children. San Francisco: Jossey-Bass, 1974.

Staddon, T.E.R., and Simmelhag, V.L. The superstition experiment: A reexamination of its implication for the study of adaptive behavior, Psychological Review 78 (1971): 3-43.

Stein, L.I., ed. Community support systems for the long-term patient. San Francisco: Jossey-Bass, 1979.

Stein, L.I., and Test, M.A., eds. Alternatives to mental hospital treatment. New York: Plenum Press, 1978.

Stein, L.I.; Test, M.A.; and Marx, A.J. Alternative to the hospital: A controlled study. American Journal of Psychiatry 132 (1975): 517-522.

Stein, R.G. Architecture and energy. Garden City, N.Y.: Anchor/Doubleday, 1977.

Stein, T.J. Some ethical considerations of short-term workshops in the principles and methods of behavior modification. Journal of Applied Behavior Analysis 8 (1975): 113-115.

Stern, G.G. People in context. New York: Wiley, 1970.

Stewart, A.; Lafave, H.G.; Grunberg, F.; and Herjanic, M. Problems in phasing out a large public psychiatric hospital. American Journal of Psychiatry 125 (1968): 120-126.

Stickney, S.B. Schools are our community mental health centers. American Journal of Psychiatry 124 (1968): 101-109.

Stokols, D. On the distinction between density and crowding: Some implications for future research. Psychological Review 79 (1972): 275-277.

_____. Readings in environmental psychology. New York: M.S.S. Information Corporation, 1974.

_____. Environmental psychology. Annual review of Psychology 29 (1978): 253-95.

Stolz, S.B. Ethical issues in research on behavior therapy. In Issues in evaluating behavior modification, W.S. Wood, ed. Champaign, Ill.: Research Press, 1975.

_____. Ethical issues in behavior modification. San Francisco: Jossey-Bass, 1978a.

_____. Ethics of social and educational interventions: Historical context and a behavioral analysis. In Handbook of applied behavior analysis: Social and instructional processes, A.C. Catania and T.A. Brigham, eds. New York: Halsted Press, 1978b.

Strauss, A.; Schatzman, L.; Bucher, R.; Ehrlich, D.; and Sabshin, M. Field tactics. In Issues in participant observation, McCall and Simmons, eds. Reading, Mass.: Addison-Wesley, 1969.

Studer, R.G. Human systems design and the management of change. General Systems 16 (1971): 131-143.

_____. Man-environment relations: Discovery or design. In Environmental Design Research, vol. 2, W. Preiser, ed. Stroudsburg, Pa.: Dowden, Hutchinson and Ross, 1973.

Studer, R.G., and Stea, D. Environmental design and human behavior. Journal of Social Issues 22 (1966): 127-136.

Suchman, E.A. Action for what? A critique of evaluative research. In Evaluating action programs: Readings in social action and education, C.M. Weiss, ed. Boston: Allyn and Bacon, 1972.

Sue, S. Community mental health services to minority groups: Some optimism, some pessimism. American Psychologist, 32 (1977): 616-624.

Suinn, R.M. Training undergraduate students as community behavior modification consultants. Journal of Counseling Psychology 21 (1974a): 71-77.

_____. Traits for selection of paraprofessionals for behavior modification consultation training. Community Mental Health Journal 10 (1974b): 441-449.

Sullivan, H.S. The interpersonal theory of psychiatry. New York: Norton, 1953.

_____. The psychiatric interview. New York: Norton, 1954.

Surratt, P.R.; Ulrich, R.E.; and Hawkins, R.P. An elementary student as a behavioral engineer. Journal of Applied Behavior Analysis 2 (1969): 85-92.

Suttmeier, R.P. Research and revolution. Lexington, Mass.: Lexington Books, 1974.

Symposium on Cardinal Utilities. Econometrica 20 (1952): entire volume.

Swan, A. Public response to air pollution. In Environment and the social sciences: perspectives and applications, J.F. Wohlwill and D.H. Carson, eds. Washington, D.C.: American Psychological Association, 1972, pp. 66-74.

Swazey, J. Chlorpromazin in psychiatry: A study of therapeutic innovation. Cambridge: Massachusetts Institute of Technology Press, 1974.

Taber, J.I. Behavior development for community placement. Program manual, V.A. Hospital, Cleveland, Ohio, 1975.

Tarver, J., and Turner, A.J. Behavior modification techniques for families of patients with behavior problems. Huntsville-Madison County Mental Health Center, Huntsville, Ala., 1974.

Taube, C.A. Consultation and education services, community mental health centers – January, 1970. Statistical Note 43, Rockville, Md.: National Institute of Mental Health, 1971.

_____. Day care services in federally funded community mental health centers, 1971-72. Statistical note 96. Rockville, Md.: National Institute of Mental Health, 1973.

Taylor, C.W. The constructed environment with man as the measure as part of the quality system in construction, Proceedings of the engineering foundation conference, New York: American Society of Civil Engineers, November, 1974.

_____. Fourteen year progress report on the architectural psychology program. Paper presented at annual meeting Rocky Mountain Psychological Association, Salt Lake City, Utah, May 7-10, 1975.

_____. Production of new manpower in architectural/environmental psychology, Summary of EdRA 7 Symposium, May 25-28, University of British Columbia, Vancouver, 1976, pp. 1-2.

Terrace, H.S. Stimulus control. In Operant behavior: Areas of research and application, W.K. Honig, ed. New York: Appleton-Century-Crofts, 1966, pp. 271-344.

Tennov, D. Psychotherapy: The hazardous cure. New York: Anchor Books, 1975.

Terrill, R. Flowers on an iron tree. Boston: Little, Brown, 1975.

Test, M.A., and Stein, L.J. Training in community living: Research design and results. Paper presented at the meeting of the American Psychological Association, Chicago, September, 1975.

_____. Practical guidelines for the Community treatment of markedly impaired patients. Community Mental Health Journal 12 (1976): 72-82.

Tharp, R.G., and Wetzel, R.J. Behavior modification in the natural environment. New York: Academic Press, 1969.

The Group for Environmental Education. Our man-made environment, book seven. The Group for Environmental Education, 1970.

Thibaut, J.W., and Kelley, H.H. The social psychology of groups. New York: Wiley, 1959.

Thomander, D. Researching psychotherapy effectiveness in mental health service agencies. Journal of Community Psychology 4 (1976): 215-238.

Thomson, T. Trends in Minnesota guidelines regulating behavior modification. In Behavior modification and ethics, J. Krapfl and E. Vargas, eds. Kalamazoo, Mich.: Behaviordelia, 1977.

Thoresen, C.E., and Mahoney, M.J. Behavioral self-control. New York: Holt, Rinehart and Winston, 1974.

Thorndike, E.L. Principles of teaching. New York: Seiler, 1906.

_____. Human learning. New York: Century, 1931.

Tinbergen, N. The study of instinct. New York: Oxford University Press, 1951.

Tornatzky, L.G., and Fairweather, G.W. The role of experimental research in a social change process: Or not reinventing the wheel. Paper presented at the meeting of the American Psychological Association, Washington, D.C., September, 1976.

Torrey, E.F. The death of psychiatry, New York: Penguin, 1974.

Toscano, P. Participant-observer behavior in the classroom: A two-year summary. State University of New York at Stony Brook, N.Y., 1974.

Toynbee, A. The study of history. New York: Oxford University Press, 1962.

Truax, C.B., and Carkhuff, R.R. Toward effective counseling and psychotherapy: Training and practice. Chicago: Aldine, 1967.

Turner, A.J., and Goodson, W.H. Programs and Evaluations, Huntsville, Ala.: Huntsville-Madison County Mental Health Center, 1971, 1972.

_____. Catch a fellow worker doing something good today. Huntsville, Ala.: Huntsville-Madison County Mental Health Center, 1975.

Turner, T.F.C. Housing by people, London: Marion Boyars, 1976.

Turner, T.F.C., and Fichter, R. Freedom to build, New York: Macmillan, 1972.

Turner, T.F.C., and Shifrin, I. Community support systems: How comprehensive? In Community support systems for the long-term patient, L.I. Stein, ed. San Francisco: Jossey-Bass, 1979.

Ullmann, L.P. Behavioral community psychology: Implications, opportunities, and responsibilities. Forward to Behavioral approaches to community psychology, M.T. Nietzel, R.A. Winett, M.L. MacDonald, and W.S. Davidson, eds. Elmsford, N.Y.: Pergamon Press, 1977.

Ullmann, L.P., and Krasner, L., eds. Case studies in behavior modification. New York: Holt, Rinehart and Winston, 1965.

_____. A psychological approach to abnormal behavior. Englewood Cliffs, N.J.: Prentice-Hall, 1975.

Ulmer, R.A., and Franks, C.M. A proposed integration of independent mental health facilities into behaviorally oriented social training programs. Psychological Reports 32 (1973): 95-104.

Ulrich, R.E. Toward experimental living. Behavior Modification Monographs 2 (1973): 1.

_____. Some moral and ethical implications of behavior modification: An inside view. Paper presented at the First Mexican Congress on Behavior Analysis. Xalapa, Veracruz, April 8-10, 1974.

_____. Toward experimental living, Phase II: "Have you ever heard of a man named Frazier, Sir?" In Behavior analysis: Areas of research and application. E. Ramp and G. Semb, eds. Englewood Cliffs, N.J.: Prentice-Hall, 1975, pp. 45-61.

Ulrich, R.E.; Stachnik, T.; and Mabry, J. Control of human behavior, 2 vols. Volume one. Glenview, Ill.: Scott, Foresman, 1966.

U.S. General Accounting Office, Returning the mentally ill to the community: Government needs to do more. Washington, D.C., 1977.

van de Wall, W. The utilization of music in prisons and mental hospitals. New York: National Bureau for the Advancement of Music, 1924.

vanWagenberg, D. Bouwkundige Ontwerptraining. Ph.D. diss. Technische Hogeschool, Eindhoven, The Netherlands. 1975.

_____. The organization and planning of the participation of the occupants in two European man housing projects, Industrialization Forum, 7 (1976): 41-46.

vanWagenberg, D., and Frsyen, H.D. Berooner participatie, Eindlroven, The Netherlands, Technische Hogeschool, Eindlroven Press, Diktaat m. 7.820., 1976.

vanWagenberg, D., and Wennekes, S. Designing a new home for mentally retarded adults with the staff and the tenants. Eindhoven, St. Jozefdal. 1975.

Vargas, E.A. Rights: A behavioristic analysis. In Behavior modification and ethics, J. Krapfl and E. Vargas, eds. Kalamazoo, Mich.: Behaviordelia, 1977.

Veatch, R.M. Does ethics have an empirical basis? Hastings Center Studies 1 (1973): 50-65.

von Neumann, J. and Morgenstern, O. Theory of games and economic behavior. New York: Wiley, 1944.

Wachtel, P. Psychodynamics, behavior therapy and the implacable experimenter: An inquiry into the consistency of personality. Journal of Abnormal Psychology 82 (1973): 324-334.

Wade, N. Sociobiology: Troubled birth for a new discipline. Science 191 (1977): 1151-1155.

Walberg, H.J. Learning models and learning environments. Educational Psychologist 11 (1974): 102-109.

Wallis, R.R., and Katf, N.Y. The 50-mile bridge: Consultation between state hospital and community mental health center staffs. Hospital and Community Psychiatry 23 (1972): 73-6.

Wapner, S.; Cohen, S.B.; and Kaplan, B., eds. Experiencing the environment. New York: Plenum Press, 1976.

Wapner, S., Kaplan, B., and Cohen, S.B. An organismic-developmental perspective for understanding transactions of men in environments. Environment and Behavior 5 (1973): 255-289.

Ward, C. Tenants take over. London: Architectural Press, 1975.

Ward, C., ed. Vandalism. London: Architectural Press, 1973.

Ward, C., and Tyson, A. Streetwork: The exploding school. London: Routledge, 1973.

Warren, J. No rave reviews for community care. American Psychological Association Monitor 7 (May 1976): 10.

Waters, J.M. Relationships among response likelihood, appropriateness, and consequence ratings. State University of New York at Stony Brook, N.Y., 1976.

Waters, J.M., and Graeff, J.A. The environmental design trends in behavior therapy: Implications for research. Paper presented at the Annual Conference of the British Psychological Society, Exeter, England, April 1-4, 1977.

Waters, J.M.; Hutchison, W.; and Graeff, J. Selecting skills to train. Paper presented at the Conference, "An Environmental Design Approach to Psychology and Education," NELP, April 6, 1977.

Watson, J.B., and Rayner, R. Conditioned emotional reactions. Journal of Experimental Psychology 3 (1920): 1-14.

Watson, R.I. The experimental tradition and clinical psychology. In Experimental foundations of clinical psychology, A.J. Bachrach, ed. New York, N.Y.: Basic Books, 1962.

Watzlawick, P.; Beavin, B.; and Jackson, F. Pragmatics of human communication. New York: Norton, 1967.

Watzlawick, P.; Weakland, J.; and Fisch, R. Change. New York: Norton, 1974.

Webb, E.J.; Campbell, D.T.; Schwartz, R.D.; and Sechrest, L. Unobtrusive measures: Nonreactive research in the social sciences. Chicago: Rand McNally, 1966.

Weber, L. The English infant school and informal education, Englewood Cliffs, N.J.: Prentice-Hall, 1971.

Weick, K. Systematic observation methods. In The handbook of social psychology, vol. 2. Research methods, 2nd ed., G. Lindzey and Aronson, eds. Reading, Mass.: Addison-Wesley, 1968.

Weiss, R.S., and Rein, M. The evaluation of broad-aim programs: Experimental design, its difficulties, and an alternative. Administrative Science Quarterly 15 (1970): 97-109.

Wexler, D.B. Tokens and taboo: Behavior modification, token economies, and the law. California law review 61 (1973a): 81-109.

_____. Token and taboo: Behavior modification, token economies, and the law. Behaviorism 1 (1973b): 1-24.

_____. Reflections on the legal regulation of behavior modification in institutional settings. Arizona law review 17 (1975): 132-143.

Whalen, C.K., and Henker, B.A. Pyramid therapy in a hospital for the retarded: Methods, program evaluation, and long-term effects. American Journal of Mental Deficiency 75 (1971): 414-434.

Wheater, D.J. Environmental design: An analysis of the field; its implications for libraries; and a guide to the literature. Council of Planning Librarians, Exchange Bibliography # 747-748, February 1975.

White, W.P., ed. Resources in environment and behavior. Washington, D.C.: American Psychological Association, 1979.

Whited, C., and Kronlolz, J. Editorial. Miami Herald, April 7, 1972.

Whyte, M.K. Small groups and political rituals in China. Berkeley: University of California Press, 1974.

Wicker, A.W. Processes which mediate behavior-environment congruence. Behavioral sciences 17 (1972): 265-277.

_____. Undermanning theory and research: Implications for the study of psychological and behavioral effects of excess population. Research in Social Psychology 4 (January 1973).

Wicker, A.W., and Kirmeyer, S. From church to laboratory to national park: A program of research on excess and insufficient populations in behavior settings. Paper presented in symposium, "Experiencing the Environment," Clark University, 1975.

Wiggins, J.S. Personality and predictions: Principles of assessment. Reading, Mass.: Addison Wesley, 1973.

Wilkinson, L., and Reppucci, N.D. Perceptions of social climate among participants in token economy and non-token economy cottages in a juvenile correctional institution. American Journal of Community Psychology 1: 36-43.

Willems, E.P. Go ye into all the world and modify behavior: An ecologist's view. Representative Research in Social Psychology 4 (June 1973): 93-105.

_____. Behavioral technology and behavioral ecology. Journal of Applied Behavior Analysis, 1974, 7, 151-165.

Wilson, E.O. Sociobiology: The new synthesis. Cambridge, Mass.: Harvard University Press, 1975.

Windle, C. Guidelines for program evaluation in community mental health centers. Draft no. 8. Rockville, Md.: National Institute of Mental Health, 1977.

Windle, C., and Scully, D. Community mental health centers and the decreasing use of state mental hospitals. Community Mental Health Journal 12 (1976): 239-243.

Winett, R.A. Behavior modification and open education. Journal of School Psychology 11 (1973): 207-214.

_____. Environmental design: An expanded behavioral research framework for school consultation and educational innovation, Professional Psychology 7 (1976): 631-636.

Winett, R.A., and Edwards, S.M. An evaluation plan for educational innovations. Journal of Community Psychology 2 (1974): 345-351.

Winett, R.A., and Nietzel, M.T. Behavioral ecology: Contingency management of consumer energy use. American Journal of Community Psychology 3 (1975): 123-133.

Winett, R.A. and Winkler, R.C. Current behavior modification in the classroom: Be still, be quiet, be docile. Journal of Applied Behavior Analysis 5 (1972): 499-504.

Winkler, R.C. Management of chronic psychiatric patients by a token reinforcement system. Journal of Applied Behavior Analysis 3 (1970): 47-55.

_____. The relevance of economic theory and technology to token reinforcement systems. Behavior Research and Therapy 9 (1971): 81-88.

_____. A theory of equilibrium in token economies. Journal of Abnormal Psychology 79 (1972): 169-173.

_____. An experimental analysis of economic balance, savings, and wages in a token economy, Behavior Therapy 4 (1973): 22-40.

Winkler, R.C., and Krasner, L. The contribution of economics to token economies. Paper presented at the annual meeting of the Eastern Psychological Association, April 15, 1971.

Wohlwill, J.F. The emerging discipline of environmental psychology. American Psychologists 25 (1970): 303-312.

Wohlwill, J.F., and Carson, D.H. Environment and the social sciences: Perspectives and applications. Washington, D.C.: American Psychological Association, 1972.

Wolf, M., and Witke, R., eds. Women in Chinese society. Stanford, Calif.: Stanford University Press, 1975.

Wollner, C.E. Behaviorism and humanism: B.F. Skinner and the Western intellectual tradition. Review of existential psychology and psychiatry 14 (1975-76): 146-168.

Wood, W.S. Behavior modification vs. civil rights and liberties. In Issues in evaluating behavior modification, W.S. Wood, ed. Champaign, Ill.: Research Press, 1975a.

Wood, W.S., ed. Issues in evaluating behavior modification. Champaign, Ill.: Research Press, 1975b.

Woody, R.H., and Woody, J.D. Behavioral science consultation. Personnel Journal 50 (1971): 382-391.

Woolfolk, A.E.; Woolfolk, R.L.; and Wilson, T.G. A rose by any other name. . .: Labeling bias and attitudes toward behavior modification. Journal of Consulting and Clinical Psychology 45 (1977): 184-191.

Wolpe, J. Psychotherapy by reciprocal inhibition. Stanford, Calif.: Stanford University Press, 1958.

Wortman, P.M. Evaluation research: A psychological perspective. American Psychologist 5 (1975): 562-575.

Wynne-Edwards, V.C. Animal dispersion in relation to social behavior. London: Oliver and Boyd, 1962.

Yen, S. Behavioral treatment to minority students: A critical review of program development. Paper presented at the meeting of the Association for the Advancement of Behavior Therapy, New York, December, 1976.

Young, C.E.; True, J.E.; and Packard, M.E. A national study of associate degree mental health and human services workers. Journal of Community Psychology 4 (1976): 89-95.

Young, M.B., ed. Women in China. Ann Arbor, Mich.: Center for Chinese Studies, University of Michigan, 1973.

Zax, M., and Specter, G.A. An introduction to community psychology. New York: Wiley, 1974.

Zeisel, J. Sociology and architectural design. New York: Russell Sage Foundation, 1975.

Zelditch, M. Some methodological problems of field studies. American Journal of Sociology 67 (1962): 566-576.

Zifferblatt, S.M. Architecture and human behavior: Toward increased understanding of a functional relationship. Educational Technology 12 (August 1972): 54-57.

Zilboorg, G. A history of medical psychology. New York: Norton, 1941.

Zubek, J.P., ed. Sensory deprivation: Fifteen years of research. New York: Appleton-Century-Crofts, 1969.

Zusman, J., and Bissonette, R. The case against evaluation (with some suggestions for improvement). International Journal of Mental Health 2 (1973): 111-125.

Zwerling, I. Racism, professionalism, and elitism: Barriers to community mental health. New York: Aronson, 1976.

Name Index

Subject Index

About the
Contributors

LEONARD KRASNER is a Professor of Psychology and Psychiatry at the State University of New York at Stony Brook. He received his B.S. degree at CCNY and Ph.D degree in psychology at Columbia University. Prior to coming to Stony Brook to establish and direct the Clinical Psychology training program in the mid 1960s he had been on the faculties of the Universities of Massachusetts, Colorado, and Stanford, visiting scholar at Educational Testing Service, and Coordinator of Training at the VA Hospital in Palo Alto, California. He currently directs the Environmental Design Program, described in chapter 8, still doggedly functioning within the context of "training clinical psychologists."

LEONIDAS CASTRO participated in the development of Children's Village in his native Bogota. He received his doctorate in psychology from the State University of New York at Stony Brook and then resumed his teaching position at the Universidad De Los Andes in Bogota, Colombia. His internship in clinical psychology was as a participant-observer in the London program described in Chapter 8.

NED COONEY is currently a graduate student in clinical psychology at Rutgers University. He received his Bachelor's degree from SUNY Stony Brook where he was a participant-observer in the Environmental Design Program in London in 1976-1977.

JULIAN D. FORD is Assistant Professor of Psychology at the University of Delaware. He received his B.A. degree from the University of Michigan in 1973 and a Ph.D. from the State University of New York at Stony Brook in 1977. His main areas of professional interest include interpersonal competence, assertiveness, problem solving and self control, design and evaluation of consultation programs in educational and medical organizations, and consumers' research on

511

methods of training, the nature of behavior therapy, family therapy, and the relationship of process and outcome in psychotherapy.

JUDITH GRAEFF received her doctorate in clinical psychology from SUNY, Stony Brook where she supervised in the Environmental Design in London program. She has been a consultant to the National Institute of Health at Bethesda, and is currently a Postdoctoral Fellow in the Division of Adolescent Medicine, University of Maryland School of Medicine, Baltimore, Maryland.

R. EDWARD HARPIN received his doctorate in clinical psychology from the State University of New York at Stony Brook in 1977 and is currently on the staff of Massachusetts General Hospital in Cambridge, Massachusetts.

CHARLES HOFFMANN was Professor of Economics and History at the State University of New York at Stony Brook. He is currently Dean of Social Science at Queens College, CUNY. He pursued his A.B. at Queens College and his A.M. and Ph.D. at Columbia University. His most recent work on China includes The Chinese Worker (Albany, N.Y.: State University of New York Press) and "Worker Participation in Chinese Factories," Modern China, July 1977. In 1973, Professor Hoffmann visited Chinese communes, factories, schools, universities, housing developments, and other social environments during a four-week stay in the People's Republic of China. He has been a frequent participant in the Environmental Design Seminar.

WILLIAM HUTCHISON received his B.A. from the University of Kansas (in psychology, mathematics, and German). He came to Stony Brook for graduate work in clinical psychology, and joined the Environmental Design Seminar at its beginning in 1972. He went to London with Ed Harpin and a small group of undergraduates in 1975 to start the London program. He received his Ph.D. from Stony Brook in 1976, and served as program coordinator in London through 1979 as the program there continues to develop. He is currently Assistant Professor in the Behavioral Systems Analysis area of the Psychology Department at West Virginia University, Morgantown, West Virginia.

ABRAHAM JEGER is currently Assistant Professor of Psychology at the New York Institute of Technology, Old Westbury, N.Y. He received his Ph.D. in Psychology from the State University of New York at Stony Brook, where he was a member of the Environmental Design Projects Group. His interests in community mental health date back to field work in the Aftercare Unit of Maimonides Community Mental Health Center (Brooklyn, N.Y.) while still an undergraduate at Brooklyn College. This interest was reinforced through a later graduate practicum in mental health program evaluation. His research interests include developing social ecological evaluation models, mental health consultation, and evaluating attitudes toward mental illness.

MIRIAM KRASNER has been teaching in an open education program for the past dozen years at North Country Elementary School. She received her B.A. degree from CCNY and her M.A. from Teachers College, Columbia University. She has been an active participant in the development of the Environmental Design Program described in Chapter 8, and has co-authored several of the research reports of the program. She has given courses, workshops, and seminars in the U.S. and abroad on open education, teacher centers, and learning centers.

GARY MCCLURE received his doctorate degree from the University of Vermont in 1970 at which time he joined the faculty of the State University College of New York, first at the Oneonta campus from 1970 to 1972 and then at the Brockport campus during the 1973-1974 academic year. From 1974 to 1977 he was Chief Psychologist at Central Islip Psychiatric Center, Central Islip, New York, and an adjunct member of the Department of Psychology, State University of New York at Stony Brook, where he was a member of the Environmental Design Seminar. He is presently Head of the Department of Psychology at Georgia Southern College.

RICHARD PARADISE received his doctorate degree in clinical psychology at the State University of New York at Stony Brook and has joined the staff of the institution. He started using assessment procedures to chart progress of mentally retarded children in an educationally-oriented behavior modification project in 1971. His internship was with the Environmental Design Program in London, where "social climate" scales were used in evaluation.

DAVID POMERANZ received his B.S. degree from Brooklyn College where he majored in chemistry, sociology, and psychology. He received his Ph.D. in psychology from the University of Rochester in 1963 and completed a post-doctoral in clinical psychology at the VA Hospital, Palo Alto, California, the following year. He came to Stony Brook in 1965 and is currently Associate Professor of Psychology and Director of the Psychological Center. Over the past five years he has become involved with the Environmental Design Program at Stony Brook and has participated in the development of the program and in the training of graduate students in it. He is currently developing the Psychological Center into a community-oriented, consultation facility which will incorporate many of the principles of environmental design.

DRIES VAN WAGENBERG is an architect trained at Eindhoven University in Holland whose interest in environmental design led him to seek a doctorate in psychology at the State University of New York at Stony Brook. He has spent one year of his graduate training as teacher and supervisor in the Environmental Design in London program. He has been consulting on the redesign of the Shoreham Middle School.

JAMES M. WATERS was born in Newark and raised in Glen Ridge, New Jersey. He received a Bachelor's Degree with honors in psychology from Hamilton College in 1974. Since September 1974 he has been enrolled in the Clinical Psychology Program of the State University of New York at Stony Brook, and has worked with the Environmental Design Projects Group there. During the 1976-77 academic year, Jim lived in London and worked as an intern helping to supervise the SUNY "Environmental Design in London" program. In addition to working toward completion of his doctoral degree, he is currently a clinical and research consultant to Infant Services of the Suffolk County Association for the Help of Retarded Children. His interests include research methodology, statistical analysis, and program evaluation.

ROBIN CHRISTOPHER WINKLER received his doctorate in clinical psychology from the University of New South Wales in Sydney, Australia, based on a dissertation which initiated a stream of research utilizing token economies to test economic theory. He spent several years at Stony Brook working with Dr. Krasner at the seminal stage of the programs described in Chapter 8. Currently Winkler is Director of the Clinical Unit in Psychology at the University of Western Australia in Perth, Australia.

Pergamon General Psychology Series

Editors: Arnold P. Goldstein, Syracuse University
Leonard Krasner, SUNY, Stony Brook

092314